1993

THE ACHIEVING SOCIETY

THE
ACHIEVING
SOCIETY

David C. McClelland

THE FREE PRESS
A Division of Macmillan Publishing Co., Inc.
NEW YORK

Collier Macmillan Publishers
LONDON

The Free Press
A Division of Macmillan Publishing Co., Inc.
866 Third Avenue, New York, N.Y. 10022

Collier Macmillan Canada, Ltd.

Published by arrangement with D. Van Nostrand Company, Inc.

FIRST FREE PRESS PAPERBACK EDITION 1967

printing number
9   10

To
ROWAN GAITHER AND BERNARD BERELSON
in gratitude for their faith in the future
of the behavioral sciences

Preface

This book grew out of an attempt by a psychologist, trained in behavioral science methods, to isolate certain psychological factors and to demonstrate rigorously by quantitative methods that these factors are generally important in economic development. The scope of such an enterprise turned out to be truly alarming for one whose background in the social sciences was slight to begin with. It required specialized knowledge on everything from population problems, to coal imports in England from the 16th to the 19th century, to methods of computing rates of economic growth, to sources of children's books, to management practices in Russia, Italy and Mexico, to the pottery of Ancient Greece and Pre-Incan Peru. Let me confess at the outset (for it will be obvious soon enough) that I have not managed to become a real professional in many of these areas of knowledge, though I have had the advantage of much expert advice and assistance. The dilemma of the "generalist" trying to acquire specialized knowledge in a hurry is nicely illustrated by what happened to me when I asked a colleague, an eminent Harvard historian, to recommend "a" book to me that would bring me up to date on English history. I also mentioned that as a budding scientist in college, I had unfortunately managed to escape all courses in history, so that my mind was practically a "tabula rasa" on the subject. He simply looked at me aghast, murmured "my God!" and turned away. Perhaps the self-taught scholar deserves such a response—at any rate he sometimes gets it—and so may this book among specialists on particular topics it had to cover in the search for the broadest possible test of the hypothesis that a particular psychological factor—the need for Achievement—is responsible for economic growth and decline.

The problem of covering so much intellectual territory is actually twofold. On the one hand, there is the strong probability of simple human error. For example, in the thousands of calculations on which this book is based, it is unlikely that no mistakes have been made. Not even the mechanical equipment that produced many of the numbers used proved infallible. It coughed at least once in some thousands of computations and refused to give one correlation it should have. Possibly in some places I have used incorrect or out-of-date data—e.g., on the electrical production of Pakistan or the location of 6th-century Greek vase remains. In others I may have overlooked an obviously better statistic or used an inadequate method of data analysis. For such errors, though I have tried hard to eliminate them, I apologize in advance and hope readers more expert than I will correct them. The only excuse is the sheer scope of the undertaking.

vii

On the other hand, and more seriously, there may be errors of conceptualization. It was hard to learn enough about so many different matters to assure a grasp of their main features. I was constantly aware of the danger of being naive about a very complex historical or economic problem. Yet I also came to feel that naiveté is not wholly a disadvantage. For example, in trying to solve the problem of how to compute comparative rates of economic growth, I was not hampered by any preconceptions. In fact, I had dropped my one course in college economics because it seemed to me such an abstract, rationalistic discipline that took so little account, at least at that time, of how men actually behave economically. So, having little formal training in economics, I did not accept so easily as most economists do by habit, the long tradition of using index numbers and estimates of national income in fixed prices. This traditional method seemed to be so objectionable that I adopted a different approach, based on sampling theory and regression analysis. I do not expect economists readily to accept such an approach, even for the limited purpose of comparing rates of growth, nor am I sure that it is entirely adequate, yet I do feel that my very lack of training in economics may have made it easier for me to break with a traditional but inadequate method of measurement and to look at the problem in a different way.

But how did I get involved in covering so much territory in the first place? Why risk being superficial? The answer lies in the general methodological approach of the book, which is in the tradition of comparative history, comparative economics or a psychology interested in generalizations that apply to all or most of the human species. In other words, the book attempts to answer *general* questions, not specific ones; it does not probe the particulars of the Industrial Revolution in England but examines the factors underlying that revolution which were common to other such waves of rapid economic development in history.

I am well aware that the search for such generalizations is often suspect. What is the point, the argument runs, in knowing what generally happens (even if it were possible to know), when the really important fact is what happened *in this case*, in this country at this particular time? For after all I am by profession a clinical psychologist where such an argument is also particularly appropriate. What good is a generalization about human nature when you really want to know what makes this particular person neurotic at this time? Why not study him as an individual, rather than waste time analyzing other people in order to discover what makes people neurotic in general?

It is perhaps because I have spent time analyzing particular cases that I feel the need for generalizations and a comparative frame of reference. It is so easy to be mistaken if you analyze only a particular case. The clinical psychologist may decide, for example, that George is neurotic because his mother mistreated him. The detailed case record makes the point very clear. Yet might not the clinician's view of the case be quite different if he knew that mothers from George's social background generally mistreated their sons and that most of those sons did not become neurotic? I have seen in writing over and over again that such and such a country, say India, cannot develop rapidly economically because it has such a high population density and/or a high net reproduction rate. The case record makes it clear: it does have a high population density, a high net reproduction rate; it is having difficulty developing. The two events would seem to be logically connected because the more mouths there are to feed, the harder it is to feed them adequately. Yet doesn't the perspective on such a case analysis change when we discover that (1) in *general* rates of population growth have not been connected with rates of economic growth (Chapter 1) and (2) India, as compared with nations in *general,* is at the present time developing rapidly despite her population problems (Chapter 3)?

Generalizations can be easily criticized. For example, some reader is almost certain to say that I have greatly oversimplified the interpretation of history, that I believe a few psychological variables can account wholly for economic development—a conclusion that can be easily demonstrated to be false for a particular country in a particular time period by someone who really understands what went on then in a more profound way than I do. Such an accusation is true but only partly true. It is justified in the sense that economic development in a particular country is a complex result of the interaction of many more factors than are considered here, but not in the sense that I am unaware of it.

It is important, therefore, to understand at the outset the simplicity of this book—what it can accomplish and what it cannot. What it does try to do is to isolate certain psychological factors and to demonstrate rigorously by quantitative scientific methods that these factors are *generally* important in economic development. Simplification is an absolute prerequisite for such rigorous scientific tests, but it is superficial only in two senses: first, it leaves out of consideration other variables which may be equally or more important, and secondly, it does not deal directly with the problem of how these variables (shown to be generally important) actually operate in a particular historical instance. It is precisely at this point, however, that the generalizations should begin to be useful to historians and economists interested in particular cases. Though it is not my purpose to deal with such cases, it is my hope that the generalizations established will help in the analysis of particular events in history, in exactly the same way that the generalizations of a physicist help an engineer design and build a particular bridge in a particular spot at a particular time.

But all of the foregoing argument tends rather to explain why I might *not* have written this book; or why I, as a psychologist accustomed to sweeping generalizations about human behavior at its simplest levels, should have hesitated a long while before applying the same approach to complex social phenomena. How then, did I happen to write it? The Ford Foundation was really responsible. It not only provided the money, but—what is far more important—the vision needed to undertake the research. The charter for the Foundation is really a remarkable document, produced as it was by some of the leading men of our generation. Its central premise is that the great need of our time is for improvement in human behavior. It then proposes operating programs aimed at such improvement in the areas of international peace, democratic political institutions, education, and the economic order. Underpinning these action programs there was to be a Division of the Behavioral Sciences to aid basic research on human behavior, so that more and better knowledge would be available for the use of the operating programs. The conception is not unlike that of a large modern corporation which has a number of operating divisions and a research division which stockpiles knowledge *over the long run* for the use of the operating divisions.

The plan for a Behavioral Sciences Division to promote the development of basic knowledge of human behavior was idealistic, perhaps visionary, partly because the behavioral sciences are only just beginning to accumulate knowledge of major social usefulness and partly because many men regard them as less useful than they really are. At any rate, the Behavioral Sciences Division of The Ford Foundation no longer exists, but while it lasted, its patronage was magnificent, and the challenge it presented raised the sights of behavioral scientists who might otherwise have been content to work on less ambitious projects.

It was my good fortune to be associated with the Division in its early days and to absorb some of its spirit of hope and enthusiasm for the role that knowledge of human behavior might play in helping man control his destiny. The research reported here was conceived in that spirit, to determine what value our psychological knowledge of human motivation might have in understanding so complex a social phenomenon as economic development. It owes its existence therefore very largely to the vision and courage of two men—the late Rowan Gaither, Chairman of the Program Committee for the Foundation, later its President, and particular patron of the Behavioral Sciences Division; and Bernard Berelson, Director of the Division, the vigor of whose imagination was largely responsible for the major impact it had on the behavioral sciences during its all-too-short existence. Later I also received valuable additional support for the study of businessmen from the Program in Economic Development and Administration of the Foundation, under the leadership of Thomas Carroll.

Neither money nor vision alone could have created it, however. The book also owes much to a corps of advisers, devoted research associates, and assistants which is unusually large because of the wide scope of the investigation. Though it is far too inadequate a recognition for the help I received,

I wish to record here my indebtedness to John W. Atkinson, to Robert Knapp and Timothy Leary for general sympathetic advice and assistance; to B. F. Hoselitz, Gerald Meier, Gustav Papanek, and Franco Modigliani for helping me acquire what little knowledge of economics I have (though they certainly should not be held responsible for my mistakes); also to Robert H. Knapp, Bernard Rosen and Joseph Veroff, for working on their own initiative on research problems related to the general theme of the investigation; and to the members of the Research Seminar at Wesleyan University who worked through the early problems of the research design—Walter Reitman, Ralph Haber, Richard deCharms, Elliot Aronson, William Morrison, David Berlew, and Roberta Cohen.

In carrying out the research reported I am particularly indebted to Thomas E. Shipley, Jr., and David Bakan for general advice and assistance; to H. W. Wendt, John Takeshita, Arrigo Angelini and P. V. Veeraraghavan for supervising the testing of adolescent boys in Germany, Japan, Brazil and India, respectively; to Julie Maehling and Robert Cohler, Ralph Haber and Richard deCharms for help in developing the coding system for the children's readers; to Salvatore Maddi, Ellen Silver, Robert Cohler, Peter Lenrow, Norman Bradburn, and David Berlew for the exacting and tedious task of applying the coding system; to Juan Cortés for his research on Spanish economic history; to Harriet Turtletaub particularly for assistance in assembling the climatological data reported in Chapter 9; to Allan Kulakow for ratings of preliterate tribes on a variety of factors; to Marc Swartz and Donald Lathrap for help on the study of pre-Incan Peru; to Evon Vogt and Frank Miller for planning and carrying out a study of n Achievement in two Mexican villages; to Thomas Fraser and the American Friends Service Committee for a similar study in Orissa Province, India; and to John and Mary Elmendorf, Elliott Dantzig and Frank Brandenburg for their help in my brief study of problems of economic development in Mexico.

For assistance in collecting and analyzing tests from businessmen, government officials, and others, I am greatly indebted to the Sloane Fellow Program at MIT and the Middle and Advanced Management Programs at the Harvard Business School; in particular to Abraham Zaleznik, James Guyot, George Litwin, Ann Litwin, John Hill, and staff members of several industrial corporations that prefer to remain anonymous. Overseas testing of businessmen and professionals was carried out through the valued assistance of Flavia Zaccone Derossi in Italy, Norman Bradburn in Turkey, and M. Choynowski in Poland. Furthermore, the data could never have been assembled, kept in order, and analyzed without the able and conscientious assistance of Vera Aronson, Dorothy Maddi, Marian Cartland, Harry Scarr, David Winter, and particularly Richard Horowitz and Bruce Finnie, who supervised the processing of mountains of figures through the IBM machines. Last, but not least, I should like to acknowledge a very special debt to my secretary, Alice Thoren, not only for trying valiantly to keep my life in order but also for preparing the final manuscript, with the able assistance of Doris Simpson.

What ultimately made it possible for me to pull together the many threads of this research enterprise and to reflect a little on their implications was a fellowship from the Guggenheim Foundation, which was the more welcome for having no strings attached. It provided the means, and Italy the sense of perspective and of leisure, that in the end made the book possible. Its final chapters have been written under the dramatic influence of the efforts of a formerly backward country to speed its rate of economic development.

DAVID C. MCCLELLAND

Florence, Italy, July 1959
Tepoztlan, Morelos, Mexico, August 1960

Contents

1

Explaining Economic Growth

The Problem

From the top of the *campanile,* or Giotto's bell tower, in Florence, one can look out over the city in all directions, past the stone banking houses where the rich Medici lived, past the art galleries they patronized, past the magnificent cathedral and churches their money helped to build, and on to the Tuscan vineyards where the *contadino* works the soil as hard and efficiently as he probably ever did. The city below is busy with life. The university halls, the shops, the restaurants are crowded. The sound of *Vespas,* the "wasps" of the machine age, fills the air, but Florence is not today what it once was, the center in the 15th century of a great civilization, one of the most extraordinary the world has ever known. Why? What produced the Renaissance in Italy, of which Florence was the center? How did it happen that such a small population base could produce, in the short span of a few generations, great historical figures first in commerce and literature, then in architecture, sculpture and painting, and finally in science and music? Why subsequently did Northern Italy decline in importance both commercially and artistically until at the present time it is not particularly distinguished as compared with many other regions of the world? Certainly the people appear to be working as hard and energetically as ever. Was it just luck or a peculiar combination of circumstances? Historians have been fascinated by such questions ever since they began writing history, because the rise and fall of Florence or the whole of Northern Italy is by no means an isolated phenomenon. In fact, as Kroeber (1944) has demonstrated, "configurations of culture growth" are the rule rather than the exception, "successes . . . occur close together in relatively brief periods within nations or limited areas" (1944, p. vii).

This book will not take as its province all kinds of cultural growth—artistic, philosophical, military—but will try to shed some light on a narrower problem, namely, the reasons for economic growth and decline. The way wealth is distributed is a matter of special interest, partly because it may well be basic to growth in other cultural areas and partly because it has become so uneven in the past century that curiosity has been aroused. Certain countries, primarily in northern Europe and North America, have accumulated wealth probably at a faster rate and certainly to a much higher average

1

level than has ever been known before in the history of the world. In the United States, *per capita* income in constant prices rose from around $244 in 1850 to around $1140 in 1950, a five-fold increase (Woytinsky, 1953, p. 383). In Great Britain average income quadrupled in the same period. At the present time, the average *per capita* income varies tremendously from one country to another, as Table 1.1 demonstrates. Thus, the average person

TABLE 1.1 SOME REPRESENTATIVE NATIONAL DIFFERENCES IN SHARES OF POPULATION AND INCOME AND IN PER CAPITA INCOME (1948), IN U.S. DOLLARS, BY REGIONS OF THE WORLD

	Per Capita Income in U.S. dollars (1948)*	Per cent of Population (1950)**	Per cent of World Income (1948)*
North America		6.8%	42.9%
United States	$1,525		
Canada	895		
Middle America		2.1	1.3
Mexico	106		
Cuba	296		
South America		4.5	2.9
Argentina	315		
Brazil	112		
Chile	180		
Europe		15.9	26.4
United Kingdom	777		
Sweden	805		
France	418		
Poland	190		
Greece	95		
USSR	181	7.3	6.4
Asia		54.9	15.7
Turkey	143		
India	75		
Africa		8.0	2.9
Belgian Congo	35		
Union of South Africa	347		
Oceania		.5	1.5
Australia	812		

* From Woytinsky, W. S. and E. S. *World Population and Production.* New York: Twentieth Century Fund, 1953. Pp. 392-394.
** From *United Nations Statistical Yearbook 1956*, p. 37.

in northern Europe or the United States has ten to twelve times as much wealth at his disposal as the average person in most of Africa or Asia. Or, to put it in its most striking fashion, approximately 7 per cent of the world's population in North America enjoy about 43 per cent of the world's wealth, while 55 per cent of the population, in Asia, have only about 16 per cent of the world's wealth. Even a quick glance at the table raises some interesting questions. Why should Argentina lag so far behind the United States or

Australia in per capita income? Is it so much less favored by climate and natural resources? Or compare France and Poland with the United Kingdom and Sweden. The differences here in climate and natural resources are by no means outstanding, and yet there is a marked difference in economic development to date. One is led to think immediately of differences in the peoples who live in those countries—in their motives and values, social and political institutions. In fact, in our time the political question has become paramount. It is widely felt that the reason why some countries have not developed as rapidly as others is because they have been improperly governed, that is, exploited either by colonial powers or by internal minorities.

One of the fundamental differences between the Communist countries and the Western democracies lies precisely in their views as to how the people should be governed so as to bring about their economic improvement. Everyone accepts the goal of economic development as of paramount importance. Certainly one of the most striking phenomena of our times is the great effort that the populous poor nations of the world—India, China, Indonesia—are making to catch up with the industrialized West. The differences arise over how best to do it, the Communists stressing centralized authoritarian rule by a minority and the Western democracies advocating a freer participation by all segments of the population in their own self-development.

For practical political reasons, then, as well as to satisfy scientific curiosity, it has become of very great importance to understand some of the forces that produce rapid economic development. It would certainly not surprise us to discover that these forces lie largely in man himself—in his fundamental motives and in the way he organizes his relationships to his fellow man. At least it should be worth a serious attempt to see what modern psychology can contribute to an understanding of why some men concentrate on economic activities and are conspicuously successful at them. Such is the primary purpose of this book. The reader should, however, not set his hopes too high. Modern quantitative psychology is young, about fifty years old to be exact, even younger than the study of economics. And the scientific study of motives and values is even younger still. Furthermore, psychology has not concerned itself much with problems of economics. The present effort should, therefore, be viewed as a first attempt by a psychologist interested primarily in human motivation to shed some light on a problem of historic importance.

General Explanations of Cultural Growth and Decline

Before we plunge into the heart of the matter, it will be worth while to consider the problem in historical perspective. After all, many distinguished men have written on the subject of why civilizations wax and wane, or more particularly on what are the forces responsible for economic growth and decline. The psychologist's contribution can best be seen against the background of such other explanations. There may be many who feel that the psychologists can contribute little because we have explanation enough already or because no general explanation is in the end really possible. Those who take the latter point of view simply avoid the whole problem. They contend that there are too many facts that no general explanation can fit. For example, Muller, who takes what he calls the "tragic" view of history, at times appears to argue that Byzantium persisted as a great, or reasonably great, civilization for hundreds of years for no good reason whatsoever. In his words, "What kept this static civilization going? Why was it preserved by a tradition that failed to preserve Rome? I can see no very good reasons, or at least none that illustrates a satisfying philosophy of history. . . . it had a strong walled capital, with an excellent location for purposes of trade and defense. . . . it had the secret of 'Greek fire,' the diabolic weapon that scattered or destroyed enemy fleets besieging Constantinople. . . . Above all, it had good luck in its emperors during its worst crises, being periodically saved by the emergence of a strong, able ruler. This looks like mere luck, because the rise of such a savior was not provided for by any peculiar wisdom in its political institutions." (1957, p. 20.)

Muller seems to be wondering in this passage, as many skeptics have before him, whether history makes any sense at all. Most historians, however, would go at least one step further, as he himself does in this passage, and search for some particular factor—a strong ruler, a military secret, a geographical location—which contributed to the growth, preservation, or fall of a particular civilization at a particular time. Many would then stop here and regard a search for any *general* explanation of the rise and fall of civilizations as useless because the reasons are uniquely different in every case.

In a sense they are right. Every event is in some respects different from every other event. No historical epoch is precisely like any other despite the ability of men like Toynbee and Spengler to see similarities. No person is exactly like any other person. No stone, for that matter, is exactly like any other stone. Yet beginning with stones, scientists have seen similarities and made generalizations based on features that events or objects have in common without denying the uniqueness of any particular event or object. Psychologists are so used to being told that they can never make generalizations about anything so complex and variable as human nature that they may be forgiven for assuming that history could hardly be more difficult to generalize about. Perhaps if we grant at the outset that all instances of economic growth or cultural flowering are unique in some respects, the skeptics might then at least admit the possibility that certain common features of many or most of them could also be identified.

Many attempts have been made to discover such common features and arrive at general interpretations. One that is only slightly less skeptical than Muller's "ironical" view of history has much in common with the anthropologist's concept of "cultural diffusion." According to this view, mankind is engaged over space and time in a variety of social or cultural "experiments" which involve different methods of economic, political, religious or social organization. Every so often a social "mutation" occurs—a particularly fortunate combination of interests or leaders or methods of organizing different spheres of activity, a new development which leads either to growth in the economic or some other cultural sphere.

In modern times, one might focus on the technological revolution, for example, starting with basic scientific developments in the 17th century which were converted in the 18th and 19th centuries into technical inventions of very great economic value. The spread of such an obviously more successful way of dealing with the world occurs by "diffusion"; that is, other people see the advantages of the new techniques and adopt them as soon as they learn about them. In a sense, such a view of economic development is little more than a description of what happened, since it does not attempt to explain why it happened in the first place.

To the extent that it relies on "diffusion" or, as the economists would phrase it, on "trade" (Buchanan and Ellis, 1955, p. 407) as a cause of economic development elsewhere, the case is certainly not a very strong one. China certainly knew about many of the technical developments in the West from the time of Marco Polo onward, yet was not recognizably eager to adopt them until the present century. Even more striking is the Moslem contact with the West, which was reasonably close in the Mediterranean throughout the entire period when the West was developing technically and economically at such a rapid rate. Yet very little of Western methods or techniques managed to "diffuse" by trade into the Middle East. By way of contrast consider Japan which, although it came in contact with Western ideas much later than did the Arab world, absorbed technological advances at a much more rapid rate. Some channels of communication along which knowledge of better techniques can be carried are undoubtedly necessary, but are not in themselves sufficient to produce economic growth in another country. Diffusion out of a "social mutation" appears to describe some cases of development but does not go far toward explaining any of them.

More strictly explanatory are two theories which, as Toynbee points out, have been favorites ever since scholars began worrying about the problem— namely, race and climate. Perhaps some peoples are simply more energetic, or some climates are simply more favorable to culture growth. For instance, one can argue that Nordic peoples have played a significant role in the rise of more great civilizations than any other group. One can assert that it was they who entered Greece from the North as the wandering Achaeans and produced the flowering of Ancient Greece, with some side-effects on India through Alexander's conquests; that they were largely responsible for the "Protestant ethic" which figured so prominently in the rise of modern capitalism (Wax, 1955); and that they are now among the richest people on earth. Even if we overlook the problem of defining "they" in statements like these, the basic difficulty remains, as with all racial theories, that such assertions do not explain why a particular people are more energetic at some times than others.

Thus it is hard to imagine, for example, that the gene pool in Florence and Northern Italy was markedly different in the 17th century from what it had been in the 15th and 16th; yet the Renaissance was largely over and the "race" was no longer productive.

It is strange how the fascination for biological explanations of economic development persists in view of such an elementary difficulty. Fanfani, a leading contemporary Italian politician and formerly a professor of economics, has written a book (1935) in which he refutes Max Weber's thesis that Protestantism had something to do with the rise of capitalism. He argues that Catholicism invented modern capitalism long before Protestantism appeared on the scene and pursued business just as energetically. But Fanfani, still faced with the obvious fact that the Protestant countries are wealthier than the Catholic countries, decides that the shape of their heads must be a factor: long-headed people make better businessmen. But even if this could be proven by careful statistical study (and it certainly never has been), how explain the fact that long-headed people did not show any particular concern for business during lengthy periods of history? The same objection appears to apply to more recent attempts by Sheldon (1940) and Morris (1948) to associate vigorous cultural activity with mesomorphy, a body structure in which muscle predominates. It is difficult to believe that the proportion of mesomorphy shifted enough in the 50-or 100-year period of the Renaissance to explain the sudden flowering of arts and sciences.

To a considerable extent, environmental explanations run into the same problem. Was the climate of Northern Italy suddenly more stimulating for one to two hundred years? Or what happened to the climate in Greece in the 8th or 7th century B.C. to stimulate culture growth there, and not in adjacent geographical areas such as the Italian or Iberian peninsulas? Climate has one advantage as an explanation over race. It is known to change rather dramatically in the same area over reasonably long periods of time. Thus, it is at least conceivable that a series of favorable growing seasons occurring in succession could produce the economic surplus necessary to stimulate a sustained period of growth. On the negative side, it is even easier to find instances of environmental calamities, such as prolonged droughts or plagues, which could seriously interfere with the continued economic development of a country.

Huntington (1915) has made perhaps the best case for the role of climate in the production of great civilizations. He points out that none of the great civilizations, at least as we understand the term today, has ever flourished in the tropics or in the far North. In fact, he argues quite specifically that the most stimulating climate for man involves a mean temperature range between winter and summer of 40° to 60°F with moderate rainfall and frequent mild storms. His classification of climates in terms of the energy they presumably evoke in man corresponds fairly closely to the climates of those regions of the world where high civilizations either now exist or have existed in the past. Climate may very well set some limits on the places where man can build a high civilization, but it does little to pinpoint specifically why growth occurs rapidly in one place rather than another in the same energy belt. Thus, both Poland and Great Britain are in the same "very high energy" belt (see Woytinsky, 1953, p. 30), but, as Table 1.1 shows, the average *per capita* income in England is some seven or eight times that of Poland. Climate is at best a gross limiting factor, and much more detailed knowledge is needed of specific variations within favorable or unfavorable environments.

Toynbee, while specifically rejecting an environmental theory of the rise and fall of civilizations, still managed to write most of *A Study of History* (1947) in terms of a modified environmental theory. For him it is the "challenge of the environment" which is responsible for the genesis of civilizations. As he employs the term, "environment" refers not only to geography, but also to social conditions. What is important is the "stimulus" which may arise from hard countries, from new soil to exploit, from living in a frontier position, from being penalized as a minority group. The stimulus must be neither too strong nor too weak, but just right. Thus the Vikings were stimulated by Iceland, but Greenland proved too severe a challenge for them. The Chinese have responded vigorously to mild social discrimination against them in Malaya but have "yielded" to a much stronger discrimination against them in California. The difficulty with Toynbee's theory is that it is so general that it cannot possibly be wrong. If a civilization has shown a creative response, it *must* have had just the right amount of stimulus. And since the stimulus may come from a large number of different sources— climate, the pressures of other peoples, internal conditions, etc.—the historian can always "prove" that the stimulus was "just right." Such a theory has very little explanatory power and certainly no predictive power. That is, if an underdeveloped country were to ask what should be done to promote its economic growth, all that one could answer in Toynbee's terms is that it should be provided with just the right amount of "stimulus." Undoubtedly this is true but not very helpful.

Spengler's general theory (1932) is even less useful. He believed that cultures are like organisms: they grow, live and die; unfortunately he is not very specific as to why some grow at particular times and not at others. Apparently it is all part of some "master plan" or Law of Nature. Kroeber (1944) is much more inductive than Spengler, but specifically disavows any intent to find a general explanation for the cultural configurations he has described. The closest he comes to a general explanation is that patterns of culture cannot achieve higher quality unless they "commit themselves to certain specializations, and exclude others." The specialized "pattern in question tends to develop cumulatively" and then "explores and traverses the new opportunities lying in its selective path until less and less of these remain, and at last none." (1944, p. 763.) In terms of economic development, which Kroeber does not specifically consider, one might argue that growth occurs when a people specializes in the means of production. Such a generalization does not get us far, but at least it narrows our attention on the more specific problem of why some people have focused their interest on economic, and in our time technological, activity.

Explanations in Economic Terms

We come, then, to more specifically economic, or psychological and social explanations of an increase in material welfare. Perhaps we can find something in the motives, customs, or institutions of men that will account for overachievement in the economic sphere. It is time to turn to the account of the process given by those who have specialized in economics. There exists by now such an extensive and thorough body of literature dealing with economic history and theory that it will be impossible to deal with it in any but the simplest terms. Our purpose is more to illustrate the approach of the economist rather than to evaluate critically his contributions to the understanding of economic development.

Basically, the economist's model of development is a rational one in which enlightened self-interest of man converts pressures acting on the economic system from inside or outside into activities resulting in greater productivity or wealth. For example, a new method of production is invented which leads to improved productivity—say the invention of the wire cable which enabled miners to get coal out of the ground without carrying it on their backs. It was "obviously" to the mine owner's advantage to develop such an invention in order to get more coal out faster and thus to have a competitive advantage over other mine owners. Likewise it was to the advantage of other owners to adopt the new technique as fast as possible to regain their competitive position. Man's self-interest and an event which changed the economic equilibrium so that he was at an advantage or disadvantage might thus explain the resulting increases in economic activity and productivity. Even today this model continues to dominate the thinking of most economists because of its great simplicity and convincing a priori reasonableness.

For example, Buchanan and Ellis, in discussing the agricultural revolution in England in the early 19th century, point out that the improved methods and techniques of cultivation which had been developed spread rather slowly "because people learn slowly even when they have for an example the evident success of their fellows. Even with the benefit of demonstrations, lectures, and reading matter, the improved agricultural techniques only gradually became general practice over the decades. It took longer still for them to spread over Europe from England. The hard economic realities of cost, income and profit, or the necessity of getting a living probably had as much to do with converting the average landlord, squire, worker, or peasant to the new practices as friendly exhortations or the gracious patronage of royalty. Yet surely this is not a peculiarity of 18th- or 19th-century England or Europe. Do not people usually change and adapt their ways only under pressure?" (1955, p. 131.)

Given such a predominantly rational psychology, the economists could focus their attention on the key events that disturbed the economic equilibrium and produced the adaptive response of increased *per capita* output. While the thinking of various economic theorists has varied in important ways, it is still possible to get a good idea of their general approach under four main headings: capital accumulation (including technological improvements), population changes, division of labor, and entrepreneurship. Since economic theory began as a serious enterprise early in the 19th century during the first part of the Industrial Revolution in England, it is not surprising that many theorists, beginning with Adam Smith, concluded that the invention of better machines and equipment was responsible for the increased productivity.

It was not just a question of wire cables for mines, but of steam engines for driving power looms, of improved techniques for refining iron which made railroads possible, which in turn improved transportation facilities, etc. Dozens of such technical improvements in England in the 19th century made production more efficient and increased profits, which could then be reinvested in the business largely through internal financing—so that more technical improvements could be made to increase productivity further, and so on in a beneficent cycle. The technological revolution seemed clearly "responsible" for great increases in material welfare in modern times. The point was stressed again, especially by the neoclassical economists in the late 19th century, who had had an even greater opportunity to observe the extraordinary effects on the economy of technical improvements. Karl Marx, writing at the same time, also stressed the importance of technology as a determining force in history. Technology, said Marx, hastened the class struggle, because the capitalists would strive to install machinery because it obviously increased the "surplus value" created by the efforts of the workers. On the other hand, the workers would soon see that machines were replacing them, forcing them to live at lower wages, and they would eventually conclude that the only way out of the vicious circle was to seize power for themselves.

Population growth also figured as a major force affecting economic growth in the early writings of economists. Smith and Ricardo both thought that in a period of rising wages "the reward of labor must necessarily encourage in such a manner the marriage and multiplication of laborers, as may enable them to supply that continually increasing demand by a continually increasing population." (Meier and Baldwin, 1957, p. 23.) In general, however, they saw an increased population not as a stimulus to growth but as a result of growth which would inevitably slow it down, leading to a final stationary state. Thus Ricardo argued that the increase in population would, of course, increase the need for food and eventually bring into cultivation less productive land, causing a rise in prices because the use of such land was less efficient. The rise in prices would be followed by a rise in wages, which would decrease profit for the capitalist, who then would invest less—and the cycle of growth would eventually slow down and stop. In the 20th century, large populations have also been seen mainly as a negative force preventing the rapid economic growth of undeveloped countries today. However, Keynes (1936) did argue that an increasing population could also affect demand, which might operate to stimulate investment and eventually facilitate growth. For example, there was some concern in the 1920's and 1930's specifically over the low birth rate and net reproduction rate in France. Could this not account for the relative stagnation in her economy? But whether it speeds or slows economic growth, population is nearly always considered by economic theorists as one of the major forces affecting rate of growth.

Division of labor or specialization and rationalization of productive functions is another such force. In Adam Smith's view, "greater division of labor and specialization lead (1) to an increase in dexterity among workers; (2) to a reduction in the time necessary to produce commodities; and (3) to the invention of better machines and equipment." (Meier and Baldwin, 1957, p. 21.) Eventually the application of this idea led to the development of the factory system in which thousands of employees performed relatively routine tasks because that was the most efficient form of quantity production. Marx and the Communists dramatized, on the one hand, the absolute necessity for the capitalists to centralize and rationalize production in this way and, on the other, the degrading effect that such production methods inevitably had on the self-esteem of the worker—and, eventually, on his economic welfare. But no one denied the importance of rationalization of productive acts to achieve maximum efficiency. Schumpeter (1934) even felt that the principle of rationalism was bound to be applied not only to the economic sphere, but to art, science, and religion as well, so that eventually the process of invention would be rationalized, and even business management itself. Consequently the modern economic system would eventually destroy the key force which produced it—namely, the creative innovating entrepreneur, for whom there would be no need in the new, completely rationalized social order.

Entrepreneurship is the fourth key force making for economic development in the view of many economists. Certainly, Ricardo thought of economic problems largely from the point of view of the capitalist, or landowner, who could invest his income in various ways, organize production, rent his land, advance wages, and the like. In fact, considerations of profit or return on investment guided his decisions to behave in one way or another. For Marx, too, the so-called "profit motive" necessarily became the "prime mover" for the bourgeois capitalist class as well as the cause of its inevitable doom, because in pursuing it so single-mindedly the capitalist class eventually forced the workers to organize and revolt. But it remained for Schumpeter (1934) to glorify the role of the entrepreneur and to make him the key figure in economic development. Schumpeter felt that the economy did not grow "naturally" or inevitably, or even steadily, but rather was pushed forward in sudden leaps by the activities of key men who wanted to promote new goods and new methods of production, or to exploit a new source of materials or a new market. The motivation was not merely profit, but also the "desire to found a private dynasty, the will to conquer in a competitive battle, and the joy of creating." In other words, Schumpeter's entrepreneur is not entirely a rational, profit-oriented human being, making his decisions to invest in one way or another solely on the basis of rational calculations. (Meier and Baldwin, 1957, p. 88.)

The Need for Psychological and Sociological Explanations

Where does the psychologist fit into this picture? Why is he needed at all? Are not the economists' explanations in such terms as the above sufficient to account for economic growth? Interestingly enough, the economic theorists themselves seem to have always felt that sources of change in the economic system lay outside the system itself. Thus it was not really clear to them why technical inventions of practical importance should appear more frequently at one period in history than in another, or why once having appeared in one country, they should spread more rapidly to country A than country B. Or consider the position of neoclassical economists like Marshall (1930). They placed great emphasis on the importance of saving so that profits could be reinvested in the expansion of business, but Marshall, at any rate, recognized that thrift is not something which people automatically practice when it is in their interest to do so. Propensities to save and invest and other attitudes necessary for economic growth appear in the end to be not economic but psychological variables. As early as 1904, the great German sociologist Max Weber was stressing the fact that such attitudes as economic rationality and the enterprising spirit of modern capitalism were consequences of certain religious world views stressed particularly by Protestant Calvinist sects. He thus laid the groundwork for efforts to understand the social and psychological origins of such key economic forces as rapid technological advances, specialization of labor, population growth, and energetic entrepreneurship.

The modern economist has become even more insistent in his belief that the ultimate forces underlying economic development lie, strictly speaking, outside the economic sphere. As Meier and Baldwin put it, half humorously, "economic development is much too serious a topic to be left to economists." (1957, p. 119.) Further, in criticizing the neoclassical economists, they point out that the neoclassical economic model simply takes for granted too many noneconomic factors, such as political stability, the "will to develop," thrift, fixed tastes, adequate supply of trained labor and managerial skill, factor mobility, rapid flow of knowledge, etc. (1957, p. 83.) While such assumptions make it possible to give a fairly adequate account of what did happen at a particular period in the growth of a particular country, they do not produce a general model which has much value for underdeveloped countries or even for different time periods in the same country when any one of these key factors is different.

Some concrete illustrations will make the point clearer. A common assumption made by economic theorists, particularly by Keynes and his followers, is that investment depends upon consumption or demand. That is, if there is demand for something, a man ought to be able to get a higher rate of interest for lending his money to someone who wants to use it to make what is needed. So the capitalist would be more likely to invest his capital, or the entrepreneur to expand his business, under conditions of rising demand. Likewise, he should not invest or expand his business when the demand is obviously falling. It was from such reasoning that the Keynesians concluded that a rising population could stimulate economic growth. But David McCord Wright questions the validity of the underlying assumption.

"Is it true that investment in the real world will be made only on a rising demand? To show how mistaken the idea is, when stated as a universal principle, let us ask ourselves under what circumstances a brewer, say, might build a new brewery even though the volume of total beer sales, or the price of beer, or both, were falling. There are three cases: the better beer, the cheaper beer, and what I have called the 'bullheaded brewer.' If a man invents a new kind of beer which he thinks is going to attract sales from other brands, it may pay him to build a new brewery even though general beer sales are falling. And the shot in the arm given by his new construction *could* raise not only general beer sales but employment in other lines as well. Next, if a man gets hold of a new and much cheaper method of brewing, it may pay to build a new brewery even though beer sales and prices are falling. For though prices are declining, say two per cent, if costs are reduced twenty per cent, a substantial profit margin remains. Finally, a businessman may simply feel that he is smarter than the market and he (the 'bullheaded brewer') may go ahead and build though things are still depressed. And it is again undeniable that his courage and the stimulus of the construction he is carrying through may start the economy once more expanding." (Wright, 1958.)

There are two interesting points about Wright's critique. First he wants to study how people actually make their investment decisions "in the real world." To the extent that he wants to know the attitudes of real people under various conditions, he is calling for the empirical techniques developed by psychologists and sociologists—for interviews and questionnaires. This represents a departure from the attitude of the traditional economist who works much more deductively starting with "self-evident" propositions like the ones criticized here and working from them logically to conclusions about economic changes. Secondly, while better beer and cheaper beer are rational economic considerations of the usual sort, the "bullheaded brewer" definitely is not. He is a problem for the psychologists, since economic considerations cannot predict whether he is going to invest or not. Under what conditions are people likely to be "bullheaded"? Can psychologists provide a measure of individual differences in "bullheadedness"? It is at such points as these the psychologist may be of some use to economics.

What Wright is calling attention to, of course, is the fact that men do not behave entirely according to rational considerations. In fact, there seems to be considerable reason for doubting that the initial impetus to economic growth is in any sense rational. Take, for example, the opening of the West in the United States in the 19th century. By what rational considerations could the building of railroads across the continent be justified when there were populations of negligible significance on the West Coast? The economic unsoundness of the venture was clearly demonstrated to thousands of investors who lost their money in railroad shares. Yet without the railroads, the United States could certainly not have developed as rapidly as it did. In the long run the venture proved sound, though it looked absolutely absurd to many reasonable men at the time. For exactly the same reasons it is hard to explain in rational economic terms why men settled in the Middle West in the 1860's and 1870's. Trollope (1862), in his travels down the Mississippi River, could never stop marveling at why people who knew better would voluntarily choose to live under such primitive conditions in caves or sod huts. He found them laboring from dawn to dark just to keep alive and with no immediate prospect of improvement in their lot. Yet they were cheerful about the future and did not want to return to "civilization," even though they were under no compelling reasons to leave it in the first place. Their behavior is the more impressive by contrast with peoples in South America and Java who have refused to leave crowded urban centers for fertile, unsettled lands not far away. Economists have sometimes felt impelled to attribute the hope of enormous material gain to migrants as the reason for their behavior, but the fact is they appear to have been motivated largely by considerations not exclusively materialistic at all. Yet, without the determination of such people, the West could never have been opened up to "rational" exploitation.

Professor Paul Lazarsfeld has illustrated the point dramatically by asking, "What rational capitalist would have invested in Gutenberg?" Suppose, he says, that Gutenberg, being much impressed by the new technique he had invented for printing books, had decided to expand his business and produce more books. Suppose further that he needed capital and asked a rich banker to supply it so that he could build a better printing press, hire more labor, or buy more materials for turning out more books. The banker, being a shrewd and rational businessman (having accumulated his money by reason of such virtues) would question the wiseness of his investment. He might then investigate a little as to the need for more books by interviewing friends and acquaintances and estimating the market for books. Even with the services of a modern market survey organization, which would have conducted a poll among a representative sample of all walks of life, he would undoubtedly have come to the following conclusions: the demand for new books was clearly not sufficient to warrant investing in Gutenberg's new technique because (1) very few people could read, (2) those who could read had all they could do to keep up with the books they had and certainly didn't have time to read any more, and (3) they were not sure that they would want to buy Gutenberg's books anyway, because they were printed by a mechanical process and therefore were certain to be less varied and aesthetically pleasing than handmade books in the long run. Quite aside from these compelling economic reasons for not investing in the enterprise, the banker, if a responsible citizen, might also hesitate to invest because the process would create technological unemployment by making less work for those who produced books by hand and because to encourage more people to read might be politically dangerous. The fable is not so fantastic as it may sound. We are accustomed to looking at inventions and technological improvements from the point of view of their subsequent history. If the invention proved an economic success, we almost unconsciously assume that the promotion of the invention was economically justifiable on rational grounds *at the time*. This clearly seems not to have been the case in many instances. It was only the simultaneous irrational efforts of many people that ultimately justified the enterprise of some of them. (Sawyer, 1954.)

Nowhere does such a conclusion force itself on one's attention more vividly than in the consideration of the current plight of underdeveloped countries. In terms of traditional economic analysis, it is hard to see how they can ever advance at all. The risks are too great for the entrepreneur, since there is no apparent demand for his products. The labor force is not trained in the skills needed for a machine world. Inventions are lacking which fit peculiar local conditions, and those from the West cannot be utilized because of lack of capital to buy them or the human or other resources necessary to use them once bought. Moreover, population is increasing faster than productivity. To an economist used to thinking in exclusively rational terms, the case indeed looks pretty hopeless; no reasonable man would invest in an underdeveloped country, any more than Lazarsfeld's banker would have invested in Gutenberg. It is precisely such considerations that have forced many modern economists to look beyond the traditional rational or utilitarian model. These economists are deeply concerned with the problem of underdeveloped areas and with the means of accelerating their growth. Realization of the difficulties involved has forced many of them to modify even the traditional economist's defense against those who argue that noneconomic forces must be also taken into consideration. This defense has been to admit that, while irrational motives, changes in taste, risk-taking attitudes, and the like may indeed modify to some extent the deductions made from the rational model, nevertheless the traditional economic considerations are *in the main* the key ones; thus the economist can, for practical purposes, neglect "irrational" factors, even while admitting they have some influence. At the very least, this defense has crumbled to the point of stating that, so far as poor countries are concerned, the irrational social and psychological factors are so important that programs for aiding development ought not to be conceived in purely economic terms. The need seems clear for help from psychologists and sociologists who specialize in such factors.

Psychological and Sociological Explanations of Economic Growth

Some theorists, of course, came to this conclusion long ago and have attempted to fill the gap with hypotheses as to what psychological or sociological factors are responsible for setting the economic forces in motion that produce development. Economists like Rostow, for example, have insisted that economic theory must be linked ultimately to sociological and psychological constructs if it is to be maximally useful. As a first step in this direction, he lists six basic "human motives" or "human propensities" which economic analysis suggests are important for development, as follows (Rostow, 1952, pp. 14, 15):

1. to develop fundamental science
2. to apply science to economic ends
3. to accept innovations
4. to seek material advance
5. to consume
6. to have children

Rostow discusses the various factors which may influence these propensities, but recognizes fully that they represent an economist's thinking about psychological characteristics which may not coincide with the way the psychologist would conceptualize human motives. That is, a propensity like willingness "to apply science to economic ends" may not be of basic importance to a psychologist, but derivable from some other motive directly measured by the psychologist. Lewis (1955) in a sense goes much further than Rostow in discussing distinctly psychological variables which he feels influence economic progress. For example, he argues that the "desire for goods" is an obvious psychological factor determining how hard people strive to increase their material welfare. He argues further that asceticism decreases the desire for goods because it ultimately lowers consumption and places a positive value on prayer and other noneconomic activities—a conclusion that on the surface seems directly opposed to the tradition established by Max Weber that Protestant asceticism increased productivity by preventing people from spending money on themselves and allowing them only to use it for productive ends. The desire for goods, Lewis further argues, may be decreased by a low valuation of economic activity, and by limited knowledge as to what is available for purchase. In other words, people don't demand radios if they prefer to spend their time meditating or if they don't know radios exist. He also discusses the importance of such nonrational psychological variables as the attitude toward work—some people clearly work harder than others—and the spirit of adventure—some people are more willing to take risks, or to hurt others in competition. In discussing such factors, Lewis goes well beyond the confines of traditional economic theory which, if it treats such matters at all, considers them as minor influences or sources of error in a predominantly rational model. He is inventing, so to speak, a psychology of wants and attitudes which would be of some help to an economic theorist. In passing it may be noticed that in doing so he is using the traditional *a priori* method of the economist. He has no concrete empirical measures of the variables he is talking about, so that the behavioral scientist would have to regard his conclusions as interesting "armchair speculation," but there is clearly no reason why the propositions he and Rostow advance could not be empirically tested.

Sociologists, as might be expected, have dealt much more explicitly with noneconomic variables than have the economists, and for a much longer time. As noted above, Max Weber started a very important tradition over fifty years ago when he traced the roots of the modern capitalist spirit to an ascetic Protestant emphasis on hard work in one's calling on this earth. He made many other important contributions to the analysis of the social structure of modern industrial and bureaucratic society which have been developed and elaborated largely by Parsons and his students (1951, 1956, 1958) in the United States. What these sociologists have concentrated on is a description of the important characteristics of the social structure of modern industrialized societies which differentiate them from traditional societies.

For example, in Parsons' terminology, developed countries are characterized by the prevalence of achievement norms, universalism and specificity, whereas underdeveloped countries are characterized by ascriptive norms, particularism and diffuseness. That is, in developed countries people are evaluated in terms of what they can do (achieved status) rather than in terms of who they are (ascribed status); anyone is at least ideally able to compete for any job (universalism), rather than being permitted only to do particular jobs as in a caste system (particularism); and the relationship of one man to another is typically more *specific*, or limited to the labor contract, rather than *diffuse* as in a traditional society where economic relationships are tied intimately to all sorts of other relationships involving kinship, political, religious and other social structures.

Such a description of types of variables introduced by the sociologists in describing the social systems of developed and underdeveloped countries is meant only to give the flavor of their approach, since their point of view permeates the rest of the book. What is in order at this point are only two general comments about much sociological thinking to date. First, it has never really seriously attempted to bridge the gap between idealized "pattern variables" as tools of analysis, and social norms as present in the minds of men. Stated another way, it is not always clear just how a characteristic of social structure like stress on "achieved" versus "ascribed" status should be reflected in the attitudes of members of that social structure so that one can check empirically whether those attitudes are in fact present in a society where they are theoretically supposed to be present. Florence Kluckhohn (1950) has made some steps in this direction, and others will be taken in the present research, but the theoretical relationship between questionnaire and interview data and the social structure variables they are supposed to be getting at has not as yet been perfectly worked out.

Secondly, sociological descriptions of developed countries as contrasted with underdeveloped ones may give rise to the belief that it is the social characteristics of the developed countries which have *caused* them to grow more rapidly. That is, if achieved status is a norm characteristic of developed rather than underdeveloped countries, is it not logical to infer that achieved status is in part responsible for economic development? Hoselitz has nicely illustrated the fallacy in this point of view in commenting on some recommendations made by United Nations experts to promote the economic development of underdeveloped areas. "These men envisage that economic development is only possible if the social relations of underdeveloped countries are reformed so as to resemble those of Western capitalist countries." He then goes on to quote from Kindleberger who comments in a similar vein on the reports of the World Bank: "Essentially, however, these are essays in comparative statics. The missions bring to the underdeveloped country a notion of what a developed country is like. They observe the underdeveloped country. They subtract the latter from the former. The difference is a program. Most of the missions come from developed countries with highly articulated institutions for achieving social, economic, and political ends. Ethnocentricity leads inevitably to the conclusion that the way to achieve the comparable levels of capital formation, productivity, and consumption is to duplicate these institutions." (Hoselitz, 1954, pp. 20-21.)

Earlier sociologists were particularly apt to make this mistake. William Graham Sumner, America's most influential sociologist at the end of the 19th century, did not hesitate to argue boldly that it was exactly the characteristics of the contemporary Protestant ideal which produced economic growth. In Hofstadter's words, he "assumed that the industrious, temperate, and frugal man of the Protestant ideal was the equivalent of the 'strong' or the 'fittest' in the struggle for existence." (Hofstadter, 1955, p. 51.) "The first fact in life," Sumner asserted, "is the struggle for existence; the greatest forward step in this struggle is the production of capital, which increases the fruitfulness of labor and provides the necessary means of an advance in civilization. Primitive man, who long ago withdrew from the competitive struggle and ceased to accumulate capital goods, must pay with a backward and unenlightened way of life. . . . Physical inheritance is a vital part of the Darwinian theory; the social equivalent of physical inheritance is the instruction of the children in the necessary economic virtues." (Hofstadter, 1955, p. 58.)

Other sociologists who criticized Sumner drew different conclusions from other aspects of the social structure of the industrializing nations, but the point is that the discussion continued largely on a level which confused what *is* with what *ought* to be—"ought" sometimes in the moral sense and sometimes in the scientific sense of necessary for economic growth. Modern sociologists did not so easily fall into this error, although their methodology and lack of knowledge of what produces cultural change sometimes makes it difficult for them to avoid it. For example, Parsons and Smelser suggest (1956, p. 252 ff.) that the separation of ownership and control may have been a structural change in the American economy that provided an impetus to further economic growth. It is undeniable that such a change did occur in the United States more than say, in France, and that the United States developed much more rapidly than France did. However, such evidence falls considerably short of establishing that the divorce of ownership and control is an essential, rather than an accidental, feature of differences in rates of growth. Parsons and Smelser recognize the dangers of generalizing too hastily from a particular case and would probably agree with Hoselitz that "we may better begin by developing theoretical models for different types of societies in different types of transition or movements from 'traditional' to more 'modern' forms of economic organization." (Cf. Hoselitz, 1955.) In other words, more description is necessary. While no one could possibly quarrel with such a conclusion, it may be possible to go beyond such descriptions to more fundamental explanations by turning to psychology and to more systematic methods for isolating causal variables.

But the psychologist has been of little help to date. He has had practically nothing to say that would contribute to an understanding of economic development. It is true that psychologists have done extensive work in recent decades on consumer preferences, on ideal working conditions, and even on the relationship of income level to saving and investment, to check some Keynesian hypotheses (see, for example, Katona, 1951 and Katona, et al., 1954). However, only the latter deals directly with a matter possibly con-

nected with economic development and then only with one specific derivation from a theoretical model in a particular country at a particular time.
The fact is that most psychologists have not been much interested in economics since it does not represent for them a field of basic science, but one
in which general psychological principles might some day be applied. Even
the present book is, strictly speaking, an accident. It was in no sense motivated by a desire to find answers to the kinds of problems of interest to
economists and sociologists of the sort just reviewed. It began with a purely
theoretical problem in psychological science—namely, the attempt to isolate
and measure quantitatively a few key human motives. Only after considerable
basic research on these motives had been done did the idea present itself
that one of them might have something to do with economic growth. The
research to be reported here was designed and carried out to follow up that
idea, to attempt to apply psychological knowledge and techniques of investigation to a problem of real interest to economists and sociologists.

Testing Explanations of Economic Growth

In our review of previous explanations of economic growth—whether
general, economic, or noneconomic—we were repeatedly critical of them
on the grounds that they were not empirically or systematically tested. The
fact is that traditions for gathering evidence for or against a general proposition in economics and history are different from what they are in the behavioral sciences and it would be well to make the differences explicit at
the outset. In a word, the behavioral scientist follows—as in this book—
the tradition of the logic of experimental design as established by R. A.
Fisher (1951) and others, whereas the economist and historian ordinarily
follow an older scholarly tradition which relies heavily on the logic of the
extreme case, on the citing of key examples, and on the opinion of outstanding authorities. Since the newer methods were developed precisely to
handle the confusion that arises from unsystematic testing of hypotheses in
biology and psychology, they should be useful in economics and history
as well. Since they are not widely used for understanding problems like
what determines economic growth, let us examine briefly what it would
mean to apply them to such a problem.

Consider first the distinction between forming a hypothesis and empirically
testing it, a distinction not always carefully observed in economic theorizing.
Hypotheses are commonly arrived at by observing a few cases or by reasoning from logical extremes. For example, it seems eminently reasonable to
advance the proposition that health and welfare have something to do with
economic productivity. One can readily imagine cases in which a people
are so undernourished or riddled with disease that they cannot work hard
or efficiently. So the hypothesis is proposed that improving health and
nutrition will help speed economic growth. Thus Buchanan and Ellis state,

"better health and sanitation, in other words, do not merely reduce mortality rates but also result in an improved factor of production—a better labor supply." (1955, p. 116.) While such a proposition is undoubtedly true for extremes where practically all the adult males and females are sick, it is not a "self-evident truth" that better health and sanitation *within the limits* in which these factors ordinarily operate in large populations will have any effect on productivity. The case of the German factory workers after World War II is enough to show the need for a careful empirical test of the hypothesis. Despite poor nutrition, they managed to achieve a higher level of productivity than many better fed and healthier people. In short, the reasonableness of a generalization or explanation is no substitute for a collection of all the instances which it is supposed to cover to see whether in fact it holds in the main or not. To my knowledge a simple test of the association between standards of health and nutrition and national rates of economic growth has never been made, although there is no real reason why it could not be made, perhaps even without great difficulty. Until it is confirmed by actual data, it would certainly seem the part of wisdom for economists and others to refrain from recommending to underdeveloped countries that if they want rapid economic growth they should emphasize better health and nutrition.

Similarly reasonable but untested hypotheses are very common in writing about economic development. Consider the following examples:

1. *Investment depends primarily on the rate of interest.* Has anyone systematically correlated the amount of foreign capital invested in various countries with the prevailing rates of interest in those countries? In fact, Simon concludes (1959, p. 264) that empirical studies show "the rate of interest is not an important factor in investment decisions."

2. *Tropical countries are not highly developed economically because peoples living in hot climates do not work as hard.* Has anyone plotted a measure of "working hard" for a culture against climatic conditions? Has "working hard" been related to economic growth?

3. *People will not demand what it is obviously foolish for them to want—i.e., ice cream will not be popular at the Poles.* As a matter of fact, Eskimos like ice cream very much and have long made it themselves.

4. *High regard for the business role (as contrasted with other occupations) is partly responsible for rapid economic advance.* Is there in fact a correlation between national rates of economic growth and prestige of business occupations in various countries as determined by standard survey techniques? Why is it that Rosenberg (1957) finds in the most economically advanced country in the world, the United States, that very few Cornell students want to enter business, and many of those who plan such careers do so reluctantly?

5. *Lack of trade barriers, i.e., a large market as in the United States,*

promotes economic growth. Is size of tariff-free trade area correlated with national rates of growth? Is Switzerland just one exception to this rule?

The point should be clear by now: reasonable hypotheses of this sort constitute the great bulk of theorizing about economic development but they cannot be regarded as self-evident. They need to be empirically checked, however reasonable they appear to be, and can, often rather easily, be tested by application of simple statistical methods.

The primary requisite of such tests is some objective measure of the variables thought to be related. That is, we must be able to compare numerically "rates of economic growth" or at least be able to decide when an economy is "growing" or "contracting." Much confusion has arisen in the past because instead of expending energy in the direction of getting simple objective measures, scholars have traditionally tried to make informed subjective estimates based on a thorough knowledge of the economy in question. From a complete knowledge of its antecedents, institutions, and its productivity in the arts or in warfare, they decide that a culture was growing more or less rapidly in such-and-such a century, that it reached its peak during such-and-such a period, and declined thereafter. The difficulty with accepting such conclusions is obvious: equally wise men who thoroughly study the same culture come to different conclusions as to when it reached its peak. Thus, in Gibbon's estimate the Eastern Roman-Byzantine Empire did not amount to much, while Muller thinks it showed "astonishing vitality. . . . Offhand, the Byzantine Empire had every reason to go down as Rome did; yet it survived the fall of the 'Eternal City' by a thousand years, maintaining a high civilization despite constant pressure from barbarians and infidels." (Muller, 1957, pp. 13-14.) Toynbee, on the other hand, decided that the Eastern Roman Empire was finished by the 7th century A.D. and that a new "imitative" empire started a hundred years or so later which lasted only a short time. Which learned historian was correct about the Byzantine Empire's cultural growth?

Or consider Toynbee's disagreement with Gibbon on the date of Rome's decline. For Gibbon the high period of Roman history was under the Antonines, whereas Toynbee feels that it had started to fall long before this time. Or when was the great period in the history of Ancient Greece? Most people would think immediately of the "Golden Age" of Pericles in the 5th century B.C., yet Heichelheim (1938) or Rostovtseff in *The Social and Economic History of the Hellenistic World* place the peak of economic development some two centuries later in the first half of the third century B.C.

The reason for such disagreements is often that different standards of judgment are used as to what constitutes growth and decline. Some of these standards refer to the arts, some to economics, and some to religion. Since an over-all synthetic judgment is often made, a particular historian or philosopher may give different weight to each of these factors, arriving at a somewhat different final conclusion. Scientists solved similar problems in dealing with natural phenomena by deciding on or creating explicitly objective measures of what they were investigating. The same approach might be used with profit here. It is difficult, but certainly not impossible (see Chapters 3 and 4) to derive quantitative measures reflecting changes in economic or other activities of a culture. For example, Kroeber's great contribution in this area (1944) is that he was able to describe cultural "bursts" of activity much more precisely than previous theorists by the simple method of counting the number of men of great distinction who flourished in a given field of human endeavor in a given time period. One may of course, quarrel over whether any particular measure is adequate, but at least it represents a distinct advance over a situation in which no measures are employed and no certain knowledge can be accumulated because every wise man's considered judgment differs as to what was happening at a specific period.

Once measures have been decided on, the next task is to collect all the instances that provide a test of the hypothesis. If they cannot all be obtained, at least a representative sample is necessary. These instances are then classified according to whether they fit the generalization or not, to see whether it holds true "in the main." It is obviously important to consider *all* types of instances because it has long been common practice for scholars to cite case after case supporting a hypothesis while failing to mention contrary evidence. Toynbee, for example, proceeds in this way in supporting by the "method of triads" his thesis that a moderate challenge from the environment leads to cultural growth. Thus he notes that European colonists were optimally stimulated by Massachusetts, but found Labrador provided too much challenge and Dixie too little. But then why did the same colonists respond so favorably to Southern Australia or Northern New Zealand, where the challenge in climatic or any other terms is not so very different from Dixie? Again, he asserts that the Scotch found their own native land offered too much challenge, the mountains of North Carolina too little, but Northern Ireland was just right. In another place, he argues that Iceland yielded just the right amount of stimulus for the Vikings; yet one asks, can its climate or other physical features be so much more like Northern Ireland than Scotland to evoke now a positive response rather than the negative one that Scotland was supposed to have induced in the Scotch? It is perhaps unfair to treat Toynbee's evidence in this way because his conception of what constitutes a challenge is sufficiently general so that it cannot be disproved by any evidence such as this. However, the point is that he simply does not check his hypothesis systematically because he is not interested in looking for negative instances, but only for positive ones that support his thesis.

A simple device for showing how an hypothesis can be systematically tested is the "two by two" table shown below with imaginary numbers of instances in the various "cells" representing what Toynbee might have

Marked economic or cultural growth

	Present	Absent	Totals
Moderate climate	10	2	12
"Non-moderate" climate (i.e., extremes)	5	10	15
Total events "considered" (cultures or periods in culture history)			27

found had he checked his hypothesis completely. Culture periods are first classified as to whether or not they show growth (perhaps according to some objective criterion such as Kroeber's indexes) and then as to whether or not they occurred in times or places where the climate could be regarded as moderately challenging rather than extremely mild or rigorous. By such a cross-classification system we might decide that the Scotch provided three instances in the cells which support the hypothesis (top left and bottom right). But then the Vikings in Iceland (assuming its climate is as rigorous as Scotland) would provide a negative instance in the lower left-hand cell; so would the Australians, and so on. If Toynbee had taken all the cases he could find and classified them systematically in this way he might have come out with the figures actually shown which have been chosen to illustrate how his hypothesis might be supported "in the main" despite exceptions in the wrong cells.

Huntington's data tend in fact to point to such a relationship. (See Woytinsky, 1953, p. 30). Statistical tests will show, of course, how many exceptions can be tolerated before the frequencies in the four cells will appear to be just random deviations from an even distribution in all of them, indicating no relationship between the two variables.

The table can be used to illustrate several other points that should be kept in mind in testing hypotheses. First, negative instances are not necessarily "fatal." One of the reasons why scholars of an older tradition either overlooked or struggled to explain away negative instances is probably that their model of causation did not permit exceptions. Yet the social scientist knows that his universe is multiply determined. Economic growth is undoubtedly a function of several factors, only *one* of which is climate. Other determinants not included in the classification in this table may combine from time to time in such a way as to outweigh the effect of climate, just as strong winds may make a leaf move upward in apparent defiance of the law of gravity. So an exception does not "disprove" a generalization any more than a "rising leaf" disproves the law of gravity. It is a question of how many "exceptions" can be tolerated. If there are too many then we must conclude that the factor we thought might be associated with economic or cultural growth is not connected with it in fact. Its influence is outweighed by other factors and we should begin searching for a new factor among the others that will separate more distinctly instances of slow from instances of rapid growth.

The effect of errors of measurement on such a test of a generalization is frequently misunderstood. They tend usually to prevent a relationship from appearing in the data rather than to create a relationship where one does not exist. Suppose we adopt a measure of economic growth which for peculiar local reasons does not "do justice" to a particular country so that we make a mistake and classify it as "growing slowly" when it is really "growing rapidly." What happens? The mistake normally will work against the hypothesis we are testing. That is, if we are checking the "moderate climate" hypothesis in a country with a moderate climate that we have wrongly classified as "growing slowly," then it provides a negative instance against the hypothesis. But what if the country had had an "extreme" climate? Then our mistake would have provided a case *in support of the hypothesis*. Isn't it possible that an accumulation of mistakes may seem to support a hypothesis that is not actually true? The question is frequently asked by social scientists who have enough detailed knowledge of particular cases to know that errors of measurement have been made in testing a generalization. The answer, however, is: "No, such mistakes seldom add up to support a wrong hypothesis (though they may obscure a right one) for the simple reason that they are more often random than systematic." That is, mistakes are usually not all of the same kind. If country A is classified wrongly for one set of reasons, country B is wrongly classified for a different set of reasons. Errors of this kind are not cumulative. No relationship appears in the "two-by-two" table. Consequently *if a significant relationship does appear*, the charge that errors of measurement have been made is pointless, unless it can be shown that they have a particular bias because the relationship has appeared *despite such errors*.

A further and more important check on whether the errors might have been nonrandom is to make an independent test of the hypothesis—say of the relationship between climate and economic development at two different time periods separated by 2,000 years. As an even better check, studies by psychologists of the direct effects of the weather on performance, long-range planning, birth rates, etc., can begin to ferret out the details of the relationship first suggested perhaps by a two-by-two table of the sort illustrated on page 23. As independent studies continue to confirm the general hypothesis, it becomes less and less likely that some nonrandom error of measurement could have created the relationship under investigation. A single test, however elegant or quantitative, does not make a scientific theory. It requires a series of tests which fit into a logical framework to confirm a hypothesis, as hopefully the remainder of this book will demonstrate.

A two-by-two table also demonstrates the weakness of dealing only with some of the cells. Suppose we had information only on cases of "culture growth" and found that 20 of them occurred in moderate climates and 9 of them in other climates. We might be tempted to think our hypothesis was supported because the cases tend to group as it would predict, but the fact is, of course, that we cannot be sure of anything without knowing how the cases not showing growth are distributed. It is possible (though not likely in this particular instance) that the other cases would distribute more or less the same way—perhaps 18 in the moderate climates and 10 in other climates, indicating not that climate had anything to do with culture growth but that there were more identifiable cultures (or more available information) from moderate climates.

Finally such a table suggests the need for some comment on the distinction between association and causation. Properly speaking, such classifications tell us nothing about causation but only about association. All we can conclude is that such and such a variable—say better health—is associated with economic growth. We do not know whether economic growth produced better health or better health produced economic growth. But we want to know what brings about rapid economic growth not just what accompanies it. We have been critical of economists and sociologists for sometimes assuming that changes that have accompanied development (like better health, specialization of labor, or disappearance of the family firm) have therefore been *responsible for* development. How can the distinction be made? Generally speaking in two ways: Sometimes logic or common knowledge decides the issue. Climate is a good case in point. It is hard to imagine how economic growth could affect climate (except in a few extreme cases) so that we would conclude from such a table that the causal relationship must go from climate to growth rather than the other way around. More often the logic is not so clearcut and it is necessary to classify in terms of what changed first. Thus we might divide countries in 1925 into those with better and those with poorer health and sanitation and then see which ones grew rapidly or slowly between 1925 and 1950. If we found a relationship, we would conclude that the differences in health and sanitation were a determinant of growth because it is hard to imagine how subsequent growth could have caused earlier differences in health. We could also of course divide the countries in terms of growth rates between 1925-1950 to see what effect they had on health and sanitation in 1950 because, of course, there is no reason why a particular factor could not be both a cause and an effect of development.

148,717

Testing a Particular Explanation: The Relation of Population Growth to Economic Development

The value of the methods advocated can best be demonstrated by using them to attack a specific problem of great interest to economic historians and theorists—namely, the association between population changes and economic development. Ever since Malthus, population growth has figured prominently in the theorizing of most economists in one way or another. To a behavioral scientist accustomed to empirical tests of hypotheses it is astonishing to read the elaborate arguments written for or against one supposed effect of population or another without a systematic classification of the facts of the sort described in the previous section. Particularly recently Malthusian fears have loomed large in the minds of those concerned with poor or backward countries. In general, these countries have high net reproduction rates, and it is often concluded that they are poor because their population is increasing so rapidly. It is true that experts like Kuznets (1956) have warned specifically against confusing association and causation. He warns against the tendency to assume that income levels are low "*because* the population follows the pattern of high birth rates and high death rates. . . . There is undoubtedly some truth in this interpretation. A population with high birth and death rates is handicapped as a body of economic producers, even if only because high mortality, particularly concentrated in the infant ages, means an exceedingly wasteful pattern of life— with energies of parents devoted to raising children, of whom only a few reach productive ages. . . . But even if the above argument is granted, the significance of these factors as *causes* of international income differentials are still to be considered. Taken in and of themselves, out of the full context of all aspects of social and economic life, differences in birth- and death-rates would scarcely have much effect on *per capita* productivity. . . . Population patterns with low birth rates and low death rates, too, are just as much consequences of a high standard of living and higher income levels as their cause." (1956, pp. 7-9.) Kuznets' skepticism (see also Hagen, 1959) appears to be based on general caution and an awareness of the complexity of factors determining economic life, rather than on any concrete empirical check of a possible relationship between the two factors. Caution is of course wise, but it is no substitute for the systematic test of a hypothesis.

In general, two types of propositions emerge from the welter of arguments and counterarguments that characterize the field. One has to do with the effect of economic development on the birth rate. Malthus and the classical economists felt that economic growth stimulated the birth rate and caused population growth. Their reason was characteristically a logical one.

As Adam Smith put it, "if this demand [for labor] is continually increasing, the reward of labor must necessarily encourage in such a manner the marriage and multiplication of laborers, as may enable them to supply that continually increasing demand by a continually increasing population." (Meier and Baldwin, 1955, p. 23.) If people can make more money by having more children, they will have more children. If wages are high, they will marry earlier and tend to have more children. It all sounds reasonable enough; furthermore there is concrete evidence at the time these men were writing that there had been a rise in the birth rate in England. From total population figures in 1750 and 1800, it may readily be estimated that the maximum net reproduction rate (birth rate minus death rate) must have been of the order of .7 to .8 per cent on the average annually. Between 1800 and 1850, on the other hand, the population rise was such that the net reproduction rate must have been at least of the order of 1.2 per cent on the average annually. In fact it was close to this when figures become available on England and Wales for 1850, when the birth rate was 33.4 per thousand and the death rate 22.6 per thousand. It has sometimes been argued that the increased net reproduction rate between the last half of the 18th century and the first half of the 19th century was due to a decline in the death rate, but this is not likely because public health measures, it has been estimated, were not sufficiently developed or widespread to cause such a significant decline in this period, and also because the decline between 1850 and 1880—when certainly there was better public health—was only of the order of .2 to .3 per cent per annum. Habakkuk (1953) has also argued convincingly for an increase in the birth rate, although he would place the rise somewhat earlier, making its connections with increased income levels as advocated by the classical economists somewhat more doubtful.

More recently the exact opposite has been argued, namely that rising income levels cause the birth rate to decline. The case again seems obvious: the Western countries have been getting richer, and their birth rates have definitely been falling. Furthermore, within these countries until quite recently when the trend inexplicably has reversed (1940-1960), the better the economic position of the family, the fewer children it produced. So Lewis is merely echoing the opinion of most people when he concludes, "there is no evidence of birth rates rising with economic growth; the evidence is rather that they fall." (1955, p. 305.) Furthermore, he has no difficulty in finding logical reasons for such a fall. When the death rate drops "people begin to feel that having so many children has grave disadvantages" (p. 312) and "what was a subject for religion and morality becomes a subject for convenience and calculation" (p. 313). Note now how easily economic utilitarianism can be invoked to support the conclusion that birth rates will fall with increasing income levels, whereas it was invoked by the classical economists to deduce the precise opposite. Some evidence as to what in fact happens in general would certainly seem desirable.

The other general proposition has to do with the effect of rapidly increasing populations on economic development, and deals therefore with the net reproduction rate rather than with the birth rate as such. Again equally reasonable but opposite conclusions have been drawn as to the relation between the two variables. The Keynesians have stressed the fact that increasing populations stimulate demand, which stimulates investment, which keeps the economic machine working in a beneficent cycle. They were apparently especially impressed by the fact that when demand fell during the depression of the 1930's, the economic machine slowed down greatly. Why shouldn't an increase in demand from an increasing population speed it up? It has been much more commonly argued, from Malthus on down to the present, that increasing populations slow development. The logic seems inescapable if development is measured in welfare terms as some kind of *per capita* ratio. If population is increasing at the rate of 2 per cent per annum, then output must increase at a faster rate if the average income per person is going to increase. And the higher the rate of population increase, the higher the rate of economic growth necessary to keep up with or surpass the growth in population. So Buchanan and Ellis (1955, Chapter 5), like many others who have considered the problem, conclude that rapidly growing populations are one of the primary factors blocking or inhibiting the growth of underdeveloped countries. They do not have any difficulty finding illustrations which support their contention.

Consider Mexico, for example. In 1930-1934 its birth rate was 44.5 per thousand and its death rate 25.6 per thousand, for a net reproduction rate of about 1.9 per annum. By 1953 its birth rate had not declined, being 45 per thousand, but its death rate had been markedly reduced by public health measures to 16.2 per thousand, for a net reproduction rate of around 2.9 per cent per annum. The inference seems clear. The reason Mexico is so poor and remains slow in its economic development is because its population is increasing so rapidly that it is difficult for the rate of capital formation to surpass it. Oddly, but characteristically in discussions of this kind, they do not present data on how rapidly Mexico actually developed economically between 1930 and 1950, although they imply that it has been developing slowly. Evidence on this point needs to be carefully sifted: Some authorities argue that Mexico has been developing very rapidly; our data on recent gains in electrical production (Table 3.5) support such a view so far as gross output is concerned but not in per capita terms. On a per capita basis Mexico has been distinctly an underachiever compared with most nations, both for the 1929-1950 and 1952-1958 time periods. Such data should have been presented before the case illustrates any point at all. What is even more important is the fact that illustrations one way or the other do not adequately test the proposition that is here being advanced—namely, that countries with rapidly increasing populations should in general grow less rapidly economically.

Let us proceed systematically to collect information to test the hypothesis according to the method outlined in the previous section. What we need is a measure of the net reproduction rate for a number of countries at a given time period and a measure of their subsequent economic rate of growth. We must consider several countries because we are trying to discover whether population *per se* has an effect on economic growth when other major factors determining growth are randomized, or held constant. Two factors known to have a major effect of growth are (1) climate and (2) the level of development of the country at the point in time in which we begin to take our growth measure. That is, countries which are already well advanced, say, in 1925 will grow on the average much more rapidly than those that were not well advanced in 1925, either because of differences in the resources they have to start with, level of technical skill, degree of business organization, or other reasons. Thus, if we were to relate population growth to crude economic growth uncorrected for initial level, we would be unlikely to detect the effect of population *per se*, since it would be outweighed by the initial difference in the capacity to grow. It would be a little like comparing the mile-per-hour speed of a man in a car with that of a man running or roller-skating. For this reason, a method has been developed, as described in full in Chapter 3, which permits a comparison of rates of growth corrected for level of development at the beginning of the time period during which the growth is measured. Furthermore, hot countries are without exception poor. If we included them, we would run the risk of biasing or obscuring our results because of the operation of a factor known to have a powerful connection with economic growth. We therefore hold its influence more or less constant by restricting our sample of countries to those falling roughly outside the limits of the Tropic of Capricorn and the Tropic of Cancer—a restriction which would be dictated anyway by the lack of data on nearly all tropical countries. The question may now be rephrased as follows: *for all countries on which data are available, and which fall roughly in the same climatic area, does a high rate of population increase slow the rate of economic growth corrected for the initial level of development?*

Table 1.2 presents the cases available for a recent time period classified as suggested earlier in the form of a two-by-two table. There seems to be no simple relationship between net reproduction rates in the early '20's and subsequent economic growth. Approximately an equal number of cases fall in each cell. Those who have viewed population growth with alarm have talked a great deal about the limiting effects of population on countries like Japan and Italy, and, to be sure, they are found in the cell where one would expect to find them—high net reproduction rates, low economic

TABLE 1.2 THE EFFECT OF RATES OF POPULATION GROWTH (1920-1924) ON
RATES OF ECONOMIC GROWTH (1925-1950)

	Countries showing *more* rapid economic growth (1925-1950) than expected[1]		Countries showing *less* rapid economic growth (1925-1950) than expected[1]	
	Net repro- duction rate,[2] %	Popu- lation density (1929)[3]	Net repro- duction rate,[2] %	Popu- lation density (1929)[3]
Countries with *higher* net repro- duction rates in 1920-24[2]	1.9	Bulgaria — .33	1.8	Argentina −1.05
	1.8	Union S. Africa — .89	1.6	Holland +2.13
	1.6	Canada −1.21	1.3	Poland —
	1.4	New Zealand −1.17	1.2	Japan +1.12
	1.4	Australia −1.19	1.2	Denmark + .01
	1.2	Norway −1.10	1.2	Portugal + .18
			1.2	Italy + .99
Countries with *lower* net repro- duction rates in 1920-24[2]	1.1	United States — .89	.9	Spain — .04
	.9	Great Britain +1.45	.9	Hungary + .27
	.9	Finland −1.04	.8	Chile —
	.8	Sweden −1.02	.7	Germany +1.34
	.7	Belgium +2.73	.6	Austria — .07
	.7	Switzerland +1.29	.3	France — .16
	.6	Ireland — .66		

[1] The method of obtaining these estimates of economic growth is fully explained in Chapter 3. They show whether a country has developed economically faster or slower between roughly 1925 and 1950 than would have been expected on the basis of its initial level (1925) of both income and electricity available per capita (see last column in Table 3.4). The combined measure of income and productivity has been used here, rather than just productivity, as elsewhere, because income more directly reflects standard of living which enters strongly into most discussions of the effect of population growth on economic growth. Bulgaria and Great Britain actually developed slightly less rapidly than average but they have been added to the left-hand column to get a more nearly equal split between more and less rapidly developing countries.

[2] Live birth rates per 100 population minus death rates per 100 population (1920-24) from *Statistical Yearbook 1956*, United Nations, New York, N. Y.

[3] Standard scores by country of persons per thousand square kilometers of standard farm land (from Clark, 1957, p. 309). $N = 33$, mean = 89.5, $SD = 71.9$. Positive scores = above-average density.

growth rates. However, such theorists typically overlook Bulgaria, the Union of South Africa, and Canada, all of which had higher net reproduction rates than Japan or Italy and nevertheless managed to grow quite a bit more rapidly. In fact, Canada had one of the highest economic growth rates of any country on which measures could be found. On the other hand, it has been common to point out that conservative countries like Sweden and Switzerland, which have low net reproduction rates (stable populations), have managed to attain very high levels of economic development. Once again these countries are where they belong in the table according to the hypothesis—in the lower left hand cell. But what about Austria and France that had even lower net reproduction rates and did much more poorly than Sweden and Switzerland economically speaking? Such a table is a healthy corrective for those who use the method of illustration to support hypotheses. Obviously, instances can be found to support various generalizations from this table, since the cases seem to be fairly evenly distributed among the four cells, but the over-all conclusion is inescapable that at least as far as this sample of twenty-six countries is concerned there has been no simple first-order relationship for the past generation between population growth and subsequent economic growth.

It is time, however, to consider some of the limitations of the table. It contains no country with a net reproduction rate of over 2 per cent. Population growth rate might be some kind of a threshold factor—if the rate rises over 2 per cent, it might begin to have a braking effect on the economy, while below that its effect might be negligible, as the table suggests. An even more likely possibility is that rapid net reproduction rates will benefit the economy, if the country is underpopulated, i.e., has a low man/land ratio, and vice versa. To check this possibility, population density standard scores have been added to Table 1.2 reflecting the number of persons in the country per thousand square kilometers of standard farm land (which appears to be a better base for economic purposes than sheer territory). That is, the deviations in density above the average for the 33 countries on which figures are available (Clark, 1957) were converted to positive standard scores $\left(\frac{X-M}{SD}\right)$ to show that such countries have more people to feed on a standard land base than the average country, and vice versa. The revised, second-order hypothesis is that rapid net reproduction rates in low-density countries and slow net reproduction rates in high-density countries will *both* tend to speed economic development, and vice versa. Such seems to be the case; all six countries in the upper left-hand cell are relatively speaking, "underpopulated"—and for them a rapid net reproduction rate is associated with rapid economic growth. Table 1.3 presents the complete classification of countries showing that the new hypothesis is confirmed at a reasonable level of statistical significance. That is, a rapid net reproduction rate appears to facilitate economic development if the country is underpopulated, and to inhibit it if the country is overpopulated—an "obvious" conclusion, some armchair observers might contend, but even obvious conclusions can and should be put to such simple empirical tests as these.

Furthermore, they need to be checked carefully because it is easy to develop plausible explanations for almost any classification of data like that in Table 1.2. For example, if the new hypothesis is checked against

TABLE 1.3 ASSOCIATION BETWEEN NET REPRODUCTION RATE (NRR) 1920-24 AND RATES OF ECONOMIC GROWTH (1925-1950) AS A FUNCTION OF POPULATION DENSITY

	Countries showing *more* rapid economic growth than expected	Countries showing *less* rapid economic growth than expected
Countries with high NRR and low density or low NRR and high density	Bulgaria Union S. Africa Canada New Zealand Australia Norway Great Britain Belgium Switzerland	Argentina Hungary Germany
Countries with low NRR and low density or high NRR and high density	United States Finland Sweden Ireland	Spain Austria France Netherlands Japan Denmark Portugal Italy

χ^2 = approximately 4.20, $p < .05$

rates of gain in electrical output per capita at another time period (1952-58, see Table 3.5) it is *not confirmed*. If anything, the trend is in the other direction, though not significantly so. More recently fewer of the countries (53 per cent) that are either sparsely populated (1955 figures) with high net reproduction rates or densely populated with low net reproduction rates have developed more rapidly in per capita terms than expected as compared with the other two types of countries, of which 73 per cent developed more rapidly than expected, despite high growth rates in densely populated countries (e.g., Pakistan, Czechoslovakia) or low growth rates in sparsely populated countries (e.g., Sweden, Austria, Ireland). The conclusion is clear: hypotheses, if they are to have any generality, must be checked a number of times. So far our search has not uncovered any dependable relationship between economic growth, population growth, and man/land ratios in recent years, although this does not exclude relationships at extremes of rates of population growth not included in our sample. At the very least it suggests greater caution than many economists or population experts have shown in generalizing about these relationships on purely "rational" grounds.

But what about the reverse relationship? Does economic development affect the birth rate? Here we can use the same classification as above—countries that advanced relatively rapidly between 1925 and 1950 and those that advanced more slowly. The question is: what happened to the birth rate in these two kinds of countries between the early 1920's and 1950? Table 1.4 supplies the answer. Again there is not much comfort in these data for either of the hypotheses that have traditionally been

TABLE 1.4   EFFECT OF ECONOMIC GROWTH (1929-1950) ON BIRTH, DEATH, AND NET REPRODUCTION RATES

| | Rates per 1,000 | Average rates for | | Average change |
		1920-1924	1950	
Countries showing *more* rapid economic growth 1925-1950 (*N* = 13)	Birth	24.5	21.5	−3.0
	Death	12.9	10.5	−2.4
	Net reproduction	11.6	11.0	− .6
Countries showing *less* rapid economic growth 1925-1950 (*N* = 13)	Birth	28.8	22.3	−6.5
	Death	18.3	11.0	−7.3
	Net reproduction	10.5	11.3	+ .8

advanced. At first glance, it might appear that there was some support for the classical economists in that the countries developing more rapidly showed *less of a decline* in the birth rate than those developing less rapidly. Thus, the wealthier a country is becoming, the less the decline in the birth rate, although there is no actual *increase* on the average, as Malthus had predicted. On the other hand, countries showing less rapid economic growth had a higher average birth rate to begin with (29 vs. 25 per thousand), and therefore it might have been easier for it to fall. The percentage decline in the two countries is very similar. So neither Malthus' view nor Lewis's summary of current opinion seems borne out by the data. The differences are small and statistically insignificant.

What is perhaps most interesting about the table is the similarity among average *net* reproduction rates between the two types of countries both in the '20's and in the 1950's, although they are obtained from very different birth- and death-rates. They all vary closely around 1 per cent or 11 per 1,000. Apparently the rate of population reproduction has been getting more efficient (reduction in both birth and death rates), but it has remained, on the average, nearly constant over the last few decades in these countries. One could also adduce from this table the fact that countries which are more inefficient in attaining a given net reproduction rate subsequently showed less rapid economic development—a hypothesis suggested by Kuznets (1956). But note that we are now moving beyond the effect of population growth *per se* on economic development to an interpretation that relates two different effects—efficiency in reproduction and efficiency in the economy—to a common psychological factor, concern with efficiency. Systematic attempts to check propositions often lead to just such an outcome—they suggest a reformulation of the original hypothesis in terms that can then be checked further (see Chapter 5). Since our purpose here is primarily methodological rather than substantive, such a hypothesis cannot be pursued beyond the present point, but it is one that might be worth investigation.

So far as our data are concerned, they do not support any of the rather extravagant generalizations that have been made for either the effect of population growth on economic growth or the reverse. The rate of population growth bears no simple first-order relationship to rate of economic growth, nor does rate of economic growth have any discernible effect on the birth rate. It therefore seems premature to use demographic measures as simple direct estimates of level or rate of economic development as suggested by Hauser (1959). They may bear a close relationship to economic variables but certainly the data provided by Hauser on 13 selected countries do not adequately test such a hypothesis or estimate the size of the relationship.

To be sure our data are limited; they cover countries most of which were already within the orbit of Western industrialization in the 1920's, and they do not answer questions about effects in *particular* countries. But they do show whether there are any discernible over-all trends that affect the relationships *despite* individual difference in the situations of the countries involved. In a sense, when such a trend is found, it seems the more impressive because it is strong enough to outweigh many local conditions, e.g., wars, depressions, changes of government, character of the people, and similar factors. Furthermore, those who are interested in a particular country can work out relationships within it using the same technique. Time series for rates of population growth can be related to time series for rates of economic growth as a function of changing man/land ratios, etc., *within* the country.

Carefully quantifying variables and relating them systematically is a tedious and difficult process, but it provides a much sounder basis for policy recommendations than the general impressions or illustrative examples that all-too-often today seem sufficient to justify the most far-reaching conclusions. Such generalizations may seem very reasonable. It appears, *a priori*, more sensible to argue that if an economy is expanding rapidly people will have more children because they can afford them and because the children can easily find work and bring in more money. The generalizations may be supported by some telling instances—e.g., in this case the expanding birth rate in early 19th-century England or in mid-twentieth-century United States. But when evidence is systematically collected, as in Table 1.4, even the most reasonable hypotheses often fail to be confirmed.

What could be more obvious than the assertion that a rapidly growing population will be a severe handicap to economic growth in a densely populated country? Yet the Netherlands—the most densely populated country in the world in 1955, with an above-average net reproduction rate—still managed to develop more rapidly economically in per capita terms (1952-1958) than many other countries in the world. Nor is it a single exception. There is no easily discernible rule covering these relationships at the present time. So facts can be a healthy corrective to the most reasonable hypothesis.

At the very least, it may be hoped that our illustrative analysis will have made two points—first, that the methods of research design and statistical inference widely used in the behavioral sciences may be usefully applied to traditional problems in economics and history; and secondly, that economists and other theorists should be more cautious than many of them have been about assuming any direct simple connections between population and economic growth.

2

The Achievement Motive: How It Is
Measured and Its Possible Economic Effects

The hypothesis that gave rise to the present study is that achievement motivation is in part responsible for economic growth. Such a statement sounds either untestable or trivial. What could be more obvious than that great achievements are motivated by strong desires to achieve on the part of at least some people in the culture? Is it really necessary to do research to prove such a point? Resolving such issues and giving real meaning to the hypothesis involves an explanation of how the modern psychologist looks at human motivation and, more particularly, of how he measures it. What precisely does the psychologist mean when he refers to "achievement motivation" or "the achievement motive"? The answer will first require a brief review of recent developments in the scientific study of human motivation.

Assessing Human Motives

At least from the time of Plato and the Bhagavad-Gītā, Western philosophers have tended to see reason and desire as two distinctly different elements in the human mind. There would be little point here in giving a history of the various ways in which the "desiring" element has been conceived in the last 2,000 years, but suffice it to say that it always represented a kind of "motivational force" often opposed to but ultimately controllable by reason. At about the dawn of modern scientific psychology, in the middle of the nineteenth century, the relationship between these two psychic elements took on a very specific meaning largely under the influence of Darwin and the wide interest he and others aroused in the theory of evolution. Man was conceived as an animal engaged in a struggle for survival with nature. It was an obvious corollary to assume that because man struggled he had a desire or wish to survive. Biologists and psychologists were quick to point out how such a desire was mechanically controlled by the organism, since unmet physiological needs ordinarily triggered certain danger signals which would irritate or disturb the organism until the needs were satisfied.

The most obvious example is the hunger need. If the organism does not get food, it does not survive; therefore, it is equipped with danger signals (controlled perhaps by contractions of the empty stomach) which would be activated in the absence of food and so cause the organism to be active until it obtains food. The more or less "intelligent" activities of the organism, representing the old reasoning element in man, were conceived as originated and guided by the hunger drive, not in the teleological sense that the organism "knows" it needs food, but purely in the mechanical sense that hunger keeps the organism going until it manages to find some food substance which shuts off the danger signals. The most important theoretical advance made by psychologists who thought of human adaptation in these terms was the conceptual distinction they ultimately made between eating and hunger (the desire to eat). Common-sense psychology might suggest that the more a man eats, the more he wants to eat, in exactly the same sense that the more a man achieves, the more he must *want* to achieve. If, in fact, the two variables are so closely connected that desire to eat can be inferred without error from eating activity, then there is no need for the motive concept at all.

Since science is a parsimonious enterprise using as few concepts as it possibly can to explain what it tries to explain, it can get along without a variable which is always perfectly associated with another. But what behavioral scientists did at this juncture in history was to establish an *independent set of operations* for defining the strength of the hunger drive— independent that is, of the activity of eating. They defined the strength of the hunger drive in terms of the number of hours of food deprivation. They assumed that the longer an organism had been without food, the hungrier it would be, and they could then go about determining how different strengths of the hunger drive, as independently measured in this way, would influence various types of behavior, including even eating. They found, not too surprisingly, that when the strength of hunger was measured by hours of deprivation, it did not correlate at all perfectly with the tendency to eat. There were, and are, many disagreements, of course, as to the best method of measuring the hunger drive, but the only point of real significance here is that the way was opened to measure motivation independently of consummatory action. So psychologists have tended by and large to distinguish between motivation and action—between hunger and eating, and between the desire to achieve and actual achievement.

Nevertheless, much remained to be done. There was as yet no interest in the unique effects of particular drives. It is true that American psychologists studied not only the hunger drive, but also the thirst drive, the pain-avoidance drive, and other basic drives. Yet all these were conceived as functionally equivalent forces acting to energize human behavior until the organism managed to remove them by something it did. As might also be expected, there was no particular interest in individual differences in the strength of various motives. In fact the model of the hunger drive suggested that motive potentialities might be pretty much alike in all people and that their actual strength was primarily determined by changes in the external environment (e.g., lack of food). There was not much interest in the possibility that some particular person might have an especially strong hunger drive either because of biological endowment or because of some special learning experiences that had reinforced it. It remained for those more directly interested in human behavior and social motives to fill out the picture somewhat.

Many of them took their cue from Freud. Oddly enough he, too, had been strongly influenced by Darwin. He recognized the importance of survival needs like hunger, but concentrated his attention on the force that perpetuated the species—namely, sexual love. His general "model of motivation" remained not unlike the one adopted by the American psychologists of the functional school. A general motive force—the libido—drives man to invent through reason a variety of techniques or stratagems for diverting or satisfying it. But while the general model stayed the same, he made important empirical contributions that markedly influenced the direction research was to take.

For one thing he destroyed forever (except, perhaps, in the minds of economic theorists) the notion that motives are rational or can be rationally inferred from action. By concentrating his attention on notable irrationalities in behavior—slips of the tongue, forgetting of well-known facts, dreams, accidents, neurotic symptoms—he demonstrated over and over again that motives "are not what they seem." In fact they might be just the opposite. It could no longer be safely assumed that a man walks across the street because he wants to get to the other side. He might, in fact want just the opposite—to enter a tavern on this side, a desire revealed indirectly by his exaggerated avoidance behavior. Since Freud, psychologists have accepted the fact that a simple act may be variously motivated. In the economic sphere, advertisers have long since taken advantage of Freud's findings in recognizing that a man doesn't buy a car just because he "needs" one in a rational sense, but because the possession of a particular kind of car may satisfy other motives—for power, prestige, or even sexual display. But how is one to know exactly what these other motives are? Here again, Freud provided us with an important clue in the method he himself used for discovering certain motives. He searched in dreams and free associations—in short, *in fantasy*—for clues to irrational motives. The limitation of his method was that it was always *ad hoc*. He proceeded, like the doctor he was, to analyze each symptom, for each person, or each dream as it came along, but did not provide scientists with measures of particular motives that would (1) enable different observers to agree what motives were operating with the degree of consensus necessary for science,

(2) permit individuals to be compared as to the strength of a given motive, and (3) provide at least crude estimates of group levels or differences in human motives that would be of use to economists and other social theorists in dealing with the behavior of large groups of people.

Measuring the Achievement Motive

The next step was to develop a method of measuring individual differences in human motivation firmly based on the methodology of experimental psychology and on the psychoanalytic insights of Freud and his followers. How this was accomplished might just as well be illustrated by reviewing briefly the history of the development of a measure of the achievement motive, since we are to study its connection with economic growth throughout the rest of the book. The procedure, which has been described in full elsewhere (McClelland, et al., 1953), may be briefly summarized as follows. First the achievement motive was aroused in a group of subjects to see what its effects on behavior might be. In this way we could avoid the mistake of assuming a priori that the strength of the achievement motive may be inferred simply and directly from some particular type of behavior. For example, actual achievement cannot be considered a safe index of the strength of the need to achieve any more than eating can be considered a safe measure of the strength of the hunger drive. In fact actual achievement is controlled by many more forces than eating—desires for social approval, power, or knowledge—to say nothing of ability factors, so that it is far less a reliable index of the need to achieve than eating is of hunger.

Instead we need some more unique index of the presence of an aroused desire for achievement. Ideally, of course, we might favor something like a "psychic X-ray" that would permit us to observe what was going on in a person's head in the same way that we can observe stomach contractions or nerve discharges in a hungry organism. Lacking such a device, we can use the next best thing—a sample of a person's spontaneous thoughts under minimum external restraints, in short, of his waking fantasies and free associations, as already used by Freud and many others to assess human motives. The question then narrows down quite specifically to: What "unique" effects on fantasy does an aroused state of achievement motivation have? If we can discover any, we can use these effects to infer the strength of "inner concerns" for achievement in subsequent studies.

Deciding how to arouse the achievement motive already involves to a certain extent at least a rough definition of the motive being investigated. It is therefore important to report just how it was done. The subjects initially were all male college students who were given a series of tasks to perform that were introduced in the following way:

"The tests which you are taking directly indicate a person's general level of intelligence. These tests have been taken from a group of tests which were used to select people of high administrative capacity for positions in Washington during the past war. Thus, in addition to general intelligence, they bring out an individual's capacity to organize material, his ability to evaluate crucial situations quickly and accurately—in short, these tests demonstrate whether or not a person is suited to be a leader." (McClelland, Atkinson, Clark and Lowell, 1953, p. 105.)

The important point about these instructions is that they stress the fact that the individual is about to be evaluated in terms of standards of excellence—intelligence and leadership capacity—which are ordinarily of considerable importance to men in American culture. It is assumed that such instructions will arouse in most of the people to whom the tests were given a desire to do well, a desire to appear intelligent and demonstrate some leadership capacity. It is, of course, unnecessary to assume that these motives were conscious, or even present, in all of the subjects tested. It is only necessary to assume that consciously or unconsciously a motive to do well was aroused in more of the subjects to whom the instructions were given than in a comparable group of subjects to whom the tests and instructions were not given. Any differences in the subsequent fantasy behavior of the two groups might then be attributed to the difference in the level of arousal of the achievement motive in the two groups.

After the above tests had been completed, samples of the subjects' fantasies were collected by having them write brief five-minute stories suggested by pictures flashed on a screen for a few seconds. The pictures represented a variety of life situations centering particularly around work, because it was not known in advance exactly what associations would be most likely to be affected by arousing the achievement motive. In non-technical language, the stories represented short samples of the things people are most likely to think about or imagine when they are in a state of heightened motivation having to do with achievement. It may be worth considering for a moment why fantasy as a type of behavior has many advantages over any other type of behavior for sensitively reflecting the effects of motivational arousal. In fantasy anything is at least symbolically possible—a person may rise to great heights, sink to great depths, kill his grandmother, or take off for the South Sea Islands on a pogo stick. Overt action, on the other hand, is much more constrained by limits set by reality or by the person's abilities. Furthermore, fantasy is more easily influenced than other kinds of behavior. Contrast it with problem-solving, for example. One might assume that how hard a person works would directly reflect the strength of his achievement motive. Yet how hard a person works is not easy to influence experimentally. Apparently most people develop a problem-solving "set" which is sufficient to keep them working at a more or less constant rate despite wide variations in feeling, such as those induced by extreme fatigue. In producing work, one motive can substitute for another so that even though the achievement motive may be weak in some people, their output may well be the same as somebody else's because of a stronger desire to please the experimenter

This points to a third advantage of fantasy over any "overt" behavioral measure—namely, the way in which it gives clues as to *what motive* is aroused. Even if working behavior were more sensitive to experimental influences, one could not determine from the mere fact that a person was working harder what his motive was in working harder. It might be the achievement motive, or it might be the need for social approval, or the desire to get out of a situation as fast as possible and do something else. It is the fantasies of the person, his thoughts and associations, which give us his real "inner concerns" at the time he is working.

The next step was to compare the stories written by subjects whose achievement motives had presumably been aroused with those written by subjects under normal conditions. Certain differences immediately became apparent. The stories written under "aroused" conditions contained more references to "standards of excellence" and to doing well, or wanting to do well, with respect to the standards. A couple of actual stories will illustrate the point best. One of the pictures frequently used shows a boy sitting at a desk with a book open in front of him. Under normal conditions, it evokes a story like this one:

"A boy in a classroom who is daydreaming about something. He is recalling a previously experienced incident that struck his mind to be more appealing than being in the classroom. He is thinking about the experience and is now imagining himself in the situation. He hopes to be there. He will probably get called on by the instructor to recite and will be embarrassed."

Nothing in this story deals with achievement or with standards of excellence, but compare it with the following story:

"The boy is taking an hour written. He and the others are high-school students. The test is about two-thirds over and he is doing his best to think it through. He was supposed to study for the test and did so. But because it is factual, there were items he saw but did not learn. He knows he has studied the answers he can't remember and is trying to summon up the images and related ideas to remind him of them. He may remember one or two, but he will miss most of the items he can't remember. He will try hard until five minutes is left, then give up, go back over his paper, and be disgusted for reading but not learning the answers."

Obviously, here the boy is concerned about doing his best on the examination ("he is doing his best to think it through" and he is "disgusted for reading but not learning the answers"). Furthermore, there are a number of aspects of an achievement sequence specifically mentioned such as the fact that it is his fault that he is not doing well ("he saw but did not learn") and that he is trying out various ways of solving his problem ("trying to summon up the images and related ideas to remind him of them"). The fact that he is not successful in his achievement efforts is *not* taken to mean that the student who composed this story has a weaker achievement motive than someone who wrote a story in which his problem-solving activities were successful. In fact, the precise advantage of the experimental method adopted is that it makes it unnecessary to make such decisions on "rational" grounds. One might make a case *a priori* for regarding images of success as more likely to be indicative of a strong and successful achievement drive than images of failure. One might also make a good *a priori* case for the exact opposite conclusion—that people who daydream about success are the very ones whose achievement motive is too weak to engage in actual attempts to do something in real life. To decide such a question on the grounds of what is most reasonable would be to fall into the error that plagued the psychology of economists and philosophers in the 19th century. The experimental approach makes *no* assumptions as to how the achievement motive is going to affect fantasy in advance: it simply takes whatever differences appear in fact between stories written under "aroused" and normal conditions so long as they make some kind of theoretical sense, and uses them as a means of detecting the presence of the achievement motive.

For example, it was thought in advance that arousal of the achievement motive might affect the outcome of the story, perhaps producing more successful or unsuccessful outcomes as compared with vague or indecisive ones. But in fact there were no differences in the frequency of various types of outcomes of the stories written under "aroused" conditions as compared with those written under normal conditions. So the outcome of the story, or of the achievement sequence in it, cannot be considered a sign of the presence of heightened achievement motivation, no matter how good an *a priori* case might be made for using it in this way. The point cannot be stressed too much. It was not logic that decided what aspects of fantasy would reflect achievement motivation. It was experimental fact. There is no need to list and define here the several different aspects of fantasy that did change under the influence of achievement arousal in college students, since they have been fully described elsewhere (McClelland et al., 1953; Atkinson, 1958). It might be questioned though how general these effects would be. Perhaps an aroused achievement motive would influence the thoughts of Chinese, or Ancient Greeks, or Navaho Indians in quite different ways. Are the results obtained restricted to the male college population on which they were obtained? Ancient Greeks have not, of course, been tested, but Navahos have and their stories change in exactly the same ways under the influence of achievement arousal (McClelland et al., 1953). So do those written by Brazilian students (Angelini, 1955), or high-school students in our culture from more unselected socioeconomic backgrounds. There may be cultural differences, but the data to date point to major similarities—inducing achievement motivation increases in all types of subjects thoughts of doing well with respect to some standard of good performance, of being blocked in the attempt to achieve, of trying various means of achieving, and of reacting with joy or sadness to the results of one's efforts.

The next step was to obtain a score for an individual by assuming that the more such thoughts he had under normal conditions, the stronger his motive to achieve must be, even in the absence of special instructions and experiences designed to arouse it. What the experiments had demonstrated was what channels peoples' thoughts turned to under achievement pressure. But suppose a person's thoughts run in those same channels without any external pressure. It seems reasonable to infer that he has a strong "inner concern" with achievement. Under normal testing conditions, the pictures used to elicit stories are sufficiently ambiguous to evoke a variety of ideas. If someone, however, in writing his stories consistently uses achievement-related ideas of the same kind as those elicited in everyone under achievement "pressure," then he would appear to be someone with a "bias," a "concern," or a "need" for achievement. So it was decided that a simple count of the number of such achievement-related ideas in stories written under normal testing conditions could be taken to represent the strength of a man's concern with achievement. The count has been called the score for n Achievement (abbreviation for "need for Achievement"), in order to have a technical term which points unmistakably to the fact that the measure was derived in a very particular way, and has an operational meaning quite distinct from estimates one might arrive at by inferring the strength of a person's achievement motive from his actual successful achievements, or from his frequent assertions that he is interested in getting ahead in the world. It remains only to say that the method just described for deriving the n Achievement measure can be applied to measuring n Affiliation, n Power (see Atkinson, 1958), and any other motive that an experimenter can demonstrate influences fantasy in regular and predictable ways.

But of what use are such measures? What good does it do us to know that a person's n Achievement score is high? The answer lies in dozens of research projects which have contrasted the behavior of subjects with high and low n Achievement scores. American males with high n Achievement come more often from the middle class than from the lower or upper class, have better memory for incompleted tasks, are more apt to volunteer as subjects for psychological experiments, are more active in college and community activities, choose experts over friends as working partners, are more resistant to social pressure, cannot give accurate reports of what their "inner concern" with achievement is, etc. (McClelland *et al.*, 1953; Atkinson, 1958). It is not necessary to review the many such findings in detail here, but it is directly relevant to consider how subjects with high *n* Achievement actually perform when confronted with a working situation.

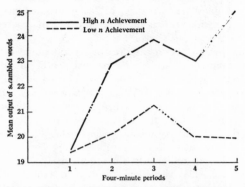

Figure 2.1   Mean output of scrambled words per four-minute period for subjects with high and low *n* Achievement scores

Figure 2.1 presents an early result obtained by Lowell. Obviously the subjects with high *n* Achievement scores, while they start at about the same level of performance as the subjects with low *n* Achievements scores, do progressively better as they proceed with the rather complex task of unscrambling words. In common-sense language, they appear to be concerned enough about doing the task well to learn how to do it better as they go along. It might, therefore, be assumed that such subjects—the "highs"—would always do better at any kind of task under any circumstances. Such is not the case. They do not ordinarily do better at routine tasks like canceling the number of "e's" and "o's" in a long string of unrelated letters where no standard of improvement with respect to the performance itself is present. That is, one can really not do such a task "better"—only faster. Furthermore, the "highs" perform better only when performance has achievement significance for them. The point can best be made with the results in Table 2.1 as adapted from an experiment by French (1955).

In the "relaxed" experimental condition, the subjects with high *n* Achievement did not do significantly better at a decoding task, presumably because the experimenter removed all achievement significance from what they were doing with the following instructions: "We are just experiment-

TABLE 2.1 MEAN PERFORMANCE SCORES AS A FUNCTION OF INITIAL MOTIVATION LEVEL AND EXPERIMENTAL CONDITIONS (*After French, 1955*)

	Experimental conditions		
	Relaxed orientation	Task orientation	Extrinsic reward
Initial motivation:			
High n Achievement	17.73	29.80	18.20
Low n Achievement	15.40	16.66	22.47
Correlations with initial motivation	.03	.48*	.02

* A correlation this large could have arisen by chance less than 1 out of 100 times ($p < .01$).

ing today and we appreciate your cooperation very much. We want to find out what kinds of scores people make on these tests." Other research has suggested that appealing for cooperation leads those in the group who have strong n Affiliation to work harder, rather than those with high n Achievement.

In the "task" experimental condition, the subjects were told that the test "measures a critical ability—the ability to deal quickly and accurately with unfamiliar material. It is related to general intelligence, and will be related to your future career. Each man should try to perform as well as possible." Under these instructions, the subjects with high n Achievement as measured some months earlier, performed significantly better than those with low n Achievement. Finally, in the "extrinsic" experimental condition, the subjects were told that "we want to see how fast it is possible to work on a code test . . . without making errors. . . . The five men who make the best scores in five minutes will be allowed to leave right away—as soon as I can check the papers. The others will have more practice periods and more tests." These instructions introduced specific pressure for speed with the extra incentive of time off from work for those who get through as fast as possible. Under these conditions, again the subjects with high n Achievement do not perform better than those with low n Achievement. If anything, the "lows" do a little better on the average, suggesting that the possibility of getting out of the working situation appeals to them the most!

All of these facts together suggest that high n Achievement will lead a person to perform better when achievement in the narrow sense is possible. If the task is just routine, or if finishing it sooner implies co-operating with someone or getting some special reward like time off from work or a money prize (Atkinson and Reitman, 1958), subjects with other motives will perform better. The achievement motive is apparently not strongly "engaged" under such conditions. Furthermore, we might legitimately expect that people with strong achievement motives would seek out situations in which they could get achievement satisfaction. They ought to be the kind of people who set achievement standards for themselves, rather than relying on extrinsic incentives provided by the situation, and they should try harder and more successfully to reach the standards they set for themselves. It does not take a great stretch of imagination to assume further that if a number of people with high n Achievement happened to be present in a given culture at a given time, things would start to hum. They might well start doing things better, as in Fig. 2.1, or what is even more important, they might start doing them differently by trying to get achievement satisfaction out of what they were doing. What had been done out of a desire to please, to make money, or to get time off from work, might now be converted into an activity in which standards of excellence were defined and pursued in their own right. Viewed in this light it would not be at all surprising to imagine that an increase in n Achievement should promote economic or cultural growth.

Forming the Key Hypothesis: The Effects of the Protestant Reformation on n Achievement

While research findings of the sort just described might well have suggested our key hypothesis, it was actually a study by Winterbottom (1953) which first pointed to a possible link between achievement motivation and economic development. She was interested in trying to discover how parents, or more particularly mothers, produced a strong interest in achievement in their sons. She first obtained n Achievement scores on a group of 29 eight-year-old boys and then conducted interviews to determine if the mothers of the "highs" had different attitudes toward bringing up children. What she found was that mothers of the "highs" expected their sons to master earlier such activities as the following (see also Table 9.1):

> Know his way around the city
> Be active and energetic
> Try hard for things for himself
> Make his own friends
> Do well in competition

Furthermore, the mothers of the "lows" reported more restrictions: they did not want their sons to play with children not approved by the parents, nor did they want them to make important decisions by themselves. The picture here is reasonably clear. The mothers of the sons with high n Achievement have set higher standards for their sons: they expect self-reliance and mastery at an earlier age. (Winterbottom, 1958, pp. 468-472.)

An interesting historical parallel suggested itself. As we have seen, the German sociologist Max Weber (1904) described in convincing detail how the Protestant Reformation produced a new character type which infused a more vigorous spirit into the attitude of both workers and entrepreneurs and which ultimately resulted in the development of modern industrial capitalism. If the Protestant Reformation represented a shift toward self-reliance training and the new "capitalistic spirit" an increased n Achievement, then the relationship found by Winterbottom may have been duplicated at a societal level in the history of Western Europe. The following diagram shows the parallel.

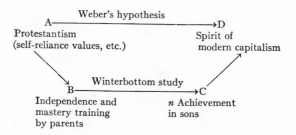

That is, the Winterbottom study suggests a psychological means by which the historical development described by Weber may have come about. The Protestant Reformation might have led to earlier independence and mastery training, which led to greater n Achievement, which in turn led to the rise of modern capitalism. Certainly, Weber's description of the kind of personality type which the Protestant Reformation produced is startlingly similar to the picture we have drawn of a person with high achievement motivation. He notes that Protestant working girls seemed to work harder and longer, that they saved their money for long-range goals, that Protestant entrepreneurs rose to the top more often in the business world despite the initial advantages of wealth many Catholic families on the Continent had. In particular, he points out that the early Calvinist businessman was prevented by his religious views from enjoying the results of his labors. He could not spend money on himself because of scruples about self-indulgence and display, and so, more often than not, he re-invested his profits in his business, which was one reason he prospered. What, then, drove him to such prodigious feats of business organization and development? Weber feels that such a man "gets nothing out of his wealth for himself, except the irrational sense of having done his job well." (Weber, 1904, p. 71.) This is exactly how we define the achievement motive in coding for it in fantasy.

In explaining how such men were produced more often by Protestantism, Weber felt that it was the intrinsic character of their religious beliefs that counted and not their particular political or economic circumstances, since these varied so much from country to country. In particular he stressed two factors: (1) the Protestant insistence on the importance of a man's "calling" which meant that a man's primary responsibility was to do his best at whatever station God had assigned him in life, rather than to withdraw from the world and devote himself entirely to God, as the Catholic Church had taught as a counsel of perfection, and (2) the "rationalization" of all of life introduced into the Protestant ethic particularly by Calvin's notion of predestination. The early Protestants had been particularly offended by the sale of indulgences and had turned against the notion that "good works" could help a man "purchase" salvation. In his sermon *On Christian Liberty*, Luther thundered that a man could be good works from the top of his head to the tip of his toe and still not enter into heaven. Calvin argued that the decision as to who were the "elect" had already been made by God and that no amount of good works on earth could alter the decision. As Weber points out, this still left the practical problem for the ordinary believer of discovering whether he was one of the "elect" or not. Only by trying *in every particular* to be like someone in the Bible who was obviously one of the elect could he hope to get rid of the fear that he was damned forever. Thus, the average Protestant had to behave well in every respect, not, as Weber points out, as a "technical means of purchasing salvation, but of getting rid of the fear of damnation. . . . In practice this means that God helps those who help themselves. Thus the Calvinist, as it is sometimes put, himself creates his own salvation, or, as would be more correct, the conviction of it. But this creation cannot, as in Catholicism, consist in a gradual accumulation of individual good works to one's credit, but rather in a systematic self-control which at every moment stands before the inexorable alternative, chosen or damned." (Weber, 1904, pp. 338-339.) Such a rigid rationalization of all of conduct when combined with the emphasis on doing one's duty in one's station in life destroyed the leisureliness, in Weber's mind, with which capitalistic enterprise had been pursued up to this time. The entrepreneur worked harder—in fact he could not relax for a moment. The Protestant labor force he recruited worked harder, and none of them could enjoy the increased fruit of their labors for fear of losing the conviction that they were saved. So profits and savings were available to be plowed back into further expansion of business which in itself was a serious calling ordained by God.

From the standpoint of our present knowledge of and interest in achievement motivation, we can add to Weber's argument. Protestantism also involved a revolt against excessive reliance on the institutional church. Luther preached the "priesthood of all believers"; the individual did not have to depend exclusively on more learned experts, but should read his Bible for himself and find divine guidance directly. There was greater stress on literacy for exactly this reason among Protestants. It seems very probable, then, that Protestant parents would stress earlier self-reliance and mastery of at least reading skills so that their children could fulfill their religious duties better. Such training, as we have seen, may well have increased n Achievement in the children according to Winterbottom's findings.

Furthermore, Calvin's description of what Weber calls "rationalization" of life is written in terms of striving continually for perfection, which would be scored very high for n Achievement. Consider the following passage, for example:

"Let us every one proceed according to our small ability, and prosecute the journey we have begun. No man will be so unhappy but that he may every day make some progress, however small. Therefore, let us not cease to strive, that we may be incessantly advancing in the way of the Lord, nor let us despair on account of the smallness of our success; for however our success may not correspond to our wishes, yet our labor is not lost, when this day surpasses the preceding one; provided that with sincere simplicity we keep our end in view, and press forward to the goal, not practicing self-adulation, nor indulging our own evil propensities, but perpetually exerting our endeavors after increasing degrees of amelioration, till we shall have arrived at a perfection of goodness, which indeed, we seek and pursue as long as we live . . ." (Calvin, I, pp. 775-776.)

In other words, the rationalization of conduct meant more than orderliness and rigidity, it meant continual striving to improve one's self, to achieve. While the achievement was supposed to be in the religious sphere primarily, Calvin made it clear that this did not imply monasticism or withdrawal from life. "Let us discard therefore that inhuman philosophy which, allowing no use of the creatures but what is absolutely necessary . . . malignantly deprives us of the lawful enjoyment of the Divine beneficence. . . ." In other words, God provided the world and what was in it "not only for our necessity but likewise for our pleasure and delight." Furthermore, we are given these earthly things as stewards. "They are, as it were, deposits entrusted to our care, of which we must one day give an account." Thus, as Weber points out, the striving to do one's best religiously was readily interpreted to mean doing one's best in the "post assigned him by the Lord," namely, in his occupation. (Calvin, I, pp. 786-790.)

So it seems reasonable enough to interpret Weber's argument for the connection between Protestantism and the rise of capitalism in terms of a revolution in the family, leading to more sons with strong internalized achievement drives. The case is further strengthened by the fact that the Protestant Church did away with the celibate priesthood and substituted what Troeltsch argues had far-reaching social consequences, namely "the Protestant citizen-pastor and his household." (Troeltsch, 1958, p. 144.) The Protestant pastor could now give concrete examples of child-rearing practices that might be emulated by his parishioners in a way that was formerly impossible under the celibate priesthood. The social mechanism was provided by which the new religious world-view could specifically affect socialization and thereby the motivation of the new generation.

Preliminary Evidence for Linkages between Protestantism, n Achievement, and Economic Development

But logic and reasonableness are one thing.[1] Evidence is another. Is there any factual basis whatsoever for the linkages among the various events shown in the diagram above? Let us begin with Weber's argument. What is the evidence that Protestantism is connected with greater economic progress? It would be difficult, indeed, to arrive at a sound opinion from the facts presented by historians and sociologists. The methods used are simply not adequate for reaching a decision. Those who accept Weber's hypothesis point to the role of Protestantism in the industrialization of England, Switzerland, Germany, and the Scandinavian countries. Those who disagree with him point out that a Catholic country like Belgium showed as strong an entrepreneurial spirit and as rapid an industrialization as any of the Protestant countries. And what about Catholic Venice, which before the Reformation reached a height of capitalistic enterprise seldom attained thereafter? It does not help particularly to point out that though Belgium was over 99 per cent Catholic, it was ruled by Protestant kings during its industrialization in the 19th century, or that Venice, in fact, very nearly became Protestant during the Reformation. The matter simply cannot be settled by the battle of instance and counterinstance. A more sophisticated method is necessary.

Are Protestant countries more economically advanced today than Catholic countries matched for natural resources? Such a question can be answered fairly precisely, although of course it is not the only question that might be asked. Table 2.2 presents the relevant data. The measure of economic development used is consumption of electricity in kilowatt-hours per capita as of 1950. While the reasons for choosing such a measure are given more fully in Chapter 3, they are basically: (1) that the figures are expressed in internationally comparable units, as contrasted with, for example, national income figures which are very difficult to translate into one another, and (2) that electricity is a form of energy on which modern industrial civilization is largely based. Anyway in 1950 kilowatt-hours per capita consumed correlated .87 with estimates of income per capita (see Chapter 3). The countries listed in the first column in Table 2.2 are all

[1] References are given at the end of each chapter.

those for which data were available lying outside the tropical zone, i.e., lying between the Tropics of Cancer and Capricorn. Since advanced economies appear to be confined more or less to the temperate zone, it seemed unfair to include the many Caribbean and Latin American Catholic countries, which lie within the tropics.

TABLE 2.2 AVERAGE PER CAPITA CONSUMPTION OF ELECTRIC POWER, CORRECTED FOR NATURAL RESOURCES, FOR PROTESTANT AND CATHOLIC COUNTRIES OUTSIDE THE TROPICS OF CANCER AND CAPRICORN

	Countries	Consumption of electricity kwh/cap[1] (1950)	Usable water power hp/cap[2] (1947) ($SD = 1.36$)	Coal produced tons/cap[3] (1951) ($SD = .99$)	Combined natural resources ($\Sigma\sigma$ scores)[4]	Predicted output kwh/cap[5]	Difference (predicted—obtained)	Rank of difference[6]
Protestant	Norway	5,310	4.182	.000	+2.73	3379	1931	1
	Canada	4,120	3.079	1.124	+2.49	3186	934	4
	Sweden	2,580	1.117	.026	− .35	908	1672	2
	United States	2,560	.388	3.431	+1.42	2328	232	9
	Switzerland	2,230	1.553	.000	+ .08	1253	977	3
	New Zealand	1,600	1.405	.675	+ .42	1526	74	11
	Australia	1,160	.164	2.505	+ .51	1598	−438	20
	United Kingdom	1,115	.023	4.529	+1.86	2681	−1566	24
	Finland	1,000	.810	.000	− .67	652	348	6
	Union S. Africa	890	.203	2.165	+ .30	1430	−540	21
	Holland	725	.003	1.238	− .58	724	1	15
	Denmark	500	.011	.121	−1.39	74	426	5
	Average	*1,983*	*1.078*	*1.318*		*1645*	*338*	*10.1*
Catholic	Belgium	986	.004	3.335	+ .96	1959	−973	22
	Austria	900	.500	.379	− .71	620	280	8
	France	790	.289	1.293	− .25	989	−199	16
	Czechoslovakia	730	.085	2.837	+ .68	1734	−1004	23
	Italy	535	.265	.033	−1.20	227	308	7
	Chile	484	.676	.381	− .53	764	−280	18
	Poland	375	.059	3.338	+1.02	2007	−1632	25
	Hungary	304	.017	1.049	− .70	628	−324	19
	Ireland	300	.156	.061	−1.29	154	146	10
	Argentina	255	.318	.003	−1.17	251	4	14
	Spain	225	.271	.418	− .91	459	−234	17
	Uruguay	165	.204	.000	−1.29	154	11	13
	Portugal	110	.070	.052	−1.38	82	28	12
	Average	*474*	*.224*	*1.014*		*771*	*−298*	*15.7*

[1] From Woytinsky, W. S. and E. S. *World population and production.* New York: Twentieth Century Fund, 1953. Table 415, p. 972. A few of the values are for Thermo- or Hydroelectric power only but in all these cases, except Chile, which has been recomputed here, the alternative source is negligible.

[2] Computed from Woytinsky, *ibid.*, Table 407, p. 952. The figures are the sum of the capacity in horsepower of existing plants and undeveloped power (ordinary minimum flow) divided by the population.

[3] Computed from *World Energy Supplies*, United Nations Statistical papers, Series J. No. 2, New York, 1957, pp. 13 ff.

[4] Sum of standard scores for water power and coal produced.

[5] Based on the regression equation computed for these 25 countries, i.e., $Y = 80.2(X + 2) − 41.5$, where Y is the predicted value in kwh/cap and X is the sum of the standard scores for water and coal resources.

[6] The probability that the higher ranks could be associated with Protestantism by chance is less than .03 (Mann-Whitney U test).

The association between level of economic development and Protestantism appears very marked in the first column of Table 2.2, as was pointed out in a previous publication (McClelland, 1955). However, further research demonstrated that some correction for differences in natural resources must be made, since the two groups of countries are not very well equated for the water power and coal supplies used in the production of electricity.[2] The disparity is most striking in the usable water power resources (column 2) which appear to be about five times as great on the average in the Protestant as in the Catholic countries, and the correlation between water power resources and electrical output is highly significant (over .50). Furthermore since 72 per cent of the electricity produced in the world in 1950 was thermal in origin, it is also necessary to include coal resources as the chief means of producing heat. Unfortunately, "coal in the ground" is not a good measure because, unlike water resources, coal cannot be used all at once and, unlike water resources, the amount available is not always accurately known. Therefore output of coal per capita was used as an estimate of coal resources (column 3), although it is a somewhat contaminated measure, since it may be higher in those very countries where people work harder and therefore reach a higher level of economic development. In predicting, for example, how much electricity should be produced per capita in England on the basis of her coal production, we may well overestimate, for the reason that coal production already includes the energy with which resources have been used. Another people living in the same country with the same coal resources might have produced less, and we would therefore predict less economic development and the country would appear to be less of an "underachiever" than Britain is in the table. The water power measure does not suffer from this defect since it represents what is available and not what is produced.

Nevertheless, some measure of available coal is necessary, since when it is combined in standard score terms with the water power reserves, the correlation of total reserves with electrical output is .75. In other words, the differences noted in column 1 might largely be due to greater natural resources in the Protestant than in the Catholic countries, since available natural resources correlate highly with production of electricity. However, it is possible to remove the effect of natural resources by a regression analysis which predicts, as in column 4, what output could be expected from a country on the basis of its natural resources. Then by subtracting the predicted output from the actual output, one can determine whether a country has done better or worse than could be expected on the basis of its natural resources. As the last column on the right shows, 9 out of 12 of the Protestant countries, or 67 per cent, have done better than expected, whereas only 3 out of 13 of the Catholic countries (Austria, Italy, and Ireland) have done substantially better than expected. If the differences are ranked from those which have done best to those which have done least well, it is clear that the ranks of the Protestant countries are higher on the average and the difference is significant according to the Mann-Whitney U test ($p < .03$). It needs perhaps to be stressed again that the measures are approximate, particularly the adjustment for coal resources,[3] but errors unless they are systematically biased in favor of Protestant or Catholic countries, can only serve to disguise a relationship, or weaken it, rather than actually to create it. So it may be concluded with reasonable confidence that, as of 1950, Protestant countries are economically more advanced on the average, even taking their differences in natural resources into account, than are Catholic countries. The question as to why the difference exists is another matter.

Granted that Weber's hypothesis has some basis in fact, what about the evidence for the other links in the key hypothesis? Do Protestants stress earlier independence and mastery training, as we have reasoned they should? Preliminary evidence suggested that they do (McClelland, Rindlisbacher and de Charms, 1955). Samples of Protestant, Irish-Catholic and Italian-Catholic mothers and fathers matched for socioeconomic status were interviewed in Connecticut using the same schedule as the one developed by Winterbottom to test various attitudes towards self-reliance training. (See Table 9.1.) Many of the parents were obtained through church groups, so that the sample perhaps included a larger number of religiously active individuals than would be obtained from a random sample. On the average, the Protestant parents expected their sons to do well in school, to know their way around the city, etc., at the age of about 6½, the Irish parents at about 7½, and the Italian parents at about 8½. The differences were significant, although the number of cases in each sample varied only between 35 and 40. As predicted, the Protestant mothers stressed earlier self-reliance than the Catholic mothers. It should also follow that Protestant boys, on the average, equating for social class, should have higher n Achievement. Such a comparison proved impossible in the United States because of migration differentials. Catholics, at least on the East Coast, represent for the most part ethnic minorities which have settled in the country within the last few decades and have generally started at the bottom of the socioeconomic ladder. Those who rise to middle-class status may well have higher n Achievement, as a considerable amount of evidence indicated. Thus it would not be possible to draw any conclusions about religious influences from a comparison of middle-class Protestant boys with middle-class Italian boys, since the Italian boys would come from upwardly mobile families with higher n Achievement than the average among not-so-mobile Protestants. Furthermore, lower-class Protestants in New England represent a peculiar minority that have failed to rise and may not, therefore, be fairly compared with lower-class Italians, more of whom may have high n Achievement because they have not had time to rise into the middle class.

To avoid these difficulties, it seemed wise to go to a place where Protestants and Catholics had lived side by side for centuries, so that comparisons would not involve complications arising out of migration differentials. The data were available on a small sample of German boys from the city of

Kaiserslautern (McClelland, Sturr, Knapp and Wendt, 1958) which confirmed the hypothesis, as Table 2.3 shows, that Protestant boys would have higher n Achievement on the average than Catholic boys where other fac-

TABLE 2.3 MEAN n ACHIEVEMENT SCORES OF A SAMPLE OF GERMAN BOYS, AGED 17-19, CLASSIFIED BY RELIGIOUS AND SOCIOECONOMIC BACKGROUND, AND LEADERSHIP STATUS

Father's educational level		Protestant		Catholic		Mean
		Leaders	Nonleaders	Leaders	Nonleaders	
University	N	15	7	3	4	
	mean	3.33	3.29	1.00	2.25	2.93
Mittelschule	N	10	12	4	7	
	mean	1.70	3.42	1.25	2.71	2.48
Volksschule	N	9	4	4	3	
	mean	2.78	6.00	1.75	1.67	2.55

Protestant mean = 3.42   Catholic mean = 1.77
Leader mean = 1.97   Nonleader mean = 3.22

Analysis of Variance

Source of variance	df	Sum of squares	Mean square	F	$p.$*
Total	11	20.19	—	—	—
Father's educational level	2	1.32	.66	.77	NS
Religion	1	8.15	8.15	9.48	<.05
Leadership status	1	4.72	4.72	5.49	~.05
Interactions	7	6.00	.86		

* Number of times in 100 that the F-value could have arisen by chance.

tors were equal. It should be stressed in view of more ambiguous findings reported in Chapter 9, that the sample is small and highly selected, consisting entirely of boys preparing for a university education in one part of Germany. The data are included because they constituted the evidence available at the time it was decided to investigate the problem on a larger scale. It was not possible to perform an analysis of variance using the individual scores because of the unevenness in subclass numbers, but the classification by father's educational level and by leadership or lack of it in the class provided enough variation to get an estimate of error from the interaction terms. Socioeconomic status as represented by the father's educational level does not contribute significantly to the variance here, probably because all the students are highly selected in the sense of aspiring to a university education. It is also interesting to note that leadership (here defined by peer nominations) is not associated with high n Achievement, but rather the reverse. The boys with high n Achievement are not regarded by their peers as likely to be future leaders. Such a finding is a healthy corrective to the view that n Achievement is a generally "good" characteristic to have, like intelligence, which leads to greater success in all spheres of life.

Finally so far as this sample is concerned significantly more of the Protestant than Catholic boys were attending a "modern language" as contrasted with a "classical language" school. That is, 67 per cent of the 60 Protestant boys and only 41 per cent of the 27 Catholic boys were attending the *neusprachliches Gymnasium* ($\chi^2 = 5.10$, $p < .03$), the remainder in both cases being in the *altsprachliches Gymnasium*. The finding is interesting because Weber argued on the basis of some data collected by Offenbacher on German school attendance in the 1890's that Protestants more often went to technical or modern schools which they found to be better preparation for business, while Catholics showed greater preference for classical humanistic studies (Merton, 1949, pp. 344 *ff*.). Thus we might infer that attending more "modern" schools becomes the means by which higher Protestant n Achievement becomes channeled into business activity in Germany. Samuelsson has recently argued that Offenbacher's figures failed to take base rates into account (Lipset and Bendix, 1959; p. 54), but this criticism does not seem to apply to our figures in the 1950's. At any rate the whole problem deserves further investigation since it suggests a means by which values and motives may affect vocational choice and eventually economic development. It is discussed below in Chapters 8 and 9, in terms of more extensive data collected subsequently.

The final link in the key hypothesis is between n Achievement and economic development. Was there any evidence to support the belief that high n Achievement would predispose individuals toward business success? Some was available, but not much. Among a group of college freshmen, a search was made to see what occupations those with the highest n Achievement (top 20 per cent) liked significantly more than those with the lowest n Achievement (bottom 20 per cent of the class). Oddly enough, the only five occupations out of one hundred in the first part of the Strong Vocational Interest Blank preferred near-significantly more often ($\chi^2 > 3.74$) by the "highs" than the "lows" were the following:

> Stock broker
> Real estate salesman
> Advertiser
> Buyer of merchandise
> Factory manager[4]

While one could expect to get five significant differences in one hundred tests of significance by chance, it is at least interesting that the five particular ones turned out to be in the business area. Since only around one-quarter of the one hundred occupations listed in the Blank relate to business, it can be estimated that the chances of getting all of the differences in the business area purely by luck are less than 1 in 1,000. Furthermore, a check was available on the same group of Kaiserslautern boys to see whether the ones among them with high n Achievement also favored these particular five occupations significantly more than those among them with low n Achievement. Such turned out to be the case, despite the fact that the German boys on the whole were much less favorable to these items than the American boys. When the average favorableness of each German toward all five of the business occupations listed above was computed (Like = 2, Indifferent = 1, Dislike = 0), it was found that those with high n Achievement favored them slightly more on the average than those with low n Achievement ($t = 2.12$, $p < .05$). The difference, therefore, did not seem to be particularly restricted to American culture. Thus, boys with high n Achievement did appear to look with more favor on business occupations as predicted by the hypothesis, though of course there was as yet no evidence that they would be more likely to enter those occupations or to perform better in them after they had entered them.

The evidence so far presented summarizes what was available at the time the present study was initiated. In general, it seemed to support the key hypothesis in enough particulars to warrant a more detailed study of what was going on. But it raised almost as many questions as it answered and left many issues entirely untouched. For example, was it Protestantism as such that led to economic development and perhaps to an increase in achievement motivation, or was it certain values which happened to be associated with Protestantism in the West? What about Japan, whose economic development seemed quite rapid, but could in no way be attributed to the Protestant Reformation? Was it higher n Achievement that led to economic development in Japan and if so what parental values produced it there? The Winterbottom study was limited to only twenty-nine middle-class families in the Middle Western part of the United States. Does earlier independence and mastery training produce higher n Achievement everywhere, regardless of cultural differences? Are there alternative sources of n Achievement?

Above all, more work needs to be done on the hypothesized connection between n Achievement and economic development. Is the connection a completely general one that applies to all societies, primitive and modern, ancient and contemporary? If so, why? Does n Achievement somehow predispose young boys to look with favor on the entrepreneurial role, or does it have this effect only when business is generally looked on with favor in the society? One of the major problems involved here is whether *n* Achievement leads to better performance in all occupational roles—from artist to priest to businessman—or to greater success only in certain roles, somehow centering around economic or rationalized activities. What is needed is a very broad attack on the problem, in which the connection between achievement motivation and economic development could be checked in a variety of times and places. It appeared likely from the outset that Weber's hypothesis represents a special case of a more general relationship that ought to be investigated fully.

Plan of the Research Investigation

At this point it seems desirable to describe in a general way the research projects designed and completed to study more thoroughly the relationships which have just been discussed, and to pursue other problems suggested by them. Such a summary will serve to indicate how we propose to try to answer the questions raised, and to provide the reader with a general orientation as detailed studies are reported one by one in subsequent chapters.

Three general types of research have been carried out: the first deals with *group* measures of *n* Achievement and other psychological variables in relation to over-all rates of economic development, the second, with *individual* measures of motives, interests, values and performance of both mothers and their sons in various countries, the third with the motives and other behaviors of actual business entrepreneurs. The first type of study was made possible by the fact that the system of content analysis developed for scoring *n* Achievement in individual protocols could just as readily be applied to imaginative products of any sort. For example, it could be applied to samples of folk tales from various primitive cultures to see whether the tales containing large amounts of achievement imagery came from tribes which showed a higher level of economic activity (Chapter 3). It could be applied along with codes for other variables to the brief, imaginative stories used to teach children to read in the third and fourth grades of school. Scores based on the children's readers could then be taken as rough indexes of the level of *n* Achievement and other variables in the country, and compared at different time periods with subsequent or concurrent economic development (Chapter 3). Similarly, the coding system for *n* Achievement could be applied to imaginative literature in the past to see whether achievement imagery was more frequent prior to rapid economic growth in countries like England and Ancient Greece (Chapter 4). In all these studies, it was possible to code the source materials not only for *n* Achievement, but for other motives, values, or variables of any sort which anyone had proposed might be associated with economic development (Chapter 5).

The second type of study was designed to get at the "microstructure" of the relationship between *n* Achievement and economic development by tracing both the origins of *n* Achievement in certain parental values and attitudes and the effects of *n* Achievement in adolescent boys on their occupational interests and performance under certain conditions. It was considered essential to replicate such a study in several widely different countries to make sure the relationships found were not due to some peculiar constellation of values or social institutions in one particular

TABLE 2.4   DESIGN OF PROJECT TO TEST THE RELATIONSHIPS AMONG MOTHERS' ATTITUDES, SONS' VALUES, *n* ACHIEVEMENT, AND ENTREPRENEURIAL BEHAVIOR

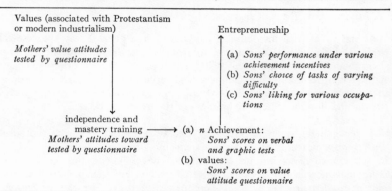

Samples	Number of sons tested	Age	Number of mothers interviewed	Other characteristics
Japan (Chief investigator: Mr. John Takeshita)	150	$M = 15.4$ $SD = 1.0$	115	Drawn from lower, middle and upper class schools in Osaka, and from a rural school
Germany (Chief investigator: Dr. Hans-Werner Wendt)	392	$M = 16.0$ $SD = .9$	300[1]	Drawn from university preparatory high schools in four West German cities[2]
Brazil (Chief investigator: Dr. Arrigo Angelini)	378	$M = 16.8$ $SD = 1.5$	130	Drawn largely from private schools of all sorts in São Paulo
India (Chief investigator: Mr. P. V. Veeraraghavan)	152	$M = 16.5$ $SD = .8$	none	Drawn from six colleges and high schools in Madras
Total	1072			

[1] Interviews conducted by the EMNID organization, a Gallup affiliate.
[2] Kaiserslautern ($N = 90$), Bad Kreuznach ($N = 67$), Bochum ($N = 88$), Münster ($N = 147$).

country. The countries decided on, the tests used, their relationship to the variables in the "key hypothesis," and the samples employed in four countries are summarized in Table 2.4. Germany was chosen for study because it represents another Western advanced economy in which social structure and values are different from those in the United States; Japan, because it was a country outside the Western tradition which had shown considerable economic development; India, because it was a non-Western underdeveloped country that has shown less economic growth to date than Japan; and Brazil because it was an underdeveloped country within the Western cultural tradition.[5] The samples of subjects are fairly comparable as to age and socioeconomic status, although they are approximately representative of the population at large only in Japan. The number of cases will vary somewhat in the statistics presented in subsequent chapters because information was not complete on every subject.

The mothers were interviewed individually and given a value-attitude questionnaire and the Winterbottom schedule asking for their attitudes towards independence and mastery training. Background information on social status, education, and the like was also obtained. The adolescent boys were tested in groups in school classes. Their n Achievement was measured in two ways—by the normal content analysis of imaginative stories, and also by a technique developed by Aronson (1958) involving scoring of spontaneous drawings, or doodles. It was considered especially desirable to use the latter method, since the former involved many difficulties in translation and in applying the code for n Achievement to very different linguistic systems. The boys were also given a values questionnaire, the scores on which might be related along with n Achievement to what we came to call "entrepreneurial behavior." For reasons described in Chapter 6, we decided that the probable common term between n Achievement and entrepreneurship was a similar interest in situations involving moderate risk or maximum opportunity of getting personal achievement satisfaction without running undue risk of failure. So an attempt was made to see whether boys with high n Achievement actually performed better under such conditions and set tasks for themselves that had these characteristics. Finally, the boys were asked whether or not they liked entrepreneurial occupations, to determine whether those with high n Achievement might favor them more as in the United States. In short the tests were designed to see whether adolescent boys in four countries with high n Achievement would be more apt to behave like entrepreneurs and to look with favor on entering entrepreneurial occupations.

The logical next step is to find out whether these boys are in fact more likely to become successful businessmen, but time considerations ruled out such a direct approach to the problem. Instead, in the third type of study, we tested businessmen themselves after they were already established in their careers to see whether they had higher n Achievement and showed more "entrepreneurial behavior" as defined for the boys than other comparable groups of men. If they did, we thought we could reason that their n Achievement had contributed to their successful career in business rather than the other way around, since boys with high n Achievement were already behaving in the same way before they got started in their careers. Again to be sure of avoiding cultural bias we studied over 750 businessmen and comparison groups of professionals in four countries—the United States (the prime example of an advanced industrial economy), Turkey (an underdeveloped country) Italy (a country well developed in some regions and not in others) and Poland (a Communist country). From these comparative studies, we hoped to be able to find out whether n Achievement is related to entrepreneurial or executive success regardless of cultural and institutional factors and the stage of economic development.

While our research plans were designed primarily to check on the importance of n Achievement in economic development, they permit also an investigation of the importance of some other factors as well. For example we have measures on our businessmen on n Power (which might be more important for business success in a really backward country) and on n Affiliation (which might be important in the United States if business here really requires "organization men"). Or in the children's stories we can also look for the sociological variables reviewed in Chapter 1 to see if they are associated with subsequent economic development. In other words, while the center of interest in these studies was originally the n Achievement hypothesis, a broad enough net was cast to discover any other variables which, along with n Achievement or without it, might precede or accompany economic growth.

Finally, our research plan stimulated some specialized studies which do not fall under any of the three general headings. Chief among these are an intensive study by Rosen (1959) on the relationship of ethnicity and social class to n Achievement and self-reliance training in the United States, and one by Rosen and D'Andrade (1959) on the interaction patterns in families of boys with high n Achievement as contrasted with families of boys with low n Achievement. Both these studies were aimed at providing more precise information on the origins of n Achievement to supplement our cross-cultural studies of mothers and sons. Still another group of studies was undertaken by Knapp (1958, 1959, 1960) to investigate the relationship of n Achievement and attitudes toward time, since the more careful management of time has frequently been considered to be of key importance in the development of modern industrial society.

It remains only to warn the reader against expecting too much. Cross-cultural research of the sort described in subsequent chapters is extremely difficult to perform under satisfactory conditions of comparability. To mention just a few difficulties we ran into: Children's readers had to be found which are really representative; the translations had to be reasonably accurate from dozens of different languages; the samples of boys and their mothers should be randomly drawn (which they clearly are not, as Table 2.4 shows); the n Achievement measure ought to be obtained under exactly comparable testing conditions in four countries, since fantasy is extremely sensitive to the atmosphere of the testing session, as is demonstrated by the way the n Achievement measure was derived; questionnaire items should tap the same attitudes in the different countries, though what constitutes "achieved status" in one country may not in another; the performance task should be equally familiar in all cultures, although what we used—namely complex arithmetic—turned out to be especially emphasized in India; the occupational titles used to measure occupational interests ought to mean roughly the same thing in the four countries (which turned out not to be the case). All these and many more such methodological difficulties will be discussed in detail in the particular chapters where the studies are reported. Those who might be discouraged by such complexities, as we have often been, can only take comfort in the thought that for the most part error is fairly random and operates to reduce relationships, rather than to create them where they do not exist. So whatever relationships are found may be taken the more seriously because they have somehow managed to "shine through" the many sources of error and confusion that undoubtedly exist in the data to be presented; nevertheless many may in the end be more persuaded, as we have been, by the over-all direction of the evidence rather than by any particular study. There is some flaw in nearly every finding reported—some alternative explanation of the result obtained. Nevertheless, the evidence *is* empirical evidence, not just armchair consideration of reasonable hypotheses, and taken as a whole it tends to support the belief that achievement motivation is an important factor affecting the rate of economic development.

NOTES AND REFERENCES

[1] Their limitations are clearly suggested by the ease with which equally plausible alternative explanations have been devised for connecting Protestantism with capitalism. For instance, Erich Fromm has argued that the capitalist has, above all, the three traits of the anal character—orderliness, parsimony, and obstinacy—so that the rise of capitalism might have had something to do ultimately with the change in toilet-training habits. Brown makes a somewhat better case for connecting both Protestantism and capitalism to a revived interest in the devil, or the destructive evil forces in life (Brown, Chapter 14, 1959).

[2] I am much indebted to V. Stefflre for calling my attention to the need for a correction for natural resources in these data.

[3] The correction for coal available seems particularly "unfair" since the countries with large coal reserves as compared to water power turn out to be nearly always "under-achievers." The reason lies probably in the fact that coal is used for many other things than to produce electricity, whereas the chief industrial use of water power is to make electricity. Nevertheless, it should be pointed out that the correction is more likely to be "unfair" to the Protestant countries if anything, since they have somewhat larger

coal production, so that the difference obtained in Table 2.2 would, if anything, be larger and more significant if the correction for coal resources could be properly made.

⁴In a previous report of this study (McClelland, 1955), two other occupations were listed—*office manager* and *sales manager*—as showing a difference. They have been dropped here because the significance of the chi-square test depended largely on differences in the "indifferent" category. It was later decided that a more meaningful test was to see what items were liked significantly more by the "highs" so that the "indifferent" and "dislike" categories were lumped together to make a two-by-two table. By this method of analysis, the differences for *office manager* and *sales manager* were no longer significant, but a new occupation—*advertiser*—reached approximately the 5 per cent level of significance. Interestingly enough, all the occupations involved are in the business field.

⁵I am greatly indebted to Mr. John Takeshita, who added our tests and questions to an investigation he was carrying out in Osaka, Japan; to Dr. Hans-Werner Wendt who organized a considerable testing operation in Germany under the kind patronage of Professor Albert Wellek, Director of the Psychological Institute at the University of Mainz, and to the many individuals who were of help on the project including Dr. Fröhner of the EMNID organization, Professors Metzger and Bornemann, Drs. Heckhausen and Ewert, Mrs. Wendt, and particularly those who participated in the school testing—i.e., E. Westrich, W. Antoni, R. Schmitt, S. Ertel, R. Petruschkat, and E. Wurmbach. I am also much indebted to Dr. Arrigo Angelini who took responsibility for the school testing and mother interviews in São Paulo, Brazil; and to Mr. P. V. Veeraraghavan who organized the Madras testing carried out through the kind cooperation of Major S. Parthasarathy, Sri P. V. Ramamurti, Mr. Syed Sathar Mesh, Sri P. Ananthakrishnan, Sri S. Krishnarathnam, Sri C. R. Paramesh, and Sri S. Santhanakrishnan.

3

Achieving Societies in the Modern World

In terminological shorthand, let us refer to those societies which are developing more rapidly economically as "achieving societies." Like most attempts at brevity, the use of this term is misleading because there may be types of societal "achievement" that are in no way dependent on an expanding economy—e.g., military, political, artistic, or intellectual achievement, or perhaps even greater achievement of peace of mind. Our choice of the term has been dictated partly to avoid a long, though more accurate periphrasis, partly to reflect the association of n Achievement with this kind of social expansion, and partly to contrast such societies with the "affluent society," popularized by Galbraith (1958) in which the emphasis is the reverse of what it is in the achieving society—namely on slowing down production rather than speeding it up. In this chapter and the next we will concern ourselves with trying to find out whether a high level of n Achievement produces achieving societies in the economic sense, first in the modern world, and then at various times in the past.

Entrepreneurship in Preliterate Cultures

The hypothesis that n Achievement is associated with economic growth was derived from a particular historical sequence of events in Western Europe—the Protestant Reformation and the rise of capitalism. However, in its most general form it might be applied to any society at any time or place. That is, a high level of n Achievement might predispose *any* society to vigorous economic activity. On the other hand, it might do so only in the West, or only under certain conditions such as a degree of free-enterprise capitalism, a certain type of open social structure, or a relatively advanced level of technology. From the logical or theoretical point of view, it is difficult to decide how general the association might be, but fortunately there is an empirical method of testing the generality of the hypothesis. Anthropologists have collected enough information on a large number of preliterate cultures so that it is possible to see whether n Achievement level is a sufficiently powerful variable to predict economic development in these societies despite major variations in other factors such as type of social organization, a particular stage in a historical sequence, level of technology, or type of economy.

The method of determining the n Achievement level of a preliterate culture relies on analysis of the content of folk tales widespread in the culture. It rests basically on the assumption that since these stories are told and retold orally by many different people in the culture, the way in which they are told will come to reflect a kind of "average level" of motivation among the people of the tribe. The stories themselves resemble in many ways the kind of simple stories written by our subjects to pictures. They can be chosen to be episodic in nature—with a beginning, a middle and an end—and also to be imaginative or fantastic in much the same way as we instruct our subjects in the laboratory to be. Factual, religious, or historical tales are specifically excluded because they may reflect existential differences among tribes rather than differences in their "inner concerns" or motivations. Child, Storm and Veroff (1958) made a careful search of folk-tale collections and were able to select on a random basis some twelve more-or-less standard tales for each of over 50 cultures. These were then coded for n Achievement in a standard manner using the scoring definitions developed for analysis of individual protocols.

It was subsequently discovered that the n Achievement scores were significantly correlated with the length of the tales in the sample so that it proved necessary to transform the raw n Achievement scores into standard scores or z-scores. In their own words, "we arranged the entire body of tales in order of length, and classified them into successive fifths (i.e., the shortest 20 per cent of tales, the next shortest 20 per cent, etc.). For the tales in each fifth, we converted one judge's n Achievement scores into normalized z-scores." (1958, p. 482.) The effect was to equate for length of story so that, for example, a low n Achievement score from a short story might actually have a higher z-score than a somewhat larger n Achievement raw score from a very long story. Child et al., pooled the scores obtained by three different judges although interjudge agreement was much lower than usual. It was therefore decided to use here only the scores obtained by the most experienced judge—Joseph Veroff—who had been one of the group that developed the original scoring system for n Achievement and who of course scored the folk tales without knowing from which culture they came or which ones might be high or low in our measure of economic development.[1]

What could possibly be used as a measure of economic growth among such widely different cultures, some of which earned their living by fishing, others by hunting, others by agriculture and gathering, and still others by a combination of several methods? Clearly the data were not available for computing measures of income per capita, even if it were possible to decide how to equate different kinds of "economic wants" across cultures. The measure finally decided on was dictated not only by practical but also by theoretical considerations. The presumed mechanism by which n Achievement level translates itself into economic growth is the entrepreneurial class. If the n Achievement level is high, there will presumably be more people who behave like entrepreneurs, acting to produce more than they can consume. It was decided, therefore, to read the ethnographic account of a given culture and try to decide what percentage of the adult males were engaged in "full time" entrepreneurial activity. An entrepreneur was defined as "someone who exercises some control over the means of production and produces more than he can consume in order to sell (or exchange) it for individual (or household) income." It was necessary to specify "full time" because nearly every household in most preliterate societies engages in some entrepreneurial activity as defined at so general a level; that is, they produce some "cash crop." On the other hand, few individuals or families would be found that got *all* of their income from entrepreneurial activities since raising at least some food for subsistence is very widespread. Therefore a full-time entrepreneur was defined as someone who received 75 per cent or more of his income from entrepreneurial activities. In practice such people turned out to be traders (who do not produce, but acquire for resale or rental, rather than subsistence or use), independent artisans (shoemakers, smiths, carpenters, and the like, when they control the means of production rather than when they work for a wage) and firm operators (e.g., innkeepers, export houses, fisheries, sheep raisers).

The cultures were also rated for their level of technology and for the way in which property was owned at the same time that the percentage of adult males in full time entrepreneurial activity was being estimated.[2] Technology was thought to be of possible importance because individuals with higher n Achievement might adopt improved techniques more quickly and more extensively as more efficient means of attaining their ends. In the broadest sense the rise of technological civilization might even be seen as an effort by people with high n Achievement to produce more than they could consume as efficiently and economically as possible. If so, even at a primitive level, higher n Achievement should be associated with higher technological development. Roughly three levels of "capital equipment" were distinguished. At the lowest level were such items present in all cultures as digging sticks, baskets, traps, knives, etc. The medium level included fishing boats, cattle, and land, if owned and worked for production. And at the highest level were such relatively modern mechanical items as tractors, motor boats, or engines of any kind. An attempt was made to estimate what per cent of the tribal income was derived by using equipment at each of the three levels. Thus, for example, the Koryak, a tribe in Siberia, was estimated as deriving 50 per cent of its income from low-level technological equipment (implements used in hunting and trapping) and 50 per cent from medium-level equipment (boats used in fishing, etc.). Furthermore, the proportion of the equipment at each level which was individually owned or community owned was estimated to determine whether or not individual ownership was more common in societies with high n Achievement levels. The issue of theoretical interest here is whether high n Achievement is more common where the institution of private property is more highly developed, as has often been maintained in the arguments over capitalism versus socialism among modern nations.

The data obtained from these various estimates are summarized in Table 3.1 for the 45 tribes on which information was available. Several method-

TABLE 3.1   ESTIMATES OF PERCENTAGES OF "FULL-TIME" ENTREPRENEURS, OF INCOME BASED ON LOW-LEVEL TECHNOLOGY, AND OF INCOME-PRODUCING PROPERTY WHICH IS INDIVIDUALLY OWNED AMONG PRELITERATE CULTURES VARYING IN n ACHIEVEMENT IN FOLK-TALES

Culture	Above median in n Ach.*	% full-time entre- preneurs	% low-level tech- nology	% indi- vidual owner- ship	Culture	Below median in n Ach.	% full-time entre- preneurs	% low-level tech- nology	% indi- vidual owner- ship
Mandan	.857	—**	50	100	Marquesan	.055	10	100	100
Aleut	.687	16	50	20	Pukan	.046	0	80	90
Comanche	.612	—	50	100	Ojibway	.043	5	33	96
Yoruba	.473	50	50	100	Ainu	.034	0	100	100
Papago	.369	10	20	55	Kurtachi	.023	0	70	70
Masai	.326	5	20	75	Teton- Dakota	.018	0	0	100
Winnebago	.273	40	—	100	Baiga	—.005	0	—	—
Jicarilla Apache	.269	50	0	100	Paiute	—.022	—	100	34
Wichita	.255	0	—	—	Tukuna	—.028	0	—	—
Crow	.229	50	80	95	Kikuyu	—.042	10	50	50
Venda	.228	0	75	100	Western Apache	—.097	0	—	—
Azande	.209	10	100	100	Lepcha	—.108	0	100	100
Cuna	.207	5	50	75	Arapesh	—.111	0	100	100
Koryak	.189	20	50	75	Tenetehara	—.119	10	80	61
Arapaho	.187	30	100	100	Klamath	—.173	—	100	6?
Chuckhee	.156	40	30	80	Chagga	—.182	0	50	75
Ifaluk (Woleans)	.133	0	90	50	Kaska	—.227	0	50	100
Aranda	.129	—	100	90	Ashanti	—.257	40	5	92
Araucanians	.128	0	100	75	Chiricahua Apache	—.258	—	100	100
Mbundu	.126	5	80	100	Chenchu	—.300	0	100	100
Muria	.115	0	—	100	Thonga	—.315	5	50	75
Navaho	.067	50	5	75	Nauruans	—.414	0	50	100
					Basuto	—.448	25	25	100

* Mean z-scores for 12 folk-tales, Veroff's scores, from Child et al., (1958).
** Information insufficient to make an estimate.

	$(N = 22)$ High Achievement n cultures, %	$(N = 23)$ Low Achievement n cultures, %	
Percentage of cultures with at least some full-time entrepreneurs........	74	35	$\chi^2 = 5.97, p < .02$
Percentage of cultures above median in technology, i.e., with not more than 50% of technology at low level........................	58	45	NS
Percentage of cultures with 100% individual ownership...............	48	50	NS

NS = not significant statistically

ological comments are in order. First, it should be noted that the sample of cultures is fairly representative, although it contains more North

American tribes than it ideally should. In round numbers 20 per cent are from Africa, 15 per cent each from Asia and the South Pacific, 10 per cent from South America and 40 per cent from North America. Secondly, a great deal should be said about the unreliability of the estimates. It was particularly difficult to estimate the proportion of the income produced by various levels of capital equipment. Percentage of low-level technology, as presented in the table, is the most reliable estimate, since the distinction between medium- and high-level equipment was harder to make. Yet even the former represents a very crude guess, as it was often difficult to decide whether a particular kind of trap, for example, was a low- or medium-level piece of equipment. The ownership estimates are also very rough, because of the difficulty of deciding where the "individual" left off and the "community" began. It seemed unwise to hold too rigidly to a criterion of individual ownership, since frequently items were the property of a family or household, but then the problem arose of how extended did a household have to be before it became the "community." Finally, many of the tribes in the table are at various stages of acculturation. In some cases the ethnographic descriptions refer to the "traditional" culture as it was more or less before contact with more advanced civilizations. In other cases the description refers to more recent times after the tribe had had a lot of such contact. The folk tales were also collected at different time periods or stages of acculturation, so that there is no assurance that the measure of n Achievement and the ratings of entrepreneurial activity refer to the same period in a culture's history.

Despite all these obvious flaws in the data, a significant relationship exists between n Achievement level in folk tales and presence or absence of full-time entrepreneurial activity in the culture. Fortunately it proved unnecessary to use the actual estimates of percentages of full-time entrepreneurs in Table 3.1, which are likely to be very unreliable. Instead it was enough to divide the cultures more simply and reliably into those estimated to have *some* full-time entrepreneurs versus those estimated to have *none*, for roughly half of them fell into each of these two categories. About three-quarters of the tribes above the median in n Achievement have at least some full-time entrepreneurs, whereas only a third of the tribes with n Achievement below the median are judged to have some entrepreneurs. The difference is highly significant ($p < .02$) and is not likely to have arisen by chance. Although these bare figures do not begin to tell the story of the differences between the tribes high and low in n Achievement, this is not the place to go into greater detail. It will suffice to say that the findings usually fit ethnographic descriptions of cultures pretty well. For example, White (1959, p. 84) in speaking of the Mandans, the tribe with the highest n Achievement in our sample, states that they "were insatiable gamblers, intensely interested in 'athletic games' " and that one of their favorite games was to see who could shoot the most arrows into the air before the first one hit the ground—a typical activity for people high in n Achievement. Nearly at the other end of the scale are the "gentle" Arapesh, so vividly described by Mead (1935).

There are only two really outstanding exceptions to the relationship, the Ashanti and the Basuto—both rated high in entrepreneurial activity but very low in n Achievement folk-tale content. In both cases a careful rereading of the folk tales suggests that the difficulty very probably lies in a defect of the scoring system for n Achievement. In both cultures stories about a trickster hero are told. They are particularly common among the Ashanti, who explain in great detail how Ananse, or the spider, is able to outwit anyone he meets. (Herskovits and Herskovits, 1937; Rattray, 1930.) Typical is a story in which elephant and Ananse have a "butting competition" to see which one can stand the blows of the other the best. The elephant tries butting Ananse first, but he manages by various ruses to get other large animals to take his place in withstanding the blows from the elephant. All these large animals are killed but Ananse is just as lively as ever, much to the surprise of the elephant. Then it is the elephant's turn to withstand blows from Ananse, who gets a steel wedge and gradually drives it into the elephant's head, killing him. The story clearly involves competition and much instrumental activity aimed at winning a competition, yet it would not be scored for n Achievement because there is no affect stated in the story indicating that Ananse *wants* to beat the elephant or is happy when he does. In other words, the scoring definition for n Achievement must be excessively literal, to avoid making complicated inferences about the motives involved in various types of activities. It was considered wiser not to make judgments about such motives, particularly insofar as other cultures were concerned, since errors might easily be made from the bias of our own culture. But in being so literal it appears likely that the Ashanti appear lower in n Achievement than they really are, because they avoid making statements of affect or desire. The argument is of course *post hoc*, but it is a fact that if n Achievement were defined in terms of the variety and quality of instrumental activity adopted to reach success, the Ashanti would score very high indeed, so that they may not be the great exception that they appear to be in Table 3.1. The main point, however, should not be lost sight of. Despite such probable errors in measurement (and there are undoubtedly others), n Achievement level is significantly associated with presence of entrepreneurial activities in a miscellaneous sample of preliterate tribes representing a wide variety of economic and social systems.

Level of technology and n Achievement levels are not significantly associated, but interestingly enough if the Ashanti and Basuto are omitted from the calculations, the rank order correlation goes from an insignificant value of .22 to a near significant value of .32. There is some ground for believing that the tribes with higher n Achievement may have adopted a higher level of technology. On the other hand, there is no evidence whatsoever that type of ownership of property, at least as it was crudely measured here, is in any way related to n Achievement levels of the various tribes.

A little further light on the relationship of n Achievement to various types of economic activity is shed by Table 3.2. Dominant or important forms of gaining subsistence (agriculture, hunting, or fishing) do not appear to be significantly related to n Achievement level, but there is a distinction in type of agriculture that makes a difference. According to Murdock's classification in his "World Ethnographic Sample," those tribes which

TABLE 3.2 TYPES OF OCCUPATIONS AMONG PRELITERATE CULTURES CLASSIFIED AS HIGH AND LOW IN n ACHIEVEMENT ON THE BASIS OF FOLK-TALE CONTENT

	Per cent in which occupation is dominant or important (from Murdock)		Significance level
	High n Achievement cultures ($N = 21$)	Low n Achievement cultures ($N = 22$)	
Agriculture,	62	64	NS
Gathering, etc.[1]	24	59	5.52 $p < .05$
Animal husbandry	43	27	NS
Fishing	33	45	NS
Hunting and gathering	71	64	NS
Religious experts[2]	48	82	5.61 $p < .05$

NS = not significant statistically.

[1] A rough index consisting of those cultures classified by Murdock as relying for food (other than meat) on gathering rather than raising cereal grains, e.g., on digging roots or tubers, or picking tree fruits.

[2] An index obtained by rating the extent to which individuals are dependent on religious experts rather than themselves in approaching the Divine or Sacred (see Chapter 9). $N = 23$ for the high n Achievement group here.

gather (dig roots or tubers, or pick tree fruits) more frequently fall below the mean in n Achievement than those that raise cereal grains, or do not engage in agriculture at all. The finding makes sense if gathering is viewed as an easier or lower level form of getting food than planting and cultivating rice, maize and the like, or getting one's food in some other way, like fishing or hunting. Thus tribes with higher n Achievement engage in more difficult forms of gaining subsistence which require a higher standard of achievement. Roughly speaking, n Achievement does not make a difference in the type of economic activity but perhaps it does in the level at which it is carried out.[3]

The final line in Table 3.2 comes from another study of the same cultures explained more fully in Chapter 9, but it is included here to show that tribes with low n Achievement may also excel in something. One theoretical possibility is that high n Achievement leads to excellence in all forms of activity and not just in the economic sphere. But this deduction does not seem to hold in at least one instance. The tribes with low n Achievement more frequently insist that individuals can come in touch with the Divine, or the sacred, only through the mediation of a specially designated priest or religious expert. So it seems safe to assume that the occupation of religious expert is more important or more highly developed in those tribes that have low n Achievement. If high n Achievement is associated with entrepreneurial activity, low n Achievement may be associated with priestly, traditionalistic activity.

Despite many flaws in the collection of such cross-cultural data, they confirm the hypothesis that the n Achievement level of a society is a variable significantly related to entrepreneurial economic activity in a culture, despite wide variations in social structure, in climate, means of subsistence, and level of technological development. The data also hint that tribes with high n Achievement are readier to adopt more efficient but also more complex and difficult means of earning a living, while the tribes with lower n Achievement appear to be more tradition-bound, particularly in the religious sphere. It does, indeed, seem possible that Weber's observation of the connection between Protestantism and the rise of capitalism may be a special instance of a much more general phenomenon. To date, of course, there is no evidence as to which came first, the change in the type of economic activity or in the level of n Achievement; nor is there any certainty that the relationship found at such primitive levels will persist among modern complex nations. To pursue these questions let us turn our attention to n Achievement levels in modern society.

Using Children's Stories to Assess Motivation Levels among Contemporary Nations

How can n Achievement level be assessed in a great modern nation like Russia or the United States? Even if the survey organization existed which could give tests to random samples of individuals in these nations, it would still be necessary: (1) to obtain a measure of motivation level some time ago before recent economic growth and (2) to determine whether the tests meant the same thing to individuals with very different cultural backgrounds and attitudes toward test-taking. For these reasons it was therefore decided to try assessing n Achievement levels from the imaginative productions of modern nations, extending the method used successfully with primitive cultures.

But what corresponds to folk tales in contemporary society where the oral tradition has almost died out? The nearest equivalent appeared to be stories for children. These, in fact, turned out to have many advantages, both theoretical and practical, for our purposes. First, they often derive from the same oral traditions that are represented in folk tales. Second, they have existed (for at least the past generation) in more-or-less standard form in school books used by second- to fourth-grade children of all lands. Such stories are simple, short and imaginative—at least in the sense that they normally do not yet deal with factual, historical events or political problems. They tell about imaginary situations, sometimes fantastic (from the world of fairies, giants and dwarfs) and sometimes realistic (from everyday life), but the intent is everywhere the same—to provide something interesting and instructive for the child to read. In this sense the stories are "projective" and tend to reflect the motives and values of the culture in the way they are told or in their themes or plots. They are less likely to reflect external or historical events in the life of a nation, since children from the age of eight to ten are ordinarily considered not yet old enough to learn much about such things. They are given fiction instead.

Children's stories have many other advantages for our purpose. The same ones are read by nearly all school children of the same age, since textbooks are widely standardized in most countries. They represent therefore "popular culture"—what is considered appropriate for all children to read, not just those from a special social class. In this sense they should be less biased than novels, for example, which may reflect the motives and values of a much narrower segment of the population. Children's stories are also less subtle, more direct in their "message," than many other forms of literature. As Margaret Mead (1951) has put it so succinctly, a culture has to get its values across to its children in such simple terms that even a behavioral scientist can understand them. Finally, and most importantly for our research design, children's readers, containing such brief comparable stories, could in fact be obtained from a generation ago for a representative sample of countries. The hypothesis could therefore be tested that *n* Achievement levels in them would *predict* subsequent economic growth.

Assembling the Sample of Children's Stories

It was therefore decided to try to collect twenty-one stories for each of two time periods (around 1925 and around 1950) from all of the nations of the world. The only arbitrary limit set on the sample of countries in the beginning was that they had to be geographically situated outside the tropics (see below). Naturally certain countries fell out of the sample early because books did not exist or could not be found. Nevertheless an attempt was made to get readers for every nation outside the tropics except the very smallest or inaccessible ones like Nepal, Kuwait, Liechtenstein, or Iceland. First, libraries in the United States were searched although they did not yield a very plentiful supply, apparently because children's textbooks are not considered important enough to keep, even in the Library of Congress. Next Ministries of Education in the various countries were asked for the names of at least three second-, third-, or fourth-grade readers widely used in the country around 1925 and 1950. Once the titles of the books were known, they could be purchased or photocopied on loan from libraries in the country. Finally, in some countries where no replies were received to such letters, individuals or book stores were able to locate the texts for us.

By all of these means we were finally able to collect completed sets of stories from 23 countries for the early period (1920-1929, centering around 1925) and from 40 countries for the later period (1946-1955, centering around 1950).[4] When a set of books arrived from a country, 21 stories were chosen at random without reading any of them. In fact they could not be read in nearly all cases by the person making the selection because they were in a foreign language. The only criteria used in selecting the stories were that they should not be less than 50 nor more than 800 words in length, and that they should if possible contain conversation—a matter that could be determined in advance nearly always by looking at punctuation marks. The latter requirement was to eliminate so far as possible stories which were simple descriptions of historical events. Next the stories were sent out to be translated with the instructions that the translations were to be literal rather than literary because we were not interested in the translator's "style." Then the stories were all typed in standard form, using code names for all the characters so that the identity of the country would not be disclosed by proper names. That is, all girls were called Mary, Jane and Judy, all boys Peter, Bob and John, all towns Big Town, Little Town, etc. The identity of the story was contained in a 6-digit code number on the back of the typewritten sheet. In the final editing and translating a few countries got lost, one translator disappeared with the stories, and no translator could be found for one language, so that the final sample of countries for 1950 was reduced to 40, but it still includes a large percentage of the major countries in the world outside the tropics with one major exception. It proved impossible to get stories from the mainland of China, and it was decided not to use Formosan Chinese stories on the grounds that they might not be representative.

The most difficult sampling problems arose in countries where there were substantial minorities which used different textbooks in a different language—for example Switzerland, India, Pakistan, Canada, and the Union of South Africa. In India and Pakistan it was decided to make up the samples of 21 stories from several of the major linguistic groups in the countries. In the case of Switzerland complete sets of stories were obtained both for the French-speaking and German-speaking cantons, and an overall "Swiss" score was computed by combining scores from the two sets of stories with double weight being given to the German score to reflect roughly the proportion of the population it represented.

A different decision was made in the case of Canada and the Union of South Africa. Canada, like the United States and Australia, has English-speaking Catholic schools which use different readers and which enroll a substantial minority of the children in certain areas. In all these countries it was decided that it was too complicated both to get samples of the parochial school readers and to determine what weight should be given them in determining the over-all n Achievement score of a country. Furthermore it was felt that the economic organization of the country was predominantly in the hands of those who supported the public schools. At the very least, government regulations concerning the economy would be predominantly managed by such people.

The same logic was applied, though admittedly with less force, to the problem of French-speaking Quebec, and to the Boer-speaking population in the Union of South Africa. That is, it was argued that at the time we were concerned with the governments and the economies of these countries, they were predominantly managed by the English-speaking population and only their readers were used in obtaining n Achievement levels for the country as a whole. Minorities of other kinds exist in many countries—for example, the native population in the Union of South Africa is much larger than the European population—but in all such cases it seemed permissible to omit them from our reader sample on the grounds that their contribution to the government and the economy was relatively small. There were a number of other special problems of this sort—Holland used many of the same textbooks in 1950 that it had used in 1925 for example—but all of them were settled before the results of any of the coding were known, so that it is hard to see how they could have biased the results in any systematic way.

Coding the Children's Stories

All the stories collected (over 1,300 in all) were then mixed together and coded for a number of different variables—three motives (n Achievement, n Affiliation and n Power) and a number of value categories. Only the results from the n Achievement coding will be dealt with in this chapter. Other findings are reported in Chapter 5. At this point the reader may find it helpful to read the illustrative stories reproduced in Appendix I so that the subsequent discussion will not seem too abstract. They were selected more or less at random to illustrate the type of material that was analyzed. They vary in length, in the time period in which they were used, in country of origin, grade level, and theme. The first story deals obviously with achievement, the second with obligations, the third with boasting, the fourth with politeness, the fifth with pride, and the sixth with "outwittery" or achievement-cleverness, a theme found fairly often in Middle Eastern countries.

The stories are obviously very different from one another and also from the spontaneous stories written by individuals or told as folk tales. What evidence is there that the stories can be coded successfully according to the *n* Achievement scoring system standardized on other materials? Two judges scored the stories for the three motivational variables, both of whom had had considerable experience in scoring other types of stories for *n* Achievement. After some practice, it was found that they could score the same material with a very high degree of agreement. Their reliability coefficients for samples of 30 stories ranged between .92 and .98 for each of the three motive variables. Regardless of how they were applying the scoring systems, they were in agreement as to how to do it. They had no real difficulty with the new material because, even though the children's stories were longer and more complex, they described motive-action sequences in the terms the scoring system was designed to cover, such as desires for success, anticipations of success and failure, various types of instrumental activity, or blocks to achievement. To get a total score for a country, each achievement-related story is given a score of +2, each further subtype of imagery in such a story a score of +1 (with the limitation that each subtype can be scored only once per story), each possibly achievement-related story a score of +1, and each unrelated story a score of 0. (See McClelland, *et al.*, 1953.)

An important question is whether stories with achievement themes are more or less randomly distributed among the various countries of the world. Common sense might readily assume that they are. Why shouldn't all countries tell some achievement stories, some dealing with power, some with obligations to others? Is there any evidence that one country focuses on one type of theme more than another? Couldn't the variations obtained from country to country in total *n* Achievement scores be due to chance? Wouldn't other samples of stories from the same countries give a very different set of scores? One way to answer such questions is to check on the internal reliability of the national *n* Achievement scores. To this end, the 21 stories for a given country were divided at random into two halves of 10 and 11 stories each, the *n* Achievement scores for each half determined, and correlations run between the scores for the two halves. For the countries in the 1925 sample, the correlation is .671, $N = 22$, and for those in the 1950 sample, it is .594, $N = 43$.[5] Both correlations are highly significant, which means that if a country scores high in *n* Achievement on one set of 10-11 stories, there is a significant tendency for it to score high on a second independent set of 10-11 stories. The scores based on the whole set of 21 stories have an even higher reliability, estimated at between .75 and .80 by the formula which forecasts what the reliability would be for doubling the length of the test.

The high correlations between alternate sets of stories from the same countries could not be due to the correlation of n Achievement with length of the stories from a given country. Although we initially tried to control for length of the stories, it turned out that some countries on the average told much longer stories than others. If the n Achievement score is likely to be greater from a longer story, it is possible that the high n Achievement scores of a country on two sets of stories could be due to the fact that all of them were longer than average. However, the correlation between n Achievement and the average number of lines per story is $-.034$ for the 1925 sample of countries and $.214$ for the 1950 sample. Both correlations are small and insignificant. Because these correlations were so low, it was decided that it was not necessary to correct the n Achievement scores for length of stories, as had proved to be necessary for the folk tales.

Comparing Levels of n Achievement in Readers and Individuals

The stories from a given country appear to be consistently high or low in n Achievement. They are measuring something, but what exactly is it? A skeptic might contend that the score merely reflects the motivation level of the authors of the children's stories in a particular country and that such people should certainly not be taken as representative of a culture as a whole. If in one place we are willing to take stories written by individuals to be diagnostic of their motivation, why must we not likewise assume that these stories merely reflect the motivation of the people writing them? Perhaps we must, and if in fact the stories reflect the characteristics of a very atypical class of people, then we cannot be very hopeful about finding a connection between such a method of assessing achievement motivation and subsequent economic development. But even on theoretical grounds, the situation is not so discouraging. After all, authors of children's stories are not primarily indulging in self-expression. They are not writing stories to demonstrate to an experimenter how imaginative they are, nor are they writing poetry to give expression to their feelings. They are writing for a particular audience—children and the adults having to do with the education of children who will decide whether their stories will be included in textbooks or not. Furthermore, they nearly always draw on a tradition of folk tales for children that is often widely known and appreciated in the country. Under such conditions, they are much more likely to produce something which is typical or at least widely acceptable within the culture than if they were merely indulging in self-expression. The extent to which this is true will depend, of course, on the extent to which authors of children's stories are not conscious propagandists. We are assuming that they usually are not, at least for such young children, but it is an assumption that the data alone can justify.

Even if it is granted that the stories are likely to be more widely representative of the nation as a whole than of the particular interests of authors of children's stories, some serious difficulties remain. One returns directly to the theoretical issue as to whether fantasy reflects what a person has or doesn't have. Does a man compensate in fantasy for what he doesn't have in real life? Or does he go on thinking in fantasy about what he is concerned with in real life? In other words, will the stories reflect the achievement motivation the people in a country have, or the motivation they don't have and wish they did? If the latter were true, we might even be led to expect a negative relationship between n Achievement scores in the stories and "real" n Achievement level in the country as measured in a representative sample of individuals. It is impossible to decide on theoretical grounds which of these two alternatives is most likely.

There is still another problem. Even if we grant that the stories are typical of more than the personal idiosyncrasies of children's authors, the question remains: typical of what or of whom? Typical of the literate classes, the government in power, the educational philosophy in vogue in the ministry of education, or what? The issue becomes particularly acute in really backward countries, where the percentage of people who even go to school may be quite small. It is nicely illustrated by a letter we received in reply to an inquiry directed to the Ministry of Education for Afghanistan. The official title of the ministry was printed in the Western alphabet in French on the letterhead! To what extent could we assume that stories would reflect local attitudes and motives as contrasted with French influences? The same is even truer of Algeria and Tunisia where the textbooks are actually printed in Paris, although they deal with North African themes. Even a quick reading of the Russian stories of the '20's shows that they were clearly designed to teach the children traits of character presumably different from those common to the great bulk of the peasant population when the communists took power. Do the stories reflect the values and motives of a small dominant urbanized class or those of the bulk of the Russian population?

Such questions are so important that every effort must be made to compare estimates of n Achievement level obtained from children's stories with those obtained by testing representative samples of individuals from the country concerned. At the present writing, a national representative sample has been tested only in the United States (Veroff et al., 1960). It permits a comparison between Protestant and Catholic n Achievement levels as estimated from readers and from scores of individuals. In general the two estimates agree that Catholics score slightly higher. The Catholic reader mean n Achievement score is higher than the mean for the readers used in the public schools (see Table 3.3) and nearly significantly so ($t = 1.55$,

TABLE 3.3 COMPARISON OF n ACHIEVEMENT SCORES FROM CHILDREN'S READERS (1950) AND FROM STORIES WRITTEN BY GROUPS OF MALE STUDENTS

Country	Mean n Ach. score from readers $N = 21$ stories	SD	A. College level samples —percentage of students telling stories with achievement imagery				Per cent of stories achievement related	Mean n Achievement scores	
			N	Picture[7]				Verbal[8]	Graphic[9]
				#2 (%)	#8 (%)	#1 (%)			
U.S. (general)	2.24	2.48	207[1]	69	51	28	49		
U.S. (Catholic)	3.62	3.14	146[2]	63	56	21	47		
Lebanon	2.71	2.68	51[3]	29	27	10	22		
India	2.71*	2.46	50[4]	56	44	18	39	3.79	—
Japan	1.29	1.77	50[4]	62	82	22	55	8.33	+.28
Germany	2.14	2.34	300[4]	34	43	21	33	4.54	−.413
Brazil	1.14	1.96	50[4]	62	64	4	43	5.22	+.095
			B. Less selective high school samples						
U.S. (general)	2.24	2.48	123[5]	41	53				
Australia	2.38	2.34	c.50[6]	41	50				

* obtained from a sample of 6 Hindi, 7 Telegu, and 8 Tamil stories.

[1] Freshmen and Sophomores at the University of Michigan.

[2] Freshmen and Sophomores at La Salle College, Philadelphia, stories told under relaxed and achievement-oriented conditions combined.

[3] From the American University of Beirut, courtesy of Dr. Levon Melikian.

[4] Samples drawn from the mothers and sons study described in Chapter 2—Madras City colleges, Osaka Senior High School (private), German Höhere Schule and São Paulo, Brazil (private schools).

[5] Waterbury (Conn.) High School.

[6] Scores by courtesy of Dr. N. T. Feather, stories told under relaxed and achievement-oriented conditions combined.

[7] Picture #2 is of two men working at a machine in a shop; #8 is of a boy at a desk with an open book in front of him; and #1 is of an older man talking to a younger one (usually interpreted as a father and son).

[8] From the mothers and sons study described in Chapter 2. Verbal n Achievement scores are based on stories written to pictures #2, #8, #1, #9 (man at a desk). (See Atkinson, 1958, Appendix III.)

[9] The graphic measure of n Achievement is the z-transformation of the D-F scores explained in Appendix III. It is not available for India because the correlation with total number of responses was not removed by the z-transformation. Ns are: Japan = 141; Brazil = 306; Germany = 372; India = 145.

NOTE: Since scoring of individual protocols was done by different people in different languages, it cannot be assumed that scoring standards are constant. Consequently only the largest differences in per cent achievement imagery are worth consideration.

$p < .15$). In the national representative sample 58.6 per cent of the Catholics are above the median in n Achievement as compared with 49.3 per cent of the Protestants ($\chi^2 = 3.03$, $p < .10$).

So far so good, but as the testing of samples of individuals gets less representative the picture gets more confusing. For the sake of the record all the estimates of n Achievement levels obtained from tests of individuals in different countries have been brought together in Table 3.3 with the estimates of n Achievement levels based on children's readers from those same countries. Again to look at the most unselected samples first, high school students in the United States and Australia write about the same proportion of stories containing achievement imagery, just as one would expect from the very comparable levels of n Achievement in Australian and American readers. However, if we then move to the special groups of college or private school students tested in some six different countries, we find no agreement between their scores and those of the readers from their country. The correlation between the two estimates based on seven samples is actually a very non-significant $-.10$.

For example, compare Lebanon and India. The mean n Achievement scores from the children's readers are identical, yet Indian students tested in Madras score significantly higher than Lebanese students at the American University in Beirut. The comparisons have to be made in terms of percentages of stories showing achievement imagery, since the same set of pictures was not administered in both countries, but 39 per cent of the stories written by individuals in India were achievement-related as compared with only 22 per cent in Lebanon ($\chi^2 = 10.49$, $p < .01$). Furthermore, the Lebanese and Indian children's books contained significantly more n Achievement than the Japanese books ($p < .05$), but stories written by Japanese students contained significantly more achievement imagery than for Indian or Lebanese students ($p < .01$ in both cases). Or for that matter consider the mean n Achievement score (derived either from the verbal or graphic measures) for the Japanese students as compared with Indian or German students. It is obviously much higher, and significantly so, yet the Japanese reader score is the lowest of the three. Finally the Brazilian stories yield a very low average n Achievement score, yet the Brazilian students score higher than either the German or Indian students who come from countries with higher n Achievement levels, according to the reader estimates.

These inconsistencies may be viewed in two ways. They may be considered as throwing serious doubt on the validity of the reader n Achievement scores, even though it is obvious that the samples are very unrepresentative. That is, they are all male, all from at least the upper-middle class, and from particular localities. For example, Osaka is considered in Japan to be one of its most business-minded, entrepreneurial cities. Thus we may have hit on a sample of boys who are atypically high in n Achievement as compared with boys in other cities like Kyoto for example. The counterargument is that it is precisely these boys (and not girls) from upper-middle class homes, from such business-minded communities from whose ranks the entrepreneurs of the next generation will be drawn. How then can we expect reader n Achievement estimates to predict rate of economic development if they do not agree with estimates of n Achievement level among those very groups that should most powerfully influence the rate of economic development?

The other way of looking at these inconsistencies is to insist that the samples of individuals may be unrepresentative in either of two ways. In the simplest or statistical sense they are clearly not random samples of the populations of the countries involved and therefore they may not give as valid estimates of national n Achievement levels as children's stories which are far more widely read and "expressive" of the "modal personality" in the country. The evidence from the one country where there is a national representative sample (the U.S.) supports this view. However, more general considerations argue against it. As Table 3.5 below shows, most of the underdeveloped countries of the world today have higher reader n Achievement scores than the developed countries. Yet, if our whole line of reasoning is correct, they are underdeveloped in part because they have not had high n Achievement in the past generation or two. Does it seem likely that the general rise in reader n Achievement has everywhere in these countries meant a general rise in n Achievement throughout the whole population? Hardly, particularly in countries like India or Pakistan which have high reader levels of n Achievement, but the great bulk of whose populations must as yet be little affected in any way significant enough to raise over-all level of individual n Achievement.

This line of argument suggests that the reader scores may not reflect n Achievement levels in *any* group of individuals in the country: in this sense any comparison with individual scores is invalid or unrepresentative. Rather, the reader stress on achievement may represent something more like "national aspirations"—the tendency of people in public (e.g., in children's textbooks) to think about achievement. What people are concerned about for public consumption may not be the same as what they are spontaneously concerned about in writing stories privately, yet it is the "public" concerns that may be more diagnostic of public achievements, as in economic development.

Comparison of reader n Achievement levels with levels obtained from individuals has raised some interesting questions as to just what the readers are measuring. It has even thrown some doubt on whether they are measuring anything of importance, but in the end, the proof of the pudding is in the eating: do they enable us to predict which countries will develop more rapidly economically?

Measuring Economic Growth in Terms of Real National Income

The next problem is to obtain a measure of economic growth. What do economists mean by such a concept? How do they measure it? Meier and Baldwin (1957, p. 2) state that "economic development is a process whereby an economy's real national income increases over a long period of time." Such a definition will do as a start. Often growth is expressed in per capita terms because it may seem contradictory to speak of economic "development" for a country in which the people are getting poorer and poorer despite an increase in real national income because of an even more rapid increase in population. Practically all nations in which population is increasing show an increase in real national income over a long period of time so that defining "development" without reference to the population base provides fairly insensitive measures of rate of growth. On the other hand expressing economic growth exclusively in per capita income terms also leads to some strange results such as that England showed no economic growth during the high point of the Industrial Revolution (1780-1840), since income per capita did not rise at that time (see Deane, 1957). We will have to return to this problem later. Growth is measured in terms of "real" national income, of course, to adjust for inflationary and deflationary price trends. Finally the definition requires "long range" increases in national income to rule out temporary upswings that may be part of business cycles or sudden shifts in the terms of trade.

But how does one measure real national income in different countries over time? In a particular country the problem is not so difficult where one can estimate the value of goods and services produced in a common unit of currency which can be adjusted for inflationary or deflationary trends. But to compare real income in different countries is much more difficult than simply converting local currency into some common currency (such as dollars) in terms of the prevailing exchange rates. The fact is that the purchasing power of money varies in different countries at different times and these differences are not accurately reflected by the exchange rate. Colin Clark (1957) has made the most determined effort to measure economic progress in various countries by means of an "international unit" (I.U.) which has the same meaning in various countries. "One I.U. of real income was taken as the quantity of goods exchangeable in the U.S.A. for one dollar over the average of the decade 1925-1934." (Clark, 1957, p. 18.) He then determined how much it would cost in terms of local currency in other countries to purchase the same goods and services as one dollar would have purchased in the United States at this time and expressed income per capita in the country in terms of the resulting standard international unit. For example, he estimates it would take 781 Italian lira in

1950 to purchase the goods and services available for $1.00 in the U.S. from 1925-34. Similarly it takes $1.64 in U.S. currency in 1950 to buy the same things. Income in both countries can thus be expressed in the same unit, in terms of "market basket equivalents." In purchasing power, 781 lira was equal to $1.64 in 1950. At current (1961) exchange rates, however, 781 lira will buy only $1.26, so that if Italian national income were expressed simply in terms of dollar equivalents it would be underestimated in terms of real purchasing power in Italy for the standard items in Clark's list.

Actually, of course, such a method of comparison works only to the extent that people in different countries want more or less the same things to the same degree. To a considerable extent such an assumption is certainly warranted: in modern nations people do want, more or less to the same degree, the standard items Clark uses in computing his indexes for purchasing power equivalents—food, housing, fuel, transportation, cigarettes, and similar goods. But, as Clark himself is the first to point out, values placed on various items do change, particularly as one goes from the Western, developed countries to the much poorer countries of the East. Rice is cheap in the Orient, but relatively expensive in the West, whereas the reverse is true of grains. Much is paid out for distributive services in the West, while in the East they are in many places nonexistent and all food that is eaten is grown locally. "And the last and most striking difference is that domestic and similar personal services, increasingly high priced and hard to obtain in the Western world, are (for obvious reasons) the one commodity which is cheap and abundant in the Orient." (Clark, 1957, p. 19). For all these reasons, Clark feels it is necessary to develop a different unit of comparison for poor countries which he calls the "Oriental Unit" and bases on the purchasing power of the Indian rupee. That is, he assumes that poor countries are similar enough in what they want to make comparisons in such a unit feasible, just as comparisons within the West are possible in terms of the I.U. For obvious reasons, I.U.'s cannot be converted directly into O.U.'s because they are, so to speak, based on different "market baskets."

Economists have been fairly skeptical of Clark's efforts to obtain measures of economic development in internationally comparable terms, partly because they do not know how safe it is to assume that people want the same things to the same extent even within Western countries, and partly because estimates he has had to make of the value of certain items in a particular country at a particular time period have often seemed to be based on insufficient information. Nevertheless, no economist has yet provided any better national income data which are anywhere near as complete in their coverage of various countries at different time periods. Interestingly enough, Watkins and Hagen (1956) independently prepared estimates of per capita income in dollar equivalents in 1953 in various countries using all the relevant information they could obtain. Their figures correlate .93 with those arrived at by Colin Clark for the sample of forty countries with which we are primarily concerned. Furthermore, by Clark's own standards, our estimates for the forty countries had to be particularly approximate since it was necessary to convert all figures into O.U. equivalents to rank them on the same scale. Such a high correlation between two independent estimates despite obviously crude approximations on both sides suggests that the estimates may indeed be dependable enough for our purposes and that Clark's figures cannot be so far off as some critics have inferred.

Alternative Methods of Measuring Rates of Economic Growth

Nevertheless, the very problem that Clark faced in trying to put a money value on various things that people want suggests that there is some ambiguity in defining economic growth in terms of growth of real national income. What exactly is to be included under income? A kind of primitive psychology of human needs is involved in the concept. People obviously need food and shelter, and if they can get more food or better shelter at less cost, their real income has increased. But don't they need leisure too? If so, what value is to be put upon it? If it is important, has an element in "income" steadily declined as people have spent more and more time working for other things? From some ultimate point of view, one could even argue that income cannot increase or decrease. If people spend more time doing one thing—say, building bridges, airplanes and skyscrapers— they must spend less time doing something else—say, sitting and contemplating the universe. Whether one regards such a shift as an increase or a decrease in income depends on one's definition of what peoples' basic needs and wants are. We in the West have felt that man "obviously" wants and needs material things—machinery, roads, buildings, and food—and our national income figures clearly reflect this conviction. We are less sure about how much he needs "services." For example, there is a major controversy among economists as to whether government expenditures (as a kind of "service") are really productive and should be included in national income estimates. (See Clark, 1957, p. 21.)

Using national income to measure rates of economic growth runs into a number of other difficulties even more serious than such "speculative" considerations. First, the figures necessary for such computations are simply not available, particularly on underdeveloped countries where they are most needed. Despite the heroic efforts of men like Clark, Kuznets, and Hagen, their figures, as they would be the first to admit, are often very rough approximations and cannot be improved and collected regularly over time for computing growth rates in all countries without very large expenditures of time and money.

Secondly, national income figures may reflect variations in natural resources in a way which defies any common sense notion of what economic development means. For example, Watkins and Hagen (1956) estimate that the average per capita income in the United States for 1953 was $1,908, while in Kuwait the average per capita income was $2,500. Are we to conclude that Kuwait is more economically advanced or developed than the United States? While oil-rich sheikdoms are perhaps rare enough not to concern us much, one suspects that natural resources may also enter in to distort the picture considerably in other countries as well. For example, Kuznets has estimated (1956) that for the Union of South Africa the average percentage increase in income per capita per decade over the past fifty-odd years is 23.8 per cent, whereas for Australia it is only 9.5 per cent. Are we to assume that the Union of South Africa has developed at a rate almost three times as fast as Australia? It is not an unreasonable assumption that at least some of the superior performance of the Union of South Africa may have been due to the fact that it happened to be richer in gold and diamonds.

Third, there is the continuing argument mentioned earlier as to whether the measure should be in per capita terms or not. It appears to be a case of "damned-if-you-do-and-damned-if-you-don't" so that most economists settle the matter by giving both sets of figures and telling the reader it is a question of whether he is interested in social welfare or not. But this does not really solve the problem. Is *any* long-range increase in national income to be considered economic growth, even if it is only due to an increase in population, let us say, in a traditional agricultural country? Or to fall on the other horn of the dilemma, are we to conclude that there was *no economic growth at all* in England during the Industrial Revolution because there was no rise in income per capita?

Such considerations suggest that the economists have too easily and uniformly concluded that rates of economic growth must be measured in terms of changes in national income. It should be possible to discover alternative methods of measurement which are theoretically less ambiguous and practically easier to compute. To begin with the theoretical issue, many of the difficulties mentioned above arise from the fact that implicit in the concept of economic growth is an idea not perfectly reflected in the national income measure, namely the idea of *technological progress*, or more generally, growth in the actual production of "economic" goods. The concept does not require that a country concentrate almost exclusively on manufacturing, but it does require that a country has developed the capacities to produce and use properly the most modern technicological innovations. For example New Zealand, though it gains more of its gross national income from agriculture than from anything else, is still an economically advanced country in this sense because it can produce, service, and use the most modern types of material culture, i.e., means of transport (automobiles, railroads), communication (telephones), sources of power (electricity), and the like. This kind of technological growth is sometimes considered more or less equivalent to growth in national income. Hagen states, for example, "Continuing rise in per capita income is due to continuing progress in techniques in production." (1959, p. 373.) But the two measures are conceptually distinct and not always perfectly associated in fact.

Thus it is because we are implicitly thinking in terms of capacity to *produce* modern material culture that we find it somewhat absurd to think of Kuwait as more developed than the United States, or the Union of South Africa as having developed several times as fast as Australia. Kuwait may be able to *purchase* more such goods in per capita terms than the United States, but until it can produce and service them we do not think of it as an economically developed country in the sense that the United States is. It is the failure to make this distinction that leads to some of the other difficulties we have encountered. We worried about whether a country could be considered to be advancing economically even though the long term rise in its gross national income was due, not to a "change in the state of the arts," but solely to a rapid rise in population. In terms of the productivity criterion just proposed it is not developing economically, though in terms of national income figures it is. Similarly the problem of whether England's economy was developing rapidly during the Industrial Revolution is solved. In terms of national income per capita it was not; in terms of production and use of the most modern types of material culture (or technological advances), it was.

The economists have run into difficulty because they became tangled up in the question of what people want or will pay for. Thus some of them would even define economic growth as an increasing capacity to satisfy human wants. But human beings may want many things—peace of mind, time to contemplate ultimate spiritual realities, as well as tangible goods like automobiles—and in the literal sense of giving people what they want, the economic systems of some of the poorest and most backward countries would have to be judged more advanced than ours. What these theorists had in mind of course was a parochial set of wants, common to the Western world, for certain material goods and services that such backward people clearly do not have. But what is interesting is the reason why the theorists were led to postulate such economic wants. They had to because they needed the price system to estimate gross national product or gross national income in terms of some common unit (e.g., money prices). And by definition a price is the amount someone is willing to pay for a product or service he presumably wants (as compared with all his other wants). This situation incidentally, creates a lot of problems in the area of wants that cannot be satisfied through the price system: how is their satisfaction to be included in national income accounts, if we hold to the "satisfaction of wants" definition of economic growth? (See Kuznets, 1956.)

The chief conceptual problems arise when economic growth is defined on the income or demand side, not on the productivity side. If we define growth in terms of rate of production and use of technological advances, fewer conceptual problems arise, but economists might regard such a distinction as absurd or at least meaningless. For, in a sense, gross national product and gross national income are identical by definition because both are estimated in the same way through the price system. If we want to keep the two concepts separate, how can we solve the problem they solved by the use of the price system—how are we to estimate gross national product if we cannot value various products in terms of what people will pay for them and then sum those values? How can we add or equate production of coal, rice, cement, automobiles, and cigarettes? What is our comparative unit of measurement if we do not employ the price system, granted that it gives rise to all the conceptual confusions and measurement difficulties already mentioned?

One answer is that we do not need to estimate *gross* national product if our purpose is only to compare rates of growth.[6] We can employ a *sampling* procedure—that is, we can select a single index of production which is *representative of* total production or economic activity. The only requirement is that the single index be representative of (highly correlated with) the total output of which it is a part. An analogy may make the point clearer. A psychologist may be interested in assessing all the mental capacities that a child of six has—ability to copy complex designs, to reason, to draw, to put puzzles together—but to get a satisfactory measure of mental growth, he does not feel that he must measure every one of these capacities. Instead he may single out one ability, such as vocabulary, which correlates so highly with the other abilities that it will provide a quick, convenient, and quite accurate measure of over-all mental growth. It is exactly in this sense that a single index may prove to be a much more convenient way of estimating economic growth than trying to combine a lot of them into an over-all measure according to the traditional practice of economists in estimating gross national product through the price system.

Electric Power Produced as a Measure of Economic Growth

After considering a number of possible indexes, the amount of electricity produced in a given country was chosen as most likely to represent economic growth in modern times, in the sense in which we have used the term. We have argued that economic growth, in its most unambiguous sense, is growth in the production, service and use of the most modern technology ("hardware") known to society at a given moment in history. Certainly in our time the production and use of electricity in a country should be highly diagnostic of the level of its technology, since it is the form into which most of the energy is converted which runs our complex civilization. Though the sources of energy may be quite varied (water power, animal power, wind, coal, oil), electricity has become the *form* in which energy is most economically stored and transmitted. Most of the productive machinery in the world would not run today without electricity; furthermore, it is spreading into every household as a consumer item, as a means of operating lighting systems and other modern appliances like radios, clocks, and washing machines.

Moreover, it avoids some of the more obvious biases that influence other measures of technological growth. For example, indexes of mining or manufacturing might weight natural resources unduly or the extent to which a country gains its livelihood from industry rather than agriculture. Consumption of electric power tends also to be biased toward industrialization but not so severely. Normally about 60 per cent of it is used in industrial and commercial establishments. Thus New Zealand, which earns the greatest share of its national income from agriculture, can still have a very high consumption of electricity per capita, since it is also used for residential, agricultural and public services. As we have already seen in Chapter 2, electricity can be produced either by water power or coal or oil, so that countries which are poor in one or the other of these resources may substitute the other. Measures of transportation facilities might also have been used, but they seem too much influenced by the geographical situation of the country—whether it is large or small, mountainous or flat, on the sea or inland. But might not electrical consumption also be influenced by geographical conditions? Northern countries certainly require more heat, but electricity has not as yet become a very economical source of heat, and it is doubtful whether they require more light since, though it is darker in winter, it is also lighter in summer.

Other advantages of using electrical output are purely practical. It is everywhere expressed in the same unit—the kilowatt-hour—so that production in various countries is directly comparable without any complex transformations of any sort. No such difficulties arise here as when one tries to equate for the purchasing power of money or to convert one commercial source of energy into another (gasoline, natural gas, and hydroelectric power into coal equivalents, for example). Also production more or less equals consumption, so that it is not necessary to go into the question of adjusting for stockpiles. Furthermore, the data on electricity consumed are more reliable than many other economic indexes which have to depend on multiple estimates from different sources. Finally, the figures on electrical output are available for about the time period in which we are interested, 1929-1950.

In the tabulations that follow, two measures of economic growth will be used—Clark's estimates of real national income, and kilowatt-hours of electricity produced. Greater stress will be put on the latter measure because it is conceptually clearer and probably has a smaller margin of error. Clark's estimates will be included largely because income per capita is the traditional measure of growth used by economists, and because the electrical measure has some weaknesses of its own which may be smoothed out by averaging in Clark's estimates of growth. In 1929 electricity consumption was not as good a measure of economic growth, or technological progress, as it is today. More nations were then in a less "modern" stage when fewer technological improvements depended upon electricity. Steam engines were much more common, so that Great Britain which had developed highly in the age of steam is probably seriously underrated using a measure of electricity alone. Other countries were predominantly agricultural, and rural electrification was still comparatively rare in 1929. The increasing importance of electrical power is illustrated by the fact that the correlation between Clark's estimates of income per capita and kilowatt-hours per capita produced rose from .60 in 1929 for the 27 countries in Table 3.4 to .73 in 1950 for the same countries. For the full sample of 40 countries in Table 3.5, the rank order correlation jumps up to .865 between kilowatt-hours of electricity per capita and the Watkins-Hagen estimates of income per capita in dollar equivalents.

These figures should provide some reassurance to those economists who are not impressed by the arguments above in favor of abandoning national income as a measure for comparing rates of economic growth. The measure we have decided to use is in any case highly correlated with the best estimates of national income available so that we are not dealing with something very special or unrelated to what they generally have in mind. Hagen's statement that increases in income per capita seem to be dependent on technological improvements is certainly true today. It may even have been as true in 1929, but electricity was then a less adequate measure of technological development than it is today. Even in the 1950's, it shows some peculiarities which a glance at Table 3.4 will show. Thus Norway in 1950 consumed twice the amount of electricity on a per capita basis as the United States, yet it does not seem altogether correct to infer that Norway is twice as far advanced technically as the United States. In fact, both in Norway and Canada, the index is inflated by highly developed pulp and paper and aluminum industries, both of which use abnormally large amounts of electric power. For all of these reasons it seemed best to compute an index which combined both national income and electrical power figures to get an estimate of economic gains.

Comparing Rates of Growth

So much for the measures of economic development, but how is *rate* of growth to be computed? Obviously the absolute size of gains cannot be used, because they are highly correlated with the initial level of development. For the countries in Table 3.4, for example, the gain in I.U. per

: capita between 1925 and 1950 is correlated .58 with the initial level of I.U. per capita in 1925. The situation is even worse so far as electricity is concerned. Gain in output between 1929 and 1950 is correlated .92 with the initial level in 1929 ($N = 34$). Apparently the rich get richer and the poor stay relatively poorer, perhaps because of marked differences in natural resources or because economic development proceeds at an accelerating rate: once a country reaches a certain level, it becomes easier and easier for it to develop more rapidly.

Economists have traditionally met this and similar problems by expressing changes as percentage increases over the base rate. Thus, gains of very different absolute size may be identical on a percentage basis so that an increase of $200 a head from $200 to $400 is equivalent to an increase of $400 a head from a base of $400 to $800. The problems involved in using such percentage transformations are very serious. For one thing they do not automatically remove the correlation with the initial level, as it is sometimes assumed that they do. The point has been fully discussed elsewhere by Cronbach (1949). In economic statistics there is often a negative correlation between the size of the denominator and the size of the percentage increase; the lower the initial level, the more likely it is that the percentage increase will be larger. Kuznets (1956) has published a table showing percentage changes per decade in national products per capita for nineteen countries. The size of the percentage growth estimate is correlated $-.34$ with the size of the denominator used in computing the percentages. The result would appear to be purely artifactual because the denominators are all expressed in terms of local currencies, the unit of measurement of which would appear to have little economic significance. While the correlation is not significant in such a small number of cases, one cannot help wondering how much of the fact that Japan has twice as high a growth rate as France is due to the fact that Japanese income is expressed in yen and French income in much more numerous francs. Furthermore, the sampling and other statistical properties of percentages are simply not very well known. Therefore it is difficult to combine them, to evaluate the significance of changes in them, or to treat them generally as other numbers are treated according to standard statistical techniques.

There is, however, a method of evaluating gains which does not have the defects of the two methods already discussed (absolute or percentage gains). It involves evaluating gains in terms of the regression line which best fits the over-all relationship between initial level and gain. The problem is analogous to the one faced by a psychologist who wants to know whether a student is doing better or worse than he should in his school work according to his intelligence level. Obviously if he does average work, he is not doing very well if he is very bright, but if he is not bright, average performance may indicate that he is "overachieving" as compared with what might be expected from one of his intelligence. The regression equation enables one to predict in the case of economic data on the basis of initial level how much a country could be expected to gain on the average. If a country gains more than could be expected for one of its initial level, it is gaining more rapidly, and if it performs less well than expected, it is gaining more slowly. The plus or minus deviation from expected thus becomes the measure of economic growth, or of relative over- or underachievement, to use the phraseology of school performance. A simple illustration taken from Table 3.4 may make the point clearer.

Country	Per capita usable water power (hp)	Coal per capita (tons)	Electricity produced in kwh/cap				% Gain
			1929	Gain to 1950	Predicted gain	Gain or loss over predicted	
Denmark	.011	.121	158	360	307	+53	228
Austria	.500	.379	380	520	531	−11	136
Portugal	.070	.052	36	74	183	−109	206

On an absolute basis, clearly Austria has the largest gain in electricity produced per capita between 1929 and 1950, but we strongly suspect that this has to do with the fact that it is much richer in water power and coal resources than either Denmark or Portugal. To know whether Austria or Denmark is developing more rapidly, we need to control somehow for the differences in resources and for the higher level which Austria started out with. Percentage gain figures do in fact show that Austria appears to have done much worse than Denmark, and also much worse than Portugal. But we suspect that Portugal may be favored in this comparison by having started at such a low level that a large percentage increase is easy to obtain. The regression which best describes the relationship of gain to initial level for electricity does take account of the fact that Portugal was initially lower than Denmark and predicts that on the average it should therefore have shown a smaller gain (183 kilowatt-hours versus 307 kilowatt-hours per capita). Nevertheless, Denmark does better than predicted and Portugal does worse, even than its much lower expected gain. Austria, on the other hand, does only slightly worse than expected and much better than Portugal, although the percentage figures do not show it.

National Levels of n Achievement in 1925 and Subsequent Rates of Economic Growth

Table 3.4 brings together the reader data and the measures of economic growth for all countries for which readers were available in the 1925 period and also for those additional countries for which readers were available in

TABLE 3.4   ESTIMATES OF NATIONAL ECONOMIC DEVELOPMENT
BETWEEN 1925 AND 1950 COMPARED WITH n ACHIEVEMENT LEVEL
IN CHILDREN'S READERS IN 1925 AND 1950

Country	n Achievement level[1]		National income in International Units per capita[2]		
	1925	1950	1924-27	Gain to 1949-52	Gain or loss over expected values in SD units (SD = 79)
Sweden	2.19	1.62	307	321	+2.35
U. S.	1.90	2.24	657	405	+1.28
New Zealand	1.48	2.05	572	313	+.63
Canada	2.67	2.29	555	252	−.04
Great Britain	2.10	1.67	504	94	−1.71
Australia	2.81	2.38	464	259	+.61
Finland	1.24	1.52	183	162	+1.10
Union of S. Africa	1.05	2.33	155	116	+.70
Ireland	3.19	2.29	297	141	+.14
Denmark	2.00	1.05	490	126	−1.23
Poland		.86	134	16	−.44
Norway	1.33	1.71	300	166	+.44
Netherlands	.29	1.48	388	112	−.78
Austria	1.57	1.86	233	18	−1.02
Hungary	1.29	1.81	128	11	−.47
Chile	1.29	1.19	173	91	+.27
Japan		1.29	170	27	−.52
Portugal		2.10	118	28	−.19
Greece	.38	2.29	187	−24	−1.28
Bulgaria		2.24	126	84	+.47
France	.81	2.38	389	101	−.92
Argentina	1.86	3.38	241	127	−.50
Italy		1.33	194	44	−.45
Uruguay	1.48	1.86			
Spain	.81	2.33	378	16	−1.93
Belgium	1.00	.43	269	240	+1.57
Germany	1.38	2.14	280	82	−.51
Mexico		1.57			
Switzerland		1.20[6]	366	265	+1.29
Russia	.95	2.10	168	99	+.39
N	23		28	28	
Mean	1.52		30	132	
SD	.72		150	108	
Regression equation:	Predicted gain = .484 initial level − 13.8				

[1] Achievement level is the sum of n Achievement characteristics per story for each country divided by the total number of stories (= 21). To get rid of negative numbers, +1 is added since in the n Achievement scoring system an unrelated story is scored −1, an achievement related story +1, and a doubtful story 0.
[2] From Clark, C., *The Conditions of Economic Progress*, 3rd ed., London, Macmillan, 1957.
[3] From Woytinsky, 1953, p. 972 and UN *Statistical Yearbook* 1956 (used also to correct Woytinsky figures occasionally). Per capita estimates are used to correct roughly for territorial changes resulting from World War II.

TABLE 3.4 (*Continued*)

Country	Electricity produced in kilowatt-hours per capita[3]			Average gain or loss in SD units
	1929	Gain to 1950	Gain or loss over expected values in SD units (SD = 247.5)	
Sweden	811	1769	+3.17	+2.76
U. S.	962	1598	+1.86	+1.57
New Zealand	484	1116	+1.86	+1.25
Canada	1855	2265	+1.73[4]	+.85
Great Britain	269	846	+1.65	−.02
Australia	359	801	+1.13	+.87
Finland	324	676	+.74	+.92
Union of S. Africa	275	615	+.69	+.70
Ireland	33	281[5]	+.33	+.24
Denmark	158	360	+.14	−.55
Poland	100	275	+.03	−.21
Norway	2850	2583[5]	−.03[4]	+.21
Netherlands	290	435	−.10	−.44
Austria	380	520	−.12	−.57
Hungary	100	214[5]	−.26	−.37
Chile	211	273	−.43	−.08
Japan	247	307[5]	−.44	−.48
Portugal	36	74	−.52	−.36
Greece	18	55	−.52	−.90
Bulgaria	15	51	−.52	−.04
France	378	412	−.55	−.74
Argentina	119	136	−.61	−.16
Italy	260	275	−.62	−.54
Uruguay	75	90	−.62	
Spain	107	118	−.63	−1.28
Belgium	505	491	−.75	+.41
Germany	475	450	−.79	−.65
Mexico	105	70	−.82	
Switzerland	1250	980	−1.26[4]	+.02
Russia				
N	34	34		
Mean	386[7]	537[7]		
SD	588	637		
Regression equation:	Predicted gain = 1.01 initial level + 147[8]			

[4] Inspection shows that the regression is not a straight line when the initial level is very high. Thus the countries with the highest initial levels (Norway, Canada, and Switzerland) should not be expected to continue to grow at the same rate because of a possible "saturation" effect, especially in the two smaller countries. Accordingly, the regression weight was reduced to .85 for Norway and .9 for Canada and Switzerland to get the predicted growth values.

[5] For these countries the base line data are for 1930, but to make them comparable to the others, one year's gain was added equivalent to the average gain per annum over the past 20 years.

[6] Average of French and German Swiss readers, in which German readers were weighted double to account roughly for population differences.

[7] Based on 34 countries for which information is available (including also Algeria, India, Turkey, Iran, and Tunisia).

[8] Although normally the growth curve is logarithmic (see Table 3.6), for this time period untransformed data yield the same results.

the 1950 period plus both economic measures. Mexican data are also shown, even though Mexico does not satisfy either of these criteria, because it seemed to fit in with this particular group of countries, all of which are part of "Western" civilization except for Japan which has been very much influenced by the West. Data for other countries like India, Turkey, Iraq, and Iran are presented subsequently in Table 3.6 for a later time period. Table 3.4 presents economic data in terms of initial levels, absolute gains, and gains relative to prediction in standard score terms so that the two independent estimates of gains might be combined as in the last column on the right in the table. The two estimates of economic performance relative to expectations (national income in I.U./cap and kwh/cap) are positively correlated ($r = .382$, $p < .05$). The trend is for deviations from predicted gains to be similar according to the two measures except for some outstanding exceptions like Great Britain and Denmark, which fell way below expectation in income per capita, but did better than expected so far as technological advance (as reflected in electrical output) is concerned. The reverse is true of Belgium and Switzerland. Such extreme differences suggest that neither measure may be telling the whole story of economic growth for the country concerned for this time period and that a combination of the two should be better than either one. Since there seemed to be no good reason for weighting one index more than the other, the two estimates of economic growth were simply averaged as shown in the last column.

The countries have been listed in the table according to gain in electrical output (1929-1950) as compared with expected gain, and even a glance at the corresponding n Achievement levels for 1925 suggests that there is a strong tendency for those countries at the top of the table which performed better than expected economically to have been high in n Achievement at the outset of the period over which growth was measured. The correlations between the n Achievement levels in the children's readers around 1925 and around 1950 with the three estimates of economic growth are shown in Table 3.5:

TABLE 3.5   CORRELATIONS OF READER n ACHIEVEMENT SCORES WITH DEVIATIONS
FROM EXPECTED ECONOMIC GAINS

n Achievement level by year	I.U./cap 1925-1950 $N = 22$	Kwh/cap 1929-1950 $N = 22$	Both combined $N = 21$
1925	.25	.53, $p < .01$ pd	.46, $p < .02$ pd
1950	−.10	.03	−.08

pd = predicted direction

The results are quite striking. The readers do not appear to have been such a poor method of estimating n Achievement level in 1925 after all, at least for these countries, and our general hypothesis is strongly confirmed. The estimates of n Achievement are positively correlated with *subsequent* economic growth and very significantly so for the electrical output measure, or for both measures combined. On the other hand, n Achievement level as estimated from the 1950 readers is *not* related to *previous* economic growth. The difference in the two sets of correlations is particularly important theoretically because it bears on the issue of economic determinism.

It is difficult to argue from these data that material advance came first and created a higher need for achievement. Rather the reverse appears to be true—high n Achievement levels are associated with subsequently more rapid economic development. Marx appears to have been somewhat premature in dismissing psychology as a major determinant in history. The relationship is quite sizeable and unlikely to be altered by various adjustments. Thus, 78 per cent of the countries above the mean in n Achievement in 1925 were "overachievers" so far as electrical output is concerned, as compared with only 25 per cent of those below the mean in n Achievement, a difference that could have arisen by chance less than 5 in 100 times. The adjustments in the regression coefficient for three countries—Norway, Canada and Switzerland—which might certainly be criticized, do not any of them change the sign of the gain. Thus Norway remains an underachiever, and the other two remain overachievers, even if no adjustments are made. Furthermore, if published figures on Russia's electrical output can be accepted at face value, it would have to be classified as doing better than expected, since it went from a kilowatt-hour per capita figure of around 40-50 in 1929 to 440 in 1950. Yet Russia's n Achievement level in 1925 is estimated to be below the mean. The Russian electrical output figures were not included in the table because both the electrical output figures and the population estimates seem more than usually open to error, but even if Russia were included as a negative instance of the predicted relationship, the over-all association would still be significant at the .05 level (Fisher's exact test).

The problem of war damage.[7] Inspection of Table 3.4 suggests that many of the countries that were "underachievers" economically speaking were crippled by World War II, either because they were conquered, occupied, or heavily bombed (e.g., Netherlands, Germany, France, Norway, Belgium). Actually, however, failure to gain in electrical output over expected between 1929-1950 is significantly correlated ($r = .46$, $p < .05$) with degree of interference by the war, when such interference is estimated as the maximum drop in electrical output (in percentage terms) in any one year during the war over any other previous year. In other words poor economic performance may not be the result of lack of motivation but of damage suffered during the war.

The crucial and rather surprising fact is that war damage as estimated above is also very significantly negatively correlated with n Achievement level in 1925 ($r = -.58$, $p < .01$). The countries low in n Achievement like the Netherlands, Belgium, France, and Germany, were in general the ones most severely damaged in the war, while the countries high in n Achievement like Australia, United States, Canada, and Sweden were not. It is difficult to be sure what such a relationship means. One possibility is to argue that it really is a once-in-a-hundred chance occurrence resulting from the historical accident that countries far removed from the European theatre of war happened to have higher n Achievement because they were largely populated by recent immigrants who tend to have higher n Achievement (see Chapter 8). According to this view it was just bad luck that countries with low n Achievement like Belgium, Holland, Norway and Finland happened to be in the way of big powers that had need of bases on their territory. They were "pawns" in European power politics, and thus it is only fair in estimating their economic gains to partial out the extent to which they were damaged by the war. Actually the partial correlation between n Achievement level (1925) and gain in electrical power output over expected to 1950 is reduced from .53 to .37 ($p \sim .05$, pd) if the correlation with extent of war damage is partialled out.

These estimates of war damage are, of course, extremely rough and are unfortunately not entirely independent of the motivational variable we are interested in. That is, we would also expect that the production of a country with low n Achievement would fall further for a standard quantity of bombs dropped than the production of a country with high n Achievement. Consider Denmark and Belgium, for example. Both were occupied fairly rapidly by the Germans under somewhat similar conditions but the Danish readers contained a higher level of n Achievement (mean = 2.00) than the Belgian readers (mean = 1.00). Danish electrical output showed a maximum drop of 18 per cent, Belgian 34 per cent. To what extent is this difference due to differences in motivation levels and to what extent to more severe treatment of the Belgians by the Germans? If we partial out such damage estimates we certainly overcorrect and take the position that *all* of such drops in output must be due to external conditions beyond the control of the people in the country. To put it another way, we are being "unfair" to the Danes in not correcting the estimate of their rate of growth as much as we do for the Belgians for the very reason that they may have worked harder to overcome the economic handicaps of German occupation and therefore showed less "damage" than the Belgians.

Adjustments for war damage can also be made that do not so directly hinge on the response of the country to such damage. For example, the 22 countries divide neatly into two halves—those that suffered noticeable damage from the outside in World War II (Great Britain, Finland, Denmark, Norway, Netherlands, Austria, Hungary, Greece, France, Belgium and Germany) and those that did not (Sweden, United States, New Zealand,

Canada, Australia, Union of South Africa, Ireland, Chile, Argentina, Uruguay and Spain). *Within* each of these groups of countries the correlation of n Achievement (1925) with gain in terms of kwh/cap is still substantial despite reduction in the number of cases and curtailment of range. In the nondamaged countries the correlation is .38 and in the damaged countries it is .56 (combined $p < .05$), confirming our suspicion that it is the *response* to the damage that is important and this response should in part at least be a function of n Achievement level in the country. Unfortunately this method does not "correct" the scores for the damaged countries but treats them separately. Accordingly, one more attempt was made to allow for destruction of plant by giving each country heavily involved in the war two more years to "make up for lost time"; the terminal date was shifted from 1950 to 1948 for the non-damaged countries and left at 1950 for the others (with two exceptions, England and Finland, terminal dates for which were set at 1949 because damage had been considerably earlier than in other countries). Such a method does not overcorrect as much as the partial correlation does because it allows all countries a fixed amount of "lost time" due to the war, independent of their actual response to it. For these adjusted figures the correlation between n Achievement (1925) and gains in kwh/cap over expected is .43, $p < .05$.

Still another approach is to move the terminal date for the growth period as far as possible (e.g., to 1957) beyond World War II to avoid its most immediately damaging effects. There are two objections to using this period generally to measure economic growth: (1) it prevents us from cross-validating our findings and checking to see whether the 1950 reader scores are beginning to predict rates of growth from around 1950 on (see next section), and (2) it yields gains in kwh/cap which are no longer linearly related to initial level in 1929. Therefore the raw data have to be transformed to produce an approximately linear regression which makes trouble because there is no rigorous way of deciding what transformation to use and because the interpretation becomes a little more complicated. However, a square-root transformation was used which permitted the usual linear regression analysis to be made. The correlation between n Achievement level and gains or losses over expected in electrical output (in square root terms) over this longer period, 1929-1957, was very close to what it had been for the shorter term, i.e., $r = .50$, $N = 22$, $p < .01$, pd. Therefore, moving the terminal date further from the war does not affect the correlation (though it does affect values for particular countries of course), despite the fact that we know from the second set of readers that n Achievement levels had begun to change sharply by around 1950.

Such corrections are all arbitrary to some extent and by making other assumptions or allowing different time periods to catch up, one could probably manage to destroy the correlation which seems to hold up fairly well despite various attempts to "adjust" it. Obviously World War

II is a problem, so far as our figures are concerned, if we try to correct for its effects. There are two ways to avoid making such corrections. First, we can go back to the period 1929-1939 before the war and see if countries that were high in n Achievement in 1925 were gaining in electrical output faster than expected over this short time period. After computing the regression equation in the same way, we find that they were: 64 per cent of the 11 above the median in n Achievement were gaining faster than expected as contrasted, with only 27 per cent of the 11 below the median in n Achievement ($p < .10$). The correlation is not significant because of a few very deviant cases, chief among them the United States, which was showing poor economic performance because it had not yet recovered from the depression. The short period of time happened to coincide with a major "business cycle," and n Achievement levels should not be expected to predict very accurately such short-range fluctuations in the economy. Instead they supposedly reflect a motivational factor which should have a long-range effect, primarily as it influences the energy with which men throw themselves into economic activity, or into coping with the difficulties that come their way in trying to reach economic objectives.

The above line of reasoning suggests the second method of avoiding correcting for war damage—ignoring the war altogether. After all, from the theoretical viewpoint (and in the historical studies in the next chapter) external events, whether for good or for ill, are turned to one account or another depending on the motives of the people involved. In a sense history is *what happened*, not what *might* have happened if there hadn't been a war, depression or an invasion. As history actually happened, n Achievement level in 1925 predicts economic growth pretty well to 1950 regardless of wars, depressions, and the like. Perhaps an analogy will help make the point clear. If a student complains to his teacher that he received a low mark because football practice kept him from studying, does the teacher adjust his grade for the lower amount of time he spent on the course? Usually not. Similarly why should we correct German economic performance because of damage in World War II? In this case certainly, if Germany had had high n Achievement, and been interested primarily in economic matters it might not have gotten into the war at all. Like the football player, it deserves the "mark" it gets for economic performance because it was busy with other things—e.g., fighting a war which proved very damaging to its economy. Sweden, on the other hand, had high n Achievement, stayed out of the war (though it might easily have been drawn in), and ended up an economic overachiever. But what about the small countries? Do they really have any choice in such matters? Weren't they "forced to play football," so to speak, so that their economic performance suffered? Apparently there was freedom of movement even for them—the Danes with high n Achievement came out of the German occupation an overachiever and much better off than the Norwegians, the Dutch and the Belgians with lower n Achievement. The latter may have struggled more against the German occupying forces, but the Danes paid more attention to what the hypothesis predicts—namely, to economic matters. If we take the hypothesis in its strongest sense, it says that people with high n Achievement will tend to focus on economic matters to the exclusion of other interests like fighting wars, so that in the end they will be better off economically. This is exactly what our data show and a strong case can be made for not giving extra credit to those countries which spent their time and resources doing other things. To be sure we would not want our terminal date for a period of economic growth to occur in the midst of a major war when there is severe destructoin of plant, but we chose 1950 as a date because it was long enough after the war for all countries to have rebuilt the damaged facilities themselves. What they "lost," economically speaking, during the war was really lost and can very properly be charged to their account in most cases, either because they did not respond vigorously enough to the destruction, or because they didn't avoid the war in the first place, or because they spent their energies in noneconomic pursuits during the occupation such as fighting their conquerors. To be sure, some injustice will be done to some countries by making no corrections for war damage, but on the whole it seems less serious than what results from trying to make such corrections. Therefore we believe the figures on economic growth in Table 3.4 are the best estimates that can be made, and have used them uncorrected in other parts of the book (Chapters 1 and 5). So far as our key hypothesis goes it is not much affected by the argument over whether to correct for war damage. National levels of n Achievement as estimated in children's readers for around 1925 predict subsequent gains in economic productivity significantly despite all reasonable corrections or adjustments for war damage.

National Levels of n Achievement in 1950 and Subsequent Rates of Economic Growth

While the result is encouraging, it is by no means conclusive. The list of countries in Table 3.4 does not include many that are really poor or outside the Western orbit, because readers and economic data were both unavailable from such countries in the 1920's. Moreover, the data in Table 3.3 suggest that readers in the 1950's may be very unrepresentative of average n Achievement levels, particularly in the underdeveloped countries not included in Table 3.4. What is therefore needed is some estimate of economic growth subsequent to 1950 to see whether the 1950 n Achievement levels also predict which countries will move ahead most rapidly in the next generation. Unfortunately at the present writing only short-range statistics are available, and these may be quite unreliable so far as an index like electrical output is concerned, since a huge hydroelectric plant may suddenly increase output in a small country in a particular year. Nevertheless electrical output figures were collected for the maximum available time period which was still removed at least a minimum time period from the date of prediction. Since the hypothesis is a *predictive one*, we ideally ought to allow several years to elapse after 1950, when the *n* Achievement levels were assessed, before beginning to measure economic growth, particularly since a number of the readers were in fact published as late as 1953. Yet the more time we allow to elapse before beginning, the less time is available to measure rates of economic growth, and the hypothesis is supposed to hold only for long range secular trends, not short-term changes due to the business cycle. As the best available compromise we chose 1952 as the starting date for measuring growth which gives at least a minimum lag from the 1950 median date for the reader data and at least a six-year period (to 1958) over which to measure rate of growth. While six years is generally speaking too short for the kind of trend we are looking for, this particular decade has an advantage that would not obtain for all such short time periods. That is, it was a time of relative peace and prosperity; there were no world-wide major wars or depressions. Therefore, one might expect that levels of achievement motivation could express themselves more directly in national economic activity than if there were major influences from the outside like the widespread depression of the thirties or World War II.

Electrical output was again chosen as likely to be the most representative measure of economic growth on which accurate comparable figures are most generally available. This time, however, there seemed to be no need to convert output into per capita terms since there were no major territorial changes in the countries concerned in the time period under study. Actually, using per capita output measures may obscure the underlying relationship because varying rates of population growth will inflate or deflate estimates of changes in rates of economic activity in a fashion quite extraneous to the hypothesis under study. For example, the population of Ireland *decreased* during this period, so that even if there had been no change in electrical output whatsoever, it would have shown an increased output in per capita terms, whatever its motivational level. Furthermore, artifacts of the reverse sort—i.e., increases in gross output attributable largely to rapid rates of population increase—are not so likely when the measure of economic growth is in terms of something like electrical output rather than national income. One of the reasons for converting to per capita terms normally is that rapid increases in population must contribute directly to rise in gross national income because the people at least produce what they consume if they are alive. But this difficulty does not arise with a measure like electrical output because people do not automatically have to produce or consume more electricity.

Therefore, absolute mean monthly electrical production figures were used for 1952 and 1958, as published in the UN *Monthly Bulletin of Statistics*. Level of production in 1952 turned out to be almost perfectly correlated ($r = .976$) with gain in production to 1958 when all figures were transformed into logarithms to insure linearity of regression and to get countries like Tunisia (mean monthly production in 1958 = 20 million kwh) on the same scale with Russia (19,400 million kwh in 1958) and the United States (60,334 million kwh in 1958). Again as in Table 3.4, the interesting question is whether a country is gaining in electrical production faster or slower than would be expected from the regression equation, as a function of its estimated n Achievement level in 1950. As Table 3.6 shows, the relationship is surprisingly high ($r = .43$, $N = 39$, $p < .01$) considering the short range nature of the electrical output figures and possible sampling errors in the selection of children's stories, particularly from underdeveloped countries. Countries high in n Achievement in 1950, generally speaking, gained more rapidly than expected in electrical output between 1952 and 1958 and vice versa. Rate of gain in the table is shown in terms of standard scores of deviations from expected gain to provide some meaningful unit of comparison. The advantage of the regression method is that it puts the countries at the same starting point, so to speak, and the standard scores show how well or poorly they have done compared to each other. Thus Russia has done very well—better than roughly 90 per cent of the countries relative to its starting point, if we convert the standard score into its percentage equivalent. Similarly, the United States is doing slightly better than would be expected, Switzerland and Belgium much worse. To a remarkable extent n Achievement levels in children's readers forecast which countries will do well or poorly.

The result is not changed markedly by expressing the output figures in per capita terms. When this is done the number of countries in various cells in Table 3.6 is altered only slightly—India, Canada, Iraq and Mexico becoming underachievers, and the Union of South Africa, Ireland, Norway, Sweden, Finland, and the Netherlands becoming overachievers. Countries like Poland and Pakistan remain overachievers even when their rates of output are divided by high rates of population increase. The difference is now somewhat less significant ($\chi^2 = 2.99$, $p < .10$), but as we have argued above, the measure of economic growth is also less pure in the sense that it is affected by differences in rates of population growth which are quite extraneous to the hypothesis.

The finding is the more impressive because it is an independent confirmation of the results for the 1925 sample of countries. More countries are involved, including many poor ones, and the countries that were high in n Achievement and rate of growth in the early period are not in the later one. The n Achievement level (1925) correlates only .26 with n Achievement level (1950) and gain in electrical output (1929-1950) corre-

TABLE 3.6   RATE OF GROWTH IN ELECTRICAL OUTPUT (1952-1958) AND NATIONAL
n ACHIEVEMENT LEVELS IN 1950

Deviations from expected growth rate[1] in standard score units

National *n* Achievement levels (1950)[2]			Above expectation	National *n* Achievement levels (1950)[2]		Below expectation
High *n* Achievement	3.62	Turkey	+1.38			
	2.71	India[3]	+1.12			
	2.38	Australia	+ .42			
	2.33	Israel	+1.18			
	2.33	Spain	+ .01			
	2.29	Pakistan[4]	+2.75			
	2.29	Greece	+1.18	3.38	Argentina	− .56
	2.29	Canada	+ .06	2.71	Lebanon	− .67
	2.24	Bulgaria	+1.37	2.38	France	− .24
	2.24	U.S.A.	+ .47	2.33	U. So. Africa	− .06
	2.14	West Germany	+ .53	2.29	Ireland	− .41
	2.10	U.S.S.R.	+1.62	2.14	Tunisia	−1.87
	2.10	Portugal	+ .76	2.10	Syria	− .25
Low *n* Achievement	1.95	Iraq	+ .29	2.05	New Zealand	− .29
	1.86	Austria	+ .38	1.86	Uruguay	− .75
	1.67	U.K.	+ .17	1.81	Hungary	− .62
	1.57	Mexico	+ .12	1.71	Norway	− .77
	.86	Poland	+1.26	1.62	Sweden	− .64
				1.52	Finland	− .08
				1.48	Netherlands	− .15
				1.33	Italy	− .57
				1.29	Japan	− .04
				1.20	Switzerland[5]	−1.92
	Correlation of *n* Achievement level (1950) × deviations from expected growth rate = .43, *p* < .01			1.19	Chile	−1.81
				1.05	Denmark	− .89
				.57	Algeria	− .83
				.43	Belgium	−1.65

[1] The estimates are computed from the monthly average electrical production figures, in millions of kwh, for 1952 and 1958, from United Nations, *Monthly Bulletin of Statistics*, January, 1960, and Statistical Papers, Series J, *World Energy Supplies*, 1951-1954 and 1955-1958.

The correlation between log level 1952 and log gain 1952-1958 is .976.

The regression equation based on these 39 countries plus four others from the same climatic zone on which data are available (China-Taiwan, Czechoslovakia, Romania, Yugoslavia) is:

$$\text{log gain (1952-1958)} = .9229 \text{ log level (1952)} + .0480$$

Standard scores are deviations from mean gain predicted by the regression formula ($M = -.01831$) divided by the standard deviation of the deviations from mean predicted gain ($SD = .159$).

[2] Based on 21 children's stories from 2nd, 3rd, and 4th grade readers in each country.

[3] Based on 6 Hindi, 7 Telegu, 8 Tamil stories.

[4] Based on 12 Urdu and 11 Bengali stories.

[5] Based on 21 German Swiss stories, mean = .91; 21 French Swiss stories, mean = 1.71; over-all mean obtained by weighting German mean double to give approximately proportionate representation to the two main ethnic population groups.

lates only .13 with the same estimate for 1952-1958. Even the major exceptions to the rule in 1950 have "explanations." For example, Poland was a decided overachiever economically speaking but its n Achievement level was very low. A recheck of the readers used, however, suggests that they may not have been representative. Polish schoolbooks had been hard to obtain and a "trade" book of children's stories and verse (usually low in n Achievement, see Table 4.2) had been substituted. Argentina turned out to be an economic underachiever despite a very high n Achievement score in 1950, but Argentinian third-grade readers, almost alone among those studied, had a very strong political slant in that most of the stories glorified the then dictator Juan Peron. The Mexican overachievement, despite its low n Achievement, was very possibly due to the presence of American top managers in significant numbers in a variety of industries, and particularly in the electric power industry.[8] Such cases serve to emphasize the fact that while the numbers look precise enough, the estimates of n Achievement level, or of economic gains for that matter, may be *unrepresentative* (subject to sampling errors) *for particular countries.* The fact that the relationship is substantial and significant, *despite such errors,* is all the more reason to take it seriously and to suspect that it may be even larger than we have been able to detect with our very crude measuring instruments.

The 1950 finding has two important theoretical implications. First of all, it suggests that the failure of the 1950 n Achievement levels to correlate with *previous* economic growth (1929-1950) is not due to the fact that children's literature is somehow less representative of national motivational levels in 1950 than in 1925. The diehard economic determinist who wants to think of motivational levels primarily as responses to economic opportunity might "explain away" the failure of rapid rates of economic development to produce higher levels of n Achievement in 1950 on the grounds that the readers in 1950 are no longer representative, particularly in underdeveloped countries where children's books may be produced by people in the Ministries of Education who are far removed in every sense from the people. Yet such a rationalization seems seriously weakened by the fact that the books do yield n Achievement levels which *predict* subsequent rates of economic growth. To put it somewhat differently, the very same scores which are uncorrelated with *previous* growth rates are correlated with subsequent growth rates.

The 1950 finding suggests in the second place that n Achievement levels in children's readers are more of a reflection of the mood or motivational level of a nation at the time than an educational influence which is affecting the next generation. On the basis of the 1925 finding one might infer that high n Achievement in the readers at that time had increased the n Achievement of the children exposed to them. These children might therefore have had higher n Achievement when they grew up some twenty years later, and their additional energy might then be held responsible for more rapid growth in certain countries. Probably the time period is too short for any such effect to have taken place, but the 1950 finding argues more persuasively against it because n Achievement levels in the readers are correlated with economic growth in the very near future or practically simultaneously. The readers, then, appear to reflect more the motivational level of the adults at the time they are published, perhaps particularly of the adults responsible for the education of children, rather than the motivational level that the children reading the books are going to have ultimately when they grow up. Such an interpretation leads to a different view of the discrepancy in the level of n Achievement in the Japanese readers and in Japanese upper middle-class boys. The former may reflect accurately a fairly low level of n Achievement among Japanese adults, whereas the latter might be reflecting a much higher level of n Achievement among the young, at least in Osaka. If so, one would predict that the n Achievement level in Japanese readers will rise over the years as these boys grow into maturity, and also that Japan will move from a status of an "underachiever" in the economic sphere to that of an "overachiever," say by 1970.

One other point in Table 3.6 is worth noting. Generally speaking, the poor or underdeveloped countries tend to be higher in n Achievement. Thus if we split the countries into those above and below the median monthly electrical output (around 42 kwh/cap) in 1952, the 20 less-developed countries had an average n Achievement score of 2.12, and the 19 more-developed countries had a lower average n Achievement score of 1.74, the difference being significant at $p < .10$. It is as if many of the backward countries realize their backwardness and are now motivated to close the gap between themselves and the more industrially developed countries. Such an interpretation will surprise no one. What it suggests once again, however, is that the n Achievement score is a sensitive barometer of the concern felt in a country for economic development. A very similar interpretation can be given the fact that the average n Achievement score for the 1950 sample of countries (mean $= 1.93$) is very significantly higher ($p < .01$) than for the 1925 sample of countries (mean $= 1.52$). If we follow the same line of reasoning, we could infer that in general there was a higher concern for economic development among the countries of the world around 1950 than there had been a generation earlier. This was true not only among the countries added to the sample in 1950—in general the poorer, less-developed ones—but also among the 23 countries included at both time periods. Their average n Achievement score rose from 1.52 in 1925 to 1.93 in 1950 ($t = 2.08$, $p < .05$). The inference that there is a growing concern for economic matters in all countries is again supported by many other facts (e.g., the better economic statistics recorded in UN publications), and our confidence in the n Achievement score as an index of that concern is correspondingly strengthened.

Characteristics of Achievement-Related Stories from Countries Growing More or Less Rapidly Economically

The code for n Achievement includes a number of subcategories which are summed to get an over-all score. It is first decided whether a story contains any achievement imagery ("concern with a standard of excellence") and then, if it does, whether it also contains additional ideas connected with the achievement sequence, such as a stated wish to succeed, obstacles to achievement, or means of gaining an achievement goal. We have so far shown that the over-all frequency of achievement imagery is higher in readers from countries developing more rapidly economically, but a second question of some interest is whether the *type* of achievement imagery is also different. We can equate for differences in the frequency of achievement imagery by taking only the achievement-related stories from rapidly and slowly growing economies and then asking the question whether the proportion of such stories containing various subtypes of achievement imagery is different for the two types of countries. Table 3.7 summarizes the relevant figures.

Since there was no real *a priori* basis for predicting which subcategories would appear more often, the differences for the 1925 sample of countries may be taken as hypotheses to be cross-validated on the 1950 sample of countries. In 1925 the achievement-related stories from rapidly developing countries contained proportionally more of all sorts of subcategories, except for a stated wish for achievement and achievement thema—a code for whether the story is centrally (as contrasted with peripherally) concerned with achievement. Of all these subcategories only two were cross-validated at reasonably significant levels in the 1950 sample of countries— namely "successful instrumental activity" and statements about obstacles either objectively present in the world or subjectively in the thoughts or activities of some person in the story. That is, several of the differences between the two types of countries observable in 1925 had disappeared or were actually reversed by 1950—notably the number of references to whether someone felt badly over failure or happy over success. But two differences held up consistently in the two independent samples: achievement-related stories from the more rapidly developing countries at both time periods were more apt to specify means that were actually successful in gaining achievement goals and were also more explicit in mentioning obstacles to be overcome, either in terms of the lack of some personal characteristic needed for achievement or in terms of some obstacle blocking the path to success.

TABLE 3.7 PROPORTION OF ACHIEVEMENT-RELATED STORIES WITH VARIOUS CHARACTERISTICS FROM RAPIDLY AND SLOWLY GROWING ECONOMIES

Characteristics	1925 Readers			1950 Readers			Combined p^3
	Rapidly growing economies $(N = 10)^1$	Slowly growing economies $(N = 12)$	Difference	Rapidly growing economies $(N = 18)^2$	Slowly growing economies $(N = 21)$	Difference	
Number of achievement-related stories	86	69		173	173		
Need stated[4]	9%	9%		14%	13%		
Instrumental activity successful	72	59	+13	74	60	+14	<.01
Instrumental activity unsuccessful or doubtful	17	9		14	20		
Anticipations of success or failure	42	26		37	32		
Positive or negative emotions	31	20		21	35		
Help by another person	23	7		11	15		
Obstacles in the self or the world	50	17	+23	44	33	+11	<.01
Themas	46	46		56	51		

[1] Based on Table 3.4, electrical output measure.

[2] Based on Table 3.6.

[3] Based on the sum of the chi-squares for the two comparisons, $df = 2$. It is probably not legitimate to treat the stories from the same country as independent, as is required for a chi-square test, but since they certainly have a degree of independence, it seems permissible to estimate significance of differences in this way, provided significance levels are raised somewhat.

[4] The labels describe briefly the various subcategories of the n Achievement scoring system, fully explained in McClelland et al. (1953).

Psychologically speaking, what such findings seem to mean is that n Achievement is not only more frequently present in stories from more rapidly developing countries but when it is present, it is more apt to be "means" oriented rather than goal oriented. The achievement sequence more often dwells on obstacles to success and specific means of overcoming them, rather than on the goal itself, the desire for it, and the emotions surrounding attaining or failing to attain it. The adaptive quality of such a concern with means is obvious: a people who *think* in terms of ways of overcoming obstacles would seem more likely to find ways of overcoming them in fact. At any rate that is precisely what happens: the "means" oriented stories come from countries which have managed to overcome the obstacles to economic achievement more successfully than other countries. We will return to this general theme again in Chapter 5.

In conclusion, if we look back over the diverse findings reported in this chapter, they confirm our general hypothesis to a surprising extent, considering the many sources of error that could affect our measures. A concern for achievement as expressed in imaginative literature—folk tales and stories for children—is associated in modern times with a more rapid rate of economic development. The generalization is confirmed not only for Western, free-enterprise democracies like England and the United States but also for Communist countries like Russia, Bulgaria or Hungary (Table 3.6), or primitive tribes that are just beginning to make contact with modern technological society (Table 3.1). It holds in the main whether a country is developed or underdeveloped, poor or rich, industrial or agricultural, free or totalitarian. In other words there is a strong suggestion here that men with high achievement motives will find a way to economic achievement given fairly wide variations in opportunity and social structure. What people want, they somehow manage to get, in the main and on the average, though as we shall see later other factors can modify the speed with which they get it.

These results serve to direct our attention as social scientists away from an exclusive concern with the external events in history to the "internal" psychological concerns that in the long run determine what happens in history.

NOTES AND REFERENCES

[1] I am very much indebted to Dr. Irvin L. Child for making the *n* Achievement z-scores available for my use.

[2] I am deeply indebted to Mr. Allan Kulakow for making these ratings. He had, of course, no knowledge of the *n* Achievement scores for the folk tales while he was making the ratings.

[3] Murdock also records whether domestic animals were not aboriginal but were introduced through European contact and were important and well integrated at the period as of which the culture was described. It is interesting to note that of the seven cultures so characterized in our sample, six of them had high *n* Achievement. In other words, they appear ready not only to accept advanced technology but also improved means of raising animals once they learn about them.

[4] I am deeply indebted to a great many people who worked hard and long on the collection, organization and coding of the sample of children's stories—to Thomas E. Shipley, Jr., Vera Aronson, and Dorothy Maddi, for their entrepreneurial efforts in getting and organizing the collection, to Marian Cartland and Alice Thoren for editorial and clerical assistance, to Thomas E. Shipley, Jr., David Bakan, Robert Cohler, Ralph Haber, Richard deCharms, and Julie Maehling, for help in devising coding systems, and

in particular to Salvatore Maddi, Ellen Greenberger, Julie Maehling, Peter Lenrow, David Berlew, and Norman Bradburn for the exacting and often tedious task of coding all the stories according to the various classifications decided upon.

[5] The number of cases is 43, because samples from Quebec, from Canadian English Catholic and American Catholic schools were included along with forty regular country samples.

[6] Another answer is that we can compute standard scores, based on deviations from average production in other countries or the same country over time, for each of the various types of production and sum them, much as psychologists get an over-all IQ score. See, for example, the method employed in Table 2.2.

[7] I am grateful to Professor Franco Modigliani for calling my attention to the necessity of dealing with the problem of war damage.

[8] In two of the largest Mexican companies associated with distribution of electric power—i.e., Cía. Mexicana de Luz y Fuerza (Valley of Mexico), Cía. Impulsora de Empresas Eléctricas (an association of companies outside the central valley)—the top management was American. For example, in 1957-1958, at least eleven key executives of the Mexican Light and Power Company—from the Chairman of the Board to the Technical Director, to the Tacubaya Diesel Plant superintendent—were Americans. Over 100 Americans held key management positions in these two companies or others associated with the sale of products consuming electricity in Mexico during the same year. Of 70 companies in the Federal District (out of 73 in all Mexico) required by law to belong to the industrial chamber covering the electronics industry, at least 23, representing by far the largest share of the business, were operated by foreigners (largely Americans). At the same time at least 85-90 per cent of the electrically operated refrigerators, radios and TV sets were produced and sold by companies managed by Americans—e.g., General Electric, General Motors, Kelvinator, Industria eléctrica Mexicana (government-controlled but a Westinghouse licensee with an American vice-president and general manager), Philco, and R.C.A. (See Fayerweather, 1960, p. 199, p. 531.) Furthermore the picture was very similar in many other industries—steel, cement, textiles, drugs, automobiles—the chief exceptions being industries connected with food (including beer and tobacco) and with oil production (a government monopoly). The Mexican government is moving to end the dominance of foreign managers by making their replacement by other foreigners more difficult so that the picture may change in the future. However, for the time period under consideration, 1952-1958, the above-average gain in Mexican electric power consumption may well have been due in part to American management and not to an error in our measurements or an unusual circumstance resulting in a country with low n Achievement apparently moving ahead more rapidly than expected.

4

Achieving Societies in the Past

Are we to infer from the data in the last chapter that *n* Achievement is always and everywhere an important factor in economic growth? The cross-cultural data do suggest that it promotes economic development in widely different cultures, but they are all more or less limited to the present type of economic development. They all deal with the extent to which a culture or a nation has adapted more or less rapidly to modern civilization with its stress on technology, the specialization of labor, or the factory system. Economic growth in the past has been of a quite different order and might have required a different motivational pattern.

The question is of particular interest because it was after all an historical case, the connection between the Protestant Reformation and the rise of capitalism, which gave rise to the general hypothesis. Can we collect any data that bear more directly on our interpretation of Weber's thesis? Was a rise in achievement motivation associated with the growth of Protestantism in the past? Or, for that matter, did a rise in achievement motivation precede economic growth in various countries in the past and did its fall precede economic decline? Fortunately the method exists for collecting data to answer such questions. The system of content analysis for *n* Achievement applied originally to individually written stories and then in Chapter 3 to folk tales and children's stories can also be applied to whatever imaginative literature has survived from past civilizations. Furthermore, with a little ingenuity our requirement for some kind of quantitative index of economic activity can normally be satisfied so that we need not get embroiled in disagreements as to whether or when a country was growing or declining in the economic sense. The present chapter brings together the efforts that have been made to date to apply the approach used in the previous chapter to historical problems, i.e., to see whether achievement imagery in imaginative literature increases in frequency prior to instances of marked economic growth and decreases prior to subsequent economic decline. The cases so far studied cover a fairly wide range of historical epochs—Ancient Greece, Spain in the late Middle Ages, England from the late Middle Ages to the Industrial Revolution, the United States from the Industrial Revolution to the present, and pre-Incan Peru. We will start with Ancient Greece, where all studies of the rise and fall of civilizations have their origin, and will present it in the most detail since the way in which the methodological problems were solved there determined to a large extent how they were solved in subsequent studies. Medieval Spain presents a sequence of events very like those in Ancient Greece but at a different time period for a totally different civilization. England is of particular importance because the data cover a longer time period and permit a more direct check on the presumed connection between Protestantism and economic growth. The Peruvian case is really an excursus into archeology, since the method of determining *n* Achievement level had to be from vase designs following a system for coding freehand drawings developed by Aronson (1958) and first applied to Greek vases.

Ancient Greece[1]

Our hypothesis more specifically stated in terms of Ancient Greece is as follows: The level of achievement motivation in Greece should have been high before its period of maximum growth and should have fallen significantly before the subsequent decline of the civilization. The level of *n* Achievement should precede and presumably determine the changes in general activity level in the culture. Presumably it takes some time for an active and energetic entrepreneurial class to build up a great civilization though it may take less time for their children and grandchildren with lower achievement motivation to "let things go" so that the civilization collapses, especially when it is under pressure from without.

Before proceeding to a description of the specific methods of testing the hypothesis, it may be worth while to take time out to consider some objections that historians are certain to raise, particularly now that the hypothesis is to be tested on a civilization which is familiar to many of them in great detail. To those who really know Greek history, it may well seem the height of absurdity to try to explain the rise of Greece in terms of any single factor like *n* Achievement. Obviously the situation is much more complex. What if iron had not been discovered which permitted individual Greeks to make their own weapons instead of relying on a central authority for bronze? What if there had been no silver mine near Athens which could be used as a regular source for money which was the basis for an expanded economy? What if Cretan civilization had not decayed? What if Athenians had not regarded the artisan, a man who worked with his hands, more highly than many of their contemporaries? What if Solon had not set up a system of laws which protected private property and thus made it more likely that people were to get the just rewards of their efforts? What if Themistocles had not tricked the Persian fleet into attacking his disorganized forces at a time and place favorable to victory for his side? So many factors seem to have been involved in the development of Greece that it seems ridiculous to single out any one factor.

Historians who raise such objections might mean several things by them. They might mean, for example, that accurate and complete descriptions of what happened in history is their business, that the history of any particular event or country is unique, and that they have discharged their duty when they have described a particular historical sequence in all its uniqueness. In other words, they are simply not interested in generalizations, in attempts to compare different civilizations, or what happened in the same civilization at two different periods in time. To such people it is simply a matter of no concern whether achievement motivation, a change in climate, or any other general factor can be associated with the rise and fall of civilizations in general. Of course not all historians fall into this group. The most notable exception in recent times is Toynbee, who has attempted to describe and compare the course of all civilizations in an effort to arrive at generalizations about stages in their rise and fall.

But some historians go beyond a mere statement of disinterest in making generalizations, as was pointed out in Chapter 1. They contend that no generalizations are really possible, that any attempt to find common factors or common stages in growth, even Toynbee's, so distorts the unique qualities of the separate events classed together that the whole enterprise is not worthwhile. There are two answers to this argument. First, any generalization, any attempt to classify two events belonging in the same category, inevitably overlooks some of the unique qualities of each event. When a biologist or anyone else, for that matter, decides to classify two individual animals as belonging to the category of "cow" he is inevitably doing violence to some of the unique characteristics of each of them—the fact that one is lovable, the other stubborn, that one has curly horns and brown spots, the other no horns and black spots, etc. The search for generalizations means the search for similarities and in finding similarities, differences have to be overlooked. So if a historian is too disturbed by the unique qualities of events which have to be neglected in the search for generalizations, his only correct recourse is to reject an interest in generalizing and stick to concrete description. Secondly, he has no right to complain that generalizations are not possible since this is a matter which can be put to the empirical test. If generalizations are really not possible, then attempts to check specific hypotheses as in the present instance must fail. That is, it will not be possible to demonstrate that high achievement motivation precedes the rise of Greek civilization and that a drop in achievement motivation precedes its fall.

Method

So once again our curiosity is sharpened as to whether our hypothesis will hold in the present instance and in particular as to how it can be tested empirically. Two measures must be found for different time periods in the history of Ancient Greece—one for the general level of n Achievement and the other for the general level of economic development. Berlew (1956), who performed the study, managed to construct useful approximations for both. To begin with the first, Berlew had to adopt the method used in Chapter 3 of scoring imaginative literature, since he could not test individuals. This was fortunate, because it would have been hard to decide just what kind of samples to draw from the Greek slave and free populations in different city states at different time periods. Instead, Berlew proceeded on the assumption that various samples of literary material would adequately represent the strivings and hopes of at least the portions of the Greek population significant for economic growth. But what samples of Greek literature should be used?

Greek literature varies considerably in style from period to period. Poetry was common early, plays in the middle period. Literature was written for different purposes—to celebrate victories or the charms of love, to urge the populace on to a greater war effort, to satisfy philosophical curiosity—and yet we know on the basis of our experimental studies that the amount of achievement imagery in imaginative material depends very much on the state of mind of the person at the time he writes it (McClelland et al., 1953). Furthermore, what right do we have to assume that material produced by a particular author (say Hesiod, Aristotle, or Xenophon) will represent the general level of achievement motivation in the population at the time? Hesiod was a farmer, Aristotle a philosopher, and Xenophon a general. Their thought patterns may have been conditioned by their position in life, by their early and different childhood training, or by what they thought their audience wanted to hear. How can their writings be compared on the assumption that each is typical of his time?

To minimize such difficulties as much as possible, Berlew selected samples of literature according to the following criteria.

(1) The samples of material chosen to represent different time periods should be written as nearly as possible for the same purpose. Table 4.1 shows how well he was able to meet this requirement. Greeks writing at different periods in their history had similar goals in mind—to describe man's relationship to his gods, to honor the dead, to describe principles for farm and estate management, and the like. The form that an author chose to accomplish his purpose might be different: Hesiod described man's relationship to the gods in narrative form, Aeschylus in dramatic form, Callimachus in the form of odes to the gods. But if the comparisons are made of material written for the same purpose, the amount of variation in achievement imagery attributable to such stylistic factors should be minimized and that attributable to internal motivational factors in the author maximized. This assumption is based on contemporary studies which show that temporary goal states markedly influence the amount of

TABLE 4.1 SAMPLES OF GREEK LITERATURE SCORED, CLASSIFIED BY LITERARY TYPE, AUTHOR, CITY-STATE, AND DATE. LENGTH OF SAMPLE REPORTED IN NUMBER OF TEN-WORD LINES

Period	Man and his gods	Farm and estate management	Public funeral celebrations	Poetry (excluding victory odes)	Epigrams (Greek Anthology)	War speeches of encouragement
GROWTH 900 B.C. to 475 B.C.	Hesiod (Boeotia) fl. 720 B.C. c. 745 lines from Theogony	Hesiod (Boeotia) fl. 720 B.C. 367 lines from Works and Days	Homer (Ionia?) fl. 9th century B.C.? c. 353 lines from The Iliad, Book 23	Sappho (Ionia) fl. c. 600 B.C. c. 452 lines Alcaeus (Ionia) fl. c. 600 B.C. c. 398 lines Tyrtaeus (Sparta) fl. 7th century c. 136 lines Solon (Athens) fl. c. 600 B.C. c. 287 lines TOTAL: c. 1273 ll.	Sample composed of works of 9 Greek writers of the 6th and 7th centuries B.C. TOTAL: c. 127 ll.	Homer (Ionia?) fl. 9th century B.C.? c. 203 lines All instances of a man encouraging others to fight in The Iliad.
CLIMAX 475 B.C. to 362 B.C.	Aeschylus (Athens) 525-456 B.C. c. 745 lines from Prometheus Bound	Xenophon (Athens) fl. c. 430-354 B.C. 367 lines from The Economist	Pericles (Athens) c. 500-429 B.C. c. 353 lines from funeral oration recorded by Thucydides, Bk II, XXXV ff.	Pindar (Boeotia) fl. c. 450 B.C. c. 400 lines Simonides (Ionia) fl. c. 470 B.C. c. 400 lines Bacchylides (Ionia) fl. c. 460 B.C. c. 309 lines Timotheus (Ionia) fl. c. 375 B.C. c. 200 lines TOTAL: c. 1309 ll.	Sample composed of works of 5 Greek writers. TOTAL: c. 127 ll.	Pericles (Athens) c. 500-429 B.C. c. 198 lines from speech recorded by Thucydides, Bk II, LX ff.
DECLINE 362 B.C. to 100 B.C.	Callimachus (Cyrene) Born 310 B.C. c. 745 lines from Hymns to the Gods	Aristotle (Athens?) 384-322 B.C. c. 367 lines from Economics and Politics	Demosthenes (Athens) 384-322 B.C. c. 353 lines from Funeral Speech	Sample composed of works of 35 Greek poets. TOTAL: c. 1260 ll. from Greek Anthology	Sample composed of works of 14 Greek poets. TOTAL: c. 127 ll.	Demosthenes (Athens) 384-322 B.C. c. 200 lines from Second Olynthiac

achievement imagery in protocols although the form of the protocol within limits does not. (See Atkinson, 1958.)

Furthermore, comparisons were made of material written for several different purposes because the culture might have emphasized achievement in connection with one goal at one time (say man's relationship to the gods in the early period) and in connection with another goal at another time (say farm and estate management in the late period). If this happened to be true, staying within too narrowly a prescribed set of literary themes might produce a distorted picture of the average level of n Achievement in a given time period. The six thematic categories represented in Table 4.1 seem to be sufficiently varied to rule out the possibility that the average level of achievement motivation for different time periods could be attributable to selecting themes more appropriate to one period than another.

(2) The literary material chosen should reflect the attitudes and aspirations of as many individuals as possible to increase its representativeness. While it is dangerous to assume that a single author, such as Hesiod, had a personality structure typical for his time, the greater the number of such authors included, the less the danger of unrepresentativeness. For example, in Table 4.1 nine different authors of epigrams from the early period are included and 35 poets from the late period. Even so, the number of individuals whose works are included is small. Are we prepared to argue that a sample of the thoughts of 15 men will give us an adequate measure of the level of achievement motivation in the Greek population from roughly 900 to 500 B.C.?

Obviously credulity would be strained to the limit if these were ordinary men. But they are not. Homer and Hesiod, who are each represented in the table twice, were extraordinary men. They captured the spirit of their times as their contemporary popularity attests, and that popularity may have actually helped *create* the spirit of the times. In other words, popularity[2] becomes another and probably better guarantee of representativeness than sheer number of authors. Homer and Hesiod were classics during the rise of Greek civilization and continued to be quoted throughout its course, though as a basis for further commentary in later centuries. Why? The assumption is that they were popular because they somehow managed to express what many of the early Greeks were feeling and wanted to hear and read about. Thus the level of achievement motivation in Homer's and Hesiod's works should be about what the audience expected. If it had not been, the members of the audience would have been less satisfied with the characters in Homer's epics or with Hesiod's comments on life and the material would have been less popular. The position taken here is that successful authors are in part successful because they manage to put into writing what is in everyone's mind, the hopes, dreams, strivings and motives of their audience. Their own motives may be less important than their ability to project the feelings of their readers.

There is a further sense in which the Homeric material may be considered especially representative. Some of it at least was almost certainly told and retold by various individuals before it was finally written down. Thus, while it was probably the work of a single author in the end, parts of it had been shaped and reshaped by many minds. Thus, as in the case of the folk tales discussed in Chapter 3, the final product available for scoring is probably already the creation of many individuals in the culture rather than of the single person who tells the final tale.

(3) The literature to be scored should be chosen for its imaginativeness rather than its realism. The reason for this requirement stems in part from the fact that n Achievement is measured in individuals at the present time from their imaginative stories and not, for example, from their autobiographical statements, but also in part from a theoretical consideration. If the material is simply a descriptive factual account of events that occurred (for example, Xenophon's *Anabasis*), there will be little opportunity for the author's motives, values, attitudes, and aspirations to show themselves. The general rule is that the more external reality determines the content of verbal material, the less the material is able to reflect internal determinants like motives.

(4) Finally, the number of lines of each sample of material within a given category should be roughly the same to equalize the opportunity for achievement imagery to appear. The number of ten-word lines in each sample is given in Table 4.1 and refers to the number of lines of English translation in the definitive Loeb Classical Library of translations of Greek literature.

Having chosen his samples of literature to be scored according to these four criteria and without having read them for content, Berlew was then ready to apply the formal system of content analysis used for determining the amount of n Achievement each sample contained. Since the scoring system had been developed to deal with brief written stories with a beginning, a middle, and an end, some adaptations of it were necessary to deal with such different material as epigrams, narrative poems, and plays, but the adaptations were not extensive. According to the usual procedure, once it has been determined that a story contains achievement imagery, a number of different subcategories are scored according to the way the achievement imagery is expressed. But these subcategories are defined in terms of the simple story form of material obtained from individuals or children's readers. So Berlew had to drop the subcategories and noted only each instance of achievement imagery as it appeared in a given passage. To give a more concrete understanding of how the scoring was done, instances of achievement imagery were scored (a) where "one of the characters in the story is engaged in some competitive activity in which winning or doing as well or better than others is *actually stated* as of primary concern"— e.g., "I am not ashamed of it; with this methinks I shall rather surpass the world"; (b) where concern for doing well in competitive activity is not explicitly stated but its importance is definitely implied by affective concern over goal attainment or references to the quality of instrumental acts (e.g., thoroughness, foresight) needed for success—e.g., "Do you, then, providently resolving that yours shall be honor in ages to come and no dishonor in the present, achieve both by prompt and zealous efforts"; or (c) where some unique accomplishment is mentioned—e.g., "It was I and none other who discovered ships, the sail-driven wagon that the sea buffets" (after Berlew, 1956). These scoring criteria are the same as the ones used for stories written by individuals today except that one other criterion sometimes used was not applicable to the Greek material— namely, long-term involvement (McClelland *et al.*, 1953). That is, in stories written by college students in our culture it is quite possible to infer that a person wants to do well if his story contains references to a series of acts over time which involve a person's career such as studying for an exam, going on to law school, and becoming a successful lawyer. This criterion could not readily be applied to the Greek literary material.

It might be objected that the scoring was done of the English translations rather than of the original Greek. Might not the achievement motivation of the translator creep in to mar the results? Of course, to the extent that it does, it will tend to introduce random error into the measurement and make confirmation of the hypothesis less likely, but there is reason to believe that the use of translations did not seriously distort the picture. In the first place, each translator was an expert on the author he was translating and did his best to give the literal meaning of the Greek in terms of his extensive knowledge of the style of that particular author. Thus he may have rendered the original meaning more exactly in English than it would have been understood by someone reading and scoring in the original Greek, but who did not understand a particular author as well. In the second place, a number of instances of achievement imagery scored in the English translation were checked against the Greek to make certain that the Greek would also have been scored for *n* Achievement. In no case was there a discrepancy.

The second major methodological problem is to get some measure of the rise and fall of Greek civilization. It is not so easy to solve as one might think. In the first place, was there any such thing as "Greek" civilization? To be sure, there was a collection of city-states spread all over the eastern end of the Mediterranean which shared a common language and religion but the differences among them might appear to outweigh the similarities. Certainly the social organization, child training practices, and economic development of Sparta and Athens were markedly different. And what did the "backwoods" Macedonians have in common with the cosmopolitan Athenians? Weren't Ionians different from Dorians who in turn differed from Aeolians? Even more serious is the fact that different city-states in Greek civilization enjoyed prosperity at quite different time periods. Generally speaking, the peak of development which occurred around Athens in the 5th century moved southeast toward Egypt in succeeding decades so that islands like Rhodes and Delos enjoyed their greatest prosperity as much as a century or so later. But since Athens was generally regarded then as the economic and cultural center of Greek civilization, it was decided to choose documents to be scored and economic indices as much as possible from Athens and the surrounding regions whose development paralleled hers, e.g., Ionia, Boeotia, and Sparta.

The next problem was to set the time limits for the periods of growth, climax and decline in the development of civilization in this area. Ancient historians are in full agreement that Athens reached her highest point of development in the 5th century B.C., during the "Golden Age" of Pericles. The development of Ionia, where Homer may have lived, was earlier and that of Sparta and Boeotia, home of Hesiod, was perhaps a little later, at least to judge by their subsequent military successes over Athens. Consequently the year 475 B.C. was chosen rather arbitrarily as the precise date dividing the period of growth from the period of climax as a time that would not be too late for Ionia and Athens or too early for Sparta and Boeotia. It also corresponds to the time when Athens succeeded in organizing the league of Delos, a great maritime federation of Greek city-states which finally succeeded in chasing the Persians definitively out of the Aegean. By the end of the 5th century Athens had lost the Peloponnesian War to Sparta and had begun her decline. Sparta in turn was defeated by the Thebans of Boeotia under Epaminondas in 369 B.C., but with his death in 362 B.C., the Thebans lost their influence to Phillip of Macedon from the "backwoods" up North. So 362 B.C. was arbitrarily chosen as marking the end of the period of climax for the city-states under consideration though it comes a little late for Athens and Ionia. These decisions set the time limits for the three periods as follows:

> Period of growth—900 B.C. to 475 B.C.
> Period of climax—475 B.C. to 362 B.C.
> Period of decline—362 B.C. to 100 B.C.

But what has happened to Alexander the Great, who expanded the Greek empire to its greatest extent in the period of "decline"—namely, from 326 B.C. to 323 B.C.? Alexander's influence was ignored in the calculations for two reasons: First, neither he nor the influence he represented came from the culture area to which it had been decided to limit attention, but from a region on the periphery of Greek city-states, namely, Macedonia; second, his influence was too short-lived to be detectable in the crude economic indices that had to be used. In any case there is some question as to whether the extent of his military power really reflected any fundamental reversal in the decline of *central* Greece as a commercial power.

The final methodological problem is to find some quantitative index of economic growth and decline in the area chosen for study. It might be thought that such an index is really not necessary because historians generally agree that the peak of Athens comes in the 5th century B.C. so that anything which occurs before then is in the period of growth and anything which occurs after in the period of decline. But the difficulty arises when one tries to discover more precisely just what the historians mean when they refer to the "Golden Age" of Pericles as the climax of Athenian civilization. Do they have economic welfare, cultural attainments, or extent of political and military achievement in mind? Although many of these developments climaxed together in 5th century Athens, it is necessary for the sake of the present argument to separate out a measure of economic development which is relatively free of judgments about other types of cultural achievement.

The scarcity of data makes the computation of most economic indexes for various periods in Greek history completely out of the question. Even crude measures like the value or volume of foreign trade, the amount of taxation or tribute, the size of cities or market places are not available. So Berlew found it necessary to derive an index in an indirect way. To understand its significance, one must remember that the economic life of the Greek city-states was organized around agriculture and overseas trade. Above all, it was maritime commerce which brought prosperity, and Athens and her seaport, Piraeus, were at the very center of Greek commerce. Here it was that the bankers and middlemen, the enterprising *naukleroi* and *emporoi*, could be found in greatest numbers making arrangements with sea captains for buying or selling cargo. Here it was that some of the strictest laws were enforced governing fairness in economic dealings, and the use of money, weights and measures. Here it was that ships laden with goods from all over the Mediterranean found their chief port of call. It is small wonder that Isocrates and Xenophon could compare Piraeus to the center of the world. (Glotz, 1925, Vol. 2, p. 419.)

What Greece had to trade was largely surplus wine and olive oil produced on specialized farms. These she sent overseas to trade for grain from Sicily, rugs from Persia, the perfumes of Arabia, foodstuffs like dried fish and salted meat, and basic materials like iron, leather, wood, ivory. Olive oil and wine were carried in large earthenware jars which, fortunately from our point of view, did not disappear as their contents were used up in the cities to which they had been transported by enterprising Greek sea captains and traders. These jars, many of which were made by potters in or near Athens, have been found in regions all around the

Mediterranean and many of them dated at least within the century of their production and use. Heichelheim in his definitive study of the economic life of Ancient Greece (1938, Vol. 1, pp. 324-325) has listed the places where jars have been found which can be classified as belonging to the 6th, 5th, or 4th centuries B.C., centuries which correspond closely enough to the periods of growth, climax, and decline of Greek civilization. From the location of these vase remains, Berlew reconstructed rough maps of the area within which Athenian Greece traded for each of these three centuries. In quantitative terms the area of trade roughly covered 1.2 million square miles in the 6th century, 3.4 million square miles in the 5th century, and 1.9 million square miles in the 4th century. In descriptive terms, Athenian trade in the 6th century B.C. covered an area beginning with Alexandria on the east and running in a fairly narrow band along the North shore of the Mediterranean westward to Spain. In the 5th century B.C. the area extended south to include the north shore of Africa, East into Persia and Northeast around the Black Sea. By the 4th century trade was lost with the Italian peninsula where the Roman Empire was developing, with the Black Sea area and with much of the Persian Empire to the East.

Area of trade is, of course, not a perfect index of economic development: loss of a trading area may be compensated for by intensity of trade within the remaining area or by shifting to manufacturing; also trade can be carried on over a wide area with little profit. But in the case of Greece, the figures on the extent of foreign trade agree rather well with estimates by historians of her economic position based on a consideration of all the factors involved. Also, if this index is not accepted, there is always the problem of finding a better one—an extremely difficult task in view of the scantiness of quantitative comparable data for the three time periods in question. So, rough though it is, the measure of the economic rise and fall of classical Greece was taken to be the area with which she traded, in millions of square miles, as determined by the location of vases unearthed in which her chief export commodities were transported. If this index seems to depend too much on commerce, it must be remembered that Greece's prosperity was based primarily on commerce, and that, in any case, her one other economic activity of any importance—namely, agriculture—depended on exporting surpluses for its profits.

The way in which measures of n Achievement and of economic development were obtained has been described, but it is certain to leave experts in the history of Greece dissatisfied at a number of points. Were all of the vase remains really from central Greece? Suppose by some mischance that all of the vases sent in trade to the Black Sea area in the 4th century were either destroyed or have not yet been unearthed? Is there not the possibility that the measure of economic activity adopted might be in error by several hundred thousand square miles because of such accidents? Similarly, not all the samples of literary material can be classified as they have been without question. There are many possible sources of error. Can Sappho really be classified as Ionian when she was born in Lesbos, a territory close to Ionian cities but probably itself Aeolian, and when she lived for a time in Sicily? Is it really right to include Tyrtaeus, a Spartan, along with Ionian and Athenian authors, when Sparta had such a unique social system and mode of bringing up its young? Or, how can Callimachus be included at all when he comes from a state (Cyrene) outside the Athenian central region and a state which at that developed much later economically than the others? Isn't it incorrect to classify Xenophon as belonging to the period of climax when he flourished and wrote after Athens had begun her fall? Is the description of the funeral games in *The Iliad* really comparable to the funeral orations of Pericles and Demosthenes? One might question scoring Pericles' funeral oration anyway since it was recalled from memory by Thucydides, although this is not a serious problem since Thucydides belongs roughly to the same historical period as Pericles, and his thoughts are therefore as valuable for our purposes as whatever Pericles may originally have said.

Many more such methodological questions could be raised, but it is unnecessary to go into them and to answer them all here in detail because the answer in every case is the same. Some methodological errors have undoubtedly been made because the requirements of the research design were difficult to meet with the data available. But errors, unless they are systematic, can only make it *less likely that the hypothesis will be confirmed by the statistical test.* They introduce random variations which make it more difficult to obtain a statistically significant association. For example, suppose Xenophon really belongs to the period of decline in Athens rather than the period of climax where he was assigned. Then his written material should lower the n Achievement score for the climax period below what it should be according to the hypothesis. Similarly, if Callimachus should have been classified in the climax period because Cyrene prospered much later than Athens, then his material should raise the n Achievement score for the "decline" period over what it should be according to the hypothesis. Ancient historians who may be shocked by the arbitrary way in which authors and their works are classified together or in which crude indexes of economic development are computed should remember that all such methodological errors, if they are truly random, should only serve to decrease the likelihood that the hypothesis will be confirmed. And the possibility of a nonrandom bias influencing the results was minimized so far as possible (1) by choosing samples of literature to be scored without knowledge of their achievement content, (2) by making completely arbitrary selections of lines from the samples, and (3) by defining the periods of growth, climax, and decline in terms of an arbitrary, quantitative index of economic influence.

Results

The results of Berlew's analysis can be presented much more quickly and succinctly than his methodology. They are summarized in Table 4.2 and Fig. 4.1. The number of instances of achievement imagery in a given sample of material was reduced to a common base by dividing by the number of lines in each sample and multiplying by a hundred to express the results

TABLE 4.2   NUMBER OF n ACHIEVEMENT IMAGES PER 100 LINES BY TYPE OF SAMPLE BY TIME PERIOD

Period	Man and his gods	Estate management	Funeral celebrations	Poetry	Epigrams	War speeches	Average
Growth 900-475 B.C.	2.01	3.54	7.93	2.87	4.72	7.38	4.74
Climax 475-362 B.C.	1.21	.82	5.94	.38	2.36	5.55	2.71
Decline 362-100 B.C.	.81	.00	2.54	.16	1.57	3.00	1.35

Analysis of Variance

	df	Sum of squares	Mean square	F	p
Total..............	17	102.15			
Time period.........	2	35.03	17.52	24.0	<.01
Type of sample......	5	59.83	11.97	16.4	<.01
Interaction..........	10	7.29	.73		

in terms of number of instances of achievement imagery per hundred lines. For example, there were 2.01 instances of achievement imagery per hundred lines in Hesiod's *Theogony* and only .81 instances per hundred lines in the hymns to the gods by Callimachus. In every category of material scored, the highest incidence of achievement imagery occurs in the growth period, the next highest in the climax period, and the lowest in the period of decline. An analysis of variance shows that the decline over time summarized in the means at the extreme right of Table 4.1 and in Fig. 4.1 could hardly have arisen by chance. It also shows according to expectation that the purpose for which the material is written makes a significant difference ($p < .01$) in the amount of achievement imagery which it contains. Obviously poems contain much less achievement imagery at any time period than do public funeral celebrations or war speeches of encouragement.

Figure 4.1 plots n Achievement score against the measure of economic development adopted. The level of n Achievement is highest in the early period when economic growth is still low. By the time economic development has reached its maximum (pushed along by the high level of n Achievement, if the hypothesis is correct), the over-all level of n Achievement has dropped, foreshadowing, as hypothesized, the subsequent economic decline. In other words, so far as Ancient Greece is concerned, the hypothesis is confirmed: a high level of achievement motivation precedes economic growth, a lower level of achievement motivation precedes economic decline.

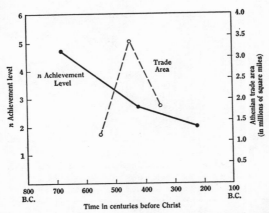

Figure 4.1 Average n Achievement level plotted at midpoints of periods of growth, climax, and decline of Athenian civilization as reflected in the extent of her trade area

While the quantitative evidence is clear-cut, it does not by itself give a very adequate impression of the changes that were going on in the way authors dealt with achievement themes during the period under study. So some qualitative illustrations may be helpful. Consider, for example, how farm and estate management is treated by the three authors compared—Hesiod, Xenophon, and Aristotle. Their spirit is very different. Hesiod, writing in the earliest period, is very conscious of man's achievement strivings. He says, for example, "For when he that has no business looks on him that is rich, he hastens to plow and to plant and to array his house: and neighbor vies with neighbor hastening to be rich: good is this strife for man. So potter contends with potter: the hewer of wood with the hewer of wood: the beggar jealous of the beggar, the minstrel jealous of the minstrel." He takes it for granted that competition—the desire to excel—is natural to man.

Xenophon, writing in the period of climax, reports a dialogue Socrates had with Critobulus on estate management. Socrates spends a good deal of his time demonstrating how difficult it is to manage an estate properly and in fact argues that even if a man does gain something, he very often wastes it. "And so hard rule these passions over every man who falls into their clutches, that so long as they see that he is strong and capable of working, they force him to pay over all the profits of his toil, and spend it on their own desires." In other words, what use is there in struggling to get ahead? He points out that while he, Socrates, is poor and his friend, Critobulus, is rich by the world's standards, still Critobulus is worse off than he is in many ways because Critobulus has much heavier responsibilities. To be sure, Xenophon attributes to Critobulus the desire to improve the management of his estate, and Socrates contends that one can always learn something especially from the bad examples of others. So there is some achievement imagery present, but it is less often mentioned than in Hesiod and most of the emphasis is on the difficulty of really achieving anything of lasting worth.

In Aristotle's treatment of estate management from the period of decline there is practically no mention of achievement striving at all. Aristotle is, as always, concerned with doing what is proper, natural, or suitable to man. A man should be careful so that others working for him will be careful, he should not give wine to his employees because it makes them insolent, he should avoid mistreating his wife as she too is part of the household. In discussing slaves he says, "Three things make up the life of a slave, work, punishment, and food. To give them food but no punishment and no work makes them insolent and that they should have work and punishment but no food is tyrannical and destroys their efficiency. It remains, therefore, to give them work and sufficient food: for it is impossible to rule over slaves without offering rewards, and a slave's reward is his food." Nothing here about potter contending with potter or the hewer of wood with the hewer of wood! No suspicion, at least so far as slaves are concerned, that food isn't everything and that a man may feel rewarded by doing a good job or by doing better than someone else. In fact, Aristotle discredits slaves who are too energetic and comes out here as elsewhere for moderation in all things: "The high-spirited are not easy to control."

In other words, the quantitative data neither here nor in the other comparisons distort the impression one gets from reading the material for qualitative differences. Despite the artificial way in which numbers of instances of achievement imagery are counted up, they reflect accurately the way in which achievement themes are handled at different times. And the advantage of dealing with numbers rather than subjective impressions is, of course, that it permits a completely objective test of the hypothesis which any observer trained in the scoring system can check for himself.

Further Evidence

Since Berlew had both selected and scored the passages himself, it is possible that an unconscious bias in favor of the hypothesis influenced his application of the scoring system, despite its objectivity. He knew what period a given selection came from and might have tended to overlook images in some passages and to search more carefully for them in others. For this reason a second judge was trained in the scoring system who had no idea what period a selection was from and who subsequently rescored all the samples of material for n Achievement. The correlation between his scores per sample of material and Berlew's scores was $+.89$; the means for the early, middle, and late periods were 3.48, 2.10, and .48, and an analysis of variance of his data shows that the differences attributable to time periods would have arisen by chance less than one in a hundred times. The second scorer systematically noted fewer achievement images in all of the material than Berlew did, but otherwise his results were identical.

There is still another possibility of error: the original selection of triads of material to be scored had to be made in many instances on the basis of some knowledge of the content of the passages. Perhaps this knowledge unconsciously influenced choices in favor of the hypothesis. But two categories of comparisons could not possibly have been influenced by such knowledge—namely, the poetry and epigrams categories, samples for which were drawn largely from the Greek Anthology simply by including all lines from the beginning until the quota for the particular time period had been filled. The variance associated with time period for these two categories alone (omitting the other categories as possibly biased) is still significant ($p < .01$) when tested against an estimate of error based either on the interaction in the whole Table or in the six cells of the restricted analysis.

But perhaps the unmistakable decline in achievement imagery over time is not its exclusive property. Perhaps almost any category one would score in these samples of material would show the same decline. Berlew (1956) actually also scored for a number of other "value orientations" (taken largely from F. Kluckhohn, 1950), results for the most important of which are presented in Table 4.3. For none of these categories does an analysis of variance performed as in Table 2, yield significant trends over time and for none of them except "future orientation" does even the same decline over time appear as in the case of achievement imagery. In Table 4.3 a somewhat different and less adequate test of significance is therefore reported based on the assumption that the total number of instances of a given category should be equally distributed over the three time periods. If such an assumption is valid, a chi-square test can be computed which will estimate the likelihood that the obtained distribution of frequencies

TABLE 4.3   FREQUENCIES OF SELECTED VALUE ORIENTATIONS FOR TOTAL SAMPLES
FROM EACH TIME PERIOD
(after Berlew, 1956)

Period	Future orientation*	Man over nature	Impulse control	Ascribed status
Growth				
900-475 B.C.	136	33	37	32
Climax				
475-362 B.C.	99	27	37	16
Decline				
362-100 B.C.	56	36	11	32
Chi-square	68.2	1.3	16.01	6.34
p	<.01	insig.	<.01	<.05

* Number of future minus past references plus 100.

deviates from the theoretically equal distribution by an amount which
could have arisen by chance only infrequently. Actually, since many of
the observations come from the same passage by the same author in each
cell, they are not independent, the theoretical distribution cannot be accurately estimated, and the chi-square test is not strictly speaking legitimate,
but it has nevertheless been included to give some idea, however crude,
of the significance of the results. The category which comes closest to
giving the same results as were obtained for achievement imagery is
"future orientation," a fact of considerable interest because other studies
have shown that subjects with high n Achievement typically look forward
more into the future (see Chapter 8).

On the other hand, a value orientation like "man over nature" shows
no trends, despite the fact that F. Kluckhohn (1950) and others have
argued that it goes with an individualistic achievement orientation in our
time. Certainly one would think that the more achievement-oriented a
person was, the more likely he would be to believe that he could control
nature rather than be controlled by it, but the results in this case do not
support the hypothesis, however reasonable it may sound. Similarly, "impulse control," or the tendency to stress self-discipline as a means to
achievement might be thought of as a prerequisite for achievement, but it
is not mentioned in our material more often during the period of growth
than during the period of climax. Actually two forms of impulse control
are perhaps unfairly lumped together in this score. During the period of
growth most of the references to impulse control had to do with ascetic
self-discipline for the purpose of character-building, while during the
period of climax the references were to moderation or avoiding excess.
Both types of impulse control tended to be mentioned less often during
the period of decline.

The results for "ascribed status" are perhaps most interesting of all theoretically. Included under this category were all references to status or rank based on factors over which the individual had no control, such as sex, age, family connections, and physical strength. The opposite of ascribed status is achieved status in which rank is accorded in terms of what the individual has actually done to merit it. During both the periods of growth and decline, Greece was more authoritarian in political and social structure than it was during the period of climax when it was more democratic. In authoritarian social systems rank is more commonly based on ascribed factors such as birth order and lineage than in a democracy where, in theory at least, anyone can achieve high rank by his own efforts, even though he may be a younger son or the son of an artisan. So the results for "ascribed status" appear to reflect fairly accurately the way the social system was organized in Greece at the three time periods in question. It is mentioned frequently in the period of growth, less often in the democratic period of climax, and with increased frequency during the period of decline when Greece became less democratic again. What is especially noteworthy is that in this case the value orientation scored simply *reflects* political and social changes and does not *precede* them, as in the case of *n* Achievement. In short, not all the elements in what might be thought of as an "achievement value complex" appear simultaneously in the thought patterns of members of a society. In this instance, a case can be made for believing that the appearance of high *n* Achievement—while the society was still fairly autocratic and evaluating people in terms of, not achieved, but ascribed, status—was the critical factor in moving the society toward a democracy in which status was awarded on the basis of actual achievement. At any rate, it is well documented (Brown, 1947; Glotz, 1925) that the rising entrepreneurial class of businessmen did force a change in the social system and it is they who were most probably the ones with high *n* Achievement (see Chapters 6, 7 and 8).

The evidence, so far as it goes, is that changes in achievement motivation and only achievement motivation or its correlate, future orientation, foreshadowed both the rise and fall of Greece in this sample of material. Yet one can still ask for more evidence despite all the tests of statistical significance because a conclusion about a whole civilization is after all being based on the analysis of 18 samples of literary material which just might have been chosen with extraordinary good luck. Fortunately a quite independent confirmation of the main result is available. Aronson (1958) has discovered that subjects with high *n* Achievement "doodle" in characteristically different ways from subjects with low *n* Achievement and has cross-validated his findings with several samples of male college students. His findings have been confirmed in other countries in their essentials in studies reported in Chapter 8 and Appendix IV. He has developed an objective scoring system for the way lines, shapes, and space are used when spontaneous doodles are produced by subjects. He found that he could apply with very little modification the scoring definitions for the shape variables and for use of space to the designs appearing on Greek vases as photographed in the *Corpus Vasorum Antiquorum*. He selected his sample of vases to be scored from Cambridge Fascicules 1 and 2 (Great Britain Fascicules 6 and 11) and from Reading Fascicule 1 (Great Britain Fascicule 12), including all whole vases from the first two Fascicules for the time periods in question which were clearly enough marked to be scored and contained at least one of the shapes associated with high or low *n* Achievement, and enough such vases from the third Fascicule to bring the total to over 100 vases for the first two time periods. The number of vases from the third period of decline is only 34 but the results for this period are less crucial for testing the hypothesis that designs characteristic of high or low *n* Achievement foreshadow economic growth or decline respectively.

Table 4.4 presents the results of his scoring the vases for four of the design characteristics he had found to be associated with *n* Achievement. It does not include data for a fifth characteristic—namely, the number of

TABLE 4.4 PERCENTAGE OF VASES FROM DIFFERENT TIME PERIODS WITH MORE THAN THE MEDIAN NUMBER OF VARIOUS DESIGN CHARACTERISTICS ASSOCIATED WITH *n* ACHIEVEMENT

Period	Number of vases	Characteristic of			
		High *n* Achievement		Low *n* Achievement	
		Diagonals 4 or more	S-Shapes 3 or more	Multiple waves 2 or more	Unused space at bottom 12% or more
Growth 900-500 B.C.	103	61.2%	68.9%	57.3%	35%
Climax 500-400 B.C.	105	41.9%	47.6%	54.3%	64.8%
Decline 400-100 B.C.	34	14.7%	14.7%	67.6%	47.1%
Chi-square		23.51	31.63	1.90	18.58
p		<.01	<.01	NS	<.01

discrete minus the number of fuzzy or overlaid lines—because this distinction could not be made with vase designs. Since the details of the scoring system cannot be given in full here, it will perhaps be enough to indicate that by "diagonals" he meant lines that were at least 15 degrees off the vertical or horizontal, and that by "S-shapes" he meant lines that reversed direction but did not continue to undulate. If either of these "forms" or the "multiple wave" form appeared in a group of two or more, they were scored twice but no more and as many sides of a vase were scored as were photographed in the *Corpus*. Both "diagonals" and "S-shapes" are characteristic of subjects with high *n* Achievement and just like the *n* Achievement scores based on literary productions, they appear most frequently in 6th-century Greece, next most frequently in the 5th century, and least frequently in the 4th century. The chi-square tests show that such differences over time could hardly have arisen by chance. The results for these categories strongly support the hypothesis that *n* Achievement was high early and declined steadily.

If the S-shape continues to undulate, it becomes a "multiple wave," a characteristic appearing significantly more often in the doodles of contemporary individuals with low *n* Achievement. No significant trend for this characteristic was found for the vase designs, although it does appear most often as predicted during the period of decline.

Since Aronson had found that subjects with low *n* Achievement tended to fill up less of the space at the bottom of a piece of paper with doodles, he also measured the amount of unused space at the bottom of the Greek vases, dividing in each instance by the vertical height of the vase in the photograph to get the *proportion* of space that was unfilled. As in the case of "diagonals" and "S-shapes," the proportion of space unused followed the *n* Achievement trend in Greek history quite closely for the first two periods. It was lowest in the period of growth (only about one third of the vases left 12 per cent or more of the bottom blank), and highest in the period of climax (about two thirds of the vases left 12 per cent or more of the bottom blank). The sample of vases for the third period is so small that with only one measure coming from each of them, the shift back toward more use of space cannot be taken to mean very much.

On the whole, the results in Table 4.4 provide independent support for the hypothesis: the signs of high *n* Achievement are most frequent (more diagonals and S-shapes, less unused space) in the period of growth, and significantly less frequent in the period of climax. In case the findings should appear too mysterious or at least too flatly empirical, it is fairly easy to give them a reasonable interpretation. The designs the person with high *n* Achievement makes are not completely meaningless: what they suggest is that in movement as in everything else he is energetic (tends to use up space, prefers "dynamic" diagonals to static verticals and horizontals) and likes variety or tends to innovate (prefers S-shapes to redundant multiple waves). Furthermore, the functional similarity between painting vases and making doodles is greater than one might at first suspect. The artist is as free as the "doodler" in many respects to make whatever designs he likes. For example, in making the figure of a man, he may want to outline the inside of an earlobe. In doing so he is producing a doodle which, so far as reality is concerned, might just as well be an "S-shape" or a "multiple wave." So whether he gives it an extra twist or not depends, as a doodle does, on an inner motivational state which has established his preference for variety or redundancy. As a matter of fact, S-shaped earlobes in vase paintings are more common in the period of the growth of Greek civilization than in the period of climax!

Finally, as with the verbal material, the quantitative results do not appear to distort seriously the qualitative generalizations art historians make in describing the styles of vase designs in these different periods. The vases of the early period are frequently described as having a geometric or dynamic quality in which diagonals, stylized figures, and S-shaped grapevines are frequent. During the period of climax the style is characterized by a striving for balance, harmony, naturalness in presenting figures, and a tendency to redundancy.

The Greek study has been presented in the greatest detail because it was the first of the several historical studies to be reported in this chapter and the kinds of solutions adopted to the many methodological problems it posed formed a precedent for later work. It also presents some interpretive problems that demand at least a short comment, although they can be dealt with more fully after material in subsequent chapters has been worked through.

What do the results mean, assuming for the moment that they can be believed? Is n Achievement a kind of "first cause" that appears and disappears out of nowhere which makes civilizations rise and fall? Clearly it is not. By now we know a good deal about what makes n Achievement levels rise and fall (see Chapter 9), and practically all of its determinants are social in origin. The simplest way to state the case is that some conditions arise in society, often based on an ideological movement (though clearly not Protestantism in the case of Ancient Greece!), which lead parents to give their children early achievement training of a certain special type. This in turn produces more boys with high n Achievement who, given at least some favorable conditions, are apt to become successful business entrepreneurs for reasons outlined in Chapters 6 and 7. In the case of early Greece, we do not know why their n Achievement level was initially high, though research can and should be done on the pottery of the various subcultures that contributed to the rise of Greek civilization (Achaean, Dorian, Cretan, etc.) to see which ones were high in n Achievement in even earlier times. We have a better idea as to why their n Achievement declined.

Democratic though the Greeks were in many ways, they never thought of extending their democracy to slaves. Slaves had probably been common in the households of great Mycenaean and other early Greek chieftains as the legitimate spoils of war, but the growing group of middle-class entrepreneurs did not become wealthy enough to purchase and maintain slaves until toward the end of the 6th century B.C. During the 5th century in the period of greatest prosperity, the son of a well-to-do Athenian family typically had a nurse of his own from birth onward to care for his wants (Glotz, 1925, vol. 2, p. 582) and a pedagogue, literally to walk him to school, to stay there with him, and to bring him home (*ibid.*, p. 591). It does not take much imagination to suppose that the nurse and the pedagogue between them, both being normally slaves and dependent on the favor of the family, would scarcely be the ones to insist on early self-reliance for the child. On the contrary, their very existence at his side tended to make the child more dependent on others for a longer period of time than perhaps his father had been, whose father had not in turn been rich enough to support so many slaves.

Much has been written about the moral degeneracy of wealthy Athens and about slavery as part of this degeneracy so that in a sense there is nothing original in this hypothesis. What is new is that there is now evidence for a very specific way in which wealth caused "character" to "degenerate." It enabled parents to provide slaves to care for their children which deprived the children of the early self-reliance training the parents may themselves have received in less wealthy homes. And certainly by the 5th century, the use of slaves was widespread in households throughout Athens so that the decrease in self-reliance training should have been general rather than restricted to a few chieftains as in earlier generations. Estimates differ as to the number of slaves in Athens, but there were probably almost as many as there were freemen and their families, although contemporary Greeks were apt to put the figure much higher (*ibid.*, p. 228).

It is tempting to speculate that one reason why practically all great civilizations of the past have declined after a few generations of "climax" is because families have nearly always used their increased prosperity to turn over the rearing of their children to slaves or other dependents who "spoil" the children or keep them dependent too long. For a time a civilization may draw its leaders with high n Achievement from the periphery, from portions of the society which have not as yet become wealthy enough to support slaves, but if prosperity becomes too general, the effect may be to diminish the number of children with high n Achievement below some critical point needed to maintain the civilization.

Such theorizing about the causes of changes in the level of achievement motivation in Greece has one important theoretical value: it serves to put n Achievement level back in its social context. Thus, we have argued that the decline in n Achievement was at least in part a function of a general prosperity and a political system which permitted and encouraged the use of household slaves. So while n Achievement modifies society, it is itself also modified by society. But the chain of influence is more of a spiral than a circle with early family life providing the means by which changes are mediated over generations in time. Social and economic conditions influence the extent to which one generation provides early self-reliance training for its children. Early or late self-reliance training presumably generates a relatively fixed characteristic in the children—n Achievement— which determines the energy and success with which they will start enterprises, particularly economic ones—that in turn will modify social and economic conditions which may affect the rearing of the next generation.

The process has been described as if it occurs in three generations, but of course in actuality it may take much longer. Child-rearing attitudes are not so easily changed. Parents try to raise their children as they were raised, slaves or no slaves. Economic wealth, no matter how high the n Achievement, cannot be built up for a whole society in one generation. But the sequence of interaction between man and society should be as described no matter how many generations it takes, if the general interpretation of the results obtained so far is correct.

Spain in the Late Middle Ages

Having noted that Spain in the 16th century, like Greece 2,000 years earlier, had shown a marked peak in economic activity, Cortés (1960) checked to see whether it was preceded by a high and steadily declining level of n Achievement as in the case of Ancient Greece. As outside limits for the historical period to be investigated, he chose roughly 1200 A.D. as a beginning point, since it was only in the 13th century that Spain had reconquered enough of her territory from the Arabs to become in any sense a "nation," and 1700-1710 as an end point since thereafter there are signs that the economic decline beginning about a century earlier had come to some kind of an end. Precise quantitative data reflecting economic trends were almost as hard to find as for Ancient Greece, but Cortés reviewed the figures over several centuries for changes in population, in the number of sheep (since wool was a cornerstone of Spanish prosperity), and in shipping from various key ports (since trade was also an essential part of her economic growth and decline).

All of Cortés' estimates point to 1492-1610 as the period when Spain reached the height of her economic prosperity and influence. The era was ushered in by the relatively stable reign of Ferdinand and Isabella and the discovery of the Americas which led to prodigious feats of exploration and conquest by Spaniards in the first half of the 16th century. On the other hand, the beginning of the end of Spanish prosperity and influence was at the very least signalled by the defeat of the Spanish Armada by the English in 1588. Cortés found that the figures collected by Chaunu and

Usher (1959) on the tonnage of ships per year cleared from Spain for the New World reflected satisfactorily the consensus of economic historians as to the periods of growth, climax, and decline in the Spanish economy in the late Middle Ages. These figures are presented below in Fig. 4.2.

In selecting literature to code for n Achievement Cortés first decided to limit his sample to the kingdom of Castile (excluding the kingdoms of Aragon, Catalonia, Navarre and Valencia) because it included more than 75 per cent of peninsular Spanish territories and almost 85 per cent of the population by the end of the 16th century. "Furthermore, Castile owned and governed the Hispanic colonies of the New World, and her language, race, and institutions have largely determined the character of modern Spain." Then selections were made without knowledge of their content according to the criteria established in the Greek study. That is, a variety of authors from each time period was included. The authors are considered to be representative of their times (i.e., were popular and well-known). The material to be scored was primarily imaginative, rather than factual or historical. He obtained selections totalling about 100,000 words (250 pages) from around 56 authors from each of three time periods: economic growth, 1200-1492, climax, 1492-1610, and decline, 1610-1710. (See Table 4.5.) The selections represented four types of literature—fiction, verse (epic poems and ballads), short stories or tales, and history. In the categories of fiction and verse, similar themes from the different time periods were chosen so far as possible. In the categories of short stories and history, bias was eliminated so far as possible by using a complete anthology and secondly, by choosing pages at random from historical accounts. Some of the better known selections he used include:

From the period of economic growth: *La Gran Conquista de Ultramar*
Poema del Mio Cid

From the period of climax: Cervantes, *El Quijote de la Mancha*
Cortés, *Cartas*

From the period of decline: Quevedo, *Buscón*
de Molina, *Los Tres Maridos Burlados*

The literary material was scored for achievement imagery as in the Greek study, except that here it was done in the original Spanish, not in translation. Furthermore, another judge who did not know the time period to which the selection belonged also scored fourteen of the selections independently to check on the reliability of the coding by Cortés. Their agreement was very nearly perfect, the rank order correlation between the two judges for these fourteen cases being .94. It seems highly unlikely

that either selection bias or coding bias produced the large differences in
n Achievement level which appeared at the three different periods in
Spanish history for all the four types of literature, as shown in Table 4.5.
The results, expressed as usual in terms of number of achievement images
per hundred lines, are identical with those obtained in the study of Ancient
Greece. Achievement motivation is highest (mean = 10.74) during the
early period and had definitely dropped (mean = 6.07) by the time of
economic climax, foreshadowing once again the subsequent economic

TABLE 4.5   NUMBER OF AUTHORS AND FREQUENCY OF ACHIEVEMENT IMAGERY BY
ECONOMIC PERIODS AND TYPE OF LITERATURE IN MEDIEVAL SPAIN

Time period		Literary form[1]				Totals
		Fiction (novels)	Verse (epic poems and ballads)	History	Legends and tales	
Economic growth 1200-1492	Authors	7	30	7	11	55
	Achievement images per 100 lines	9.64	18.44	10.72	4.16	10.74
Economic climax 1492-1610	Authors	7	30	8	12	57
	Achievement images per 100 lines	2.72	11.64	6.76	3.16	6.07
Economic decline 1610-1730	Authors	8	30	7	11	56
	Achievement images per 100 lines	.84	3.48	4.96	1.40	2.67

(from J. Cortés, 1960)

[1] The samples for a literary type in a given time period were each approximately 25,000 words
(2,500 lines) in length.

decline. An analysis of variance based conservatively on the cell means in
Table 4.5 (ignoring within-cell variance) shows that the variance by time
period and by literary type are both significant at less than the .05 level.
Actually, of course, such an estimate of significance is definitely on the
conservative side since an F test based on the within-cell variance with its
much larger number of degrees of freedom would almost certainly be much
larger, indicating even less likelihood that the results could have arisen by
chance.

In short, the means in the final column of Table 4.5, also shown graphically
in Fig. 4.2, may be considered a fairly trustworthy index of what was

happening to the *n* Achievement level in Spanish society between the 14th and 17th centuries. This level was high initially and it declined sharply and steadily thereafter. Figure 4.2 plots this information along with the figures on shipping cleared from Spain for the New World which Cortés considers a representative index of what was happening to the Spanish economy as a whole. The initial high level of *n* Achievement is followed some time later by a wave of economic growth which subsides fairly abruptly after the level of *n* Achievement has decisively dropped. The result is very like that obtained for Ancient Greece and confirms the connection between achievement motivation and economic growth in

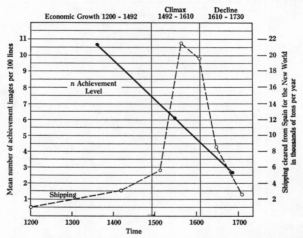

Figure 4.2   Average *n* Achievement level in literature at midpoints of periods of economic growth, climax, and decline in Medieval Spain

another time period for a totally different culture. Furthermore, this time the coding was done in the original language, eliminating the possible objection to the Greek study that the results might have been dependent in part on the *n* Achievement of the translators. The results of these two studies are sufficiently encouraging to warrant a closer examination of the relation between successive "waves" of achievement motivation and "pulses" of economic growth within the same country. The case of England provides us with an opportunity for such a study.

England from Tudor Times to the Industrial Revolution

The economic history of Great Britain is of special interest for several reasons. For one thing it provides the longest and most intensively studied record of economic development available for any society. In fact, the record is long enough so that one ought to be able to detect more than one wave of growth of the sort already investigated in Ancient Greece and Spain. Furthermore, England was at the very center of the Industrial Revolution which ushered in the modern most impressive phase of economic growth. It should therefore be of special interest to see what was happening to the level of achievement motivation in England in the eighteenth century. Finally, English literature is available for coding from 1400 on, so that it should be possible to push the assessment of n Achievement level back well before the first major wave of economic growth. In doing so, we may be able to detect the actual *rise* in achievement motivation which presumably occurred both in the Greek and Spanish cases but which the data do not actually show. In both instances n Achievement starts out high and drops off steadily.

Presumably if we had been able to measure it earlier, the n Achievement level would have been lower, but one of the lessons a student of human behavior learns early is to take nothing for granted. An alternative explanation of the Greek and Spanish findings is that n Achievement decline precedes economic growth, since all we have actually measured is such a decline and we do not know whether the initial point is high or low relative to what it had been earlier. It may always be difficult to measure the earliest levels of presumably low n Achievement, for the simple reason that if a culture is really low in n Achievement, it may in fact not produce enough literature to be scored. Nevertheless it becomes of the greatest importance to demonstrate if possible that *rises* in n Achievement level precede waves of economic growth in a way that was not possible in the Greek or Spanish case so that such an alternative interpretation of the data may be more decisively eliminated. The length of the literary record in England and the care with which it has been assembled and dated provide us with better opportunities for detecting rises as well as declines in n Achievement level.

Therefore Bradburn and Berlew (1961) who made the study, set out to get a continuous record of n Achievement level in England from around 1400 in half century periods up through the beginning of the Industrial Revolution (around 1830). In other words, they wanted to start well before England began to stir under the Tudor kings, back in the days when it was still largely pasture and woodland, when "from Blacon Point to Hillbree a squirrel may jump from tree to tree," and to carry the record continuously up through the time when England was largely a concentration of great industrial cities that became the workshops and commercial capitals of the world. In making their literary collections they were guided by the same principles already discussed in the two previous historical studies. They succeeded in finding 40 to 50 authors and 150 pages of comparable text to represent each time period (usually a half century). The literary material used was of three general kinds: drama, accounts of sea voyages, and street ballads. The choice of these particular literary forms was again dictated by the fact that they represented popular imaginative literature through the time period under investigation rather than the production of only an "off beat" literary or élitist minority.

Only authors whose productive years fell largely within the limits of a given time period were included. Under these restrictions it proved possible to get adequate samples for all three literary types for six time periods beginning with 1501-1575 and ending with 1776-1830. In the case of drama it was possible to get an earlier sample also representing the 15th century. (See Table 4.6.) Among the better known plays used in part for coding were the following for each of the time periods:

1400-1500
1. Anonymous: *Everyman*
2. Anonymous: *Noah's Ark. A Newcastle Play*
3. Medwall, Henry: *Fulgens and Lucres*

1501-1575
1. Robert Wever: *Lusty Juventus*
2. John Skelton: *Magnificence*
3. Richard Edwards: *Damon and Pythias*

1576-1625
1. Christopher Marlowe: *Tamburlaine*, First Part
2. William Shakespeare: *King Richard II*
3. Ben Jonson: *The Alchemist*

1626-1675
1. George Digby: *Elvira*
2. John Milton: *Samson Agonistes*
3. Janes Shirley: *Gamester*

1676-1725
1. Thomas Southerne: *The Fate of Capua*
2. William Congreve: *The Way of the World*
3. Joseph Addison: *Cato*

1726-1775
1. David Garrick: *The Guardian*
2. Samuel Johnson: *Irene: A Tragedy*
3. Oliver Goldsmith: *She Stoops to Conquer*

1776-1830
1. William Wordsworth: *The Borderers*
2. Richard Sheridan: *The Critic; or, A Tragedy Unrehearsed*
3. Percy Bysshe Shelley: *Prometheus Unbound*

The coding of the samples for *n* Achievement was done by one of the investigators who did not know what time period a work represented or for the most part who wrote it. Furthermore, the investigator who made the literary selections knew nothing about the economic data which had been collected, to minimize the possibility of bias entering into his selection of the materials to be scored. Actually such bias is particularly

TABLE 4.6 NUMBER OF AUTHORS AND FREQUENCY OF ACHIEVEMENT IMAGERY BY TYPE OF LITERATURE FROM THE 15TH TO 19TH CENTURIES IN ENGLAND

Time period	Sample size per period:	Literary form			Totals 6,048 lines
		Drama 2,240 lines	Sea voyages 2,500 lines	Street ballads 1,308 lines	
1400-1500	Authors	14			
	Achievement images per 100 lines	4.60			
1501-1575	Authors	14	11	20	45
	Achievement images per 100 lines	6.16	2.76	6.34	4.79
1576-1625	Authors	14	10	18	42
	Achievement images per 100 lines	4.20	3.04	9.25	4.81
1626-1675	Authors	14	9	27	50
	Achievement images per 100 lines	2.50	2.64	4.59	3.01
1676-1725	Authors	14	10	27	51
	Achievement images per 100 lines	2.28	2.08	5.96	2.99
1726-1775	Authors	14	10	25	49
	Achievement images per 100 lines	3.48	3.92	6.12	4.23
1776-1830	Authors	14	10	34	58
	Achievement images per 100 lines	2.67	6.24	11.24	6.00

(from Bradburn and Berlew, 1961).

unlikely to have entered into the selection of street ballads, since in this instance large numbers of short selections were coded wholesale with the single criterion for selection being that they were accurately dated. Both coders were highly experienced, having worked on the coding of children's stories presented in Chapter 3, but to check on their reliability both of them scored one-third of the total sample of selections. The correlation coefficient between their two estimates of n Achievement present in the same material was .93 and periodic checks with shorter samples throughout the scoring showed that their agreement reliability coefficient never dropped below .92. The results of their scoring, presented as usual in terms of average number of achievement images per hundred lines, are presented in Table 4.6 and Fig. 4.3. They show a high point at the beginning of the period of investigation, a drop in n Achievement to a low point between 1626 and 1725, followed by another sharp rise thereafter. The meaning of these changes can best be understood after a discussion of how a measure of rate of economic development in Britain was derived.

The problem of getting a quantitative estimate of economic development in Britain was especially complicated by the fact that growth was more or less continuous from 1600 on. That is, unlike the waves of development in Ancient Greece or Medieval Spain, England has shown no marked or prolonged drop in *absolute* level of economic activity or prosperity since around 1600. So the problem becomes one much more like that dealt with in Chapter 3; that is, one of comparing *relative rates* of growth, to discover times when the English economy was growing more rapidly or more slowly than at other times. Deane (1955) has collected some national income estimates beginning with Gregory King's figures in 1688, but they do not go back early enough nor are they continuous or accurate enough to use. Furthermore, Bradburn and Berlew decided that since the problem was to compare rates of growth, rather than the absolute levels of development that might be represented in national income figures, it was only necessary to find a quantitative series, much like the electrical output figures used in Chapter 3, which could be regarded as representative of what was happening in the economy as a whole. They examined several such series and found that coal import figures at London collected by Nef (1932) and Jevons (1906) in general followed quite closely whatever other evidence was available on changes in rate of economic growth. The reason appears to be that coal then, like electricity now, provided the power for many key economic activities, both commercial and domestic. The only question that might be raised would have to do with the earliest period for which coal figures are available, from around 1585 to 1650, since it might be contended that coal at that time was still largely for domestic rather than commercial use. Coal had been burned as domestic fuel for several centuries earlier, but it did not come into wide use until early in the 16th century when brick chimneys were invented that would cheaply and efficiently draw up the "noxious fumes" that had formerly made it unpopular. Still by the end of the century, or by 1585 when the figures begin, it was used quite generally, not only for domestic fuel but for the dressing of meat, washing, brewing, and dyeing. (Woytinsky, 1953, p. 867.)

But the figures are only for one method of entry of coal into one city. How can they represent adequately what was going on in the country as a whole? Two considerations may help explain why they do. London was during all this period (roughly 1600-1800), perhaps even more than later when the Industrial Midland developed, the hub and commercial center of the country. What happened in London was a good barometer of what was happening all over the country. Furthermore, the port figures are so important because London was not near coal fields and had to get its coal primarily by sea up until the middle of the 19th century when railroads came into wide use. Fortunately this is after the period under consideration.

Granted for the moment that the coal import figures provide probably as accurate an index as is availabile of the level of economic activity in England over this time period, how can they be used to get estimates of rate of growth? The normal procedure economists use is to express the gain from one time period to the next as a percentage of the level at the first time period. The objections to such a procedure have already been outlined in Chapter 3. Suffice it to say again here that such a method tends to inflate enormously the percentage gains at the early stages of growth when the initial levels are very low. For example, in the present instance the percentage gain in coal imports for the first 20- to 30-year time period in the series is 363 per cent, a figure considerably higher than the highest percentage gain ever recorded in a similar time period, even at the height of the Industrial Revolution in the early 19th century when coal imports were leaping upwards by millions of tons rather than thousands as in the earliest time period. The best and simplest solution to such problems appears to be to use a regression analysis similar to the one adopted in Chapter 3. One can estimate on the basis of the general trend relating level of coal imports to gains in imports, what the gain for a given time period should be and then see whether the actual gain was more or less than expected.

The exact method by which this was done by Bradburn and Berlew (1961) for the coal import figures is as follows. The starting point was taken to be the first year for which figures are available, namely 1585-1586. Next, they decided to get estimates of coal imports for every third of a century thereafter to get enough points to plot a reasonably stable regression line. Rather than use the figure for any given year, such as 1618, 1651, etc., they averaged all figures available for the third of a century in question to get an approximation of imports *over* that period. Such averages were used for two reasons: figures were often not available for a particular year needed and also yearly figures sometimes show much fluctuation due to short-range changes in the condition of business which are not of interest in a long-range study of trends. So the figures available for years between 1605 and 1637 were averaged to get an estimate for around 1618-1620, those between 1634 and 1667 to get an estimate for around 1650, and so on. Then gains in roughly equal time periods of approximately 33 to 35 years could be obtained simply by subtracting each level from the preceding one (i.e., the level for 1618-1620 subtracted from the level for 1585-1586, etc.).

Inspection showed that if level is plotted against subsequent gain in logarithmic terms, the relationship is clearly linear and very close ($r = .82$ for the 8 time periods under consideration). In other words the gain (in log units) is higher the higher the initial level (also in log units). The regression formula for the straight line relationship (log gain = .671 log level + 1.6389) predicts what the gain should be from one time period to the next. Then this predicted value can be compared with the obtained value and the deviation expressed in standard score units, as in Chapter 3, to see how fast the economy was expanding or contracting in terms of its average performance over this time period. The standard score values obtained in this way by Bradburn and Berlew (1961) are plotted in Fig. 4.3 at mid-points in the intervals over which the rate of gain took place. That is, they plotted the gain between 1585 and 1618-1620 at 1600, simply because it had to be plotted at some point and the mid-point seemed more represent-ative than the end point for a rate of gain taking place over the whole period. Actually if the plotting were done at the end points, no differences in the interpretation of the relationship between n Achievement and economic changes would be necessary.

Although the estimates are admittedly crude, they nevertheless show three rather well-defined phases in the economic growth of England to the Industrial Revolution. The first period, centering in the years 1600-1690, is one of moderate overachievement (mean standard score for the first three estimates of gain = + .33). This is followed by a period of stagnation or underachievement centering in the years 1700-1780 (mean standard score for the three estimates of gain in this time period = − 1.11). Finally, by 1800 the third phase of phenomenal economic growth culminating in the Industrial Revolution is already well under way (mean standard score for the two estimates of gains in this time period = +1.17).

Now the question is: how well do these estimates of the three phases in economic growth in Britain agree with historical accounts and with the hypothesis that n Achievement levels should foreshadow such changes at an earlier date? Figure 4.3 plots for easy visual comparison the motivational scores for a 50-year earlier time period along with the economic gain figures. Obviously the fit between the two curves is fairly close, the main point being that the motivational changes *precede* the economic ones by 30-50 years. Let us consider in detail the evidence at each stage in development.

First, the figures show an above-average rate of economic development at the first point in time when an estimate is really possible, namely, around 1600. The most likely possibility is that the earlier rate of development was average. So a line has been drawn pointing downwards to indicate that the rise to the "overachievement" represented by the estimate for 1600 occurred most probably in the last half of the 16th century. Does other evidence support such an inference? Bindoff states that the 15th century in England represented a period of economic decline—"The area of land under

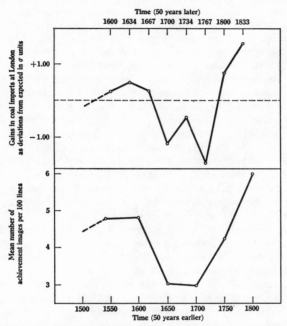

Figure 4.3   Average *n* Achievement levels in English literature (1550-1800) compared with rates of gain in coal imports at London 50 years later

cultivation instead of continuing to expand underwent a contraction. . . . Its industrial and commercial life exhibits the same tendency towards stagnation." (Bindoff, 1950, p. 13.) Subsequently, however, during the reigns of the Tudor kings Henry VII and Henry VIII, England pulled herself together and showed a great burst of energy in the last half of the 16th century, symbolized by the exploits of Drake and Hawkins on the sea and the decisive defeat of the Spanish Armada in 1588. "In the sixties and early seventies England had shaken herself free of that excessive dependence upon the Netherlands' market which had earlier exposed her economy to such severe crisis. Her merchants had opened up new markets, in Europe,

Asia, and Africa, which they served with a wide range of goods. By about 1575 the nation began to reap the reward, and the next ten years, which saw Antwerp go down to irreparable ruin, were by contrast a boom period for English trade, and through trade for her industry and agriculture." (Bindoff, 1950, p. 285.) The growth of trade and the expansive mood of the times are nicely illustrated by the foundation in 1599 of "the most famous of the English trading corporations, the East India Company. . . . Thus there was planted, in the last year of the Tudor century, the seed of trade and dominion far exceeding the wildest flights of Tudor fantasy." (Bindoff, 1950, p. 288.) There is little doubt that economic historians would agree with the estimates in Fig. 4.3, which show that England was advancing very rapidly economically around the turn of the 17th century. The figures indicate that the rate continued above average until well toward the end of the 17th century. While we have been concerned strictly with economic data, it is perhaps worth noting that Kroeber's figures (1944) also show the whole of the 17th century to have been remarkable in England for its production of men eminent in literature, music and science. The scientist figures are of particular interest because of the contention by Weber, Merton (1949) and others that interests in business and in science tend to occur together. Certainly together they produced the technological revolution in England a century later. If one accepts the argument that they are two aspects of the same type of culture growth, then Kroeber's figures provide independent confirmation of the "above-average" rate of growth in this culture area in the 17th century.

   Was the economic peak preceded by a peak in n Achievement? The over-all estimate of n Achievement level, as shown in Fig. 4.3, is high in the period 1500-1575, though not higher than in the succeeding 50-year period. The simplest summary of the data is that n Achievement level was high from 1500 through 1625 and that this high level definitely appeared *before* the rapid economic growth that extended from 1600-1675. However, the figures for plays (Table 4.6) are especially interesting because they go back 50 to 75 years earlier, into the 15th century. They show that so far as this literary form is concerned, n Achievement level was lower earlier in the mid-15th century (mean = 4.60) than it was later, around 1525 (mean = 6.16), confirming our hypothesis that our over-all measure starts (1540) at a high point in the n Achievement curve. The difference in the mean scores for the first two time periods in the drama curve is unfortunately not statistically significant ($p < .15$, pd). Nevertheless, the result is an interesting and potentially important confirmation of the theoretical expectation, not tested in Greece or Spain, that n Achievement has to *rise* to the high point at which it appears at the beginning of the phases of economic growth that have been chosen for study.

   It is interesting to note, also, that the other two literary forms—accounts of sea voyages and street ballads, also show a rise in n Achievement but at a later time period (1576-1625 instead of 1501-1575). If the p values for each of the rises considered separately are combined, using one-tailed significance tests throughout because all the trends are in the expected direction, the tendency for n Achievement level to rise from the first to the second period for which the literary forms are available is fairly dependable statistically speaking $(p < .05)$.[3] At least this result fairly effectively disposes of the notion that n Achievement level is always highest in the earliest period of a literary form. Why it should rise at somewhat different historical time periods in the different types of literary forms is an interesting question. It is tempting to speculate that literary forms represented the thoughts and aspirations of different social classes in England in the 16th century, which showed a rise in n Achievement at somewhat different time periods. Perhaps, for example, the plays represented the feelings of the London population or of the more educated classes. The street ballads and accounts of sea voyages, on the other hand, may have represented the aspirations of the common people or the people from the smaller towns outside London. Then one could argue that the wave of n Achievement hit the better educated city people first and then spread out to the provinces and to the less educated. But such speculations will have to be left to closer students of English history in the 16th century.

Do qualitative data support the finding that n Achievement level was high in England between 1500 and 1625? To begin with, it is certainly in accord with the best historical judgment that a wave of expansive energy reached England a century or more after it had reached its highest point in Spain. Comparison of Figs. 4.2 and 4.3 shows that Spain's level of n Achievement had dropped off significantly by the middle of the 16th century when England's was at a high point. The fact that Spain's absolute level was still higher than England's means nothing because absolute levels depend on the types of literature scored in the two countries which were not comparable. Neither epic poems nor history were scored in England, both of which in general give a very high level of n Achievement. Here, as in Chapter 3, we find again that a country at a low point in n Achievement (Spain) suffers a major defeat at the hands of a country high in n Achievement (England) during the battle with the Spanish Armada (1588).

Even more interesting, in the light of the presumed connection between Protestantism and n Achievement, is the fact that the period 1500-1625 is precisely the time when Protestantism and eventually Puritanism was growing most rapidly in strength and numbers both in England and Scotland. In mid-century John Knox led the Calvinist revolution to a successful outcome, with the help of the English, in Scotland. In England the century began under the leadership of a king, Henry VIII, who certainly in his youth set an example of high n Achievement for his people. "He could bend a bow with the best forester in the realm, and when complimented on his archery by the French ambassador could reply, 'It was good for a Frenchman.' His colossal suit of tilting armor in the Tower reminds us that once he flashed through the lists like Lancelot, laying low his adversaries and calling for more. He was a champion at tennis and a mighty hunter. . . . Among other accomplishments this Admirable Crichton was no mean musician, and played well on all known instruments." (Trevelyan 1926, p. 292.) Henry, while orthodox enough himself in the beginning in religious matters, encouraged the "new learning" brought over from Renaissance circles in Europe. Eventually he broke with Rome over the question of his remarriage, but certainly the rupture would not have lasted without the ground swell of support in public opinion led by the scholars he had encouraged and two great religious reformers—Cranmer, who translated the Prayer Book into English, and Latimer "the soul of the popular movement," who "by his rough, homely sermons, set the standard of that English pulpit oratory which, together with the Bible and the Prayer Book, effected the conversion of the people to Protestantism in the course of the next hundred years." (Trevelyan, 1926, p. 313.) The basis for the Protestant Reformation had been laid decades before by Wycliffe's translation of the Bible into English, but the popular movement which had failed then gained decisive momentum during the very years when our evidence shows that n Achievement level in England was high. So far as this period in history is concerned, the rise of Protestantism and n Achievement are closely connected, as they should be if our interpretation of Weber's hypothesis in psychological terms is correct.

To turn to the next decisive phase in the development of the British economy, the coal import data show a definite period of slower economic development roughly from 1700 to 1790. Do historians agree that this was a period of relative economic stagnation in England? Unfortunately they do not. While most of them would have agreed that the nation was developing slowly then as compared to her very rapid development subsequently in the Industrial Revolution, Deane's national income figures (1955) show a slow but steady rise in national income per capita between 1700-1770 and a slight decline thereafter which persisted through the early stages of the Industrial Revolution. Must we then conclude that England was developing rapidly early in the 18th century and slowly thereafter, instead of the reverse as the data in Fig. 4.3 show?

On the face of it to call the Industrial Revolution in England a period of relative economic decline seems absurd. The difficulty arises from using national income per capita as a measure of economic development. As Colin Clark also concludes on the basis of his estimates "the first half of the nineteenth century, with all the tremendous changes brought about, only just succeeded in maintaining real income per head constant." (1957, p. 218.) It is the "tremendous changes," the "speeding up" of economic activity, that we need a measure of and that economists, at least part of the time, really have in mind when they speak of economic development, as we pointed out in Chapter 3. Therefore we can hardly regard Deane's national income figures as a decisive contradiction of the inferences based on the coal figures that the English economy was developing more slowly between 1700-1770 than it had earlier or would later.

Deane (1957) also presents figures on trade volume which increased steadily throughout the 18th century, though the rate of increase cannot be compared with the rate of increase in the 17th century to judge which is faster or slower. However, in one key direction British overseas trade languished in the first half of the 18th century—in respect to her trade with her American colony. In absolute pound volume it showed no consistent increase between 1690-1745, yet during this time period the number of colonists in America was increasing fourfold, from around 250,000 persons to about one million (see Wright, 1949, p. 128). Certainly British traders were not taking advantage of the greatly increased market. On a per head basis, trade with the American colonies fell from around two pounds per head per year in 1690 to around half a pound per head per year in 1745. Yet American trade was valued by the English. "I state to you," said Chatham, "the importance of America; it is a double market: a market of consumption and a market of supply." (Trevelyan, 1926, p. 444). And trade with the Colonies could increase rapidly as the sudden spurt in volume after 1745 clearly demonstrated. The inference seems clear: English businessmen were not as enterprising in the first half of the 18th century as they had been earlier or would be later.

It is extremely hazardous to draw inferences about economic life from what happens in other spheres of human activity, yet it is perhaps worth mentioning that the first half of the 18th century in England might well be described by some such term as "stagnation" or "consolidation" in many fields of endeavor. Politically, Walpole was primarily interested in peace and compromise, in letting sleeping dogs lie (Trevelyan, 1926, p. 504). The universities and the Royal Navy languished. Kroeber notes "a definite dip in the first half of the eighteenth century in the production of eminent men of science in England, and other eminent men as well." (Kroeber, 1944, p. 148.) He identifies "two growths, one from 1600 to 1700, culminating in Newton; the other from 1750 to the present. . . . The interval of slump was real. The single figure of note in the interregnum was a Scotchman. The emphasis of the time was on 'politeness'; which, earlier developed in France than in England, and perhaps contributed to the premature ending of the great Descartes—Fermat growth. . . . That the interregnum was profound though short is indicated also by the miscellaneous origins of the participants when British science began producing again after 1750." (Kroeber, 1944, p. 149.) The one really outstanding achievement during this time was the firm establishment of parliamentary rule and the codification of English law, culminating in Blackstone's famous Commentaries. But other evidence (Knapp and Goodrich, 1952) strongly suggests that interest in law, in codification of the traditional, is antithetical to interests in exploiting the new fields represented both by science and business. In general, then, aside from Deane's national income figures which we have questioned on other grounds, the historical evidence does support the slump in economic development clearly shown in the coal import figures in Fig. 4.3.

To turn now to the n Achievement data, there is no question but that the economic slump characterizing the first half of the 18th century was preceded by a fall in n Achievement level beginning in the period 1625-1675 and continuing through the next 50 years to 1725. The drop appears in all three forms of literary samples. The simplest statistical comparison is between the level for 1500-1625 versus the level for 1626-1725. T tests were computed for the comparison for each of the three types of literature separately, and their p values combined by the chi-square technique. The results show that the chances of the drop arising from sampling fluctuations are less than one in a hundred, i.e., the drop in n Achievement is marked and statistically highly significant. What produced it is really not a question for detailed examination here, but it may be noted in passing that these were years of great internal stress and civil war in Britain, of struggles between kings and Parliament as to who should rule. Apparently the generally unsettled conditions of ordinary life affected the motives and the values of the people at the time more than it did England's economy, which continued to thrive throughout the 17th century, a finding which may come as a surprise to some historians who look to more direct and immediate connections between political and economic developments. If our argument is correct, the political instability of the 17th century did affect the economy not at the time, but a generation or two later and then only indirectly by affecting the motives and aspirations of people.

Fortunately the third phase in the development of the English economy is not likely to be questioned seriously by anyone except those who are trapped by their belief that national income per capita is the best measure of economic development. A marked increase in the rate of growth began near the end of the 18th century and continued on through the Industrial Revolution. The coal import figures in Fig. 4.3 show that the gains from around 1770 to 1833 were well above average and reached a magnitude several times as great as the earlier spurt in Elizabethan times. Between the mid-18th and mid-19th centuries the British economy was transformed "in a way which no country had ever before known." (Meier and Baldwin, 1957, p. 149.) The chief agent of change was the rapid growth in technology brought about by the marriage of science and industry. The last third of the 18th century saw the practical application of many technological improvements which made greatly increased productivity possible—the spinning "jenny," the power loom, Watt's steam engine, new applications of chemistry to industry, improved methods of producing pig iron, and the use of iron wire rope for winding up coal. (Meier and Baldwin, 1957, pp. 152-153.)

Did a rise in n Achievement level precede this striking economic development? Once again the answer must be in the affirmative. All three types of literature showed a rise in n Achievement between 1700 and 1750. The simplest statistical comparison again is to check the low point in n Achievement from 1625-1725 with the level in the succeeding century, 1725-1825. All three measures of n Achievement show a rise from one to the other of these time periods and the probability of such increases occurring by chance is less than one in a hundred using the combined chi-square technique as in previous comparisons. Accounts of sea voyages and street ballads both show a continuous and marked rise on up to 1800, foreshadowing the continued and spectacular economic development in the first half of the 19th century. On the other hand the plays show a rise followed by a small but insignificant drop around 1800 which might be attributed either to sampling error or to the fact that plays at this time may have represented less adequately the motivations of the men who were remaking England than they were in Elizabethan times.

The Wesleyan Revival, n Achievement, and Economic Growth

Once again there is an opportunity to check the connection between n Achievement and the rise of Protestantism. Was the increase in n Achievement between 1700 and 1750 accompanied by a Protestant revival? Certainly yes. It was precisely during this period beginning in 1729 at Oxford that John Wesley sparked the religious revival that culminated in the foundation of the nonconformist Methodist Church. Trevelyan notes that "the dissenting bodies of the Bunyan tradition which had been founded in the heat and zeal of the Cromwellian era" had tended to become more respectable and less enthusiastic (roughly from 1680-1730). (Trevelyan, 1926, p. 519.) The zeal of the first Methodists like John Wesley and George Whitefield "was opposed in every respect to the characteristic faults and merits of the eighteenth century attitude of mind" (1926, p. 519), and put new life in the dissenting bodies. Furthermore, Methodism was influential precisely among those commercial and industrial classes that spearheaded the Industrial Revolution. History appears to have repeated itself. Once again in the first half of the 18th century as in the first half of the 16th century a strong Protestant movement coincides with a high n Achievement level and both are followed in a generation or so by a greatly increased rate of economic growth.

Our interpretation of Weber's hypothesis in Chapter 2 has two specific implications for developments in England at this time: (1) the higher n Achievement reflected in the literary samples was more heavily concentrated in the nonconformist Protestant group and (2) the nonconformist group, because of its higher n Achievement, was more responsible for the increased entrepreneurial activity that sparked the Industrial Revolution from around 1770 on. Direct quantitative evidence on the first hypothesis is not available as yet, although it could be obtained by comparing, for example, the n Achievement levels in nonconformist vs. Anglican sermons or in other personal documents produced by key individuals of the two religious persuasions. But indirect evidence strongly supports the hypothesis. The twin keynotes of Methodism were stress on constant personal communion with God and on Christian perfection in this life. The one promotes self-reliance in establishing and maintaining continuous contact with God and the other, high standards of excellence in judging one's own conduct. These happen also to be the key elements in the formation of n Achievement.

Both are nicely expressed in a verse from one of the well-known hymns of Charles Wesley.

> Heavenly Adam, Life divine
> Change my nature into thine
> Move and spread throughout my soul
> Activate and fill the whole.

The singer is, in effect, making a direct personal approach to God to help him be more perfect. And the perfection of the individual's relationship to God is "known by its fruits," by right conduct. Wesley's insistence on the importance of Christian perfection was so strong that it got him into serious trouble with the established church: "Christians are saved in this world from all sin, from all unrighteousness, that they are now in such a sense perfect, as not to commit sin." Whatever its political or theological implications, such an uncompromising stress on excellence (as the very name Methodist implies) seems almost certain to have acted to promote the development of achievement motivation in Methodist children (see Chapter 9). And the picture was similar in other nonconformist bodies in England in the 18th century. It is one of the ironies of history that while the religious revivalists were almost exclusively concerned with man's relationship to God, they defined it in such a way that it tended to promote a trait of character—high n Achievement—that led in turn very often to marked business success. Wesley himself was puzzled and somewhat alarmed by the fact that Methodists tended to grow rich since he also believed that it was harder for a rich man to get into Heaven than for a "camel to pass through the needle's eye." [4]

Evidence for the second hypothesis—that nonconformists sparked the Industrial Revolution in England—is more direct. Historians and economists have long accepted the point without much question, illustrating it with a number of striking examples like the Quakers in the iron industry, but only recently has Hagen (1961) collected the figures which permit a systematic test of the hypothesis. Relevant data are summarized in Table 4.7 which

TABLE 4.7   BIRTHPLACE AND RELIGIOUS AFFILIATION OF BRITISH INNOVATORS IN THE INDUSTRIAL REVOLUTION 1725-1850 (After Hagen, 1961)

Birthplace	Population estimates (around 1800)	Number of innovators	p
England and Wales	9,187,000	55	
Scotland	1,652,000	18	
Per cent Scottish	15.2%	24.6%	<.05
Unknown or other		9	
Religious affiliation			
Anglican	—	27	
Unknown	—	27	
Nonconformist	650,000	28	
Per cent nonconformist	6.0%	34.1%	<.001

shows the origins of innovating entrepreneurs in the Industrial Revolution. Hagen took all the names of such entrepreneurs mentioned by T. S. Ashton (1948) in his book *The Industrial Revolution* and tried to track down their nationality and religious affiliation. The advantage of such a technique is that it starts with a presumably unbiased sample of industrial innovators and then attempts to see whether they are drawn in greater numbers from different segments of the population than would be expected on the basis of the proportion of that segment to the whole. The breakdown by birthplace is of interest here because the established church of Scotland was more Protestant in Weber's Calvinistic sense than the established church of England. And it is true that the percentage of known Scotchmen among the innovating group is significantly higher than it should be based on the estimate of the per cent of Scotchmen in the total British population. However, the finding loses some of its force when it is noted that four of the eighteen Scotchmen were actually Anglicans. If they are eliminated, the difference in percentages becomes insignificant and it is doubtful that a case can be made for Calvinism being a more effective breeder of industrial entrepreneurs than other forms of Protestantism, at least so far as this comparison is concerned.

The situation is quite different so far as the nonconformist bodies are concerned. They formed at the very most around 1800 six to eight per cent of the total population of England, Wales and Scotland, yet they produced at least a third of the innovators in the sample, a difference over the expected per cent which is highly significant statistically. Unfortunately it is not possible to compare very precisely the yield of the nonconformist and established churches in numbers of innovators because no figures are available on what proportion of the population belonged in any real sense to the Anglican church. If one argues that everyone who was not a dissenter was an Anglican, then of course the yield of the nonconformist bodies was much greater than that of the established church, but it is doubtful if being an Anglican meant very much religiously to a considerable percentage of the population. That is, an unknown percentage of the population ought really to be considered not religious, rather than included with the Anglican population. But even if one assumes that only half of the population belonged to the Anglican faith in any real sense, it can be seen from Table 4.7 that this 50 per cent of the population produced a significantly smaller percentage of the industrial entrepreneurs than it should have on a proportional basis. The connection of the particular form of Protestantism common to the dissenting bodies (Methodism, Quakerism, Unitarianism, etc.) with the innovating leadership of the Industrial Revolution seems firmly established. The presumptive reasons for the connection—a higher n Achievement level among the dissenting groups—has not been directly checked but is strongly supported by an analysis of the nature of religious revivals like Methodism in the 18th century and by inferences based on contemporary evidence (see Chapter 10).

In summary, Bradburn and Berlew's findings provide three separate confirmations of our basic hypothesis in the course of English economic development between 1600-1800. A rise or at least a high level of n Achievement in the 16th century preceded the first wave of economic growth in the early 17th century; a fall in n Achievement concentrated in the years 1650-1700 preceded the economic stagnation of the early 18th century; and a decisive rise in n Achievement beginning around the middle of the 18th century preceded the spectacular economic growth of the Industrial Revolution. The curves when juxtaposed so as to eliminate time lag, look very similar (Fig. 4.3). Furthermore, both the 16th and 18th century increases in n Achievement level were accompanied by strong popular Protestant movements within the church, and the fall in n Achievement corresponds to a time when Protestantism in England was not very active but was becoming "respectable." Finally, there is even some evidence that the rise in n Achievement at the end of the 18th century was significantly higher as it should have been than the rise in the 16th century which had preceded the first—and lesser—wave of economic growth. For the scores based on street ballads and accounts of sea voyages, the mean n Achievement in 1800 is significantly higher than it was at its previous high point between 1500-1625 ($p < .05$ and $< .02$ respectively).

The picture is complicated a little bit by the fact that the n Achievement in drama around 1800 is significantly lower ($p < .02$) than it was at its high point earlier. Combining the p's to get an over-all estimate of whether the second peak in n Achievement is higher than the first is not very meaningful under the circumstances, though on balance it would suggest that the greater average height of the second peak would not often have arisen by chance ($p < .15$, if a one-tailed test is permissible). Thus our hypothesis would certainly have to predict that since the second wave of industrial growth beginning around 1770 was considerably larger than the first one, the level of n Achievement preceding it should also be higher than the level of n Achievement preceding the first economic spurt. Rather than combine the results in this way, it is probably more meaningful to argue that plays written between 1775-1830 were less representative of the aspirations of the middle and lower classes than they had been in Shakespeare's time and that they were almost certainly less representative than the street ballads and the accounts of sea voyages were. Such a line of reasoning would lead to the inference that the second wave of n Achievement was stronger in the larger segment of the population represented by the lower middle classes than it had been in the 16th century. Even if the plays at both time periods are accepted as representing the interests of the "better" classes equally well, we are still left with the suggestion of class differences in the effects of the two "waves" of n Achievement: during the first one, the effect was greater in the "better" classes (represented by the "drama" figures) and during the second it was greater in the much larger middle and lower classes (represented in the figures for "sea ballads" and "letters"). Such a hypothesis must be considered highly tentative until it is confirmed by further evidence, but the main argument of Bradburn and Berlew's study seems fairly well established. Major stages in the rates of English economic development between 1600-1800 were foreshadowed and presumably determined at least in part by corresponding developments in n Achievement levels, as reflected in imaginative literature.

Achievement motivation in the United States: 1800-1950

What has been happening to achievement motivation in the United States in the past century is not only of great topical interest, it also fills an important gap in the Western historical record which, as presented in this and the preceding chapters, runs more or less continuously from 1300 to the present time. First, we noted a brief wave of achievement motivation in Spain in the late 15th century, followed by a similar wave of somewhat longer duration in England in the mid-16th century, then a pause and a very much larger wave preceding the English Industrial Revolution. There the record leaves off until we pick it up again around 1920 in the study using children's readers and find a major wave of achievement motivation occurring primarily in the underdeveloped countries of the world in the decade 1950-1960.

But what happened between 1800-1920? Obviously a number of countries experienced the "take-off" into rapid economic growth—e.g., Germany,

France, the United States, Japan. In all of them, our theory would have to predict, a wave of achievement motivation should have preceded the economic "take-off." For one of them—the United States—de Charms and Moeller (1961) have obtained very good evidence that such was indeed the case. They sampled every third page of four American reading textbooks typical of each twenty-year period from 1800-1950, and obtained achieve-

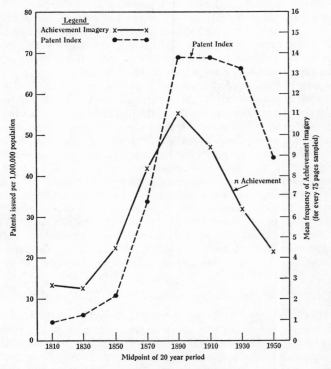

Figure 4.4 Mean frequency of achievement imagery in children's readers and the patent index in the United States, 1800-1950

ment imagery scores as plotted in Fig. 4.4. A characteristic wave of achievement motivation appears very clearly in the data: it rises from 1800 to a peak in 1890 and drops significantly and regularly thereafter. The figures disagree slightly with those in Chapter 3 in that they show a further decline between 1930 and 1950, whereas our data showed no change. However, the time periods are not the same: our first one runs from 1920-1929; theirs from 1920-1939; our second one from 1945-1955; theirs from 1940-1959. Probably their figures are less subject to sampling error, as their focus was on changes over gross units of time within one country, while ours was on international comparisons.

They also obtained a rough index of rate of economic growth in terms of the number of patents granted per 1,000,000 population as plotted in Fig. 4.4. This index is of particular interest, both for the theory of economic growth and for the theory of how achievement motivation affects behavior. Economists have agreed with surprising unanimity that technological innovation—here reflected in the patent index—sparked the Industrial Revolution in the West. The question has always been: what accounts for increases in the rates of technological innovation? Figure 4.4 suggests an answer: perhaps an increase in achievement motivation is responsible. At any rate, the two curves coincide very closely; if anything, changes in the achievement imagery curve occur somewhat ahead of similar changes in the patent index curve. The time difference, however, is not in itself distinctive enough to make a case for a causal connection between *n* Achievement and technological innovation. What is somewhat more convincing is evidence discussed in Chapter 6 that high *n* Achievement leads individuals to be interested in concrete knowledge of results, or more specifically in "constructional" activities (Moss and Kagan, 1961; Table 7.3 below). From "constructional activities" to "technological innovations" is not a great step, nor is "technological innovations" to "rapid economic growth." Certainly a reasonable case can be made from existing data for *n* Achievement producing an interest in constructional activities which lead to technological innovations and on to rapid economic growth. However, the question remains: why doesn't the achievement imagery curve "lead" the economic growth index by a longer period of time as in previous studies? The answer probably lies in the nature of the economic index used: it takes time usually for patents to be reflected in gross consumption or production measures of economic growth. Patents, as they reflect technological innovations, are in a sense the "seeds" of rapid development, but it often takes time, a decade or more, before they become used widely enough to affect more general economic growth measures. Thus, if higher *n* Achievement is producing more technological innovations from the people who have it, indexes reflecting these two factors should be closely associated in time and both should precede general increases in economic productivity. Such seems clearly to be the case so far as the United States is concerned, as Fig. 4.4 makes very clear. The psychological and technological basis for American prosperity in the early 20th century appears in the records of the late 19th century. The recent "take-off" into economic growth in the United States was preceded by a marked rise both in *n* Achievement level and in innovating activity. So the de Charms and Moeller study fills an important gap, not only in our historical knowledge but also in our understanding of how *n* Achievement comes to be associated with subsequent economic growth. The link appears to the "innovating entrepreneur," as we shall see in Chapters 6, 7, and 8.

An Archaeological Investigation: Pre-Incan Peru

The successful use of vase designs to predict *n* Achievement level and economic development in Ancient Greece suggested that the method employed might be of use in archaeological investigations where written records have not survived in sufficient quantity to be scored by the usual verbal technique. Nearly all great civilizations of the past have left a record frozen in ceramic patterns of the way in which their people tended to doodle. It seemed worth at least one attempt to look for the designs characteristic of high *n* Achievement in the pottery surviving from a civilization that left no written history. Such an investigation would show to what extent coding vase designs for *n* Achievement might be a useful additional tool to the archaeologist in piecing together what had happened to such civilizations.

The civilization chosen for study centered in the north coast of Peru and flourished roughly between 800 B.C. and 700 A.D. The dates are necessarily approximate because they are based on carbon-14 determinations. McClelland, Lathrap, and Swartz (1961) chose this culture area because, within the broad limits set by carbon-14 dating, a carefully worked out pottery sequence exists and because Willey's detailed work in the Virú valley (1953) provides a basis for making a quantitative estimate of cultural growth in terms of volume of public buildings constructed at time periods associated with certain points in the pottery sequence. The vases selected for scoring were primarily funerary urns, since they are generally the best preserved and most elaborately decorated, from two neighboring valleys on the north coast of Peru (Virú and Chicama). Some 254 urns in all were scored, about 30 from each of eight style periods which had been matched roughly as to time period in the two valleys. (See Table 4.8.) The actual coding was done by one of the investigators (Swartz) who did not know what time period a particular urn represented. He found it possible to use the conventions adopted in scoring Greek vases with a few modifications necessitated largely by the fact that Peruvian pottery is much more often modeled than is Greek pottery.

The first result obtained produced a complication not present in the scores for the Greek vases. There turned out to be a huge difference in the number of units scored per urn at different time periods. Thus in Sample C (Moche V) about 47 units per urn were scored as compared with only 6 for Sample F. Obviously then, all designs would be more frequent in Sample C than in Sample F. Again the simple solution of converting all scores to percentages could not be adopted because it distorts the results. For example, when the number of designs on the pot was small, percentages tended to be high even though only one or two examples of an S-shape might be present, about either of which the judge might have

TABLE 4.8 DEVIATION SCORES FOR SHAPES CHARACTERISTIC OF n ACHIEVEMENT ON FUNERARY URNS ON THE NORTH COAST OF PERU, 800 B.C.-700 A.D. (*from* McClelland, Lathrap and Swartz, 1961)

Sequences	B.C.←		→A.D.					
Time:	c.800	c.200	c.100	c.250	c.350	c.450	c.550	c.700
Virú:	Guañape	Gallinazo		Huancaco				
Chicama:	Cupis-nique	Salinar		Moche I	Moche II	Moche III	Moche IV	Moche V
Sample designation:	G	B	D	H	F	A	E	C
Number of urns	30	28	32	32	31	36	33	32
Mean units scored per urn	8.43	7.21	6.91	8.97	6.06	10.00	17.42	47.03

Mean Deviation Scores[1]

S-shapes	+.06	+.02	−.09	+.03	−.02	+.08	+.01	−.09
Diagonals	+.01	+.06	+.07	−.19	+.01	+.03	+.09	−.06
Multiple waves (reversed sign)	+.07	−.16	+.09	+.07	−.02	−.02	+.11	−.16

F values for time periods ($df = 7/246$) Diagonals $F = 3.06$, $p < .01$
S-shapes $F = 2.38$, $p < .05$ Multiple waves $F = 4.10$, $p < .01$

[1] Deviation scores are obtained by subtracting the mean transformed scores for a given sample from the mean transformed score for the whole sample for that characteristic. The transformed score is the deviation of the logarithm of the number of given characteristics on an urn from its predicted value based on the regression of that characteristic on the logarithm of the total number of units on the urns.

been in serious doubt anyway. When the number of units was large (and some pots contained over 100 scorable units), certain types of designs appeared less likely to increase proportionately than others. For example, multiple waves are more likely than S-shapes to be repeated over and over again contributing disproportionately more to the total score the larger the number of scored units.

Since the distribution of units per urn scored was badly skewed with relatively few urns containing a large number of scored units, it was decided first to transform all scores into log units. Then the regression of the log scores for a given characteristic on the log of the total number of units was computed just as in other parts of the research where similar problems have arisen.[5] The regression equation then permits determination of how many S-shapes, multiple waves, or diagonals would be expected on the average for a pot containing a given number of scored units (in log terms). Then, as usual, the actual number of obtained units can be compared with the expected number and the difference score, whether positive or negative, used in subsequent analyses. These differences from expected values will be referred to as transformed scores.

Table 4.8 presents a summary of the results in terms of the deviations of the mean transformed scores for a sample from the mean transformed score for the whole population of urns. In other words, the score of +.06 for S-shapes in Sample G should be read to mean that the urns in Sample G were this much above the average deviations from regression for all samples so far as S-shapes were concerned. The fact that the absolute values in Table 4.8 are small does not mean, of course, that the variations from sample to sample were necessarily small. It results from transforming the raw scores so many times—first into logarithmic units, then into differences between expected and obtained values, and finally into deviations of sample means from means for the total. Analyses of variance actually show that the fluctuations due to time period are significant statistically for each of the three design characteristics measured.

The general picture of what happened to n Achievement level as indicated by these design changes is sufficiently clear. All three measures indicate an above average level of n Achievement at the earliest period. The sign of the deviation for multiple waves has, of course, been reversed since they indicate low n Achievement. In other words, during the time represented by Sample G, S-shapes and diagonals were more common than expected, and multiple waves were less common. For the next four periods in the time series (samples B, D, H and F), the picture is more confused, but in every case there is an indication that n Achievement is now lower than it was in the earliest period. Next, there seems to be a rise in signs of n Achievement beginning with Moche III and culminating in Moche IV. Finally, there is a distinct drop in signs of n Achievement in Moche V.

To summarize these trends more simply, it seemed desirable to get one over-all index which would somehow combine the indications given by the various design characteristics. Furthermore, the amount of space unused at the bottom of the urn, which was also scored as in the Greek study, should be included in such an over-all index to increase its reliability. A method of combining the scores was therefore decided upon, which was quite a bit cruder than the regression analysis, but which permitted including the scores for unused space and which seemed to yield results quite consistent with those obtained in Table 4.8. A new set of scores was determined by plotting the number of diagonals, S-shapes, and multiple waves on a vase against the total number of units scored on the vase, by connecting the median number of diagonals, etc., for different totals with a straight regression line, and by computing the proportion of vases in a given time period above the line (for diagonals and S-shapes) or below the line for multiple waves. Instead of transforming scores into log terms and computing the actual distance from the regression line, it was simply determined whether a vase had more or less of a given characteristic than the median number for vases with its total number of scored units. Then the percentage of vases in a sample with more or less of the characteristic than the median can be computed. The objection to using percentages is not here serious because the denominator (the number of urns scored in each time period) is roughly the same in all cases. The percentage of vases in each time period with no unfilled space at the bottom was then determined. It will be recalled that the tendency to use up space is characteristic of high *n* Achievement, so that the proportion of vases in which the space was entirely used up with designs would be indicative of higher *n* Achievement.

The next step was obviously to combine these four percentages to get an over-all index of *n* Achievement level. However, the S-shapes were so infrequent that it proved impossible to draw any regression line that would yield as many urns above the line as were obtained for the other two design characteristics. Consequently a simple average of the four percentages would weight the S-shape determinant about half as much as the other two determinants. Consequently, the percentage values were multiplied by 1.5 for the S-shapes to make them more nearly equal to the percentages for the other three determinants, all percentages were transformed into arc-sine equivalents, averaged, and the percentage equivalents of the averages plotted in Fig. 4.5, along with the increase in the volume of

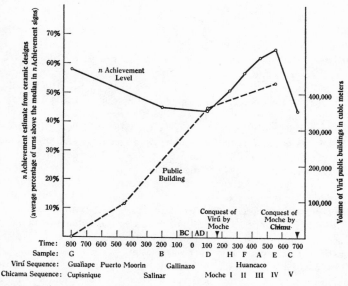

Figure 4.5 Estimates of *n* Achievement in ceramic designs from the North Coast of Peru plotted against time and volume of public building in the Virú valley

public buildings in the Virú valley from one time period to the next. Although the method of arriving at the estimate of n Achievement level was, unfortunately, quite complicated and must be considered very rough and open to methodological criticisms, nevertheless, the resulting picture given by the estimates so obtained is reasonably clear.

The n Achievement curve shows the initial high level characteristic of so many studies in this chapter which corresponds, so far as the archaeological evidence is concerned in the present case, to the moving in of the Chavin civilization from the North. This initial high level is succeeded by the slow growth of civilization in the area, rising to the Gallinazo climax reflected in the great increase in public building in the Virú valley around the time of Christ. The n Achievement curve has in the meantime, as in our other cases, been showing a slow, but steady, decline which is followed, according to the best archaeological evidence, by the conquest of Virú somewhere between Samples D and H and by a new cultural wave from the North, generally called the Moche civilization. This conquest shows up in a decline in the amount of new buildings constructed in Virú in the following Huancaco period. The n Achievement estimate for Moche I pottery is higher than for the Gallinazo sample from Virú, which one would think it should be if the Moche culture was at this point vigorous and enterprising enough to overwhelm Virú. Nevertheless, the difference is small and does not appear in the more refined data of Table 4.8, so that this conclusion must be regarded as highly tentative.

Next we are on firmer ground in noting the sharp and steady rise in n Achievement level through Moche IV. There is, unfortunately, no direct quantitative evidence available such as exists for the Virú valley to measure the effect of this high level of n Achievement in economic terms (size of buildings in the Moche valley), or in the spread of the Moche influence throughout the area. Nevertheless there is little doubt that the Moche climax was, if anything, greater than the Gallinazo climax in Virú. "It would be of some interest if the great structures in the Moche valley, *Huaca del Sol* and *Huaca de la Luna,* could be assigned to a specific period of Moche. The *Huaca del Sol* was probably the largest single construction in aboriginal Peru. There is reason to believe that neither of these structures is pre-Moche in the major part of its construction." (McClelland, Lathrap and Swartz, 1961.) Building during the Moche climax would undoubtedly show a very marked increase if precise data were available. One note of caution, however, should be sounded about using increase in the volume of public building as a measure of rate of development. Its defect is obviously that there must be some upper limit of construction, particularly in small valley civilizations, because buildings from all earlier periods can ordinarily continue to be used. Thus the fact that there is less new building undertaken between the Gallinazo and Huancaco periods in Virú is somewhat misleading since, of course, the amount of public building actually used in the

Huancaco period was much greater even than it had been during the Galli-nazo period. Ideally, some other measure of development should be used, such as the "spread of influence" index obtained by the geographical location of vase remains in the Greek studies. But lacking these more precise data, we can only argue that there were two waves of n Achievement which shaded off into each other and produced, in all probability, two successive waves of economic and cultural growth that were related to each other in a way as yet not altogether clear.

On the other hand, the drop in n Achievement in the last period of Moche civilization is decisive and is followed, according to archaeological evidence, by the conquest of the Moche kingdom by the Chimu civilization invading from the South. So on balance the n Achievement estimates from ceramic patterns support quite well inferences as to what was happening in this culture area based on other evidence. Two high levels of n Achieve-ment are followed by marked cultural growth, and two low levels are followed by conquest by outside civilizations. Thus the technique de-veloped appears to have promise as a tool to help archaeologists puzzle out what happened in extinct civilizations which left no written record of their history. It should be useful in helping decide which cultures were growing and which declining in energy and who was most likely to have conquered whom. In the present instance, probably the chief contribution of the technique to knowledge of the history of this culture area is strong support for the inference already based on other evidence that there were two distinct waves of cultural energy or high n Achievement: one in Cupisnique times, which started off the cultural growth, and another in the middle of the Moche kingdom. As far as our key hypothesis is concerned, the data confirm for another culture area, as different from the traditions of Western civilization as it is practically possible to get, that n Achievement is a key factor in the rise and fall of the economic base of civilizations.

NOTES AND REFERENCES

[1] This section is based on a thesis by Berlew (1956) and has already been published substantially in its present form as Chapter 37 in Atkinson, J. W. (ed.) *Motives in fantasy, action, and society.* Princeton: D. Van Nostrand Company, Inc., 1958.

[2] We have avoided in this discussion the question of popularity *with whom*. Actually for our purposes it is popularity with an educated or an élite group that matters since we know from contemporary studies that the n Achievement score distribution is skewed with relatively fewer people classified as "high" than as "low." Furthermore, these few tend to come more often from families which because of their energy and emphasis on mastery have achieved at least moderate status in the community. Consequently, even if songs which have not come down to us were *more* popular with the masses than Homer and Hesiod, they would probably not be as representative of the motivation of the middle-status group from which subjects with high n Achievement tend to be dis-proportionately drawn.

[3] The t's were combined by finding chi-square equivalents for the p values for the

obtained t tests, summing the chi-squares, and obtaining the p value for the combined chi-square with three degrees of freedom.

⁴ The Wesleyan revival was probably not the only source of a higher level of n Achievement. Ryerson (1960) in a historical study of medical advice on child-rearing has shown that the mid-18th century represented a "really startling point of change" in respect to a new stress on freedom in all physical activities stemming in part from the spirit of Rousseau. Such stress (including as it did much emphasis on self-reliant achievement) should certainly have stimulated the development of n Achievement (see Chapter 9).

⁵ Unfortunately, there is a serious defect in applying the regression method of correcting scores in the present instance because the total is the sum of the three contributing subscores, when ideally it should be independent of them. However, since no alternative solution appeared feasible, it was decided to proceed with this method as the best available.

5

Other Psychological Factors in Economic Development

It is time to broaden the scope of our inquiry. In the last two chapters we have concentrated on the role of n Achievement in economic development to the exclusion of other factors. But what of all the other explanations of economic development reviewed briefly in Chapter 1? Are they wrong? Can they be "derived" from changes in achievement motivation? Or are other factors of genuine importance in promoting economic development quite independently of n Achievement? Certainly it is unlikely that any complex social event like economic growth would be the result of a single "prime mover," and if our demonstration of the importance of n Achievement has tended to create this impression, it is time it was corrected. The fact that n Achievement may be important tells us nothing as to how important other factors may be.

Fortunately, the material assembled to test the n Achievement hypothesis can also be used to discover the importance of other variables according to the methods of analysis developed in Chapter 3. That is, nations have already been classified as growing relatively rapidly or slowly between 1925-50 and between 1952-58, and the children's stories from these two sets of countries can be searched for clues as to what other motives, values, or aspects of social structure differentiate those which have grown more rapidly from those which have grown more slowly. Furthermore, it will be possible by appropriate statistical techniques to see whether such other variables operate independently of n Achievement or only in association with it. Since the problem of exposition of findings on a host of other variables is formidable, the simplest method of procedure seems to be to organize the presentation around the two other major techniques used for coding the children's stories: i.e., (1) further motivational analysis, using the scoring systems previously developed for n Affiliation and n Power, and (2) value analysis according to a scheme specifically designed to study as many as possible of the variables thought to be of importance by historians, economists, and sociologists who have concerned themselves with the problem of explaining economic development. A somewhat more integrated view of how all the variables found to be of importance empirically interact to produce economic development will have to be postponed to a later chapter when all the evidence is in.

n Affiliation and Population Growth

It was not anticipated that n Affiliation would be related in any way to economic development. The stories were coded for this variable simply because the scoring system was available and could be easily applied. As it turned out, n Affiliation bears a rather complex and interesting relationship to economic development that sheds light on why economists, historians, and others have for so long regarded population as somehow important in economic growth. But the relationship was certainly not predicted in advance. One of the advantages of collecting and analyzing data systematically is precisely that doing so will sometimes suggest a new way of ordering events which had seemed hopelessly complex before.

What exactly is the need for Affiliation, as the psychologist understands and measures it? The scoring definition will serve to introduce the variable: "Affiliation imagery is scored when the story contains some evidence of concern in one or more of the characters over *establishing, maintaining, or restoring a positive affective relationship with another person. This relationship is most adequately described by the word friendship.* The minimum basis for scoring would be that the relationship of one of the characters in the story to someone else is that of friendship. Certain interpersonal relationships, in or of themselves, do not meet this criterion. For example, father-son, mother-son, brothers, lovers, etc., are all descriptive of a relationship between two people, but they do not necessarily imply that the relationship has the warm, companionate quality implied in our definition of affiliation. These must further be characterized by concern about maintaining, or restoring, a positive relationship. Sex, achievement, dominance, or other motives might better describe the nature of the relationship in cases of this sort when there is no explicit statement of the precise nature of the relationship. Affiliative concern is also readily inferred from some statement of how one person *feels* about another or their relationship. Some statement of *liking*, or the *desire to be liked* or *accepted* or *forgiven* reveals the nature of the relationship." (Heyns, Veroff, and Atkinson, 1958, pp. 205-207.) It remains only to be said that the scoring definition was arrived at empirically as in the case of n Achievement, by a comparison of imaginative stories written by subjects in whom the affiliation motive had been aroused as contrasted with subjects in whom it had not been aroused, and that persons with high n Affiliation tend to be "approval-seeking," "to select faces rather than neutral stimuli in a perceptual task" (Atkinson and Walker, 1958), to be considered likely to succeed by peers (McClelland, Sturr, Knapp and Wendt, 1958 and Groesbeck, 1958), and to choose friends over experts to work with them on a performance task (French, 1956). Thus a high *n* Affiliation indicates a concern in fantasy and in action for warm, close relationships with other people.

The judges had no difficulty in scoring the children's stories for *n* Affiliation (the interscorer reliability coefficient was around .95), but the measure for a given country turned out to have two distinct drawbacks as contrasted with the *n* Achievement measure. In the first place, the split-half reliability coefficient was only .32, and in the second, the *n* Affiliation score turned out to be substantially and highly significantly correlated with the length of the stories in the sample for the country ($r = .41$, $N = 63$, $p < .01$). Thus the split-half reliability is further reduced to .27, $p < .05$ by the correlation of each of the halves with story length, a value which is much lower than for the *n* Achievement measure and which when estimated for doubling the length of the test reaches only .43. In short, for some reason the measure of *n* Affiliation is much less reliable than the measure of *n* Achievement: one cannot conclude with the same assurance that just because a particular sample of stories yield a high *n* Affiliation score, that therefore any other sample of stories from the same country at the same time will also yield a high score. Nevertheless, the reliability is sufficient to warrant use of the measure, though it should make it more difficult to find significant relationships to other variables.

The influence of length of the stories on the *n* Affiliation score was eliminated by the same method used by Child *et al.* (1958) in dealing with folk tales from primitive cultures. The samples of stories from both time periods were arranged in order of length, then divided at the median into samples of longer and shorter stories. Then the raw *n* Affiliation scores were converted into standard scores within each of these two groups of different lengths. In effect what the procedure does is to show how high a given *n* Affiliation score is relative to the length of the sample of stories on which it is based. Thus it can turn out that a raw score which is lower than another may have a higher standard score because it is based on a shorter set of stories. This procedure reduced the correlation of the *n* Affiliation standard scores with length of the stories in the sample to insignificance.

When the *n* Affiliation standard scores were set over against measures of economic growth, an unexpected relationship appeared. In the 1950 sample the countries with high *n* Affiliation scores were gaining less rapidly in electrical output between 1952-1958 ($r = -.32$, $N = 39$, $p < .05$). Furthermore in 1925 the relationship is *positive* ($r = .26$) or significantly different from what it is in the later time period. As might be expected from such results, the *n* Affiliation level for a country in 1925 is not highly nor significantly related to the level of *n* Affiliation in 1950. The correlation of +.22 is very similar to the one obtained for *n* Achievement, indicating that motivational levels reflected in readers can change quite markedly in a generation.

What is going on here? Why should *n* Affiliation be related to economic growth at all? One hypothesis that comes readily to mind is that *n* Affiliation might have some relationship to the propensity to have children—to the birth rate—and that the birth rate should logically be connected with population growth, which in turn may be related to economic growth. Our preliminary treatment of the problem of population and economic growth in Chapter 1 should have taught us to be somewhat cautious about assuming that "logical" relationships are necessarily empirically true, but the data are available for checking all the links in such a hypothesis. Testing the first link suggests that there may be something to the argument: *n* Affiliation turns out to be positively related to the birth rate in 1950 ($r = +.41$, $N = 26$, $p < .05$) and *negatively* related to the birth rate in 1925 ($r = -.41$, $N = 17$, p around .10). The difference between the two correlations is highly significant, as measured by z-transformations ($t = 2.59$, $p < .02$). But why should high *n* Affiliation lead to having *fewer* children at one period in history and *more* children at another period in history?

A clue to an answer lies in the fact that prior to the introduction of large-scale public health measures, the birth rate appears to have been largely controlled by the death rate. For sixteen European countries around 1880, the correlation between the birth rate and death rate was .74, $p < .01$, whereas for a group of 20 similar countries in 1953 the correlation had dropped to .19, which is not significant. Furthermore, for a group of 20 Asian countries in 1953, the correlation between the birth rate and death rate was .52, suggesting that these countries were in a transitional stage in which public health measures might have rapidly reduced death rates without the birth rates having as yet had time to adjust themselves to new conditions. Of course the correlation does not establish the direction of causation, but it seems reasonable to conclude that if parents expect and know on the basis of experience that a certain proportion of their children are likely to die, they will have more children. If this reasoning is correct, infant mortality rates should be particularly closely associated with the birth rate, and in fact such is the case for the 16 of the 22 countries in our 1925 sample on which data are available ($r = .82$, $N = 16$, $p < .01$). By 1950 for 26 of the same countries, the correlation between birth rate and infant mortality had dropped to .51, $p < .05$, a drop which reaches near significant levels of statistical significance ($p < .10$).

The correlation is largely accounted for by three countries which have not as yet moved into the modern public health era—namely, Poland, Chile, and Mexico, where birth rates and high infant mortality rates continue high. On a cruder classification basis, the relationship disappears altogether. That is, 42 per cent of the countries with high birth rates have high infant mortality rates, and 50 per cent of those with low birth rates have high infant mortality rates. So it seems quite reasonable to conclude that infant mortality is dropping out as an important factor determining how many children people have, as public health measures are more and more widely introduced.

Instead how many children people have may now be determined by how many they *want*, and how many they want appears to be a function of their need for Affiliation, as demonstrated by the significant positive correlation between n Affiliation and the birth rate in the 1950's. Further support for this argument can be found by examining what happened to the birth rates between 1925 and 1950 for 17 countries on which we have n Affiliation figures for 1925 and also birth-rate figures. Generally speaking, most countries showed a drop in the birth rate during this period, but those with high n Affiliation in 1925 showed less of a drop; that is, the correlation between n Affiliation in 1925 and birth rate drop to 1950 is $-.51$, $p < .05$. The birth rate was sustained at a higher level among those countries high in n Affiliation in 1925. During this same period infant mortality was dropping from an average of 107 per thousand live births in 1925 to an average of 54 per thousand live births in 1950. In short, as infant mortality drops out as a reason for having more children, n Affiliation moves in.

But why should n Affiliation be *negatively* related to the birth rate in 1925? Strictly speaking, all our statistics require is that the relationship be different in 1925 from what it is in 1950, a difference which can readily be attributed to the greater importance of infant mortality in determining the birth rate in 1925. Nevertheless, treating the negative relationship to the birth rate in 1925 as significant carries us one step further in understanding how all of these relationships bear on the problem of economic growth. For n Affiliation turns out to be negatively associated with infant mortality in 1925 ($r = -.45$, $N = 17$, $p < .10$), whereas it is not significantly related to infant mortality in the 1950's. Now everything falls into place: in the prepublic health era, how many children survive of those born would appear to depend more on how much care and attention the parents give them. The parents with higher need for Affiliation care more for their children, fewer of them die, and there is therefore less need for "excess" children to take the place of those who die off. In other words, those countries with a high n Affiliation have a lower infant mortality rate, and a lower birth rate. Furthermore, a lower birth rate is associated with rapid subsequent economic growth in electrical output per capita ($r = -.41$, $p < .05$), but *not*, as some theorists have assumed up to now, via the connection of the birth rate with population growth (see Table 5.1). For one thing, even as recently as 1925 in the fairly advanced nations we are dealing with, birth rates are not so highly associated with population growth as one might assume ($r = .58$, $p < .05$); and furthermore, as we demonstrated in Chapter 1, rapid population growth may have either promoted or inhibited economic growth depending on whether the country was sparsely or densely settled. The connection of the birth rate with economic growth in this time period appears to be mediated by a different factor—by what Kuznets has referred to as a greater "reproductive efficiency," or more precisely, by a more efficient attitude toward life which was reflected in greater

TABLE 5.1 SUMMARY OF RELATIONSHIPS BETWEEN *n* AFFILIATION, BIRTH RATE, AND ECONOMIC DEVELOPMENT IN VARIOUS COUNTRIES AROUND 1925 AND 1950

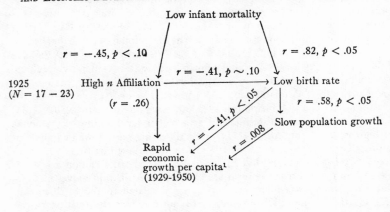

[1] Electrical output gains over expected from Table 3.4.
[2] Electrical output gains over expected (see Table 3.6) recomputed on a per capita basis.

reproductive efficiency. That is, the simplest explanation of the complex series of relationships laid out in the top half of Table 5.1, is not in terms of population growth, but in terms of a concern over the wastage of human life. The countries with higher *n* Affiliation showed a greater concern for infant mortality, had fewer children and took better care of them, and were, therefore, more efficient in reproducing themselves; apparently, the same economizing attitude was reflected also in the economic sphere, so that they developed more rapidly. In other words, low birth rate and rapid economic growth appear to be related in this time period because they both reflect a fundamental attitude of efficiency toward the organization of human activity, and not because of any direct connection. Furthermore, this fundamental attitude is not present just in those countries with high *n* Achievement, but in fact seems to be quite independent of *n* Achievement, since the correlation between *n* Achievement and *n* Affiliation scores in the 1925 sample is only .12. Apparently we have here stumbled across, in quite a roundabout way, a fundamental value attitude which promoted economic development in the '30's and '40's quite independently of *n* Achievement.

By the 1950's the picture had changed quite radically and become much simpler in the process. (See the bottom half of Table 5.1.) For the countries under consideration infant mortality shows much lower correlations both with *n* Affiliation and with the birth rate. It no longer inverts the relationship between liking people and bearing children. Now *n* Affiliation leads quite simply to having more children, since better medical care practically insures that they will all live, and for the same reason, a high birth rate is now much more significantly associated with rapid population growth ($r = .95$, a highly significant increase over the .58 value for the 1925 period).

But does having more children slow down the rate of economic growth, thus explaining the negative correlation between *n* Affiliation and economic growth in the 1950's? It seems fairer to compute economic growth in *per capita* terms where the effects of rates of population growth are at stake; so the electrical output figures for 1952 and 1958 have been converted to per capita terms and economic performance estimated in terms of deviations from the values predicted for the country from the per capita regression equation (log gain 1952-1958 = .8339 log 1952 level −.0165). This reduces the negative correlation between *n* Affiliation and economic performance slightly (from −.320 to −.284), but the difference is probably due to the fact that the U.S.S.R. had to be omitted from the calculations for lack of adequate population figures, since it is almost certainly an economic overachiever even in per capita terms, and is low in *n* Affiliation.

The expected negative relationships, however, between birth rate or net reproduction rate and economic growth, even in per capita terms, did not appear. They are in the expected direction but do not approach accepted levels of statistical significance. What is the explanation? Why is it that countries with rapidly growing populations are not economic underachievers even in per capita terms, as so many have argued they should be? And if *n* Affiliation does not inhibit economic growth via its effects on the birth rate, what does account for this relationship?

Could the factor complicating matters be population density, the man/land ratio, or more generally the amount of resources available per capita? For example, Finland has a fairly high net reproduction rate (1.5 per cent, tied for 9th and 10th place out of 29 countries in 1950), but presumably has managed to have an above expected rate of economic growth (standard score in per capita terms = +.58) in part because the country is sparsely settled or is high in land resources per capita. However, the relationship to resources is not close. (See Chapter 1.) What matters more is what the people are like, what interests them, how much n Achievement they have, etc. Consider Israel. Of all the 39 countries in the 1950 sample, it has the second highest net reproduction rate. It has, in fact, an "Oriental" birth rate (33 per thousand), and an "Occidental" death rate (around 7 per thousand), a combination which is supposed to be especially bad for creating population pressures on scarce resources (i.e., the net reproduction rate = 2.6 per cent). Furthermore, Israel was absorbing as many immigrants as wanted to enter the country during this time period. Yet without question it must clearly be placed among those countries which performed better economically in the 1950's than could have been expected from its 1952 level of development (standard score in per capita terms = +1.05). Or consider the Netherlands as another example. It is well below average in water power resources per head, about average in coal reserves, and is more than twice as densely populated as China or India and Pakistan (around 335 vs. 150 persons per square kilometer of standard farm land as of 1955). Also its net reproduction rate is higher than for most European countries (1.5 per cent) and it lost many of its colonies in this period. Yet its rate of economic growth in per capita terms (1952-58) was slightly above average for the countries studied (standard score in per capita terms = +.19). The *quality* of the people—their values and motives—apparently can outweigh many handicaps.

So population growth, even when measured against resources, does not of itself appear to be a strong factor influencing economic growth. It depends on *what kind of people* are increasing more or less rapidly. If they have the attitudes and values that promote economic growth, a rapid increase in their numbers might actually be considered a positive gain in capital resources (in skills, n Achievement, etc.), as in the case of Israel. But if their personality structure does not lend itself to efficient economic productivity, then of course a rapid increase in their number would have to be counted as a liability.

If we are not to account for the negative relationship between n Affiliation and economic development in the 1950's by a more rapid population growth, how else might we account for it? A clue to an answer may lie in the fact that n Affiliation is significantly *negatively* related to n Achievement in 1950 ($r = -.46$, $N = 39$, $p < .01$). Apparently in more recent times a concern for affiliative relationships with people has meant *less* concern for achievement. In the 1950's it is as if people with high n Affiliation are busy enjoying other people and spend less time in trying to get ahead. One of the ways they enjoy people is to have more children ($r = .41$, $p < .05$), but having more children does not *directly* slow economic growth by creating more mouths to feed: the correlations are simply too low to support such an argument. Instead having more children is normally just a *symptom* of an affiliative rather than achievement concern in life. When it is not—as in the case of Israel which is high *both* in *n* Achievement and *n* Affiliation —then neither a high birth rate nor *n* Affiliation has much, if any, connection with economic growth, at least at the present time.

It may seem as if the argument is inconsistent since *n* Affiliation had one effect in 1925 and another in 1950, but actually the paradox is more apparent than real. One would argue that *n* Affiliation has always meant a greater concern for people, or more particularly, for children, but that such a concern in 1925 because of the hazards of child-rearing led to greater reproductive and economic efficiency, whereas in 1950 it meant a greater enjoyment of people and children as an *alternative* to concern with economic achievement. What obviously caused the big shift in the relationship of *n* Affiliation to economic development between 1925 and 1950 was the great improvement in public health medicine, which introduced a major new factor (low infant mortality) into the network of relationships among motivation, population, and economic growth.

To consider the findings in another way for a moment, the one relationship which is duplicated both in the 1925 and 1950 time periods is the negative correlation between birth rate and economic growth (combined $p < .10$). At both time periods a high birth rate does not appear to slow economic development primarily because of a simple first-order population pressure on resources. Instead, a high birth rate is better regarded as a *symptom* in both cases of different attitudes which are not conducive to promoting economic growth—i.e., carelessness and inefficiency in the 1920's and a concern with affiliation rather than achievement in the 1950's.

Consideration of the policy implications of these findings must necessarily be postponed to the final chapter. But at the very least they suggest that attempts to manipulate population growth directly are not likely to be very effective in influencing the course of economic growth because they deal with a symptom rather than a cause. The capital resources needed to affect population growth might be more efficiently used in an attempt to influence the psychological factors which more directly control economic growth, and perhaps indirectly affect population growth.

n Power and Dictatorship

The stories from the children's readers were also scored for *n* Power, which is defined in the coding manual as a concern "with the control of the means of influencing a person." Such concern may be inferred from emotional reactions to a dominance situation (e.g., pleasure in winning or anger in losing an argument, "statements of wanting to avoid weakness," etc.), from dominance activities—"disputing a position, arguing something, demanding or forcing something, trying to put a point across, giving a command, trying to convince someone of something, punishing someone"

—or from a description of "an interpersonal relationship which in its execution is culturally defined as one in which there is a superior person having control of the means of influencing another one who is subordinate (e.g., boss-worker, judge-defendant)." (Veroff, 1958, pp. 220-225.)

Much less empirical work has been done with this measure than on the other two and less is therefore known about its relation to other types of behavior. The split-half reliability coefficient for the n Power score based on the children's stories was only .24 and, as in the case of n Affiliation, the scores correlated with length of stories in a given national sample significantly $(r = .29, p < .05)$. Inspection showed that the correlation was entirely due to the fact that very short samples of stories tended to have low n Power scores: once they got above a certain length there was no longer any correlation of length with n Power. Therefore, the story samples were arranged in order of length and the raw n Power scores were converted to standard scores separately for the bottom one-third and the top two-thirds of the distribution of story samples by length. This effectively made the n Power scores independent of the length of the story sample on which they were based. The split-half reliability coefficient when corrected for correlation with story length, in this way was reduced to .19, which is not statistically significant, although the estimated reliability for a total score based on a sample of twice as many stories is .32, $p < .01$. In other words, the n Power measure is very much less reliable than the n Achievement measure, and even less than the n Affiliation measure. Nevertheless, it was tested against various economic criteria, partly because it does have some marginal reliability, and partly because its validity (relationship to other measures) *might* be greater than this estimate of its reliability would indicate that it would be.

It was not anticipated that n Power would be related to economic development, nor in fact did it turn out to be. In the 1925 sample of those showing subsequently rapid and slow economic gain, exactly the same percentage (55 per cent) scored above the mean in n Power. In the 1950 sample, 61 per cent of those developing rapidly thereafter had high n Power, whereas 43 per cent of those developing more slowly had high n Power, but the difference is not at all significant and could easily have arisen by chance.

What n Power does appear to be related to, as might have been expected, is the political means used to achieve economic or other ends. In particular, a combination of low n Affiliation and high n Power is very closely associated with the tendency of a nation to resort to totalitarian methods in governing its people. Every one of the more notorious "police state" regimes in our sample of countries (with one possible exception) was above the mean in n Power and below the mean in n Affiliation, as the standard score values in Table 5.2 show. Thus in the 1925 sample, the pre-Hitler readers show this pattern, as do the pre-Franco readers in Spain,

TABLE 5.2 THE MOTIVATIONAL PATTERN IN
READERS OF TOTALITARIAN REGIMES

Country and year		Standard scores	
		n Power	n Affiliation
1925	Austria	+1.37	− .30
	Germany	+ .49	− .42
	Japan	c.+ .50[1]	c.−2.00[1]
	Russia	+1.16	−1.42
	Spain	+1.06	−1.33
1950	Argentina	+ .40	− .09
	Iraq	+3.39	−1.62
	Pakistan	+ .57	−1.00
	Russia	+ .29	− .91
	Spain	+1.65	−1.51
	U. So. Africa	+ .10[2]	− .42[2]
	Portugal	−1.17	+ .72

[1] Estimated from scores on 13 stories only, not included in the main analysis.
[2] Based on English readers only.

the early Communist readers in Russia, the readers in Japan before the military coup in the '30's, and even the readers in Austria which "produced" Hitler and at the very least welcomed Hitlerism later on. In the 1950 sample, the association is no less striking: Peronist Argentina shows it, as does Iraq before the recent bloody military revolution, Pakistan before its turn to military government, contemporary Communist Russia and Fascist Spain, and even the Union of South Africa which has recently turned to fairly totalitarian methods. The one exception is Portugal, which at least in some limited sense has been ruled by a dictatorship for a generation, although it may be doubted that it ever has been as ruthless as most of the other totalitarian regimes on the list.

Excluded from consideration have been three totalitarian regimes—those in Bulgaria, Hungary, and Poland—on the grounds that the totalitarianism is, strictly speaking, not "indigenous." Instead these countries appear to have more of an occupied status in which the totalitarian regimes are supported by a foreign power, rather than by the motives and/or values of the people locally. At any rate, they do not show the low n Affiliation-high n Power pattern that characterizes the remaining countries with authoritarian governments. Such a motivational pattern seems in fact like a psychological prerequisite for political authoritarianism or *ruthlessness*. It implies that a people (or that portion of them whose motives are reflected in the readers) has a strong desire to dominate and control others unchecked by a friendly interest in those others. In some cases, the average level of n Power can be high, as it is in the United States in 1950, but be without totalitarian effects presumably because it is checked by a high n Affiliation which limits the extent to which people are willing to override the interests of particular others. Apparently on the other hand if n Affiliation is low, if the concern for individuals is not strong, a high power drive is not effectively checked and individuals may be used as means rather than as objects of friendly interest in themselves.

Among the 51 remaining nontotalitarian governments, from both time periods, the low n Affiliation-high n Power pattern is extremely rare. In fact, only nine (or 18 per cent) of them show it. The figure is markedly and very significantly lower than the 92 per cent value obtained for the totalitarian regimes (chi-square = 21.4, $p < .001$). Furthermore several of these cases do not appear to be major exceptions to the rule that low n Affiliation and high n Power are particularly likely to give rise to totalitarian governments. Three of the instances (Australia 1925, Denmark 1950, India 1950) show the pattern by such slight deviations from the mean that they might easily be regarded as within sampling error. Another "exception" is Finland which showed the pattern in 1925, but some might regard the government that it had subsequently as being of a fairly authoritarian military character. Still another exception is Germany which showed the authoritarian pattern in 1950, as it did in 1925, but it is at least legitimate to ask whether Germany in the 1950's was as yet completely free to choose its form of government. On the basis of all the other data, one would have to predict that as soon as it gets a chance Germany will move back into a totalitarian form of government of some kind in which the drive for power will tend to override the rights of individuals. Finally, the German-Swiss readers show the authoritarian pattern, but it is almost perfectly balanced by the French-Swiss readers which show a very low need for power. This leaves only three or four real exceptions—in 1925, Hungary (but wasn't Admiral Horthy a dictator?) and Chile, and in 1950, New Zealand. Certainly the association is very close, highly significant statistically, makes good theoretical sense, and demonstrates once more that children's stories appear to be revealing with remarkable validity the motives and aspirations of the people who give them to their children to read.[1]

The motive scores for a given country at a given time period suggest many more fascinating hypotheses as to subsequent political or other developments in the countries concerned, but to develop them here would be well beyond the scope of this book. All the scores are reproduced in Appendix II for those who will want to pursue these possibilities further. It is sufficient for our present purpose to conclude that a combination of low n Affiliation and high n Power is particularly likely to lead a country to pursue its economic or other ends by totalitarian means.

The Values Coding Scheme

The values coding scheme for the children's readers had to satisfy two requirements: (1) it had to fit the story sequence well enough for coders to make their judgments with reasonable reliability, and (2) it had to include within it measures of as many variables as possible that various theorists have contended are important in producing economic development. Table 5.3 shows how it met the first requirement, and Table 5.4 the second.

TABLE 5.3   OUTLINE OF VALUES CODING SCHEME FOR CHILDREN'S READERS

I. The action sequence from the viewpoint of "ego"

Influences on ego——→	Ego———→	Ego's response———→	Object of response——→	Outcome of response——→	Evaluation of ego
(a) Fate	(a) Superior	1. Impulse control or expression	1. People	Successful, unsuccessful or doubtful	Achieved or ascribed norms
(b) Nature	(b) Peer	2. Type of instrumental act (deceit, intelligence, strength, hard work, etc.)	2. Nature (a) over (b) in (c) under		
(c) Man, etc.	(c) Inferior	3. Motives for acting (Biological needs or other)			

II. The "interaction" sequence from the viewpoint of "alter" (society)

Source of interaction pressure———→	Means of exerting pressure——→	Ego's motives for interacting——→	Outcome from alter's viewpoint
1. Impersonal Material, institutional, moral, etc.	1. Love-rejection	1. Self-interest	Successful, unsuccessful or doubtful
2. Personal (a) Superior (b) Peer (c) Inferior (d) Group	2. Asking, demanding or sharing 3. Material, reward or punishment	2. Self-esteem 3. Love 4. Nurturance 5. Cooperative work or play	

As Table 5.3 shows, the coding was done from two points of view—that of "ego" (or a leading character) doing something, and that of "alter" (society or another person) trying to get "ego" to do something (to conform, cooperate, or more generally to interact in some way). The basis of this distinction is a crude functional analysis made first elsewhere (McClelland *et al.*, 1958) of the two key problems involved in the relationship of the individual to society. On the one hand, certain norms or values must deal with the individual's obligation to himself (since it seems functionally impossible for him to be *utterly* passive, with *no* capacity for individual choice, no will of his own) and other norms with his obligation to society, since no society can function without regulating in some way the conduct of its members toward others or the whole group.

At any rate, such a distinction can be applied fairly readily to most children's stories. First, the coder takes the point of view of "ego" and codes who he was (whether superior, peer, or inferior), what happened to him (what the source of various influences was), how he responded to such influences (both affectively and instrumentally), what was the main object of his response, its outcome, and how the person was evaluated in the end (whether in terms of achieved or ascribed status norms). The coder then takes the point of view of "alter" and codes who or what tried to get "ego" to cooperate or conform, what methods of exerting pressure were used, what motives are ascribed to "ego" for cooperating or interacting, and finally again how successful the attempt to get cooperation was. Obviously many of these categories represent "values" only in the "normative" sense—in the sense that the culture or individuals see the world as *existing* in particular ways without implying that it *should* exist in those ways. The details of the entire scoring code with illustrations of how it was applied to various stories may be consulted in Appendix III. More precise meanings of various coding categories will be discussed as the results are presented, when they will be more directly relevant to understanding more fully the rather small number of findings obtained with the values coding scheme. Two judges read each story together and made some 65-70 decisions as to whether a given element was present in a story or not. With so many decisions to make a judge working alone could easily overlook some aspect of the story. Even with two judges working together, coding reliability was not nearly so high as for the motive scoring schemes. Two pairs of judges were trained in the coding system and divided up the work of scoring over thirteen hundred stories. From time to time the two teams scored the same stories and their percentage agreement was computed by the following formula:

$$\frac{2 \times \text{the number of categories checked by both Team A and Team B}}{\text{number of categories checked by Team A} + \text{number of categories checked by Team B}}$$

This formula yielded percentage agreement figures for the two teams which fell somewhere between 64 per cent and 73 per cent on various occasions. The values err on the conservative side because the formula does not include the agreement on the number of categories which were *not* present in the stories (by far the largest number). Nevertheless, in what follows, it should be kept in mind that the reliability of the coding is not as high as it ideally should be, especially for certain categories. Other discriminations, on the other hand, such as the superior, peer or inferior judgments for "ego" and "alter" were made with much higher coding reliability.

Value Attitudes that Should Promote Economic Development

Table 5.4 lists on the left hand side some five major variables thought by various theorists to be associated with economic development and on the

TABLE 5.4   RELATION OF VALUES CODING SCHEME TO SOCIAL VARIABLES THOUGHT TO BE OF IMPORTANCE FOR ECONOMIC DEVELOPMENT

Social variables thought to be important for economic development	Corresponding items in reader value code which should characterize more rapidly growing economies
1. "Modern" vs. "traditional" social structure	1.* Institutional (traditional) interaction pressure *less frequent*
(a) Universalistic vs. particularistic norms	2. Peer status of "ego" *more frequent* (a society of equals)
(b) Specificity vs. diffuseness of role relations	3.* Ego's relation to others more often "contractual" (e.g., motivated with an outcome)
(c) Achieved vs. ascribed status	4. Achieved status *more frequent;* ascribed status *less frequent*
(d) Collectivity vs. self-orientation	5.† Peer pressures for interaction *more frequent*
	6. Self-interest, self-esteem, and nurturance *less frequent* as motives for interaction
2. Affective neutrality (asceticism, thrift)	7. Impulse control and/or punishment for impulse expression *more frequent*
3. Rationality, planning, orderliness	8.† Deceit and magic as instrumental acts *less frequent;* hard work and "intelligence" *more frequent*
	9. Fate and magic as influences on ego *less frequent*
4. Man *over* nature, optimism, belief in progress	10. Man *over* nature *more frequent*
	11. Ego's actions *more often* successful
5. Material needs over other concerns	12. Biological needs *more frequent* as a motive for "ego"
	13. Material reward *more frequent* as means of exerting interaction pressure
	14.* Impersonal cooperation pressure *more often* of a material sort

* Hypothesis confirmed.
† Hypothesis indirectly or partly confirmed.

right hand side some fourteen different specific hypotheses as to elements in children's stories which should be associated with them. The first three sets of variables (1-3 in the Table) derive from Max Weber's treatment of the association between the Protestant ethic and the rise of capitalism (1904), though the particular form in which they are stated here owes most to Parsons' various reformulations and developments of Weber's ideas (Parsons, 1951, 1958). Briefly they state that economic advancement is associated (1) with a "modern" social structure (a) in which human resources are allocated according to universalistic criteria of efficiency, ability, etc., rather than by such particularistic criteria as race, creed, caste, kin or color, (b) in which there is increasing "division of labor" or specificity of a person's relations to others, (c) in which people are evaluated in terms of what they can accomplish rather than in terms of "who they are," and (d) in which the élite, and eventually, the people, become increasingly concerned with the "common good," the market, the nation, rather than their private ends (as a sign of increasing inter-dependence); that economic advancement is also associated with (2) affective neutrality, a tendency to become more "coldly rational" or impersonal in the pursuit of economic ends which also may show itself as decreased self-indulgence and increased saving and investment; that economic advancement is associated with (3) rationality or increased concern with planned and efficient use of resources, (4) optimism and belief in the possibility of progress and (5) an increased concern with material needs and their satisfaction ("economic" wants) as against "spiritual" needs, for example. I have followed Hoselitz in separating out "affective neutrality" from the four other aspects of modern industrial social structure [1 (a), (b), (c), (d)] with which it is often associated. The reason is that he believes its status as an essential variable in "modern" industrial social structure is much less certain: "The degree and frequency of affective orientation toward social objects is not demonstrably correlated with levels of economic advancement. . . . This set of pattern alternatives, although of great relevance in describing and classifying certain structural relations . . . has no relevance in sorting them out in terms of per capita productivity." (Hoselitz, 1953, p. 13.) This summary of a vast literature on sociological and other types of variables presumed to be of importance in economic development is woefully inadequate, but it will have to suffice as an introduction to the tests that could be made of such ideas within the limits of stories for children.

Three shortcomings of the methodological procedure outlined in Table 5.4 are immediately obvious. First, the hypotheses dealing with coding variables listed on the right-hand side of the table can by no means be derived rigorously from the concepts they are designed to test (listed on the left-hand side of the table). It is very doubtful if sociological theorists would be willing to accept the elements of the children's stories listed as reasonable tests of their hypotheses. In a sense, however, they have nothing to lose. If the operational measure in the children's stories confirms their hypothesis, they can accept it as evidence that they were right. If it does not confirm their hypothesis, they can argue that the derivation from the hypothesis to the children's stories was improperly made. Difficulties arise only if certain hypotheses are confirmed and not others, since it might be hard to maintain that children's stories are satisfactory for confirming some ideas but not for rejecting others.

Secondly, children's stories are obviously not the best place to look for certain social structural characteristics or values theoretically associated with economic development. It was decided to use such stories primarily because they were the kind of fantasy production which had been found best for assessing human motivation in individuals. By the same token it might be argued that aspects of social structure would be most readily revealed in "reality-oriented" literature. A case in point is our attempt to find a way of measuring in children's stories, the very important social structural variable described in part by Adam Smith as "division of labor" or, in the Parsonian terminology in Table 5.4, as "specificity vs. diffuseness of role relations." What is meant by the concept is the shift from "status" to "contract"—the tendency for men to have specific contractual relations to others (as in working for wages) rather than diffuse ones (as in working on a feudal estate or in a caste system). How could such a shift in the relationship of people to others be reflected in stories for children? Would it not be much more appropriate, for example, to do content analysis of such "reality-oriented" social products as legal documents to measure the effect of changes of this sort on economic development? It might very well be. The simplest defense of the use of children's stories is that they were available in large numbers of countries and might as well be scored because they had already been collected for other purposes. Beyond this it can be argued that such stories may actually reflect how far legal and structural changes in the society have begun to be understood or become part of the thinking of people in the society.

A third obvious limitation of the values scoring system is that many variables were not included in it, partly because we did not learn of them in time, partly because we could think of no way of testing them in children's stories, and partly because some of them have been advanced only since the coding was completed. Among the variables of possibly great importance for economic growth not included in Table 5.4 are the following: an economizing rather than efficient attitude toward work (Shils, 1958), the breakup of the extended family (Shils, 1958, Levy, 1955, and others), and the role of subordinated groups in leading the way to economic change (Hagen, 1961, and others). Also, we might easily have included a measure of how often machinery or other bits of technology such as toys, appeared in the stories, but simply failed to think of it in time. Such a variable might only reveal the *level* of technological development of a society, but with sufficient subtlety it might also detect that "favorableness toward technological innovations" which has long been supposed to precede rapid economic development. So the scoring scheme has its definite limitations, but in its defense it might be said that any scoring scheme would have some limitations, that the judges were already strained to the limit in the number of discriminations they had to make per story, and finally that we were also concerned to include a number of other categories, not particularly related to anyone's theory, on the chance that an exploratory study of this empirical sort might turn up some new ideas that no one had really considered seriously before.

The method of checking the association of a given scoring category with economic development followed the procedure adopted in studying the role of the achievement motive in Chapter 3. Countries were classified as developing more or less rapidly than expected in terms of the electrical output data in Tables 3.4 and 3.6 for the earlier (1929-1950) and later (1952-1958) periods. The question that can be investigated then is whether any of the variables on the left hand side of Table 5.4 as represented in the values coding system appeared more often in 1925 children's stories of countries that grew more rapidly than expected economically between 1929-1950, and in 1950 children's stories of countries that grew more rapidly than expected between 1952-1958. Many of the variables are not treated by sociologists in any sense as *causes* but rather as accompaniments or *results* of economic development. So an appropriate test of them is rather a comparison of their representation in readers from advanced and backward countries, say in 1950. But for the moment we are focusing on the question of whether any of them could *predispose* or help speed up the rate of economic development, as n Achievement apparently does.

The stories from the economies developing more rapidly than expected were therefore pooled and contrasted with those from the economies developing more slowly than expected to see whether certain story elements appeared in a greater percentage of the stories from one set of countries than from the other. Differences in frequencies of story characteristics from the two groups of stories were then checked for significance by the chi-square technique. Such a procedure has some methodological weaknesses that must be recognized. In the first place it tends to inflate the number of degrees of freedom by an unknown amount since the number of cases becomes the number of stories rather than the number of countries, as in the motivational analysis in Chapter 3. To make the point more concrete, let us consider the Australian stories which contain numerous references to nature. On the basis of Australia's economic performance (1929-1950), all 21 of the Australian stories are thrown into the sample of stories from more rapidly developing economies, yet strictly speaking these are not 21 *independent* tests of whether concern with nature will appear more frequently in countries which develop rapidly. A procedure with fewer objections would be to decide whether Australia was above or below average in its references to nature in its whole sample of 21 stories; then we could test whether the countries that developed more rapidly were more often above average in their concern with nature. However, such a procedure limits the possibility of getting any results at all much more than in the case of the motive scores, which were a summation of separate characteristics. Since we are dealing with infrequent separate characteristics, both the scores themselves and the cutting points into "above" and "below" average are likely to be very unreliable, and more refined statistical techniques like correlations can hardly be used. Therefore it seemed better to pool all the stories from countries in a group rather than to use the country as the unit of measurement. Furthermore, while the 21 stories are probably not completely independent, they are *somewhat* independent in the sense that they come from different books by different authors, and may well represent different viewpoints in the country. Therefore we will probably be on the safe side if we consider that the number of independent measures is somewhat less than the raw number of stories and are accordingly stricter in establishing levels of statistical significance.

A second difficulty with the method of analysis adopted results from the fact that since some 65 to 70 different discriminations make up the values code, several significant differences should arise by chance alone. To avoid the danger of interpreting chance differences and also to take account of the somewhat inflated N, we decided to take seriously only those differences in frequencies which could be cross-validated at least at a moderate level of significance between the 1925 and 1950 samples of countries. That is, a difference in the stories of more and less rapidly developing countries found to be significant at the .10 level either in 1925 or 1950 had also to show up in the comparison at the other time period in the same direction and at a reasonable level of significance so that the combined chi-squares ($df = 2$) would be significant.

Finally, we want to know whether any differences in the stories of rapidly and slowly developing economies are independent of n Achievement scores or merely accompaniments of them. In other words the search is for factors not related to n Achievement which have a connection with economic growth. In fact, if the differences are closely associated with n Achievement scores, we might suspect that they are the result of some contamination or lack of independence in the scoring systems. To check on such a possibility the differences were computed separately for countries high and low in n Achievement to see if the differences were independent of this variable.

Value Attitudes Actually Associated with Economic Development

As Table 5.4 has indicated, only five of the 14 or so hypotheses made in advance were confirmed, two of them in a somewhat different way than expected. Table 5.5 summarizes the significant differences that were obtained. They will be discussed along with negative findings in order of the hypotheses listed in Table 5.4, then related to differences in n Achievement (the two columns at the right of Table 5.5), and finally reviewed in terms of the general picture they present. In the course of the discussion we will deal with the further issue of whether the value attitudes are causes or consequences of economic development.

Hypothesis 1. *Anti-traditionalism.* Probably the most widely accepted general notion that theorists have as to why some nations have developed more rapidly than others is that they are *anti-traditional,* that they are more willing to break with insititutional survivals of an earlier period and to accept the social and technical innovations which are part of the new industrial order. The first hypothesis attempts to get at the stress on traditional ways of doing things by a measure of the frequency with which institutional pressures are brought to bear on an individual in the story to get him to conform, cooperate or interact. That is, in the scoring scheme the very first distinction made in the interaction sequence is whether the source of interaction pressure is impersonal or interpersonal. Impersonal sources of pressure are further broken down into various types, one of which is "institutional" pressure, defined as "a force for conformity which is highly generalized, superindividual, persistent over time, and supplying to the actor a set of rules for his behavior." The following are to be considered institutions in this classification: the church, the state in its political, economic or legal aspects, business, the educational system, and the family. All of the above supply "ego" with guideposts for action and conformity. The pressure may come from an individual acting in *an institutional role*—i.e., the butcher, the priest, the policeman—but not from any one specific individual acting toward ego in terms of his unique personality or relationship with him.

As the first set of results in Table 5.5 shows, it is the institutional type of impersonal interaction pressure that appears more frequently in stories from the slowly growing economies. The difference is significant both for the 1925 and the 1950 samples and it is not significantly associated with national n Achievement levels (see the last two columns on the right of Table 5.5). However, there is a significant interaction effect: it is as if "traditionalism" has more of an inhibiting effect on economic growth when n Achievement is high than when it is low. When n Achievement is low 20 per cent of the stories from slowly developing countries show "institutional" interaction pressure; when it is high about 30 per cent of them do. The high drive to achieve might have moved these last somewhat atypical countries into the "rapidly growing" category, had they not been held back by traditionalism—which we can interpret here as an attitude of respect for impersonal insitutional rules and roles, which is not so immediately and flexibly responsive to the person, place or situation.

Hypothesis 2. *Universalism vs. particularism.* As a more specific aspect of modern society, Parsons and others have stressed the importance of universalistic as contrasted with particularistic norms for regulating behavior. Perhaps the best single illustration of universalism is the development of a code of laws which applies equally to all individuals regardless

TABLE 5.5 STORY CHARACTERISTICS AROUND 1925 AND 1950 FROM ECONOMIES SUB-
SEQUENTLY DEVELOPING MORE OR LESS RAPIDLY

Percentages of stories with various characteristics

hypotheses	1925 readers	1950 readers	Nations with low n Ach. (1925 + 1950)[1]	Nations with high n Ach. (1925 + 1950)[1]
Hypothesis 1: *Institutional interaction pressure:* Total	17.9	20.1	18.5	20.0
Rapidly growing economies[2]	a[3] 11.3	c 15.4	e 13.8	g 14.1
Slowly growing economies[2]	b 22.7	d 24.2	f 20.0	h 29.8
Difference ($R - S$)	−11.4	−8.8	−6.2	−15.7
$p < .02, df = 2$[4]	$p < .05$	$p < .05$	interaction $p < .05$[5]	
Hypothesis 3: *Ego motivated to interact:* Total	88.4 *	95.5	90.4 *	95.5
Rapidly growing economies	94.0	97.6	87.4	99.9
Slowly growing economies	83.2	93.7	91.4	87.1
Difference ($R - S$)	+10.8	+3.9	−4.0	+12.8
$p < .001, df = 2$	$p < .01$	$p < .01$	interaction $p < .01$	
Hypothesis 3: *Interaction outcome specified:* Total	86.8 *	91.4	89.4	90.3
Rapidly growing economies	90.3	93.2	91.0	92.5
Slowly growing economies	83.4	89.9	88.8	85.9
Difference ($R - S$)	+6.9	+3.3	+2.2	+6.6
$p < .05, df = 2$	$p < .05$	$p < .15$	interaction NS	
Hypothesis 5: *Peer interaction pressure:* Total	38.8 *	45.7	40.2 *	46.4
Rapidly growing economies	43.5	48.5	43.4	47.9
Slowly growing economies	33.9	43.3	39.0	43.1
Difference ($R - S$)	+9.6	+5.2	+4.4	+4.8
$p < .10, df = 2$	$p < .10$	$p < .20$	interaction NS	
Hypothesis 5: *"Demands"*[6] *successful as means of interaction pressure:* Total	39.0	43.9	40.5	44.1
Rapidly growing economies	43.5	47.5	40.9	48.2
Slowly growing economies	35.1	41.0	40.3	36.1
Difference ($R - S$)	+8.4	+6.5	+.6	+12.1
$p \sim .05, df = 2$	$p < .15$	$p < .10$	interaction NS	
Hypothesis 8: *Hard work as means to end:* Total	22.5	21.3	19.8	23.6
Rapidly growing economies	27.8	24.9	23.2	27.0
Slowly growing economies	17.3	18.3	18.6	16.3
Difference ($R - S$)	+10.5	+6.6	+4.6	+10.7
$p < .01, df = 2$	$p < .01$	$p < .05$	interaction NS	

TABLE 5.5 (*Cont.*) STORY CHARACTERISTICS AROUND 1925 AND 1950 FROM
ECONOMIES SUBSEQUENTLY DEVELOPING MORE OR LESS RAPIDLY

Percentages of stories with various characteristics

hypotheses	1925 readers	1950 readers	Nations with low n Ach. (1925 + 1950)[1]	Nations with high n Ach. (1925 + 1950)[1]
Hypothesis 14: *Nature as source of interaction pressure:*				
Total	10.0	12.1	10.9	11.1
Rapidly growing economies	13.8	17.1	24.1	13.6
Slowly growing economies	7.3	7.7	6.8	7.0
Difference $(R - S)$	+6.5	+9.4	+17.3	+6.6
$p < .01, df = 2$	$p < .15$	$p < .01$	interaction $p < .05$	

* Differences between percentages from 1925 and 1950 or from nations high and low in n Achievement are significant at least at $p < .05$.

[1] To get a sufficient number of countries with low n Achievement which showed rapid economic development (and vice versa), the samples of countries for the 1925 and 1950 time periods have here been combined. For example, the countries which showed low n Achievement in 1925 and above average economic performance 1929-1950 have been combined with the countries which showed low n Achievement in 1950 and above average economic performance 1952-1958 to get the figure 13.8%.

[2] The classification into rapidly and slowly growing economies is based on gains in electrical output over expected 1929-1950 (per capita, Table 3.4) and 1952-1958 (Table 3.6). For the earlier figures the division into more and less rapidly developing countries was made between Norway and Holland.

[3] The percentages represent the number of stories with the characteristic in question out of the total number of stories in the category (sum of the number of stories coded per country). Percentages in each category are based on the following numbers of stories, drawn from the numbers of countries listed in parentheses:

$a = 80\text{-}215\ (11);$ $b = 110\text{-}226\ (11);$ $c = 169\text{-}369\ (18);$ $d = 194\text{-}429\ (21);$

$e = 56\text{-}159\ (8);$ $f = 192\text{-}453\ (22);$ $g = 191\text{-}425\ (21);$ $h = 114\text{-}202\ (10).$

Numbers vary between all the stories from a given set of countries and all the stories from those countries coded in a given way. For example, of the 215 stories from countries developing rapidly after 1925, 80 contained instances of some kind of impersonal interaction pressure; 9 of these 80 or 11.3% were instances of institutional interaction pressure, etc.

[4] Combined p values for the sum of the chi-squares for the 1925 and 1950 samples, two-tailed test.

[5] From the interaction chi-square, i.e., sum of chi-squares for low n Achievement and high n Achievement countries separately minus chi-square for the two sets of countries combined.

[6] "Demands" represents the sum of instances in which *alter* "asks" and either demands or shames the person into interacting (cooperating, obeying, complying, etc.). See Table 5.3.

of who they are in particular. Individuals do not enjoy special rights or privileges due to their status in life nor are they penalized from birth as, for example, members of the Untouchable caste were in India. Instead they are "equal before the law." It was predicted that such a value would appear in the readers as a tendency to make the hero of the story a "peer" rather than a superior or inferior. Perhaps the coding definitions will make the reason clearer. "By *superior* is meant any individual who is in a position of authority or superiority relative to others around him. Age, size, social status, or strength are the characteristics which mark off a superior individual. By *inferior* is meant any individual who is in a position of lesser age, size, social status or strength with regard to others interacting with him. *Peer* is to be used under two conditions: the first of these is when ego's position is not explicitly superior or inferior, the second when ego is 'one among equals'—namely, someone of the same age, size, social status, strength as the others in the story." It was predicted that societies which valued equality or universalism would tend not to tell so many stories with marked status distinctions among the protagonists. While both in 1925 and 1950 slightly more stories in which "ego" was a "peer" appeared in the more rapidly developing countries, the differences are nowhere near significant. The prediction is not confirmed. The reason very possibly lies in the fact that universalism need not be reflected in who initiates action in the stories. That is, people can be "equal before the law" and yet be frequently perceived as differing in rank, though this seems somewhat unlikely psychologically speaking.

Hypothesis 3. Specificity of role relationships. One of the chief characteristics of modern society, according to social theorists, is its stress on contract rather than status, in particular, on the wage contract, an arrangement in which an individual carries out a limited service for another as a laborer or professional in return for money. Often the two individuals have no contacts with each other outside such specific role relationships as teacher-student, employer-employee, doctor-patient, etc. Traditional societies are often characterized, by way of contrast, as consisting of diffuse networks of relationships that individuals have with each other which are not *functionally specific*, not entered into with a specific objective to be accomplished on each side, as in the doctor-patient relationship, for example.

Are societies able to adapt more quickly to the demands of a modern economy if they show evidence of thinking in terms of specific rather than diffuse relationships among people? The problem is to find some method for detecting such a way of looking at relationships in a story for children. Tables 5.4 and 5.5 show under Hypothesis 3 how the coding problem was solved: we decided that if a motive was assigned to "ego" for interacting with another person (or reacting to social influence), then "ego" had a specific *reason* for relating to others and was not relating in the vague, diffuse ways theoretically characteristic of traditional societies. In other words, if the story assigns a reason for the interaction, in a sense it is almost by definition making the role relationship *specific*, i.e., motivated. If no motive is given, then it seems logical to infer that neither the author nor the audience thinks it so necessary to give reasons why people relate to each other.

As Table 5.5 shows there is a significant increase in the frequency of specifying ego's motives from the 1925 to the 1950 time period, as indeed there should be, if this is a measure of specificity of role relationships and if such specificity is increasing everywhere as the world becomes "modernized." Furthermore at both time periods the stories from the more rapidly developing countries specify ego's motives significantly more often. However, the variable is not independent of n Achievement, since it occurs more often in stories with high than low n Achievement. Could it be then that it is simply a scoring artifact due to the fact that specifying achievement motivation, as a subtype of motivation for "ego," is more common, as we have already shown, in countries developing more rapidly? Not necessarily, because the achievement motivation in the scoring system is practically always part of the *action* sequence, not the *interaction* sequence (see Table 5.3). It refers to what ego is trying to accomplish and how, not to what others are trying to accomplish and ego's motives for responding to such social pressure.

Therefore the result is not likely to be a scoring artifact but may be interpreted as a sign that countries high in n Achievement are more apt to be successful if they stress functional specificity. The most interesting finding with this variable is the significant interaction: among countries low in n Achievement, functional specificity makes no difference to subsequent economic growth, but among countries high in n Achievement it apparently makes a considerable difference. Can we hazard a guess that functional specificity is something like an efficiency factor which reflects the extent to which people's relationships to each other are directed to efficient ends? That is, it may show the extent to which there is no "waste" (or play?) in human relationships, no unmotivated interaction. If so, then the results may be interpreted as follows: if countries are not driving toward achievement, then efficiency in role relationships has little effect on or association with rate of growth. But if they are high in n Achievement, the more definite they are in specifying why people relate to each other, the more orderly their social organization and therefore the more rapid their economic growth. At any rate practically *all* of the stories (99.9 per cent) in the countries with high n Achievement which developed rapidly specified ego's motives in the interaction sequence. It is interesting too that the *type* of motive attributed to "ego" made no difference: it was just whether he had any motive at all. There is no evidence here for the supposed greater materialism of economically successful societies: at least material rewards and selfish ends were not more frequently mentioned in stories from such countries.

A related scoring category treated in the next row in Table 5.5 also under Hypothesis 3 is whether the outcome of the interaction is specified as being successful or unsuccessful. It seems reasonable to infer that if the outcome of the social relationship (i.e., the interaction sequence) is left "up in the air," then the role relationship is less specific or more diffuse, again almost by definition. In such cases, we do not know how "alter's" attempt to influence "ego" came out, or more precisely the basis of the relationship of alter to ego is not sufficiently well defined to begin with so that an "outcome" has any real meaning. One might expect that diffuse role relationships would no more have an "outcome" than a specific reason for being in the first place. In any case the results are very similar to those obtained for the category just discussed covering "reasons (i.e., motives) for being." Interaction outcomes are specified more often in 1950 than in 1925 in line with the growing modernization of nations and more often in rapidly growing economies both in 1925 and 1950. This time, however, there is no significant association with n Achievement nor is the interaction significant, though it is in the same direction as for the previous category. In general these results confirm those just discussed and strengthen our conviction that these rather simple story characteristics do reflect an increasing concern for the specific contractual nature of role relationships, their reasons for being and the extent to which they achieve them, a concern which tends to precede and presumably facilitate economic growth, as many social theorists have argued it should.

Hypothesis 4. Achieved vs. ascribed status. All sociological theorists agree that *achieved* status distinctions should be more frequent in rapidly growing economies, whereas *ascribed* status distinctions should be more common in slowly developing, societies. However, the results do not strongly confirm the prediction: at both time periods achieved status distinctions were more common in stories from the rapidly developing economies (23.6 to 20.2 per cent in 1925 and 26.6 to 20.3 per cent in 1950) but only the second difference is significant ($p < .05$) and the combined significance estimate does not permit us to put great faith in this trend ($x^2 = 5.18$, $df = 2$, $p < .10$). Furthermore, achieved status appears significantly more often in stories from countries high in achievement motivation at both time periods as would be expected since it would be part of the information used in deciding whether achievement imagery is present or not. To some extent then the result is not independent of the findings for n Achievement. The fact that it is considerably *less significant* than the n Achievement score suggests that social evaluation in terms of some standard of excellence (i.e. achieved status) is by itself less important than when it is combined with some involvement on the part of "ego"—some *concern* over whether one is evaluated well or poorly (which is the remainder of the scoring definition for n Achievement).

But what about *ascribed status?* Is it mentioned less often in the more rapidly developing economies? It has the advantage of not being positively or negatively associated either with n Achievement scores or with the *achieved status* category. Unfortunately it shows no relationship with economic development either. In 1925 it appeared slightly less often in stories from the more rapidly developing economies, as predicted, but in 1950 it showed just the reverse trend.

These results are rather puzzling in the light of the widespread agreement among sociologists as to the importance of these two changes in social structure for the "modernization" of society. Perhaps *achieved status* can be scored as an important element for modern social structure by adding to it the notion that people must *want* to be evaluated in terms of some standards of excellence, when it becomes *n* Achievement. Note, however, that the "standards of excellence" in the *n* Achievement definition can be achieved or ascribed! And furthermore the results for *ascribed status* cannot be handled in this way at all. What could have happened? Since this is just one of a number of rather important hypotheses that are not really confirmed by the data, it is worth following out in some detail some of the possible explanations of such negative findings.

One simple possibility is that the characteristic in question does not *precede* (or cause) but *accompanies* more rapid economic development There is even some evidence that such may be the case with achieved status as a norm, since we reported earlier (Table 4.3) that stress on achieved status was greatest *during* the peak of prosperity in Ancient Greece, rather than before the peak as in the case for *n* Achievement. Fortunately a simple method exists for checking such a possibility with the present data. The countries can be reclassified in terms of level of economic development rather than in terms of rate of gain. Do the wealthy industrialized countries in 1950 show more instances of achieved status and fewer instances of ascribed status in their readers than the backward underdeveloped countries? The answer is a clear "no"; if anything, the nonindustrialized countries show a slightly higher emphasis on achieved status. The same comparison made also in 1925 reveals no difference.

A second possible reason for the results not coming out as predicted is that the readers are simply not reflecting this aspect of social structure accurately. But studying the results for particular countries does not lend much support to such a point of view. Instead it suggests, if anything, that there may have been some "selective perception" among theorists of comparative social structure. For example, in 1925 a number of modern industrialized societies like Sweden, Canada, New Zealand, Australia, Netherlands, were high in achieved status in the readers just as they should have been according to students of comparative sociology. On the other hand, at least three other wealthy "modern" societies were quite high in the stress they placed on ascribed status—namely, England, Belgium, and France. Once the two particular groups of countries are put over against each other, it is not difficult to find support for the view that in England and France, for example, there has been a greater stress on the importance of the "aristocratic tradition" than in such countries as Australia or the Netherlands. But if the former countries can support modern industrial economies and at times develop rapidly economically, how can we argue that low stress on *ascribed* status is a *necessary* cause or accompaniment of economic development? We cannot of course reject completely the possibility that the readers may be inadequate measures of this value; it is just that inspection of the scores for particular countries suggests that they do not seem to be notably inaccurate, when judged by outside evidence for the cultures concerned. So the fault may not lie with the children's stories but with the theorists who may have focused on one set of rapidly developing countries which have stressed achieved status to the exclusion of other countries which have not.

The third possible reason for failure to confirm the hypothesis is that the achieved-ascribed status distinction was not properly formulated in the scoring code. The actual definitions are as follows: "*Achieved status:* the individual is evaluated in terms of his accomplishments or achievements, rather than in terms of his fixed characteristics, given by birth. *Ascribed status:* the individual is evaluated by fixed characteristics which are given by birth, rather than in terms of his accomplishments." Consider its application in the following story. "Then they were sure that she was a real princess, since through twenty mattresses and twenty feather beds she had been able to tell the pea. Only a princess could be so sensitive. Then the prince married her for now he knew that he had a real princess." The story of the Princess and the Pea appears to be a clear example of ascribed status, but it contains a possible source of confusion. In order to be consistent, it was thought necessary to score any characteristic given by birth—e.g., intelligence, beauty, unusual sensitivity—as an instance of "ascribed status" since the person does not "achieve" intelligence or beauty or sensitivity. However, it is clear that the princess gets her unusual sensitivity not so much from heredity as from her social position, from the fact that she is a princess. In other words there is a kind of "social heredity" in the notion of ascribed status which in the coding, for the sake of simplicity, got converted into "biological heredity." And there is a certain sense in which modern society has substituted one kind of ascribed status for another: the aristocracy of intelligence (an ascriptive characteristic of the individual) has replaced the hierarchy of social position (an ascriptive characteristic of a class or family). So it may be that in scoring "intelligence" as an ascribed status characteristic we have departed from what sociologists mean by the term and have failed to confirm the hypothesis for that reason. In fact, defining ascribed status in terms of socially prescribed roles exclusively (leaving out biological characteristics like strength, beauty, and intelligence) would make the category very similar to "institutional interaction pressure" which *is* more common in slowly developing countries (see Hypothesis 1 above).

While this is possibly the best explanation of the failure to confirm the hypothesis, it leaves the further problem of what exactly should be included as an instance of "ascribed status." Certainly many definitions to date have been too imprecise in seeming to cover *individual* biological inheritance ("who one is"), when probably they should include only biological characteristics supposedly inherited by the individual because of his *group* membership, e.g., intelligent because Jewish, sensitive because a princess, etc. In fact the "achieved-ascribed" dimension appears to be rather imperfectly named. It might better be described more awkwardly, though more correctly, in terms of whether the individual is evaluated in terms of group membership characteristics or in terms of his own personal characteristics, whether given him by nature or achieved by his own efforts. Such a coding definition might have yielded the expected results. Nevertheless we are left with the impression that the way in which a person is evaluated is by no means as central an issue in moedrn economic society as has been commonly assumed. What is important is whether he cares about evaluating his performance or himself in terms of any standards of excellence, no matter what their source—which is another way of saying that what matters is whether n Achievement level is high or not.

Hypotheses 5 and 6. Collectivity vs. self-orientation. The fourth key aspect of modern society described analytically by Parsons is the extent to which it must, at least to some extent, put the goals of the collectivity (i.e., the town, the region, the nation) above those of personal interest. In contrast to underdeveloped countries, "governments in economically advanced countries, even with totalitarian constitutions, maintain collectivity-oriented relations to economic goods, or at any rate, officially and publicly proclaim their adherence to the maxim that they exercise their function in the public interest and for the benefit of the public." (Hoselitz, 1953, p. 14.) In fact, the specialization of modern machinery requires a greater degree of public coordination than was formerly necessary at lower levels of technological development. Consider just the problem of regulating transportation networks involving railroads, highways, and airlanes.

Two very crude measures of collectivity emphasis were available in the stories—the extent to which pressure for conformity came from "peers" or "the generalized other," and the extent to which motives for cooperation were "selfish." The former showed a difference in the expected direction at both time periods, the estimates of significance for which reach a moderate level ($p < .10$) when combined. (See Table 5.5, Hypothesis 5.) One might suppose that collectivity orientation in the democratic countries would be likely to be maintained by "peer" pressure, whereas in statist countries it would more often come from centralized authorities almost by definition (i.e. "superior" pressure). That is, one could argue that there is no reason to expect a greater peer orientation among more economically successful authoritarian societies. Quite the contrary: we should expect more "superior" orientation. However, the findings are if anything the reverse of such a "rational" hypothesis.

Sixteen countries were selected out as having totalitarian governments or for being so underdeveloped (less than 100 kwh/per head per year in 1950) that they had to be centralized or "statist." [2] Of these, ten developed more rapidly than expected (U.S.S.R., Greece, Bulgaria, Iraq, Pakistan, Turkey, India, Portugal, Spain, Poland) and six less rapidly (Lebanon, Tunisia, Algeria, Syria, Hungary, Argentina). Oddly enough the difference in the proportion of stories mentioning "peers" as a source of personal interaction pressure between the more and less successful economies in this statist group of countries is even larger (50.0 to 42.1 per cent) than it is for all countries, suggesting that "peer" orientation is just as important to authoritarian countries as it is to democratic ones. And "superior" orientation actually occurs more often ($p < .15$) among *slowly* developing statist societies (48.4 per cent) than among more rapidly developing ones (39 per cent) or than among slowly developing democratic societies (39 per cent). In other words stress on pressure from superiors to get ego to conform is a handicap *particularly* in authoritarian societies.

It should be noted also that peer pressure is significantly associated with higher n Achievement level but that there is no interaction with that level, the differences being about the same for countries high and low in n Achievement.

Further support for Hypothesis 5 (now seen as orientation toward a *peer* collectivity) is also listed in Table 5.5 which shows that *asking* or *demanding* cooperation from someone is more often sufficient for successful interaction in stories from rapidly growing economies. To put it differently, other means of exerting pressure for conformity—either psychological (use of conditional love or rejection) or physical (using material reward or punishment)—are less often successful. A simple interpretation of these findings is that the peer "collectivity" or "public opinion" more successfully forces the individual into line in the more rapidly developing economies. It does not appear necessary to people in these countries to resort to "psychological" pressures like threats of loss of love or physical punishment. Instead simple requests or demands—public pressures—work. They are mentioned as being successful more often at both time periods in stories from the more rapidly developing countries. "Other directedness," more or less in Riesman's sense of term (1950), seems to be correlated with rapid economic development.

Hypothesis 6, that selfish motives for cooperating would be more common in slowly developing economies, was not confirmed; that is, it was thought that characters in the stories from the more slowly developing countries would be more often looking out for their own interests or be interested in their own self-esteem. It was further expected that they might more often show the kind of charity or interest in helping the helpless (nurturance) which seems to be peculiarly characteristic of societies where status distinctions are important. But none of these predictions was confirmed.

Hypothesis 7. Affective neutrality. One of the key characteristics of radical Protestantism, particularly in its early days, was the stress it placed on hard work, saving, asceticism, and the renunciation of worldly pleasures. Weber argued that it was this very asceticism which made it possible or even necessary for Protestant businessmen to plough their profits back into the firm causing further expansion. It might therefore be supposed that nations which were developing rapidly economically would stress the importance of controlling one's impulses and leading a disciplined thrifty life. However, such an expectation was not clearly confirmed in the children's stories. At neither time period are there differences in the frequency with which impulse expression is punished. On the other hand, in 1925, 8.5 per cent of the stories from the more rapidly developing countries mentioned impulse control with favor as contrasted with 6.8 per cent of the stories from the more slowly developing countries. The difference does not approach significance. It is somewhat larger (13.0 to 6.3 per cent) in 1950 and more significant ($p < .10$), but the combined estimate of significance ($p < .20$) falls well below levels ordinarily accepted as sufficient to reject the assumption that there is no real difference. Furthermore it does not matter whether the countries are classified by the rate of growth or by level of development. In neither case is asceticism associated with the economic variable. Possibly children's stories touch on impulse control too infrequently or what is more likely, theorists have confused asceticism as a means to an achievement goal and asceticism as an end in itself (as in certain types of religious fasting, for example). The former seems likely to be associated with more rapid economic development via its link with the capacity of subjects with high n Achievement to reject immediate rewards for longer range, larger ones. [See Mischel (1960) and Chapter 8.] On the other hand, in at least the most simple and obvious meaning of the words, impulse denial or asceticism is not directly associated with more rapid economic growth and Hoselitz is confirmed in his judgment that degree of economic advancement is not "correlated with an increase of affective neutrality." (Hoselitz, 1953, p. 13.)

Hypotheses 8 and 9. Rationality and planning vs. magic. Weber also made a great deal of the "rationality" of modern society in which magic and superstition have been largely done away with. Certainly the modern machine or the coordination and operation of a number of machines in a modern factory requires a degree of rationality and planning much greater than is absolutely necessary, say, in traditional agriculture. If a job is broken up into a number of different parts, as in the specialization of labor, then planning is necessary to put them together to get the finished product. Therefore, countries which stress rationality in planning ought to be able to adapt to such a system of production more readily and move ahead more rapidly. Hypothesis 8 concerns rationality of action in children's stories. The question is: how often does "ego" use means to gain his ends which may be classified as rational—involving intelligence and hard work—as opposed to irrational, involving deceit and magic. As Table 5.5 shows, only one of these four characteristics, hard work, appears more often, as predicted, in the stories from the more rapidly developing countries, at a significant level both in 1925 and 1950. Not too surprisingly countries which "get ahead" faster are the ones that have stressed "hard work" in their stories for children. The finding is very similar to the greater frequency of instrumental activity in achievement-related stories in such countries reported in Table 3.7. In fact there may be some scoring overlap so that they are not really two independent findings. However, as the figures in the right-hand column of Table 5.5 show, hard work is not closely or significantly related to national n Achievement levels, though it might be supposed it would be, since a logical method of pursuing an achievement goal is to work hard.

Oddly enough, none of the other characteristics associated with rationality showed the predicted relationship to economic growth. Irrational factors either as means (deceit and magic) or as forces acting on "ego" (fate and magic—Hypothesis 9) did not appear any less often in stories from countries which were developing more rapidly, nor did a stress on intelligent action appear any more often. Possibly even in the most rational societies, appeals to magic are considered "good" for children and treated in such a way that the children know that they belong in the world of fantasy rather than real life.

Hypotheses 10-11. *Optimism.* Hypotheses 10-11 deal with attempts to check the very widely held hypothesis that more rapidly developing countries have tended to have greater faith in their ability to conquer nature, more belief in progress, and a more optimistic attitude toward the future. The results do not strikingly confirm expectations. Man is not pictured as more powerful than nature, acting to conquer it more often in the rapidly developing economies. If anything, the trend is slightly the reverse at both time periods, with more stories representing man as *under* nature coming from the more rather than the less rapidly developing countries (50.4 to 46.2 per cent in 1925 and 44.4 to 41.4 per cent in 1950), although the differences do not approach significance.

The other prediction under this heading, namely that "ego" would be more often successful in his endeavors in the more rapidly developing countries, also turned out not to be confirmed. So there is no real evidence in the children's readers of a greater faith in one's ability to succeed or conquer nature among those countries which subsequently developed rapidly in the economic sphere. Here is a clear case of an eminently "reasonable" psychological hypothesis not being confirmed in fact. What could be more "self-evident" than that men who have in fact advanced economically should have had confidence in their ability to advance before they started? Such confidence would seem to be practically a prerequisite of their working hard and effectively for progress, but we find no evidence of it in their stories for children. Instead we find just as much "fatalism" and belief in the dominant forces of nature as in the more backward countries which are often assumed to be backward because of just such beliefs. Children's stories are not the only way of measuring such beliefs, of course, but they do serve to make one sceptical as to whether what is so "logical" and self-evident is necessarily true.

Hypotheses 12-14. Material needs emphasized over other concerns. Concern with the material world did not show up in more frequent mention of biological needs (i.e., "economic wants") attributed to "ego" or in the greater use of material rewards (money, food, presents, etc.) to get "ego" to conform (Hypotheses 12 and 13). On the other hand, there is evidence that nature appears more often in the stories as a reason for cooperating (Hypothesis 14). (See the last rows in Table 5.5.) The type case here is provided by Dutch stories dealing with the necessity for the members of a community to work together to construct dikes to keep out the sea. Such stories appear more frequently among rapidly growing economies both in 1925 and 1950. The emphasis appears to be on the *salience* of nature as something to be dealt with rather than on material needs and their satisfaction *per se*. In other words, it is not *any particular attitude* toward the material world (such as a desire to conquer nature) that is more common in the rapidly developing countries but rather the *salience* of nature as something with which men must deal by working together. Oddly enough this attitude, unlike all the others in Table 5.5, appears to favor economic growth particularly in countries with low n Achievement (last figures in the bottom right-hand corner of Table 5.5). The other value attitudes in the table interact with n Achievement level, if at all, in such a way as to promote economic development even more if n Achievement is also present, but nature as a force making for interaction or cooperation among men works the other way. Apparently if men lack n Achievement or the entrepreneurial spirit, stress on the need to cope with the forces of nature is even more effective in promoting economic growth.

On the other hand, failure to confirm Hypotheses 10-13 tends to throw doubt on the "rational" model of human psychology which argues that those countries will develop more rapidly where men stress the importance of economic wants and the material means of satisfying them, and have faith in their capacity to shape the material world to such an end.

Summary: The Achievement Syndrome, Nature as a Source of Cooperation, and Market Morality

In examining the results of the value analysis as a whole, one gets the impression that a number of well-known and eminently reasonable theories about economic development did not come off particularly well. Thus the more successful countries economically speaking did not stress ascribed status less, affective neutrality more, man's ability to conquer nature more, the importance of satisfying material needs, or perhaps even economic rationality or planning. In all of these cases, as in the case of ascribed status, there is no evidence that the factor *accompanies* rather than precedes economic development and not much comfort in the thought that the readers must not be measuring the variable in question very well. To consider a further example of the last point, inspection of the findings for individual countries shows, entirely as expected, that the Scandinavian and Anglo-Saxon countries stress the importance of impulse control. In general they have also developed more rapidly than other groups of countries. But only a completely systematic survey such as ours shows that impulse control is also stressed in countries like Spain, France, and Chile, which did *not* develop so rapidly (1929-1950). If we are seriously interested in general propositions as to what aspects of social structure or national values are responsible for economic growth, we must cast a very broad net and consider all the cases.

The chief burden of the methodological argument in Chapter 1 was precisely that students of comparative social structure have ordinarily not had the means of comparing systematically and quantitatively the presence of certain factors in a representative sample of countries. Only by such a method is it possible to discover the central forces in economic growth and to eliminate those which are accidental features of certain economies which have developed more rapidly. Those who still believe that many of these factors are of key importance—and certainly one cannot deny that many of them sound as if they should be—would at the very least seem to have the burden of proof shifted to their shoulders. Other methods of measurement can certainly be devised than children's stories. And all that remains to be done is to apply them to a representative group of countries differentiated in terms of their rate of economic growth. If one has doubts as to whether such an undertaking would in fact be worthwhile they arise from a general suspicion of "rational" psychological explanations of human behavior as much as from the particular failure of characteristics of the children's stories to confirm such explanations.

On the positive side, the findings of the value analysis are quite interesting and may be dealt with under three headings, two minor and one major. To begin with the minor results, the stress on hard work is neither novel nor particularly surprising. It appears clearly to belong in the achievement syndrome along with *n* Achievement level. To rephrase these results in common speech: countries which get ahead economically are those which are concerned with getting ahead and stress hard work as a means of doing so.

Secondly, nature is more salient among such countries as a force to be reckoned with, above all as a source of pressure for cooperative action among men. Again the result is not surprising since practically anyone would have predicted that at the very core of modern technological society lies a concern with nature as something which requires manipulation, management or cooperative action. What is surprising is that this concern with nature is not unambiguously a faith in one's ability to conquer or subdue it, nor is it associated with the achievement syndrome. In fact it seems to be most often associated with rapid economic development in those countries which are low in *n* Achievement.

The major proposition supported by these findings is that in societies which subsequently develop rapidly economically *the force which holds society together has shifted from tradition, particularly impersonal institutional tradition, to public opinion which helps define changing and functionally specific interpersonal relationships.* The first five sets of results in Table 5.5 can be interpreted as supporting some such generalization. More rapidly developing societies have begun to stress institutional traditions less (Hypothesis 1) and specific interpersonal relationships more (Hypothesis 3). They see requests and demands from others, particularly peers (Hypothesis 5) as more often sufficient to get people to relate to others. Or to interpret these findings a little more, rigid prescribed ways of relating to others have begun to give way to more flexible ones which are seen as arising out of the specific needs or demands of particular others, especially peers. Society is somehow less "fixed" and more open. Individuals enter into relationships with others for specific reasons and the relationships are generally controlled by the opinions and wishes of the "others."

It is to this last point that we should direct particular attention, because it may be an important new source of morality or social cohesion in rapidly changing societies. What it suggests is that "other-directedness" is an essential feature of rapid economic development even in its early stages, rather than a special feature of advanced urban culture in the United States as Riesman (1950) suggests. The social facts that support the hypothesis are well known; all modern nations are characterized by increasing literacy and intensive development of the mass media—newspapers, radio, public address systems, television. The simplest interpretation of our finding is that in the more economically successful countries, people have been trained to pay more attention to what other people are saying through such mass media. Just as characters in the children's stories are guided no longer by institutional norms, but by specific demands from other people, particularly peers, adults in economically progressive societies appear to be guided more in their conduct by what they read in the papers, hear on the radio, or see on television. Why should such an attitude promote economic development particularly?

One can think of several reasons without much difficulty. In the first place, coming to value the opinion of the "generalized other" as it is reflected in the mass media, tends to promote the shift of one's loyalties away from traditionalistic norms which in many backward countries impede rapid development. If a man is bound by a caste system, or by a near exclusive loyalty to his kin group, or to a set of other-worldly religious goals, he is likely to act in "maladaptive" ways so far as generalized economic goals are concerned, as any number of theorists have pointed out. But how does he discover new ways of behaving? An individual Indian may see, for example, that the norms governing the joint family system are not particularly conducive to economic development or to modern society, but if he gives them up, how will he know what social obligations to substitute for the old ones? Where will he turn for guidance? What the data suggest is that those countries will develop most rapidly which succeed in getting such people to pay attention to new norms dramatized in the newspapers, in local political party meetings, or on the radio. The value of using the mass media for educational purposes lies precisely in the fact that they come to represent a new "voice of authority" replacing the authority of tradition. Westerners who may cringe at the thought that any authority is needed in such matters should remember that norms governing social behavior must exist, must come from somewhere, if the society is not to become disorganized. Our data suggest that the more successful societies are those which have prevented such disorder by switching loyalties most effectively from tradition to organized public opinion as represented in the mass media.

In the second place, paying attention to the opinion of others as a way of guiding one's behavior has the advantage of greater flexibility. One of the features of traditional norms is that they generally change very slowly over time, which means that they may persist long after the time when they were functionally adaptive. Thus, for example, the tradition of dividing land equally among one's children might at a certain stage in a nation's history be a useful way of avoiding family dissension and promoting ideals of equality, yet when the land fills up beyond a certain point, as has happened in a number of countries, it may lead to a very uneconomical process of trying to farm productively very tiny and scattered bits of land. Yet such a tradition may be very slow to change so long as it is common throughout the community and so long as it is difficult for an individual or groups of people to get an overall view of its detrimental effects. On the other hand, once the flaw in such a system is recognized, its bad effects can be dramatized and spread throughout the public rapidly through the mass media if they have been developed as a source of attitude change. Such traditions may die fairly slowly even under the impact of a dramatic mass media campaign, but it seems safe to assume that they will die more rapidly than they would have without such a campaign. The main point is that public opinion can be more quickly responsive to changed conditions and can be mobilized more rapidly than oral or religious tradition to support needed social innovations.

As our data also suggest, what a modern society needs for successful development is flexibility in a man's role relationships. His entire network of relations to others should not be traditionally determined by his caste or even by his occupational status. Instead he enters into relationships for particular reasons which should provide for greater efficiency in working out the network of relationships among people. To use the unpleasant language of Marxism, interpersonal relationships are reduced to a "cash basis"; they have a particular reason for being, so that in a sense they seem calculated rather than warm and diffuse. The danger to a social order made up of such specific transactions is anarchy or disorder. Who knows what to expect of whom when traditional diffuse role relationships or interpersonal obligations no longer exist? The transition to the new order is certainly likely to be helped if people can learn to listen to what "other people" say is the right thing to do. To be specific, if the traditional role of being a parent is no longer accepted, then it certainly helps parents to have child-rearing information given them in the mass media so that they can be guided in what to do. Relying on such information also serves to narrow the parental role from a typically diffuse one to one dealing more specifically with the functional problem of child-rearing. This in turn may free it from traditional "adhesions" like loyalty to one's parents, which may have been adaptive in a former day, but which in a modern society may serve only to prevent a free and efficient flow of labor in the market. (See Strodtbeck, 1958.)

The third advantage of increasing reliance on public opinion as a source of guidance in social behavior is perhaps the most important of all. All economists agree that the growth of the market is at the very center of modern economic society. In fact one can measure the maturity of an economy by the absence of "imperfections" in the market mechanism, "by the degree of openness, freedom, and absence of other obstacles to the smooth allocation of resources among competing uses." (Hoselitz, 1958.) The market must be considered as a social as well as an economic institution governing allocation of resources. "Who meets whom, under what conditions, in what surroundings, for what kinds of contractual arrangements, are some of the questions which appear paramount in the institutional analysis of the market. And even more important, what are the commodities which are customarily traded on the market, and what prohibitions or impediments exist against the market being allowed to intervene as a mediator of certain exchanges? How universalistic are market criteria, with respect to persons transacting business on a market?" (Hoselitz, 1958, pp. 2-3.) In other words how advanced an economy is depends on how near the market is to the ideal in economic allocation of resources and how near the market is to this ideal type depends on social institutions and values restricting its use as a "rational" mechanism in one way or another. What then tends to create market imperfections and what to remove them? In the most general sense possible, market imperfections are the result of commitments of individuals to trade certain goods or offer their labor only under certain conditions to certain people at certain times, etc. These restrictions, in turn, are the result of traditional values or norms governing their behavior to particular groups of "others" (relatives, strangers, friends, superiors, inferiors). The most generalized solution, then, to the problem of particularistic commitments is to transfer the individual's loyalties to the "generalized other." This is exactly what reliance on public opinion permits and promotes.

Let us turn to a specific example, since the argument in its most general form appears unnecessarily abstract and vague. A market imperfection which is still a handicap in many underdeveloped countries is the variable price system in which an article sells for one price to a friend, another to a stranger, or to someone who is a sharp bargainer versus someone who is not. In fact the code of business practice in traditional societies is often quite different for friends and relatives, for kin groups, and for strangers whom one may never meet again. Yet the very essence of the market system is production and exchange involving unknown "others," so that the functional social problem in its most general terms is to get the individual to behave toward strangers (or toward anyone) as he would toward friends and relatives. For example, so long as one operates on a kinship or even a neighborhood basis, an inferior piece of merchandise or a sloppy piece of work will have direct and immediate repercussions for the individual. People will know who was at fault and will be in a position to apply sanctions directly to him. However, when the producer begins to do things for impersonal others, for the market, sanctions are not so obviously or immediately applied and individuals may be tempted to "get away" with inferior goods or services for the immediate rewards they sometimes bring. In terms of social norms, the problem is to establish a new value pattern which extends the morality governing particularistic economic relations to those involving unknown "others." In Brazil an ingenious partial solution to the problem has been discovered by Japanese immigrants (see Kuznets et al., 1955). They realized that the social institution of *compadre* (serving as a godfather to someone) could be put to business use. That is, anyone to whom one had served as a godfather should ideally treat his adoptive parent henceforth as a member of the kin group, in business as well as in other relationships. Thus, the Japanese businessman, by serving as godparent to a number of individuals, could extend the circle of people whom he could trust in business relationships. As a relative, they would not cheat him as they might a stranger. Such a solution is of course only a partial one to a much larger problem: how can a society get individuals to be honest, to set fair prices, to do a good job of work—for an unknown other?

One way of accomplishing this end is obviously to make the individual sensitive to what the "generalized other" is thinking, i.e., to public opinion. Then he does not cheat or try to get away with poor workmanship because of what "people" will think. In psychological terms, he no longer worries just about what particular others will think, such as his friends and relatives, but about what more or less "anonymous" others will think. The mass media can strongly support him in his notion that "they" will find out economic "wrong-doing" by giving publicity to trials of individuals caught for various offenses (charging too much, giving differential prices to friends, etc.). An individual may best learn from the newspapers sometimes what is considered by the "generalized other" to be improper behavior. Public officials in the United States might have had some doubts as to how far it was proper to accept gifts or favors from friends until the newspapers publicized so vividly the trials of a few officials punished for receiving such gifts, that no one could longer entertain any doubts as to what his behavior should be if he didn't want to undergo similar punishment. Quiz show contestants may have had honest doubts as to how much coaching beforehand was ethical until the newspapers exposed and public opinion severely punished anyone who had had any coaching. Such "trials by public opinion" are common in countries, both democratic and totalitarian, which have become "other-directed" in the sense that they rely on such sanctions (rather than more traditionalistic ones) for controlling deviant behavior and establishing new social norms. Thus the most important social function fulfilled by the tendency to shift responsibility for social control from tradition to other people is the greater guarantee that it provides that there will be morality in the anonymity of the marketplace. Reliance on public opinion is the social mechanism which tends to supply and enforce *market morality*, and market morality is essential to removing market imperfections that slow economic progress.

So far our argument sounds as if it might apply only to democracies where public opinion admittedly and consciously plays a part in social control. What about the "statist" societies where an enlightened and informed public opinion might play less of a role? Do they develop rapidly without shifting social control from tradition to public opinion? If we turn to the 16 countries identified as "statist" or centralized in authority, in discussing Hypothesis 5 above, we find no evidence of any difference in this respect. The statist countries developing more rapidly, as pointed out in that connection, are, if anything, even more peer-oriented than the democratic countries developing more rapidly. Furthermore they are also less tradition-oriented: only 11.5 per cent of the stories mention *institutional* interaction pressure from more rapidly developing statist countries as contrasted with 31.3 per cent from the less rapidly developing statist societies ($\chi^2 = 8.90$, $p < .01$). The interesting fact is that the more successful of the statist countries, those that have grown most rapidly economically, are exactly those that have moved in the direction of *relying less* on traditional institutional authority. It is perhaps the more remarkable when it is remembered that the stories come from such highly bureaucratized countries as Bulgaria, Spain, Russia, Iraq, and Poland. What appears to be happening is that such countries clearly recognize the power of public pressure as mobilized in the mass media for producing conformity. So the general argument remains the same even for statist societies: those countries will tend to advance most rapidly economically which have been most successful in getting their people to look for guidance not to traditional institutions but to the opinion of others.

How Other-Directedness Is Learned

Since the value analysis of children's stories has uncovered a second factor independent of and perhaps as important as the achievement syndrome, a word about its origins seems in order. In particular the following question arises: nearly all countries today have a public press and other channels of mass communication that try to be influential or educational in the broadest sense. How is it that in some countries, if we are to believe the reader data, people tend to pay more attention to opinions emanating from such sources? When all peoples could be other-directed, how is it that some are more so than others?

The way children are brought up in the United States should provide us with a clue, since Americans are certainly among the most other-directed people in the world. To cite just one or two factual illustrations, they agree much more than Britons or Austrians with an item like "parents should be guided primarily in what they do by what other parents do in their neighborhood so as to avoid bringing up their child differently" [3] or more than Germans with items like "the negative opinion of others often keeps me from seeing a movie or play I had planned to attend" or "my political opinion is easily swayed by editorials I read." (McClelland, Sturr, Knapp and Wendt, 1958.) How do Americans get that dependent on the opinion of others? McClelland *et al.* (1958) found a very large difference in the social behavior of German and American boys of high school age, which may provide the answer. They administered a questionnaire which asked the boys to list any activities outside of school in which they were engaged. The American boys listed on the average five *group* activities (interest clubs, school publications, religious associations, team sports, etc.), whereas the Germans listed one on the average, with very little overlap between the two distributions. The Germans, on the other hand, listed slightly more individualistic activities (walking, collecting stamps, playing music). The finding nicely highlights the fact that German schools are not the beehive of extracurricular activities that American schools are, that children there do not participate, as American children do from the earliest grades, in group activities—in plays, interest clubs, in producing school papers, in service organizations and the like.

It has, of course, been noted by many observers that Americans are a nation of "joiners," that a prominent feature of American life is the large number of voluntary organizations in which people get together for group activities. What is perhaps not so well known is that these organizations, particularly those in school, may serve the very important social function of training people to pay attention to the wishes and opinions of others. It is by constant practice in groups that Americans learn to cooperate and to be responsive to what others expect of them. On the other hand, the German boys appeared to have a much more clearly worked out formal code of obligation to others and to stress more the importance of sociocentric virtues. The questionnaire also asked the boys to list "the three things you would most like to teach your children." What they answered was then coded as "egocentric" or "sociocentric." "Egocentric" is not here a value term but includes the development of individual capacities (to be intelligent, to appreciate music, to enjoy life). Sociocentric virtues, on the other hand, refer to one's obligation to others, to friendship, honesty, and loyalty. The Americans stressed egocentric, or self-development virtues more, and the Germans sociocentric ones. So, while the German engages in more individualistic activities, he has a great sense of his obligation to others, whereas the American has a greater sense of obligation to himself which is held in check by participation in many group activities.

If other-directedness is in fact related to the kinds of group experiences that children have in school, then the U.S. children's stories should show more other-directedness than the German stories do. To check such a hypothesis, it is necessary to calculate at least a rough over-all measure of other-directedness from the variables in Table 5.5. Three of these variables seem directly or indirectly related to other-directedness: (1) the *absence* of institutional interaction pressure, (2) the presence of peer interaction pressure and (3) the number of instances in which simple requests or demands are successful in initiating interaction. In other words, an other-directed society should be one in which ego is not motivated to interact by traditional institutional pressures, but by pressures from others, particularly peers, whose requests or demands are respected enough to produce compliance. The actual index was constructed by computing the percentage of stories from each country showing each of the three characteristics in question in the 1950 sample, ranking the percentages separately, summing the three ranks and reranking the sums.[4] According to this index the United States ranks 5th and Germany 17th in other-directedness out of a sample of 39 countries. In short, the hypothesis is confirmed: American children's stories are considerably more other-directed than German stories, as they should be if our argument is correct that American children are trained to pay more attention to the opinions of others through participation in many group activities.

Fortunately the hypothesis can be checked further because the same questionnaire items used in the earlier study of German and American boys (McClelland *et al.*, 1958) were included in our comparative study of attitudes and interests of boys in four countries—Japan, Germany, India and Brazil. The relevant data have been assembled in Table 5.6 which shows the

TABLE 5.6 INDIVIDUAL AND GROUP ACTIVITIES AND VALUES AMONG BOYS IN THE UNITED STATES, JAPAN, GERMANY AND INDIA

Countries	Percentage of boys listing *at least one*		Difference	Percentage of boys listing as desirable *at least one*		Difference
	individual activity	group activity	(group − individual)	egocentric virtue	sociocentric virtue	(sociocentric − egocentric)
A. More other-directed[1]						
United States						
(N = 73)	58.9%	93.2%	+34.3%	93.1%	75.0%	−18.1
Japan (N = 172)	68.0	82.0	+14.0	71.5	47.7	−23.8
Combined (N = 245)			85.3		55.7	
B. Less other-directed[1]						
Germany (N = 392)	88.8	76.3	−12.5	72.7	68.9	− 3.8
India (N = 151)	85.4	77.5	− 7.9	58.9	93.4	+34.9
Combined (N = 543)			76.6		75.7	

[1] Classification based on sum of ranks for absence of institutional interaction pressure, peer interaction pressure, and "demands successful" as a means of interaction pressure (see Fig. 5.1). Final ranks (out of 39) are: United States, 5; Japan, 6; India, 13; Germany, 17.

comparative frequencies of egocentric and sociocentric activities and values mentioned by boys in four countries classified as higher or lower in other-directedness according to the system just described for coding the content of their children's stories. Brazil could not be included because its stories were not coded for these variables. But the Japanese stories rank high in other-directedness (rank 6) like the U.S. stories and the Indian stories rank lower (rank 13) like the German stories.

Because of gross differences in the frequency of mentioning outside activities of any kind, it was necessary to use the rather crude nonparametric statistic shown in Table 5.6—namely the proportion of subjects who mentioned *at least once* either an individual or a group activity, and either an egocentric or sociocentric virtue. The U.S. data are from the earlier study and show the trend to be checked elsewhere—more stress on group *participation* and less stress on group or sociocentric values or virtues. Japan shows the same trend, as its high rank on other-directedness in its children's stories would predict.

The German data, just as in the earlier study, show a reverse trend—more stress on individualistic *activities* and a more nearly equal stress on sociocentric virtues. The Indian boys react similarly. More of them report individualistic activities and stress the values of obligations to others (loyalty, friendship, etc.). The same interesting contrast occurs between Japan and India as between the United States and Germany.

Probably the simplest way of testing the significance of these differences is to note that of the 245 boys from the more other-directed countries (United States and Japan), 209 or 85 per cent listed at least one group activity in which they participated as contrasted with only 416, or 76.6 per cent, of the 543 boys from the less other-directed countries (chi-square = 7.79, $p < .01$). On the other hand sociocentric virtues are mentioned as desirable by more of the boys in the less other-directed countries (Germany and India). Of these, 75.7 per cent listed at least one sociocentric virtue as contrasted with only 55.7 per cent of the boys from the more other-directed countries (chi-square = 31.64, $p < .001$). Thus participation in group activities is associated with stress on self-development virtues (United States, Japan), whereas participation in individual activities is accompanied by stress on sociocentric virtues (Germany, India).

To summarize: In more other-directed countries stress on self-realization is checked and disciplined by much practice in learning to be sensitive to the opinions of others through participation in group activities. In less other-directed countries the process is reversed. Society or traditional institutions are the primary focus of attention. The person is part of a social organism who asserts his individuality in solitary pursuits. The difference in point of view between the two kinds of societies, one beginning with the individual and the other with society, is nicely illustrated by the contrasting ways in which German and American psychologists induce frustration in their human subjects. The Germans typically do it by "Überforderung" (Klauer, 1959)—literally demanding too much of the individual —whereas the Americans do it by blocking or interfering with something that the individual is trying to do (Dollard *et al.*, 1939). In other words, the Germans start from the viewpoint of society and see frustration as demanding too much from a person, leaving him in the most general sense too little individuality. The Americans, on the other hand, start from the viewpoint of the individual and see frustration as anything which interferes with his wishes, making the ultimate problem here not individuality but "socialization," or fulfillment of one's social obligations.

It is premature to draw any firm conclusions based on a study of boys in only four countries, yet the evidence points to an interesting conclusion.

At least in the countries studied, other-directedness may well be learned by relatively greater participation in peer group activities which is accompanied by stress on self-development values. In more traditional societies, there is less dependence on the opinion of others, therefore less need for group activities to make people sensitive to such opinions, and correspondingly greater stress on such sociocentric virtues as kindness, loyalty, and obligations to others as defined and prescribed in traditional social institutions.

Predicting Rates of Economic Growth from n Achievement and Other-Directedness

Since n Achievement and other-directedness are both related to economic development and unrelated to each other, they should, taken together, have a very marked effect on the rate of economic development. A double classification by both factors in the 1925 and 1950 readers does, in fact, reveal some impressive differences, as illustrated in Fig. 5.1. To prepare this figure, the rough measure of other-directedness described in the previous section was used. That is, the countries were ranked on each of three variables mentioned there, first in the 1925 sample and then again in the 1950 sample, and the ranks summed to obtain an over-all rank on other-directedness. They were then classified as above or below the median on this dimension and also as above or below the median in n Achievement both in 1925 and 1950. Then the average gain or loss in sigma units of electricity produced between 1929 and 1950 and between 1952 and 1958 was computed for countries falling below the median on both variables, above the

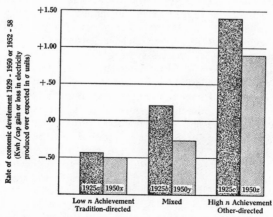

Figure 5.1   Relation of n Achievement and other-direction in the 1925 and 1950 readers to subsequent economic development

median on both variables, or below on one and above on the other, with the results shown in Fig. 5.1. Obviously the countries which were high in *n* Achievement and other-directedness greatly outperformed those which were low in both variables, both in 1925 and in 1950, whereas those that were high on one and low on the other showed an average gain somewhere in between.

Perhaps the most striking way to state the results is to note that *every country*, with but a single exception, developed at a faster rate than expected which had high *n* Achievement and high other-directedness in its children's readers either in 1925 or 1950. The exception is Ireland in 1950, which developed a little less rapidly than expected in the 1950's in terms of gross electrical power consumption. However, Ireland alone of all the countries decreased in population during this time period so that a gross consumption measure may be "unfair" to it. In per capita terms it was definitely an overachiever in the 1950's as these psychological measures would predict. On the other hand, very few of the countries which were both low in *n* Achievement and high in "tradition-directedness" (none in 1925 and only Austria, Mexico, and Poland in 1950) grew more rapidly than expected. Again at least two of the exceptions in 1950 seem easily explicable on other grounds—Mexico because it had the largest rate of population increase so that it is really an underachiever in *per capita* terms, and Poland because as we have already pointed out there is reason to doubt the representativeness of the children's readers used. When it is recalled that the psychological indexes for a particular country are based on only 21 stories, which in the case of several countries should by chance be unrepresentative, the results are quite remarkable.

It may come as something of a shock to realize that more could have been learned about the rate of future economic growth of a number of these countries in 1925 or 1950 by reading elementary school books than by studying such presumably more relevant matters as power politics, wars and depressions, economic statistics, or governmental policies governing international trade, taxation, or public finance. The reason apparently lies in the fact that the readers reflect sufficiently accurately the motives and values of key groups of men in a country which *in the long run* determine the general drift of economic and political decisions and their effects on productivity. Economic and political policies are of course the means by which economic change is brought about, but whether policies will be implemented, or even decided on in the first place, appears to depend ultimately on the motives and values of men as we have succeeded in detecting them in the stories they think it is right for their children to read.

What has been true in the past should also be true in the future, if we have, in fact, succeeded in isolating certain key variables influencing the rate of economic development. We would predict that within the normal limits of human history (barring near total destruction of a country by atomic attack), those countries which show high n Achievement and high other-directedness in their stories for children for 1950 should be the ones that continue to grow more rapidly economically between 1960 and 1970. Furthermore, countries in this group that also have high n Power and low n Affiliation scores should more often adopt dictatorial methods of obtaining their ends (as represented by more totalitarian forms of government). What is missing from such predictions is, of course, any consideration of extrinsic factors which influence n Achievement or n Power levels or the extent to which a nation becomes other-directed. To judge by the low correlations between the motive levels in 1925 and those in 1950, we must conclude that changes may occur quite rapidly and they must be taken into account in any long-range predictions. The way in which one of the variables— n Achievement—may be influenced by various historical events is outlined in some detail in Chapters 9 and 10. Furthermore, national policies might even be affected by the findings presented in this book! One of the problems that the behavioral scientist has in predicting the course of human events is that people may be influenced by what he finds out about them, a possibility that puts behavioral science in quite a different category from physical science. But all such considerations aside, we should have to predict that in general those countries which are high in n Achievement and highly other-directed, should, on the average, continue to develop more rapidly economically in the next generation. Time alone will tell whether the prediction is correct.

NOTES AND REFERENCES

[1] As might be expected on theoretical grounds, n Affiliation and n Power scores are negatively related, the correlations being $-.47$, $p < .05$ for the 1925 sample; $-.28$, $p < .06$ for the 1950 sample, or for both samples combined $r = -.33$, $p < .01$, $N = 67$. Apparently it is difficult to want to order people about and to like them and want to be approved by them at one and the same time. To round out the picture, n Power scores are unrelated to n Achievement scores, the correlation being $.05$ for the 1925 sample and $-.04$ for the 1950 sample.

[2] The following countries were considered "statist" in the 1950 sample: (1) because their governments were totalitarian: Argentina, Spain, Portugal, Russia, Hungary, Poland; (2) because they were backward with a kwh/cap output in 1950 of less than 100: Turkey, India, Lebanon, Pakistan, Greece, Bulgaria, Tunisia, Syria, Iraq, Algeria.

[3] This finding is from an unpublished study in which the same questionnaire was administered to 60 to 70 lower middle-class adults around 1950 in the United States, in England, and in Vienna, Austria. The item in question reads, "a boy about eight years old has been punished by his parents for lying. They discover afterwards that he was not lying after all." The respondents were requested to indicate their degree of agreement or disagreement with various alternative responses of the parents to this situation on a scale going from $+3$ to -3. The average agreement with the "guided by other parents" alternative was $+2.57$ for the Americans, -2.50 for the Britons, and -2.14 for the Austrians, the differences being highly significant.

⁴ The three rank orders are, practically speaking, independent. In the 1950 sample ($N = 39$), the rank order correlation between variable A (absence of institutional interaction pressure) and variable B (peer interaction pressure) is .24; between variable A and variable C (demands successful as a means of interaction pressure) it is −.01 and between variables B and C it is .11. None of the values is significant suggesting that each variable is measuring an independent aspect of what we have been calling "other-directedness." It should also be remembered that the rank on a particular variable is highly unreliable based as it is on the presence or absence of a single characteristic that appears rarely in the stories in any case. It was for this reason that rankings on as many variables as seemed related to other-directedness were combined to build as much reliability into the measure as possible.

6

Entrepreneurial Behavior

The research studies so far reported deal exclusively with estimates of the importance of certain motives or values for a whole nation or culture. They are not, therefore, very illuminating as to the process whereby a motivational level affects economic development. Certainly we are not likely to be satisfied with some such vague concept as a "group mind" which somehow expresses its feelings and aspirations in vigorous economic activity. It should be possible to trace the motivational connection in much more detail. How specifically does a high level of n Achievement result in more rapid economic development? The link is obviously the entrepreneur —the man who organizes the firm (the business unit) and/or increases its productive capacity.

In its most general terms, the hypothesis states that a society with a generally high level of n Achievement will produce more energetic entrepreneurs who, in turn, produce more rapid economic development. But such a simple statement is loaded with difficulties. What, exactly, is an entrepreneur? In what sense is he crucial for economic development? It is true that ever since Schumpeter revived interest in entrepreneurship, many if not most economists and sociologists interested in economic development insist on the importance of the entrepreneur. Thus Hoselitz can write, "If the theorists of capitalism agree on anything, they agree on the fact that with the rise of capitalist production a new class or group of men—call them bourgeois, or entrepreneurs, or businessmen—attained first positions of leadership in the economy and later also in the political and other élites." (Hoselitz, 1953.) But what about Communist States like Russia? Is the entrepreneur just as important for them? For that matter, what about the classical economists who discuss economic development in terms of inputs and outputs, referring to entrepreneurship, if at all, only vaguely and in passing, possibly because they have as yet found no way to quantify its "quality." Even if we can succeed in defining an entrepreneur and obtaining agreement that he is a key figure in economic development, will he necessarily have higher n Achievement than people in other occupations of equal prestige and importance? If entrepreneurs do have higher n Achievement, did they develop it after entering into their occupation as a response to its pressures or did n Achievement lead them to enter and/or perform successfully in the occupation? If the latter be true, why should a high level of n Achievement lead people to perform entrepreneurial activities better rather than those required in other occupations? Finally, what about other factors which may be just as important as n Achievement for developing successful entrepreneurship? Is the "other-directedness" discovered in the last chapter, for example, likely also to be a key part of the entrepreneurial role?

The issues are obviously complex and interrelated. Our plan for dealing with them will be as follows: first, in the present chapter we will try to define analytically and theoretically the key components of the entrepreneurial role—that is, we will try to discover what it is that a man does which makes theorists call him an entrepreneur. Then we shall check to see whether boys with high n Achievement in various countries of the world behave as an entrepreneur should before they have entered entrepreneurial positions and had a chance to be influenced by them. In this way we may hope to find out whether n Achievement leads people to behave in an entrepreneurial way, or whether an entrepreneurial position increases n Achievement, thereby leading to more vigorous entrepreneurial activity. Finally, we present data as to whether high n Achievement in various countries causes boys to be interested particularly in entrepreneurial occupations, or whether its relationship to occupational choice is random. Then, in the next chapter, we can turn to a study of men having the status of entrepreneurs in various countries to see whether they in fact have the characteristics assigned to them by theorists and the higher n Achievement required by our central hypothesis.

It might be thought that the last step should be taken first. Why bother with analytical distinctions as to what makes up the entrepreneurial role if actual entrepreneurs do not behave as they should according to theory? The answer lies in the very important distinction between status and role. *Status* is used here to refer to a position in society, and *role* to the behavior required, by definition, of an occupant of that status. Therefore, it is theoretically possible, though empirically not likely, that all the occupants of a given status will not behave according to the role requirements of their position. An illustration may make the point clearer. The status, or position in society, of "garbage man" carries with it the role requirement, by definition, of collecting and somehow disposing of garbage. Yet some or all of the occupants of this position in a given town may not fulfill the role requirement. Instead of collecting garbage they may sit in the shade and play dominoes. If one began with an empirical study of the actual behavior of garbage collectors, rather than a theoretical analysis of role requirements, he might conclude on the basis of this sample of garbage collectors that playing dominoes was part of the role. Thus a study of the "behavior of entrepreneurs" is conceptually distinct from a study of "entrepreneurial behavior." Entrepreneurs, or those occupying entrepreneurial status, need not show entrepreneurial behavior, just as garbage collectors may not always collect garbage. Furthermore, it is quite possible for individuals occupying other statuses to behave in an entrepreneurial way, just as a parent may occasionally collect garbage when the regular garbage collector is not available. Thus a politician, a physician, a university professor or a ditch-digger may show all of the components of entrepreneurial role behavior, even though his status is not primarily that of an entrepreneur. From this discussion, it should be apparent that our primary interest is in entrepreneurial role behavior as an ideal or analytical type and that it is a secondary problem, although one of great importance, to discover whether holders of entrepreneurial status in a given country do, in fact, behave as they should according to the ideal type analysis.

The Entrepreneurial Role

Table 6.1 provides a more detailed outline of our plan of attack. On the right-hand side are listed some key components of entrepreneurial role

TABLE 6.1 POSSIBLE DETERMINANTS AND CHARACTERISTICS OF ENTREPRENEURSHIP AS CONSIDERED IN CHAPTERS 6 AND 7

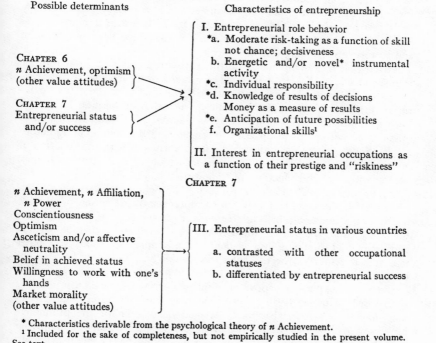

Possible determinants

Characteristics of entrepreneurship

CHAPTER 6
n Achievement, optimism
(other value attitudes)

CHAPTER 7
Entrepreneurial status
and/or success

I. Entrepreneurial role behavior
*a. Moderate risk-taking as a function of skill not chance; decisiveness
b. Energetic and/or novel* instrumental activity
*c. Individual responsibility
*d. Knowledge of results of decisions Money as a measure of results
*e. Anticipation of future possibilities
f. Organizational skills[1]

II. Interest in entrepreneurial occupations as a function of their prestige and "riskiness"

CHAPTER 7

n Achievement, n Affiliation, n Power
Conscientiousness
Optimism
Asceticism and/or affective neutrality
Belief in achieved status
Willingness to work with one's hands
Market morality
(other value attitudes)

III. Entrepreneurial status in various countries

a. contrasted with other occupational statuses
b. differentiated by entrepreneurial success

* Characteristics derivable from the psychological theory of n Achievement.
[1] Included for the sake of completeness, but not empirically studied in the present volume. See text.

behavior, including interest in entrepreneurial occupations, as dependent variables to be related in this chapter to personality characteristics, particularly n Achievement, in adolescent boys in four countries. In Chapter 7 we will go on to see whether occupants of entrepreneurial status—particularly more successful occupants—will show the attitudes and behaviors listed on the right-hand side of the Table. Also, in Chapter 7, as shown in the bottom half of the Table, we can check a variety of other hypotheses which have been put forward to explain why some people are drawn to or are successful in entrepreneurial activities. Unfortunately the design is not perfectly symmetrical, because it was to a certain extent determined by research findings rather than a master plan which guided the selection of research instruments before any work was begun. Thus, for example, in Chapter 7 we will be able to discover whether "willingness to work with one's hands" is a key characteristic of business entrepreneurs (or more successful ones) as some theorists have argued (Hoselitz, 1952). But unfortunately, we did not include in our value attitude questionnaire given to adolescent boys in various countries any items dealing with this value, so that we cannot determine whether the interest led to entrepreneurial behavior or resulted from occupying an entrepreneurial status. The only variable for which the design is perfectly symmetrical is n Achievement, the key variable being studied. Other variables were included in a more or less wholesale attempt to check various theories that have been put forward and to turn up anything else of interest.

Arriving at the components of the entrepreneurial role listed on the right-hand side of Table 6.1 was not easy, nor is the particular list of characteristics likely to please everybody. As Lazarsfeld says, there is a "practically inexhaustible literature" on entrepreneurship or business leadership. Hoselitz sums up the literature nicely as follows: "A study of economists' opinions on entrepreneurship leads to strange and sometimes contradictory results. Some writers have identified entrepreneurship with the function of uncertainty-bearing, others with the coordination of productive resources, others with the introduction of innovations, and still others with the provision of capital." (Hoselitz, 1952, p. 98.) Schumpeter argues in contradiction to the last point that the entrepreneur by definition bears none of the risk, a function which he reserves for the capitalist owner. Following this distinction somewhat, Redlich makes "a tripartite division of the entrepreneurial function into *capitalist*, i.e., supplier of funds and other non-human resources for the enterprise, *manager*, i.e., supervisor and coordinator of productive activities, and *entrepreneur*, in the narrow sense of the term, i.e., planner, innovator, ultimate decision-maker in a productive enterprise." (Hoselitz, 1952, p. 98.) One may, also, of course, make distinctions based on a somewhat more detailed breakdown of the productive process from start to finish, beginning with the function of supplying capital, then proceeding to the function of buying or obtaining materials, to the function of supervising actual production, and finally to the function of selling or distributing the finished product.

The difficulty with such distinctions is that they confuse role and status, or rather they try to define the entrepreneurial role in terms of a particular status (e.g., purchasing or selling). While such a procedure is justified in a rough sort of way, it necessarily leads to disagreements as to which status is really the entrepreneurial one and is therefore not sufficiently precise for our research purposes. Thus, if we adhere to the distinction between role and status, it is quite possible to conceive of a capitalist, or a manager, or a technical innovator who behaves either in an entrepreneurial or non-entrepreneurial way. There is no necessary one-to-one relationship between status and role. The point becomes particularly clear when business functions are studied from a cross-cultural or historical perspective, because they are carved up in different ways, at different times, in different places. Thus, in the early days of capitalism in the West, one man often performed all of the functions—getting capital out of his own earnings, managing his own enterprise, innovating, selling, etc. Yet, as Pelzel (1954) makes clear, the contemporary situation in Japan is quite different. The typical Japanese "entrepreneur," if such he may be called, runs a small shop in which he maintains freedom of action only in the production sphere, being totally dependent on others for financing, buying and selling. In many respects he is what Redlich calls a *manager* (not an entrepreneur), yet it appears to be his *entrepreneurial activity* which is in many respects responsible for Japan's fairly rapid economic development in the past hundred years.

To avoid such confusions and also to obtain a more precise definition of entrepreneurial activities than status labels provide, it was decided to hold as rigorously as possible to defining entrepreneurship in terms of entrepreneurial role behavior, eliminating so far as possible distinctions based on the *type* of business position involved. In theory such a decision opens the field a little too wide, since any human activity might be performed in an entrepreneurial way, from making love to writing poetry or leading an army in battle. If we had to consider all these areas of human life, it might become increasingly difficult to isolate exactly what we mean by the phrase "in an entrepreneurial way." So in practice, primary attention was directed at business activity as it is normally understood, although within that sphere, different *types* of business activity—whether buying, selling, producing or providing capital—were considered more or less equivalent. Looked at in this way, the problem narrows itself down to the following question: What do theorists (economists, sociologists or others) mean when they say that someone engaged in any aspect of a business or economic enterprise is behaving "like an entrepreneur" or "in an entrepreneurial way"? If the issue is so defined, it turns out that there is a fairly high degree of agreement on the role characteristics listed on the right-hand side of Table 6.1. Let us consider each of them in turn and see whether *n* Achievement leads people to behave in that particular way. A great deal of our attention will be focused on the first characteristic, risk-taking. Subsequent characteristics are identified by letters referring back to Table 6.1.

(a) RISK-TAKING

Practically all theorists (e.g., Schumpeter, 1934, Lazarsfeld, 1959, Sawyer, 1954, Meier and Baldwin, 1957) agree that entrepreneurship involves, by definition, taking risks of some kind. Sutton is speaking for all of them when he says: "Characteristically, the factors determining the outcome of business efforts are numerous, and difficult both to assess and control. The sale of goods on a more or less free market is, of course, one major source of these difficulties; the dispositions of buyers are subject to only limited control and prediction. They in turn are influenced by those diffuse but important factors which go under the label of general business conditions. Even within the context of a given firm there may be conditions and possible courses of action (such as personal appointments, or the performance of certain equipment) which may be beyond ready prediction and control. A great part of the efforts of business executives is directed toward minimizing uncertainties." (Sutton, 1954, p. 19.) "It is characteristic of executive roles that they are specialized for the handling of situations which call for something more than routine action. When business executives are asked what is the essential content of their roles, they characteristically say, 'We make decisions.' This emphasis on decision-making is symptomatic of a specialized concern of executives with situations in which there is significant uncertainty as to the results of proper courses of action. (One does not make a 'decision' when there is a predictable, correct outcome, as in getting the sum of a column of figures.)" (Sutton, 1954, p. 20.) Many of these uncertainties exist for the Russian plant manager also, although they may arise more on the procurement than the marketing side at the present time (Granick, 1960).

In short, the executive or entrepreneurial role appears to call for "decision-making under uncertainty." If there is no significant uncertainty, if the action called for involves applying a known procedure, however complicated, to produce a known and predictable result, then entrepreneurship cannot be said to be involved. To be sure, all human activities involve decisions and usually some uncertainty—even those of the highly skilled and experienced surgeon or the plumber making repairs—but the degree of uncertainty is measurably less than for the business executive who must decide under the variable conditions described by Sutton. On the other hand, businessmen are not ordinarily considered to be gamblers, although gamblers certainly "make decisions under uncertainty." The distinction here is an important one analytically, and it does not really depend on the fact that the gambler is operating under longer odds than the businessman. The chances of success of some business decisions may be on the average less than the odds under which some gamblers play. The real point is that the gambler can exercise no control over the outcome, unless he uses loaded dice, whereas the businessman can influence by his actions whether his decisions will turn out in the long run to be successful or unsuccessful. As Sutton puts it, there is "a strong tendency among businessmen to emphasize that their decisions are based on 'facts' and thus to make favorable outcomes the consequence of perspicacity and 'judgment' rather than good fortune." (Sutton, 1954, p. 23.) They may overemphasize the extent to which it was their skill or lack of it which affected the outcome of a decision, but it is a fact that skill plays *some part* in the decision process, as implied by Ambrose Bierce's witticism that "the gambling known as business looks with austere disfavor on the business known as gambling."

Thus one may describe a continuum running from a situation of little or no risk in which actions are prescribed by tradition (as in religious ritual), or specialized knowledge (as in science), to situations in which there is no precedent or knowledge for deciding what to do as in the case of the gambler who flips a coin or bets on the turn of a card. On such a continuum the business executive falls clearly somewhere in the middle; he is called upon to make calculated or moderate risks in which some skill and some luck are involved. The crucial fact is that in such moderately risky situations the outcome depends more clearly on his skill—on his achievement, if you will—than in the case of either extreme. For at the safe or traditional end of the continuum, he need do only what anyone with the proper skills or knowledge can do, whereas at the gambling end nothing he decides to do will make any difference as to the outcome, since by definition it depends entirely on factors outside his control.

Attitudes toward risk-taking in games of skill and games of chance

It follows that people who are attracted to or perform well in an entrepreneurial role should be people who like working under the conditions just described, or who perform better under such conditions. That is, they should have personality characteristics which should lead them to "blossom" under conditions of moderate uncertainty where their efforts or skills can make a difference in the outcome. Much laboratory work demonstrates that this is precisely the working situation which individuals with high n Achievement prefer and work best under. Consider, for example, the findings presented in Fig. 6.1 taken from a study of the distances from a peg at which five- and six-year-old children stand when they are playing a game of ring toss. The children with high n Achievement choose to stand predominantly at a moderate distance from the peg, whereas children with low n Achievement do not show any marked preference. In fact they throw more often from very near the peg or from very far away than do the children with high n Achievement. In other words, the children with high n Achievement are taking "moderate risks" and standing where their skill is most likely to pay off in subjective feelings of success. If they stand close to the peg, they are much more likely to throw the ring on as the smoothed probability-of-success curve shows, but they are less likely to get any feelings of achievement satisfaction from doing so. If they stand too far away, they are both much less likely to succeed and more likely to regard success as "luck," than if they stand a moderate distance from the peg. In fact they are behaving like the business-man who acts neither traditionally (no risk) nor like a gambler (extreme risk), but who chooses to operate in a way in which he is most likely to get achievement satisfaction (moderate risk, in this case about one chance in three of succeeding).

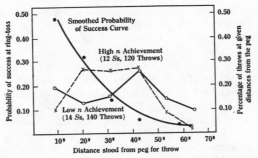

Figure 6.1 Percentage of throws made by 5-year-olds with high and low "doodle" n Achievement at different distances from the peg and smoothed curve of probability of success at those distances. (McClelland, 1958a)

The finding in Fig. 6.1 has been replicated in the United States for college students by Atkinson and Litwin (1960) for a ring-toss game, by Atkinson, Bastian, Earl and Litwin (1960) for a shuffleboard game, and by Litwin again (1958) for a ring-toss game, for pitching pennies into different sized holes, and for pencil maze puzzles of varying degrees of difficulty. In all these situations the subjects with high n Achievement chose to work on tasks of moderate difficulty more often than the subjects with low n Achievement. An attempt was made to check the findings cross-culturally in Germany, Brazil and India, using as subjects the boys studied intensively to discover the "universal" correlates of n Achievement. (See Chapter 2.) Since they were tested in groups, it was not possible to use the ordinary ring-toss or shuffle board games, but a pencil-and-paper modification was adopted in the hope that it would yield the same results.

The boys were presented with a piece of folded paper, asked to draw a circle on it, then to turn it over and place a cross in the center of the circle. Obviously, if the boy drew a very large circle, it would be extremely easy for him to put a cross in the center of it without seeing it, whereas the smaller the circle the harder it would be for him to succeed. The dynamics of the situation were supposed to be analogous to ring toss in which success is easier or harder depending on how far away from the peg a person stands. It was predicted that, as in the ring toss, the boys with high *n* Achievement would choose to draw circles of moderate size, setting a task from which they would gain the most achievement satisfaction from succeeding, whereas the boys with low *n* Achievement would show no consistent preferences. The diameters of the circles were all measured, and the tendency of a boy to choose moderate risk measured by determining the deviation of the diameter of his circle from the average diameter for all boys in his country.[1] The smaller the boy's deviation score, the more he had chosen to draw a circle of average size representing medium difficulty so far as his group of peers was concerned. The correlation of the deviation scores with *n* Achievement was in the predicted direction in all three countries, but reached significance only in Brazil, where it was $-.13$ ($N = 367$, $p < .02$). In Germany, however, the correlation was only $-.001$ ($N = 386$) and in India $-.07$ ($N = 150$).[2] The combined probability does not quite reach the .05 level, so that confirmation of the hypothesis provided by these data is at best weak.[3] On the other hand, the task itself was almost certainly too simple to interest sixteen-year-old boys, and only a single measure from each boy was used so that it might reasonably be argued that a good solid test of the hypothesis was not made. Perhaps the best way of summarizing the situation is that there does seem to be some evidence that boys with high *n* Achievement in other countries choose tasks of moderate difficulty more often and that the relationship would be stronger if less trivial tasks were used, such as those on which the findings had originally been obtained and confirmed in the United States.

So much for risky situations in which skill of the actor is clearly involved. What about betting situations in which the outcome depends entirely on luck? Here the evidence is not so clear-cut. Atkinson, Bastian, Earl and Litwin (1960) found that subjects with high *n* Achievement showed a definite preference for bets under intermediate odds as compared with very short or very long ones. They used the Edwards' betting preference schedule (1953) in which subjects are asked to indicate which of two alternative bets, such as the following, they would prefer: 3/6 to win $600 vs. 5/6 to win $360. In this schedule all the "utilities" (probabilities times amounts to be won) are equivalent and every set of odds from 1/6 to 6/6 is paired with every other set of odds to see which the subject consistently prefers. They found that 53 per cent of their subjects with high *n* Achievement, as compared with only 17 per cent of those with low *n* Achievement preferred intermediate risks (4/6, 3/6, 2/6), once the no-risk options (6/6) preferred most by all types of subjects were discarded. The difference was significant, but the number of subjects was small; it was not significant when the expected payoffs were increased from 30¢

to $300, even though no actual money was involved. Litwin (1958) also found that subjects with high *n* Achievement showed a greater preference for intermediate odds in a horse race game in which the outcome depended not at all on skill, but on the turn of a card. But Littig (1959) has found a quite different trend in a more typical gambling situation in which players are bidding for poker hands and actual money is at stake. Here the subjects with high *n* Achievement definitely and consistently preferred the shortest odds they could get (the safest bets). Thus, in a true gambling situation subjects with high *n* Achievement preferred the highest probability of success. The behavior of the subjects with low *n* Achievement was also particularly interesting. In Littig's words, "these subjects like a long shot and they especially like it when there is a large amount to be won." In this carefully controlled experiment in which betting preferences were measured over a long period of time on the same individuals, the subjects with low *n* Achievement behaved just as many people do in underdeveloped countries. They place small amounts of money on lotteries where they are taking a very long shot at winning a huge prize. The subjects with high *n* Achievement, on the other hand, are reacting like the businessmen in Ambrose Bierce's remark: they don't like pure gambling and show their "disapproval" by choosing the shortest odds they can possibly get.

Littig's results are more in accord with our general theory and the only problem that remains is to explain why in two other experiments the subjects with high *n* Achievement chose intermediate risks in situations where the outcome depended on chance. One likely explanation is that in these experiments the "games of chance" were mixed in with games of skill in an achievement context where the gambling nature of the game was further minimized by the fact that no actual money was involved. Furthermore, it should be remembered that preferences for moderate risks with the Edwards' betting schedule appeared only when the choices of the safest odds had been eliminated. The greater preference that subjects with high *n* Achievement have for situations involving moderate risk in all likelihood appears only when they have some chance of influencing the outcome through their own skills or abilities. In games of pure chance they normally prefer the safest odds they can get.

Atkinson's model of the interaction of n Achievement and risk-taking

Why should subjects with higher *n* Achievement show a preference for tasks of moderate difficulty? So far we have talked in terms of their being able to get more achievement satisfaction in such situations, but Atkinson has described what may be going on much more precisely in the theoretical model illustrated in Table 6.2. He assumes first that "the incentive values of an achievement, i.e., the relative amount of satisfaction to be experienced in any personal accomplishment, is a positive function of the difficulty of the task." Difficulty is represented in the model as decreasing probability of

TABLE 6.2 PREFERENCE AS A JOINT FUNCTION OF MOTIVES TO ACHIEVE (M_a)
PROBABILITY (P) OF SUCCESS AND INCENTIVE VALUE OF SUCCESS (I_s) WHERE
$I_s = (1 - P_s)$.

	Higher n Achievement					Lower n Achievement				
	M_a	$\times$ P_s	$\times$ I_s	$=$	Approach	M_a	$\times$ P_s	$\times$ I_s	$=$	Approach
Task A	8	$\times$ .10	$\times$ .90	$=$	.72	1	$\times$ .10	$\times$ .90	$=$	.09
Task B	8	$\times$ .50	$\times$ .50	$=$	2.00	1	$\times$ .50	$\times$ .50	$=$	.25
Task C	8	$\times$ .90	$\times$ .10	$=$	.72	1	$\times$ .90	$\times$ .10	$=$	.09

After Atkinson, 1957.

success (P_s). Thus in Table 6.2, Task A is difficult (1 chance in 10 of succeeding, or 9 in 10 of failing) whereas Task C is quite easy (9 chances in 10 of succeeding). Incentive value is then assumed to be a simple inverse function of the probability of succeeding, or $1 - P_s$. "When the probability of winning is high—an easy task—the amount of satisfaction experienced in winning is low. When the probability of winning is low—a difficult task—the amount of satisfaction in winning is high." (Atkinson, 1957, p. 298.) He next assumes that "the extent to which motivation is aroused to approach any goal is a joint function of the probability of goal attainment (P_s) and the incentive value or amount of satisfaction accompanying attainment of that goal." Thus the tendency to prefer or approach the difficult Task A for subjects with a high motivation to achieve (M_a) is the product of the probability of success (.10) times the incentive value of success ($1 - P_s$ or .90) times the strength of the motive (e.g., $= 8$) or .72.

From such assumptions it follows, as Table 6.2 demonstrates, (1) that the tendency to prefer or approach a task will be greatest when it is of moderate difficulty and will be less for either very easy or very difficult tasks and (2) that the stronger the motive to achieve the greater the differential preference for tasks of moderate difficulty. A subject with a motive score of 8 has a theoretical preference value for Task B of 2.00 and for Task A of .72 contrasted with values of .25 and .09 for the subject with a motive score of 1. For the latter the difference in "pulling power" of the two tasks might be so small that in a forced choice situation he chooses more or less randomly, whereas for the former the "pull" of Task B is so much greater in absolute terms that he should choose it more often. The model provides a concise description of what appears to be going on, although it may have to be modified in some detail when precise measures of all the variables assumed to enter into the determination of action are available. Already Littig's results show clearly (as Atkinson's first principle implies) that the incentive value of success is only a simple inverse function of probability of success ($1 - P_s$) *in achievement situations*. In a gambling situation the results can best be explained by assuming that incentive value of winning is not $1 - P_s$ but a constant which, when multiplied times probability of winning, yields the obtained preference for shorter odds among subjects with high n Achievement. That is, in Table 6.2, I_s does not equal $1 - P_s$ but 1.00, so that the greatest preference is for the situation represented by "Task C" where the $P_s = .90$, and the least for "Task A" where $P_s = .10$. But the point is that we have now moved from a "task" to a "gambling" situation, the difference between which lies precisely in whether the subject can influence the outcome by his efforts. Thus the lack of fit of Littig's results with the Atkinson model makes good sense: the incentive value of achieving to a person with a strong achievement motive should vary with the difficulty of the task *only* when "winning" at the task can be interpreted as a personal achievement.

Efficiency of performance under different probabilities of success

So far we have been reporting findings that have to do with the *preference* of subjects with high n Achievement for tasks of moderate difficulty. Do they not only prefer them, but work harder and more efficiently at them, than they do at tasks which are extremely easy or extremely difficult? And what about the subjects with low n Achievement? Do they work equally hard under all probabilities of success, or perhaps more effectively when the odds are either for or against them? At first glance, the literature on the relationship of n Achievement to performance appears rather confusing. Sometimes it is significantly associated with better performance (French, 1955, Klauer, 1959, Atkinson and Reitman, 1956) and sometimes not (Miller and Worchel, 1956, Atkinson and Reitman, 1956, and Reitman, 1960). Failure to find significant positive correlations may, of course, be due to a number of factors such as the unreliability of the n Achievement measure and the nature of the incentives in the task situation, but one theme runs throughout the apparently contradictory results that bears directly on our problem. In general n Achievement appears less likely to be positively related to performance when that performance is routine or almost mechanical, such as in putting X's in circles or decoding. On the other hand, high n Achievement appears more likely to be associated with better performance at tasks which require some imagination, mental manipulation, or new ways of putting things together, as in anagrams, the French problem-solving tasks, or complex arithmetic operations (see Wendt, 1955). This generalization, while it has not yet been decisively confirmed in a carefully controlled experiment, tends to support the hypothesis that subjects with high n Achievement tend to do better than subjects with low n Achievement only at nonroutine tasks that require some degree of personal initiative, or even inventiveness, for solution. The incentive value of success is greater in such tasks because they require more of a personal achievement for solution.

Atkinson has also reported some preliminary results which bear more directly on his theoretical model. Using college females as subjects in two tasks (complex arithmetic and putting X's in circles), he found that all his subjects performed better under moderate odds than they did under extremely short or extremely long odds. The odds in the situation were defined for the person by giving her instructions like the following: "You are one of a group of four persons. The three persons in your group with the highest scores will win $2.50. In other words, your chances of winning $2.50 are three out of four." (Atkinson, 1958, p. 290.) In addition to the "three out of four" (3/4) condition which provided the greatest probability of success, other subjects were told that the best two out of a group of four, or one out of a group of three, or one out of a group of 20 would win, so that he set up conditions which provided expectancies of winning of 1/20, 1/3, 1/2, and 3/4. The subjects performed under these conditions as his model (in Table 6.2) would predict. That is, the subjects performed better under moderate chances of winning (1/3 and 1/2) and more poorly under longer (1/20) and shorter (3/4) odds. He further found that the subjects with high n Achievement performed significantly better than the subjects with low n Achievement at longer odds, particularly the 1/3 condition, whereas there was no difference between the two types of subjects at shorter odds (1/2 and 3/4).

A major effort was made to replicate these findings among the adolescent boys in the four countries included in our cross-cultural study—Germany, Brazil, Japan and India. To avoid possible complications from using a routine task like marking X's in circles, only Atkinson's complex arithmetic test was used. Otherwise the instructions for creating various expectancies of winning were the same, except that no money prizes were offered because Atkinson had found that the use of larger money incentives tended to wipe out the effect. The task employed is sometimes referred to as the Pauli arithmetic test in which the subject must sum three numbers with positive or negative signs on one line, then do the same for three numbers on a line below it, and finally subtract the second sum from the first if it is smaller or add it if it is larger. Obviously, the task is complex rather than routine, and requires considerable mental manipulation, since the subject is not allowed to write down any of the intermediate steps in the process. Its use was further dictated by the fact that verbal tasks like anagrams are not so easily adapted to a language like Japanese and the fact that still other tasks cannot easily be performed in groups. Finally, it was expected that simple arithmetic knowledge of the sort needed for solution of these problems would be taught to more or less the same degree all over the world. This expectation turned out to be incorrect in one important particular. While the mean numbers of problems solved in the fifteen minutes allowed did not differ seriously for Germany (mean = 41.10, $SD = 15.93$, $N = 372$), Brazil (mean = 33.69, $SD = 15.00$, $N = 306$), or Japan (mean = 40.92, $SD = 20.30$, $N = 141$), the mean number correct for the Indian students was clearly of a different order of magnitude (mean = 64.63, SD = 27.46, N = 145). Several Indian students solved over 150 of the problems in 15 minutes, for an average of 10 problems a minute, or something over five or six seconds apiece. Such a level of performance far exceeds that obtained in the other countries or in the United States with the same test. Obviously, this kind of arithmetic performance is a highly developed skill in Indian students, as subsequent inquiry among Indian educators confirmed. Consequently, it is doubtful if the task presented the same kind of challenge to ingenuity and the sense of personal accomplishment that it presented in the other countries or in the United States. Rather it would appear to fall clearly in the category of a task calling for highly overlearned routinized skills. At any rate, for whatever reason, the relationships of performance to varying expectancies of winning and to n Achievement scores were somewhat different in India from what they were in the other three countries, and the logical explanation appears to be that the task had a totally different character there.

TABLE 6.3   CORRELATIONS OF n ACHIEVEMENT (GRAPHIC) WITH PERFORMANCE UNDER VARYING EXPECTANCY OF WINNING IN JAPAN, BRAZIL, AND GERMANY

Country		Expectancy of winning (probability)				p value*
		$\frac{1}{20}$	$\frac{1}{3}$	$\frac{1}{2}$	$\frac{3}{4}$	
Japan	N	47	26	26	26	.10
	r	−.16	.01	.28	−.10	
Brazil	N	70	75	81	80	.01
	r	.07	.17	.22	−.14	
Germany	N	88	98	92	94	.17
	r	.10	−.07	−.06	−.05	Combined < .02

* Probability that a difference between the r at $\frac{3}{4}$ and the largest positive r to the left could have arisen in the obtained direction by chance.

Table 6.3 presents the results for the other three countries in terms of the correlations of graphic n Achievement scores (see Appendix IV) with number of problems correctly solved under varying expectancies of winning ("odds groups"). The number of subjects in each condition is considerably larger than in Atkinson's study, but this advantage is probably outweighed by the fact that conditions of testing were much more variable in the several groups tested in each country. Subjects belonging to various odds groups were always tested together by the simple expedient of stapling different instruction sheets to the arithmetic test telling them how many people were in the group and how many could be expected to "win." It is not really known how meaningful or effective these statements were in the various countries because obviously they are pretty vague. The boys might well have wondered who the "others" were that they were competing with and what, for example, three out of four of them would "win," since there was nothing in the way of a money prize. Nevertheless the correlations in Table 6.3, although small,[3, 4] do show a rather consistent pattern. In all three countries they are negative at the shortest odds, indicating that those with low n Achievement do better when the chances of winning are greatest; then in Japan and Brazil they move to a positive value when there is a 50-50 chance of winning (1/2) and fall off regularly thereafter. In other words, the subjects with high n Achievement perform better than those with low n Achievement in these countries under moderate risk, or expectancy of winning, but their superiority declines as the risk gets more extreme. In Germany, however, the superiority of the subjects with high n Achievement shows up only under the longest odds (1/20). So only the most general hypothesis appears to be confirmed by these data, namely, that high n Achievement will lead to better performance at some degree of challenge greater than that provided by almost certainty (3 chances out of 4) of winning.[5]

The particular pattern of correlations could, of course, be obtained in a number of different ways—by subjects with low n Achievement doing more poorly under longer odds, or by subjects with high n Achievement doing better under longer odds, or by some irregular fluctuations in the efficiency of either group. Figure 6.2 represents our best estimate of how

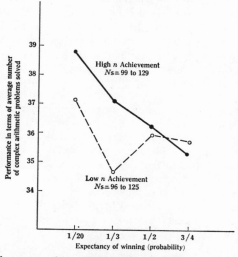

Figure 6.2 Performance of boys high and low in graphic n Achievement under varying expectancies of winning (Japan, Brazil and Germany combined).

the two groups were responding to varying expectancies of winning. They were obtained by breaking the n Achievement (graphic) distributions at the median separately in the three countries and pooling the scores obtained by the high n Achievement and low n Achievement subjects in all three countries. Unfortunately, none of the differences between the two curves or between two points on the same curve is significant, despite the large number of cases, and an over-all analysis of variance is not really practicable because of unevenness in subclass numbers. Furthermore, the results do not conform particularly well to what might be expected on the basis of the correlations in Table 6.3, probably because of the necessarily coarse grouping of subjects into the high and low n Achievement categories. On the basis of Table 6.3 one would expect the largest difference in the performance of the two groups to occur at a 1/2 expectancy of winning, whereas in Fig. 6.2 the largest difference appears at the 1 out of 3 odds.

Nevertheless, the following analysis permits us to draw a simple conclusion from Fig. 6.2. Suppose we set up the hypothesis that performance gets better the longer the odds under which the subjects are working; then the mean score at 1/20 should be greater than the mean at 1/3, which should be greater than the mean at 1/2, which should be greater than the mean at 3/4. There are six possible comparisons of means in each country, each of which can be classified as either conforming to the hypothesis or not. In Germany and Brazil the pattern is clear. In nine out of twelve comparisons between the mean scores for the subjects with high n Achievement, the means are greater under longer odds, whereas in only two out of twelve comparisons for the "lows" are the means greater under longer odds (chi-square corrected $= 6.04$, $p < .02$). In Japan there was no difference in the response of the subjects with high and low n Achievement to decreased expectancy of winning (i.e., longer odds). Both groups tended to perform better under longer odds; in 4 out of 6 comparisons for the "highs" and 5 out of 6 comparisons for the "lows," average performance under the longer odds was better. Since Japanese boys were significantly higher in n Achievement than the Germans or Brazilians, either by the graphic or verbal measure (see Chapter 8), this result is not really inconsistent. Many subjects classified as low in n Achievement in Japan would have been classified as high in n Achievement in Brazil or Germany, particularly the latter. Yet we could not divide the subjects into high and low n Achievement in terms of the whole sample because of between-country differences in testing conditions. Yet because in 13 out of 18 comparisons in three countries the subjects with high n Achievement performed better under the longer odds, it seems highly likely that the curve plotted in Fig. 6.2 for the high n Achievement subjects represents the "true" state of affairs. They perform better and better the greater the "challenge" of the task and the harder it is for them to win. The curve for the low n Achievement subjects is somewhat more problematical and in particular is distorted at the 1/20 odds by the excellent performance of the Japanese "lows" (who were probably not really low on a cross-national basis). The best guess as to the real shape of the low n Achievement curve is that it is a straight line showing no particular trend in response to varying expectancies of winning.

These results are not in conformity with Atkinson's previous results or with his theoretical model in that they do not show a dropping off in performance at the longest odds, either in the group as a whole or in the high n Achievement group in particular. The inconsistency may be due to the fact that the quoted odds had different meanings in other countries or the fact that we used male rather than female subjects. Fortunately, however, Atkinson's results and the present ones do not differ in one important respect. In both experiments subjects with high n Achievement performed better under longer odds than subjects with low n Achievement, whereas there is no difference between the two (or the situation is actually reversed) under shorter odds. Chances of succeeding of the order of 1/3 and 1/2 present more of a challenge to work harder for subjects with high n Achievement not only in the United States but in Germany, Brazil and Japan as well. It is not entirely clear what happens at still longer odds but this seems to be a question of greater importance for psychological theory than for the understanding of entrepreneurial behavior.

Perceived probability of success

We have demonstrated that subjects with high n Achievement prefer tasks involving some objective risk and work harder at such tasks. Does this make them suited to be better business entrepreneurs? Do businessmen like to take risks? Do they see themselves as taking greater risks? As a matter of fact they do not. Sutton quotes an interesting passage from the autobiography of Alfred P. Sloan, describing the decision of General Motors to continue the production of Chevrolets after World War I, after expert advice had been sought:

"The most illuminating recommendation was that the whole Chevrolet operation should be liquidated. There was no chance to make it a profitable business. We could not hope to compete. I was much upset because I feared the prestige of the office might overcome our arguments to the contrary, so I went to Mr. Pierre Du Pont. . . . We urged . . . that it was an insult to say that we could not compete with anyone. It was a case of ability and hard work. He listened most patiently and finally said, 'Forget the report. We will go ahead and see what we can do.' Mr. Du Pont was always that way, he had the courage of his convictions. *Facts were the only things that counted*."

Sutton goes on to say that "the logical reader can only conclude that had Mr. Du Pont been as devoted to the facts as Mr. Sloan alleges, he would have been paralyzed in indecision, or even more, he would certainly have discontinued the production of Chevrolets." (Sutton, 1954, p. 23.) Although the objective risk of continuing to produce Chevrolets must have been considerable, neither Sloan nor Du Pont felt, at least in retrospect, that they were taking any great risk. Sawyer calls particular attention to a similar phenomenon which he calls "the entrepreneurial accelerator." He argues that certain factors in 19th century American culture "repeatedly induced entrepreneurs and investors to overrespond to existing market stimuli and in effect overleap existing economic realities in the scale of their plans and in the scope and timing of investment decisions; and that in the special circumstances of 19th century America their individual and collective overestimations operated to accelerate the processes of growth and often, in varying measure, produced the result that, *ex post*, made 'economic' their initial overestimates. . . . I emphasize the nonrational component, for it is the increment over and beyond any rational estimate of the situation that I am concerned to pursue." (Sawyer, 1954, p. 4.)

What both Sutton and Sawyer are stressing is the famous "self-confidence" of the businessman, his ability to believe that he can do better than the facts warrant. Sawyer is going farther and arguing that possibly self-confidence is an essential component of the entrepreneurial role in a strictly economic sense in that it leads people to take ventures that taken individually would not be economically sound but taken together in large numbers may turn out to be. A good case in point is the building of railroads across the American continent: when they were built they could hardly be justified in economic terms, as the subsequent ruin of many stockholders demonstrated. Furthermore, they would never have been economically justified if the country had not been "swarming," to use Sawyer's terminology, with thousands of small entrepreneurs who repeatedly overestimated their chances of success, but who collectively managed to settle and develop the West while many of them individually were failing. If these men were taking risks, they often hardly realized it subjectively in their confidence that with their skill and present opportunities they would win out in the end.

In psychological terminology the variable under discussion is known as the "perceived probability of success." And once again we have fairly good evidence that subjects with high n Achievement tend to perceive their probability of success as greater, particularly when there are no facts to justify their estimates. Atkinson originally called attention to the fact that subjects who are high in n Achievement "tend to feel that their chances of winning are actually better than the stated odds." (1958, p. 299.) For example, they "state higher levels of expectation for performace of a task at which they have had no previous experience" (Pottharst, 1955), and when the objective evidence is conflicting as to how well they are doing in a course, they tend to overestimate more the grade they will get in it than do subjects with low n Achievement (McClelland *et al.*, 1953). Atkinson, Bastian, Earl and Litwin (1959) asked their subjects to estimate how many of the 125 people in their class they expected to beat at a shuffle board game they were playing. The question was obviously quite open-ended because the answer involved picking a number all the way from 1 to 124. They found that about two thirds of the subjects with high n Achievement felt that they would do better than average (beat more than half the people in the class), whereas only one third of the people with low n Achievement felt that they would do better than average, the difference being highly significant. Furthermore, Litwin (1958) found the same tendency in an experiment purporting to measure extrasensory perception. He told his subjects that he had a deck of special cards, a certain number of which he had designated as "winning cards." The subjects were to try to guess when a winning card would turn up. The experimenter would concentrate on a card and attempt to send them a "message" as to whether it was the winning or losing card and the subject then simply circled the word "win" or the word "lose." "The purpose of this game was to attempt to measure subjective probability of success when no cues about the objective probabilities were present." Litwin found that his subjects with high n Achievement in this unstructured achievement situation tended to circle the word "win" more often than the subjects with low n Achievement.

However, there are situations in which subjects with high n Achievement do not overestimate subjective probability of success. When they have pretty good knowledge on the basis of past performance how they will do in a course, they base their estimates on that knowledge (McClelland *et al.*, 1953). Furthermore, Litwin (1958) found that in the ring-toss game when his subjects were asked to estimate how many hits they would make from each line *after practice*, they did not show a greater perceived probability of success than the subjects with low n Achievement. The difference between these situations and the earlier ones seems to lie in the greater number of cues in the latter situations on which the subjects can base a realistic estimate of how well they will do. In other words, the more unknown the situation which demands their achievement, the more self-confident they are as contrasted with the subjects with low n Achievement. But as reality cues become available, they tend to base their judgments on these cues. They are not impractical "dreamers" overestimating their chances of success at everything; instead they rely on facts so far as they are available, and then fall back on generalized self-confidence. In this respect they are behaving just the way Sloan and Du Pont behaved, at least as Sloan perceived the situation.

The difference can readily be explained in terms of Atkinson's model (Table 6.2). When there is accurate knowledge of the difficulty of the task for them, they choose moderate risks or perceive themselves as able to do a little better than they have done. When there is no real knowledge of how well they can do, it is as if difficulty (P_s) and hence incentive value of success $(1 - P_s)$ are based on generalized expectations, divorced from their own performance potential. Further it is as if this generalized knowledge of difficulty (P_s) continues to determine incentive value (I_s) but does not itself enter into the equation in Table 6.2, so that the resultant approach value is a simple product of $M_a \times I_s$. Since M_a is higher for the subjects with high n Achievement, they should be more self-confident, or show a greater approach tendency whatever the perceived difficulty of the task. When they know better how well they can do, the part of the P_s value affected by their performance potential enters in, and their preferences become more modest and realistic. Obviously such an interpretation requires modification of the Atkinson model in the direction of splitting the P_s factor into a component based on general knowledge of the difficulty of tasks and another component based on knowledge of one's own competence at a particular task. The formula would have to be revised somewhat along the following lines:

$$\text{Approach} = M_a \times P_{s_1} \times I_s$$

$$\text{where} \quad I_s = 1 - \frac{P_{s_1} + P_{s_2}}{2}$$

and P_{s_1} = probability that I will succeed, based on my past performance

P_{s_2} = general estimate of difficulty of the task

Thus when P_{s_1} is unknown, approach becomes in effect a simple function of M_a and P_{s_2}.

One other finding deserves mention. Subjects with high n Achievement do not overestimate their chances of winning in a gambling game (Littig, 1959). The reason must be different from the one just discussed, since obviously it is not the presence of reality factors that keeps them from being overconfident. Instead it seems to be just the reverse—the absence of any basis in reality for making an estimate of future winnings. Once again this serves to underline the fact that the overconfidence of the man with high n Achievement is based on his conviction that he can modify the outcome of an uncertain situation by his own personal achievements. If the outcome depends on luck (as in gambling) rather than skill, he has no basis for overconfidence. If the outcome is clearly predictable on the basis of his past performance, he also has no basis for overconfidence. It is only in relatively new situations where the outcome depends on him that his overconfidence shows up most clearly.

The fact that he warps the perceived probability of success may also explain better why he works harder under longer objective odds. To return to Table 6.2 again, it is clear that if preference is a function of *subjective* probability of success times the incentive value of success, then in Task A, the most difficult one, subjects with higher n Achievement may actually estimate their probability of success at .30, say, rather than the objective probability of .10. In such a case the attraction to Task A would have a theoretical value of 2.16 rather than .72, and they would be more attracted to the most difficult task than they are to the one of moderate difficulty (Task B). In some such way it would be quite easy to account in terms of Atkinson's model for the regular increase in performance of the subjects with high n Achievement as a function of decreasing expectancy of winning (Fig. 6.2). But whatever the final explanation in psychological terms of their behavior, the subjects with high n Achievement certainly act, point for point, here as elsewhere in the risk-taking area, as they should if they are to be successful entrepreneurs as theoretically described by economists and sociologists.

(b) ENERGETIC AND/OR NOVEL INSTRUMENTAL ACTIVITY

The second component of the entrepreneurial role frequently mentioned is energetic, innovating activity (see Table 6.1). Certainly businessmen, especially American businessmen, are described as conspicuously overactive. Starch found that two and one-half times as many top executives "had records of working hard and long hours" as lower level executives (Roe, 1956, p. 184). Although they give no precise comparative data, the editors of *Fortune* in *The Executive Life* (1956) conclude that "executives are working as hard as they ever did. It is difficult to see how they could possibly work harder." In their sample they report an average work week of some 57 to 60 hours, which "can easily go to seventy or eighty hours" in an emergency (p. 5). But men in other occupations work long hours, too. Do business executives really work longer hours than doctors, lawyers, or even civil servants? Is working long hours an *essential* component of the entrepreneurial role, or is it characteristic of all more successful people? Sutton *et al.* contend that the overactivity of the businessman can, in fact, be derived from a theoretical analysis of the strains inherent in the uncertainty with which he has to deal. "The enormous power ascribed to executive action by the definition of the businessman's responsibility seems to imply that in any situation there must be something he can do. Hence the executive's reaction in the event of strain is not to evade action, but to 'do something.' " (1956, p. 335.) Nevertheless, it is still not clear that this characteristic can be ascribed to the role as such or to the philosophy of Americans who fill it. Certainly it appears to be a general reaction of Americans when in difficulty to "do something," whereas in other cultures, the common reaction to strain or difficulty is to "do nothing." Contrast, for instance, the Navaho (Kluckhohn and Leighton, 1947).

The case for innovational activity is somewhat better. It can be said with much greater confidence that the entrepreneurial role involves almost by definition doing things in a new and better way. In fact, this is the chief way in which the distinction can be made between holding entrepreneurial status and fulfilling the entrepreneurial role. A businessman who does not innovate but simply behaves in traditional ways is not, strictly speaking, an entrepreneur as normally defined. (Lazarsfeld, 1959; Redlich, 1958; Hoselitz, 1952.)

How about the subjects with high n Achievement? Do they always work harder and show more "innovational" activity? The picture provided by the evidence reviewed in the previous sections is not one of n Achievement leading to harder work under all conditions. On the contrary, people with high n Achievement appear to work harder only when it counts for personal achievement or, more precisely, when there is a chance that personal efforts will make a difference in the outcome. Specifically, they do not work harder under all probabilities of winning, but only when there is some challenge in the situation, some chance of losing. Furthermore, they do not work harder at routine tasks, but only at tasks which appear to require some degree of "mental manipulation," originality, or a new angle of approach for successful solution.

Consider some further data presented in Table 6.4, in which the subjects high in n Achievement are contrasted with those high in "optimism." The optimism score was obtained by summing the degree of disagreement of the boys in the four countries studied to the following four items which, according to a previous factor analysis (see Strodtbeck, 1958a), had appeared as a well-defined factor both in the United States and Germany:

Planning only makes a person unhappy, since your plans hardly ever work out anyway.
There is no such thing as a really permanent friendship. Your friends change with circumstances.
There are some people like great artists and musicians who can be forgiven for not being considerate of others, kind to the poor, etc.
When a man is born, the success he is going to have is already in the cards, so he might as well accept it and not fight against it.

A cluster analysis of these four items showed that the six intercorrelations among them were almost invariably positive (23 out of 24 for the four countries), the mean intercorrelations being .14 for Japan, .24 for Germany, .17 for Brazil, and .11 for India. In fact, of the 20 items in the questionnaire given the boys, these were the only four which consistently covaried. A boy who disagrees with these items is less resigned to fate, more progressive or optimistic about the future. He believes in planning, and fighting against fate.

Now he is the boy, interestingly enough, who is obviously a good, hard-working, outstanding pupil, as Table 6.4 shows. In all countries, he

TABLE 6.4 CORRELATIONS OF n ACHIEVEMENT (GRAPHIC) AND OPTIMISM SCORES WITH PERFORMANCE, OUTSIDE ACTIVITIES, AND LEADERSHIP PROMISE

Country	Complex arithmetic performance under all conditions		Number of outside activities		Votes received as most likely to succeed	
	n Ach	Opti-mism	n Ach	Opti-mism	n Ach	Opti-mism
Japan (N = 140-150)	−.01	+.35	−.15	+.11*	−.04	+.19*
Germany (N = 367)	+.01	+.08	−.15	+.08*	−.01	+.12*
Brazil (N = 386)	+.05	+.14	−.05	+.07*		
India (N = 151)				+.08*		
Combined p, $df.$ = 2-4	NS	<.001	<.01	<.05	NS	<.01

Correlations in *italics* are significant at $p < .05$ or better.
* Average correlations of the four items in the optimism scale.

solved more arithmetic problems irrespective of the odds under which he was working (1/20 to 3/4); he is involved in more outside activities (hobbies, clubs, etc.), and in the two countries where the measure was taken, he was voted by his classmates the most likely to be "a leading member of the community in thirty years." In comparison, the boy with high n Achievement makes a poor showing: he is marked in general only by a tendency to participate in *fewer* outside activities and by a tendency to work harder only when there is an achievement challenge in the situation (Fig. 6.2). A careful check was made of other variables in the questionnaire to see if any of them related to performance in the same way that n Achievement did, but without success. Apparently n Achievement, and only n Achievement, at least within the limits of the variables measured, relates to performance in this peculiar way.

The difference in the characteristics of the two types of boys seems quite analogous to the distinction that Shils has made between the efficient and the economical person, or that Hoselitz has made between the manager and the entrepreneur. That is, the optimistic boys appear to be conscientious, efficient, forward-looking, *managerial* types. They may well be the ones described by Shils as bureaucrats primarily concerned with efficiency. In his words, "the bureaucratic variant of ambition—namely, efficiency—is not conducive to economic progress. Ambition . . . involves a boundless aspiration; its goal is not fixed in quantity at a particular point. . . . The more that can be achieved, the better. . . . Each triumph leads to another goal a little further off." (Shils, 1958, p. 8.) The terminology is a little different from what we have been employing here, but it is easy to translate in terms of n Achievement. Ambition describes the goal of the person with high *n* Achievement precisely because what he is interested in is something that will give him achievement satisfaction. As soon as he solves one problem, he loses interest in it because he can no longer get achievement satisfaction from it (see Table 6.2). If there is no challenge, he doesn't work so hard: in this sense, he would make a poor bureaucrat. He must constantly be seeking novelty or new solutions to old problems because that is the only way he can get a sense of personal achievement. According to Atkinson's model in Table 6.2, as the task becomes easier and easier or more routine its incentive value declines for the person with higher *n* Achievement until it theoretically fails to arouse any approach motivation in him at all.

It is obvious, of course, that any country needs some of both kinds of boys—the efficient, conscientious ones and those with high *n* Achievement. The chief contribution of the research findings in Table 6.4 is the way in which they demonstrate that there are two distinct types of achievers, just as Shils has argued: the person who works hard and efficiently at everything more or less indiscriminately and the person who works hard only at those things which because of their challenge will give him a sense of personal accomplishment. It is presumably because such things don't "count" that boys with higher *n* Achievement list fewer outside activities. The two achievement syndromes are quite unrelated in these four countries, the correlations between the optimism and *n* Achievement scores being $-.12$ ($N = 150$) for Japan, $-.02$ ($N = 386$) for Germany, $+.02$ ($N = 367$) for Brazil, and $-.06$ ($N = 150$) for India (verbal *n* Achievement). There is some evidence, however, that in the United States the two syndromes are positively related, since boys with high *n* Achievement do report more outside activities in college and at least in one experiment (Rosen, 1959) disagreed significantly more often with one of the items in the optimism scale ("when a man is born . . ."). There is no reason, of course, why a particular boy should not be high on both variables or why in a particular country they shouldn't be closely associated. However, they are conceptually and empirically distinct and apparently have quite different consequences for society, the one leading to conscientious performance and the other to the innovating activity essential to the business entrepreneur. The fact that the American businessman is so hyperactive, if in fact he is more so than other Americans, would not then be considered an essential part of the entrepreneurial role, but either the result of a general American philosophy of life or of the fact that the *optimism, conscientiousness* variable tends to be positively associated with *n* Achievement in America.

(c) INDIVIDUAL RESPONSIBILITY

The entrepreneurial role has also generally been assumed to imply individual responsibility. In fact some people would define an entrepreneur as he who is ultimately responsible for making a decision, although it is recognized of course that decisions of varying complexity are made at all levels of responsibility. As Sutton puts it, "The key definitions for the businessman seem to center around the concept of *responsibility*. . . . Businessmen have not shied away from the responsibility implied in Emerson's famous definition of a business as the lengthening shadow of a man. They have readily brushed aside complications and assigned crucial importance to the decisions of the guiding executives. . . . Responsibility of this sort implies individualism. It is not tolerable unless it embraces both credit for successes and blame for failures, and leaves the individual free to claim or accept the consequences, whatever they may be." (Sutton, 1954, pp. 21, 22, 25.) There is a sense, of course, in which such a situation is ideally suited to the needs of a man with high *n* Achievement. All our evidence reviewed to date points to the fact that he wants to operate in a situation where he can get a sense of personal achievement. He is conservative in games of chance, more daring in games of skill, overestimates his chances of doing well, works harder under competition, etc.

Yet there is another issue involved here which centers around the issue of "selfishness versus altruism" or working for oneself versus working for others. How "free" must the entrepreneur be in making his decisions? American ideology has tended to stress a large amount of freedom and individual responsibility because of the history of the owner-entrepreneur who did everything for himself in the development of Western capitalism. Yet the Japanese case, already cited, suggests that entrepreneurs can still function quite successfully with much less freedom in decision-making. According to Pelzel (1954), they have individual responsibility only within the shop for production, being quite dependent on others for capital, supplies and sales. In the Western capitalist sense, they are working "for themselves" only in a very restricted sense. This is even truer of the Russian executive (Granick, 1960).

The problem may be clarified by considering what happens when people with high *n* Achievement work for themselves as contrasted with when they are working for others. Data already presented in Chapter 3 provide us with a clue. In the cross-cultural study of preliterate tribes, it was found that the cultures with high *n* Achievement did not stress private as opposed to public ownership more than those with low *n* Achievement. The results of two experimental studies point to the same conclusion (de Charms, 1956, and French, 1958). In both experiments subjects were assembled in groups to work on a common task. French's instructions are typical: she gave each of the members of the group some parts of a story to be assembled. In some of her groups she arranged it so that the individual could submit his own solution to the total task after discussion with the other members, and in other groups she permitted only one final solution to be given *by the group*, to which each person could contribute. In the first condition the subject could get individual credit for successful effort, and in the second condition he could get credit only indirectly to the extent that he had contributed to a successful solution given by the whole group. Under these two different orientations there was absolutely no difference in the efficiency with which the subjects with high n Achievement worked; they worked just as hard for a group goal as they did for an individual goal. De Charms (1956) reports substantially the same results.

But note that in the task the individuals were still free to decide how they would work on or discuss their part of the total task. The difference in treatment was not in terms of *responsibility for action*, but in terms of whether the person was working for himself or for others. Apparently the subjects with high n Achievement are not so interested in public recognition of their individual success that they must work for themselves in order to be sure to get it. On the other hand, they do need some measure of how well they are doing (see below) and they do need to be able to make the decisions as to what is to be done or they can feel no satisfaction in success. The subjects with high n Achievement would probably have done less well if they had been told exactly what to do rather than who they were working for—themselves or the group, for several studies have shown either directly or indirectly that they do not respond positively to suggestions from others as to what they should do, or think, or believe (McClelland et al., 1953; de Charms et al., 1955). In situations evoking conformity from others, they are apt not to go along.

The evidence is not as directly to the point as it might be, but it strongly suggests that the *achievement satisfaction arises from having initiated the action that is successful*, rather than from public recognition for an individual accomplishment. The distinction is an extremely important one so far as the theory of business enterprise is concerned, because it has been so often and so emphatically stated that to be in business for oneself is necessary to keep an entrepreneur really "on his toes." To be sure, the hard-working executives for large U.S. corporations or for Russian state-owned corporations would seem to contradict such a belief. But here we have evidence that permits us to restate the issue more precisely. If we are correct in our belief that behaving in an entrepreneurial way is practically an alternative way of saying that a person has high n Achievement, then it is true that the individual must retain some individual freedom and responsibility for generating and choosing among courses of action if he is to get any achievement satisfaction, but it is not true that he must therefore work for himself rather than some group enterprise. Individual responsibility for action and working for oneself must not be confused, although they often go together. A man may get achievement satisfaction from having contributed to the success of a group enterprise, so long as it is he who made some of the decisions contributing to a successful outcome and he therefore has some way of telling how well he has done.

(d) KNOWLEDGE OF RESULTS OF ACTIONS

An entrepreneur ordinarily has definite concrete knowledge as to whether he has done a good job, or made a series of correct decisions. "The focusing of a business firm's activities on well-defined, tangible ends, such as the profitable manufacture and sale of piston rings or toothbrushes, implies a focus on the *concrete outcome* of complicated processes of action. Businessmen seem to mean something like this when they stress that business is 'practical.' " (Sutton, 1954, p. 18.) "In contrast to such organizations as governments and universities, the prime criteria of business achievement are relatively definite and tangible. These standards include profitability, percentage control of the market, size of firm, and rate of growth." (Sutton *et al.*, 1956, p. 328.) A person acting in an entrepreneurial capacity almost by definition cannot avoid knowing in concrete terms how well he has done—in the United States, in terms of profits and sales, in the Soviet Union, in terms of whether he has met his production quota or not.

Parsons (1949) has also emphasized that in other professions as well there are definite criteria of achievement. The doctor knows whether his patients get well or not, the lawyer whether or not he wins his case. However, a teacher, a clergyman, or a civil servant may have only the most general kind of feedback as to how well he has accomplished what he set out to do. (In fact, a university professor may often wonder, meeting his students years later, whether he taught them anything at all!) In such cases a man must often be satisfied with the conviction that he has acted as he should have acted according to the established traditions of his occupation, or according to the norms generally approved at the time. But he cannot have the kind of definite concrete feedback that the businessman often has in the form of quantified knowledge of profitability, percentage control of the market, rate of growth, etc.

From the psychological point of view, it does not automatically follow that all kinds of people like to have concrete knowledge of results of their choices of action. Such knowledge is a source of anxiety because it cuts both ways: it provides not only proof of success but also inescapable evidence of failure. Consequently, some people ought to prefer functioning in an occupation in which a person can rest assured that he is doing a good job if he follows established traditions closely. To want more definite feedback is to run a greater risk of being wrong. Contrast a businessman and a priest, for example. A businessman can operate according to the best established business practices—good personnel policies, good sales policy, efficient production procedures, etc.—and still fail. Despite doing everything "correctly," his product may not sell or may not bring in sufficient return to keep the business going. His success is determined by "results," not by following established practices. A priest, on the other hand, knows only that he is being a better priest if he obeys more rigorously the rules of his profession, or more scrupulously follows its prescribed rituals. He cannot "fail" in the same concrete sense that the businessman can.

By this time it should be no surprise to discover that people with high n Achievement have been shown to perform significantly better under well controlled experimental conditions when they have positive and definite feedback as to how well they are doing. In the experiment described earlier, French arranged for two different kinds of feedback for her groups of subjects working on a common task. After the subjects had been working for a while she stopped them and introduced a two-minute discussion period for half of them with the words, "This group is working very efficiently." She then drew their attention to various specific behaviors displayed previously by members of the group that were useful in solving the problem, such as "reading off all cards immediately, trying to rough out possible plots, making use of grammatical cues, identifying characters in the story, etc." (French, 1958, p. 403.) For the other half of the subjects her introductory phrase was, "This group works very well together." "The specific behaviors mentioned included: praising each other for making good suggestions, giving everyone a chance to contribute, not becoming impatient with poor suggestions, failing to argue or keeping arguments friendly, etc." (p. 404). She found that her subjects high in n Achievement worked subsequently more efficiently in the "task feedback" condition than they did in the "feeling feedback" condition. Definite knowledge of correct methods of solving the problem facilitated their subsequent performance, whereas knowledge that they were behaving nicely and properly according to the best rules of cooperative interaction did not. Furthermore, the reverse was true of the subjects high in n Affiliation: they later worked more efficiently after "feeling feedback" than they did after "task feedback." In still another experiment, French (1956) has demonstrated that subjects with high n Achievement will choose an expert over a friend as a working partner, whereas the reverse is true of subjects with high n Affiliation. The evidence is strong that the person with high n Achievement wants problem-solutions more than friendly interaction.

Quite independent confirmation of his interest in concrete feedback comes from a totally different source. Moss and Kagan (1961) report in an important longitudinal study of n Achievement that in boys it is highly correlated, both in adolescence ($r = .31$) and young adulthood ($r = .63$) with rated mechanical achievement—or the "degree to which the subject attempted to master mechanical skills and manifested involvement in activities such as carpentry, construction of model vehicles, engines and motors and craft work." The significance of this finding in the present context is readily apparent: construction, mechanical or carpentering activities ordinarily give excellent knowledge of results. If a boy is trying to build a tower or make a table, the object itself "tells him," so to speak, how well he has done. The tower either stands firmly, leans or falls, the table likewise. There is every theoretical reason to suppose that if subjects with high n Achievement like situations with direct feedback as to how well they are doing, they should be drawn to mechanical or constructive activities in which they have a chance to show *objectively* how well they can do, as this study shows. We will return to the question of whether this mechanical interest is present in business executives and important for economic development in the next chapter.

For the present, we may conclude that the person with high n Achievement is oriented, as the businessman must be, toward concrete feedback on how well he is doing and should therefore be happier and perform better in the entrepreneurial role.

The "Profit" Motive and the Achievement Motive

Knowledge of achievement for businessmen is nearly always expressed in money terms. In fact, as Marx and Engels observed years ago in *The Communist Manifesto,* growing specialization in the economy, as represented, say, in the factory system, tends to destroy the *intrinsic* (nonmonetary) worth of what is being done. The "dignity of labor" of the traditional artisan is lost. Instead, achievement is measured by the one simple quantitative standard of how much money it is worth. The "money value of labor" replaced its "intrinsic" value. As Sutton *et al.* put it, by quantitative money criteria "pills are as good as poetry, and a hat factory may be more successful than a book store. A firm making sewer pipes, cheap dresses or artificial flowers, may be more successful than one producing elegant china." (1956, p. 328.) Since businessmen had obviously shifted their concern from intrinsic worth to money worth, Marx and other economists endowed man with a psychological characteristic known as the "profit motive." The capitalist, at any rate, was pictured as being driven by greed, by the necessity of making money or keeping up his rate of profit.

That such an assumption is a typical oversimplification of rational or armchair psychology has recently begun to be realized by historians in particular who have studied the lives of actual business entrepreneurs in the nineteenth century. Oddly enough, many of these men did not seem to be motivated primarily by a desire for money as such or what it would buy. If they had been, many of them ought to have quit working sooner, after they had made all the money they could possibly use. Many others should not have risked large sums of money they had accumulated by ploughing savings back into further business expansion. Still others, the Quakers and Dissenters in England, for example, must have had a very peculiar kind of interest in money indeed, since they were prevented by religious scruples from spending it in any of the many delightful ways employed by the continental nobility at the time, for example. Furthermore, a little comparative study has tended to throw some doubt on the importance of the "profit motive" as such. Who could reasonably argue that the capitalist of England or America, for example, had a corner on greed or the desire to make money? Certainly the Italian nobility or the Greek trader was just as interested, if not more so, in making money as the Anglo-Saxon capitalist. Why then didn't Greece and Italy or many other such countries develop as rapidly as northern Europe or the United States? Or to consider some underdeveloped countries today, it would be hard indeed to argue that the money lenders of India, for example, have a lesser desire to make money than British capitalists of the nineteenth century, yet the money lenders' "profit motive" has so far had nothing like the effect on the Indian economy that it is supposed to have had in England according to Marxian and other economic theorists.

Furthermore, on the positive side, if one is to believe what the Western entrepreneurs said their motives were, they were very often interested in such generalized achievement goals as bringing about the Kingdom of God on earth more rapidly, improving the general social welfare of mankind, perfecting themselves in the eyes of God, mastering "Brute Nature," or extending the influence of their nation (Wilson, 1954). Perhaps they were rationalizing an unconscious greed, perhaps even deceiving themselves as well as others. But it is at least interesting to the psychologist to observe that some of the most successful "empire builders" were apparently among those most deceived as to what their motives were, whereas those who were most openly and honestly devoted to accumulating money often appear to have contributed somewhat less to the general economic development of the country.

Yet obviously no one would want to argue that these men had no interest in profitability. That interest can now be understood, not in terms of the naive psychology of the "profit motive," but in terms of a need for Achievement which is interested in profitability precisely because it gives definite knowledge of how competent one is. As expressed by Sutton *et al.*, "Personal money income plays a highly important role in our society as a *symbol* of achievement. A man with a large income is likely to gain respect —not because of the income itself but because of the presumption that it is an index of his importance or competence." (1956, p. 331.) But so far this is only speculation, a reasonable hypothesis. What evidence is there that people with high n Achievement behave towards money as we have argued that businessmen do? Are they interested in it, not for its own sake, but as a measure of their achievement?

On the first point the evidence is quite clear, at least as far as American students are concerned. If they are high in n Achievement, offering them money incentives makes them work no harder and, in fact, may even lower their performance slightly. The reverse seems to be true of subjects with low n Achievement. For example, Atkinson and Reitman (1956) measured arithmetic performance under an "Achievement" orientation and also under a "Multi-incentive" orientation, in which the subjects were told the following: "Since we are interested in seeing your very best performance when you are actually putting out, we are going to award a prize of five dollars to the person having the highest score on each of the tasks. So you could stand to walk off with ten dollars for your efforts today." When there was no money reward, the subjects with high n Achievement did better than the subjects with low n Achievement, as is usually the case. However, when the money reward was introduced, they fell off somewhat in performance while the subjects with low n Achievement improved so that there was no net difference in the performance of the "highs" and "lows" when a money reward was offered. Atkinson reports (1958, p. 294) a similar effect in another experiment: when a financial incentive was increased from $1.25 to $2.50 a difference in performance favoring those with high n Achievement was wiped out. Finally Douvan (1958, p. 513) found that offering a ten-dollar reward had quite different effects on the n Achievement scores of senior high school students from middle as contrasted with working class backgrounds. After they had been made to fail in an achievement situation, the n Achievement scores of the middle class students were definitely higher than those of working class students provided no material reward was offered. However, when a ten-dollar prize had been offered for the best performance, the working class students showed just as high n Achievement scores after failure as did the middle class students. In other words, subjects normally high in n Achievement (those from the middle class) were not influenced by the introduction of a ten-dollar prize, but those normally low in n Achievement (those from the working classes) were definitely influenced by the introduction of such a reward. All three studies point to the same conclusion: people with high n Achievement are not influenced much by money rewards; they are interested in achievement. People with low n Achievement, on the other hand, are influenced by money and can be made to work harder for money or other such external incentives. (See also Table 2.1 above which deals with the same point.)

As for the second issue—the value of money as a measure of success— some data collected by Litwin (1958) and presented in Fig. 6.3 appear quite definitive. In a ring-toss game he asked his subjects to state how much money reward a person should get (up to one dollar) for making a "ringer" at successive distances from the peg. The average amounts reported by subjects with high and low n Achievement have been plotted in Fig. 6.3 together with the best-fitting straight lines for the two groups. Clearly the slope of the amounts awarded by the subjects with high n Achievement is steeper than the slope for the subjects with low n Achievement. The difference in the regression coefficients of the two lines of best fit is highly significant. Litwin had also asked his subjects to estimate the probability of success from each of the lines and found first, as expected, that estimated success decreased in an almost linear fashion with increasing distances from the peg and second, that there was no difference in the estimated probabilities of success between high and low n Achievement groups. Thus the conclusion is quite clear: for tasks perceived as growing increasingly difficult, subjects with high n Achievement believe the rate of pay for accomplishing

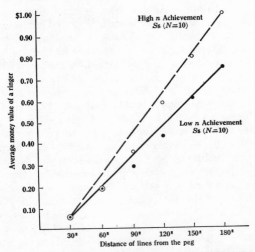

Figure 6.3   Average money reward assigned for hits from different distances in a ring toss game by subjects with high and low n Achievement

more and more difficult tasks should increase more rapidly than do subjects with low n Achievement. Achievement means more to the "highs" and they like greater concrete recognition of it in money terms. Note that this is exactly what would be predicted from Atkinson's model in Table 6.2. Here the subjects are not being asked where they would stand which involves the probability of *their* succeeding, but how valuable a success would be for tasks of different difficulty. Such a value should therefore be a simple product of motive strength × difficulty of the task $(1 - P_s)$. For a subject with a motive score of 8, the values should be $8 \times .90$ or 7.20, and $8 \times .10$ or .80 for the hard and easy task respectively, a much steeper gradient than for a subject with a motive score of 1 for whom the values would be .90 and .10 respectively.

Here, at last, is evidence for what economists and others have been calling for so long and so inaccurately the "profit motive." If we can assume, as all our evidence indicates, that Western capitalists were actually motivated primarily by the achievement motive, we can now understand why they were so interested in money and profit, although not, paradoxically, for its own sake. Money, to them, was the measure of success. It gave them the concrete knowledge of the outcome of their efforts that their motivation demanded. Even among college students who have had no extensive experience with the business world, money rewards have come to symbolize for those with high n Achievement in particular the measure of success. Yet these same students paradoxically do not work harder for money; they want it primarily as a symbol of higher achievement. What gallons of ink and acres of paper might have been saved if economic and political theorists had understood this distinction sooner! [6]

(e) and (f). LONG-RANGE PLANNING AND ORGANIZATIONAL ABILITIES

Two entrepreneurial role components listed in Table 6.1 have not yet been explicitly treated—namely, long-range planning and organizational abilities. Both, in a sense, relate to the planning activities of the entrepreneur. As to the first one, several theorists have maintained that entrepreneurship, particularly perhaps in the industrial field, requires long-range planning—anticipation of future possibilities. They have arrived at this conclusion by looking at the entrepreneur's job as one involving decision-making. Theoretically an economic agent should consider all the alternatives facing him, rank them in order of utility, and choose the course of action which maximizes this utility. "Simon points out that this scheme has to be made more realistic in two respects. For one, the actor does not really know all the alternatives; he must find them out, and for this purpose, a period of search is necessary. Secondly, the actor does not know all the consequences, and he has neither the time nor the skill to figure them out." (Lazarsfeld, 1959, p. 23.) The successful entrepreneur in these terms is by definition someone who considers more alternatives and their consequences before they actually happen to him. In more ordinary language, he anticipates future possibilities.

The same conclusion has been reached from quite a different point of view by Hoselitz, who points out, "A moneylender, or banker, deals in that commodity that has the widest currency, that is accepted by anyone, that can easily be transported, hidden, and that—if need be—can be directly used to bribe officials or other persons in power. An industrial entrepreneur has usually more property tied up in his plant for longer times than either a trader or a banker; he depends upon the smooth functioning of the market to sell his output; his property is exposed to a series of dangers—destruction by fire or other accident—which the others may escape." (1952, pp. 106-107.) In other words, the nature of industrial entrepreneurship appears to require more investment in the future, a longer time span, more planning ahead rather than just reacting to emergencies as they arise.

Consequently, if people with high n Achievement are to make good entrepreneurs, they should "think ahead" more. In fact they do. They tell stories that deal more often with the remote future (Ricks and Epley, 1959);

they think more in terms of anticipatory tenses (Zatzkis in McClelland *et al.*, 1953, p. 250); they tend to anticipate a future event before it occurs (Green and Knapp, 1959). Their whole attitude toward time is so interesting in itself that it deserves more extensive treatment than can be given here. The problem is fully discussed below in Chapter 8.

The final entrepreneurial role characteristic has to do with another kind of planning—namely, organizing human activities in the firm. If an entrepreneur is ever to accomplish more than he can by his own efforts, he must organize the activities of other persons. Hoselitz, Lazarsfeld, and many others all emphasize the *coordinating* function of the entrepreneur. Only two comments need be made here on this component of the entrepreneurial role. In the first place, there is some confusion in the theoretical literature as to whether this function belongs, strictly speaking, to the entrepreneurial role or to the managerial role. Secondly, there is no direct experimental evidence to show that subjects with high *n* Achievement have superior organizational skills. On the other hand, they do have a characteristic which should lead to greater organizational efficiency. French (1956) has shown that in choosing working partners for a problem-solving task, subjects with high *n* Achievement prefer experts over friends. That is, they would rather work with someone who can help solve the problem than with someone they know and like. This is an attitude which should promote business success in firms in the sense that choosing personnel in terms of their task-oriented skills should contribute more to business efficiency than choosing them in terms of other personal qualities. And, in fact, Godfrey, Fiedler, and Hall (1957) have demonstrated that more successful managers are both more distant and more discriminating in judging their staff members. Their measure of discrimination is different from French's, but like hers it seems to involve judging people in terms of their capacity to achieve or contribute to success in problem-solving.

For the present, it must satisfy us to have learned that high *n* Achievement leads people to behave in most of the ways they should behave if they are to fulfill the entrepreneurial role successfully as it has been defined by economists, historians and sociologists. The achievement motive should lead individuals to seek out situations which provide moderate challenge to their skills, to perform better in such situations, and to have greater confidence in the likelihood of their success. It should make them conservative where things are completely beyond their control, as in games of chance, and happier where they have some opportunity of influencing the outcome of a series of events by their own actions and of knowing concretely what those actions have accomplished. Contrary to the expectations of extreme economic individualists, the achievement motive should not lead them to perform better when they are working for themselves than when they are working for a group. And finally, it should encourage them to value money not for itself but as a measure of success. The parallel between the behavior evoked by high n Achievement and that required for the entrepreneurial role is so close that one can understand much better how a high n Achievement level in a society can produce more rapid economic development, as demonstrated in earlier chapters. The high n Achievement might be regarded as a sign that there are more men in key positions in the society behaving in all the ways that define successful entrepreneurial behavior.

Interest in Entrepreneurial Occupations

There is still a missing link in our analysis, however. If we have succeeded in showing that people with high n Achievement are likely to behave in an entrepreneurial way, we have not yet demonstrated that such people are likely to end up occupying entrepreneurial *status* in a particular society. Perhaps all the boys with high n Achievement in a Buddhist society will become monks and not businessmen. They may behave vigorously like entrepreneurs so far as that is possible within the limits of Buddhist monastic life, but how is the economic life of the country likely to be affected? What guarantee is there that people with high n Achievement will be attracted to business occupations? Is it not theoretically possible to have a society with a very high level of n Achievement in which, for reasons of prestige or other considerations of social structure, most of the boys with high n Achievement are drawn into occupations that have little or nothing to do with economic productivity? Clearly such an eventuality is theoretically possible. Economic development must depend not only on the level of n Achievement, on the number of vigorous entrepreneurs, but also on their distribution in various occupational statuses. Yet the data presented in the first part of the book suggest that as a rule, so far as large complex modern nations are concerned, a high level of n Achievement does affect the economic sector. Consequently, one might infer that *on the average* in most countries more boys with high n Achievement, or high entrepreneurial potential, end up occupying positions of business leadership.

But to understand just how this happens will require some complex analysis. Suppose we begin with the simplest possibility. Occupational choice is still largely determined in most societies traditionally. A son tends to do whatever his father does. Even in the United States, Warner and Abegglen report (1955, p. 46) that 63 per cent of the fathers of their business leaders were in business as of 1928 and 60 per cent as of 1952. In other words, as other studies also show (Bendix and Lipset, 1959), over half the businessmen, even in a presumably mobile country like the United States, come from business families and choose their occupations traditionally. In other nations the percentages may be still higher. If the average level of n Achievement in a country is raised by some of the influences to be considered in Chapter 9, the simplest assumption would be that the percentage of people with high n Achievement would increase in all occupations, because choice of occupations is still largely determined traditionally. Thus, even though most young men going into business were reluctant about it because of the higher prestige of other professions, they would nevertheless behave more vigorously as entrepreneurs because of their higher n Achievement. From this point of view, occupational choice and the prestige of various occupations has very little to do with the matter. Raising or lowering n Achievement level in a society simply affects business performance as it affects performance in all roles, but it is peculiarly adapted to leading to more effective performance in the business sector for the various reasons enumerated in the previous sections.

On the other hand, it is equally true that in every society there is some freedom of choice of occupation. One might argue for a kind of "natural selection" process by which a man with high n Achievement discovers through trial and error that he is happiest in an entrepreneurial occupation. He might, in fact or in imagination, consider the occupation of being a priest or a civil servant and discover it to have characteristics that did not give him the achievement satisfactions he desired. Even assuming very little occupational information, a man may try out several roles and discover the one that suits him or the one at which he is most successful. Business activities may be undertaken "on the side" in an experimental or tentative way in combination with almost any occupation. In fact Bendix and Lipset report (1959, p. 162) that men who end up owning their own businesses have worked in a greater variety of other occupations than men in any other occupational group. Consequently we might expect in the area of free choice that individuals with high n Achievement would, on the average, tend to "drift into" or "find" themselves in the business world because it requires those very characteristics that they possess.

We do not as yet, however, have data on the "career lines" of men with high and low n Achievement so that we can see whether some such "natural selection" process takes place. What we do have is the occupational preferences of boys with high and low n Achievement which may give us some idea of the occupational directions in which they may head in life. Then in the next chapter we can look backward into the histories of men who have ended up in various occupations and try to figure out the route the businessmen, as contrasted with others, followed. Between the starting points and the outcomes we may be able to piece out a picture of how business leadership is recruited from among boys of high and low n Achievement in various countries.

Nature of the Occupation as a Determinant of Preferences

Again suppose we start with the simplest assumption that boys with high n Achievement will tend to be attracted to business occupations more, because they *perceive* the occupations as calling for the characteristics which they possess. For example, they may realize that they are challenged by moderately risky enterprises, that business involves this kind of challenge, and therefore that they would like being in a business occupation. This rather simple idea was put to the test in our study of adolescent boys in India, Brazil, Germany and Japan because some preliminary data, reported in Chapter 2, had seemed to show that in the United States boys with high *n* Achievement did prefer business occupations.

The boys were asked to record their attitudes toward twelve occupations. The instructions used were the same as those in the *Strong Vocational Interest Blank* and since they may have had an effect on these results, they are reproduced here in full:

> Indicate after each occupation listed below whether you would like that kind of work or not. Disregard considerations of salary, social standing, future advancement, etc.
>
> Consider only whether or not you would like to do what is involved in the occupation. You are not asked if you would take up the occupation permanently, but merely whether or not you would enjoy that kind of work, regardless of any necessary skills, abilities, or training which you may or may not possess.
>
> Draw a circle around L if you like that kind of work.
> Draw a circle around I if you are indifferent to that kind of work.
> Draw a circle around D if you dislike that kind of work.
> Work rapidly. Your first impressions are desired here.

After they had given their reactions to each of the twelve occupations the boys in India and Germany were asked to "go back and check all those occupations which you feel are risky (as contrasted with secure or safe)." Four of the occupations in the list had to do with various business functions —*stockbroker* for the financial function, *buyer of merchandise* for purchasing, *factory manager* for production, and *advertiser* for selling. These occupations were chosen on the basis of the preliminary research in the United States reported in Chapter 2, which had shown that these occupations tended to be preferred more often by American boys with high *n* Achievement. In contrast, four traditional occupations were included—*civil service employee, clergyman, poet* and *lawyer*. Finally, four additional occupations were interspersed among the others which were included partly to get a somewhat broader coverage and partly to include some other occupations which are generally perceived by American boys to be moderately risky. That is, it is possible the American boys with high *n* Achievement liked certain business occupations not because of their "business" quality as such, but because of their "riskiness," since research findings presented earlier in the chapter show that people with high *n* Achievement tend to seek out challenging or moderately risky tasks. That is, by analogy with the ring-toss results (Fig. 6.1), they might prefer occupations perceived to be moderately risky as contrasted with safe or very risky ones. Therefore the following non-business occupations, judged moderately often to be risky (by 30-60 per cent of the boys) in Germany and India, were included: *explorer, politician, scientific research worker.* The business occupations judged to be moderately risky were: *stockbroker* and *buyer of merchandise.*[7] *Auto racer* was included as an example of an occupation judged very often to be risky (by 72 per cent of the German boys and 73 per cent of the Indian boys). Several of the traditional occupations were, on the other hand, regarded as safe—e.g., *civil service employee* and *clergyman.* While the rationale for choosing these occupational titles was clear enough in terms of previous research findings, as so often happens in cross-cultural research, it did not take into account sufficiently the meaning of these titles in other countries. Thus the term *advertiser* was almost certainly not understood by boys from countries where the Madison Avenue approach has not yet created such a profession. *Stockbroker* has a very ambiguous and low-level reference group in Japan, *clergyman* in India, etc.

Nevertheless, for what they are worth, Table 6.5 presents the correlations of *n* Achievement scores in five countries with liking for each of the 12 occupations on a numerical scale running from 0 (for "dislike") to 1 (for "indifferent") to 2 (for "like"). The fact that all the correlations are small should not obscure the fact that we can use them to estimate *whether* a relationship exists, although error and unreliability prevent them from providing a valid estimate of its extent.[3] Those for two United States samples are included, the larger one consisting of the top and bottom fifths of the *n* Achievement distribution for three successive entering freshman classes in a small liberal arts men's college in New England. Since these boys were a year or a year-and-a-half older, on the average, than the boys in the samples from overseas, data from a smaller United States sample of high school and preparatory school seniors are also shown.

Since a positive correlation means that the boys with high *n* Achievement like the occupation more, the table shows that they do tend to be drawn more to business occupations in the United States samples as predicted and possibly in Japan, but not significantly elsewhere. The most that can be said about other countries is that 11 out of the 16 correlations with the business occupations are positive, a deviation from the equal number of positive and negative correlations expected (and practically obtained for the remaining occupations) which approaches significance ($\chi^2 = 2.25$, $p < .10$ *pd*). There is no indication that boys with high *n* Achievement are more attracted to the occupations judged moderately often to be risky (i.e., *explorer, politician, scientific research worker,* and *stockbroker*) and less attracted to safe occupations (i.e., *civil service employee, clergyman*) or very risky ones (i.e., *auto racer*). On the other hand, boys with high

TABLE 6.5 CORRELATIONS OF n ACHIEVEMENT (GRAPHIC) WITH LIKING FOR VARIOUS OCCUPATIONS AMONG BOYS IN FIVE COUNTRIES

Occupational title	U.S.[1,2]		Combined p value	Japan	Brazil	Germany	India[1]
	$N = 70$	$N = 254$		$N = 140$	$N = 351$	$N = 367$	$N = 151$
A. Business							
1. Stockbroker	.27[3]	.25	<.001	.13	−.07	.04	.10
2. Buyer of merchandise	.00	.21	<.01	−.08	−.04	.03	.04
3. Factory manager	.09	.16	<.02	.11	.01	.08	−.08
4. Advertiser	.25	.09	<.02	.14[1]	.04	−.14	.15
Average r	.15	.18	<.01	.075	−.015	.00	.053
p value				<.10			
B. Traditional							
1. Civil service employee		−.04		−.09	−.09	.09	.01
2. Clergyman		−.00		.04	−.04	.09	.09
3. Poet	.00	−.14		.06	−.09	.08	.09
4. Lawyer	−.16	.14		−.04	−.04	.02	.10
Average r		−.01		−.01	−.065	.07	.073
p value					<.02	<.02	<.10
C. Other (risky)							
1. Scientific research worker		.02		−.11	.02	−.08	−.02
2. Explorer		−.08		.12	−.08	−.04	.08
3. Auto racer		.09		−.02	−.01	−.08	.00
4. Politician		.02		.02	.02	.03	−.14

[1] Based on verbal n Achievement scores. All other correlations are based on graphic n Achievement scores. The graphic n Achievement correlation with liking for advertiser was lost in the IBM calculations for Japan and the correlation with verbal n Achievement substituted.

[2] All U.S. correlations are point-biserial r's computed from the top and bottom fifths of the n Achievement distributions.

[3] All correlations have been corrected for coarse grouping.

n Achievement are significantly more attracted to "traditional" occupations in Germany and India, although the correlations are very small and the trend is reversed in Brazil.

What is to be made of these findings, scattered and inconclusive as they are? The most obvious conclusion is that the hypothesis which guided the research is wrong: boys with high n Achievement do not universally like business occupations because they perceive these occupations as involving characteristics like moderate risk-taking, which they like. As a matter of fact boys probably do not have enough information on what occupations are like to be guided by such considerations. At any rate, La Cava has demonstrated in a carefully conducted study that attitudes and beliefs about each of nine occupations freely expressed in nondirective interviews are *in no way* related to the *n* Achievement scores of the subjects interviewed. For example, subjects with high *n* Achievement were not more concerned with the work side of an occupation, with its promise of self-fulfillment or with its degree of challenge. In general in these interviews when subjects were asked, "What is your image or conception of a lawyer (engineer, etc.)? What images or associations come to mind?" very few of them "referred to the specific nature of the work in which a member of the occupation is involved." (Beardslee and O'Dowd, 1958.)

Prestige as a Determinant of Occupational Preferences

If the nature of the work is not a key part of occupational images, what is? According to the La Cava study and many others, it is the *prestige* of the occupation which is one of its most salient dimensions. So we move to another hypothesis: Could the prestige of business occupations determine whether people with high *n* Achievement are attracted to them? Certainly the idea has ample support among economists, historians, and sociologists, nearly all of whom concur in stating that it is the relatively high prestige of business occupations in the Western industrialized countries which is in part responsible for their rapid development, since abler people will be attracted to business if it has higher prestige. For example, Wilson (1954) feels that the industrial revolution in England was made easier by "the long familiarity with and high prestige of commercial activities." Harbison and Myers state that "in the United States, the social status of entrepreneurial and business groups has always been relatively high, and this has been an important factor in attracting the high level human resources needed for our own economic development" (1959, p. 124). Shils has generalized the point by arguing that business activities have always been to a certain extent outside the area of the "sacred"—unconnected "with the ultimate powers and mysteries of the universe, such as life and death and sovereignty over them" (1958, p. 10)—and therefore have not appealed to the ablest people in traditional societies.

Do the correlations in Table 6.5 support this view? That is, if we assume that boys with high *n* Achievement are abler, at least in the sense of better qualified to pursue business activities successfully, are they more attracted to business in countries where its prestige is higher? Unfortunately we have no direct measure of prestige, but we have several indirect ones. We can reason, following the argument above, that countries which are more industrialized should give higher prestige to business. Then U.S. boys with high *n* Achievement should be more attracted to business (which they are) and so should German boys (which they are not). Or if we take current *rate* of economic growth (Table 3.6) as an index of business prestige, then the correlations should be higher in Germany, India and the United States than they are in Japan, which they are not in any consistent way. Or finally we may consider the average liking for various occupations as presented in Table 6.6 to be an indirect index of the prestige of business.

TABLE 6.6   AVERAGE LIKING (SCALE OF 0-2) FOR VARIOUS OCCUPATIONS AMONG ADOLESCENT BOYS (AGE 14-18) IN FIVE COUNTRIES

Occupational title	U.S.			Japan		Brazil		Germany		India	
	$N = 70$[1]	$N = 254$[2]	Rank	$N = 140$	Rank	$N = 351$	Rank	$N = 367$	Rank	$N = 151$	Rank
A. Business											
1. Stockbroker	1.17[3]	.96	7	.75	12	.74	7	.49	12	.38	12
2. Buyer of Merchandise	.97	.95	8	1.50	3	.58	11	.63	8	.96	8
3. Factory Manager	1.12	.97	6	1.14	5	1.28	2	1.47	1	1.38	3
4. Advertiser	1.28	1.19	4	.82	9.5	.62	10	.62	9	.76	10
Average		1.02		1.05		.81		.80		.87	
B. Traditional											
1. Civil Service employee		.78	12	1.19	4	.71	8	1.12	4	1.10	7
2. Clergyman		.88	11	.87	7	.69	9	.58	10	.56	11
3. Poet	.49	.94	9	1.10	6	.77	6	.56	11	1.30	5
4. Lawyer	1.43	1.36	1	.82	9.5	1.00	4	1.10	5	1.11	6
Average		.99		1.00		.79		.84		1.02	
C. Other (risky)											
1. Scientific research worker		1.30	3	1.52	1	1.55	1	1.46	2	1.70	1
2. Explorer		1.49	2	1.51	2	1.18	3	1.40	3	1.45	2
3. Auto racer		.90	10	.76	11	1.03	5	.89	6	.94	9
4. Politician		1.18	5	.84	8	.51	12	.80	7	1.32	4

[1] Boys about 16 years of age drawn from college preparatory classes in a public high school and a New England boys preparatory school in about equal proportions.

[2] College Freshmen at entrance about 17-18 years of age drawn from the top and bottom fifths of the n Achievement score distribution in three successive entering classes at a New England men's college.

[3] The standard deviation for the average liking for a particular occupation varies around .75 so that differences in mean favorableness scores of .15 to .17 and .18 to .20 are significant at the .05 and .01 levels respectively depending on the size of the samples between which the comparison is made.

There are several points of interest in this table. To begin with, the most popular occupations in all five countries are *scientific research worker* and *explorer*. They probably also enjoy high prestige, although *explorer* is not usually included in prestige rankings. Aside from these two occupations however, there is no consistently high cross-national agreement on popularity rankings. For example, the intercorrelations of the popularity ranks vary from .10 for the U.S. and Japan to .75 for Germany and India. While *civil service employee* is disliked most by college students in the U.S. the occupation has moderate to high popularity in other countries. The disagreement is greater here than in other cross-national studies (see Inkeles and Rossi, 1956) probably because unusual occupations (like *auto racer* and *explorer*) were included and because the range of occupations included here is limited (i.e., there are few low-status occupations).

The four business occupations are only *moderately* liked in all countries, the average ranks of popularity varying between 6.25 (for the U.S.) and 8.00 (for India). Actually the pattern of liking is very different for different business occupations. The U.S. students like the occupations of *stockbroker* and *advertiser* significantly more than the students in any of the other four countries, possibly because the latter understood the occupational titles less well. On the other hand, the pattern for *buyer of merchandise* is not at all clear and *factory manager*, perhaps the most typical and well understood business role of all, is actually liked *less* well by the U.S. boys than by boys in other countries. There is no strong support here for the often expressed notion that business occupations enjoy higher prestige among more rapidly developing or more developed economies, at least to the extent that popularity gives an indication of prestige. Furthermore there is no evidence that the abler boys—i.e. those with higher n Achievement— are drawn more to business occupations, the better liked those occupations are. Consider the occupation of *factory manager*, for example. While it is significantly less well liked in the United States than it is in India, nevertheless, boys with high n Achievement are more often attracted to it in the United States ($r = .16$) whereas the reverse is true in India ($r = -.08$). The over-all relationship was checked specifically for the business occupations as follows: the popularity ranks of the four business occupations within each country were re-ranked from high to low, a step that was necessary because the general favorableness toward all occupations was greater in some countries than others. This gave a final ordering of the relative standing of business occupations in the four countries. Then the correlations of n Achievement with liking for these occupations in all four countries were ranked from high to low and the correlation run with the prestige (or favorableness) ranking. It turned out to be $-.19$, $N = 20$, a value which is not significant and which points in a direction opposite to the hypothesis. That is, boys with high n Achievement, (if anything) prefer business occupations more when those occupations are in general less well liked! It would seem to render highly unlikely the hypothesis, so often stated in the literature, that making business occupations more popular will succeed in attracting *more* entrepreneurial talent to enter them.

Occupational Preferences as a Joint Function of Prestige, n Achievement, and Class Status

How then are we to make sense of our findings if the two most obvious hypotheses do not account for them? Why is it that the boys with high n Achievement are more attracted to business occupations in the U.S. and possibly the Japanese samples, but not elsewhere? It is evident that we need a more analytical approach to the problem now that we cannot explain the results in terms of the image of the business occupation or its popularity. Once again Atkinson's model (Table 6.2) is helpful. Both he (in personal communications) and Litwin (1958, 1959), have pointed out that the value placed on an occupation should be analogous to the value placed on getting a ringer in a ring-toss game for tasks of greater difficulty (i.e., standing further away). See Fig. 6.3. Valuation for the occupation should be the product of motive strength times difficulty of achieving success in the occupation $(1 - P_s)$. Occupations which are perceived as more difficult to achieve, such as the professions, should therefore be valued more highly than those which are not difficult to achieve, such as clerical or semiskilled jobs, and as in the ring-toss game, the gradient of valuation between the "easy" and "difficult" occupations should be steeper for the subjects with high n Achievement because of the multiplicative nature of the relationship. Since more "difficult" occupations are ordinarily more prestigeful, Atkinson and Litwin have used prestige rankings as rough measures of difficulty, and checked to see if subjects with high n Achievement have a steeper gradient of preference or liking for occupations varying in prestige, as predicted. First results indicate that they do. For example, Atkinson has pointed to the differential slopes of satisfaction with occupations of varying prestige shown by Italian and Jewish boys, as reported by Strodtbeck, McDonald, and Rosen (1957). The boys were asked to indicate whether they would be pleased or disappointed should they eventually end up in certain occupations. The percentage of "pleased" responses for middle-class boys was as follows for occupations ranked from high to low prestige or status:

	Italians	*Jews*
1. Doctor, advertising executive	57%	71%
2. Druggist, jewelry store owner	47	55
3. Bank teller, bookkeeper	37	17
4. Carpenter, auto mechanic	40	19
5. Mail carrier, bus driver	5	2
6. Night watchman, furniture mover	3	1

The preference gradient is much steeper for the Jewish boys as it should be if they are higher in n Achievement, which is highly likely (see Table 9.7).

Litwin (1959) has conducted the most systematic analysis of the problem using the data on the Japanese sample from the present study. He was hampered by not having clear-cut status or prestige ratings available, but by putting together information contained in a number of sources and by analyzing the nature of the job he was able to arrive at four distinguishable occupational levels as shown in Table 6.7. The figures in the table are the average liking for the occupations, as in Table 6.6, broken down for middle-class subjects of high and low n Achievement (verbal).[8] Obviously again the slope of preferences for occupations increasing in prestige is steeper for the subjects with high n Achievement than for those with low n Achievement. Litwin obtained the regression coefficients for each subject separately to get an estimate of the variance and was able therefore to infer that the difference between the two mean regression coefficients was unlikely to have arisen by chance ($t = 1.77$, $p < .05$, pd). Furthermore he found in

TABLE 6.7   MEAN OCCUPATIONAL PREFERENCES (SCALE OF 0-2) OF JAPANESE MIDDLE-CLASS BOYS IN THE EIGHTH GRADE WITH HIGH AND LOW n ACHIEVEMENT (VERBAL) (From Litwin, 1959)

Levels	high n Achievement $N = 15$		low n Achievement $N = 14$	
Occupational level 1		1.56		1.43
Scientific research worker	1.67		1.43	
Explorer	1.80		1.43	
Poet	1.20		1.43	
Occupational level 2		1.11		.67
Factory manager	1.27		.57	
Politician	.67		.50	
Buyer of merchandise	1.40		.93	
Occupational level 3		1.00		1.04
Clergyman	.87		1.00	
Civil servant	1.13		1.07	
Occupational level 4		.70		.93
Auto racer	.80		1.00	
Stockbroker	.60		.86	
Mean regression coefficient		−.272		−.129

three other groups of boys—from the upper class, the working class, and a rural school—that in every case the preference slope for the boys with high n Achievement was steeper. Consequently, the difference in slopes for all the "highs" ($N = 62$) as compared with all the "lows" ($N = 58$) is highly significant ($t = 3.22$, $p < .001$, pd). The prediction from Atkinson's model seems amply confirmed: liking for an occupation appears to be a product of achievement motivation and difficulty (or prestige) of the occupation.

But so far the findings appear to lead to an impasse since we have just finished demonstrating that n Achievement is *not* more positively correlated with liking for occupations of higher prestige in most of our samples. The way out of the impasse is indicated by a study of the preferences of a class of Harvard students for three prestige levels of occupations. Level 1 included *lawyer, medicine: specialist,* and *research scientist;* level 2, *druggist, factory manager,* and *building contractor;* and level 3, *civil service employee, clerk,* and *mail carrier.* Here there was no difference in preference slopes between subjects high and low in n Achievement for level 2 occupations over level 3 occupations, but there was for level 1 over level 2. To put it in terms of the correlation coefficients we have been using, there is a positive correlation between n Achievement and liking for the highest prestige occupations but not for the middle-prestige occupations (which include two of our business occupations). In fact, at the middle-prestige level 2 the correlations are *negative*. In this sample of students the correlation between n Achievement scores and the sum of liking for four business occupations (*business:*

advertising, factory manager, stockbroker and *building contractor*) is − .39, $N = 21$, $p < .10$.

But these are the same occupations for which we have reported an average correlation of +.18 in Table 6.5 for another group of college students. What explains such a striking paradox? The chief difference between the two groups of students is their class status, the Harvard students being more upper-class in fact or in aspiration than the others, who had furthermore been tested on the day they arrived at college before they had a chance to begin to think of professional careers like the Harvard students who were tested in their junior year. Now at last an hypothesis presents itself that makes sense of our data on *n* Achievement and occupational aspirations: The relationship depends on prestige *and also on the status of the person involved*. Again this flows directly from Atkinson's model, which states that probability of success must also enter into the equation to determine the *actual aspiration* of the person (as opposed to his *valuation* of various occupations).

Let us return to the ring-toss analogy. Motivation and difficulty alone are enough to predict what value (in money terms) subjects with high and low *n* Achievement will put on success at different distances. But if we want to know *where the subject will stand*, we must take probability of succeeding into account, or more particularly the subject's own estimate of what his chances are at different distances. It was in this way that Atkinson derived the preference of subjects with high *n* Achievement for *moderate* risks even though they placed greater value on success under extreme risk or difficulty.

Now by analogy boys of middle-class background should have a lower estimate of their probability of success at high-level occupations than boys of upper-class background. Therefore if their occupational preferences *include* any element of their own ability to achieve in the occupation, then boys of middle-class backgrounds with high *n* Achievement should prefer middle-level occupations representing "moderate risk" for them. Since business occupations are moderately difficult (middle-level prestige in all societies—see Table 6.6), it follows that *n* Achievement should be positively correlated with liking for such occupations primarily in middle-class boys. In upper-class boys, it should be negatively correlated because business occupations are "easy" for them or, if anything, represent a step downward in the prestige hierarchy.

The hypothesis is confirmed by the much greater preference the middle-class Japanese boys with high *n* Achievement show for middle-level occupations, including two of our business occupations (see Table 6.7). Let us bring this fact together with others mentioned into a single table to sharpen up the point. Table 6.8 shows how the correlations vary depending both on the prestige of the occupation and on the status of the boys. *N* Achievement scores correlate with liking for a high-prestige occupation

TABLE 6.8   CORRELATIONS OF n ACHIEVEMENT SCORE (VERBAL) WITH LIKING FOR OCCUPATIONS OF HIGH AND MIDDLE PRESTIGE AMONG BOYS OF UPPER AND MIDDLE STATUS

| Classification | N | Occupation with | |
		High prestige: research scientist	Middle prestige: factory manager
Upper-status boys			
U.S. (Harvard Juniors)	21	+.46	− .37
Japan	30	+.22*	.05*
Middle-status boys			
U.S. (Table 6.5)	254	.02	+.16
Japan (Table 6.7)	29	.15*	.47*

* Biserial estimates based on mean differences.

(*research scientist*) among high status boys and with liking for a middle-prestige occupation (*factory manager*) among middle-status boys, in both countries. The middle-status boys of high n Achievement do not aspire to the highest-level occupation (research scientist) any more than such boys try to make a ringer from as far away as they can stand from the peg in the ring-toss game. On the other hand, they do aspire more to the highest-level occupation, i.e., *factory manager, that is within their reach.* The comparison of the correlations for *factory manager* for the upper-(.05) and the middle-status (.47) Japanese boys is particularly illuminating so far as the rest of Table 6.5 is concerned, for *only* in Japan and the United States were there an appreciable number of middle-class boys in our samples. In the other countries the correlations between n Achievement and liking for business occupations should be and are more like the .05 value found for the upper-class Japanese boys. In Germany and India, as has been pointed out elsewhere, the boys were a *highly selected* group preparing for a university education which is attained by a much smaller percentage of boys there than in the U.S. (See Lipset and Bendix, 1959, p. 94.) One would expect therefore higher correlations of n Achievement in these two countries with liking for occupations of the highest prestige, not for the business occupations. Such seems to be the case if we consider the "traditional" occupations in Table 6.5 as having higher prestige. In both countries n Achievement is positively correlated only with liking for these occupations. We are not, to be sure, relying on popularity as an index of prestige in this case, but we seem justified in not doing so on the basis of other information from the countries that such occupations as *poet* and *clergyman* enjoy high prestige despite the fact that they may not be popular among adolescents. As for Brazil, the sample is again highly selected but more heterogenous as to class background, age of subjects, intention to get professional training, etc. So the lack of any pattern to the correlations in Brazil may be explained on this basis.

Interestingly enough, Mahone (1958) has obtained results which confirm the conclusion drawn from Table 6.8 and from Atkinson's model. He used estimates by the individual of his own ability and the ability required to succeed at various occupations. He predicted and found that the subjects with high n Achievement would then actually aspire to occupations representing small discrepancies between the two estimates ("moderate risks") as contrasted with the subjects with low n Achievement who were more unrealistic in their vocational aspirations. The individual's estimate of his ability is equivalent in Table 6.8 to the social status of the boys and his estimate of the difficulty of the occupation is equivalent to the prestige of the occupation. So the two sets of results are quite analogous and both confirm the prediction from Atkinson's model that occupational aspiration will be a multiplicative function of n Achievement, prestige (or difficulty) of the occupation, and probability of success, as affected by the social class status of the respondent.

Thus, the new hypothesis seems to account for our findings reasonably well. That it does not do so better is due to the fact that we did not collect our data with the hypothesis in mind, so that there were no careful controls for class background of the boys tested—or for the prestige of the occupations in various countries or for the way in which the question of occupational preferences was put to them. According to Atkinson's model, one result should be obtained if they are asked for prestige rankings—i.e. higher rankings by those high in n Achievement, the greater the prestige of the occupation—and another if they are asked some preference question that involves an estimate of their own ability to achieve in the occupation—i.e., greater preference by the "highs" for occupations just above their own estimated level of ability or opportunity. Our way of putting the question (see above) asks the boys to disregard "salary, social standing, future advancement" which suggests that we are asking them the second question— namely, whether they could succeed at that kind of work. But then they are told to disregard whether they have "the necessary skills, abilities or training" which should tend to eliminate the probability of success factor and move them back toward a preference in terms of prestige. The instructions are confusing in terms of the theoretical model we have now adopted, and considering the other failures in our research design, it is surprising that we were able to draw any inferences at all from our data.

Fortunately, however, other theorists have come to quite similar conclusions based on quite different data. For example, Lipset and Bendix state: "This emphasis on business ownership in occupational aspirations has been shown to vary with class position among adolescents as well, with those from lower-income groups aspiring to business ownership, and those from higher-income groups hoping for professional careers." (1959, p. 178.) The point is also made in statistics collected by Rosenberg (1957) at Cornell, a relatively high-status university where only 6 per cent of the students want and expect to go into business; another 5 per cent are planning to enter the field reluctantly. The bias against business among such student élites is shown up by the fact that around 20 per cent of the graduates of all colleges in the United States chose a business career (Pierson, 1959). What we have added to this fact is that those among the élite who are endowed with more of the entrepreneurial spirit—with higher n Achievement—will seek the higher-prestige professional occupations even more, with a net loss to the business community.

Yet the picture is just the reverse at the other end of the income or social status scale. Lipset and Bendix report that in the United States and Sweden aspiring to own a business is predominantly the "mobility path of manual workers and low-status, relatively unskilled salespeople" (1959, p. 178). Sixty-seven per cent of the manual workers in their sample had business aspirations, 35 per cent had made an attempt, and 23 per cent had been in business at least for a time for themselves. As a middle-prestige occupation which is easy to enter at a low level, business should get the lion's share of the people with high n Achievement from lower-status backgrounds. In most cases it is the occupation of highest prestige that they realistically *can* enter (whatever their perception of their own ability) because they do not have the funds or family backing to support the long period of education necessary for the higher-prestige professions.

A further attractive feature to a business career for people with high n Achievement from low-status background is that it provides possible outcomes in prestige that rank almost all the way to the top. That is, *high level business executive* ties in prestige rank with *architect* for ninth and tenth place (out of 40) in Mahone's study (1958), just below the professions of law, medicine, research science, etc. Yet a person can start in at the very low level of difficulty (and prestige) of retail sales and conceivably rise nearly to the top. Few other careers provide such a range of possible vertical mobility. So the person with high n Achievement who starts life relatively low in social status can by pursuing a business career satisfy both factors that influence him—he starts with a moderate risk which is important to him because of his tendency to be influenced by his realistic chances of success, and if he succeeds, he can pursue the higher prestige within the business career which is more important to him than to the person with low n Achievement. To be sure, few of the highest-level executives start at the very bottom, as other figures in Lipset and Bendix show (Chapter 4) but the argument applies particularly well to the son of a businessman who has done only moderately well, a class from which the business élite seems largely to be drawn. In such cases, the son with high n Achievement may not yet aspire to the highest-prestige occupations

—the professions; so he chooses business as the next best bet to reach high status; he also has the opportunity to learn about business at first hand (perhaps discovering that it satisfies his needs in the process), to enter it directly and to expand it still further with the start his father has already made.

It is interesting to note that it is precisely this same group of lower middle-class families that in general also produces the highest n Achievement in its sons (Table 9.7) in the United States. So long then as there is freedom to enter business in a society, there appears to be a built-in recruiting mechanism for getting boys of lower status with higher n Achievement into business. It is the career with the highest potential prestige in which they have at least a moderate probability of succeeding, both because of opportunity and personal ability factors. Thus if the n Achievement level in a society rises, it should not affect all occupations equally, but business occupations more since they tend to recruit particularly boys with high n Achievement from the more numerous middle and lower classes, at least in many countries that have already developed.

What happens in underdeveloped societies and in Communist countries like Russia where entry into business occupations may be controlled by a different mechanism can best be saved until after we have looked at the origins of businessmen in the next chapter.

Attitudes Associated with Business Interests among the Young Élite in Germany, India, Japan and Brazil

It may be worth pursuing a little further, however, the question of who does aspire to and enter business occupations from the upper classes, since generally speaking those with high n Achievement do not. In terms of the data we have collected, the problem boils down to trying to discover what other attitudes we measured are correlated with business interests, particularly in countries like Germany and India where our samples were drawn largely from the adolescent élite. The search proved not to be simple because some 400 correlations were involved—i.e. approximately 25 attitude or background items (see Appendix VI) correlated with interest in each of four business occupations for each of four countries. In a matrix of such size a number of significant correlations can arise by chance, but fortunately they could here be cross-validated from country to country. Actually, when this was done, the chief impression gained was that the attitudes associated with interest in business were quite specific to the country involved. Very few variables appeared to have a cross-national association with business interests.

Only two factors had any discernible generality—the optimism score (see above) and a single item diagnostic of authoritarian ideology. The more optimistic boys tend to avoid the business occupations somewhat, the correlations with liking for the four business occupations being —.12 for Japan, —.04 for Brazil, —.01 for Germany and —.08 for India (combined $p \sim .10$). Or to put it the other way, boys from élitist backgrounds with an interest in business seem to be slightly more often resigned, pessimistic, or cynical in their outlook toward life. However, the optimistic boys show a more marked preference for the four occupations checked moderately often (30-60 per cent of the time) by boys in Germany and India as risky—e.g., *explorer, politician, scientific research worker,* and *stockbroker* (although the latter contributes little to the correlations). The correlations of liking for these occupations with optimism score were .11 for Japan, .11 for Brazil, .06 for Germany, and .16 for India (combined $p < .01$). The forward-looking, progressive boys in all countries tended to be attracted to "progressive," challenging occupations like *scientific research worker* and *explorer,* a not-too-surprising outcome which fills in our picture of these boys as models of conscientiousness and "correct" attitudes and behavior. They are not, however, drawn to business.

The single attitude positively associated with an interest in business in all countries involved agreement with the following item:

> There is hardly anything lower than a person who does not feel a great love, gratitude and respect for his parents.

The correlation between endorsing this sentiment and liking for being a *factory manager* was .132 for Japan, .022 for Brazil, .187 for Germany, and .220 for India. The combined p value is $< .01$ for the four countries taken separately, and the correlation for the entire sample of boys is .136, $N = 1,009$, $p < .01$. The finding is of particular interest because this item has the highest discriminatory power on the well known F-scale, a measure of authoritarianism (Adorno *et al.,* 1950, p. 260). In other words, agreement with it is most likely to go with conservative political, economic, and social attitudes, personality rigidity, and racial prejudice, at least in the United States.

What is even more interesting is that the correlation is higher in those countries where the boys represent a more selected upper-class sample— namely, Germany and India. The average r for these two countries is .196 as contrasted with an average r of .063 for Japan and Brazil, where more of the boys are not part of the educational élite. The difference between the two correlations is significant ($p < .05$) indicating that boys from the upper classes who are interested in business tend to be *more* conservative than other boys interested in business. The point can be further documented: the difference in the size of the correlations exists not only in relation to liking for the occupation of *factory manager,* but for all four business occupations. The average of the eight correlations for Japan and Brazil combined is only .011 as contrasted with .098 for Germany and India, a difference which is highly significant ($p < .01$). Note that in all countries conservative ideology goes with interest in the most traditional and highest-prestige business occupation, that of *factory manager*, but when other business occupations are added, it is associated with business interests only among the most upper-class student groups.

One final fact before interpreting these findings: the students with business interests in Germany and India are much less involved in extra-curricular activities than those in Japan and Brazil (average of eight correlations $= -.034$ vs. .124 respectively, the difference between the two being highly significant, $p < .01$). In other words, the students with business interests from among the more élite student groups in Germany and India are not only more conservative, they tend to mix in student activities much less than students with business interests who are not so definitely upper class from Japan and Brazil. These findings fit in well with similar ones obtained by Rosenberg (1957) in the United States, when he studied Cornell students with business interests, since such students are also part of the educational élite in the sense in which we are using the term here. He reports that they have a greater concern for status and extrinsic rewards, low faith in people, and a conservative ideological viewpoint on the importance of capital over labor. Avery (1959) also found in studying another group with business interests from a student élite that they showed more authoritarianism, tough-minded aggressiveness, and concern with status. The U.S. studies have so far not shown what we appear to have found here—that upwardly mobile students with business interests may be conservative, but *less so* than those who go into business from an upper-class status. The latter, on the other hand, appear everywhere to be a picture of authoritarian conservatism. They are somewhat disillusioned, want to hang on to what they have, do not participate in student activities, and have strong feelings of family loyalty.

The picture suggested by these findings is one that makes good sense in terms of the general understanding of the business community and how it is recruited. In countries like the United States, as we pointed out above, there appears to have been a recruitment pattern that in ideal form ran somewhat as follows. The father moved from the country to the city and established himself perhaps as a skilled or semiskilled worker. The son was one of the 67 per cent of such people who not only wanted to but succeeded in establishing a small business, possibly because he had high n Achievement. He reached the lower middle class. The grandson, if he too had high n Achievement, expanded the business and eventually moved up into the business élite (see Lipset and Bendix, 1959). But *his* son, the great-grandson, is now part of what we have been calling the student élite. He goes to an Ivy League college and if he has high n Achievement, he aspires to one of the professions. If not, or if his school work is not good enough, or if he is made to go into the family firm, he goes into business and *takes with him a much more conservative ideology* than his upwardly mobile father or grandfather had. The reasons for having a conservative ideology are strong, much stronger than in his father's case, for he must maintain the family position, the capital, the business that his father established. He is also more often than not less suited for the business role than his father because he has less of the entrepreneurial spirit—that is, lower n Achievement. Certainly it is a widely accepted belief that sons who inherit their businesses have in general less "drive" than those who created them, though we do not as yet have factual evidence on differences in their n Achievement scores.

Such an idealized picture also helps explain the vicious circle that many underdeveloped countries are caught in. Because they are often low in n Achievement, they do not have a steady flow of entrepreneurial talent upward from the lower middle class which creates new businesses, and must recruit their business leaders primarily from the upper classes where the capital and opportunity to go into business exist. Kahl (1960) presents a good picture of this recruitment pattern as it operates in Mexico, a country currently below average in n Achievement (Table 3.5). By far, fewer of the factory workers than in the U.S. had ambitions to go into business on their own and the top management positions were open only to those from the educational and social élite. But these men are often conservative in ideology, believing strongly in family solidarity (see the F-scale item above), so that they set up family firms into which their sons are expected to go whether or not they have talent or motivation for business activity. Thus opportunity to rise in the business world is often denied even to the small flow of people with high n Achievement from the middle and lower classes. Such countries not only have a short supply of entrepreneurial talent, they do not even recruit efficiently the supply they have (see Harbison and Myers, 1959).

The ultimate question of how to affect such recruitment patterns in different types of societies will have to be saved until later, after we have studied the origins of businessmen (Chapter 7) and n Achievement (Chapter 9). For the present, it is enough to have learned something of why n Achievement promotes behavior particularly suited to the entrepreneurial role and how it leads young men to aspire to a business career if they are of a middle- or lower-class background but not if they are of an upper-class background.

NOTES AND REFERENCES

[1] It was necessary to use a square root transformation of the deviation scores because they were badly skewed.

[2] Graphic n Achievement scores were used in Germany and Brazil, and verbal n Achievement scores in India for reasons given in Appendix IV. Combined probability was estimated by summing chi-squares equivalent to p values for the various correlations.

A second attempt with the same subjects to check the same hypothesis by asking them to put down as many dots as they thought they could connect in a few minutes failed completely, possibly because this task was even further removed from the dynamics of the ring-toss situation. For one thing, it certainly was clear to the brighter boys that almost an indefinitely large number of dots could be connected very rapidly simply by arranging them in straight lines or geometrical shapes. The task had been used successfully by McClelland (1958) to check the hypothesis with younger boys (age 9) who apparently were less able to figure out this way of "solving" the problem.

[3] Here and at many other places in this chapter (see Tables 6.3 and 6.5) we may seem to be stretching the reader's patience to the limit in paying attention at all to such trivially low correlations of no intrinsic significance whatsoever. Many of them, even though unlikely to have arisen by chance, could account for no more than 1 per cent of the variance in the relationship of the two factors correlated. The justification for paying attention to them runs more or less as follows: the purpose of this research was not to design experiments which would reduce error variance to a minimum in each country so that the main effects could affect the outcome strongly. In fact such experiments in so many different countries under such differing conditions would have been prohibitively expensive in time and money. Experimenters would have had to be trained, the local culture would have had to be studied, etc. One can, of course, raise the correlations obtained theoretically to a marked extent by correcting for attenuation due to unreliability of the measuring instruments which was extreme in most of these instances. Or to put it another way, one can argue that the relationship must indeed have been a strong one to appear *despite* so much error or "noise" in testing conditions, measuring instruments, experimenter attitudes, etc.

But the point of the research was *not to estimate the extent or size of the relationships* theoretically expected, but rather to gather empirical evidence across a number of countries as to *whether or not the relationships existed at all* and were, so to speak, sufficiently worthy of belief to merit more detailed study as to the extent of the relationship. Many examples exist in this chapter of relationships which are lower in a country when they are tested under conditions standardized for cross-cultural comparisons than under conditions peculiarly adapted to the country. See Note 4.

[4] It is surprising that the correlations between the measure of n Achievement and arithmetic performance are so low under all conditions in view of earlier results. For example, Klauer (1959) has reported in an independent investigation in Germany, a correlation of .62 ($N = 100$, $p < .01$) between n Achievement (verbal) and performance on the same task. In the present experiment the correlations in Germany between the verbal measure of n Achievement and performance were all negligible and formed no particular pattern. The two chief points of difference between the two experiments appear to be that in Klauer's case the administrator was a teacher from their own school, rather than an outsider, and that the boys were 10–15 years old not going on to "höhere Schule." For them the complex arithmetic task may have been a challenge more like the 1/20 chance of winning for our older and more intelligent boys.

[5] As a matter of fact, the Indian results also fit in with this hypothesis to a certain extent. The correlation of performance with n Achievement (verbal) at the shortest odds (3/4) is —.09 and rises to .31 ($p < .10$ that the difference in r's is significant) at the next degree of uncertainty (1/2) just as in Japan and Brazil, but thereafter the correlation pattern becomes meaningless, being —.26 at odds of 1/3 and .01 at odds of 1/20. The Indian correlations are, of course, particularly likely to be unstable because of the much larger variance in the scores. Nevertheless, taken as a whole, the results in all the countries tend to support the hypothesis that subjects with high n Achievement perform better as contrasted with subjects with low n Achievement when the chances of winning are somewhat reduced so that personal effort is likely to make more difference.

⁶ The conclusion supported here by empirical evidence is by now quite generally held in the United States. "Apparently a strong motivation to make profit is not enough." (Hoselitz, 1952, p. 106.) "The profit motive itself is but a historical category and is always coupled with other motives." (Redlich, 1958, p. 187.) See also Lauterbach (1959).

⁷ In Germany, *stockbroker* ranked 5th in riskiness (30 per cent of the boys checking it as risky) and in India 3rd (40 per cent of the boys checking it as risky). *Buyer of merchandise*, on the other hand, ranked 7th in Germany (15 per cent considering it risky) and 4th in India (38 per cent considering it risky).

⁸ Unfortunately, he made the analysis before it had been decided that the graphic measure of n Achievement was in general more valid. But, as has been pointed out several times, in Japan the verbal and graphic measures of n Achievement generally gave similar group results, despite the fact that they are uncorrelated.

7

Characteristics of Entrepreneurs

The previous chapter has laid the groundwork for the present one. Its main theme was that high n Achievement suits men particularly for the entrepreneurial role. At least students with high n Achievement behave in many of the ways that theoretically should lead to successful entrepreneurship. But again, theory alone is not satisfactory. Do men with high n Achievement in fact more often become entrepreneurs and are they more successful in that role, as they should be if their motivation peculiarly fits them for it? Of course, there is no guarantee that society will make it easy for men with high n Achievement to enter business. However, as the previous chapter demonstrated, there is a built-in mechanism which tends to bias occupational choice toward business among boys of middle (but not upper) class status with high n Achievement. We might, therefore, expect in general to find more of them in business than, say, the professions. Furthermore, if n Achievement really adapts a man to perform the entrepreneurial role well, we should expect that those with lower n Achievement would on the average perform less well and would tend to be weeded out of managerial positions, leaving the n Achievement level in such positions higher than in other occupations.

So in a mobile society where an occupational position is somewhat dependent on performance (rather than on family or political connections), managers, executives, or entrepreneurs should have higher n Achievement than men in other comparable occupations. But what constitutes a comparable occupation—teaching, medicine, the law, the ministry, accounting? One can think of objections to all of them. For professionals must also behave in an entrepreneurial way at times. Probably the best comparison group would be a random sample of men of the same age and education from all other types of occupations. But we were able to approximate it only in the United States as shown in Table 7.1. Fortunately, two of the pictures used in our study of the motivation of businessmen in four countries were also used in the national survey of motivation on a random U.S. sample conducted by Veroff et al. (1960). Thus it was possible simply to compare achievement imagery scores on the two pictures for the 153 male college graduates in the sample with the scores made by a fairly representative group of successful middle level executives who were part of the Middle Management Program at the Harvard Business School or

TABLE 7.1 MEAN ACHIEVEMENT IMAGERY SCORES[1] FOR BUSINESS EXECUTIVES COM-
PARED WITH A NATIONAL SAMPLE OF MALE COLLEGE GRADUATES

Conditions		Business executives[2]	Male college graduates	Diff.	t	p
Picture #28[3]	N	50	153			
(man seated at	Mean	1.140	.758	.382	3.06	<.01
drafting board)	SD	.80	.57			
Picture #83[3]	N	50	153			
(conference table)	Mean	.900	.647	.253	2.16	<.05
	SD	.73	.65			

[1] Imagery scores only in which a score of +2 is given for achievement imagery, +1 for task imagery, and −1 for unrelated imagery.

[2] 28 executives (including some executive engineers) from the M.I.T. Sloane Fellow Program and 22 executives from the Harvard Business School Middle Management Program.

[3] The picture numbers refer to Atkinson's master code (1958a), #28 and #83 appearing in serial position 2 and 3 for the executive group and 4 and 5 for the national sample.

the M.I.T. Sloane Fellow Program. As predicted the stories written by the business leaders for each of the pictures contained significantly more achievement imagery than the stories written by the college-educated comparison group from a variety of occupations. The finding is not absolutely conclusive because the pictures might be considered more appropriate to a business group and because the test was administered individually (not in groups) by female interviewers in the national sample which may have lowered achievement imagery by suggesting other thoughts to the respondents. Still, finding the expected difference is encouraging enough to warrant investigating the matter further.

n Achievement Levels among Managers and Professionals in Four Countries

Since such random comparison samples were difficult to obtain, particularly in foreign countries where we wanted to check differences found in the United States, we decided that the most practicable alternative was to test comparison professional groups. While it is true that professionals must at times behave in entrepreneurial ways, they probably need do so less than a business entrepreneur. That is, by definition, their job requires primarily application of specialized knowledge to problems that fall within their province—whether medical, legal, educational, or theological. They should be most satisfied when they are able to solve a problem with the knowledge they have systematically acquired or memorized. The businessman, as we have argued in the preceding chapter, is more apt to be involved in new, risky or challenging problem situations in which there are many unknowns and he must improvise new solutions rather than apply existing specialized knowledge. Business and the professions overlap in what they require of a man, but business should require more of the behavior found to be characteristic of people high in n Achievement so that average differences in n Achievement levels should not be entirely obliterated. And testing professionals has some practical advantages. They are at least of equal status to business leaders and they can be rather easily tested while still attending professional schools, at an age not too much below that at which young business executives are already identifiable. It was therefore decided to compare average n Achievement levels among business leaders and professional groups using a standard set of six pictures representing men in a variety of common but ambiguous situations—e.g., an older man talking to a younger man in an office (which suggests a law office if anything), a man in his shirt sleeves sitting at a drafting board with a photograph of a woman and children in the background, several men talking around a conference table, a man working at a desk in a business office alone, a "father" talking to his son in a rural setting, and an obviously satisfied man relaxing in an easy chair, possibly in an airplane.[1]

A question of considerable interest is whether managers have higher n Achievement not only in a highly industralized country like the United States but also in less highly developed countries or in a Communist country that does not rely on the free enterprise system. One could easily make a case for the fact that in underdeveloped countries, the odds against business success are so great that an entrepreneur must be a real Schumpeterian "hero" to get ahead, a buccaneer perhaps with a high n Power. Or cultural relativists might argue that the motivation required for business success is different in every country depending on the structure of the business enterprise. For example, might it not require a different set of motives to get along in the typical French or Italian family firm than in a large U.S. corporation? Even more probably, why should a Communist plant manager have higher n Achievement, if, as many have argued, initiative is stifled by state capitalism because the manager cannot own the plant and, therefore, receive additional financial returns for expanding his business?

Such considerations led us to make the comparison not only in an economically advanced country, the United States, but also in a moderately developed country, Italy, both in the more developed North and the less developed South, in an underdeveloped country, Turkey, and in a Communist country, Poland. All tests (over 800) administered in these countries to managers,[2] usually attending management training courses, and to professionals were scored for n Achievement by the same person in a random order in English (after translation where necessary) without knowledge of the background of the person taking the test. The results as summarized in Table 7.2 are extremely interesting. The managers are higher in n Achievement than the professionals in every country except Turkey. In

TABLE 7.2   AVERAGE n ACHIEVEMENT SCORES OF MANAGERS AND PROFESSIONALS
IN THE UNITED STATES, ITALY, TURKEY, AND POLAND

Country and conditions	Managers	Professionals	Difference (Mgrs.-Prof.)	p
United States N	31[1]	31[1]		
Mean age	42.1	42.7		
Mean n Achievement score	6.74	4.77	1.97	$< .025\ pd$
SD	4.49	4.54		
Italy N	68[2]	107[3]		
Mean age	27.6	21.7		
Mean n Achievement score	4.18	2.31	1.87	$< .01\ pd$
SD	4.13	4.31		
Turkey N	17[4]	48[5]		
Mean age	33.1	27.2		
Mean n Achievement score	1.76	3.52	-1.76	NS
SD	3.99	5.81		
Poland N	31[6]	48[7]		
Mean age	35.9	27.2		
Mean n Achievement score	6.58	4.85	1.73	$< .10\ pd$
SD	5.22	4.98		

[1] Matched pairs of unit managers and specialists of same position level, age, educational background and length of service from the General Electric Company. See Behavior Research Service, 1960.

[2] 41 junior managers from various Italian companies attending IPSOA management training course in Torino (North Italy), 27 attending a similar course at ISIDA in Palermo (South Italy).

[3] 56 students of law, medicine, and theology from Torino and 51 of law and medicine from Palermo.

[4] Junior managers employed in private companies attending the Middle Management training programs of the Institute of Business Administration of the University of Istanbul (Bradburn, 1960).

[5] Students in the pedagogy program of the Gazi Institute, a higher teacher training college in Ankara (Bradburn, 1960).

[6] Managers from various Polish firms tested through the kind assistance of Dr. M. Choynowski, head of the psychometric laboratory of the Polish Academy of Sciences, Warsaw.

[7] Priests and educators also tested through the courtesy of Dr. Choynowski.

the United States a very careful comparison was made by the Behavior Research Service of the General Electric Company by matching 31 Unit Managers with staff specialists of the same position level (8), age (42 years), educational background (college graduates), and length of service (18 years). The specialists are professional in function though not exactly in the same sense as the professionals in the other countries. The managers scored significantly higher in n Achievement ($p < .025$ pd, using the differences between matched pairs). See Behavior Research Service (1960). Furthermore, the higher n Achievement level is not limited to managers in the General Electric Company. A group of middle level managers from many different U.S. companies scored significantly higher (mean = 8.90, see Table 7.9) than the G.E. managers or professionals, as did a comparable group of U.S. government middle managers (see Table 7.9).

In Italy the difference is even more significant and appears in the Southern as well as the Northern comparisons. The IPSOA management trainees (from Torino) scored higher than Northern professionals (4.12 vs. 2.66, $p < .05$ pd) and the ISIDA management trainees (from Palermo) scored still higher than comparable Southern professionals (4.26 vs. 1.90, $p < .025$ pd). Contrary to some expectations the managers from the more industrialized North did not show more "drive," i.e. more concern with achievement, than their Southern counterparts. The result, of course, is not conclusive because neither group is a random sample of businessmen in Northern or Southern Italy. It is therefore possible that, since ISIDA is a newer less widely known and accepted organization in the South, a more highly selected group of especially forward-looking, energetic young Sicilian businessmen enter it than in the North. Because the businessmen are nearly 6 years older on the average than the professionals, might not the age difference somehow account for the difference in n Achievement levels? However, if we consider only the 42 medical students in the professional group who are only three years younger on the average (mean age = 24.8), the difference in average n Achievement scores is even larger (4.18 vs. 1.24), or to make assurance doubly sure, smaller samples matched for age and social status of parents were drawn from the larger populations, and still the managers scored significantly higher in n Achievement than the professionals.

The case of Turkey is interesting because it reverses (although not significantly) the general trend. Does it suggest that outside of more developed countries like the U.S. and Italy, business managers in an underdeveloped country like Turkey do not have higher n Achievement than professionals? Such an eventuality is theoretically quite possible in the sense that the business community may not recruit men with high n Achievement for a variety of reasons, some of which we will discuss below when we look into the origins of these businessmen. Bradburn (1960), who collected the test data has evidence that the comparison group of educators was probably atypically high in n Achievement for Turkey because it drew from a sample of boys, an unusually large percentage of whom (over half) had left home by the age of 14 to attend Village Institutes (i.e., teacher-training schools). Both on theoretical and empirical grounds, a strong case exists for the fact that freeing a boy from the influence of an authoritarian father tends to favor the development of his n Achievement (see Chapter 9). The Village Institutes may unintentionally have raised the n Achievement level of the teacher population in Turkey by freeing boys from the repressive influence of their fathers.

But another possibility of considerable theoretical importance exists. Suppose it is not a question of just happening to choose a comparison professional group unusually high in n Achievement. Suppose it is not a question either of ineffective recruitment of young men with high n Achievement into business in Turkey. Suppose that, instead, here is a genuine exception to our whole line of reasoning—*that in Turkey it does not require high* n *Achievement to be a successful businessman*. Is this not a possible interpretation of the result? It is, but there is other evidence that makes it a highly unlikely one. Bradburn (1960) also tested 23 leading Turkish businessmen of a much higher level of success and prominence than the middle managers whose average score is presented in Table 7.2. These senior managers averaged 3.87 in n Achievement (see Table 7.9), nearly significantly higher than the private middle managers ($t = 1.65$, $p < .10$), and very significantly higher than all middle managers, including those from the government, ($N = 42$, mean $= 1.11$, mean difference $= 2.76$, $t = 2.91$, $p < .01$). In other words, the men who were outstanding businessmen in Istanbul were significantly higher in n Achievement than a group of less successful younger managers attending a middle management program at the University of Istanbul. Apparently in Turkey, too, n Achievement is associated with business success, and there is no reason to believe that in such underdeveloped countries n Achievement is no longer peculiarly adapted to the entrepreneurial role. So to explain the results obtained, the most likely remaining possibility is that the lower ranks of business management in Turkey, at least to judge by the sample attending this school, are not attracting efficiently the men with high n Achievement. The men training to be teachers are significantly higher in n Achievement than public and private middle managers combined (3.52 vs. 1.11, $t = 2.44$, $p < .05$).

In Poland the pattern is just like it is in such capitalist countries as the United States and Italy. The managers have higher n Achievement than the professionals. Even though the job of a manager in a Communist society differs in some respects from a similar job in a capitalist society, it must be similar enough to require the same type of motivation. Our finding fits in well with Granick's thesis (1960) that the Soviet executive is in fact under many of the same pressures to produce as his American counterpart. Apparently, ownership of the means of production is not crucial to people with high n Achievement, as was suggested by our data on preliterate tribes in Chapter 3, and, also, by French's finding cited in Chapter 6 that it made no difference in the performance of such people whether they were working for themselves or the group. Analysts of the American business scene have frequently made a similar point in stressing the increasing separation in this country between ownership and management. The psychological situation of a manager working for a very large company like General Electric, which he cannot be said to own in any real sense though he may own a few shares in it, would not appear to be very different from that of a Polish manager who is working for the state. Both are responsible to some higher board (one private, the other public) representing the ownership; neither has "pride of possession"; both have "knowledge of results," of how well they are doing by increased production, more pay, or promotion, and both must take risks to succeed. It is, therefore, not so surprising after all to find that Polish industry like General Electric is able to recruit and keep men with higher n Achievement for its managerial posts.

Although there are few places outside the public sector for such men to work in Poland, they might have entered the professions where they might have had more autonomy and "pride of possession." In the United States, they can leave General Electric and go start smaller companies which they can own in large part themselves. Perhaps, the large company is a sign of "decay" in the free-enterprise capitalist system in the sense that it destroys the initiative of its managers or, to speak more precisely, forces out more of those with high n Achievement who leave in disgust to found their own firms. The fact that the n Achievement levels of managers for General Electric and for Polish state industry are almost identical might be taken as a sign, not that Communism requires so much of the entrepreneurial spirit, but that large U.S. corporations require so little. Perhaps the men with highest n Achievement in the U.S. are still the owner-managers, the ideal type of the capitalist entrepreneur. At first sight a figure cited earlier might seem to support such a view: the mean n Achievement score for middle-level business executives from assorted companies, many of which were much smaller than General Electric, is significantly higher than for the G.E. managers. But the comparison is not fair because there were a number of salesmen in the executive group, and none in the General Electric sample, and as we shall see in a moment, salesmen score higher in n Achievement. A fairer comparison can be made by dividing a large sample of senior executives in the Advanced Management Program at Harvard into those who were getting the top or nearly the top salary in their company vs. those who were not. Since the Program does not recruit the top executives from major U.S. firms in this age group (35-50), the former were largely owner-managers of small companies receiving lower salaries (median around $18,000 a year) than the executives from larger firms (median around $28,000 a year) who, however, were much further "down the line" in power and ownership than those from small companies. The mean n Achievement score for the 26 "owner-managers" of smaller companies was 5.4 (for a four- instead of a six-picture test) as contrasted with 5.8 for the executives from the larger organizations, a difference of no statistical significance. Once again there is no evidence that ownership is of importance to the man with high n Achievement, though it may be to the man of high n Power (see below). Owning and operating smaller businesses is not the special refuge of the man with high n Achievement even in a capitalist society where he is free to make such a choice.

A final point about Table 7.2 of considerable interest is the average level of n Achievement among managers in the four countries and how it compares with reader estimates of national n Achievement and recent rates of economic growth. The average for an assorted sample of U.S. managers (8.90, Table 7.8) is significantly higher than for a similar sample of Polish managers (6.58), which is significantly higher than for a sample of Italian managers (4.18), which in turn is significantly higher than for the Turkish junior managers (1.76) but not for the Turkish senior managers (3.87). The U.S.-Italian difference agrees both with the reader estimate of n Achievement and the differential rate of economic growth in the two countries (Table 3.6). But Poland and Turkey present problems. Poland was developing considerably more rapidly than average in the period 1952-1958, but the reader estimate of n Achievement level was well below average. We argued at the time that the books used were not representative and the present data showing the high level of n Achievement among Polish managers strongly support that view. Turkey presents a more serious paradox. Its reader level of n Achievement is the highest recorded in 1950; its rate of economic growth is also well above average. But the n Achievement level among its managers is the lowest recorded. No simple explanation comes to mind. We can reasonably infer that the schoolbooks may be atypically high in n Achievement because as we have seen, the teachers in Turkey seem to be especially high in n Achievement. But then we must reason that Turkey's rapid economic growth was, at least in part, due to some outside factor, rather than its own high level of entrepreneurial spirit. One such factor could certainly have been the large amount of foreign aid (including technical and managerial assistance as well as grants and loans) given Turkey during this period by the United States (Higgins, 1959, p. 606). But unless our sampling of Turkish executives is markedly atypical, one would have to predict that the future of the Turkish economy looks bleak, particularly if foreign aid is withdrawn, unless some way can be found of drawing more of the men with high n Achievement into managing the economy, either in the private or public sector.

With the possible exception of Turkey then, our data on the n Achievement levels of managers in various countries fits fairly well our general hypothesis that reader n Achievement levels reflect the determination to move ahead economically among those élite groups most responsible for managing a nation's economy.

n Achievement Levels in Various Types of Business Occupations

Is n Achievement more suited to some business occupations than others? Our extensive testing of businessmen in four countries permits us to answer the question at least so far as five general types of business activity are concerned, i.e., general management, sales and marketing, finance, engineering, and personnel. Among the U.S. senior managers from various companies, the 24 men who classified themselves as in marketing were clearly above average in n Achievement (75 per cent above the median, $\chi^2 = 6.00$, $p < .02$) as contrasted with the remaining 54 men classified either as in production and engineering (somewhat below average) or control and finance (average). A more general comparison involving men from all four countries also shows the salesmen to be higher. That is, the average n Achievement score for 184 general managers is 5.43, $SD = 5.10$ as contrasted with 7.53, $SD = 6.05$ for 40 salesmen, when both samples are drawn in equal proportions from the four countries, e.g., 45 per cent from the United States (not including the senior managers just mentioned), 24 per cent from Italy, 23 per cent from Turkey, and 8 per cent from Poland. The difference of 2.10 is significant ($t = 2.02$, $p < .05$) and cannot be attributed to different proportions of men from different countries. The sample of 27 finance men in the group is somewhat less comparable (41 per cent U.S., 37 per cent Turkish, 11 per cent Italian, 11 per cent Polish) but for what it is worth, their average score is very similar to that for the general managers (5.32, $SD = 5.91$).

Adequate samples for engineers and personnel men were available only in the United States. Their average scores in no case (for the senior managers or for the middle managers from the government or private industry) differed significantly from the average for the general managers, although the government engineers were somewhat higher (mean = 9.2) than the government managers (7.7).

The most general conclusion to be drawn from this analysis is that only the men involved in sales and marketing tend to have higher n Achievement within the business community. Such a result does not come as a great surprise since the marketing role certainly requires to an unusual degree the kind of entrepreneurial activity (risk-taking, knowledge of results of sales campaigns, etc.) that we have found to be characteristic of high n Achievement.

n Achievement and Managerial Success

So far all our data have dealt with the higher level of n Achievement in more entrepreneurial as compared with less entrepreneurial occupations. But *within* the entrepreneurial occupations, higher n Achievement should in general lead to greater success, if our general line of reasoning is correct. Some data that we have collected point in this direction, although not without qualifications. For example, in an early study we argued that older men in the Harvard Business School Middle Management Program might be regarded as less successful since they had taken longer to reach approximately the same level of distinction, assuming that being sent to the Program was a mark of distinction. At any rate the 23 men 36 years of age and older had an average n Achievement score of 7.61 as contrasted with 9.73 for the

33 men under 36 (diff. = 2.12, $t = 1.58$, $p < .10$ pd). The finding is not completely unambiguous because n Achievement may generally decline with age. If so, however, the greater n Achievement of senior managers in Turkey already reported takes on an even greater significance. There the more successful Turkish business leaders (who were also older) had significantly higher n Achievement than the less outstanding middle managers.

A more detailed analysis is available on the relationship between salary level and n Achievement among the U.S. senior managerial group already mentioned. It was first necessary to separate the men into those who were more or less the top executives in small businesses and those who were important executives in large businesses, because the salary levels in the two types of companies were not comparable. The distinction was arbitrarily made on the basis of the top salary reported for the company, with $65,000 a year or more being the cutting point distinguishing a large business from a small one. For the 22 men from smaller companies on whom there was full information, it was hard to get a good measure of success, but the results tended in the predicted direction. The 10 who could be classified as receiving the top salary in their company had a mean n Achievement score of 6.60 as contrasted with 4.33 for the 12 who were not receiving the top salary, a difference of 2.27, $t = 1.23$, p < .15 pd. But further adjustments in this comparison are really justified. That is, there were several older men in the group (age 46-50) who were getting the top salary in the company but it was in the lowest bracket (less than $15,000 a year). These could reasonably be classified as less rather than more successful. On the other hand, there were some relatively young men (age 36-40) who were not earning the top salary yet who were earning high salaries for their age. If these men, too, were reclassified—i.e., placed in the more rather than the less successful category—the difference between the two groups is larger (2.73) and more significant ($p < .10$ pd). So men with higher n Achievement are likely to be more successful in small companies.

In large companies the situation is considerably more complex, as Fig. 7.1 shows. Oddly enough it is those in a middle salary bracket that have the highest n Achievement. They are significantly higher than those in the lowest salary bracket ($t = 3.59$, $p < .01$) and than all those being paid more than they are ($t = 2.46$, $p < .02$). The four cases in the sample over 50 were omitted because they were all low in n Achievement and the three under 35 were also omitted because they were all high. Within the age range of 35-50 there is no interaction effect of age × salary level × n Achievement. The men earning between $20-25,000 a year are always higher in n Achievement whatever their age. Probably the best way to describe the result is to say that n Achievement has a decisive effect in raising people out of the lowest salary brackets into a middle bracket. If we consider only the men earning $25,000 a year or less 83 per cent of those with high n Achievement (score of 7 or more) are in the higher income bracket. But with men paid even more the picture changes in the opposite direction. A greater percentage of men in the low n Achievement group are earning over $25,000 a year. The result is curious and raises a host of interesting questions. Does increasing money income above a certain point tend to satisfy achievement needs and lower n Achievement scores? Are salaries in large U.S. corporations above a certain point no longer so directly a function of entrepreneurial drive, but of other variables such as specialized knowledge or personal leadership characteristics? In particular, what role does kinship play in the higher levels of executive salaries in U.S. corporations? Is it possible that some of these high

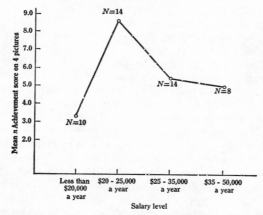

Figure 7.1 Relationship of n Achievement and salary level among middle-aged executives (age 35-50) in large U.S. corporations (top salary $65-250,000 a year)

salaries are a function of the relationship of a man to an owner of the company rather than his entrepreneurial drive? Unfortunately we can only raise these questions, not answer them at the present time. We must be satisfied with the finding that at least at the lower levels n Achievement seems to contribute to managerial success in large U.S. companies.

To turn to some evidence from abroad, we had enough information to be able to divide the Polish managers into those who were supervising 1-30 subordinates and those who supervised over 30. The 13 in the former group, who might be regarded as being less successful in the sense of having less responsible jobs, had a mean n Achievement score of 5.62 as contrasted with 8.83 for the 12 men occupying more responsible positions. The difference of 3.21 is significant at $p < .10$ pd. Similarly in Italy, where the sample included lower level supervisors, we were able to find 7 men supervising 1-5 subordinates as contrasted with 8 men supervising 6-30 subordinates. Again the mean n Achievement score of the former group occupying less responsible positions is lower (3.5) than for the latter occupying more responsible positions (6.4), the difference being 3.1, $p < .10$ pd. If we combine the probabilities from the two samples, we can feel reasonably confident ($p < .05$ pd) that the differences did not arise by chance. To the extent then that managerial ability is measured by the number of men the manager is put in charge of, there is evidence that n Achievement is associated with managerial success.

But not all such evidence is positive. Hill (1959) made a study of U.S. government managers carefully matched for age and type of occupation (engineering, personnel, accountants-auditors, general administration, purchasing) but differing in civil service grade. He found that those with higher rank (GS—14 and 15) scored only slightly and not significantly higher than those of similar age and job type but lower rank (GS—12 and 13). Apparently speed with which high rank is attained in the U.S. civil service is not related to n Achievement. Unfortunately this finding could not really be checked abroad, although for what it is worth, it can be reported that the average n Achievement score of 5 Italian government managers supervising 6-30 employees also was not higher than the average n Achievement score of 4 other managers supervising 1-5 employees. At the present writing there is no evidence that managerial *success* in the public sector is associated with higher n Achievement, except, of course, where practically all managers are public employees, as in Poland.

Furthermore, a study has been made of beginning life insurance salesmen to see whether those with higher n Achievement perform better. They do not. Forty-four per cent of the men classified as "successes" ($N = 25$) had high n Achievement as contrasted with 54 per cent of the men classified as "failures" ($N = 26$). The "failures" included many who found that they did not like the business of continually trying to make contacts with complete strangers over the phone—a very special ability that may not be related to the kind of managerial talent we have been studying—but the finding serves to emphasize the fact that the theory does not require that high n Achievement will lead to greater success in all types of managerial or sales jobs in all types of organizations under all conditions. Basically the theory as presented in detail in Chapter 6 predicts only that n Achievement promotes success when the job presents some challenge or risk to which the person can respond with appropriate problem-solving activities, discover how well he is doing, etc. A particular job, though classified as managerial, might not permit a man to exercize his entrepreneurial skills and hence discourage people from staying in it with high n Achievement. Or an organization might reward people with higher salaries or more responsibility, not on the basis of accomplishment but on the basis of seniority, kinship, or other such factors. In such cases and many others, one should not expect a relationship between n Achievement and managerial success. It might even be argued that the evidence so far presented, both theoretical (in Chapter 6) and practical (in Chapter 7), makes such a strong case for the association between n Achievement and entrepreneurial success that when the association is not obtained, it can be considered *prima facie* evidence that one or more of the conditions defining the entrepreneurial role in the theoretical sense has not been met.

Entrepreneurial Success in Rural India

One way to escape the complexities of modern business organizations and the way they define occupational roles or reward their incumbents is to seek out the "pure case," the small-time entrepreneur who has little or nothing to work with but his own skills. It is here that we should see the effects of higher n Achievement most clearly, uncomplicated by organizational factors, differential access to managerial jobs, etc. Fraser (1961) has collected some fascinating data from potential, small-time entrepreneurs in a rural village in Orissa Province, India. He tested a number of mechanics trainees for n Achievement, using the graphic expression method described in Chapter 8 and Appendix IV. He then waited over a year and checked to see which of them had made use of their training in the sense of functioning more or less as independent artisans in work related to their training (i.e., as mechanics, carpenters, masons). Table 7.3 summarizes his findings. It also has the advantage of giving some concrete case detail on how men with high and low n Achievement behave whereas in previous studies we have dealt only with "impersonal" average scores.

Even though exact classification of individuals into those more or less actively engaged in skilled labor related to their training is difficult and in several cases questionable, obviously the men with high n Achievement show more entrepreneurial spirit and less involvement in traditional cultivation of the soil than those with low n Achievement ($p < .05$ pd). Three of the four men with the highest scores run very active and successful shops for such a backward rural setting. The fourth may well do likewise eventually if he goes to work in a nearby town as he is thinking of doing: mobility is one of the characteristics of people with high n Achievement (see Chapter 8). The six with lowest scores are without exception not engaged in anything like full-time work related to their training. It may be objected that two of them are in school and may turn out to be active later, but it is wise not to count on it in advance since further schooling may be an alternative to entrepreneurial activity, particularly for those with low n Achievement. It should also be noted that while Dhansingh must be classified with the "less entrepreneurial" group, he might easily move into the "more entrepreneurial" group if he leaves his small village for better opportunities elsewhere, as he is currently thinking of doing. In a sense he is an "untapped manpower resource" so far as the economy is concerned, because of the limitations of his immediate environment.

One final point about these findings: the men in class B at the bottom of

TABLE 7.3 SUBSEQUENT EMPLOYMENT OF INDIAN VILLAGE MECHANICS TRAINEES
VARYING IN n ACHIEVEMENT (GRAPHIC)

A. Employed more or less fully in work related to construction

Name	n Ach score[1]	Description of employment 12-18 months later
Parmanand[2]	23	Does cycle welding, diesel work, soldering, masonry; takes orders from government agencies (e.g., cement hume pipes); owns no land.
Chungilal	16	Has set up shop in his village, taken on assistant, invested in considerable supply of lumber for future work, makes doors, door frames, loom parts.
Trilochen	16	Has been in charge of construction of several houses in his village, will build weeders for the cultivators during monsoon; when such work unavailable supports himself by silversmithing.
Chandra	13	Full-time making bullock cart wheels for sale (expensive items locally); more demand than he can fill.
Chaitanga	13	Small backward village does not provide many jobs but has repaired pumps, helped on construction of school building.
Khadia	11	Full-time carpenter's helper, fair pay.
Panika	10	Earns fair income from cot-making and loom repairs, also engages in cultivation and priestly duties.
Premanand	9	Full time work as assistant in shop of Barpali Village Service; also helps village carpenter.
Pandaba	7	Takes housebuilding, carpentry jobs whenever he can get them, has specialized in doors and windows, cultivates for lack of demand for furniture, etc.
Average	**13.1**	7 out of 9 high in n Achievement.

B. Not employed more or less fully in work related to construction

Name	n Ach score	Description of employment 12-18 months later
Dhansingh	16	Most of the time busy cultivating, has made plows for his family, doors for several houses, is considering getting a carpentry or masonry job in nearby towns.
Kasinath	13	Comes from a family of carpenters, but generally does more agricultural work than others in the family. Takes carpentry jobs when available.
Jageswar	10	Only child of well-to-do, landed family. Has constructed clothes closet, plow, brick cattle feeding trough, latrines, for use of own family.
Kama	7	Too busy with local agricultural cooperative to do much carpentry.
Chaturbhuj	5	Worked as a clerk, now studying blacksmithing.
Bipin	5	Studying carpentry in government school.
Dhaneswar	5	Tried carpentry at low pay, left, has been out of work for some months, supported by brothers.
Dadhi	4	Main occupation is cultivation, but when time permits he does private carpentry and masonry jobs.
Kartikeswar	1	Full-time cultivation; aside from building and repairing own tools (as do most other cultivators) has not used his training at all.
Surendra	−13	Has done no work related to his training; currently a dyer for a local weaving organization.
Average	5.3	3 out of 10 high in n Achievement.

$p < .05$ pd that higher n Achievement is associated with greater occupational activity related to construction.
[1] D-F score; see Appendix IV. In case of re-tests, the highest score is reported.
[2] Full names are not given to avoid easy identification. (After Fraser, 1961).

Table 7.3 can in no sense be considered "failures," except possibly Dhaneswar. For instance, Kama, who is busy with the local agricultural cooperative, is a useful and valuable member of his community. The point is rather that his low achievement motivation simply does not fit him well for entrepreneurial craft activities involving constructions that provide concrete knowledge of results (see Chapter 6 and Moss and Kagan, 1961). He undoubtedly has strong other motives that fit him for the work he is doing. The table simply supports the theoretical argument of Chapter 6 that n Achievement fits people for entrepreneurial jobs, particularly those with concrete knowledge of results, here represented in the construction activities of mechanics, carpentry, masonry and the like. One cannot help wondering what would happen if men like the first four in the table were given financial and technical assistance to expand their businesses, and if Dhansingh were helped to get started in town. Certainly it is such people who would be most likely to make the best use of outside help and to contribute to the economic development of this backward rural area.

Recruitment of Italian Entrepreneurs and Professionals

In the preceding chapter we presented some evidence to show that students with high n Achievement would be more likely to aspire to business occupations if they were of middle or lower-middle class origin than if they were of upper class origin. In the latter case they should be more likely to aspire to the professions as being both accessible to them and more prestigeful. Using the motivational data already collected, we can now classify managers and professionals according to their social class background and attempt to see whether the recruitment patterns in fact approximate expectations based on the aspirations of youth. There is some reason to think they might, since Moss and Kagan (1961) have demonstrated that n Achievement is reasonably stable from adolescence into early adulthood. Italy is the only country from which the sample was large enough to permit this kind of analysis, and Table 7.4 represents an attempt to tease out the main factors influencing professional and career choices there.

It shows in the first row the social class origins, by father's occupation of the 259 men in the entire Italian sample and also the number and percentage of men from each of the three social classes that were high in n Achievement (above the median of 2.5). Obviously the middle class is higher in n Achievement (chi-square $= 4.05$, $p < .05$) as it is in the United States (Table 9.7). Next a random sample of 61 professionals was drawn (37 from the North and 24 from the South) to match the 61 middle managers on whom we had full information, and Table 7.4 shows the number of each group from each type of social background and the number and percentage of each group from each social class that were high in n Achievement. Before interpreting the results it should be stressed (1) that the social class

TABLE 7.4 PROPORTIONS OF ITALIAN BUSINESSMEN AND OTHERS WITH HIGH
         n ACHIEVEMENT DRAWN FROM DIFFERENT SOCIAL CLASSES

Occupations	Lower middle class (4)[1]			Middle class (5)[2]			Upper class (6)[3]		
	N	n (high)[4]	% high[4]	N	n (high)[4]	% high[4]	N	n (high)[4]	% high[4]
Total[7]	135	64	47	77	46	60	47	20	43
A. Business managers[5]	35	22	63	16	13	81	10	5	50
% of "highs" from class		(34%)			28%			25%	
B. Professionals[6]	35	13	37	10	5	50	16	4	25
% of "highs" from class		(20%)			11%			20%	

[1] Father's occupation: chiefly clerical and small business (level 4) or less (i.e., level 1-3, 28 blue collar families).

[2] Father's occupation: level 5, minor professional, medium business.

[3] Father's occupation: level 6, major professional or business executive.

[4] Number (n) and per cent above the median in n Achievement (score = $+3$ or more), e.g., $64/135 = 47\%$.

[5] Thirty-seven students of medicine, law and theology from Torino and 24 students of medicine and law from Palermo.

[6] Thirty-seven middle managers from Torino (IPSOA training program) and 24 from Palermo (ISIDA training program).

[7] Ninety-seven professionals plus 61 businessmen plus 52 students of commerce (Torino and Palermo), and 49 government employees in a special training course at Bologna.

information was often not very adequate, so that the classification by social class contains more than the usual margin of error, and (2) the total sample tested bears an unknown relationship to the true distribution of men and n Achievement by social class in Italy. It is not a random sample, but one biased toward occupations that draw heavily from the upper end of the social class scale. With these cautions in mind, let us see if we can make sense of the results in terms of general theoretical expectations.

Professionals should be drawn more frequently from upper social status (class 6) and businessmen from middle social status (class 5) because professional parents are put in class 6 and business parents more often in class 5 and, in general, there is a strong tendency for sons to stay within their father's occupational classification (Warner and Abegglen, 1955, p. 54). This is, in fact, what happens. Of the 26 men in the business sample from classes 5 and 6, 16 or 61.5 per cent come from class 5, whereas, the situation is exactly reversed for the professionals, the majority coming from the upper class ($\chi^2 = 2.8$, $p < .10$). The larger absolute numbers for both groups coming from the lower middle class or below are, of course, deceptive because they are drawn from a much larger population base than is represented in our total sample. Since our concern was primarily with business and professional groups, we have oversampled heavily from the upper end of the social class scale. But there is no reason to believe that the samples from classes 5 and 6 are markedly unrepresentative. For example, in the total sample 70 per cent of the sons from class 6 backgrounds were classified as being either in business or the professions as contrasted with 42 per cent of those from class 5 backgrounds. As expected, many more of those from class 5 backgrounds were following careers of lower status such as commercial courses, or government employment. It is easier and more common for sons of upper status to go into fairly high-level managerial positions and the professions than for sons of middle status.

The distribution of high n Achievement among these various groups is a little more complicated and harder to interpret. From our analysis of the aspirations of youth in Chapter 6, we would expect that the ones with high n Achievement from the lower classes should aspire more often to business careers. We have made an attempt to check this hypothesis by showing in Table 7.4 what proportion of the total number of men with high n Achievement from a given social class end up in business or the professions. From classes 4 (and below) and 5, a greater percentage of the "highs" are in business, as predicted. The percentages for class 4 (34 vs. 20 per cent) are particularly dubious because we have probably overestimated the number of highs in this class by including in our sample only fairly upwardly mobile men. However, for class 5, the difference is somewhat more trustworthy (28 vs. 11 per cent) and statistically significant ($p < .05$). More of the supply of entrepreneurial talent (high n Achievement) is drawn into business rather than the professions from a middle class background.

So far so good, but for class 6 the results do not fit in easily with the vocational aspiration findings in Chapter 6. There we found that young men with high n Achievement from upper class backgrounds preferred the even higher prestige professions more. If they followed out their aspirations, more upper class men with high n Achievement should end up in the professions, but such is not the case according to the data in Table 7.4. In Italy, at least, about the same proportion of those high in n Achievement (25 and 20 per cent) end up in business and the professions respectively. But even more remarkably a much higher percentage of the men from class 6 with low n Achievement are in the professions (44 per cent) as compared with business (19 per cent) so that there remains a differential in n Achievement between businessmen and professionals as for other social class backgrounds.

How can this anomaly be explained? It is tempting to speculate. Perhaps since it is easy for men with professional (class 6) fathers to slide into the professions, it is the course of least resistance for men with low n Achievement. For men from class 5 homes, on the other hand, a professional career involves more of a challenge, hence includes more of the more venturous young men (i.e., 50 per cent of those in the professions from class 5 are high in n Achievement vs. 25 per cent from class 6).

Business recruits an even higher percentage of "highs" (81 vs. 50 per cent) from class 5 backgrounds because it is a more feasible career for such young men to pursue. Or perhaps there is a strong *selective* factor in managerial occupations that markedly changes the pattern one would expect on the basis of vocational aspirations. Consider the men from class 6 background. It is conceivable that 30 of them *started out* in business, including, let us say for the sake of the argument, only 5 with high *n* Achievement or 16 per cent—a lower proportion (as predicted) pursuing business careers than a professional career (25 per cent). Then we must suppose that out of this 30 only 10 rose into the managerial group we sampled including all 5 of those high in *n* Achievement, since we have shown that *n* Achievement is specific to managerial success.

On the other hand, it is not specific to professional success so that a similar process of "weeding out" those with low *n* Achievement from class 6 in the professions does not take place. Such speculations can not be tested conclusively with the data at hand, since the numbers are small and many of the differences nonsignificant. They are useful in pointing to many of the social complexities that intervene between the aspirations of youth and the careers they ultimately follow. What is abundantly clear from the data is that Italian businessmen have higher *n* Achievement than Italian professionals whatever their social background, but that the difference is most marked for men from what we have labeled the "middle" class, where *n* Achievement is also higher.

Social Class Background of Managers in Various Countries

Warner and Abegglen (1955), Lipset and Bendix (1959), and others have intensively pursued the question of what types of social background American business leaders have been drawn from. They have been largely interested in determining whether the proportions drawn from different sources have changed throughout the history of the United States. The question is important for economic development because it deals with the sources of managerial talent at different stages or levels in development. The U.S. studies show in general that 50-80 per cent of the business élite has come from a middle to upper status background in a fairly stable proportion over the last 150 years (Lipset and Bendix, 1959, pp. 134-135). The variation in proportions depends on how the social class categories are defined. Since the percentage of fathers enjoying such high status was smaller several generations ago than today (see Warner and Abegglen, pp. 40, 45), this means in effect that business leaders were drawn from a smaller élite group then than now. Warner and Abegglen (1955, p. 68), also note that the proportion of business leaders who were sons of laborers increased from 7 per cent in 1900 to 15 per cent in 1950, despite the fact that the percentage of such people in the total population remained fairly constant. There is evidence that as the United States has developed, business leaders have been drawn more widely from a less élite group.

What about the countries we have studied? Are the business leaders in the less developed countries drawn disproportionately from more upper class groups than in the more developed countries? Table 7.5 summarizes

TABLE 7.5 SOCIAL CLASS BACKGROUND OF MANAGERS IN TURKEY, MEXICO, ITALY, U.S. AND POLAND

Social class	Turkey		Mexico* private $N = 69$ %	Italy		U.S. private $N = 158$ %	Poland $N = 25$ %
	Private $N = 39$ %	Public $N = 24$ %		Public $N = 49$ %	Private $N = 61$ %		
1-3. Lower	0	4	12	2	8	22	40
4. Lower middle	18	54	30	53	49	26	56
5. Middle	28	25	39	22	26	32	4
6. Upper middle and upper	54	17	19	22	16	20	0

Unclassifiable cases not included (e.g., military or government service backgrounds) or inadequate information.

(1) Unskilled, (2) semiskilled and (3) skilled laborers, foremen, public service workers, and tenant farmers.

(4) Clerical or sales occupations, small farm owners, small business.

(5) Minor professional (e.g., high-school teachers, medical technicians) medium business, and large farms with paid help.

(6) Major professionals, executives, and owners.

* 22 salesmen (including managers) from a management course at Mexico City College and a random sample of 47 middle-level executives provided through the courtesy of Dr. Elliott Dantzig of Dando, Mexico City. Median age = 33. All other samples as presented in Table 7.8.

what data we were able to collect on the point. As far as the most underdeveloped country is concerned, Turkey, the expectation is borne out. A very high proportion of the business leaders in the private sector (54 per cent) come from the tiny segment of the Turkish population enjoying the highest occupational status (class 6). Alexander's figures for the Izmir region are not easy to compare directly with these. His industrialists from the private sector also appear to be drawn heavily from the upper end of the socioeconomic scale, but not to such an extreme degree: 17 per cent came from our classes 1-3 and probably somewhere between 50-70 per cent from our classes 5 and 6 (Alexander, 1960, p. 352). The government middle managers from the Istanbul region are drawn more democratically and predominantly from the much more common class 4 background as in other countries. To look at the other extreme for a moment, business executives in the United States, the most developed country, seem to be drawn in fairly equal proportions from all class groups. Our sample from the Advanced Management Program at the Harvard Business School is possibly somewhat less élite than the business leaders studied by others, but it is more comparable to our foreign businessmen. Even so, the percentages do not differ by much from those obtained by other investigators. In the Warner and Abegglen sample 19 per cent of the business leaders come from a blue-collar background (including foremen) vs. 22 per cent for our sample, and 26 per cent were from a class 6 background (professionals, owners of large businesses, major executives) vs. 20 per cent here. Bendix and Lipset report a stable percentage of such men coming from "manual" backgrounds of around 12 per cent (1959, p. 134) which is precisely what our percentage would be if we subtracted the 10 per cent of the group whose fathers were foremen.

The other two non-Communist and less developed countries, Mexico and Italy, are like Turkey in having a smaller percentage of men from blue collar backgrounds than in the United States. They are unlike Turkey, however, in drawing businessmen largely from the middle and lower middle classes. Thus there is support in these data for the commonly held view that outside the United States "access to managerial positions is rigidly restricted" (Harbison and Burgess, quoted in Fayerweather, 1959, p. 100) but not in the extreme form in which the proposition is sometimes stated. The rigidity of restriction is much greater in Turkey than in Italy or Mexico. In fact, it is tempting to see a trend in these data, as the italicized figures show, for increasing proportions of business leaders to be drawn from lower and lower status groups as the country develops more. Going from less to more developed countries the largest percentages of business executives in the private sector are drawn from class 6 for Turkey, class 5 for Mexico, and class 4 for Italy. Then in the most developed country, the United States, significantly more (though not the largest number) are drawn from class 3 and below. However, the trend is no more than suggested by the data because comparable social class identifications in different countries are very hard to make and, furthermore, it is not certain that the managerial groups are exactly comparable.

Poland stands alone among the countries in that a very high proportion of the managers report a working-class background. Probably they exaggerate somewhat since many such men would probably hesitate to admit an upperclass background in a Communist country. But the same bias should in fact be operating somewhat against the employment of such men as managers so that Polish managers may very well be drawn in greater proportions from the lower classes just as the data show. That is, Communist ideology may succeed to some extent in doing what it sets out to do—namely to create a "workers'" state which draws less on men of bourgeois origin. Granick reports (1960, p. 55) similarly that 55 per cent of a group of Russian factory department superintendents (comparable to our middle management groups) stated that they came from blue-collar families (our classes 1-3).

The interesting question is whether this or any other method of recruiting business managers is most likely to draw more efficiently on the supply of entrepreneurial talent (high n Achievement) in a country. Figure 7.2 has been drawn up in an attempt to shed some light on the problem.

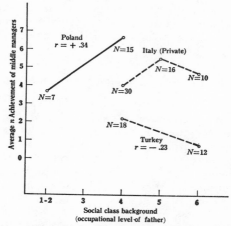

Figure 7.2 Average n Achievement levels of middle-level managers in Poland, Turkey and Italy as a function of class background

Interestingly enough, it shows that the Poles have not gained anything in n Achievement of their managers by recruiting them more from the lower classes because these men have lower n Achievement. The same thing is true of the Turks but in reverse. They recruit managers more heavily from the upper classes but these men also have lower n Achievement. The trends for the private and public Turkish middle managers are identical and have here been combined to give a more stable result. To put it in another way, the correlation between n Achievement and higher social status is positive ($r = .34$) in Poland and negative ($r = -.23$) in Turkey, the difference between the two correlations being significant ($t = 2.15$, $p < .05$). The findings agree fairly well with those for Italy which also show a peak in the n Achievement of managers from a "middle status" background, though it is at a different point (class 5) than in the contrast between Poland and Turkey (class 4).

While the findings are not conclusive, they suggest that the best place to recruit business managers is from the middle classes because they are more apt to have higher n Achievement from that background than if they come from a lower or an upper class background. If we add our tentative generalization for Table 7.5 to this one, it follows that countries at very low levels of development, like Turkey, are apt to recruit n Achievement talent inefficiently because managers are drawn in such large proportions from the upper class. In a sense they have to create a larger middle class before they can draw such talent from it. So a vicious circle is involved: development is necessary to create a larger pool of middle-class entrepreneurial talent which makes development possible. The Communist technique of recruiting more heavily from the working classes does not seem to be more efficient, to judge by the Polish data, although Communist ideology may have played a part in raising over-all n Achievement levels in Russia (Chapter 3) and here among the Poles.

Recruitment of Business Leaders from Disadvantaged Minority Groups

Hagen (1958, 1961) has made a special point of the importance of disadvantaged minority groups in supplying business leadership in times of economic growth and change. There are many historical examples—the Dissenters in England, the Protestants in France, the Samurai in Japan, the Jews in many countries, and the Parsees in India. His argument is that men in these groups feel discriminated against and compensate in the best and often the only way open to them—by succeeding in business. Put in the context of our present analysis, the argument makes good sense, provided the minority group has predominantly middle class status and reasonably high n Achievement. Young men with high n Achievement from such groups should normally aspire to the high prestige professions (Chapter 6) or positions of political or governmental leadership, but they may be blocked from entering such careers by discrimination against them. If so, they should turn to business as the next best alternative for high achievement. In this way the high percentage of business leaders from minority group backgrounds in many countries can rather easily be explained.

It should, however, be clear that the explanation works *only* if there are an appreciable number of young men with high n Achievement in the group, and if the group has reached at least lower middle class status. Thus there are a number of disadvantaged minority groups—the Catholics in England, the Negroes in the United States—that have not supplied a high percentage of business leaders. Since measures of n Achievement are not usually available on such groups, one can predict that they will supply more than their share of entrepreneurs only (1) if they are predominantly middle class, assuming on the basis of Fig. 7.2 and Table 9.7 that the middle class is higher in n Achievement and also has sufficient *opportunity* to start businesses, and (2) if they are prevented from entering higher prestige occupations.

The Individual as Promoter of His Own Career

All the discussion on how individuals with high n Achievement start out from various social classes, with various aspirations, and end up more often in positions of managerial leadership has been excessively abstract. It gives very little notion of the *processes* which intervene between the starting and end points in a career. Fortunately Dill, Hilton and Reitman (1961) have provided us with a good description of how an individual with high n Achievement acts in the pursuit of his career. They do not intend their description to apply only to such people, but it nevertheless fits them particularly well, in terms of all we know about n Achievement (see also Chapter 8). For example, they discuss the early stages in the career of a young American whom they call Olin Larson, a graduate of a school of Business Administration. He joined a large company as an administrative assistant and was put in charge of a file—not a very exciting task for someone who had aspirations of being an executive. But he decided the file needed a better index so that it could be more useful to management. He also made some changes as to what information should go into the file, after talking with various executives to find out what kind of information they wanted from it. Finally, "he took some of the responsibility of finding people to make changes and additions to the file, and he was ready himself to help them carry these through." (Dill *et al.*, 1961.)

They focus here on the *strategies of advancement* that Larson used. He (1) wanted to do a good job, to get ahead, (2) developed better strategies for noting relevant features of the job environment (found out what people wanted from the file), (3) adapted his strategies to fit what he perceived (changed what went into the file), (4) did not let the organization define his job for him (did not simply accept the file-supervision job as it was presented to him), and (5) was willing to take reasonable risks (changed the file, even though someone might have liked it better the way it was). Larson was what they call an "agent of his own progress." He took an active attitude toward his environment, even to the setbacks that it had in store for him. He was, not surprisingly, soon considered a very useful and enterprising junior executive by the company. It is in some such ways that we can best imagine how young men with high n Achievement pursue their careers and end up more often in positions of business leadership.

Value Attitudes of Entrepreneurs and Professionals

So far we have focused exclusively on n Achievement, but in Chapter 6 we discussed extensively other characteristics that entrepreneurs should have, either derived from the theory of n Achievement or from an analysis

of the structural demands of the business role. None of these characteristics bears directly on n Affiliation or n Power but be it noted in passing
that the fantasy tests were scored for these variables as well as n Achievement. The results (see Appendix Table VII.1) showed no differences between managers and professionals on these two motives across countries.
Many of the businessmen and professionals in various countries were given
in addition to the fantasy test, a questionnaire designed to tap the other value
attitudes supposedly characteristic of entrepreneurs summarized in Table
6.1. The question to be answered is whether the business men showed
certain expected attitudes more strongly than men of comparable status,
again represented by professionals as the most easily obtainable group. But
because the questionnaire was not administered to professionals either in the
United States or Poland, comparisons must be based on the Italian sample plus
a reduced Turkish sample. Since there were 50 items in the test, a number
of significant differences might arise by chance and it was therefore decided
to apply a fairly strict criterion for deciding that an attitude characterized
the managers more than the professionals. A difference between the two
occupational groups had to appear in the same direction for three samples
(Northern Italy, Southern Italy, and Turkey) and also be significant when
the three samples were combined. The combined figures only are given
in Table 7.6 for simplicity's sake along with the figures for a U.S. managerial
group for comparison, which are generally nearer the figures for the foreign
managers than the foreign professionals. By this criterion 10 items showed
significant differences and they have been classified in Table 7.6 under
headings which correspond to characteristics attributed to the entrepreneur
in our previous discussion (Table 6.1).

As to *risk-taking and decisiveness* (see Table 6.1), it should first be noted
that the Edwards Betting Preference Test used to check on the preference
of students with high n Achievement for moderate odds was also administered
to the General Electric managers and specialists. As predicted more of the
managers (52 per cent) than of the specialists (32 per cent) preferred intermediate odds, the difference being significant ($p < .05$). In our questionnaire
there were four items that seemed to touch on risk-taking, two of which
showed the expected differences and two of which did not. The two which
did are both from the answer key for Presidents of Manufacturing Concerns
for the Strong Vocational Interest Test, as are all the items marked with a
$+3$ in Table 7.6. That is, these are items answered in the given direction
significantly more strongly by such Presidents than by Men-in-general in
Strong's standardization of his test in the U.S. in the 1930's. To simplify
presentation the responses of the subject which are given as either "Like,"
"Indifferent," or "Dislike" have been changed to a scale of $+3$, $+2$ and
$+1$, with $+3$ indicating the direction of the answers given by the Presidents.
The two items also accepted more by the foreign managers than professionals
suggest a kind of willingness on the part of the managers to take chances—

TABLE 7.6   AVERAGE AGREEMENT WITH VARIOUS ATTITUDE ITEMS AMONG MANAGERS AND PROFESSIONALS IN THE U.S., ITALY, AND TURKEY

Attitudes	Item No.	U.S. mgrs.[1] N = 102	Italian and Turkish		diff (M − P)	p
			Mgrs.[2] N = 85-129	Professionals[3] N ~ 185		
1. Moderate risk-taking; decisiveness	17,31[4]	(no significant trends)				
Prefer selling 10% above competitor (+3)	24	2.30*	2.04	1.79	.25[6]	<.05
Start activities of my group (+3)	25	2.44*	2.58	2.28	.30	<.05
2. Individual responsibility						
Work for self in small business (+3)	22	1.87*	2.49	2.33	.16	NS
Work for self vs. respected superior (+3)	21	2.35*	2.31	2.57	−.26	<.05
Won't sacrifice autonomy to join group (+7)[5]	38	2.10	3.44	4.02	−.58	<.05
3. Knowledge of results	30	(no significant trend)				
Commission preferred to salary (+3)	20	1.61*	2.16	1.86	.30	<.05
Incentive pay good (+7)	34	6.26	5.46	4.28	1.18	<.01
4. Belief in achieved status	33, 36, 39, 48 (no trends; see Table 7.7)					
Approve careers for married women (+7)	41	3.02	4.48	3.77	.71	<.01
Leave home for better job (+7)	45	6.76	5.95	5.30	.65	<.01
5. "Other-directedness"						
Like being an advertiser (+3)	1	2.12*	2.42	1.86	.56	<.01
Demands determine worth of an article for sale (+7)	32	3.70	4.56	3.45	1.11	<.01

* Preferred significantly ($p < .07$) more often by presidents of U.S. manufacturing concerns than by men-in-general, according to the answer key for the Strong Vocational Interest Blank.

[1] Senior managers from various companies, Advanced Management Program, Harvard Business School, average age = 45.

[2] Forty-one Italian managers from IPSOA management training course in Torino; 27 from ISIDA management training course in Palermo, average age = 28; 17-42 Turkish middle managers from management training course in Istanbul, average age = 34 and 0-19 Turkish senior managers, average age = 41.

[3] Eighty-five students of law, medicine, and theology from Torino, Italy, and 50 of law and medicine from Palermo, Italy, average age = 21; 50 Turkish educators, average age = 27.

[4] Item numbers refer to the questionnaire reproduced in full in Appendix VII which can be consulted for complete wording. Some items have been reversed scored for this table in the direction of expected greater agreement among managers to make findings easier to understand.

[5] Items are marked +3 or +7 to indicate whether maximum agreement was +3 (Like, Indifferent or Dislike) or +7. In the latter case the respondent indicated agreement on a scale of −3 (for complete disagreement) to +3 (for complete agreement), which was converted to a scale running from +1 to +7.

[6] Differences have been computed only when they were in the same direction for three independent comparisons: (1) North Italian managers vs. professionals, (2) South Italian managers vs. professionals and (3) Turkish managers vs. professionals.

to sell *above* competitors and to start activities of a group. Of the two items showing no differences, one deals with competition ("being pitted against another in a race") and one with "risking a little to make a lot." Oddly enough, competition was *disliked* more by American Presidents of Manufacturing Concerns, suggesting it should not be considered as part of the risk-taking complex anyway. Finally the risk-taking item itself suggested gambling as much as an achievement situation—i.e., winning one time in five—and, as Chapter 6 pointed out, managers and men with high n Achievement avoid pure gambling as much as they are challenged by risky achievement-related situations. So the cues given by the item may have been ambiguous enough to wash out any difference between the two groups. On the whole, there is mild support here for the notion that managers are somewhat more willing to take chances and to start things going.

The evidence on *individual responsibility* is much more confusing. In fact, if anything, it is the reverse of expectation. The American Presidents wanted to work for themselves in a small business and not to work for a respected superior, as might be expected from the positions they held. On the other hand the American senior managers, mostly from various large companies, took a different stand, as again might be expected from their occupational status. They didn't want to work for themselves in a small business, although they did want some autonomy within a large one. The foreign managers reversed this pattern: they were somewhat (but not significantly) more interested in running their own businesses, less interested in autonomy within a large one than the professionals. Finally both the American and foreign managers agreed on one point: they do not mind "sacrificing decision-making at the individual, personal level" to join an organization as much as the professionals do; such a difference seems to follow from the structural difference of the two types of occupations. Businessmen are usually part of organizations and must sacrifice some autonomy to the group, whereas professionals more often work alone and can be more individualistic. It is interesting to observe that the American executives are significantly *more* group-minded, more willing to sacrifice individual autonomy, than their foreign equivalents in Italy and Turkey.

The results look somewhat paradoxical. How can a man say in one breath that he "starts activities of his group" and the next that he is willing to sacrifice "individual decision-making" to the group? Perhaps the answer is the formula Americans have developed to handle their desire both for freedom and for conformity (see McClelland, *et al.*, 1958)—namely, "I want to freely choose to do what others want me to." Or, "decisions are made by me, activities are started by me, but they are in accordance with what is wanted by or is best for the organization." In this way the individual retains both a sense of personal freedom and organizational responsibility: government is both *by* the people and *for* the people. If this is in fact the stance of the business manager, then questions have to be very carefully phrased to avoid bumping into one part or the other of this complex value attitude and hence giving the impression that the businessman doesn't know what he thinks. On the one hand he wants initiative but on the other he is guided by the welfare of his organization and is quite willing to sacrifice his autonomy to it. Fayerweather (1959, p. 195) has made a similar distinction between the freedom an individual has "to seek his own groups" once he is "free from fixed groups." He finds that the pattern of *voluntary* curtailment of individualism for the interests of the group is more characteristic of American than foreign managers. Our findings agree in showing the pattern very distinctly for American executives but also demonstrate that it is more characteristic even of foreign business executives than professionals in the same countries. Apparently there is something about the business role that helps create this dual attitude.

The findings as to desire for *knowledge of results* are quite consistent with expectations, with one exception. Normally managers believe more that pay should be tied to performance—either in the form of commissions for executives or incentive pay for workers—presumably so that men can get direct feedback on how well they are doing. The exception is the group of senior executives from various U.S. firms who, unlike the American Presidents of Manufacturing Concerns, prefer salaries to commissions. This reflects either a shift in attitude in U.S. business in the last generation or the fact that the former were mostly salaried executives themselves. The item that did not show a difference was rather badly phrased and attempted to check on willingness to leave home and friends to work on a project that was really "getting somewhere." Aside from this, the evidence seems fairly conclusive that businessmen believe more in the famed profit motive—in the sense that men will work better if their pay is determined by how hard they work.

Most of the items dealing with *achieved status* showed no differences between managers and professionals and will be discussed below in contrasting the attitudes of American and foreign managers. The two that did show a difference both stress the desirability of pursuing a career, despite ascribed status handicaps—i.e., kinship ties. The managers are more willing for a son to leave his parents for a better job and for a married woman to work— although surprisingly enough the American managers believe significantly less in careers for married women than their foreign counterparts. To look ahead for a moment, the managers are more favorable to letting people pursue their careers despite ascribed status obligations but are no more favorable to the idea that they will or should be rewarded strictly according to how they achieve in those careers. (See the other achieved status items in Table 7.8 below.) In a word, they seem to be more *against* ascribed status than they are *for* achieved status. The distinction is reminiscent of the one we established between the children's stories from the more and less rapidly developing countries in Chapter 5. Those from the more rapidly developing countries stressed tradition—which involves ascribed status—less but did not stress achieved status more.

Finally the managers are more in favor of what we have, with some license, labelled *other-directedness* in Table 7.6. They are more consumer-oriented in the sense of being more interested in being an *advertiser* and of believing that an article is worth what people will pay for it.

While these results are encouraging in the sense that they lend support to several widely held notions as to characteristics of businessmen, it is time to point out that a number of other such notions also from Table 6.1 were not supported by the questionnaire results. Perhaps the simplest way to draw attention to these negative findings is to list the expectations along with the questionnaire items designed to test them as in Table 7.7. The interested reader can then check the items in Appendix VII and decide whether they provided anything like a fair test of the hypothesis. That is, as always with negative results, one must decide whether the hypothesis is wrong or the test of it inadequate. The most one can say about the failures to find differences between managers and professionals is that they render the hypothesis they were designed to test somewhat less likely than those supported by the positive results in Table 7.6. Of all the characteristics not confirmed, only the last one listed in Table 7.7 has any support in the

TABLE 7.7   EXPECTED CHARACTERISTICS OF MANAGERS NOT CONFIRMED BY
QUESTIONNAIRE FINDINGS

Characteristics expected more often in managers than professionals.	Questionnaire items that failed to show the expected difference. (See Appendix VII for complete wording.)
Energetic or novel instrumental activity	23. Prefer variety in work
	29. Stimulate ambition of associates
	40. Good luck created by effort
	47. I work like a slave
Optimism or planning	42. Plans do work out
Functional specificity	43. Prefer a doctor or lawyer who is not a friend (see also 35)
Market morality	35. Can trust strangers in business
Business is for success not money	37. Wealth created by those who worked for success, not money
	50. Corporation not just for profit
Rationality	49. Prayer ineffective (see also 40)
Time conscientiousness	27. On time with my work
	44. I don't waste time
Working with one's hands	9. Like to be a mechanical engineer
	14. Like operating machinery
	26. Have mechanical ingenuity

data. All three items dealing with machinery were answered more positively by the managers than the professionals in all three samples, but the combined difference did not approach an accepted level of statistical significance. So the hypothesis that business managers have generally a greater interest in mechanics or in construction because they yield good knowledge of results, is listed as not confirmed, although actually the differences are all in the predicted direction. Since the hypothesis has strong theoretical support in view of the connection of n Achievement with skill in such mechanical activities (Moss and Kagan, 1961, and Table 7.3), it deserves about as much acceptance as those supported by the positive findings in Table 7.6.

All the results in this section must be regarded as more tentative than usual. It is very hard to frame questionnaire items that really tap a single theoretically derived characteristic and nothing else. It is even harder to translate such items into foreign languages without a real shift in meaning.

Cross-validation is weak because professionals were not given the questionnaire in the United States or Poland. Finally, even the classification of the items under various hypotheses can be questioned in a number of instances. That the results are presented at all is only because they render a little more or less likely certain commonly held notions about what characterizes business managers in contrast to others, and because, thin though they are, they are more substantial than the generalizations arrived at in this area that are based on little or no systematic tabulation of evidence.

Contrasting Motives and Attitudes of Managers in More and Less Developed Countries

Much has been written (see Fayerweather, 1959, 1960; Harbison and Myers, 1959) on how the American business executive differs from his foreign counterpart. The assumption is usually also explicitly or implicitly made that the American's attitudes are by and large representative of the best management practices because he is from the country which has been most successful in the economic sphere. We are in a position to see how his attitudes compare with those of managers abroad and we can to some extent escape the charge of ethnocentrism by arranging countries in order of their level of economic development to discover if the U.S. attitudes are shared most by the next most developed area (Northern Italy), somewhat less by the next developed (Southern Italy), and least by the most underdeveloped country (Turkey). Poland should perhaps be considered in a separate category because good management practices in a Communist-managed economy might conceivably be different.

Table 7.8 brings together the motivation scores and the attitude items that showed significant trends for the managers from the five areas. To consider the motivational differences first, the decline in n Achievement scores from the U.S., to Italy, to Turkey, has already been commented on. It agrees with the level of development of those countries, while the high level of n Achievement among the Polish managers suggests that some force, probably patriotism or Communism or both, has been at work to raise it. As for n Affiliation, the U.S. executives are lower (combined $p < .05$) than their foreign counterparts (again except for Poland). The finding nicely confirms observations of Fayerweather and others that foreign executives in countries like Mexico and Italy often seem more concerned with adjusting relationships among people than with solving a problem more efficiently, whatever the cost in personal relationships. For example, Fayerweather reports how an American executive working for a U.S. subsidiary in Mexico tried to get his Mexican purchasing agent to do something about the poor quality of some of the parts supplied and the erratic way in which they were delivered. Both problems were costing the company money because the production manager insisted on keeping a high inventory of parts against a rainy day. The difficulty did not seem great to the American: it was a simple matter of getting tough with the supplier, or finding another one. To the Mexican, however, it was more complicated because he was more interested in the personal relationships involved. He wanted to please the American and understood the efficiency problem, but he also felt that the American did not understand how loyal and helpful the supplier had been in a pinch in the past and how much the

TABLE 7.8 AVERAGE MOTIVE SCORES AND AGREEMENT WITH VARIOUS ATTITUDE ITEMS AMONG MANAGERS IN THE U.S., ITALY, TURKEY, AND POLAND. (Scale = 1 to 7)

Attitude items	Item No.[1]	U.S. $N = 102$	Italy (North) $N = 41$	Italy (South) $N = 27$	Turkey $N = 17\text{-}42$	Poland $N = 31$
Mean age		44.8	26.6	29.1	33.5	35.9
Achieved status						
Merit more important than seniority in giving promotions	33	6.67[2]	6.07	5.74	5.41	4.58
Qualified workers should be promoted to managerial jobs	36	6.90	5.85	6.19	4.71	4.74
Pay scale not determined by education	39	5.21	4.78	3.74	3.51	3.06
Average for business items		*6.26*	*5.57*	*5.22*	*4.54*	*4.13*
A man with money can learn good manners without proper upbringing	48	5.52	2.68	3.15	3.93	2.06
Planning, optimism						
Plans work out	42	6.69	5.63	4.52	5.76	4.35
"Market morality"						
Can trust strangers in business	35	6.70	5.41	5.07	6.12	5.97
"Profit" motive						
Corporation not exclusively for profit	50	3.97[3]	1.71	2.56	2.26	3.33
Mean n Achievement score[4]		8.90[3]	4.12	4.26	1.12	6.58
Mean n Affiliation score[4]		4.25[3]	5.15	5.70	5.31	2.16
Mean n Power score[4]		7.01[3]	6.61	5.59	5.93	5.48

Note: The U.S. sample consists of senior executives in the Advanced Management Program at the Harvard Business School (except as noted in note 3 below). The remaining samples are as described in Table 7.2, except that the Turkish sample includes some middle managers working for the government and a few senior managers (see Table 7.9).

[1] Item numbers refer to the questionnaire reproduced in full in Appendix VII. Items have been paraphrased and scored in the direction of "better" management practice for easier comprehension.

[2] Standard deviations for these distributions vary normally between 1.7 and 2.1 so that usually differences between means of the order of magnitude of .7 to 1.0 and 1.2 and up are significant at the .05 and .01 levels respectively.

[3] Middle managers from various companies in the Harvard Business School and the MIT Sloane Fellow Program. Mean age = 34, $N = 38$ for item 50, $N = 67$ for motivation scores.

[4] Standard deviations for the distributions of motivation scores vary around 4.00 ± 1.5 so that differences between the means for different countries of the order of 1.2 to 1.5 and 2.0 are significant at the .05 and .01 levels respectively.

production manager just wanted a high inventory to feel better (Fayerweather, 1959, pp. 1-3). The data in Table 7.8 clearly explain the source of these contrasting attitudes, if we compare Italian (in place of Mexican) managers with American ones. Among the latter, concern for achievement is almost double the concern for affiliation whereas among the Italians, the concern for affiliation is significantly higher than the concern for achievement.

Again to quote Fayerweather (1959, p. 73): "In Mexico, very few people are actively opposed to being on time, following plans, or obeying any of the other rules of industrial discipline. When they do not obey them, it is because some conflicting avenue of action appeared and they felt it was more important." One of the main conflicting avenues of action in Mexico he feels is "the maintenance of personal alliances." If we translate the latter into n Affiliation and Mexico into Italy, our results strongly support this view. So do the reader data in Appendix II. In both Mexico and Italy n Affiliation is higher than n Achievement; there is some evidence that these two needs tend to be complementary. In a random sample of 119 cases out of the 760 men tested in all four countries, n Achievement score correlates negatively with n Affiliation score ($r = -.32$, $p < .01$). Similarly it will be recalled that there is a significant negative correlation between the two variables in the children's stories in 1950 (Chapter 5). People who are concerned about interpersonal relationships tend generally to be less concerned about achievement and vice versa.

But we must be wary of overgeneralizing about managers in different foreign countries. While it is true the Turkish managers also show a much greater concern with affiliation than with achievement (although the Turkish children's stories do not), the Polish managers are even less concerned with affiliation than the Americans. Probably the situation will be different in each country and Fayerweather's attempt to treat foreign executives as having a similar personality configuration represents a useful, but demonstrably limited oversimplification. The low n Affiliation of the Polish executives reminds one of descriptions of the severity of Communist production quotas to which interpersonal considerations may have to be sacrificed (Granick, 1960). People with low n Affiliation and high n Achievement might survive better under such pressure. The conclusion is marred, however, by the fact that in retouching the pictures for Polish use, the small family photograph in the draftsman's desk in the second picture was omitted, thus removing an important cue for affiliation-related stories present in the other countries.

The American executives are significantly higher in the need for power, the desire to control the actions of others, than the executives in any other place except Northern Italy, the next most developed region economically speaking. Perhaps here we find a reflection of the popular image of the business tycoon who is interested in building an empire and above all beating the competition. Compare W. H. Whyte's description of his training as a salesman for the Vick Chemical Company in 1940:

"Fella," he [the supervisor] told me, "you will never sell anything until you learn one simple thing. The man on the other side of the counter is the *enemy*." It was a gladiators' school we were in. Selling may be no less competitive now but in the Vick program, strife was honored far more openly than to-day's climate would permit. Combat was the ideal—combat with the dealer, combat with the "chiselling competitors," combat with each other. (Whyte, 1956, p. 117).

The word "combat" as an image nicely combines the concern for achievement and power characteristic of American businessmen, according to our results. Sutton *et al.* point out (1956, p. 98) that the American business creed "resists in various ways any image of the business executive as an authoritarian figure of high status" because of the democratic value atmosphere in the United States. In fact it probably masks the power drive in the concept of competition which suggests the image of achievement which is less suspect. Whether n Power is an essential ingredient in managerial success, as we have argued n Achievement is, or an accidental feature of the private enterprise system cannot be settled with the information available. The first view is favored by the fact that managers from the next most successful region economically, Northern Italy, may also have a higher n Power ($p < .20$) than executives from less economically successful regions; the second is favored by the lack of evidence that managers are higher in n Power than professionals and by the evidence presented below that n Power is more apt to go with managerial responsibility in the private than the public sector.

To look now at various attitude differences in Table 7.8, it is clear that belief in rewarding a man directly for what he has accomplished in business (achieved status) is closely associated with the stage of economic development of the region from which the managers are drawn. The average belief in reward solely for performance in business decreases sharply from left to right across the table as level of economic development of the region or country decreases. To take an extreme case, American executives believe to nearly the fullest possible extent that deserving workers should be promoted; Italian managers share the belief almost as fully, especially from the industrialized North. But among the Turks and Poles there is considerable doubt about whether workers should be promoted, because if they are, "it would destroy the respect for authority which the workers must have toward management." Similarly the U.S. managers reject seniority, education, and family upbringing as determinants of a man's standing more firmly than the Italians, who reject them more than the Turks who reject them more than the Poles. The results strongly suggest that belief among managers in a man's right to make his way in the world is at least a strong accompaniment or result of economic development, even if we could not find evidence in Chapter 5 that it helped speed up economic growth.

The traditional optimism of Americans is also apparent. They strongly believe in making plans because they usually work out while managers abroad are less optimistic, perhaps because in fact their plans don't work out as often. There is something of a vicious circle in scepticism about planning: if you have doubts about its worthwhileness because others don't plan and wreck your plans, then *you* may not plan and may wreck theirs. On the other hand an irrational or unjustified faith in the future may justify itself by creating confidence all around.

The item labeled "market morality" is particularly interesting in view of the importance we assigned to this factor for economic growth in Chapter 5. It reads in full: "In business you can only really trust friends and relatives." The Americans disagree almost completely with this sentiment, or (as it is rephrased in Table 7.8) they believe that you can trust strangers significantly more than do managers in any of the other countries. To refer again to our discussion of Chapter 5, fair dealings in the market with impersonal, unrelated "others" (i.e. strangers) is one of the necessities of advanced economic organization. If on the other hand, prices, contracts, supplies, etc. are a function of a multiplicity of particularistic relationships with friends, enemies or *compadres*—in a word, of personal alliances—then economic efficiency is bound to suffer. It is interesting to note that this factor, like n Achievement, differentiates the more from the less rapidly developing countries, not only in stories for children but in the attitudes of business executives.

Finally the Americans are less convinced than foreign executives that corporations are *exclusively* for profit. What do they think corporations are for, if not just for making profit? Possibly they are giving some implicit recognition to our point that corporations also satisfy achievement strivings or to a commonly held notion that they have a public service function. Actually the issue should be somewhat complicated for the ideal-type entrepreneur if our psychological analysis of his state of mind is correct. In the pure case, he should be primarily interested in achievement, not money—and not in selfish achievement at that. For if he is interested only in money or personal gain, he is likely to gamble, break the rules of the game or generally act like the competitive individualist that Fayerweather (1959) contends spends his time avoiding, competing with, and out-maneuvering others and thereby creating considerable inefficiency in a firm. If he idealistically expresses no interest in profit, he loses the main measuring stick by which he judges whether the organization is operating efficiently or not. This point is frequently misunderstood both by friends and foes of the private enterprise system. Both imply that profit is important as an *end*, or as an incentive, when actually its major importance is as a criterion or value in terms of which the efficiency of business operations can be judged. The conflict is unconsciously reflected by Fayerweather when he writes:

"Business leaders are generally inclined to accept many responsibilities, both as good citizens and as part of the job of assuring conditions which will be profitable over the long term. But that is not the same as viewing their enterprises as public instruments. Unfortunately, many well-meaning people do harm to their causes by forgetting the profit element and pushing business to act as though contributions to public objectives were its primary concern. . . . [The businessman's] first duty to the public is to keep his business strong" (Fayerweather, 1960, p. ix).

Fayerweather seems to be saying, somewhat paradoxically (just as our American executives say in Table 7.8), that business is for profit, but not exclusively. That is, if businesses are pushed to place other values (i.e. public service) above the profit motive, then they become weak, by inference because they have lost the yardstick that creates efficiency, not because they have lost an incentive system. Despite this emphasis on the importance of profit, he too mentions the businessman's "duty to the public" and the importance of over-all business conditions. Thus there are implicit sanctions invoked against the man who acts exclusively for his own profit to the disregard of all others. The conflict is just as we would expect it to be based on in theoretical analysis of the meaning of profit or money reward to students with high *n* Achievement in Chapter 6. It is and should be not exclusively an end in itself but the *measure of achievement*.

Motives and Attitudes of Managers in Public and Private Enterprise

No problem has interested sociological and popular students of social organization more than how enterprise is affected by public vs. private control. Frequently in the United States public control is associated with bureaucracy which is often defined as directly opposed to the entrepreneurial spirit. For example, Dimock (1959) reports that in his interviews, many criticisms of bureaucracy centered on its tendency to create *security-mindedness* and to *decrease risk-taking*, as in these comments:

Excessive red tape created by complicated and often obsolete rules and regulations.
A feeling of security in a situation devoid of challenges. Timidity due to an urge to play it safe.

Other comments suggest that the critics felt bureaucracy lowers n Achievement or drives out people who have it, e.g.,

Lack of sales motive when competition is restricted.
Complacency and inertia resulting from a long period of success.
Mediocrity resulting from a belief that leveling is the best policy.
Waste and carelessness due to a lack of employee interest.
Lack of ambition because of grooving.

While it is increasingly recognized that bureaucracy is a "disease" that may affect big business, many apologists for the free enterprise system feel that its chief locus is the government. As Sutton *et al.* (1956) put it, according to the American business creed,

"the activities of governments involve first the politician, who buys votes for the party in power; then the impractical theorist in the civil service—usually a professor in disguise—who conceives grandiose and unworkable plans; finally these are executed and administered by the hidebound bureaucrat. The characteristic views of these three species of homo politicus differ, but they share a common feature: the absence of those personal virtues possessed by businessmen. Their heads are neither clear, hard nor level; none of them is really honest; all of them lack practical imagination and the desire to get things done" (Sutton *et al.*, 1956, pp. 192-193).

Such traditional skepticism about the efficiency and drive in governmental activity has recently run head on into two facts: (1) many underdeveloped countries must make extensive use of public enterprise to accelerate economic development because it is the only sector far enough advanced to use at all, and (2) Communist countries like Russia have developed with extraordinary speed in the past decades entirely by means of public enterprise. In fact by our index of the rate of economic growth, i.e., electricity produced (or consumed), Russia is now developing at a considerably faster rate than the United States. The remarkably linear equations are: $Y = .0325 X + 4.5690$ for the U.S. and $Y = .04869 X + 3.9517$ for the U.S.S.R., where Y = predicted monthly output in log kwh and X = the number of years from 1952, the base date from which the calculations were made. The regression coefficient for the U.S.S.R. (.05) represents a considerably faster growth rate than for the U.S. (.03), which means that Russia should reach the present level of U.S. development by 1967 and surpass it by 1990. Can it be that public enterprise is always as inefficient and lacking in drive and practical imagination as pictured?

It seems particularly important therefore to get some factual information on the enterprise and attitudes of managers working for government as contrasted with private business. Fortunately we have the data, not only

294 THE ACHIEVING SOCIETY

for the United States, where the differences should be greatest if the popular image of the bureaucrat is correct, but also for Italy and Turkey. We can also compare the Polish managers working in the Communist type of bureaucracy with private and public managers in other non-Communist countries. Are government managers everywhere less enterprising, more security-minded, more impractical than their private counterparts? The relevant facts are presented in Tables 7.9 and 7.10. They do not lend themselves to easy generalization across countries.

TABLE 7.9 MOTIVE SCORES OF MIDDLE MANAGERS IN THE PUBLIC AND PRIVATE SECTORS IN THE U.S., ITALY, TURKEY, AND POLAND

Country	N	Mean age	n Achievement		n Affiliation		n Power	
			Mean	SD	Mean	SD	Mean	SD
United States								
A. Private[1]	67	34.0	8.90	5.22	4.25	3.29	7.01	3.09
B. Public[2]	66	34.9	9.23	5.40	3.50	2.73	5.47	2.89
difference (A − B)			−.33		.75		1.54*	
Italy								
A. Private[3]	68	27.6	4.18	4.13	5.37	3.53	6.21	3.27
B. Public[4]	50	29.0	2.56	3.17	6.76	3.89	5.60	2.99
difference (A − B)			1.62**		−1.39**		.61	
Turkey								
A. Private (Sr.)[5]	23	40.6	3.87	3.78	4.22	2.86	6.83	2.51
B. Private (Jr.)[6]	17	33.1	1.76	3.99	4.18	2.30	5.65	3.11
C. Public[6]	25	33.7	.68	2.55	6.68	2.96	6.12	3.83
difference (B − C)			1.08		−2.50*		−.47	
Poland								
"Public"[7]	31	35.9	6.58	5.22	2.16	2.41	5.48	2.84

* = p < .01, ** = p < .05

[1] Men from various companies attending the middle management program at the Harvard Business School or MIT as Sloane Fellows.

[2] Middle level U.S. government employees (GS Grades 12-14) from the Departments of Defense, Treasury, and Health, Education and Welfare. Protocols obtained through the kind assistance of James Guyot.

[3] Forty-one middle managers attending a management training program at IPSOA (Torino) and 27 attending a similar program at ISIDA (Palermo).

[4] Seventeen administrators and 33 administrative assistants in government employment attending a training course at Bologna in 1960.

[5] Leading businessmen in Istanbul, tested by Bradburn (1960).

[6] Middle level managers from public or private enterprises attending management training courses at the University of Istanbul, tested by Bradburn (1960).

[7] Managers tested through the kind assistance of Dr. M. Choynowski, head of the psychometric laboratory of the Polish Academy of Sciences, Warsaw.

As far as n Achievement is concerned, "bureaucrats" have less "drive" than private executives as expected in Italy (p < .05) and in Turkey, particularly in comparison with the more successful private managers ($p <$ .01). According to all our findings on n Achievement then, government managers in these countries should be less enterprising than private ones. However, the surprise is provided by the United States where very carefully matched samples of junior executives in the public and private sectors are compared. There is no significant difference in n Achievement between the two groups. If anything, the government managers score a little higher on the average. Furthermore the Polish managers, also from the public sector, score significantly higher than the Turks or Italians from the private sector. Apparently it varies from country to country whether men with high n Achievement work for the government or not. There is nothing *intrinsic* to public employment which universally lowers n Achievement or tends to select those with low n Achievement. This conclusion strongly supports a similar inference based on the conspicuous economic achievements of governments relying heavily on the public sector.

The Italian and Turkish public managers are also significantly higher in the need for Affiliation, while the reverse appears to be true of the American and Polish managers, since the latter are lower than the only Polish comparison group we have, the professionals (see Table 7.1). What can we make of these shifts? In part they reflect the tendency already noted for n Achievement and n Affiliation to be negatively correlated. The men who are less interested in achievement tend to be more interested in affiliation and vice versa. As far as the U.S. comparison is concerned, it lends support to Whyte's argument that the American business executive, at least compared with his public counterpart, is becoming increasingly an "organization man" concerned with "togetherness" and the "intellectual hypocrisy of the leadership group" (Whyte, 1956, p. 55). But Whyte need not worry too much as yet: the American business executive is still much lower in n Affiliation than his European counterpart.

To look at the other side of the coin, both American and Polish bureaucratic managers would appear to be nearer to Weber's ideal type (1922) in the sense that they are less concerned with people, and therefore presumably more guided by impersonal universalistic rules and regulations. The difference becomes more marked for the U.S. government managers who are particularly successful. Hill (1959) found that they are even lower in n Affiliation ($p < .001$) than others of comparable rank, but lower civil service grade. On the other hand, one would expect the Turkish and Italian bureaucracies to be more concerned with "personal alliances," with particularistic interpersonal relationships. While systematic data do not exist, it is certainly a widely held belief based on many personal experiences that dealing with these two bureaucracies involves precisely this kind of interpersonal as opposed to impersonal relationships. One's success depends on who one knows and what favors (or bribes) have been passed on to whom, rather than on universalistic rules which are impersonally enforced regardless of the particular situation and person involved. Bureaucracies can apparently vary a good deal in the extent to which administration is personal (high n Affiliation) or impersonal (low n Affiliation).

Nevertheless, they may all generally recruit managers who are lower in n Power than those in the private sector. The difference is very significant in the United States and in the same direction in Italy. Turkey is not a major exception if the public managers are compared with the more successful private managers. And the Polish "public" managers are as low in n Power as any other group. Perhaps working for the government requires enough obedience to arbitrary dictates from above (often for task-unrelated or political reasons) to make such employment unpleasant for men with high n Power. As Hoselitz puts it, the public official "is merely an instrument implementing policies which were not designed by him, but imposed upon him" (1954, p. 7). Whether this is always the case does not matter: it is probably more often the case in government or in large bureaucratic organizations than elsewhere so that the man with high n Power, who wants to impose his will, not be imposed upon, migrates to other employment.

One point is cleared up by the findings for the United States. It is no wonder that American private executives feel strongly hostile to the encroaching power of government (Sutton et $al.$, 1956). Since they are very high in n Power themselves, they do not want any threat to their position of influence from an outside force. It also helps explain why they think private $ownership$ is so important for an efficient economy. For ownership, as we have shown above, does not seem to be crucial for men with high n Achievement, but it might well be for men with high n Power, because by definition it implies the $power$ of disposal of what is owned.

Table 7.10 presents the relatively few differences in the attitudes of public and private managers that were obtained with the questionnaire when a fairly strict cross-validation criterion was applied. That is, only a few items were administered to the U.S. public managers, none of which showed differences. Therefore the main reliance had to be on a comparison of public and private managers in Italy and Turkey (where the number of cases was small). Since we have argued that bureaucracies in these countries are different from those in the U.S. and Poland, we felt it necessary to confirm the results obtained in those two countries elsewhere. So for the U.S. we decided that working for General Electric was a little more similar to working for the government than working for the various companies represented in the Harvard Business School Advanced Management Program, since many of the latter were small. We could then require that differences between the public and private managers in Italy and Turkey must be in the same direction for the G.E. managers vs. the other U.S. managers. And finally we could require that the attitude of the Polish public managers differ from the attitude of the Italian and Turkish private managers in the same way as the attitude of their own public managers. In this way

TABLE 7.10 CONTRASTING ATTITUDES OF MANAGERS IN MORE AND LESS "BUREAUCRATIC" ORGANIZATIONS IN THE U.S., ITALY, TURKEY, AND POLAND.
(Scale = 1 to 7.)

Item	Organization	U.S.[1]	Italy[2]	Turkey[3]	Poland[4]	Total Italy and Turkey
Universalism						
34. Incentive pay is bad, produces overwork, poor health, etc.	More bureaucratic	1.74	4.18	4.11	3.87	4.17
	Less bureaucratic	1.54	2.41	1.88		2.35
	diff.	.20	1.77	2.23		1.82 $p < .01$
Ascribed status						
36. Qualified workers should not be promoted, creates disrespect	More bureaucratic	1.41	2.32	3.33	3.26	2.47
	Less bureaucratic	1.10	1.96	3.25		2.09
	diff.	.31	.36	.08		.38 $p = .20$
41. Disapprove careers for married women	More bureaucratic	5.30	4.20	4.00	4.81	4.17
	Less bureaucratic	4.98	3.59	2.37		3.46
	diff.	.32	.61	1.63		.71 $p < .10$
45. Son should not leave parents for a better job	More bureaucratic	1.37	2.74	1.92[5]	2.77	2.47
	Less bureaucratic	1.24	2.29	1.53[5]		2.14
	diff.	.13	.45	.39		.33 $p < .20$
Irrationality						
40. There is such a thing as good luck beyond human control	More bureaucratic	3.33	3.02	2.56	2.35	2.95
	Less bureaucratic	2.97	2.69	1.50		2.57
	diff.	.36	.33	1.06		.38 $p \sim .20$
49. Remarkable how prayer influences things	More bureaucratic	4.81	5.04	5.56	omitted	5.12
	Less bureaucratic	4.59	4.01	4.13		4.03
	diff.	.22	1.03	1.43		1.09 $p < .01$

[1] Twenty-seven managers from General Electric, average age = 43, and 102 managers from the Harvard Business School Advanced Management Training Program, average age = 45, at least one-third of whom are from small businesses.

[2] Fifty administrators and administrative assistants from the Italian government, average age = 29, and 68 managers from private industry in training at IPSOA in Torino and ISIDA in Palermo, average age = 28.

[3] Nine Turkish managers from the public sector and 8 from the private sector, average age = 33.

[4] Thirty-one Polish managers having public status as in a Communist society, average age = 36.

[5] For these values $N = 17$ private managers and $N = 25$ public managers.

there is a kind of four-way check on a finding, to see whether it is a fairly universal characteristic of men working for large scale, bureaucratic or public organizations as contrasted with smaller private ones.

The first finding in Table 7.10 is scarcely a surprise in view of the large amount that has been written about universalism in bureaucracies and the obvious fact that bureaucrats are seldom, if ever (except plant managers in Communist countries, Granick, 1960), on an incentive or bonus pay system. "Bureaucrats" believe men should be paid regular wages or a salary. The same attitude crops up decisively as a large preference for a "definite salary" vs. "commission" ($p < .01$) among public vs. private managers in Italy, the only place where this item was administered. Bureaucrats do not, in general, believe that financial reward should directly and immediately be tied to effort or productivity.

The next three items all reflect a kind of conservatism among managers in "bureaucracies": they believe less in promoting qualified workers because authority lines must be maintained, disapprove more of careers for married women, and believe in greater loyalty from a son for his parents. Technically all of these attitudes represent greater respect for *ascribed status*, for behavior fixed by social tradition rather than initiated by the individual. It is partly for the same reason that they did not want pay so directly tied to performance. They tend to think more in terms of universal, fixed principles or social positions: salary schedules, managers vs. workers, women vs. men, fixed ties of kinship, etc. Such an interpretation is clearly in line with the theory of bureaucracy which pictures it as concerned with rational universalistic principles, clear legal claims, and impersonal regulations rather than a system of flexible rewards depending on the achievements of particular men. Oddly enough, the Italian and Turkish bureaucrats accept *values* that appear related to the universalistic principles of bureaucracy but their high n Affiliation (Table 7.9) would lead us to expect that they might administer them particularistically. The trouble is that the particularistic administration is likely to be in terms of affiliation rather than achievement criteria. That is, it is one thing so far as efficiency is concerned if rules are waived or applied selectively in terms of the achievements of an individual and another if they are similarly adjusted for the sake of personal friendships, kinship ties, or bribes.

Thus there is evidence here that the fixed requirements of a bureaucracy or a large organization may create an attitude of mind (or recruit managers who already have it) which is not so much in favor of flexible rewards for differential achievement. If the latter is essential to efficient operation of an organization and to economic development—which does not appear to have been conclusively demonstrated—then relying too heavily on the public sector has some disadvantages. Still within this framework of values, regulations are likely to be particularistically administered according to the dominant motivations of the public officials involved. If they have high *n* Achievement, they are likely to make adjustments that are not so different from what would be made in the private sector. If they have a high *n* Affiliation, they are likely to make the kinds of personalized adjustments that will make the organization even less efficient than one in the private sector, with less universalistic standards. So the question of whether it is more efficient to rely on the public or private sectors to promote economic development depends very much on the motives of the people employed in the two sectors.

The final two items in Table 7.10 come as a real surprise. The bureaucratic managers (except for the Poles) believe more in irrational, non-instrumental processes—sheer good luck and prayer. The surprise derives from the fact that bureaucracies are by definition "rationalized." They represent an attempt to organize and systematize behavior to the highest possible degree. There should be reasons for everything. Why then should men involved in such a system believe more in such nonrational elements as good luck and prayer? The answer possibly lies in the feeling of powerlessness that a man has in a large impersonal organization where it is hard for him to exercize the same personal control over the outcome of events as a man may feel he has in a smaller organization. Certainly many U.S. public officials concerned with a particular appropriation must often feel that it was a sheer lucky combination of events that determined what his department was voted by Congress in a given year. What he did to try to influence the appropriation may have seemed pretty ineffective, but a Senator suddenly died or was called away on business; another appropriation was defeated for other reasons that gave his a better chance, etc. The impersonal workings of a bureaucracy must often seem like forces completely beyond a man's control.

Is this bad? It would be if it led men in large organizations to give up trying to influence the course of events and to await passively what fortune has in store for them. It is just for such reasons that many Americans and Russians criticize bureaucracies. They are felt to be too large and unwieldy, too hard to influence and consequently believed to promote resignation and passivity. But it is possible to regard this reaction as an irrational response to a difficult situation which reflects the public manager's state of mind more than it influences what he will do. A pilot may utter a prayer before he lands his plane because he knows there are many things that might happen, but he does not then give up flying the plane and wait to see what will happen. Belief in luck and prayer are not necessarily *substitutes* for action.

So there seems to be no compelling reason to alter the judgment we have already made: the framework of large organizations (e.g., government) does tend to create certain value attitudes which might interfere with efficient enterprise if put into action, but how they are put into action seems to depend more crucially on the *motivations* of the men working for the organization. Thus public enterprise if run by men of high *n* Achievement is very likely to be effective because the men will find a way to apply the regulations in a way that will lead to greater efficiency. The crucial issue does not seem to be public vs. private, but what kind of men are in which sector. This issue is the main point of the whole chapter. What kind of men are available for leadership positions in economic organizations in various countries? For in the long run it is they, and their primary concerns, whether for achievement, affiliation, power or something else, that determine the rate at which the economy of their country develops.

NOTES AND REFERENCES

[1] This set of pictures is numbered 5, 28, 83, 9, 24 and 53 respectively in Atkinson's master list (1958, Appendix III, p. 831 ff.). It is fairly well balanced for the three motives it is designed to measure. In the present study the mean scores for each motive are as follows: $N = 760$ males; 238 from the United States, 162 from Turkey, 281 from Italy, 79 from Poland. Average age $= 32$. All of business or professional status. Mean *n* Achievement $= 4.69$, $SD = 5.42$. Mean *n* Affiliation $= 4.64$, $SD = 3.74$. Mean *n* Power $= 5.86$, $SD = 3.52$.

[2] Throughout the chapter, the terms *entrepreneur, executive, manager,* and the like will be used interchangeably, despite the ease and clarity with which these roles have been distinguished by economists and sociologists. The reason is a simple practical one: while we were able to distinguish clearly in Chapter 6 what we meant by the *entrepreneurial role,* when it came to picking particular individuals to test, we had no refined instruments of job analysis available to decide who was really acting in an entrepreneurial way. Instead we were forced to fall back on job titles, or on occupational statuses; and, in the jumble of terminology used in firms, both here and abroad, we were able to distinguish only a single very generalized managerial status in which we could not pick out sub-types with any degree of success. The confusion adds to error, of course, and once again stresses the fact that while our groupings, though crude, are generally sufficient to establish the existence of a relationship, they are by no means precise enough to provide a valid estimate of its extent.

8

The Spirit of Hermes

People with high n Achievement have been around for a long time, at least ever since the cave paintings at Lascaux (the earliest scorable imaginative productions) were made, and probably from the beginning of human history. They also obviously behave in ways that are quite distinctive so that others should be able to recognize their personality type. We ought therefore to be able to find the type celebrated in song and story, or at the level of myth. Discovering the mythological type is not only an interesting search in its own right; it also has some possible immediate advantages in suggesting some further characteristics of the entrepreneur which may derive from his high n Achievement, but which may promote less directly, or possibly even hinder, his success as a businessman.

One of the first mythological types that comes to mind is Spengler's "Faustian spirit." For a long time we felt there were many similarities between Spengler's description of the Faustian will and n Achievement. He argues, for example, that the Faustian culture gives priority consistently to "time, direction and destiny over space and causality" (1932, I, p. 308) and exerts its "will to overcome and break all resistances of the visible" (1932, I, p. 185). He constantly contrasts this *dynamic* spirit with the *static*, timeless, and "will-less" spirit of Classical Greece. Certainly dynamic restlessness and concern with time would appear to go with high n Achievement and static "classicism" with low n Achievement, but on closer examination many flaws in the analogy are evident. For one thing, it is obvious from the study of Classical Greece reported in Chapter 4 that a great deal depends on which period in Greek history Spengler is talking about—in our terms the sixth century B.C. was certainly dynamic in the sense of having high n Achievement—and not static and unconcerned with time. Moreover, Spengler's concern with *will* and his description of the Faustian spirit contains as much or more *power* imagery as it does achievement imagery, and in our scoring systems these two motives are quite distinct and uncorrelated with each other. They may be combined in a given country at a given time, as they appear to be in Russia at the present time (Appendix I), but if we want the pure "mythological type" for n Achievement we will have to look for something more analytically "pure" than the Faustian will. While Spengler's ideas stimulated some of the research reported in this chapter, it was ultimately in Greek mythology, as so often in such matters, that we found the image of the man with high n Achievement fully pictured in all his strengths and weaknesses.

The member of the Greek pantheon who fits the n Achievement personality type best is Hermes. His characteristics as a thief, a trickster, a shepherd, an athlete, or a messenger underwent a number of changes throughout Greek history (Brown, 1947), but the image of him we want to focus on is that provided in the *Homeric Hymn to Hermes*. The reason is twofold: First, it is in this hymn that he appears most clearly, if Brown's interpretation is correct, as the patron of the upwardly mobile Athenian merchant entrepreneurs and reflects their aspirations and characteristics, as seen both by themselves and others. Second, if Brown's dating of the *Hymn* is correct, it was written at a time when Athenian n Achievement was high (around 520 B.C.) as compared with later periods, so that the projected image of the "merchant businessman" should reflect the characteristics of high n Achievement.

How does Hermes appear in the *Hymn*? Basically the story deals with how he steals the cattle of his older brother Apollo on the day he is born. He clearly has high n Achievement: "It did not take him long to prove his prowess to the immortal gods. Born in the morning, in the noonday he performed upon the lyre, in the evening he stole the cattle of the archer-god Apollo." [1] The achievement imagery is of two general types. Great stress is laid on how cunning a schemer Hermes is to outwit his powerful older brother, even though he is only a baby. "He is litigious, skillful at making the worse appear the better reason. He lies brazenly to Apollo. He tries a mixture of trickery, bluffing, flattery, and cajoling to persuade Apollo to let him keep the cattle, and it succeeds. These are the essential traits of the impudent and smooth-talking self-seeker that haunted the Athenian agora" (Brown, 1947, pp. 77-78). They are also the essential traits of the "trickster hero," physically weak but smart enough to defeat powerful rivals, who appears again and again in mythology all over the world—Bre'r Rabbit, Coyote, Reynard the Fox, Ananse the Spider, etc. But Hermes also displays the achievement satisfaction of the Attic craftsman. He is delighted over his idea of making a lyre out of a tortoise he sees in the doorway of his cave and over some wicker sandals he invented for himself to avoid having to leave his footprints on the road. He not only wants to get ahead in the world; he gets real pleasure out of the schemes he devises for doing so.

There is no doubt either that his n Achievement is connected with business. "He discovered a tortoise from which he made an immense fortune: it was Hermes who first made the tortoise into a singer" (by constructing the tortoise-shell lyre). Here is a simple straightforward instance of the technological innovation that is the defining characteristic of entrepreneurship, especially when it is involved with the ability to make money out of it. Hermes' skill as an inventor is stressed in other places. The sandals he made are described as "a unique invention, marvellous past telling, past belief." So is his interest in money. When his mother scolds him for stealing Apollo's cattle, "he tells her that her scruples about his activities are childish; that he intends to put his own interests first, and follow the career with the most profit in it; that a life of affluence and luxury would be better than living in a dreary cave." (Brown, 1947, p. 76.)

Finally Hermes is described as an outrageous liar and a thief. He swears, after stealing his brother's cattle, both to Apollo and Zeus that he is as innocent as the newborn babe he is and that he has not seen the cattle. Nobody believes him—in fact they seem rather to be amused and impressed by his prowess. But why should the ideal type of the businessman be given such negative characteristics? Are they peculiar to the self-seeking merchants that "haunted the Athenian agora" at the time? Perhaps, but, as Brown (1947) points out, the real point of the story is its realistic reflection of the conflict which was going on between the traditional propertied classes, represented by Apollo, and the *nouveaux riches* merchant classes, who adopted Hermes as their patron. In such a conflict the merchants were clearly the aggressors, just as Hermes is, in their demands for a greater share of both wealth and higher social status. Their behavior could be regarded by them as well as the upper classes only as aggressive, as an attempt to force the traditional landed gentry to share wealth and privilege. In this respect, the *Hymn* again touches on a universal theme—the relation of a growing and successful entrepreneurial class to the traditionally wealthy. The fast-talking salesmen certainly, and perhaps even all business types, have never been very highly regarded and are not now (see Table 6.6). Furthermore as the data in Chapter 5 show, economic development has proceeded most rapidly in countries where the entrepreneurial spirit (*n* Achievement) has met the least resistance from traditionalism (Fig. 5.1).

So in many ways the *Homeric Hymn to Hermes* sums up the characteristics of the entrepreneur and his relation to the traditional social order as we have uncovered both in our own researches. Does it suggest anything new? Suppose we take a second look at Hermes. What is his essential spirit? He is in effect a "little dynamo" of energy—always on the move, in a hurry. He doesn't waste a moment's time, but starts out into the world to get ahead the moment he is born. He makes his technological innovations and pursues his career in a spirit of restless energy in which there is much motion and little waste of time. Most of the research in this chapter is an attempt to see whether these characteristics of the spirit of Hermes also characterize people with high *n* Achievement. In other words, we broaden the scope of our inquiry here beyond what it was in Chapters 6 and 7 where we were trying to find out if *n* Achievement fitted a man peculiarly for success in his work as an entrepreneur. Now we want to know what "manner of man" a person with high *n* Achievement is—in particular whether he shows the dynamic attitude toward time and motion attributed to the entrepreneurial type in the *Homeric Hymn to Hermes* and more or less ever since. In pursuing such a question, we are not abandoning our interest in economic development altogether because it can be argued that the restless quality of the entrepreneurial spirit is not incidental but an essential part of its success in producing economic growth.

Restless Expressive Movements

Our first set of researches deals with the question of how a person with high *n* Achievement quite literally moves. Is he "brisk," energetic, restless, dynamic as we might expect or is he no different from other people in this respect? The technique used to answer this question was invented by Aronson (1958), although at the time he started his work he had no hypothesis as to what he would find as clearly formulated as we have stated it here. His goal initially was purely exploratory; he wanted to see whether subjects with high *n* Achievement made characteristically different expressive movements from those with low *n* Achievement. As a matter of convenience, he observed those movements as they were "frozen" in doodles or scribbles made by the subjects on a piece of paper. To get his subjects to doodle freely, he showed them very briefly a slide with a number of abstract designs or scribbles on it and asked them to reproduce what they saw. Since there was not time enough to see much of anything, what they produced presumably represented the way they characteristically expressed themselves in movement. At any rate, he found significant differences in the doodles of subjects with high and low *n* Achievement. The "highs" used significantly more "discrete" rather than fuzzy or overlaid lines. That is, they made more single, unattached lines, and did not scribble back and forth over the same place as often. Furthermore, they "drew more S-shaped (two-directional, non-repetitive) lines"; fewer multiple waves (S-shapes continued so as to give "two or more crests pointing in the same direction"), and more diagonals as opposed to vertical or horizontal lines (Aronson, 1958, p. 256). Finally, they tended to leave less blank space at the bottom of the page. These findings were all cross-validated in several different groups of American subjects. Looked at as a whole, they do appear to define a "dynamic" approach to movement. That is, the "highs" seem to avoid repetition (fewer overlaid lines and multiple waves), and to fill up more of the space available with discrete and *different* lines, which more often than among the "lows" take the form of diagonals which physiognomically appear to be "going somewhere." They move or doodle restlessly, seeking variety rather than sameness in what they draw.

To see whether Aronson's findings are restricted to American college students, or to people using Western cursive writing, they were checked on the samples of boys from Japan, Germany, Brazil and India, already described and studied for other purposes relating to our general research objectives. The boys saw briefly the same two sets of stimulus material and produced two pages of doodles which were subsequently coded by Aronson for the same variables he had found differentiated subjects with high and low n Achievement in the United States.

When the scores for the various graphic characteristics were correlated with the verbal n Achievement scores also available on these boys, none of the coefficients of correlation for any of the characteristics in any of the countries departed significantly from zero.

Such a result, unfortunately, may mean several things. It may mean that people with high n Achievement do not express themselves in movement in the same way in other cultures as they do in the United States. It may mean that the relationship still exists but that one or the other, or both, of the two measures was not obtained under testing conditions enough like those in the United States. While every attempt was made to keep testing conditions constant, because expressive behavior is easily influenced by situational factors, even a preliminary look at the data demonstrated the attempt had not been successful. So far as the graphic expression measure is concerned, the average number of scored units in every one of the four countries was significantly larger than it had been in Aronson's sample of U.S. college students. (See Appendix IV.) The protocols were not comparable as to the number of responses they contained. This was particularly true of the Indian protocols, which averaged nearly 56 scored units as contrasted with 22 scored units on the average for the United States protocols, with almost no overlap in the two distributions. A possible reason for the difference lies in the fact that the stimulus materials were not presented in India by photographic projection, which allowed exact control of viewing time, but by hand, as hectographed sheets held up for a few seconds for small groups of students to see. Thus they may have had more time to observe and therefore had seen more to reproduce in the time allowed. Whatever the reason for the larger number of scored units in the Indian protocols, it was decided that they had been so strongly influenced by some situational factor that they should be discarded as unlikely to be comparable to what had been obtained elsewhere.

So the lack of correlation of verbal n Achievement scores with these signs of "restless" expressive movements may have been due to errors in the way the graphic expression test was administered. For example, producing a large number of responses may increase differentially the frequency with which certain specific expressive characteristics appear in the record. Then these characteristics may no longer correlate with verbal n Achievement, if, as in the present instance, n Achievement is completely uncorrelated with number of responses in the graphic expression protocols. Nevertheless, rough methods of correcting for number of responses, by partialling their influence out or omitting the longest records, did not appreciably increase the correlations with verbal n Achievement. Attention was therefore turned to possible influences affecting the imaginative stories written by the subjects.

The testing conditions for obtaining the measure of *n* Achievement from brief written stories are known to be of the utmost importance because studies in the United States have demonstrated that if the stories are obtained under conditions of achievement arousal, the scores are no longer valid measures of individual differences in *n* Achievement. (McClelland *et al.*, 1953.) That is, if testing conditions are achievement-oriented enough —if the students feel under enough achievement "pressure"—even those with low *n* Achievement will fill their stories with achievement imagery, thus tending to wipe out differences between the "highs" and "lows" which appear under more relaxed testing conditions. Perhaps some of the testing in the various countries was done under "aroused" conditions and some under more "relaxed" conditions, so that the resulting distribution of *n* Achievement scores would not reflect validly individual differences in *n* Achievement level. A detailed examination of the mean *n* Achievement scores for the 13 groups tested in Germany seemed to confirm this suspicion. For instance, there were marked and significant differences in the mean *n* Achievement scores obtained among different administrators, among different test groups, and among the correlations with the graphic expression variables. The evidence is summarized in Appendix IV.

An alternative explanation of the lack of correlation of verbal *n* Achievement with expressive movements is that the testing conditions abroad were somehow less relaxed and more achievement-oriented than in the United States. This theory needs some direct support, however, if it is to be taken more seriously than a strictly *post hoc* rationalization for the failure to find some predicted relationships. The idea was pursued a little further: if the explanation is correct, then the predicted relationships should still obtain among boys abroad who manage to remain more relaxed like the U.S. boys despite greater achievement pressure. Appendix IV describes in detail how the questionnaire administered to the boys was searched for answers that would pick out the relaxed ones among whom the relationship of verbal *n* Achievement to the graphic expression variables should still exist as in the United States. Suffice it to say here that failure to agree almost to the maximum possible extent with the following two items apparently indicated a more relaxed attitude towards life like that held by boys in the U.S. samples.

> I work like a slave at everything I undertake until I am satisfied with the results

> A child should never be asked to do anything unless he is told why he is asked to do it

At any rate among such boys—whom we have called "low" in achievement conscientiousness—the correlations of the verbal *n* Achievement score with the graphic expression variables, while small, more or less follow the same pattern as in the United States, not only in Germany where the scale was derived but also in the cross-validating groups in Brazil and Japan. (See Table 8.1.) That is, the less "conscientious" with high n Achievement

TABLE 8.1 CORRELATIONS BETWEEN VERBAL n ACHIEVEMENT SCORE AND GRAPHIC EXPRESSION VARIABLES AMONG SUBJECTS LOW AND HIGH IN "ACHIEVEMENT CONSCIENTIOUSNESS"[1]

(S_s with D-$F \leq 40$ omitted because of excessively long protocols)

Correlations between n Achievement and	Germany[2]		Brazil		Japan		Average	
	Low[3] N = 197	High[3] N = 162	Low[3] N = 175	High[3] N = 130	Low[3] N = 84	High[3] N = 71	Low N = 456	High N = 363
Discrete-Fuzzy lines (D-F)	.11	−.09	.09	.01	.12	−.10	.10 *	−.06
Diagonals (D)	.07	.05	.10	.06	.15 *	−.18	.10	.01
S-shapes (S)	.16 *	−.19	−.04	−.02	−.07	.12	.04	−.07
Multiple waves (MW)	−.10	.08	−.05	.13	.02 *	.40	−.06 *	.16
D + S − MW[4]	.13 *	−.13	.06	−.05	.04 *	−.32	.09 *	−.14
Space unused	−.02 *	−.23	.09	−.08	−.05	−.10	.02 *	−.15
Total quartile score[5]	.16	−.04	.08	.02	.05	−.17	.11 *	−.04

Correlations in italics are significant at .05 level or beyond.

* Indicates difference between correlations is significant at .05 level or beyond.

[1] Achievement conscientiousness is operationally defined as the sum of agreement to the following two items (on a scale of −3 to +3): (18) I work like a slave at everything I undertake until I am satisfied with the results, and (19) A child should never be asked to do anything unless he is told why he is asked to do it.

[2] The correlations for Germany are the *averages* for three administrators. The degrees of freedom are correspondingly reduced.

[3] High achievement conscientiousness in Germany and Brazil means at least one +2 and one +3 agreement with the two items; "low" means lesser agreement. In Japan, since there was generally less agreement with the items, to get about the same split, the criterion for the "highs" was lowered to at least two +2's.

[4] Total shape index: Diagonals plus S-shape minus Multiple Waves.

[5] Total graphic measure of n Achievement: the sum of quartile scores for D-F, Diagonals, S-shapes and (reversed) for Multiple Waves and Space unused.

scores draw more discrete as contrasted with fuzzy lines, more diagonals, possibly more S-shapes (though only in Germany), and fewer multiple waves (only in Germany and Brazil). What is even clearer is that the correlations are significantly reversed in almost every case for the boys high in "achievement conscientiousness." That is, if a boy is extremely conscientious and also has a high verbal n Achievement, he tends to draw more fuzzy lines, perhaps trying to be more careful in his reproductions. He also makes more multiple waves and consistently uses up more space on the page. Oddly enough, only the last correlation is in the same direction as the one obtained by Aronson for all the boys in the United States sample. It creates problems because, unlike the line or shape characteristics, unused space is more related as it "should" be to verbal n Achievement in the highly conscientious boys. No ready explanation of this reversal comes to mind, though perhaps one could argue that the use of space is especially influenced by an achievement anxiety factor in n Achievement, accentuated in the German boys high in "conscientiousness," present in enough of the American boys to produce the same relationship, and more or less eliminated in the German sample of boys low in "conscientiousness."

What does it all mean? Apparently some conscientiousness or achievement anxiety factor, more frequently present in boys overseas, modifies the relationships between verbal n Achievement and the graphic expression variables found in the United States. It might affect the verbal n Achievement scores, the graphic expression test, or both. It might be either a factor present in the boys, in the testing conditions, or in the interaction of the two. Since every attempt was made to keep test administration conditions constant, the most likely explanation is that these conditions were differently perceived by the boys in these countries, more of whom as their questionnaire responses show, have a conscientious attitude toward achievement. They are more easily aroused to thoughts of achievement, so that the same testing conditions could represent more "achievement-orientation" than in the United States. We can then assume that only among those less aroused (as suggested by their low conscientiousness scores) do the n Achievement scores represent valid indexes of individual differences in n Achievement (as has been repeatedly found in the United States, cf. McClelland et al., 1953). Among such boys a high imaginative concern with achievement is associated with what we have called restless, "dynamic" expressive movements in so far as they are reflected in the types of lines and shapes drawn, though not so far as the use of space is concerned.

The argument just used tends to cast doubt on the validity of the verbal measure of n Achievement for many of the boys tested overseas. While the problem is not crucial to the theme of this chapter, it is to the reporting of results on these boys elsewhere. Obviously the verbal concern with achievement can be considered a valid index of spontaneous concern with achievement only in the absence of specific situational pressures—when fantasy is relaxed or spontaneous.

How does such a generalization help in the present instance? We can eliminate the boys with high achievement conscientiousness in all our samples, but to do so greatly reduces their size and places more weight on a very imperfect measure of possibly invalid n Achievement scores than it deserves. Or we can derive a measure of n Achievement from the graphic expression characteristics, as suggested by Aronson (1958), on the grounds that it remains a more spontaneous reflection of inner needs, despite situational pressures, than the verbal measure does. Table 8.1 presents the correlations with verbal n Achievement of the total quartile score suggested by Aronson as one possible over-all measure, though the rationale for this combination of scores is not good in the overseas sample because of the reversal in the correlations with unused space. Appendix IV describes in detail how various considerations suggested in the end that the best measure of n Achievement for all the boys in these three countries is the Discrete-Fuzzy line count, corrected for length of protocol. It satisfies criteria both of internal consistency and validity. In fact, it turned out to be much more meaningfully related to other variables as predicted than the verbal measure of *n* Achievement, and is consequently used throughout the book wherever an estimate of individual *n* Achievement in these samples is reported. So in the end we decided that restless, nonrepetitive expressive movements are not only symptomatic of high *n* Achievement, they may also be the best way to measure individual differences in *n* Achievement cross-culturally when it is difficult to control and reduce the situational pressures that affect and invalidate verbal measures of *n* Achievement.

Preference for Sombre Colors

So far we have shown that people with high *n* Achievement—imbued with the spirit of Hermes—appear in expressive movement to be restless or active in producing change or avoiding repetition (scribbling over the same space). Knowing this, Knapp reasoned (1958) that they should prefer sombre blues and greens because they are less "intrusive" than reds and yellows. He took his cue originally from Spengler, who contends that blue and green are the "Faustian will" colors, associated with great distances that do not "press in on us," whereas red and yellow are "the colors of the material, the near, the full-blooded." (1932, I, p. 246.) Although, as we have seen, the Faustian will has a strong power component, it still seems reasonable to infer that the person with high *n* Achievement might prefer colors like blue and green which he can "act on," as background, so to speak, as contrasted with reds and yellows that act on him. At least this was the hypothesis tested by Knapp.

Recognizing that color associations are largely determined by cultural convention (e.g., bricks are most often red), he chose a type of stimulus material which could, properly speaking, be any color of the rainbow—namely, Scottish plaids or tartans. Their colors vary widely from sombre blues and greens to rich reds and yellows and may appear in almost any combination. When he asked his subjects to pick out the ones they most preferred and those they least preferred, he could be reasonably sure that they would not be picking what is conventionally accepted as good or bad colors for a tartan, but would be expressing preferences based more on personal needs. He found that only one of the ten tartans most preferred by the subjects with high *n* Achievement contained any significant amount of red, whereas of those least preferred, seven out of ten contained red. On the other hand, the reverse was true of blue, a majority of the tartans most preferred by subjects with high *n* Achievement containing blue and none of the least preferred. He interprets his results in somewhat more common sense terms than Spengler uses. He notes first the "psychophysical fact that red is inherently brighter than blue, more rarely found in nature, more commanding of attention generally. Beyond this . . . blue is a 'soft' color and red a 'hard' color, as Liebmann designated them some thirty years ago. . . . Blue holds form poorly, is malleable and is a preferred 'ground' color. Red, by way of contrast, is 'figure' color, resists perceptual distortion, and imposes itself as figure in the perceptual field" (1958, p. 372). He concludes that it is therefore reasonable to find that people with high n Achievement prefer blues as opposed to reds, "for such persons require that their environment be soft while they are 'hard'; they wish to exert their will effectively—to manipulate, not be manipulated." He goes on to note an historical parallel. "The Puritans, imbued with very strong achievement motivation, eschewed all but the somberest of dress and ornament, imposed fines for the wearing of bright colors, destroyed the stained glass windows of churches, and cultivated unconditional austerity in dress and decor. They stand in dramatic contrast to the Cavaliers with their feudal and chivalric traditions of ascribed status, colorful dress, and fondness for indulgent living." (1958, p. 372.)

This comment suggested a further hypothesis that could easily be tested—that blues should be more preferred in the Northern part of the United States where the Puritan tradition was strong than in the South where the Cavalier tradition was stronger. The colors of State flags confirm the hyopthesis, possibly because they were adopted within a fairly short period of history when major differences in religious tradition (and presumably associated n Achievement levels) continued to exist. Twenty-one of the flags from the Northern States are predominantly blue-green, whereas only two, or 9 per cent, are predominantly red-yellow. The remainder involve other colors or are equally divided between the two types of colors. Of those which can be definitely classified one way or the other in the South, only six are predominantly blue-green, whereas nine, or 60 per cent, are predominantly red-yellow. The difference is highly significant statistically ($p < .01$). It tends to confirm the belief that high n Achievement is associated with preference for blue and greens over reds and yellows because of various kinds of indirect evidence that n Achievement has been higher in the North than the South—the greater economic development in the North, its closer association with the kind of radical Protestantism that was associated with high n Achievement (Chapters 4 and 10), and the presence of household slaves in the South which should lower n Achievement in the children they rear (Chapter 9).

Nevertheless some more direct test of the hypothesis seems highly desirable, particularly for non-Western countries where color associations are quite different. Previous research has tended to emphasize that colors mean different things in different countries; what seems lively to Spengler, the color for "noisy, hearty market days and holidays" may be the color of other-worldliness, withdrawal, and holiness for another people. Is it really likely that people with high n Achievement would be attracted and repelled by the same colors the world around?

The graphic expression test provides a means of finding out in the four countries where it was administered, two of which—India and Japan—

should have quite different and definitely non-Western traditions of color associations. McClelland (1958) had previously demonstrated that children in a U.S. kindergarten tended to choose colored crayons to make their doodles with, for the same test, in accordance with Knapp's hypothesis. That is, the children who were classified as high in n Achievement in terms of the line, shape, and space variables tended to use blues and greens more frequently and those classified as low in n Achievement by the same measure tended to use reds and yellows more frequently. The correlation between n Achievement score (graphic) and preference for blues and greens over reds and yellows was actually a substantial .45, $p < .05$ (McClelland, 1958, p. 317). So in obtaining measures of expressive movements for the test the adolescent boys in four countries were each given a red, a yellow, a green, and blue pencil, and told that they could reproduce the designs seen using any or all of the pencils. The instruction did not make a great deal of sense, since the stimulus material was not in any particular color, but, nevertheless, the boys fell in with the suggestion and most of them used several colors in making their graphic designs.

The preference for blues and greens over reds and yellows was positively correlated with verbal n Achievement among the boys low in achievement conscientiousness in Germany, Brazil, and Japan, but the correlations were all low and not significant even when combined. However, the picture is dramatically different if the graphic expression estimate of n Achievement $(D - F$ z-score) is used which, on the basis of evidence in Appendix IV, appears likely to be a more valid measure of individual differences in n Achievement in these countries. The relevant figures are summarized in Table 8.2, which also includes the correlations for India using the verbal measure of n Achievement which is the only valid one for that country. Of the 16 correlations in the table, 13 are in the predicted direction. The

TABLE 8.2 CORRELATIONS BETWEEN n ACHIEVEMENT MEASURES (GRAPHIC) AND COLOR PREFERENCE AMONG ADOLESCENT BOYS IN FOUR COUNTRIES

Item	Japan[1] $N = 175$	Brazil[1] $N = 378$	Germany[1] $N = 411$	India[2] $N = 151$	combined p values[3]
Number of *red* designs (R)	−.017	−.026	−.050	−.091	
Number of *yellow* designs (Y)	.075	−.102	−.135	.000	
Number of *green* designs (G)	.094	.090	.079	.026	<.02
Number of *blue* designs (B)	.033	.025	−.040	.123	
BG − RY	.069	.094	.084	.183	
p values (one-tailed)	.18	.03	.04	.01	<.01

[1] The correlations for these countries are with the graphic measure of n Achievement $(D - F$ z-score), with the influence of $D + F$ partialled out.

[2] Correlations are with verbal n Achievement, with the influence of $D + F$ partialled out.

[3] Obtained by adding the chi-square equivalents of p values for the individual correlations and obtaining the p value for the sum of the chi-squares, $df = 4$.

only correlations that are significant for a particular color involve the tendency of subjects with high n Achievement in all countries to choose to make their designs more often with the green pencil. Perhaps the association of *green* with *envy* (competitiveness) has some foundation in fact as well as popular fancy. In any case, a combined measure for each subject showing the general preference for making blue and green over red and yellow designs shows the over-all trend of the individual correlations better. It correlates positively with the n Achievement estimate in all four countries and significantly so in the predicted direction for three of them. The correlations do not differ significantly from each other from country to country and may reasonably be combined to yield the inference that on a world-wide basis there is a highly significant tendency for subjects with high n Achievement to prefer blues and greens over reds and yellows.

Knapp's hypothesis seems nicely confirmed by these data in countries where cultural associations to color are quite different from those in the West. Apparently, so far as such fundamental distinctions as the "figural" quality of red and the "ground" quality of blue and green are concerned, one need not be a complete cultural relativist and hold that it is equally easy for people to see these colors one way as the other. Instead, the simplest interpretation of the significant results is that blue and green are universally perceived as less "intrusive" than red and yellow, and that subjects higher in n Achievement prefer them for this reason. They simply want a less stimulating or vivid environment since they are oriented toward "acting on" the environment rather than being acted on by it, just as Knapp argues.

The conclusion bears on the question discussed briefly in Chapter 5 as to whether entrepreneurially minded people are more ascetic. Weber started the discussion by vividly describing the asceticism of Protestant sects which played such an important role in economic development of the West. However, other authors have argued that such asceticism was an accidental, rather than an essential, attribute of these successful entrepreneurs, particularly since successful entrepreneurs in other parts of the world—say in Japan or in parts of India—were not particularly characterized by worldly asceticism. Furthermore, in our study of children's readers, we found no evidence of greater stress on impulse control in those countries which had developed more rapidly as compared with those that had not.

The present results, however, suggest that if the term "asceticism" is differently defined, it may be a more nearly universal characteristic of the entrepreneurial spirit or high n Achievement. Asceticism, as Weber and others discussed it, had to do with renunciation of pleasures in this life, or with denial of libidinous impulses in the interest of maintaining a completely rationalized social and moral existence. In this sense, asceticism certainly has not characterized the Japanese businessman, and in fact even in the West, it has seemed to characterize certain Catholic brotherhoods as much as, or even more than, Protestant entrepreneurs. But if asceticism is taken to mean *avoiding intrusive stimuli*, so that one may *act on* rather than be acted upon by the environment, then the issue is stated more clearly in psychological rather than in social or moral terms, and the attitude may more nearly universally characterize entrepreneurs. The question is no longer whether entrepreneurs deny their impulses, or even whether they avoid excess, but rather whether they *avoid a situation in which they are no longer in control* and are "pushed" about, as it were, by sights and sounds from without, by strong stimuli in the environment. It is easy to see how such an attitude might lead to renunciation of certain worldly pleasures (those involving vivid sights, tastes, sounds, etc.) but not others. The point can, perhaps, be made clearer by an illustration. Quakers sternly prohibited wearing bright colors. They assumed, as did everyone else, that they did this for highly moral and religious reasons. They were avoiding "vain and worldly display" and concentrating on things of the spirit. Yet even the famous ascetic "Quaker gray" could be, and was, converted into a luxurious dress of costly material to be worn by the wife of a wealthy Quaker merchant. What had become of their "worldly asceticism"? The usual answer given is that they were hypocrites, that they were denying a worldly impulse at one level and giving full expression to it at another. But hypocrisy is not an explanation for a psychologist. He would like to know why they behaved this way. The problem is greatly simplified if we assume that the avoidance of bright colors for the Quaker had a psychological significance over and beyond the religious one of rejection of worldly display. If we may assume, as seems reasonable on the basis of all the historical evidence, that Quakers were somewhat higher on the average in n Achievement, then they may have avoided bright colors in order to maintain the posture of acting on the environment rather than being acted upon by it, and then found a moral explanation for a posture which they vaguely felt was right. The subsequent step of making clothing out of rich and sumptuous material, though of sombre hue, contradicted the religious rationalization (worldly asceticism), but not the psychological basis for it. They were still avoiding strong intrusive stimuli.

Travel

According to the *Homeric Hymn to Hermes*, the infant Hermes started traveling the day he was born. He was off to find the cattle of Apollo almost as soon as he jumped out of the cradle. In Greek mythology, and later as Mercury in Roman mythology, he was depicted as the winged-foot messenger of the gods and the patron of travelers. If we are right in thinking that Hermes is the mythological projection of the entrepreneurial spirit and that the entrepreneurial spirit means high n Achievement, should we not predict that high n Achievement leads people to travel more? Actually such a prediction seems an eminently sensible extension of the findings for expressive movements: people who are restless in movement, seeking variety and avoiding repetition, should also move about in space more.

Historical evidence does in fact suggest that waves of high n Achievement were accompanied by extensive geographical exploration. Certainly the period in Classical Greece, which in our data is characterized by the highest n Achievement level, was both preceded and followed by extensive traveling. Sometime before the dawn of Greek literary history when the n Achievement level is highest, the Athenians appear to have moved into the Greek peninsula from long distances away to the North and East. In the sixth and fifth centuries B.C. they pushed far to the westward in the Mediterranean area, as the figures on the trade area show (Chapter 4). The even more extensive traveling to the East as far as India under Alexander in the later Hellenistic Period (when our index of n Achievement is at its lowest level) would appear to contradict the generalization. The contradiction is, however, not decisive because (as we have argued in Chapter 4) economic and other developments in the Hellenistic Period must be considered a separate phenomenon, perhaps due to a subsequent "pulse" of n Achievement not detected in the largely Athenian documents we were coding. Certainly the high point of n Achievement for Medieval Spain (see Chapter 4) was closely followed in the 16th century by extensive geographical explorations in the New World. Furthermore, the somewhat later wave of n Achievement in England also was associated closely with a marked increase in English sea travel under the leadership of Drake and Hawkins. These examples are suggestive but not in themselves conclusive. Not enough measures of n Achievement level in various historical periods exist as yet to put the generalization to a crucial test.

Somewhat more systematic information is available, however, on the primitive cultures for which measures of n Achievement have been obtained from folk tales (see Chapter 3). Kulakow found it possible to make ratings on 21 of these cultures in terms of the following rough rating scale of the normal range of distances traveled by the tribe or an appreciable number of individuals from it.

    1 = very little travel (from practically nothing up to 100 miles
        at the most)
    2 = a moderate amount of travel (within a 100-300 mile range)
    3 = extensive travel (a range of over 300 miles)

The average travel rating for the ten cultures highest in n Achievement in this sample was 2.40—representing a travel rating between moderate and extensive. The average rating for the 11 cultures lower in n Achievement was 1.73, and the difference is statistically significant ($t = 2.09$, $p < .05$). Furthermore, if the distribution is broken slightly differently into the eleven highest and the ten lowest in n Achievement, the difference is even more significant ($t = 2.74$, $p < .02$). So far as this sample of cultures is concerned, those with higher n Achievement in folk tales travel significantly more.

It would be gratifying to check such a finding on the modern nations for which we have n Achievement scores based on children's readers. If the hypothesis holds true generally, it should follow that people from nations with a high estimated level of n Achievement should travel more than those from nations with a low estimated level of n Achievement. Unfortunately, it is extremely difficult to get a measure of travel that is not markedly influenced by the geographical location of a country. For example, if we use the figures on tourist travel which exist, large countries and isolated countries will be at a disadvantage because the tourist figures are obtained from information as to the nationality of people crossing borders. To take an extreme case, a Swiss citizen can hardly move without crossing a border, whereas an Australian or a citizen of the United States can do much more extensive traveling without ever appearing in the tourist figures. Figures on travel by sea, railway, or automobile are also suspect for purely geographical or historical reasons. The Swiss could not be expected to do as much traveling by sea as the Norwegians, and trying to compare the number of miles traveled by car or railroad in the two countries would involve so many assumptions and adjustments that it would probably be meaningless.

Air travel is less open to these objections. The air is equally accessible to all nations, and the topography of a country has relatively little effect on the ease of air transportation. Furthermore, figures are available on passenger kilometers flown not only within a country, but outside it on airlines originating in the country. Whereas automobile and railroad figures would have to be adjusted for size of a country because they exist only within the country, air traffic figures need not be. The passenger kilometer figures for KLM Royal Dutch Airlines, for example, include the flying that Dutchmen do at home and all over the world. It would be wrong to assume, of course, that only Dutchmen use the Dutch airlines, but it does seem reasonable to expect that its traffic figures will not be wildly erroneous in estimating how much Dutchmen fly or are interested and enthusiastic about air travel. To a certain extent a national airline ought to reflect the interest that the people in that counry have in travel in the modern air age. If they are not interested in travel, they don't have to support an airline just to get around because there are plenty of other countries that are willing to provide them with air service in the mid-20th century.

The major factor that affects passenger kilometers flown is the wealth of the country. The correlation between national income per capita (Watkins-Hagen estimates, 1956) and monthly passenger kilometers flown per 1,000 inhabitants in 1958 is .85, even omitting the three poorest countries

(India, Pakistan, Iraq)[2] on which statistics are available. Table 8.3 compares the air travel figures for countries of approximately the same economic level but differing at least .5 in n Achievement score for 1950 (see Table 3.6), and answers the question whether, given equal wealth or opportunity, people from a country high in n Achievement fly more (or develop their airlines more) than people from a country low in n Achievement. In general they do, although the difference is not as statistically reliable as it might be

TABLE 8.3   PASSENGER KILOMETERS FLOWN PER MONTH PER THOUSAND INHABITANTS (1958) BY n ACHIEVEMENT LEVEL AND INCOME PER CAPITA

Income/cap[1]	Countries higher in n Achievement	Monthly pass. km flown/1000[2]	Countries lower in n Achievement	Monthly pass. km flown/1000[2]	Difference
$1000+	United States} Canada }	20.0	Switzerland	16.3	+3.7
$900-1000	New Zealand	13.8	United Kingdom	6.6	+7.2
	Australia	18.5	Sweden	9.5	+9.0
$700-800	Norway	13.4	Denmark} Belgium }	10.2	+3.2
$600-700	France	7.8	Netherlands	14.8	−7.0
$400-500	Israel } Ireland}	9.4	Finland	3.4	+6.0
$300-400	Argentina	2.7	Italy	1.3	+1.4
$250-300	Lebanon Portugal } Union S. Africa}	4.6	Chile	4.4	+ .2
$200-250	Spain } Turkey}	1.1	Mexico	2.4	−1.3
$100-200	Greece	1.4	Japan	.6	+ .8
Average		9.27		6.95	2.32 $p < .10\ pd$

[1] From the Watkins-Hagen estimates, 1956.
[2] From civil aviation figures, Monthly Bulletin of Statistics, United Nations, New York, January, 1960.

and all the special factors that influence particular figures are hard to control. In eight out of the ten comparisons, the countries with higher n Achievement show greater interest in flying ($\chi^2 = 3.60$, $p < .05\ pd$). Here indeed is a modern confirmation of the Greek image of the entrepreneurial spirit—Hermes—as having wings on his feet: apparently the results obtained on a small sample of preliterate tribes apply also to modern nations. Peoples characterized by a high n Achievement level tend to travel more.

Another form of travel is emigration. One might expect that peoples characterized by high n Achievement would also send out more emigrants. The usual explanation of emigration is that famines or other difficult conditions in the homeland "force" people to go to a new country. But obviously some people are "forced" more easily than others. Some people have not emigrated even when it has been clearly disadvantageous for them to stay in their homeland. Consequently it might well be n Achievement level which determines how "positive" the response is to the challenge of difficulties at home. To get a large enough sample of countries or cultures to test such a hypothesis fairly is almost impossible. However, figures do exist on the number of people who emigrated from various European countries during the decade 1921-30, for which we also have estimates of national n Achievement levels. During this period Europe generally was a source of emigrants to various parts of the world, so that it does seem reasonable to ask whether certain countries produced a larger number of emigrants in per capita terms as a function of n Achievement level. The Woytinskys supply figures (1953, p. 75) for 12 countries for which we also have n Achievement estimates. For the 6 of these higher in n Achievement the average number of emigrants per 1,000 inhabitants was 29, whereas the same figure for the 6 countries lower in n Achievement was only 18 emigrants per 1,000 inhabitants. Or, somewhat more dramatically, the correlation between n Achievement level in 1925 and emigration per capita during the decade 1921-30 is .74, $N = 12$, $p < .01$. The hypothesis is clearly confirmed so far as this small sample of countries is concerned. Peoples of higher n Achievement tend to send out more emigrants. Naturally it does not follow that n Achievement is the sole cause of emigration. Rather, it appears more likely to determine the response of people subjected to various pressures at home to move.

What is so far lacking is a test of the hypothesis at the individual level. We do not yet know whether individuals with higher n Achievement tend to travel more, but all these data suggest that they do. If they do, we may have uncovered another clue as to why people with high n Achievement tend to make successful entrepreneurs: they travel more and by traveling are exposed to more information that might be put to use in their business. By definition it is the entrepreneur's job, particularly in the early stages of economic development, to put various pieces of information together in a plan for a new undertaking. He may notice that there is a market in Place A for a product made in Place B. If he has been in both places and also knows something about how to transport goods from A to B, how much easier it is for him to put two such ideas together! The restless spirit that leads to avoiding the familiar, to seeking new information, and above all to traveling should be functionally adapted to successful entrepreneurship; it is exactly this spirit that people with high n Achievement show, just as their mythological prototype Hermes did.

Social Mobility

A major theme of the *Homeric Hymn to Hermes* is the upstart who challenges the established aristocratic order: The infant Hermes steals the cattle of his noble brother Apollo, but ultimately through a bargain at the end is recognized more or less as an equal with his brother. It is the old story of the *nouveaux riches* trying to make their way into "society," reminiscent, as Brown points out, of the passage where Plato "compares 'those who associate with culture though unworthy of her' to a little bold tinker who has made a fortune and takes a bath and puts on a new suit, preparatory to marrying his master's daughter" (1947, p. 97). In more conventional terms, do we find that individuals with high *n* Achievement are more "upwardly mobile" socially like Hermes?

To begin with, moving up in social status frequently implies the geographical mobility we have found to characterize high *n* Achievement. If people with high *n* Achievement are more willing to move about physically in space, they might also be more willing to leave home and to adapt themselves to the requirements of upward social mobility. Strodtbeck (1958) and Rosen (1959) have developed and applied the following questionnaire item which nicely illustrates the point: "A good son would try to live near his parents even if it means giving up a good job in another part of the country (Agree, Disagree)." Strodtbeck reports (1958) that upwardly mobile Jewish boys in the United States disagree much more with this item than boys of South Italian extraction who, generally speaking, are much less mobile in American society. That is, the less upwardly mobile Italian boys are less willing to leave home. Similarly, Rosen found that more mobile upper-class Protestant boys are more willing to leave home (54 per cent) than lower-class boys (27 per cent), $p < .03$. Social mobility is thus associated with disagreeing with this item or willingness to travel away from home. Is high *n* Achievement also associated with it in the same way? In Rosen's sample it was but not significantly: 42 per cent of the "highs" as contrasted with 32 per cent of the "lows" disagreed with it. Somewhat more convincingly, in a random sample of 119 businessmen and professionals from four countries, reported in Chapter 7, the correlation is $-.12$, $p < 10$ *pd*. The higher the *n* Achievement the greater the tendency to disagree with this item or to accept the desirability of leaving home for a good job. Such a willingness to move should be an essential part of the "rationalization" of society needed to promote economic development, since it permits the most efficient use of manpower resources.

Accordingly, we might expect that boys with high *n* Achievement being more willing to move about and try new things and also having more interest in getting ahead in the world would in fact show greater social mobility. Some indirect evidence on the point is available from our study of the *n* Achievement levels of boys in Brazil, India and Germany. In these three countries the boys tested were all attending highly selective schools attended by very small fractions of boys of their age. In India they were perhaps most highly selected in the sense that they were all attending Madras city colleges; in Brazil the boys were drawn not from state schools but nearly all from private schools, where the standards of education were definitely higher. In Germany they all were attending *Höhere Schule* (University preparatory) as contrasted with the *Volksschule* or *Mittlere Schule*, which most German boys attend. It becomes meaningful to ask whether the boys in these schools from poorer backgrounds have higher *n* Achievement than boys from better backgrounds. For boys of poor background, attendance at such good schools represents greater social mobility than it does for boys of better background. The measure of background used was the sum of the number of years of education reported for the boys' father and mother together. The correlation between the amount of parental education and boy's *n* Achievement score was −.113 in Brazil, −.034 in Germany and −.140 in India, graphic measures of *n* Achievement being used for the first two countries and the verbal measure for India as usual. The average correlation for the entire sample of boys from the three countries is −.084, *df* = 860, *p* < .05. Boys in these selective schools whose parents have less education therefore tend to have higher *n* Achievement. While correlations ought not to be interpreted in terms of causation always, it seems logical to interpret the relationship as meaning that the higher *n* Achievement of these boys of poorer background has made them more upwardly mobile and led them out of the schools they could normally go to and into more selective schools. In Japan the schools were chosen to represent three different socioeconomic levels (upper, middle, and lower class status). Consequently, according to the hypothesis, there should not be any correlation between parental education and *n* Achievement; in fact there was none.

The same general line of reasoning produces some further support for the hypothesis if the boys in our cross-cultural study are classified as to whether they come from Catholic or Protestant backgrounds. It has been argued that Catholics do not stress higher education for everyone as much as Protestants do. If so, it may be further reasoned that Catholic boys who attend such specialized advanced schools as we studied in Germany and Brazil should be more upwardly mobile than the Protestant boys in them and should, therefore, have a higher level of *n* Achievement than the Protestant boys.

The argument depends crucially on demonstrating that Catholics are not so interested in higher education for the masses. On historical and doctrinal grounds one could easily understand why this might be so. If there was in fact to be a "priesthood of all believers," it was necessary for the average, ordinary Protestant to be able to read his Bible and find his way to God, to some extent through his own efforts. Consequently, one of the first things the Protestants did was to translate the Bible into the vernacular so that people could read and understand it. The Catholic church, on the other hand, had always stressed the importance of an educational élite which would thoroughly understand religious and doctrinal matters that were beyond the comprehension of the average Catholic believer, whose primary duty was not to understand the rituals and dogmas of the church so much as to obey them. Even if one grants that such a difference in the orientation toward education of the two churches existed at the time of the Reformation, it does not follow automatically that it still exists today in the attitudes toward higher education of Catholic and Protestant populations, although the evidence all points clearly in that direction. For example, let us consider the per capita consumption of newsprint for the Protestant and Catholic countries in Table 2.2 on which data are available for the year 1954 (UN *Statistical Yearbook* 1956, pp. 604-605). Consumption af newsprint should reflect the level of education of the masses more sensitively than mere illiteracy figures and it is significantly higher in the Protestant countries. However, the Protestant countries are wealthier on the average and can afford more newspapers, books, and journals so that we must remove the correlation of .92 between income per capita (Watkins-Hagen figures, 1956) and newsprint consumption per capita by the usual regression technique. When this is done,[3] it appears that the 11 Protestant countries use slightly more newsprint per capita than would be expected on the basis of their wealth (mean deviation from prediction = +1.30 kgm/head) whereas the 10 Catholic countries use less than predicted (mean deviation from prediction = −1.29 kgm/head). The difference is statistically significant ($t = 2.04$, $p < .025$ pd). According to this index at any rate, people in Protestant countries appear to read more than in Catholic countries even allowing for differences in wealth, and differences in amount of reading very probably reflect differences in interest in better education for the masses.

More directly relevant to our problem are figures for Germany, where the two religions have existed side by side for centuries enjoying more or less equal prestige. Wendt has adapted some figures given by Heckel (1959) to show that the percentage of pupils in *Mittelschule* or *Hochschule* as contrasted with *Volksschule* is almost perfectly negatively correlated with the proportion of Catholics in the different West German States ($\rho = -.91$, $N = 11$, $p < .01$). In other words, the larger the proportion of Catholics in the State, the smaller the proportion of the students in more advanced schools. The difference persists at the university level. Zieger (1953) took the entire university population of 112,000 students in the year 1951-52 and calculated that 56 per cent of them were Protestant and 40 per cent Catholic as compared with the expected percentages of 52 per cent and 44 per cent respectively, based on the figures for the West German population as a whole. The differences between the obtained and expected frequencies are, of course, highly significant ($p < .001$), since the number of cases is very large. Furthermore, in some data made available by the EMNID organization (a Gallup affiliate) on a representative sample of German housewives, about 30 per cent of the Protestants had had 10 years or more of education, as compared with 19 per cent of the Catholics (chi-square

$= 5.73$, $p < .02$). (See Fröhner *et al.*, 1956, for sample characteristics.) It may be objected that such differences merely reflect the fact that Protestants in general in Germany have higher socioeconomic status than Catholics do and can therefore afford to send their children on to higher schools. The argument is somewhat circular because Protestants may, of course, have higher socioeconomic status as a result of being more interested in higher education. So far as our problem is concerned, it does not matter *why* Protestants go on more often to more advanced schools. The question is simply one of fact—whether they do or not.

More detailed figures have already been presented in Chapter 2 for a small and possibly atypical sample of schoolboys in Kaiserslautern. Nevertheless the findings there and in the surveys just reported are all supported by more extensive figures collected by Dr. Hans-Werner Wendt for the city of Mainz and presented in Table 8.4. The city is fairly typical of Western Germany

TABLE 8.4 PERCENTAGES OF PROTESTANT AND CATHOLIC BOYS AGED 15-17 IN HÖHERE SCHULE IN MAINZ (1955)

Item	Protestants	Catholics	χ^2	p
1. Total number in sample	101	123		
per cent in *Höhere Schule*	55	33	11.87	<.001
2. Number from occupational levels 4-6 (nonmanual)	51	56		
per cent in *Höhere Schule*	78	54	7.22	<.01
3. Number from occupational levels 1-3 (manual)	43	62		
per cent in *Höhere Schule*	21	8	3.71	<.06

with respect to its religious composition. Catholics and Protestants live side by side representing all socioeconomic levels, and religion is not associated with attendance at private religious schools or with ethnicity as it often is in the United States. Yet, as Table 8.4 shows, Protestant boys are significantly more often to be found in the more advanced schools rather than the *Volksschule*, particularly among boys of better background (with fathers in nonmanual occupations) but even among boys whose fathers are manual workers. The results incidentally support Weber's conclusion for the 1890's even though the data on which he based it seem to have been faulty (see Lipset and Bendix, 1959, p. 54).

So far as Germany is concerned, then, the evidence from many different sources points clearly to the fact that Catholics are less interested in higher education for everyone. Therefore Catholic boys who go on to better schools ought to be more socially mobile, more achievement-oriented. They should have higher *n* Achievement scores than the Protestant boys in such schools, more of whom should be there because of a stronger parental value placed on education than because of an individual motive to get ahead. And, in fact, the 125 Catholics in our sample of boys from *Höhere Schule* appear to have a somewhat higher level of n Achievement (graphic) than the 251 Protestants ($t = 1.41$, $p < .10$ pd). In Brazil, substantially the same result was obtained, although we could not prove that Catholics in Brazil are less interested in higher education than Protestants. For our sample of Brazilian boys, all of whom were in better schools, the 262 Catholics had a higher n Achievement (graphic) than the 101 Protestants ($t = 1.48$, $p < .10$ pd).[4] If the tests of significance are combined for the two countries using the chi-square technique, the probability is less than .05 that Catholics have a higher level of n Achievement in these selective schools. The evidence is certainly not as direct as it might be but it does suggest that higher n Achievement leads to upward educational mobility in German and Brazilian Catholic boys.

Fortunately Gurin and Veroff (1959, p. 29) have obtained much better data which bear directly on the problem of occupational mobility. In a nationwide representative survey for the United States, they report from a dissertation by Crockett (1960) that respondents from low prestige backgrounds who are upwardly mobile significantly more often have higher n Achievement scores than those who are not upwardly mobile. All the evidence supports the inference that boys with higher n Achievement are apt to be more upwardly mobile in society, particularly if they are at a fairly low socioeconomic level to start with.

Athletic Games

Hermes was also an athlete, and in later vase representations is pictured as "the image of the perfect young gentleman, the ideal ephebe, the flower of physical and mental culture." (Brown, 1947, p. 96.) He became the patron of gymnasia and athletic contests among the *nouveaux riches*. If he is the embodiment of the spirit of high n Achievement and entrepreneurship, as we have argued, then we might expect those with high n Achievement to be more interested in competitive athletics both as spectators and participants. The association is not unreasonable: by definition people with a high level of n Achievement show much inner concern with doing something well, with striving to achieve or surpass some standard of excellence. Shouldn't they, then, be interested in competitive games where they will have a chance to achieve (or watch others achieve) standards of excellence? Certainly cases can be found where a high level of n Achievement would appear historically to have corresponded with bursts of interest in competitive sports. The Olympic Games, for example, were started during a period in the history of classical Greece when n Achievement level was high according to the evidence in Chapter 4.

Yet a clear statistical test of the hypothesis does not confirm it so far as modern nations are concerned. An effort was made to determine how interested a nation was in competitive athletics by converting the unofficial team scores for the International Olympic Summer Games in 1928 and 1932 and again in 1952 and 1956 into per capita terms. It was expected that the number of points won by representatives of a given nation in these international athletic competitions might be an index of the extent to which people in the country devoted themselves to competitive athletics. However, the correlation between n Achievement scores (1925) and points won per head in 1928 and 1932 proved to be insignificantly positive, and the similar correlation for the 1950 n Achievement measure (democratic countries only) and points won per head in 1952 and 1956 was insignificantly negative. *Post hoc* objections may be raised to the use of Olympic Games team scores as a measure of national interest in competitive athletics. Throughout the history of the Games it has been clear that considerations of power and national prestige have played as much of a part in the success of the teams as an interest in athletics for its own sake. For example, the Italians scored more points than usual in 1928 when Mussolini's prestige was at stake, the Germans in 1936 when Hitler was determined to make a superb showing, the Russians in 1952 and 1956 when they first entered the games. The host country nearly always does better on its own territory than abroad. Furthermore it is not clear whether or how much team scores should be corrected for the population base. Several small countries like Finland have consistently done as well as or better than other countries many times their size. If scores are converted to a *per head* basis Finland's score becomes many times as large as its nearest competitor, yet its success may have been largely due to one or two extraordinary athletes like Nurmi who might have been born anywhere. Nevertheless, the figures, so far as they go, do not support the hypothesis. Probably the difficulty lies in the fact pointed out in Chapter 7 that "competitiveness," especially between individuals, implies a striving for power or dominance as well as achievement. American private entrepreneurs who stress the competitive nature of business are high both in n Achievement and n Power. Moreover, in the international sample of businessmen and professionals from Chapter 7, liking for "being pitted against another as in a political or athletic race" is correlated .17 ($N = 119$, $p \sim .05$) with n Power and only .09 with n Achievement. Another difficulty lies in the fact that the hypothesis deals with competitive *games* which should include intellectual games like chess along with interest in athletics.

Nevertheless, positive evidence for the hypothesis was found in a comparative study of the preliterate tribes on which we had folk-tale measures of n Achievement (Chapter 3). Kulakow made extensive ratings of the kinds of games played (including nonathletic games) in each of the cultures for which any information is available. He classified the games as competitive or noncompetitive, group or individual, and noted whether they were played by children or adults, males or females. Thus for each culture he checked which, if any, of the 16 different types of games were played and how often (never, sometimes or often). (See Appendix V for details.) Information was available on 21 of the 26 cultures classified as high in n Achievement on the basis of folk-tale content and on sixteen of the 26 cultures classified as low in n Achievement. The figures obtained, therefore, probably err on the conservative side, since lack of information which was more frequent among the "lows" more probably means that the culture doesn't play games at all. The largest difference obtained for a single category of games appeared in the frequency with which boys played group competitive games in the two types of cultures. In 76 per cent of the cultures high in n Achievement, such games were played as contrasted with 50 per cent of the cultures low in n Achievement (chi-square $= 2.78$, $p < .10$). The reverse trend was observed for group noncompetitive games, 44 per cent of the cultures with low n Achievement playing such games and only 19 per cent of the cultures high in n Achievement (chi-square $= 2.54$, $p < .15$). The interaction chi-square $= 5.30$, $p < .03$, which supports the hypothesis that it is the competitive character of games which characterizes the cultures high in n Achievement.

A general index was devised to summarize all the information checked in each of the 16 cells representing the various types of games. A scoring weight of $+2$ was assigned to games that were both competitive and individual, $+1$ to games that were competitive and group, 0 to games that were noncompetitive but individual, and -2 to games that were noncompetitive and group. The scoring weight was multiplied by .5 if the game occurred sometimes and by 1 if it occurred frequently. The weighted scores for each cell were then summed and divided by the number of entries in the 16 cells, to get the over-all index of competitiveness of games played in the culture. The divisor was the number of cells for which there was information, rather than the total number of cells, because absence of a check mark in a given cell might simply mean that information was incomplete rather than that that type of game wasn't played. Such a scoring system yields an average value of .88 for the 21 cultures high in n Achievement and .35 for the 16 cultures low in n Achievement, a significant difference in the expected direction ($t = 2.31$, $p < .05$). Thus an index combining all the information available on types of games played demonstrates that preliterate cultures higher in n Achievement tend to play more competitive, individualistic games as contrasted with group, noncompetitive ones.

Attitude Toward Time

At least since the *Homeric Hymn to Hermes*, the entrepreneurial spirit has been associated with "hustling." "As soon as he leaped from the immortal thighs of his mother, he did not lie long in the sacred winnowing basket that was his cradle; instead he jumped up, and was off in search of the cattle

of Apollo." Hermes wastes no time and hurries off. Once again if we identify
n Achievement with the entrepreneurial spirit, we might expect that individuals with high n Achievement would have a special attitude toward
time—in particular that they would not want to waste it, would perceive
it as moving swiftly, would generally be in a hurry or busy, etc. Hall (1959)
has performed a useful service in outlining the way time is generally perceived in the United States, a high n Achievement country, as contrasted
with other, low n Achievement countries. Here it is regarded as valuable
(not to be wasted), tangible (a commodity to be bought, sold, and saved),
urgent (passing slowly or rapidly), "monochronistic" (permitting only one
thing to be done at a time), etc. Hall's description adds much to our understanding of the stance of the "entrepreneurial spirit" toward time.

Knapp has devoted himself directly to finding out how subjects with high
n Achievement perceive time in a series of ingenious experiments. Using the
method of assessing n Achievement level in individuals through preferences
for various Scottish tartans described earlier in the chapter, he has demonstrated that subjects with high n Achievement do appear to be more acutely
aware of the rapid passage of time. Green and Knapp (1959) asked subjects
to indicate when certain events of recent history, such as the outbreak of
the Korean War, had occurred. They found that those subjects who preferred the Scottish tartans characteristic of high n Achievement tended to
recall the past events as nearer the present. The subjects also were asked
to estimate how long a moving point would take to reach a certain target
after it was hidden from their view. Again, the subjects presumably with
higher n Achievement tended to say that the moving point would reach
the target before it actually did, i.e., they anticipated a future event before
it occurred. For them time appears to be "short," to be passing "rapidly,"
so that the past is near the future and the future is "upon us before we know
it." Knapp and Green (1960) demonstrated a somewhat similar effect in a
different way when they asked subjects to judge how much time had passed
when the intervals were filled with music. They found that the subjects with
high n Achievement kept better track of the time whereas those with low
n Achievement seemed more passively absorbed in the music so that they
underestimated the time that had passed. The time consciousness of subjects
with high n Achievement is even clearer in a further study by Knapp (1960)
of attitudes toward and practices with respect to time characteristic of subjects who prefer the tartans that the subjects with high n Achievement
prefer. He factor-analyzed a questionnaire consisting of 23 time attitudes
and practices and discovered a factor which is characterized by such attitudes
as the following:

Annoyance "to find your watch has stopped or does not run properly"
Feeling guilty "if you sleep late in the morning"
Feeling that "you waste time or spend it uselessly"
Feeling anxious "when you are not certain of the time"

Negatively loaded on the factor were statements dealing with having lots of leisure time or being frequently early for an appointment. The correlation of agreement with items in this factor with the estimate of n Achievement based on tartan preferences was .34, $p < .01$. American subjects with high n Achievement appear to be anxious about the passage of time and to feel that they do not have enough time.

Knapp and Garbutt (1958) in a further study checked to see what kind of metaphors for time were preferred by subjects with high n Achievement, using the standard method for obtaining n Achievement scores from imaginative stories. When they correlated preference for a given metaphor with n Achievement scores, they found that eight of the ten metaphors more preferred by subjects with high n Achievement were characterized by swift movement, whereas none of the ten metaphors most preferred by the subjects with low n Achievement suggested swift movement. (Chi-square with Yates' correction = 10.2, $p < .01$.) Gurevitch checked these results on another group of college students and found that the pattern of preferences for individual time metaphors was fairly unstable, since several of the metaphors more preferred by subjects with high n Achievement in Knapp and Garbutt's study were less preferred by the subjects with high n Achievement in the second study. However, the same general trend still persisted in the preferences. If the hypothesis is that subjects with high n Achievement will prefer metaphors suggesting motion and vice versa, then 13 out of 17 correlations in Knapp and Garbutt's study are in the direction predicted and 11 out of 17 in the replication. However, the classification is rather crude since only five of the metaphors they used suggest no motion at all and 12 implied motion which might either be simply repetitive ("a whirligig") or directional ("a bird in flight"). Much more revealing is a study of the metaphors consistently preferred by the subjects with high and low n Achievement in both studies, as shown in Table 8.5. They present a very clear picture.

TABLE 8.5 TIME IMAGES PREFERRED BY U.S. SUBJECTS WITH LOW AND HIGH n ACHIEVEMENT IN TWO EXPERIMENTS

Time images	Correlations with n Achievement				
	Exp. A[1]		Exp. B[2]		Combined p[4]
	$N = 73$	p	$N = 47$	p[3]	
A galloping horseman	+.32	<.01	+.19	=.10	<.02
A bird in flight	+.30	<.02	+.31	<.02	<.01
A fleeing thief	+.22	<.06	+.36	<.01	<.02
A quiet motionless ocean	−.41	<.01	−.32	<.02	<.01

[1] Original data of Knapp and Garbutt (1958).
[2] Cross-validating data obtained by Gurevitch; correlations are biserial r's.
[3] In the predicted direction.
[4] Obtained by summing chi-square equivalents of p values, $df = 2$.

The subjects with high n Achievement like images of time that represent it as "going somewhere in a hurry"—*a galloping horseman, a fleeing thief, a bird in flight*—whereas they do not think *a quiet motionless ocean* is a good image for time. An independent confirmation of this finding has been obtained by Cortés, who conducted the following simple but ingenious behavioral test of the attitude toward time of subjects with high and low n Achievement. Having first checked his watch carefully, he interrupted a class session of a group of high school senior boys at one point with the following remarks: "It is now *exactly* X o'clock. Please raise your hand if your watch is fast by any amount. Now please raise your hand if your watch is slow." Of the 31 in the class of 97 who had watches which were clearly fast or slow and on whom n Achievement scores were available, 13/15 or 87 per cent of those high in n Achievement reported that their watches were fast, as contrasted with 7/16 or 44 per cent of those low in n Achievement ($\chi^2 = 6.14$, $p < .02$). For the individuals with high n Achievement time is almost literally moving faster. They are, so to speak, always a little "ahead of themselves."

Knapp and Garbutt also report that "in one study employing ratings of the concept of time on dichotomous adjectival scales, individuals with high n Achievement are characterized by describing time as 'clear,' 'young,' 'sharp,' 'active,' 'tense,' 'fast,' etc. Individuals of low n Achievement describe time as 'empty,' 'soothing,' 'sad,' 'cold,' and 'deep.'" (1958, p. 433.) So far as individuals in the United States are concerned, the evidence from a variety of sources strongly supports the hypothesis that individuals with high n Achievement are acutely aware of time passing rapidly.

An independent set of studies by Ricks and Epley (1960) has demonstrated that subjects with high n Achievement also have a longer time perspective on the future in the imaginative stories they write. For example, in the sample of 138 senior business executives referred to in Chapter 7, 68 per cent of those with high n Achievement were above the median in length of time span in their TATs as contrasted with only 37 per cent of those low in n Achievement ($p < .01$). Heckhausen (1960) reports a similar result for German university students—namely, a correlation of $+.46$, $p < .01$ between n Achievement score and the length of future time perspective. To a certain extent, such a finding is implicit in the scoring definition for n Achievement. One part of the scoring definition of n Achievement refers to "long-term involvement"—to situations described in the stories in which an individual is involved over a long period of time in achieving some occupational goal. Another part of the scoring system gives credit for anticipations of successful or unsuccessful outcomes of achievement efforts. Still another gives credit for various types of "instrumental activity" which nearly always take place "over time." So to a very considerable extent the person getting a high score for n Achievement has had to introduce more references to time, at least in the achievement area, to get such a score. What is new about the

Ricks and Epley findings is that the subjects with low n Achievement who are presumably high in other needs have not had to introduce equally long time spans to write about other matters such as Affiliation, Power, etc. Also Götzl has demonstrated (reported by Heckhausen, 1960) that longer future time perspective is not limited to the same fantasy material from which the n Achievement score is derived. School children in the ninth grade with high n Achievement ("hope of success") showed better recall in 24 hours for tasks to be reported on in eight weeks than for tasks to be reported on the following day, even though both sets of tasks had already been completed. The subjects high in fear of failure (lower in n Achievement), on the other hand, concentrated more on the tasks to be reported on in the near future and remembered them better. It is as if thinking in terms of achievement implicitly invokes "action forward in time" or simply thinking ahead. The notion of "action forward in time" even shows up grammatically, as Zatzkis has demonstrated. Subjects with high n Achievement tend to use more "anticipatory tenses" (McClelland et al., 1953, p. 250), phrases indicating a "forward orientation" in the writer's mind. In such terms it is certainly not surprising to find that Western cultures have primarily a Messianic (whether socialist or Christian) conception of history as "going somewhere" as contrasted with Eastern countries, which at least traditionally should have had a lower level of n Achievement, and have certainly been characterized as thinking of time as a "quiet motionless ocean."

The longer forward time perspective of individuals with high n Achievement may be in part the explanation for their superior ability to delay gratification. Mischel (1960) has conducted a series of studies on delayed reward in which children are given the choice between a small reward now (e.g., a candy bar) and a larger one a week later. In Trinidad he found among predominantly lower-class Negro children a strong tendency for those with higher n Achievement to choose more consistently the larger but delayed rewards. Also, when asked what they would want to be, if a "magic man" could change them into anything they wanted, the ones with high n Achievement much more frequently mentioned an occupation (e.g., policeman, pilot, doctor, priest) or achievement-related traits (e.g., important, bright, successful) as contrasted with answers not related to achievement (e.g., nice, same, a baby, brother, honest, etc.). (Mischel, 1960.) In other words, they are thinking in terms of longer-range occupational goals rather than other more immediate gratifications. Possibly the achievement fantasies help them bridge the gap when they must do without in their pursuit of larger but delayed rewards. But whatever the explanation, the data all indicate that individuals with high n Achievement tend to be oriented forward in time toward longer-range goals, even when that means foregoing immediate pleasures. In a certain sense this may define more precisely what Weber and others observed in businessmen and classified as asceticism. In Chapter 5 we found no evidence that "impulse control" was a value characterizing more rapidly developing countries which raised doubts along with information on successful but not ascetic business castes in India (Lamb, 1958), as to whether asceticism was generally associated with business success. What the present data suggest is that one should distinguish between asceticism *as a means* to long-range goals, and asceticism as an end in itself. High *n* Achievement and successful entrepreneurship may lead to behavior that looks ascetic in the former sense (i.e., in the sense of capacity to forego immediate pleasures for longer range ones) but not necessarily in the latter. So the famous asceticism of the Protestant ethic may either have been dictated by a desire to "act on" the environment, as suggested earlier, or by a preoccupation with long-range goals that blocked out pleasures of the moment.

There is still much research on the time orientation of individuals with high *n* Achievement to be done—particularly in other countries, to see whether our findings are peculiar to the United States. What evidence there is, however, does fit the picture of a man hurrying forward with his attention focussed on the more distant future so that present time seems to be slipping past him rapidly, just like his mythological prototype, Hermes.

Trickery and Dishonesty

Above all else Hermes was dishonest. He lied outrageously to his brother Apollo and his father Zeus; he stole his brother's cattle; he wore special sandals backwards to try and conceal the way he had really gone; he boasted untruthfully of his exploits. All in all he was a pretty unethical trickster and thief. We have left this characteristic until last, not because it is unimportant, but because we have not collected much information on it in the present group of studies.

The matter might perhaps be dismissed as the natural reaction of the aristocracy to the commercial upstarts to whom they owed money. Brown (1947) points out that the image of Hermes in the Homeric Hymn is a fairly accurate reflection of how the rising entrepreneurs were regarded— i.e., looked on with mixed envy and dislike—around Athens at the time. Yet to treat the image solely as a projection of the dislike of the "better" classes for people "in trade" is to overlook a possible realistic basis for the prejudice. Many entrepreneurs then and ever since have been dishonest "thieves" and tricksters (for a portrait, see Lewis, 1959). For example, not all the prejudice against the Jewish money lenders in the Middle Ages or the Marwaris in India today can be attributed to the fact that people were in debt to them or envied their wealth. Some of it was justified in the sense that money lenders often charged exorbitant interest (up to 33⅓% in parts of India today) and did not hesitate to demand high security and foreclose at a moment's notice if it seemed to their advantage. The image of the evil businessman pursuing only his own wealth to the total disregard of human feelings and values, which was taken over *in toto* by the Marxists, is not wholly without foundation.

Yet it is clear that such entrepreneurs have by and large not been the ones responsible in a major way for economic development. It was a new type of businessman, as Weber suggested, who sparked the Industrial Revolution. His prototype was the Calvinist, Methodist or Quaker whose religious outlook somehow managed to curb the tendency to use *any* means to gain his achievement goals. In Chapter 7 we found more group consciousness among businessmen than professionals and more among those of the managers who came from more developed countries (Tables 7.6 and 7.8). The key theoretical question then is: What determines how ethical an entrepreneur will be? Does high n Achievement by itself tend to encourage men to use any means, however unscrupulous, to seek a sense of personal achievement, as the Hermes myth suggests? Is it necessary to have some other ingredient, such as the universalistic ethics of the Quakers and the Marxists or other-directedness to make certain that n Achievement expresses itself through socially legitimate channels? Or are there different types of n Achievement?

We can do little more than raise such questions at the present time. There is some evidence in Chapters 5 and 7 that what we called "market morality" or "other-directedness" will facilitate economic development, particularly when added to high n Achievement; so some such "outside" factor may control the expression of n Achievement and tame the trickster into an ethical entrepreneur. There is also a little indirect evidence that some entrepreneurs may be unscrupulous or "antisocial" because of a slight variation in the way in which their n Achievement was acquired.

Again the clue lies in the Hermes myth. The *Hymn* makes it clear that Hermes is a love child, the product of a casual liaison between Zeus and Maia. He lives with his mother, and his father is almost entirely out of the picture. Thus Hermes comes in effect from what the anthropologists call a mother-child household. Whiting and his associates have found that mother-child households cross-culturally are associated with homosexuality, poorly developed superegos (low self-blame over illness), and high frequency of personal crimes (Monroe, 1960). Furthermore, high frequency of this "psychopathic syndrome" occurs also among lower-class Negroes where mother-child families are common, because of what is sometimes known as "serial" monogamy. "Fathers" come and go but the child stays on with his mother. According to Whiting, the conditions are poor for superego development in such families because the boy does not have any strong, stable male figure to identify with. Consequently he is apt to grow up with weak moral standards and turn out to be as unscrupulous, tricky and dishonest as Hermes is pictured. However, normally mother-child families are associated with low n Achievement (see Chapter 9). If this line of reasoning is correct, there must be some as yet unknown variant of training in the mother-child family which produces sons with high n Achievement but without the ethical code that comes from living in intact or strongly moral families.

But here we must leave the problem on a speculative note. We do not know at the present time what makes an entrepreneur more or less ethical in his dealings but obviously there are few problems of greater importance for future research. The answer to the problem may come in part from a careful study of how n Achievement develops, particularly in the mother-child family.

The Lack of Fit between Beliefs and Action

So far the picture presented of individuals or groups high in n Achievement has been fairly consistent. It suggests a forward-looking, active, restless, entrepreneurial spirit, reminiscent of the spirit of Hermes. Certain negative findings, however, have been purposely saved for presentation in one place to give them greater emphasis. They all point in one direction: the entrepreneurial spirit is *not* necessarily reflected in the beliefs and attitudes, as verbally expressed, of people known to be high in n Achievement in terms of their fantasies or graphic expressive movements. The data all indicate that one must make a very sharp distinction between what people *say* their attitude toward life is and what their attitude appears to be in terms of what they *do*.

Let us review some evidence on this point. To begin with, it should be recalled that *conscious reports* of a strong need for achievement are *not* related to n Achievement as measured in fantasy (de Charms *et al.*, 1955). Two items included in our four-country study of adolescent boys gave them an opportunity to express such desires for achievement.

> I set difficult goals for myself which I attempt to reach.
> I work like a slave at everything I undertake until I am satisfied with the results.
> [To be answered +3 (complete agreement)
> to −3 (complete disagreement)]

In none of the four countries was agreement with either of these statements significantly related to the measures of n Achievement based on fantasy or graphic expression, nor was there any over-all trend for the four countries together. Furthermore, agreement with the second of the two items was not significantly correlated with n Achievement score among the managers and professionals in three other countries ($r = .06$, $N = 119$). The evidence is fairly decisive in view of the large number of subjects tested in many different countries. Questionnaires dealing with conscious reports of achievement striving are simply not measuring the same thing as n Achievement in fantasy, either verbal or graphic. People do not know whether they have high n Achievement or not in the technical sense of the term. Their beliefs on the subject are not related to their scores for n Achievement.

Recall for a moment the "optimism" score derived also from the questionnaire and discussed in Chapter 6. Boys who are optimistic, who believe that planning is worthwhile, that man's fate is not "in the cards" at birth, or at least who say they do, are not consistently higher in n Achievement in any of the countries studied. This is odd because these are all sentiments or beliefs one would expect in a person having the restless entrepreneurial spirit our research findings have gradually defined. Apparently beliefs are *not* directly determined by motives. In India there is quite a consistent tendency for the subjects with high n Achievement (verbal) to be somewhat more fatalistic, i.e., to believe that the wise person lives for today and lets tomorrow take care of itself (item 2, $r = .16$, $p < .05$), or that a man with money "cannot really learn how to behave in polite society if he has not had the proper upbringing" (item 14, $r = .23$, $p < .01$). Beliefs and attitudes must be a function of nonmotivational factors, more specifically of the social situation in which people with high n Achievement find themselves in a given country at a given time.

Consider another example. Two of the attitudes toward time found by Knapp (1960) to characterize college students with high n Achievement in the United States were also tested in our international studies. The first one is incorporated in the following item:

I feel I waste time and spend it uselessly.

In the study of businessmen and professionals from four countries (Chapter 7), agreement with this item did not correlate significantly with n Achievement estimates, though it had in Knapp's study. Another of his items was phrased as follows in the questionnaire answered by the boys in four countries:

It would irritate me very much to have a watch or clock which
was off by several minutes every day or so.
[To be answered +3 (complete agreement)
to −3 (complete disagreement)]

Knapp's comparable item states:

Does it annoy you to find your watch has stopped or does
not run properly?
(To be answered on a 5-point scale from "yes" to "no")

In none of the four countries abroad is agreement with the former item significantly correlated with n Achievement scores (graphic or verbal).

Possibly the difficulty lies in a subtle difference in the way the two items are phrased. Knapp's item suggests that the trouble with the watch is that it has "stopped" or runs slow. It stands to reason that a person with high n Achievement would be unhappy with such a watch. Our item, on the other hand, only mentions that the watch is "off by several minutes," but, as we have seen earlier, people with high n Achievement more frequently have watches that are "off" in the sense of being "fast." So they might be unhappy about a slow watch but not necessarily about one that was "off" because it was fast. Desire to have a watch that keeps *exact* time is significantly correlated in all four countries with items reflecting a social concern, e.g., with item 14: knowing how to behave in polite society (average r for the four countries = .14, $p < .01$); with item 5: being influenced by the negative opinion of others in deciding whether to go to a movie or not (average $r = .13$, $p < .01$); and with item 19: giving reasons to a child before asking him to do something (average $r = .11$, $p < .01$). (See Appendix VI.) Worrying about having a watch that keeps poor time apparently reflects a concern about what others will think, about being late for appointments, or about living up to one's social obligations. The result highlights the difficulty of phrasing attitude items which will be consistently correlated with high n Achievement. Sometimes the item doesn't quite express the significant attitude correctly. Sometimes translation changes the intent of the item. And sometimes the attitude is not affected by the motive in the same way because it is more influenced by the realities of the social situation —as in the case of the fatalism of the Indian boys with high n Achievement. So far as attitudes toward time are concerned, we can only conclude that we didn't phrase our item correctly, and that even if we had we might not have found the expected relationship to n Achievement score. For people in various countries with high n Achievement may have quite different *beliefs* about time, though we would continue to argue for the moment that they would act *as if* it were passing more rapidly whatever they *said* about it.

Illustrations of the same point could be multiplied many times over. For example, all the 400 items in the Strong *Vocational Interest Test* have been checked a number of times to see whether American subjects with high n Achievement consistently have certain likes or dislikes more often than subjects with low n Achievement. Occasionally significant differences are found, but except for the preferences for business occupations discussed in Chapter 6 (which appear only in the U.S.), they do not consistently hold up even within successive samples drawn from what appear to be similar populations. Subjects with high n Achievement therefore do not express greater interest in such competitive sports as chess, or poker, or in reading the sporting pages (Item 171), nor do they consistently say they like "being pitted against another as in a political or athletic race" (Item 222). Nor are they especially interested in travel movies (Item 183), as one might expect if our argument that they travel more is correct. In one way or another nearly every one of the types of behavior supposedly characteristic of people with high n Achievement discussed in this chapter can be demonstrated not to be consciously preferred by subjects with high n Achievement. One would have to predict from all this that subjects with high n Achievement, if asked, would *not* say that they prefer blues and greens to reds and yellows: it should be remembered that our measure of this preference was a behavioral one in the sense that the subjects had a choice of various colored pencils with which they could actually make their designs.

It is not merely attitudes that should characterize people with high n Achievement that they fail to show in practice. It is any attitude at all, at least within the limits tested by our 20-item questionnaire (see Appendix VI). These items were drawn up to represent as many different possible value attitudes that might characterize people with high n Achievement as could be imagined on the basis of either theory or previous evidence. Yet *not one single item* out of the 20 was consistently answered one way or the other by subjects with high n Achievement in all four countries. Although a number of significant correlations were found within a given country which could be discussed and interpreted in terms of the social psychology of that country, no attitude consistently characterizes the subject with high n Achievement across all countries. It should not therefore be concluded, of course, that attitudes are trivial: we demonstrated in Chapter 6, for example, that optimism as expressed in attitude items is significantly related to performance in all four countries. Attitudes and beliefs are apparently not simply and directly influenced by fantasy concerns for achievement or what we have been calling throughout the chapter the "entrepreneurial spirit."

Nonetheless we have found a number of types of behavior which do characterize high n Achievement across cultures. It is associated with greater frequency of certain types of expressive movements, with better performance under achievement incentives, with the preferred use of blues and greens over reds and yellows, with greater geographical and social mobility, with fewer outside social activities in school, and perhaps with greater emphasis on competitive games, and different images of time. People with high n Achievement behave in certain characteristic ways, but if asked, they do not consistently respond with the attitudes and beliefs their behavior seems to imply. It is for this reason that we have chosen a mythological figure, Hermes, as the symbol for the entrepreneurial spirit characteristic of people with high n Achievement. For mythical figures are unself-conscious: they act out what they are, independently of their opinion of themselves or life, or the opinion of them held by others. So the spirit of Hermes, the entrepreneurial spirit, has been abroad in the world since the beginning of man, expressing itself in his fantasies and actions, but seldom in his opinions. It will likewise persist as long as man persists—with this difference: we are now in a position to detect its presence in men and nations—the elusive spirit has been caught in the scientist's bottle where it can be weighed and measured as the *n* Achievement score.

NOTES AND REFERENCES

[1] The quotations from the *Homeric Hymn to Hermes* are from the translation of N. O. Brown, based on his interpretation in *Hermes, the Thief* (1947).

[2] West Germany was omitted because it got a very late start (1955-56) in civil aviation and Pakistan, India, and Iraq partly because their income level on a per capita basis is so low it should invalidate such an expensive travel measure, and partly because there are no nations of comparable low income level with low *n* Achievement on which air travel figures are available.

[3] The formula is: $Y = .206 \ X - 1.41$, where Y is predicted consumption of newsprint/head in kgm/head and X is national income/head in dollar equivalents as computed by Watkins and Hagen (1956).

[4] In Germany the verbal measure of *n* Achievement yielded the same result at a higher level of statistical significance ($t = 2.38$, $p < .05$), but oddly enough, the situation is reversed in Brazil for the verbal measure of *n* Achievement, which shows the Protestant boys to be higher on the average ($p < .05$). However, a more detailed analysis reveals that the two measures of *n* Achievement in Brazil do agree in the most important particular—e.g., in demonstrating that the Protestant boys of higher socioeconomic status have lower *n* Achievement than the other three groups (i.e., Catholic boys of higher or lower status, or Protestant boys of lower status). The detailed findings are therefore consistent with the main argument in the text. Attendance at these specialized advanced schools apparently represents upward mobility for all Catholics and for Protestants of lower socioeconomic status, and therefore boys from these backgrounds have higher *n* Achievement on the average. The only group for which attendance at such schools does not reflect upward mobility is the upper-class Protestant boys who are more often there, if our argument is correct, because of the Protestant emphasis on better education for everyone rather than because of an individual achievement orientation.

9

Sources of n Achievement

Suppose we accept, for the sake of the argument, that a part of the "push" for economic development comes from a psychological characteristic which is roughly reflected in our measure of n Achievement. What then? Why do some people have more n Achievement at some times than other people? Is it a question of racial heredity, challenge from the environment, or perhaps certain economic, political or social disadvantages?

The problem is not merely one of academic interest. If it should turn out, for example, that n Achievement itself is a rather simple psychological response to certain economic or social conditions, then the historians and economists could, perhaps with a sigh of relief, continue thinking as they always have in terms of environmental rather than psychic events. They might accept the fact that the psychologist has a legitimate interest in trying to understand what happens in the minds of men as history unfolds, but still argue that the unfolding of history can be understood perfectly well in terms of relations between external "visible" events without reference to inner, psychic states.

In more abstract terms, suppose an economic historian is trying to understand how a country gets from condition A (a low level of economic development) to condition D (a high level of economic development). Ordinarily he explains and "understands" the process in terms of concrete historical, political or economic events (B and C) which intervene between A and D. The psychologist argues that such an understanding must necessarily be inaccurate and incomplete if it leaves out the effects of such events on certain intervening factors in the minds of men, on n Achievement level, for example. However, if it turned out that social event B always has a certain effect such as raising n Achievement level, then psychological analyses might be safely by-passed. They would be interesting but not essential. But even to know whether psychological analyses are necessary requires a study of how inevitably certain conditions give rise to psychic states like n Achievement. Only after it has been completed can we decide how much psychology must be introduced into studies of economic development.

The issue is also of more than academic interest because so many countries consciously want to develop rapidly at the present time. They might, for the sake of the argument, be willing to grant that some mysterious psychological quality that the psychologists label n Achievement is somehow needed for rapid economic growth, but then they would naturally want to know how to produce more of it. Is it something that can be increased by conscious efforts, or perhaps by economic and political policies affecting incentives to work? A whole new perspective is opened up—the possibility of social planning in terms of its psychological effects as well as in terms of its more rational economic or political effects. It is even conceivable that a given investment policy should be judged as much in terms of its effects on people, i.e., on n Achievement level, as in terms of more strictly economic objectives. The shortest way to achieve economic objectives might turn out to be through changing people first. Such possibilities will be investigated in the next chapter. But first it is clearly necessary to understand as fully as possible what conditions do change n Achievement levels.

Race and Environment

Our search must begin with a very important distinction—that between factors *essential* to the development of n Achievement and other factors *associated* with it because they are related to the essential factors. To use a medical analogy, night air (i.e., having the windows open) is definitely associated with the incidence of malaria, but "night air" is not an essential factor in the production of malaria. It is simply associated with something else (the malaria-carrying mosquito) which *is* essential to the production of the disease. In exactly the same way certain factors appear to have been related to high n Achievement levels, not for intrinsic reasons, but because they have been associated with factors which are more truly intrinsic. Chief among the former, at least in terms of popular psychology, are race and climate. Certain peoples have been assumed, since the beginning of written history, to be more energetic than others—whether it be the ancient Greeks or the English during the 19th century. If one asks why they are more vigorous, the answer is simple: they were born that way. Some races are supposed to have a combination of genes that produce greater energy.

A variant of this theme is found in the works of Sheldon (1940), Morris (1948) and others, who argue that the key factor is body type: Peoples genetically so constituted as to produce more mesomorphs, that is, more people with strong muscular bodies, are the ones that are more vigorous and enterprising. So far as n Achievement is concerned, however, there is one very compelling argument against the belief that the genes or body type are directly responsible for its variations in strength. Changes among nations in n Achievement level demonstrated in previous chapters have simply occurred much too rapidly to be attributed to genetic factors. The genetic constitution of the Greeks could not have changed radically between 550 B.C. and 400 B.C. when there was a marked drop in n Achievement level, nor could some genetic mutation have occurred in England in the

18th century which produced the marked rise in n Achievement recorded at the end of the century in Chapter 4.

To a considerable extent, the same argument applies to the hypothesis that climate is the important factor affecting the vigor of a people's response. In Chapter 3 we noted that the correlation between national n Achievement levels in 1925 and 1950 was not significantly different from zero, indicating that a number of nations shifted quite radically in their n Achievement levels in a single generation. Could all these changes be attributed to changes in climate? Take Denmark, for example, which in standard score terms was well above the mean n Achievement level in 1925 (standard score $= +.66$) and way below the mean in 1950 (standard score $= -1.27$). Did the climate of Denmark change sufficiently in this twenty-five year period to account for a near significant drop in n Achievement level? It is doubtful, although Huntington (1915) has produced a good deal of evidence that climatic changes can occur quite dramatically in given places over just such time periods.

Those interested in climatic or racial explanations of energy will, of course, be quick to point out that the specific measure of "energy" which we are speaking of here, namely, n Achievement, is not necessarily what they had in mind at all. There are several answers to this objection. First, if they don't want to measure energy this way, they should provide some alternative objective measure. Secondly, n Achievement does in fact appear to be associated with many of the energetic characteristics such theorists have talked about. And thirdly, it is a fact that high n Achievement level has often been associated with those peoples and climates that it should have been associated with if it were the source of energy that the climatic theorists were talking about. For example, a glance at Table 3.4 shows that around 1925, when many of these theorists were writing, it was precisely the Anglo-Saxon and Scandinavian countries that were high in n Achievement. It is easy to see how observers might have been led to believe that these peoples were intrinsically more energetic at the time. Also, as we shall see later in the chapter, it does turn out to be true, very much in accordance with Huntington's argument, that cultures living in temperate climates have higher levels of n Achievement. But the association in both cases appears to be extrinsic rather than intrinsic, as so many theorists assumed. That is, neither Nordic heritage nor temperate climates have anything directly to do with the production of n Achievement, but both were associated with other factors which *are* intrinsically connected with the production of n Achievement. So let us examine first some of these intrinsic factors.

A more analytical version of environmental theories would assert that challenges from without can *arouse* achievement motivation in peoples. After all, our measure of n Achievement is at bottom based on a technique for challenging and stimulating individuals so that they think more in terms of achievement. Why should not climate, or for that matter any type of social challenge, increase over-all levels of achievement motivation? A popular explanation for why a people show the energy characteristic of high n Achievement is that they have somehow been subordinated or discriminated against. Don't people who are suppressed try to strike back, to compensate in some way for their inferiority? Hagen has used the idea explicitly in trying to account for the way economic growth begins. He speaks of the *law of group subordination* which "states that major social change, including the type of social change being discussed here, will come about only if some group in the society regards itself as 'subordinated'. . . . the group must feel itself 'looked down upon' or socially discriminated against by the dominant groups in the society, and must feel that this attitude is improper." (1958, p. 380.) As we pointed out in Chapter 7, the fact that Hagen's law attempts to explain—namely the high proportion of business leaders from minority groups in many countries—may be accounted for in another way. The young men with high n Achievement in such groups, provided there are some and they have at least moderate means, may be forced to go into business because the higher prestige professions are closed to them. Also some of the minority groups have an ideology which strongly favors the development of n Achievement in children, as we shall make clear later in the chapter. But Hagen here seems to be making a different point—that subordination will directly increase or arouse achievement motivation in members of the minority group. In a sense Toynbee's whole theory of just the right amount of *challenge,* discussed in Chapter 1, is another variant of this general explanation.

The idea has an element of truth in it, but as we have repeatedly pointed out, the response to subordination depends on the initial level of achievement motivation in the group. If it is high, as among Jews in the United States (Table 9.7), then the response will be vigorous; if it is low, as among Negroes in the United States (Table 9.7), the response is likely to be one of apathy and withdrawal. Degree of challenge also makes a difference. Atkinson's model (Table 6.2) was designed to account for the joint effects of variation in n Achievement level and degree of challenge or risk. Different responses will occur according to the model, depending on which of the two factors is held constant while the other is varied.

Suppose, first, that n Achievement is held constant at a high level; then, according to the model, the degree of challenge will determine the vigor of the response. If the challenge from the environment is moderate (.50 probability of success), then the approach response will be maximal, but if it is too great or too little, just as Toynbee argues, the response will be somewhat less. In this way it is possible to account for the "decline" of a civilization even with a high level of n Achievement if the people in it for any reason find their tasks too easy (not challenging enough). They simply respond less vigorously because there is less incentive value for them in performing the easy tasks left for them to do. What is unfortunately not known is how far n Achievement level determines the level of difficulty of tasks that people set for themselves. As Fig. 6.1 shows, there is a tendency for children with high n Achievement to set tasks for themselves which are just beyond their reach.

A civilization that finds its problems solved may simply be one whose n Achievement level has dropped to the point where it no longer creates challenging tasks to perform. Yet we cannot exclude altogether the objective fact that it is harder for a rich country (for example) to see challenging tasks to perform than for a poor country. Similarly it is certainly conceivable, and in fact appears to have happened in the case of certain primitive cultures with high n Achievement levels (like the Yoruba, Table 3.1), that a people can have a high level of n Achievement but be blocked from any very effective economic development by the overwhelming difficulty of the tasks they have to perform to succeed. In this sense, degree of environmental challenge can be considered an *intrinsic* factor affecting the degree of achievement motivation which is aroused.

Suppose next that the other factor—degree of challenge—is held constant. Then, according to the model, the vigor of response will depend on n Achievement level. The Jews in the United States respond vigorously, the Negroes as a whole less so. Or to return to Weber's initial example, the Protestants in France and the Catholics in England in the 18th century were more or less equally discriminated against. But the former responded much more vigorously, at least in business. Why? An explanation in terms of degree of subordination alone seems hard to maintain and more especially to test objectively without resort to *post hoc* reasoning. Yet the difference in response is readily accounted for in terms of a presumed higher level of n Achievement among the Protestants than the Catholics—an inference which can be directly checked by the methods used in Chapter 4. In short, degree of challenge from the environment is an important determinant of aroused achievement motivation, but its effect is greatly influenced by initial levels of n Achievement.

Child-Rearing Practices

Both for theoretical and empirical reasons research on "intrinsic" determinants of n Achievement has concentrated on the family. Psychoanalysis has taught us that the inner concerns of fantasy life have their roots in early parent-child relations. Infantile images of the parents, jealousies, and competitive strivings appear to persist into adulthood less modified by the realities of later life which shape conscious beliefs and attitudes. On the empirical side, meaningful individual differences in n Achievement level have been detected as early as the age of five (McClelland, 1958) and, furthermore, Winterbottom (1958) has shown that such differences may be traced to the attitudes of their mothers at least at a somewhat later age (8-10). Something apparently happens in the family in childhood, beginning at least as early as the fourth or fifth year, which produces differences in n Achievement level, and much research attention has focused on trying to find out exactly what it is. More recently some efforts have been made to find influences later in life which might alter n Achievement, but these findings, meager as they are, seem best saved for the next chapter which deals more directly with attempts to induce changes in n Achievement.

The results of Winterbottom's initial careful study deserve review because the themes running through them have essentially been confirmed in further more extensive work. She was interested in the ages at which mothers made certain demands and placed certain restrictions on eight- to ten-year-old boys she had previously classified as to their n Achievement level. She interviewed the mothers and asked them at what age they expected their sons to have learned such things as those listed in Table 9.1. The particular

TABLE 9.1 ITEMS USED TO ASSESS MOTHERS' ATTITUDES TOWARD INDEPENDENCE, MASTERY, AND "CARETAKING" (after Winterbottom, 1958)

General question to the mother: At what age would you expect a son of yours to have learned:

Independence and mastery (achievement)

A-1. To try new things without asking for help—at about what age would you think a son of yours should have learned that? ————years.
A-2. To be able to lead other children and assert himself in children's groups?
A-3. To make his own friends among children his own age?
A-4. To do well in school on his own?
A-5. To make decisions for himself, such as how he spends his pocket money, what books he reads, what movies he sees?
A-6. To know his way around the neighborhood so that he can play where he wants without getting lost?
A-7. To be active and energetic in climbing, jumping, and sports?
A-8. To try *hard* things for himself without asking for help?
A-9. To have interests and hobbies of his own? To be able to entertain himself?
A-10. To do well in competition with other children? To try hard to come out on top in games and sports?

"Caretaking"

C-1. To be able to undress and go to bed by himself?
C-2. To do some regular tasks around the house?
C-3. To be able to eat alone without help in cutting and handling food?
C-4. To hang up his own clothes and look after his own possessions?

A-1 to A-5 (A-1 modified), A-7 to A-10, and C-1 to C-4 used to compute indexes in United States (Rosen, 1959); A-1 to A-9 and C-1 to C-3 used in Japan, Brazil, and Germany.

items listed are the ones selected from her schedule for use in subsequent, more extensive studies to be reported below. Note that the items deal with attitudes toward three overlapping but distinguishable matters—i.e., independence, mastery, and caretaking. For example, "to do well in school on his own" includes attitudes toward "doing well" and toward self-reliance ("on his own"). Similarly, "doing some regular tasks around the house" may refer to achievement demands or it may touch on the extent to which the mother tries to shift responsibility to the child for taking care of himself or doing things for the parents—an attitude related to what Child *et al.* (1958) more properly call "responsibility" training. These distinctions become of importance in subsequent studies, although in the middle-class American families with which Winterbottom initially worked, the three types of attitudes tend to hang together as a unitary syndrome. She also was interested in the restrictions the mothers placed on their boys—that is, in the ages at which the boy was expected *not* to do certain things, such as "not to run and jump a lot," "not to depend on his mother for suggestions of what to do," "not to try to beat other children in play," etc. (Winterbottom, 1958, p. 457). In subsequent studies the "caretaking" items listed at the bottom of Table 9.1 were used as a substitute for the "restriction" items to shorten the interview, although the two kinds of items are by no means identical. What they do appear to be getting at in common is the mother's "authoritarianism," the extent to which she insists that the boy look after himself and not "get in the way," though it should be clear that her attitudes may not be dictated by her values but by practical necessity, as in the lower-class families discussed below.

Winterbottom's findings may be briefly summarized: the mothers of sons with high *n* Achievement tended to expect "self-reliant mastery" at earlier ages than mothers of sons with low *n* Achievement. They also placed fewer restrictions on their sons than did the mothers of the "lows," but the restrictions they did insist on were to be observed at an earlier age. Even so, the self-reliance training was expected still earlier by these mothers. It *preceded* the age at which the restrictions were imposed. The boys were encouraged to master something, and once they had done so, held to it by restrictions against "regressive" behavior. The mothers of the "lows," on the other hand, make more restrictions altogether, and do not expect their sons to show independence and mastery so early. In a word, their sons remain more *dependent* on adults, both for achievement help and for restrictions, for a longer period of time.

Attempts have been made to generalize Winterbottom's initial findings in two ways: (1) through cross-cultural studies of the association between various child-rearing practices and *n* Achievement in folk-tales (see Chapter 3), and (2) through testing groups of mothers and sons drawn from different social classes and various countries. The cross-cultural studies first suggested on a small sample of American Indian tribes that it is self-reliance or independence training which is closely associated with achievement imagery in folk-tales (McClelland and Friedman, 1952). Later work on a larger group of cultures (Child, Storm and Veroff, 1958) did not confirm the earlier result for self-reliance training,[1] but did reveal that, in a sample of 33 cultures, positive training for achievement is associated with n Achievement in folk-tales ($r = +.34$, $p < .05$ pd). Apparently it is the achievement rather than the self-reliance aspect of Winterbottom's child-training variable which is more universally associated with achievement fantasies.

The cross-cultural study by Child *et al.* also yielded some further results on the effect of "restrictiveness." They found that cultures which were "rigid" in the sense of punishing their children for "sins of omission" (i.e., for failure to be obedient, responsible, self-reliant or nurturant), tended to produce folk-tales containing less achievement imagery ($r = -.56$, $p < .01$). Again as in Winterbottom's study, restrictiveness in parents seems to be in general associated with low n Achievement. However, *within* the cultures high in rigidity, the greater the stress placed on achievement training the higher the level of folk-tale n Achievement (1958, p. 487) suggesting that if a culture makes a lot of demands on its children, it must put even greater stress on achievement, if it is to produce high n Achievement. The finding is somewhat like the tendency of the mothers of the "highs" in Winterbottom's study to set earlier (though fewer) restrictions and then to set achievement demands even earlier still. Within the cultures low in rigidity, some process other than achievement training seems responsible for high n Achievement, but while Child *et al.*, speculate that it may be identification, neither they nor others have as yet collected enough data to confirm such a possibility.

As to checking Winterbottom's results on other groups of mothers and sons, Rosen (1959) succeeded in getting a large sample from some six different ethnic backgrounds (French-Canadian, Italian, Greek, Negro, Jewish, Protestant) of varying social status. Winterbottom had worked with 30 white middle-class families. The question Rosen sought to answer was: how general are her findings? Would high n Achievement in boys be associated with the same family attitudes in different social classes and different cultural subgroupings? His over-all results were not particularly encouraging. A single score was derived for each mother, based on the average age which she put down for nine of the ten achievement items listed in Table 9.1 (omitting item A-6). Then an analysis of variance was performed in which the major determinants were the six ethnic groups, three social classes (see Table 9.7) and early versus late independence and mastery training, the mothers having been divided at the median on this variable. The F-value obtained for the achievement training variable was 1.92, df 1/423, $p \sim .10$ pd. That is, there is a slight over-all tendency for the mothers of sons with high n Achievement to put down earlier ages for expecting achievement in their sons but it is not very large or reliable. Further, more detailed analysis, however, tends to confirm Winterbottom's initial findings and to reveal what is complicating the picture. For the white, Protestant, middle-class families in Rosen's sample, the correlation between average age of mastery expected by the mother and son's n Achievement score is substantially the same as in Winterbottom's sample ($r = -.30$, $N = 32$, $p \sim .05$ pd). Furthermore, for the middle-class families in all the ethnic groups the correlation is $-.19$ ($N = 106$, $p \sim .05$ pd).

However, for boys from upper-class families the correlation is only $-.07$, and for the large sample from the lower-class families (Classes IV and V) the correlation is, if anything, positive (.04), suggesting that the later the mastery training the higher the boy's n Achievement.

What is so different about the lower-class families? For each mother the ages which she had given for the caretaking items had also been averaged and a study of these values revealed that in the lower-class groups, caretaking is expected relatively earlier than independence and mastery, as contrasted with families from other social statuses. If "caretaking" can be taken to reflect the "authoritarianism" measured by Winterbottom's restrictiveness items, it should promote low n Achievement, since Winterbottom had found that mothers of "lows" were more restrictive. To check on this possibility, the 18 social class and ethnic groups in Table 9.7 were ranked separately for the average age at which caretaking was expected and the average age at which achievement was expected. For six of these groups— four from the lower-class (French-Canadian, Italian, Greek, Negro), one from the middle-class (Negro), and one from the upper-class (Italian)— the caretaking rank was higher than the mastery training rank, indicating that caretaking for these families was demanded relatively earlier than achievement. Note that ranking the two sets of means separately automatically takes care of social class differences in average ages at which these items of behavior are expected to be mastered. For example, in absolute terms, lower-class Jewish mothers put down early ages both for achievement and for caretaking, but in the ranking of achievement training they stand much higher than in the ranking of caretaking training, indicating that they stress achievement relatively even earlier than caretaking. The reverse is true of lower-class Negro mothers, who also put down fairly early ages for both variables, though the rank for the caretaking variable is higher than for the achievement training variable. The average n Achievement score of the boys drawn from the six groups which stressed caretaking over achievement is 3.47 ($N = 177$), whereas it is 5.69 ($N = 247$) for the boys from the remaining twelve groups. The difference of 2.22 is highly significant ($t = 4.11$, $p < .001$). Furthermore, in only one of the six groups which placed earlier stress on caretaking, is the correlation between achievement training and sons' n Achievement score even in the right direction, whereas for nine out of eleven of the remaining groups,[2] the correlations are in the predicted direction ($p < .05$, by Fisher's exact test). Finally, the same result was obtained on an individual basis. It was possible to find 77 cases where the mothers actually put down earlier ages on the average for the achievement items than for the caretaking items, though ordinarily, of course, the caretaking mean is earlier because it includes feeding one's self. For these 77 cases the mean n Achievement score of the boys was 5.82 as compared with 4.53 for all the rest of the boys ($N = 347$) in the sample ($t = 2.05$, $p < .05$).

In short, the complicating factor appears to have been identified: early mastery training promotes high n Achievement, *provided* it does not reflect generalized restrictiveness, authoritarianism, or "rejection" by the parents. In other words, putting down an early age for expecting a boy to "make decisions for himself" may indicate a genuine interest in self-reliance and mastery on his part, or it may be part of a general push to get the boy to look after himself so that he will not be a burden or trouble to his parents. If it is the latter, the boy does not develop higher n Achievement, and we can determine if it is in the present study indirectly by checking to see whether caretaking is expected even earlier than achievement. Or to look at it in another way, the boy can be put on his own either too early, as in the predominantly lower-class, early caretaking families, or too late, as in the predominantly middle-class families that expect achievement and independence quite late. Neither condition is optimal for producing high n Achievement. Instead, what is desirable in somewhat idealized terms, is a stress on meeting certain achievement standards somewhere between the ages of six and eight (at least according to the mothers' reports), neither too early for the boy's abilities nor too late for him to internalize those standards as his own.

Child-Rearing and n Achievement Outside the United States

Except for the very general cross-cultural type of study reported by Child *et al.* (1958), all of the evidence on the origins of n Achievement in childhood discussed so far has been derived from studies conducted in the United States. How can we be sure that what Winterbottom or Rosen found applies to Japanese families, for example? Perhaps family structures or cultural values differ so much in other countries that quite different parental behavior would lead to high n Achievement. To provide a rough check on such a possibility, samples of mothers were interviewed in three of the countries where we had studied their sons' n Achievement and related behavior. Table 9.2 reports the relationship between mothers' reports of achievement training demands and sons' n Achievement in Brazil, Japan and Germany. Achievement pressure was measured by using the same items as those originally used by Winterbottom and also subsequently by Rosen in the United States. (See Table 9.1.) The only difference is that the mothers have sons who are on the average five to six years older than the boys whose mothers were questioned in the United States.

At first sight the correlations appear quite inconsistent since later

TABLE 9.2 AGE OF MOTHERS' ACHIEVEMENT DEMANDS AND SONS' n ACHIEVEMENT
(GRAPHIC) IN BRAZIL, JAPAN, AND GERMANY

Age and correlations	Brazil $N = 118$	Japan $N = 115$	Germany $N = 300$
Average age of mothers' } M achievement demands[1] } SD	7.70 1.46	8.27 1.39	8.52 1.37
	diff. $= .57$ $t = 3.04, p < .01$	diff. $= .25$ $t = 1.64, p \sim .10$	
Correlations Achievement demands $\times$ son's n Achievement (graphic)	$+.32, p < .01$	.00	$-.13, p < .02$

[1] Averages for items A-1 to A-9, Table 9.1.

achievement training is significantly associated with higher n Achievement
scores in Brazil, earlier achievement training with higher n Achievement
scores in Germany, and no relationship at all exists in Japan. However,
a glance at the mean ages at which the mothers expect their sons to
achieve various things in the different countries, suggests that these
apparently contradictory results are in fact consistent with and provide
further support for the general hypothesis that low n Achievement can
result *either* from too much or too little achievement pressure. Thus, the
Brazilian mothers on the average expected mastery significantly earlier
than the Japanese mothers or the German mothers ($p < .01$). Apparently
still earlier pressure from these mothers signifies the rejection and dominance
that repeatedly in other studies have been found to be associated with
low n Achievement.[3] In Germany, however, achievement training tends
to come much later (even later than is shown in Table 9.2, where the
mean appears at least half a year earlier because of coarse grouping in the
coding of the ages reported by the mothers). The German mothers much
more often put down ages in the teens than had been expected on the
basis of reports from other countries, so that the code adopted which
stopped at "twelve or older" was not sensitive to such late expectations for
independent achievement.

In a culture that, like Germany, generally expects self-reliant achievement
quite late if at all, earlier stress on mastery leads to higher n Achievement.
The Japanese mothers, on the other hand, fall exactly between the Brazilian
and German mothers in the average age at which they expect self-reliant
mastery of certain activities, and their attitudes are not correlated at all
with their sons' n Achievement scores. Neither the Japanese mothers who
expected achievement earlier (like the Brazilian mothers) or later (like the
German mothers) had sons with higher n Achievement. The Brazilian
mothers who expected achievement later (at the same average age the

Japanese mothers expected it) or the German mothers who expected achievement earlier (again at the same average age as the Japanese mothers) had sons with high n Achievement.

The relationship is curvilinear with the optimum average expected age for self-reliant mastery (so far as n Achievement is concerned) around 8 years of age, an optimum expected "right on the nose" by the average Japanese mother in our sample from Osaka. Consequently, earlier or later stress on achievement is not significantly related to higher or lower n Achievement in Japan. Such an interpretation of the data is, of course, supported strongly by the fact that the n Achievement scores are in fact considerably higher for the Japanese boys than for the boys either in Brazil or Germany (see Table 3.3).[4] Furthermore, Moss and Kagan (1960) report some independent evidence that an optimum age exists for producing n Achievement by maternal achievement pressure. In their study of middle-class white American families, ratings of maternal acceleration during ages 0-3 correlated .11 with male adolescent n Achievement scores (median age, 14 years 6 months), while similar ratings during ages 3-6 and 6-10 correlated .37 and .51 ($p < .01$ pd) respectively with the adolescent n Achievement scores. Acceleration pressure (which by their definition is very similar to what we have been calling achievement pressure) is more effective in producing high adolescent n Achievement if applied to boys between the ages of 6-10 than if applied earlier.

Attempts were also made in these countries to study and partial out the effects of "authoritarianism" by getting a rough estimate of it, as we did earlier in the Rosen study, from early pressure for caretaking (see Table 9.1). Caretaking pressure in these three countries has essentially zero order relationships with sons' n Achievement scores, and therefore partialling it out has little effect. However, it does have some rather interesting relation-

TABLE 9.3 CORRELATIONS OF MOTHERS' CARETAKING PRESSURE[1] WITH SON'S BEHAVIOR IN BRAZIL, JAPAN, AND GERMANY

Son's behavior variable	Brazil $N = 118$	Japan $N = 115$	Germany $N = 300$	Average
Arithmetic performance	.05	.13	.11	.101, $p < .02$
Optimism score[2]	.03	.09	.05	.054, $p < .20$
Number of scored units in graphic expression test	−.05	−.11	−.16	−.126, $p < .01$

[1] Caretaking pressure is the average age at which the child is expected to eat, go to bed, and do chores by himself. The earlier they are expected the higher the pressure. Signs of the correlations have thus been reversed to make the table easier to read.

[2] Extent of disagreement with four items dealing with the hopelessness of struggling against fate. See Table 6.4.

ships to the "conscientiousness" syndrome described in Chapter 6. As Table 9.3 shows, mothers in all three countries who urged their boys to look after themselves early tended to produce sons who performed better at arithmetic no matter what the odds of "winning" were, who were more optimistic toward life, and who were less "spontaneous" in the graphic expression test in the sense that they produced fewer scoreable units. Furthermore, in Japan and Germany, where the mothers were given the same questionnaire as their sons, mothers who were optimistic (see Table 6.4) tended to stress early caretaking ($r = .05$ and $.16$ for Japan and Germany respectively; combined $p < .01$). The mothers who believed there was some point to planning, to struggling against fate, tended to urge their sons to look after themselves early and to bring up sons who are conscientious, hard-working and optimistic, if somewhat restricted or "unspontaneous" in their expressive behavior. The relationships are limited, but they point to the existence of another type of achievement-oriented boy who, as suggested in Chapter 6, should perform well regardless of the challenge of the task. He may indeed form the backbone of the civil service, but he is not likely to be found in the front line of entrepreneurs in the country.

What about the effect of the mother's own n Achievement on her son's n Achievement? Oddly enough this study has yet to be made in the United States using the standard verbal measure of n Achievement on both mothers and sons, although parents and children have been studied that do not come from the same families (e.g., Veroff and Gurin, 1960). The only data available are graphic estimates of n Achievement obtained from mothers and sons in Germany and Japan. Figure 9.1 represents the best estimate that could be obtained from these data as to the "true" relationship between mothers' and sons' n Achievement. In general, the mothers did not doodle as spontaneously as did their sons, and it was necessary to eliminate a fairly large number of records on the grounds that they did not contain enough scoreable units to provide any kind of a reliable estimate of the mothers' n Achievement. All scores were transformed to $D-F$, z-score equivalents as described in Appendix IV.

The mothers' z-scores were then tabulated and the distribution divided into quartiles, so that sons' n Achievement estimates could be plotted as a function of four different levels of mothers' n Achievement. Curves were drawn separately for German Protestant mothers, German Catholic mothers and for the Japanese mothers. In all three cases the relationship was curvilinear, with the high point of sons' n Achievement occurring in the second or third quartile of the mothers' n Achievement scores and the two low points occurring at the extremes. Different degrees of significance were associated with increases and decreases in sons' n Achievement score as a function of mothers' n Achievement in the three subgroups. For example. the increase in sons' n Achievement score from the first to the second quartile of the mothers' *n* Achievement scores was significant for the German Protestant group, whereas for the German Catholic group there was a decrease in sons' *n* Achievement score from the second to the fourth quartile, which was significant.

Because the data are not refined enough to demonstrate that these differences among the subgroups differed significantly from one another, it was finally decided to treat them as sampling variations and to throw all the data together with the results shown in Fig. 9.1. For the combined data the

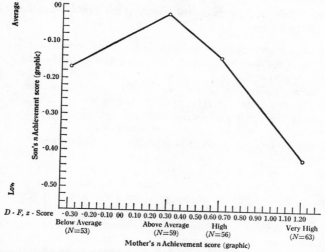

Figure 9.1   Son's *n* Achievement (graphic) as a function of mother's *n* Achievement (graphic) Japanese and German data combined

increase in the sons' average *n* Achievement scores is not significant, though the decrease from the second to the fourth quartile is ($t = 2.21$, $p < .05$). We may therefore conclude with some certainty that a very high level of *n* Achievement in mothers is likely to lead to lower *n* Achievement in their sons. Such a conclusion actually makes good sense in terms of all the evidence that has so far been reviewed. The mother with too high a level of *n* Achievement may make too early demands on her son, or she may be too concerned with her own success to be interested in her son's. On the other hand, the mother with too low a level of *n* Achievement may not set high enough achievement standards for her son. This trend might well have been more significant if we had proceeded in getting in our sample more mothers with really low *n* Achievement. Note that on the whole the mothers score higher on *n* Achievement than their sons in this sample (i.e. there are fewer with negative or "below average" z-scores)—probably because we had a selected sample of "high-power" mothers who had succeeded in getting their sons into high level schools, and who had been able to cooperate in performing the somewhat bizarre graphic expression test. In a less selected sample containing more mothers of really low n Achievement, the left-hand side of the curve in Fig. 9.1 would in all likelihood drop more sharply, supporting more definitely the theoretical expectation that low maternal concern with excellence leads to low concern with excellence in the son.

Parent-Child Interaction for Boys with High and Low n Achievement

Thus far all the evidence bearing on the relationship of child-rearing practices to n Achievement has been indirect, based largely on the reports of mothers (even in the ethnographic data) as to how they behave toward their children. Rosen and D'Andrade (1959) were not satisfied with such information; they state: "Interviews can be a valuable source of information, but they are often contaminated by interviewer and subject biases, particularly those of perceptual distortion, inadequate recall and deliberate inaccuracies." They are speaking here particularly of interviews or questionnaires for parents, although the same types of errors undoubtedly affect information gathered from sons about the way their parents treated them. Boys' reports of parental practices, unlike the parents' own reports, appear to have no consistent relationship to their n Achievement scores (Child, Frank and Storm, 1956).

Rosen and D'Andrade propose to remedy this situation by checking what "parents *say* their child-rearing practices are . . . against more objective data . . . acquired under controlled experimental conditions, that . . . permit us to *see* what they do." They observed parent-child interaction in the homes of 40 families, 20 of which contained a son in the highest quarter of the n Achievement distribution and twenty of which contained a son in the lowest quarter of the n Achievement distribution. The boys were all between nine and 11 years of age and were further matched for social class, race, and intelligence. The experimenters wanted to see how each of the parents reacted to their sons when they were working on certain tasks. Their description of the first of these will serve to describe the social and experimental situation.

"The boys were asked to build towers out of very irregularly shaped blocks. They were blindfolded and told to use only one hand in order to create a situation in which the boy was relatively dependent upon his parents for help. His parents were told that this was a test of their sons' ability to build things, and that they could *say* anything to their sons, but could not touch the blocks. A performance norm was set for the experiment by telling the parents that the *average* boy could build a tower of eight blocks, and they were asked to write down privately their estimate of how high they thought their son could build his tower. The purposes of this experiment were (1) to see how high were the parents' aspirations for and evaluations of their sons, e.g., did they set their estimates at, above or below the norm, (2) to see how self-reliant they expect or permit their son to be, e.g., how much help did they give him."

The boys were given a number of tasks to solve and, in general, three types of measures were obtained, as shown in Fig. 9.2. First, there were the levels of aspirations set privately by each of the parents for their sons. These represent the "standards of excellence" that they expected for his problem-solving behavior. The data in Fig. 9.2 have been rearranged slightly from

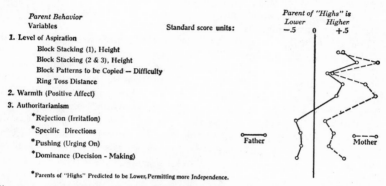

Figure 9.2   Mean differences in the behavior of parents of sons with low and high n Achievement working in task situations

Rosen and D'Andrade and show the difference in the behavior of the mothers and fathers of sons with high and low n Achievement. Raw score differences have been converted to standard scores to make the scale units comparable for different measures. What the chart clearly demonstrates for the level of aspiration measures is that both the mothers and fathers of the boys with high n Achievement set higher standards of excellence than did the mothers and fathers of boys with low n Achievement. They tended to expect their sons to build higher towers, to copy block patterns of greater difficulty, and to stand further away from the peg in the ring-toss game. This finding clearly confirms all the evidence already cited that one of the ways in which a child can develop low n Achievement is through having careless or indulgent parents who do not expect great things of him.

The second measure is derived from the voluminous record of the things the parents said to their boys during the experimental session. Rosen and D'Andrade labelled it "warmth," because it involved a "combination of positive tension and positive evaluative acts, indicating generally pleasant, happy, anxiety-relieving, laughing-joking behavior . . . and provides a measure of the amount of positive affect the parents put out while the boy is working." Again, as Fig. 9.2 makes clear, the parents of the sons with high n Achievement also showed more of this type of behavior, particularly the mothers. The finding is especially interesting because it confirms a difference in the reaction to success reported by mothers of sons with high and low n Achievement in Winterbottom's study. There, too, the mothers of the "highs" reported that when a son succeeded at something they more often "kissed or hugged" him, presumably showing, as here, their greater emotional involvement in his success. Furthermore, the finding fits in well with the general theory as to the origins of motivation proposed in *The achievement motive*, which states that motive intensity is acquired as a function of the "amplitude of affective change" associated with the achievement situation (McClelland *et al.*, 1953, p. 69).

The third group of measures have been lumped together under the heading of "authoritarianism," because they all have the character of "pushing" or "dominating" the child and all show markedly different effects depending on whether they originate from the father or the mother. In general, the mothers of the "highs" also show more authoritarianism towards their sons, just as they showed more "warmth." They appeared to be much more actively involved than the mothers of the sons with low n Achievement. The fathers of the "highs," on the other hand, differ quite markedly from their wives in that they show *less* dominating behavior than do the fathers of the "lows." Here again is clear evidence for the inference found repeatedly in other studies—namely, that very high rigidity or authoritarianism, apparently particularly if it comes from the father, is likely also to lower n Achievement.

Consider the "decision-making" variable. It was measured by asking the father, mother and son to agree, for example, on how high the boy should try to stack the blocks after each had made a private estimate of how high he should do it, following a procedure used by Strodtbeck (1958). In such a situation someone has to state the final decision, and what the data show is that the fathers of the boys with low n Achievement more often made such decisions than the fathers of the boys with high n Achievement. Psychologically speaking, boys with more powerful fathers would appear more likely to come to depend on their fathers for decisions as to what they should do and how they should do it. Note, for example, the greater tendency of the fathers of the "lows" to give more specific directions as to how they should approach their work. All such dominating behavior makes the boy more dependent and perhaps more obedient and responsible, but it does not encourage him to set his own standards of excellence and to strive for them on his own.

What is new and significant about these findings is not only that they are based on actual observation, but also that they show that such dominating behavior does not interfere with development of *n* Achievement if it comes from the mother, but only if it comes from the father. The explanation probably lies in the fact that the boy is more likely to get his conception of the male role from his relationship to his father rather than his mother and, therefore, to conceive of himself as a dependent, obedient sort of person if his father is strong and dominating.

The interviews with mothers in Japan, Germany, and Brazil also provided some data which bear on the three child-rearing variables regularly found to be related to *n* Achievement, and with particular clarity in the Rosen and D'Andrade study. The results are presented in Table 9.4 and can best be discussed under each of the three variables as a way of drawing attention at the close of this section to the main findings of this type of research to date.

Standards of excellence. When the mothers were asked what kind of a job they felt their sons should have when they grew up, the mothers of the "highs" both in Germany and Japan put down occupational titles that more frequently suggested higher status. The difference appeared at occupational level 6 for Japan, where in general the *n* Achievement level was higher, and at occupational level 5 for Germany, where the level of *n* Achievement was considerably lower. Once again mothers of sons with higher *n* Achievement hold out higher expectations of success for their sons, here in the occupational area.

Warmth. The mothers were also asked to tell the interviewer what they did when their children did what they were "supposed" to do. The alternatives were the same as those used by Winterbottom (1958, p. 455), although in her study the reactions were more specifically connected with achievement behavior than here. She had found that the alternative "kiss or hug him to show how pleased you are" was checked more frequently by the mothers of the "highs" than by the mothers of the "lows." Unfortunately in the present study—possibly because their sons were on the average six or seven years older—the mothers in other countries checked this alternative very much less frequently than did the American mothers (only 11 per cent in Germany, 20 per cent in Japan, and 31 per cent in Brazil). Interestingly enough in Brazil where the reaction occurred most frequently, 37 per cent of the mothers of 67 boys classified as "high" in *n* Achievement (graphic) chose the "kiss or hug" alternative as contrasted with only 24 per cent of the 66 "lows." (chi-square = 2.67, $p < 10$ *pd*) Table 9.4 shows the results when this alternative is combined with two others suggestive of achievement pressure. The combination was made by inspection of the Brazilian data, and then checked in the other two countries with one-tailed tests. In general, there is some slight support in all three countries for the notion that affective involvement on the part of the mother, to the extent that it is reflected in checking these three alternatives, is associated with higher *n* Achievement in the sons.

Low authoritarianism. Finally, from the German interview data, which

TABLE 9.4 PERCENTAGES OF MOTHERS OF SONS WITH HIGH AND LOW n ACHIEVEMENT
(GRAPHIC) REPORTING VARIOUS FACTS ABOUT THEIR SONS

| Reported facts | Percentage of mothers reporting, when sons are classified as | | | p |
	high N Achievement, %	low N Achievement, %	difference, %	
Mothers' job expectation for son				
Japan (professional or big business)[1]	29 % $N=32$	7 % $N=27$	22 %	<.03 pd
Germany (managerial or better)[1]	73 $N=132$	66 $N=144$	7	<.15 pd
Mothers' first reaction to doing what he is supposed to do is: kissing or hugging, "show you expected it" or "show he could have done better"				
Brazil	60 $N=67$	52 $N=66$	8	.34
Japan	27 $N=52$	16 $N=44$	11	.09
Germany	27 $N=142$	22 $N=153$	5 Combined p <.20[2]	.16
Germany only				
Nicest things about little children: "obedience, cleanliness, politeness, niceness" among 2 choices out of 7[3]	77 $N=269$	83 $N=293$	−6	<.03 pd
Mother says father has most influence over son	42 $N\sim142$	49 $N\sim153$	−7	<.15 pd
Problems son has:				
(a) worried about not doing what he should "sometimes" or more[4]	54 $N\sim142$	63 $N\sim153$	−9	<.15
(b) Troubled by nervous habits (nail biting, etc.) "pretty often" or more[4]	29 $N\sim142$	19 $N\sim153$	10	∼.05

[1] The occupations chosen by mothers for their sons were classified into the usual 6 point scale. The cut-off point in Japan was level 6 (Professional or major executive) and in Germany level 5 (Minor professional, managerial, medium business, etc.).

was more extensive, there are several suggestive bits of evidence pointing to the fact that greater authoritarianism or restrictiveness lowers sons' *n* Achievement as in the several studies previously reported. Mothers were asked to look over a list of seven possibilities and to check two things that they had "found nicest about little children." Four of these, suggesting interest in obedience and conformity were combined and predicted to be more frequent among mothers of sons with low *n* Achievement. These alternatives are "when they listen to what you tell them to do," "when they are clean and neat," "when they are polite and well-behaved with other people," and "when they play nicely with other people." The remaining three alternatives are: "when they hug and kiss you," "when they learn to do something after a long time," and "playing with them." Choosing from among the first set of alternatives was more common, as predicted, among the mothers with sons having low *n* Achievement. These mothers stressed obedience, niceness and conformity more than the mothers of sons with high *n* Achievement.

Next the mother was asked whether she would say that she or her husband had the most influence over their son. The mothers of the sons with low *n* Achievement named the father as more influential more frequently, as would clearly be predicted from Rosen and D'Andrade's results (Fig. 9.2) showing that more influential fathers tended to have sons with lower *n* Achievement. Then the mothers were asked to check how often their sons had "different problems that children have." In the list of six problems, two showed differences that would have been predicted. The mothers of the "lows" stated that their sons more often worried about not doing what they should, i.e., worried more about conformity and obedience problems. The mothers of the "highs," on the other hand, stated that their sons were more often troubled by nervous habits such as "biting his nails, picking his nose, pulling his hair, etc." Research by Mackinnon (1938) and others, has shown that these so-called "nervous habits" are a form of self-aggression or intropunitiveness associated with stronger feelings of guilt, psychological discipline from the parents, etc. Greater intropunitiveness among boys with high *n* Achievement is quite consistent with what one would expect if one assumes they have acquired a kind of inner-directed achievement orientation as contrasted with the authority-oriented conformity orientation of the boys with low *n* Achievement.

---

[2] Since the particular combination of answers was not predicted, the results from Brazil were used to set up the hypothesis, which was then checked in the predicted direction for the other two countries. Combined *p* is obtained by summing chi-square equivalents with $df = 3$.

[3] Item taken from a United States nationwide survey conducted by the Institute of Social Research at the University of Michigan. (See Veroff *et al.*, 1960.)

[4] These problems, the phrasing for which is also taken from the United States Survey mentioned in footnote 3, were checked by the mothers as characterizing their sons "nearly all the time," "pretty often," "not very much," "never." "Sometimes" refers to a check in one of the first three categories.

By way of summary one can conclude that moderate child-rearing pressures on several dimensions are optimal for producing n Achievement. To begin with, let us list the "extremes" that do *not* develop n Achievement. First, father dominance is one extreme in which the son develops low self-reliance and n Achievement because the father makes the decisions and little pressure is put on the son to work out high standards for himself. Secondly, another extreme is simply low standards of excellence and an indulgent attitude toward the son that obviously should not promote his n Achievement. Still a third "extreme" is very early achievement demands (as in the Brazilian case and in certain lower class United States groups) where the son is, so to speak, thrust out of the nest before he is ready to fly. What lies in the middle of all these extremes is reasonably high standards of excellence imposed at a time when the sons can attain them, a willingness to let him attain them without interference, and real emotional pleasure in his achievements short of overprotection and indulgence. In brief, the picture emerging from all these data as to the type of parental attitudes which facilitate development of n Achievement is quite clear and consistent, although it is obscured at times by the crudity of the measuring instruments that have been applied to develop it.

Protestant and Catholic Values, Child-Rearing Practices, and n Achievement

Having made some progress in identifying the types of parental behavior which are associated with the development of n Achievement in boys, we turn next to the problem of why some parents behave in this way and others do not. In doing so we are expanding the scope of our inquiries from what we have called "intrinsic" factors directly associated with the development of n Achievement, to "extrinsic" factors which have an effect on n Achievement because they modify child-rearing practices. Obviously the number of such extrinsic factors is potentially very large and will differ from time to time and place to place, so that to keep our inquiry within bounds we must restrict ourselves to only a few of the most important of such influences. Let us start with what is most likely to affect directly child rearing—namely, parental values—and then move out to remoter extrinsic factors like birth order, family type, occupation of the father, and climate.

From the very beginning we have been assuming that parental values as represented in their religious world view, would affect child-rearing practices and therefore n Achievement level. It was in this way that we argued in Chapter 2 that the Protestant Reformation may have been responsible for a change in child-rearing practices which increased n Achievement and eventually brought about the Industrial Revolution. Logically the case for such a change is quite convincing. To produce sons with high *n* Achievement, both parents should set moderately high standards of excellence, and respond emotionally, especially positively, to his performance. Furthermore, authoritarianism, restrictiveness, particularly interference by the father, should produce low *n* Achievement. In many ways it appears as if the Protestant Reformation would have produced precisely this family type. It stressed perfection (high standards of excellence) in every detail of performing one's duty in this world, tending to be anti-authoritarian at least in its initial impulse.

In similar fashion it may be argued that other worldly religions like Hinduism or Buddhism stress values that would hardly be expected to lead parents to behave in ways that would induce high *n* Achievement in their sons. For example, Hinduism explicitly teaches that concern with earthly achievements is a snare and a delusion. The ultimate goal is to become "nonattached," to act without a concern for the consequences of action. If all parents were devout Hindus, it is hard to see how they would set high standards of excellence for their sons' performance, or show great pleasure over his achievements or displeasure at his failures. Furthermore, for the traditional Hindu the world is not moving toward some ultimate Messianic goal as in Judaism and Christianity, so that the individual's achievements can have little long-range significance anyway. Similar analyses can be made of the other great religions of the world—Moslem, Buddhist, Greek Orthodox, etc.—in terms of the extent to which their world view would favor parental attitudes that would lead to the development of high *n* Achievement. Such a study might well reveal that Christianity, particularly in its Protestant form, promotes more of the attitudes or values conducive to the development of high *n* Achievement than most other religions. It would then be a short logical step to the conclusion that Protestant Christianity was largely responsible for producing the great improvement in the standard of living everywhere in our time.

The problem, however, is much more complicated. It is one thing to argue that Protestant parents should behave in such and such a way because of their religious beliefs, but quite another to demonstrate that they actually do behave that way, and that their sons have higher *n* Achievement. Furthermore, support can easily be found for the opposing point of view that Lutheranism was in many respects more authoritarian than Roman Catholicism, and that the latter stressed standards of achievement every bit as much as the former. Such issues can be settled not by logic or by appeal to various church doctrines but by empirical tests. Do Protestant parents in fact differ from Catholic parents consistently in their attitudes toward life and child-rearing? Such a question cannot be answered in terms of church doctrine but in terms of the way that doctrine is understood and practiced by members of a particular religious group.

In the United States, early results suggested that Protestants favor earlier independence and mastery training than do various Catholic groups. Table 9.5 summarizes some of the relevant figures obtained in independent studies

TABLE 9.5　DIFFERENCES IN PROTESTANT, JEWISH, AND CATHOLIC ATTITUDES TOWARD CHILD-REARING IN THE UNITED STATES

Attitudes	Protestant	Jewish	Catholic			p diff. P vs. C
			French-Canadian	Italian	Irish	
Average age independence and mastery expected						
Rosen (1959)	N = 122 6.87	N = 57 6.83	N = 62 7.99	N = 74 8.03		<.01
McClelland et al. (1955)	N = 42 6.64	N = 45 6.59		N = 35 8.42	N = 33 7.66	<.01
Veroff et al. (1960)	N = 139 6.73[4]		N = 63 6.89[4]			NS
Importance of knowledge (7 items)[1]	4.39	4.67			3.78[5]	<.001
Children better on their own (3 items)[2]	4.98	4.77			4.35[5]	<.05
Activistic value complex[3] (Rosen, 1959)	5.16	5.54	3.68	4.17		<.01

[1] Another part of the questionnaire administered by McClelland et al. (1955). Average agreement (on a scale of 1 to 7) with such items as the following: "A child who asks too many questions is likely to end up not believing anything" (disagree); "A child should never be asked to do anything unless he is told why he is being asked to do it" (agree); "If a child gets a reasonable and logical explanation for everything, he will lose reverence and admiration for the mysteries of life" (disagree). Items marked (disagree) were reverse-scored. On every one of the seven items the Protestants and Jews answered more in the direction of favoring understanding than did the two Catholic groups. An analysis of variance showed no significant effects for sex or educational level of parents or for any interactions. The F-value for religion was 12.50, df 2/138, p < .001.

[2] Average agreement with the following items: "Children should have free unsupervised periods when they can really let themselves go" (agree); "Children are often better when they are on their own than when they are with their parents" (agree); "I believe that children's free time should be planned for them to prevent mischief" (disagree). F-value for religion = 3.17, df 3/131, p < .05; no other effects significant.

[3] Average agreement with seven items reflecting activism (vs. passive acceptance of life), individualism, and planning. See Rosen, 1959.

[4] National representative samples, regular church attenders only because they should be most influenced by religious values.

[5] Average for Italian and Irish samples combined.

by McClelland, Rindlisbacher and deCharms (1955), Rosen (1959), and Veroff et al. (1960). The items used for obtaining ages at which parents expect achievement are the same as those listed in Table 9.1. Both mothers and fathers were interviewed from different social class backgrounds. Clearly the Protestants and Jews expect mastery at least a year earlier on the average than do French-Canadian, Italian or Irish Catholics in the first two studies conducted in New England. More recent results reported by Veroff and Gurin (1960) for a nationwide sample show a greatly reduced and no longer significant difference in the expected direction, suggesting that the earlier results may have been due to ethnicity or the less complete assimilation into the U.S. pattern of the immigrant Catholic groups tested in New England. The attitudes associated with Catholicism in Europe may change, as they are subjected to the pressure of the American achievement ethic. Miller and Swanson (1958) supply direct evidence for the existence of two types of Catholics. In their very carefully drawn sample from the Detroit area equal percentages of Catholic and Protestant families are classified as "entrepreneurial" vs. "bureaucratic" in occupation and outlook *in the middle class,* but in the lower class, 60 per cent of the Protestant vs. 40 per cent of the Catholic families are classified as entrepreneurial ($\chi^2 = 7.48$, $p < .01$). Since their entrepreneurial classification is very close to what we mean by achievement-oriented, we can reasonably infer that lower-class Catholics are less influenced by the American achievement ethic, but that middle-class Catholics have assimilated it to the point where they are indistinguishable from other groups. So the rest of the findings in Table 9.5 should be interpreted as applying more to *traditional* Catholicism as represented in lower-class and immigrant groups rather than to "modern" middle-class American Catholicism.

Other data in Table 9.5 show that the Protestant parents are somewhat more anti-authoritarian in two respects: they stress more the importance of knowledge, of an individual's finding out things on his own, and they also believe that children should be by themselves, away from their parents, and are often better when they are on their own. Protestant interest in education, science, and individualistic inquiry also appears in the figures collected by Knapp and Goodrich (1952) demonstrating that Protestant colleges have produced many more eminent men of science, relatively, than Catholic colleges have in the United States. Finally, as the last line in Table 9.5 shows, Rosen also found the Protestants to believe more in the worthwhileness of planning and achieving, whereas the Catholics were somewhat more fatalistic in their attitude toward life. He used several of the same items included in our questionnaire study of mothers' and sons' value attitudes in four countries, in fact the ones which we combined to get an "optimism" score in Chapter 6. American Protestants appear to be more optimistic or activistic than various traditionalistic groups of American Catholics.

The difficulty with these data is that they may reflect degree of Americanization more than religious differences *per se.* The Catholics have more recently arrived in the country and are more frequently less educated so that the results are very probably not a simple result of religion as such. The matter deserves study in a country where such marked differences in ethnicity, education, and degree of assimilation do not exist.

Germany is such a country. Protestantism and Catholicism have existed side by side since the Reformation. Neither is now a "disadvantaged" group. Protestants and Catholics are of the same ethnic stock and come more or less equally from all social classes. Table 9.6, therefore, brings together some

TABLE 9.6   PROTESTANT AND CATHOLIC ATTITUDE DIFFERENCES IN GERMANY
(after Wendt, 1960)

Attitudes	Protestants $N = 190$	Catholics $N = 102$	Chi-square and p values
* Average age independence and mastery expected	8.53	8.58	NS
* Planning useless (% agree)	33.0	46.1	$\chi^2 = 4.87, p < .03$
* Success in the cards at birth (% agree)	13.2	30.4	$\chi^2 = 9.65, p < .01$
* Reaction to son's being good (%)			
Verbal approval	43.8	58.1	
Indifferent	35.8	32.4	
Special attention (kiss, hug, special treat, show that he could have done better)	20.4	9.5	$\chi^2 = 8.04, df = 2, p < .05$
** Bible phrases (% recalled)	$N = 822$	$N = 612$	
(1) Power of God, the commandments	23	28	
(2) Consolation, dispelling doubt in salvation	28	16	$\chi^2 = 50.18, df = 3, p < .001$
(3) Proverbs, historical statements, etc.	18	30	
(4) None, no answer, etc.	31	26	

* From the interviews with mothers of sons in higher schools studied for the project discussed in Chapter 2 and elsewhere. See Appendix VI for exact wording of questions.
** Males and females, representative of ages 15-24, rearranged from EMNID survey in Germany, 1955.

relevant data on differences in Protestant and Catholic attitudes in Germany. The first item in the Table shows that there is no average difference in attitudes toward independence training between the German Protestant and Catholic mothers in our sample. This is a little surprising in view of the fact that these Catholic mothers produce sons with higher n Achievement presumably because they are atypically ambitious for their children to have higher education (see Chapter 8). Furthermore, in the next two items they more frequently subscribe to fatalistic sentiments just as their Catholic counterparts in the United States do. (The two items are negatively weighted in Rosen's "activistic value" score used in Rosen's study, *cf.* the last line in Table 9.5.) They believe less in the value of planning "because your plans hardly ever work out anyway" and that "when a man is born, the success he is going to have is already in the cards, so he might as well accept it and not fight against it." Why then do they press early independence training as much as Protestant mothers? Again we are more or less forced to an explanation in terms of a group which is moving away from traditional Catholic attitudes. These mothers we know are more interested in higher education than is traditional for the average German Catholic (see Chapter 8) so that we may infer this somewhat atypical interest has generalized to attitudes toward independence training but not yet to attitudes toward the value of activism.

Table 9.6 also adds information not available for the United States. The Protestants more frequently say they respond emotionally to their sons' being good in the way that Rosen and D'Andrade found to be characteristic of the parents having sons with high n Achievement. Furthermore, just as Weber and others have argued, Protestants appear to be more concerned with achieving individual salvation (to judge from the type of Biblical phrases recalled), whereas Catholics focus more on the power of God and church tradition. Wendt (1960) has collected some futher data demonstrating that the Catholic concern for power and authority reflects itself in Germany very concretely in the purchase of equipment for controlling the activity of very young children. The correlation of the proportion of Catholics in thirty German cities with the sale of playpens in the city is .67, $p < .01$, and with the sale of walking harnesses .61, $p < .01$. Catholic families apparently buy more equipment designed to circumscribe the young child's activity. Here is a nice illustration of what might be called the "unintended consequence" of a religious world view. Certainly there is nothing in Catholic doctrine or Catholic educational advice to parents that tells them they should buy more playpens and walking harnesses. But the view toward authority and control which is consciously promoted by the church, has had what is probably an unintended consequence on the child-rearing practices of Catholic parents. These practices may in turn have as yet unknown important influences on their children's motives and values, which in turn may well color their attitude towards politics, economic activity, etc.

Two conclusions stand out from the much too brief survey of contrasting Protestant and Catholic values and child-rearing practices: (1) more traditional Catholics do appear to have some of the values and attitudes that would be associated with lower n Achievement and (2) other groups of Catholics exist at least in the United States and Germany which have moved away from some of these traditional values toward the "achievement ethic." Catholicism, while it may have been associated with attitudes promoting low n Achievement, is today a complex congeries of subcultures, some of which are traditional and others modernist in outlook.

The Interaction of Religion and Social Class

What then are the differences in n Achievement levels between the two religious groups? As would be expected, they turn out to vary greatly depending on what groups are compared. It depends on what social classes are being compared, whether the Catholics are devout or not, and what kind of Protestant is involved. Possibly the best way to summarize the evidence existing at the moment is that in truly representative samples of the world population of Catholics and Protestants, Protestants might have a

TABLE 9.7 MEAN n ACHIEVEMENT SCORES CLASSIFIED BY ETHNICITY AND SOCIAL CLASS IN THE UNITED STATES (after Rosen, 1959)[1]

Ethnicity	Social class			N	Mean	SD
	Upper	Middle	Lower			
	I-II	III	IV-V			
French-Canadian	5.00[2]	5.92	3.26	61	3.85	4.27
Italian	4.43	7.94	3.75	74	4.78	5.76
Protestant	6.85	6.00	4.03	120	5.19	5.04
Negro	6.36	4.00	2.67	65	3.40	5.04
Jew	5.06	5.41	6.00	57	5.53	4.24
Greek	4.17	7.13	4.67	47	5.81	6.39
N	77	106	241	424		
M	5.69	6.34	3.78		4.76	
SD	5.32	5.31	4.92			5.11

Analysis of variance	df	F	p
Ethnicity	5	2.13	<.07
Social class	2	10.76	<.001
Ethnicity × Social class	10	.42	NS

[1] The analysis is based on the same data reported somewhat differently elsewhere by Rosen (1959). The figures differ slightly because (a) they are reported here without the constant of +5, (b) there were very slight variations in numbers and classification of cases, and (c) Classes IV and V are combined here to simplify the presentation.

[2] 1 case only; all other cells contain from 6-61 cases.

slightly higher average n Achievement because more of the Catholics live in traditionalist societies. Consider the data in Table 9.7 for example, provided by Rosen (1959). The boys from the Italian and French Canadian samples combine to give a Catholic mean n Achievement score of 4.36 versus 5.19 for the Protestant boys, $p < .10$ pd. But the table also shows that social class is a much more important determinant of n Achievement score than is ethnicity (or religion plus ethnicity). Does the difference reflect anything more than the fact that 67 per cent of the boys in the Catholic sample are from social classes IV and V, as contrasted with only 51 per cent of the boys in the Protestant sample? To take a more extreme case: the Protestant boys have a higher mean n Achievement score than do the French Canadian boys ($p < .05$ pd), but even more of the French Canadian boys are in the lower classes (77 per cent). Does this mean that more Catholics are in the lower class groups because traditional Catholicism leads to low n Achievement or that the lower n Achievement of Catholics is due simply to the fact that more Catholics are recent immigrants and therefore lower class and therefore lower in n Achievement? One could as easily demonstrate that middle-class Italian and French Canadian boys have higher n Achievement scores than lower class Protestant boys. What is a fair comparison? If Protestant and Catholic samples are carefully matched for the proportion of cases in each of the social classes, then Catholics will have a higher average n Achievement score, because upwardly mobile Catholics (those in social classes I to III) have distinctly higher n Achievement scores, as both Table 9.7 and Chapter 8 demonstrate. Furthermore, Veroff et al. (1960) have shown that in a truly representative sample of the United States population Catholics score high in n Achievement more often ($p < .10$), but particularly those who do not attend church regularly! Which are the truly "representative" Catholics? Which, for that matter, are the truly representative Protestants? The Negroes in Table 9.7 are also Protestants but have significantly lower n Achievement scores than the Italian Catholics, for example. Nevertheless certain meaningful statements can be made. Predominantly traditionalistic, devout Catholic groups like the French Canadians almost certainly have a lower average n Achievement level than the general average among the white Protestant population. Similarly, upwardly mobile, rapidly assimilating Catholics almost certainly have higher n Achievement than the general white Protestant population. But general over-all differences are very small and depend almost entirely on the exact composition of the two groups compared.[5]

So far as childrens' stories from Protestant and Catholic countries are concerned, they show the same trend as obtained for large representative samples of individuals—namely, a slight but insignificant difference in favor of the Protestant groups. The average n Achievement scores for the readers are as follows: in the 1925 sample for 12 Protestant countries, 1.70, for 9 Catholic countries, 1.47; in the 1950 sample for 13 Protestant countries 1.82, and for 14 Catholic countries 1.75. These mean differences do not even remotely approach significance statistically at either time period or when combined. Furthermore, the mean n Achievement scores from English

Catholic readers in Canada and the United States are significantly higher. The French Canadian readers for the Province of Quebec, Canada, on the other hand, have a somewhat lower average n Achievement score than for either the general Canadian readers or the Catholic readers for the English-speaking population. Once again, we are forced to the conclusion that while the Protestant and Catholic religious labels may have been significantly associated with certain value attitudes, they are not associated in any marked over-all way with n Achievement. More careful discriminations must be made within each of the religious subgroups before one can arrive at any consistent differences in n Achievement scores.

n *Achievement among Jews*

One can argue that Jews should have high n Achievement on religious grounds. Judaism is a Messianic religion which stresses that living up to God's Commandments (i.e., being perfect in everyday conduct) will ultimately help bring about the day when God will reward his Chosen People. It involves an attitude toward time as an independent means of regulating local events (Wax, 1960) which is somewhat analogous to the attitude toward time that we found to be characteristic of people with high n Achievement in Chapter 8. Furthermore, it stresses above all, knowledge of the Law, a knowledge which every individual is supposed to have in some detail. Rabbis are technically teachers who are supposed to know more about the Law, but every individual is supposed to understand it himself and he may go to the rabbi for help only on a particularly debatable point. So the religion in a sense stresses perfection in conduct for everyone and insists on a measure of self-reliance for the sake of understanding the meaning of God's relationship to man. Furthermore, Strodtbeck's careful study of American Jewish families (1958) has shown that in many ways they approximate the ideal type shown by Rosen and D'Andrade (1959) to produce high n Achievement in sons. They set high levels of aspiration for their children; the mother in particular tends to be very warm toward her son, and the father less authoritarian, at least in the sense that the mother has more of a voice in family matters than the Italian mother does.

The prediction based on these facts that Jewish boys should have higher n Achievement is clearly supported by the facts. In Rosen's data in Table 9.7 the Jews have the second highest average n Achievement score, which is significantly higher than the mean for the Catholic or Negro groups, though not higher than the Protestant or Greek samples. In the national representative sample tested by Veroff *et al.* (1960), the Jews again are significantly higher than the rest of the population, although the N is quite small. Furthermore, Strodtbeck (1958) and McClelland (1958) summarize evidence which demonstrates that Jews are generally overachievers on the American scene in ways that would strongly suggest that they have higher average levels of *n* Achievement. Finally, it should be noted that the Jews are the only group in Table 9.7 which does not show a drop in average *n* Achievement level for the lowest socioeconomic classes. Apparently the influence of American Jewish culture is sufficiently powerful to wipe out the effects of differences in class status which are very marked for the other ethnic groups. In short, there is very little doubt that the average *n* Achievement among Jews is higher than for the general population in the United States at the present time.

It would be fascinating to know whether Jews generally, in other times and places, have tended to have higher levels of *n* Achievement than their contemporaries in the various nations of the world where they have lived at one time or another. The association of the Jew with financial and economic matters is proverbial in the Western world. Shakespeare's Shylock is typical of the folk image of the Jewish concern for money, at least in the Middle Ages. Persecution of the Jews, from the time they were thrown out of England during the reign of Edward I in the 13th century down through their expulsion from Spain in the 15th century and from Poland and Germany in the 19th and 20th centuries, has nearly always been based on their real or alleged financial success. The legend keeps cropping up all over the world. It is claimed that the most influential and successful Turkish businessmen are really Dönme (converted Jews), that the Antioqueños in Colombia, South America, are so successful in business because they are descended from Jews expelled from Spain at the time of Isabella, that a successful business group in Southern Rhodesia today is descended from one of the lost tribes of Israel. The truth of these assertions is extremely difficult to establish one way or the other. When persecuted and forced to change their religion, the Jews have often concealed their Jewish origins to prevent further discrimination. The rest of the community, believing that the Jews represent an inferior race and religion, are loath to admit that Jews could be especially responsible for economic or any other outstanding success. One anecdote will serve to illustrate the extreme difficulty of making sense out of historical records on such matters. Gabriel Mejia (1942) has made a careful study of the genealogies of Antioquia and Caldas in Colombia and demonstrated to his own and a lot of other people's satisfaction that the amount of Jewish ancestry in Antioquia is quite small, certainly no greater than in other communities in Colombia, like Bogota. Thus many writers, including Hagen (1961), have concluded that the common belief in Colombia that the Antioqueños are Jews is not based on fact, but based on their undoubted economic success. In terms of the popular image, they must be Jews because they are so rich.

However, a Hungarian Jewish refugee in Colombia, checking over the records on which Mejia bases his book, reports that the primary source material is not very trustworthy. For example, she ran across one reference that went like this: "Family Charem: Don Angel Charem de Mates, natural of the kingdom of Galicia (Spain), came to Antioquia in the last part of the eighteenth century to establish himself in the province in business and commerce. This is a family of old Christians." She comments: "I couldn't help but have an inward smile regarding the fate of the Charem family. With that name I couldn't possibly believe that they were a family of old Christians, and it seemed tragic to me when I thought about how worried Mr. Charem must have been when he came to the New World and how pleased he must have been when he 'passed' as a Christian here. Yet it is on the basis of such 'data' that Mejia concludes 'that the first inhabitants of our mountains were Spanish by birth, Christians, notorious old noblemen and not Jews brought by Robledo, nor outcasts or jailbirds escaped from Spain.' " [6] The anecdote does not prove, of course, that there were more Jewish settlers in Antioquia than in other parts of Colombia, but it does show how difficult it will always be to arrive at the truth in matters where feelings have run so high in the past.

All that the present research adds to the controversy is that if the Jews had higher n Achievement in the past, as they appear to have now in the United States, then their concern with business and commercial matters could be predicted on the basis of all the findings reported in this book. It would be unnecessary to assume, as many writers have, that they went into business because they were blocked from going into other activities and because, unlike Christians, they were permitted to charge interest on loans. There were undoubtedly other minority groups like the Gypsies present in most of these countries at the same time the Jews were, who like the Jews would have had no scruples about charging interest and who were blocked from other types of occupational careers. So if persecution and freedom to charge interest were the "causes" of Jewish commercial success, why didn't they operate on other minority groups as well?

Yet there is reason to doubt that Jewish groups have always everywhere had a higher level of n Achievement. Kroeber points out that at least in noneconomic fields the Jews have produced significant numbers of eminent men only at a few time periods with long intervals in between. Thus there was a burst of Jewish activity in the Middle Ages in Arab-Spanish culture and again at a very much higher level beginning from about 1850 on. (Kroeber, 1944, p. 740.) Furthermore, Oriental Jews have never been so conspicuously successful for their economic success, nor is it the impression of Western Jews in Israel that they have very high levels of n Achievement. Finally it can be argued that the religion itself is basically authoritarian, at least in its traditional orthodox form, and that a content analysis of the Pentateuch reveals practically no achievement imagery whatsoever in the sense in which it is defined in our present research; instead the emphasis is definitely on purification and cleanliness. The argument is not going to be decided by claims and counterclaims, but only by careful content analysis of Jewish documents from different times and places in Jewish history.

Core Religious Values: Positive Mysticism

Dealing in terms of the religious labels of Protestant, Catholic and Jew has not gotten us very far in our search for the basic values associated with the development of n Achievement. It is obviously necessary to go behind the labels to elements within each of the religions which may be more closely associated with achievement training. A more promising place to begin is with the religious attitudes of sects within all religions that have been conspicuously successful in the business world.

The original impulse to the Protestant Reformation was certainly anti-sacerdotal and individualistic. It may have come at least in part from the Scandinavian ethic of the Vikings, as Rosalie and Murray Wax (1955) have argued, for the Vikings were rather defiant of supernatural powers and showed the interest in trade and travel that we have found to be characteristic of a people with high n Achievement. But both in England in Anglicanism and in Germany in Lutheranism, the impulse was curbed by the weight of Catholic tradition and produced churches that as institutions were compromises between the old and the new. They relied, at least to some extent, on tradition and on centralized church authority and ritual as the Roman church did. The individualistic spirit persisted in purer form in some of the minor Protestant sects, like the Anabaptists on the Continent or the Quakers and later the Methodists in England, and the Unitarians in the United States. Oddly enough, it is these smaller Protestant bodies which were generally more revolutionary than the established Protestant churches and which were especially associated with business success. For example, eight out of the 82 industrial innovators in Hagen's list (see Chapter 4) were Quakers, a much larger number than would have been predicted on the basis of the proportion that the Quakers were of all the nonconformist sects. Likewise, Quakers in Philadelphia, were showing a remarkable talent for business (see Tolles, 1948). It may, therefore, be rewarding to look for a moment at the religious characteristics of these sects.

First, they were nearly all more strongly against traditional church authority than even the larger Protestant denominations had been. The Quakers went all the way: they were even opposed to having sacred places of worship—churches, which George Fox referred to contemptuously as "steeple houses." They discarded all outward signs of religious authority—sacraments, priestly robes, religious pictures and sacred music—and revolted even against the notion of a special class of men whose duty it was to look after religious matters. They were strongly opposed to the "hireling ministry." On the positive side, they emphasized the mystical strains in

Christianity which had stressed direct communion of the individual with God. Rufus Jones, in describing the religious character of mystics of all kinds, succeeds, as a good Quaker, in giving a vivid picture of the positive mysticism characteristic of Quakerism at its best:

"They [the mystics] had saved Christianity from being submerged under scholastic formalism and ecclesiastical systems, which were alien to man's essential nature and need. They have been spiritual leaders, they are the persons who shifted the levels of life for the race. They have been able to render these services because they felt themselves allied inwardly with a larger personal Power than themselves, and they have been aware that they were in immediate correspondence with Some One—a Holy Spirit, a Great Companion—who is working with them and through them. This *furtherance of life* by incoming energy, the heightening of power by correspondence with what *seems* to be God, is, however, by no means confined to a few chosen spirits and rare geniuses; it is a widespread fact to be reckoned with everywhere." (R. M. Jones, 1919, p. xxx).

As the quotation demonstrates, this particular type of mysticism was not world-renouncing, in the sense of the asceticism of the Catholic or Buddhist monk, nor was it confined to a few "rare spirits." Rather, everyone could get renewed energy by direct contact with the Divine. The Methodists certainly also belonged to some extent in this tradition in that they, too, stressed spiritual union with Christ for every believer, so that man's will becomes God's will through Perfect Love. Furthermore, for many of these people, mysticism implied a reverence for life which took the form of renunciation of violence, or pacifism.

The fact that these mystical religious sects happened also to be unusually successful in business might be regarded as an accident except for a curious fact. In India, where the religious traditions have been totally different and entirely outside the stream of Christianity, the picture is amazingly similar. In northern India, for example, the conspicuously successful business communities again represent small, minority religious sects—the Jains, the Vaishnava Hindus and the Parsees (Lamb, 1958). All of these religious groups, like the minor Protestant bodies in the West, are characterized by opposition to dominant traditional religious authority—in this case Hindu Brahmanism. Furthermore, both the Jains and the Vaishnavas practice *ahimsa* or "nonviolence toward living beings," which in the case of the Jains "issues in peculiar practices such as straining one's drinks to avoid swallowing organisms, filtering one's breath by a respirator for the same reason, and wearing no clothes to avoid crushing vermin in their folds" (Bouquet, 1954, p. 155).

It is at least an odd coincidence that an attitude of nonviolence or reverence for life should be associated with business success both in the East and the West. The connecting link seems to be the mystical reverence for life rather than asceticism. Both the Quakers and Jains are notorious ascetics, but the Vaishnavas, if anything, are epicurean in their tastes. But "reverence for life" may not be the psychologically significant variable running through all these religions either, for the Parsees do not practice *ahimsa*. They are a remnant of Persians who fled to India centuries ago who were Zoroastrians. The key doctrine in Zoroastrianism is psychologically somewhat akin to the key notion in Calvinism: every single act that a man makes has eternal significance for his salvation as it contributes either to the forces of good or evil fighting for control of the universe and his individual soul. Thus a man's life "is, in spite of dangers and temptations, a responsible one" (Bouquet, 1954, p. 104), in which there is no "remission of sins" or divine forgiveness for very human foibles. If a man does something evil, it is never wiped out in the eternal accounting books, although it may be outweighed by corresponding good deeds. Psychologically speaking, what all of these religious viewpoints appear to mean for the individual believer is a sense of being religiously "on his toes," so to speak. He must consider the religious significance of every act, not in the ritualistic Brahman sense but in the sense of having to make a responsible decision as to whether he is showing reverence for life or contributing to his eternal salvation. In the negative sense, the picture is even somewhat clearer; these are all sects which do not hand over religious authority exclusively to experts or traditions that prescribe minutely for them how they should behave ritually. Rejection of the priestly caste was by no means as extreme in the East as it had been in the West under Quakerism, but in all three of the Indian religious groups, the laity participated much more in the regulation of religion than in traditional Brahmanism. Thus Lamb states (1958) that "some scholars attribute the survival of Jainism to the greater organization and participation by the laity in the support and regulation of the Jain religion," and that among the Hindu Vaishnavas the Gujarati businessmen "established the principle of the dispensability of their priests by their successful assertion that household worship without benefit of priests was on a par with temple worship."

The number of similar cases could be multiplied: the rise of the business class in Japan in the 19th century was associated with a special form of Buddhism—Zen, which again is a form of positive mysticism which is definitely individualistic and against many ritual religious forms. It stresses individual enlightenment or *satori* which is to be attained not by ritual or by "verbal implantation from the outside" but by the growth of "one's inner life" (Suzuki, 1959, p. 10). "Zen discipline is simple, direct, self-reliant, self-denying." (*Ibid.*, p. 62.) Its similarity to Quakerism has been suggested by many, but oddly enough in Japan it was the religion predominantly of the military caste—the *samurai*. And it was precisely from the *samurai* class that the "new economic leaders" were drawn in the late 19th century in Japan (Hagen, 1958, p. 389).[7] Hagen feels that it was the "psychological frustrations" of the *samurai* arising from their increasingly "subordinated status" that drove them into business. Our view does not so much contradict as supplement and extend his. Presumably the *samurai* class would not have felt "frustrated" and reacted by counterstriving *unless they had had high* n *Achievement*, as their association with the mystical Zen Buddhist movement suggests to us that they did have at the time. Other groups have certainly been subordinated from higher status (e.g., the Catholics in England in the 18th century) without reacting by counterstriving, presumably because they had low n Achievement at the time.

Or finally, to take just one more example, it is a curious fact that the distinct business success of Jews within the past few generations has been associated with a strong antirabbinical mystical movement within Judaism known as Hassidism (see Scholem, 1941). Hassidism, like all these other religions, was an attempt to escape from "formalism and ecclesiastical systems" and to encourage the individual believer to feel that he could directly and joyously feel the presence of God. But, as we have repeatedly argued, multiplication of instances is not proof. What is needed is a careful and systematic test of a hypothesis suggested by these cases.

If we assume that these business communities were successful because of a higher average level of n Achievement, then it follows that their religious ideas should in some way be connected with a higher level of n Achievement. A simple summary of the evidence just reviewed would then run something as follows: institutionalized individualistic approaches to God (represented usually by some strain of positive mysticism) should be associated with higher levels of n Achievement. The data already systematically collected on the n Achievement levels of preliterate tribes permitted a systematic test of such a hypothesis. Four codes were developed for describing the nature of the religious views of each of these cultures. Each is described fully in Appendix V, but a brief summary will suffice here. The first recorded the extent to which the religions stress *individual vs. ritual contact with the Divine*. Individual contact includes private prayer, or group contact (as in Quaker silent meetings, group trances or revival meetings, etc.), or individual interpretation of oral or written tradition (as in the traditional Protestant practice of encouraging individual members to read the Bible and figure out the meaning of particular verses for their own lives). Ritual contact with the Divine, on the other hand, stresses exact memorization of ritual formulas which gain their religious potency, so to speak, from being repeated often exactly as prescribed, as in Navaho, Buddhist, or Roman Catholic chants. Many religions, and certainly complex ones like Roman Catholicism, stress both approaches to the Divine to a certain extent, so that it was necessary to weight the order of importance of each of the approaches in each of the religions, which was done, of course, without any knowledge of the n Achievement content of the folk tales for the culture. The resulting distribution of scores was broken at the median, and as Table 9.8 shows, the cultures high in *n* Achievement folk tale content were significantly more often above the median on individualism in their approach to God.

TABLE 9.8 RELIGIOUS ORIENTATIONS OF 45 PRELITERATE CULTURES CLASSIFIED AS HIGH AND LOW IN *n* ACHIEVEMENT ON THE BASIS OF FOLK-TALE CONTENT

Orientations	High *n* Achievement cultures N = 23	Low *n* Achievement cultures N = 22	Chi-square	*p*
I Per cent above median in individual over ritual contact with the Divine	65	23	8.30	<.01
II Per cent below median in dependence on religious experts	52	18	5.61	<.05
III Per cent placing high emphasis on ethics as opposed to self-improvement or worship as goals of religion	57	45		NS
IV Per cent having high internalization as opposed to externalization of the Sacred	48	45		NS

The second code dealt with the extent to which *religious experts are necessary* in religious activity. For example, Jewish rabbis are useful and very important in the religious life of the Jewish community, but they are strictly speaking not *necessary* in the individual's performance of his religious duties. On the other hand, Roman Catholic priests have special powers directly granted them through the "laying on of hands" from the first heads of the church down to the present. At the other extreme are the Quakers who had practically no ministry at all and refused to believe that any person could perform a religious function for somebody else in a way that would substitute or be better than the person's doing it for himself. Every Quaker is at least theoretically qualified to perform all religious duties. Again, on this dimension, Table 9.8 shows that the preliterate cultures characterized by higher *n* Achievement also less often stressed the importance of religious experts, as *necessary* adjuncts to performing religious duties.

Two other codes, perhaps less directly related to the key hypothesis, did not show differences. The primary goal of the religion was also determined so far as possible in terms of three general objectives—ethical conduct of one man toward another, self-improvement (peace of mind, personal salvation, etc.), and, more strictly speaking *worship*, in the sense of *do ut des* or *do ut abeas*. Since many of the mystical sects described above appear to be characterized by interest in "good works" and an interest in man's relationship to his fellow man, it had been predicted that high n Achievement cultures would more often stress ethics as a goal of religion, but the prediction was not confirmed. Finally, since these same sects also appeared to be generally opposed to "externalization of the sacred," to the use of idols, sacred images, fixed places of worship, etc., it was also predicted that the cultures with high n Achievement would more often stress "internalization" of the sacred, as in the purely mystical forms of religion. Again, the hypothesis was not confirmed among these preliterate religions.

On the whole, however, our research has refined much more closely the core religious values associated with high n Achievement than a general comparison of such large amorphous religious bodies as contemporary Protestantism and Catholicism permitted. The key religious attitude is not unlike the general one we found to be associated with n Achievement in Chapters 6 and 7; that is, the person with high n Achievement wants to be responsible for his own decisions and the very act of making a decision implies some uncertainty as to the outcome. He is therefore "on his toes" in the same sense as the believer is in individualistic religions. In formal ritualistic ecclesiastical systems, on the other hand, the individual is "safe" if he does exactly what he is supposed to do, performs correct rituals, says his prayers often enough, calls in the right priest at the right time, etc. But here we run into the old chicken-and-egg problem: which came first, individualistic religion or n Achievement? No clear answer to the question can be given that would cover all cases, although some evidence on the point will be presented in the next chapter. However, theoretically either factor could "come first" and influence the development of the other. That is, Quaker parents with the religious views just described would certainly tend to behave toward their sons in ways that would be conducive to the development of high n Achievement. In this case the religion clearly comes first, and in fact since religion is one of the more stable persistent elements in many societies, it may often have "come first."

However, if n Achievement level should happen to be increased through the mediation of any of the other variables discussed in this chapter, it appears highly likely that the religious world view or practices of the church of which these people were members would be likely to undergo changes in the direction of greater individualism as defined above. To take just one contemporary example to illustrate the point, let us suppose that orthodox Communism represents a "religious" world view which institutionally, at least, is ecclesiastical and formalistic. It would certainly score high on the second variable in Table 9.8 in the extent to which it relies on experts who have absolute authority in matters of dogma. But if our data based on children's readers is to be taken seriously, n Achievement level in

Russia has been rising between 1925 and 1950. Consequently one might expect and predict over the next twenty-five years a shift toward more individualism in Communist orthodoxy.

Indirect Influences on n Achievement Levels

Let us now turn to more indirect influences that may affect n Achievement levels. For convenience these will be discussed briefly under four main headings: physique, the family, the economy, and the physical environment. The distinguishing feature of all these variables is that they influence acquisition of n Achievement indirectly rather than intentionally and directly, as in the case of some religious value attitudes.

Physique. As we have pointed out above, physique could not very well be the sufficient cause of n Achievement because of relatively rapid changes in group n Achievement levels; it could still be a factor in individuals which makes it more or less likely that a given person will acquire high n Achievement under standard child-rearing conditions. Starting from this basic assumption, Cortés has obtained preliminary data showing that n Achievement is *significantly positively* associated with mesomorphy (strong, muscular physiques) and *negatively* with ectomorphy (thin, fragile physiques). He classified 97 boys, aged 16-18, from a Catholic High School in Boston according to the somatotyping system developed by Parnell (1958) after Sheldon *et al.* (1940), in which the individual is rated on a scale of 1-7 for the strength of endomorphic, mesomorphic, and ectomorphic components. Of the 50 boys above the class average in mesomorphy (rating = 4.0 or better), 34 or 68 per cent were above the median in n Achievement (obtained and scored independently without knowledge of the somatotype) as contrasted with 13/47 or 28 per cent of the boys above average in ectomorphy ($p < .001$). There was no difference in the n Achievement scores of boys high and low in endomorphy.

The interpretation of this result is not perfectly straightforward. It may simply mean that in an achievement-oriented society the boys with stronger physiques are more likely to have the early success experiences which according to theory (McClelland *et al.*, 1953) strengthen the achievement motive. Or it may mean that boys with stronger physiques are likely to be able to surmount challenges or risks more successfully (see Chapter 6). It may even mean that boys with higher n Achievement exercise more, engage in more competitive sports, etc., and therefore develop stronger, more muscular bodies. But whatever the final interpretation it seems clear that physique does not *produce* achievement motivation in any simple fashion. Instead it is probably one of the environmental conditions which makes it more or less likely that a strong achievement motive will be acquired, given other more direct influences.

The Family Structure. What family set-up is most likely to promote the development of n Achievement? It is difficult to generalize because family variations mean different things in different cultures. Consider birth order as a typical variable. In the United States Atkinson and Miller (1956) have obtained evidence showing that first-born children tend to have higher n Achievement, presumably because their achievement-oriented parents can set higher standards, be more affectionate, etc., with one child than with several. But in our sample of Indian students from Madras, the correlation between n Achievement (verbal) and birth order is actually $+.10$ ($p \sim .20$), suggesting that younger children may have higher n Achievement in India. Furthermore, Abegglen's study of Japan (1958) indicates that there it may also be the younger sons who get more independence and achievement training so that they leave home and go into business in town while the first-born son stays home and responsibly continues the family traditions.

Consider next the question of broken homes. Veroff *et al.* (1960) report for the United States that men more often have low n Achievement ($p < .05$) if the family is broken because of divorce, separation or death of parents. Yet Bradburn (1960) has found that separation from the father in Turkey is associated with higher n Achievement in the son, as we shall see below.

Nevertheless, the family variations most likely to influence n Achievement in the same way cross-culturally are those in which the father is absent or the son lives with the mother. A check of our data on the family types of the tribes on which we have folk tale n Achievement scores shows that mother-child households are associated with low n Achievement. Any type of polygyny, for example, favors household units in which a mother lives with her own children. If the 42 cultures on which data exist are classified as to whether they permit or encourage *any* type of polygyny or not, it appears that only 48 per cent of the 21 cultures high in n Achievement as contrasted with 77 per cent of the 21 cultures low in n Achievement are characterized by some form of polygyny (chi-square $= 4.08$, $p < .05$).[8] Presumably polygyny promotes mother-son households in which the son stays dependent on the mother longer and does not get the strong emphasis on independent achievement needed to develop n Achievement. Further evidence in support of this interpretation is provided not only by the data on effects of broken homes in the U.S. already cited but also by knowledge of family types among lower-class Negroes known to be low in n Achievement (see Table 9.7). In many such families the mothers are the consistent breadwinners, and the fathers may come and go in a fashion which creates a family type sometimes known as "serial monogamy." The young children typically stay with the mother as the more consistent provider of nurturance so that opportunities for strong mother-son ties are present just as in polygynous societies. Again it does not seem far-fetched to infer that n Achievement is low in such groups because the institution of serial monogamy tends to favor the creation of mother-son dependency. At any rate

Mischel (1960) has reported direct evidence that in Trinidad where serial monogamy is common among lower-class Negroes, father absence is significantly associated with lower *n* Achievement.

On the other hand, Bradburn has obtained some very striking evidence from Turkey showing that father absence is associated with *higher* *n* Achievement (see Table 9.9). In three separate samples, the Turkish men

TABLE 9.9 PERCENTAGES OF TURKISH MEN WITH HIGH AND LOW *n* ACHIEVEMENT
WHO HAD BEEN SEPARATED FROM THEIR FATHERS

Sample	High *n* Achievement, %	Low *n* Achievement, %	Chi-square and *p* values
1. Education students: Lived apart from parents before age 14	$N = 24$ 67	$N = 23$ 35	$\chi^2 = 4.78, p < .05$
2. Business students: Lost father or lived apart from parents before age 18	$N = 22$ 45	$N = 25$ 12	$\chi^2 = 6.51, *p < .02$
3. Senior executives: Lost father or lived apart from parents before age 18	$N = 12$ 50	$N = 12$ 17	$\chi^2 = 2.95, *p < .05 \, pd$

* Corrected for continuity. (After Bradburn, 1960.)

show higher *n* Achievement more often if they had escaped their father's influence, as contrasted with continuing to live in the intact family after the age of 14 or 18. Isn't this contradictory to what has just been argued? Shouldn't "father absence" tend to create mother-son families which supposedly inhibit the development of *n* Achievement? The paradox nicely illustrates the importance of determining how environmental conditions work through the factors more directly influencing *n* Achievement level. It can be resolved by remembering that low *n* Achievement can be produced in several ways—i.e., either by overindulgence (lack of high standards) particularly early and in the mother or by authoritarianism in the father, particularly later in the boy's development. The mother-child family follows the first path in which the son is unlikely to develop high standards of excellence at all. The Turkish family follows the second path in which the son may be exposed to high standards but fails to develop high *n* Achievement because his authoritarian father stands in the way. Consequently, in Turkey, getting the boy out from under the father's influence should promote his *n* Achievement *so long as it does not occur so early as to promote the development of a mother-child household*, which, of course, may be unlikely in Turkey for other cultural reasons or because the boy escapes his father not to live with his mother but away from home altogether. Variations in family type are important as they modify the key factors responsible for the development of n Achievement—e.g., high standards of excellence, warmth, and low father dominance—and so far, mother-son families and father absence (perhaps especially from around age 8 on) seem most likely to have consistent effects in this respect; father absence, because it cuts down father dominance, and mother-son families, because they tend to lower stress on high standards of excellence for the son.

Slavery. Previous theorizing about economic development has tended to stress the direct influence on men of environmental conditions. The whole thesis of this book is that the influence is not direct, but is tempered and altered by the character of the men on whom the external factors operate. The environment may yet, however, be the final determinant of man's response in that it shaped his character even earlier. In the present context such a general question becomes: does the environment, or more particularly the type of economy, determine the n Achievement level which in turn determines the level of economic activity?

The answer is: "Yes, but not directly, in the sense of opportunity automatically creating the n Achievement needed to exploit it." Consider the institution of slavery, to start with. It has been a major way of organizing economic activity for millennia, in fact up to very recent times, in many if not most nations. Does slavery promote or inhibit economic development? The question might be hard to answer from a purely economic point of view, but from the psychological standpoint, the answer is unequivocal both on theoretical and some empirical grounds. It impedes economic development because it is an economic institution which indirectly affects child-rearing practices which affect n Achievement level which affects economic development! Psychologically speaking, slavery is a form of symbiosis, which should lower n Achievement both in the slave and the slaveholder, though for somewhat different reasons. The slave is by definition put in a position of being more or less completely dependent on his master. He and his children will get the responsibility and obedience training which Child et al., found to be negatively related cross-culturally to n Achievement. All his rewards come, not from individualistic achievement, but from dependent compliance (see Dollard, 1937, for example). Furthermore, slaves are nearly always "decultured" in the sense of being removed from their own culture and thrown with slaves from quite different cultures. This was certainly true among Negro slaves in the South. Thus the economic and social conditions surrounding the institution of slavery became dominant in determining their life adjustment, since they shared no cultural values to oppose or mold the effects of such conditions. Negro slaves should, therefore, have developed child-rearing practices calculated to produce obedience and responsibility not n Achievement, and their descendants, while free, should still show the effects of such training in lower n Achievement—which in fact is exactly the case, as Table 9.7 shows. The lower class Negroes in the North, presumably those least removed from Southern lower caste Negroes, have the lowest average n Achievement level of any of the minority groups tested, in fact. The Negroes as a group are significantly lower than practically all the other groups tested, although middle and upper class Negroes are conspicuously high in n Achievement level, reflecting once again the fact that individuals who have managed to move out of a low n Achievement group tend to have exceptionally high n Achievement.

The slaveholders should also tend to develop low n Achievement over the generations because they nearly always use slaves as personal servants responsible for the more disagreeable aspects of child-rearing. The child of a white Southern plantation owner normally had several slaves to take care of all his needs. Even though parental standards of achievement for him might be theoretically high, they would tend to be constantly undermined by the empirical fact that there was a slave whom the child could order to his rescue whenever he got into difficulty. Servants are not, strictly speaking, in the same category, since they can always technically leave their employment if too much is demanded of them. Slaves, on the other hand, can "get ahead" best by ingratiating their masters, by doing them favors, or more simply by "spoiling the young master." It is difficult to see how high standards of individualistic achievement for young children could be maintained in families where slaves were used to rear the children. The evidence is all indirect as far as the South is concerned, but it supports the inference that n Achievement level, which may have been high initially among those who founded the plantations in the South, tended to decrease in succeeding generations. Certainly it was the non-slaveholding North which excelled in all forms of business and even non-slaveholding portions of the South, like North Carolina, which took the lead in commercial enterprise.

What is most fascinating about such a possibility is that it suggests a rather simple, if ironic, account of the rise and fall of many great civilizations in the past. The argument runs as follows: a people with higher level of n Achievement tend to pursue business enterprise more vigorously and ultimately to become more wealthy. Nearly always in the past such wealth has been used to support slaves. Certainly this was the case in Ancient Greece. Beginning around 525 B.C. when a much larger proportion of Athenian families were wealthy enough to support slaves, each child of good family was ordinarily assigned two slaves—a nurse and a pedagogue to go to school with him (Glotz, 1925). Furthermore, in our sample of which leads to more household slaves. But in Greece the more general use preliterate cultures, 45 per cent of twenty cultures with high n Achievement versus only 19 per cent of 21 low in n Achievement had slaves (chi-square $= 3.29$, $p < .10$).[9] In short, high n Achievement leads to increased wealth, of such slaves preceded by a generation or two the marked drop in n Achievement recorded in Chapter 4 (Fig. 4.1). Is it unreasonable to infer that the slaves undermined the achievement training of their masters' children, although probably not consciously? So, ironically, the masters were undone by the very instrument that demonstrated, they thought, their mastery—namely, their enslavement of those they had conquered. The irony lies in the fact that what happened was certainly not *intentional* on either side. Explanations of the decline of slave civilizations in terms of the "decay of moral fibre," although vague and *ad hoc*, do have at least this kernel of truth in them: the institution of slavery in all probability undermined achievement training, which in turn lowered general n Achievement level and made civilizations less enterprising in business and more vulnerable to economic decline and ultimately attack and destruction from without.

Occupational status. What about economic and social conditions less extreme than slavery? Do they have an effect on n Achievement level? Clearly, socioeconomic status of the parents is an important determinant of n Achievement in children, as Rosen's data in Table 9.7 show, at least as far as the United States is concerned. Middle-class children are significantly higher in n Achievement than lower-class children. Furthermore businessmen and professionals in several countries tend to have higher n Achievement if they come from middle class families than if they come from upper or working class backgrounds (Table 7.4, Fig. 7.2).

Some insight into how their family background might condition their motivational level is given in a study by Douvan (1958) in which she found that both failure and possible loss of money were necessary to mobilize the same amount of n Achievement in lower-class children that failure alone produced in middle-class children. An explanation runs as follows: several studies have shown that middle-class families work for longer range goals and think in terms of longer time spans (LeShan, 1952). Middle-class children are more willing to work for a delayed reward than working-class children (Mischel, 1960). In behaving in these ways, the children seem to be conditioned by the nature of the occupations in which their fathers are predominantly engaged. Middle-class occupations require more planning ahead, as in the case of small business; they may require a longer period of education before financial rewards begin to be available, as in the minor professions like secondary school teaching; and even the pay for such occupations tends to come only once or twice a month, as compared with weekly for lower-class occupations, so that more planning ahead is required in terms of household expenditures. Consequently, children of middle-class background may find failure sufficient to arouse their achievement striving, because they recognize its long-range significance in terms of deprivation of possible future rewards. For children from the working classes, however, who are used to thinking in terms of a bird in the hand rather than two in the bush, it is only when the "bird-in-hand" or the actual financial reward is threatened that their n Achievement is aroused.

In a wider frame of reference, n Achievement is itself a somewhat irrational concern in that it is not tied to immediate present rewards but has to do with much longer range goals of personal significance, as the data in Chapters 6 and 8 have demonstrated. Such "irrational" long-range achievement concerns should appear more often among families whose occupations and economic positions "require" or promote the development of just such concerns.

One must be constantly wary, however, of falling too easily into a Social Darwinist position of arguing that the social environment inevitably tends to produce the character structure or motivational level "best" adapted to it. Consider some results from Japan in Table 9.10 for example. They

TABLE 9.10   RELATIONSHIP OF n ACHIEVEMENT TO SOCIAL CLASS IN JAPANESE BOYS AGED AROUND 14

School population	Measure of n Achievement					
	Graphic expression (D-F, z-scores)			Verbal		
	N	Mean	SD	N	Mean	SD
A. Upper middle class or higher	24	.588	.62	30	9.07	4.01
B. Lower middle class	24	.075	1.03	29	7.83	5.01
C. Working class	31	.321	1.03	33	7.55	5.08
D. Rural	27	.181	.78	30	7.87	5.12
Groups B, C, D, combined	82	.203	.79	92	7.74	5.11
Difference $A - \Sigma(B, C, D)$		.385			1.33	
t		2.48			1.45	
p		<.02			<.20	

are only vaguely similar to the American results. Among these samples, the boys from the upper-middle and upper classes attending a private school in Osaka have the highest n Achievement level, whereas boys drawn from a middle-class district of small shops, from the working-class district, or from a rural area appear not to differ significantly in n Achievement level. There is a hint in the graphic measure of n Achievement, which has generally been more sensitive than the verbal measure of n Achievement, that the working-class boys in Japan have the second highest level of n Achievement of the four groups tested. Since socioeconomic status is clearly an "extrinsic" factor which is only indirectly connected with n Achievement development in boys, it follows that theoretically it should be quite possible to find situations, particularly in a less mobile society perhaps, where the lower classes might have higher n Achievement than the upper or middle classes. We mentioned this possibility in dealing with the class differences in n Achievement level reflected in different types of literature in English history. Wesleyanism in England appeared to affect primarily the upper-lower and lower-middle classes and, if our general interpretation is correct, it probably raised the n Achievement level there above what it was in the middle classes at the time. Members of these "lower" classes then tended to rise and to become middle and upper-middle class themselves, but if testing had been done before their upward mobility, a result not unlike that suggested by the working-class data for Japan would doubtless have been obtained. The upper-lower classes would have had as high (or higher) n Achievement as those above them. Our test data from the three other countries—India, Germany, and Brazil—shed no further light on this problem, since the boys from lower-class backgrounds in these samples from élite schools were obviously unrepresentative and highly mobile.

On the whole, however, one would expect that social class status would be an imperfect indicator of n Achievement level, since it does not group occupations together in terms of their motivational requirements. Miller and Swanson (1958) have proposed an alternative way of classifying occupations that should relate more directly to n Achievement levels. They distinguish "entrepreneurial" families, in which the husbands are self-employed, or work for fees or commissions, or in small businesses, from "bureaucratic" families, in which the husbands predominantly work for salaries or wages in large corporations. One would expect that the entrepreneurial families should stress the self-reliant achievement training that produces n Achievement, but the evidence they present on the point is not clear-cut. Most of the information they collected in interviews with these families is not directly relevant to what produces n Achievement; the one item that is relevant ("agree that a child should be on his own as soon as possible to solve his own problems") does not show a significant difference in the expected direction. The entrepreneurial families agree more (48 per cent) than the bureaucratic families (41 per cent) but the difference is small and not significant (Miller and Swanson, 1958, p. 241). We must always be cautious about assuming that a particular environmental condition (here the entrepreneurial role) will automatically produce the type of child-rearing that produces the type of child best suited to functioning in that environment.

More direct data on the relationship of parental occupation to child's n Achievement level is available from rural India. In many ways India provides an ideal test of the connection, because its occupations are more rigidly separated by the caste system than they are in a complex industrialized country like the United States, where a man may actually fill several occupational roles and every man, regardless of his occupation, is expected to be something of an entrepreneur. At any rate, some data collected by Fraser (1959) in India are amazingly clear-cut. He tested a large number of school children for *n* Achievement (graphic) in villages in Orissa Province, with the results as classified by father's occupation (caste) as shown in Table 9.11. The children whose fathers were members of the

TABLE 9.11   MEAN *n* ACHIEVEMENT SCORES (GRAPHIC) OF INDIAN SCHOOL CHILDREN (ORISSA PROVINCE) BY CASTE (after Fraser, 1961)

Occupation	D-F scores		
	N	Mean	*SD*
A. Production and sale of commodities Teli (oil pressing), Gaud (milking)	18	8.22	6.34
B. Weaving Ganda, Bhulia, Kuli	33	6.39	4.64
C. Cultivation Sahara, Binjhal,[1] Kulta, Gand	80	4.35	6.52

Mean differences		*t*	*p* value
A − B	1.83	1.05	.30
A − C	3.87	2.32	< .02 *pd*
B − C	2.04	1.85	< .05 *pd*

[1] Village priests but in this sample exclusively cultivators.

Teli or Gaud castes—the only real "entrepreneurial" castes in this section of rural India—had higher *n* Achievement than the children whose fathers were engaged in traditional agriculture. The children from the weaving castes fell somewhere in between, as in fact they should, since the weavers are somewhat entrepreneurial in function—certainly more so than the traditional cultivators but less so than those in the Teli or Gaud castes. One would have to predict, on the basis of our theory, that fathers engaged in the production and sale of commodities would have higher *n* Achievement than those engaged exclusively in traditional agriculture. And the fact that their children have higher *n* Achievement tends to confirm the prediction that the parents do and also the inference that the parents have managed to bring up their children in a way to give them the same higher level of *n* Achievement that they have.

There are also indications in our cross-cultural comparisons of preliterate societies that traditional agriculture is negatively related to *n* Achievement level. Our entire picture of the person with high *n* Achievement, gathered from the data in Chapters 6 and 8, would not lead us to expect him to be the kind of person who would stay on the land, raising food in the same traditional ways. As Table 9.12 below shows, the low *n* Achievement cultures are much more often physically located where the soil is at least fair or good, permitting successful agriculture. Barry, Child, and Bacon (1959) report that high food accumulation has a strong negative relationship ($-.60$) to achievement training and Child, Storm, and Veroff (1958) have reported elsewhere that achievement training is correlated positively ($+.34$) with n Achievement content in folk tales. What is associated with high food accumulation (e.g., herding) is *compliance training,* or training for responsibility and obedience rather than achievement and self-reliance. The results make good sense in terms of the view that a culture adopts the child-rearing practices suited to its economy. "Pressure toward obedience and responsibility should tend to make children into the obedient and responsible adults who can best insure the continuing welfare of a society with a high accumulation economy, whose food supply must be protected and developed gradually throughout the year. Pressure toward self-reliance and achievement should shape children into the venturesome, independent adults who can take initiative in wresting food daily from nature and thus insure survival in societies with a low accumulation economy" (i.e., in societies that live by hunting and fishing).

It would be logical to assume from the very high correlation between food accumulation in the economy and compliance versus assertion training that economies high in food accumulation ought to be significantly lower in n Achievement folk tale content. But, oddly enough, there is no relationship that even remotely approaches statistical significance. Thus, of the ten cultures high in food accumulation according to Barry *et al.,* six are below the median in n Achievement folk tale content; whereas, of the 13 classified as very low in food accumulation, seven are above the median in n Achievement scores. The trend is in the predicted direction but it is nowhere near significant.

Such a finding can mean either one of two things. First, there is plenty of opportunity for sampling error to distort the true picture. The number of cases on which we have both n Achievement and food accumulation data is quite small; the number of folk tales was also small and may have been unrepresentative in particular cases. One might therefore continue to believe that there is really a relationship between food accumulation in the economy and low n Achievement, but that it was not found empirically because the measuring instruments were too crude.

Second, there is an interesting possibility of much theoretical importance. If, as Barry *et al.* argue, people tend to adjust their child rearing to the social and economic requirements of their life situation, this does not mean they will automatically know how to raise their children to give them the characteristics most adaptive to that life situation. The low food accumulation societies may well realize that they should stress achievement and self-assertion, but they may do it in ways that do not produce high n Achievement necessarily. To assume that they would generally know how to produce the qualities in their children that they realize are necessary is to take a Social Darwinist or functionalist point of view that gives parents everywhere the credit for knowing more psychology than even those modern psychologists know who have studied the problem in detail. Moreover, our data suggest that there is a particular error that parents trying to induce n Achievement and self-reliance in their children may commit. They may undermine the very characteristic they want to produce by becoming so authoritarian in demanding it (precisely because they realize it is needed) that a boy will not develop his own standards of achievement but continue to rely on those imposed on him by his parents, particularly his father. Previous data have shown that the father must not be too demanding (Fig. 9.1) nor the mother either (Table 9.3, Fig. 9.2) if the son is to develop high n Achievement.

Finally, specific studies by Strodtbeck (1958a) of American families suggest that one of the reasons why parents of upper socioeconomic status do not always produce an overachieving son is precisely because they may stress the importance of achievement too much for him. The father in particular continues to make too many suggestions, so that in the end the son finds it more adaptive to be passive and dependent. Here as elsewhere, we must be very cautious about concluding that the environment automatically produces certain adaptive characteristics in people, or that a society always gets the character structure it deserves.

Climate. Lastly, we arrive at the most extrinsic determinant of human achievement—man's physical habitat. Is there any basis for believing that climate modifies n Achievement level? Once again let us remember that changes in n Achievement level, at least in modern nations, probably also in ancient ones, occurred too rapidly to be accounted for exclusively in terms of climatic changes. Nevertheless, granted that other factors can influence n Achievement level, is there any evidence that people living in temperate climates have higher n Achievement levels? Huntington's argument runs as follows: "Climate influences health and energy, and these in turn influence civilization. . . . On an average the men of genius in the North Sea countries would be more energetic than those of other regions because they would enjoy better health, even though the medical service were everywhere equally good. They would be continually stimulated by their cool, bracing climate, and would feel like working hard all the year, whereas their Southern and Eastern colleagues in either hot weather or cold would be subject to periods of depression which are a regular feature of the less favored parts of Europe. Because of their strength and energy the men of genius in the North Sea region would cause civilization to advance. . . ." (Huntington, 1924, p. 233.) Or, as the Woytinskys summarize his view, "Huntington held the following conditions to be most stimulating to mind and body: mean temperature of approximately 40° F in winter and 64° F in summer, relative humidity of about 60% at noon and high enough at night so that dew is precipitated, and variability of weather with frequent but not extreme changes." He then classified various regions of the world in terms of the extent to which they met these criteria and was able to map climatic regions of high and low energy. (Woytinsky and Woytinsky, 1953, p. 29.) In general, advanced modern and ancient civilizations appear to have occurred predominantly in Huntington's regions of high climatic energy.

Huntington's thesis was checked so far as *n* Achievement was concerned, by studying the physical habitat of the preliterate tribes on which we had *n* Achievement folk tale scores. Their location in the world is given in Murdock's World Ethnographic Sample (1959) in terms of latitude and longitude; temperature and rainfall figures were obtained from the records of the nearest weather station to that point. Altitude, quality of the soil, and nature of the habitat (desert, forest, sea coast, rivers) was obtained from various geographical atlases (Reed, 1942, also Hann, 1908, 1910, 1911). The chief findings are summarized in Table 9.12 according to the criteria considered important by Huntington.

TABLE 9.12 ECOLOGICAL CHARACTERISTICS OF PRELITERATE CULTURES CLASSIFIED AS HIGH OR LOW IN *n* ACHIEVEMENT ON THE BASIS OF FOLK-TALE CONTENT

Climate conditions	High *n* Achievement	Low *n* Achievement	Chi-square	*p*
Mean annual temperature,	$N = 26$	$N = 26$		
% between 40°-60° F	50	19	5.44	<.05
% between 75°-85° F	15	42	4.58	<.05
Mean daily or monthly temperature variation				
% >15° F	92	50	11.34	<.01
Mean annual rainfall				
% up to 20 in.	46	19 ⎫		
% 20-60 in.	46	50 ⎬ 6.53, $df = 2$, $p < .05$		
% over 60 in.	8	31 ⎭		
Altitude over 2,000 ft	54	48	NS	
Quality of soil	$N = 24$	$N = 23$		
% poor (vs. fair or good)	38	8	5.49, $p < .05$	

First, it is clear, as Huntington's theory would predict, that high *n* Achievement is more common in areas of moderate temperature. The limits of temperatures considered "moderate" were established by reviewing the mean annual temperatures in various parts of Europe included by Huntington in his zone of high climatic energy. The mean annual temperature runs from 39° F in Moscow to 60° F in Rome, London falling almost exactly in the middle at 50° F. Table 9.12 does not give all the data, which are perhaps most easily summarized in graphic form as in Fig. 9.3, which shows exactly the results predicted by Huntington; that is, the highest average n Achievement level occurs for tribes living in climates where the mean annual temperature falls between 40° F and 60° F. As the heat increases, n Achievement level falls off steadily until it reaches its lowest point in tropical climates, where the mean annual temperatures fall between 75° F and 85° F. Furthermore, as temperatures get colder, n Achievement level also falls off, although the trend cannot really be checked for significance since only four cases were available of cultures living in habitats where the mean annual temperature was below 40° F.

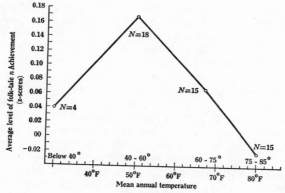

Figure 9.3   Average level of folk tale n Achievement in preliterate cultures plotted against mean annual temperature

In addition, the association of high n Achievement with daily or monthly temperature variation is, if anything, even greater. The measure of temperature variation was computed as either the maximum difference between mean temperatures at different seasons of the year or the median variation of the mean daily ranges in temperatures at different times of the year, whichever was larger. Temperature variation can occur either daily or seasonally, and either one would provide the kind of "stimulating" environment that Huntington considers desirable for producing an energetic response. Of the 26 cultures classified as high in n Achievement, only two—the Yoruba in Africa and the Ifaluk in the South Pacific—did not have at least 15° F of daily or seasonal variation in temperature, whereas, one-half of the cultures classified as low in n Achievement did not have even this much temperature variation. The relationship is not linear, the correlation between amount of temperature variation and n Achievement score being only .24, $p < .10$, but the theory does not in fact predict that it should be. Huntington would argue that there is some minimal degree of temperature variation which is desirable, and either too much or too little would be less desirable for producing high energy.

Rainfall tends, of course, to go with lack of temperature variation and with tropical heat so that it, too, shows the same general effect. Cultures with high *n* Achievement live more often in relatively dry climates, whereas those with low *n* Achievement live more often in areas of heavier rainfall. Thus the general picture is quite clear. Low *n* Achievement is associated particularly with tropical climates which are hot, humid and show little temperature variation. High *n* Achievement is associated with moderate, dry climates which also tend to have poor soil, so that growing conditions for agriculture are not optimal.

Should we therefore conclude that Huntington's interpretation of such findings is correct—that climatic conditions invigorate people and encourage them to think more about achievement? Perhaps, although cases like the Yoruba give us pause since they have one of the highest *n* Achievement levels recorded. Atkinson's general model of the way external and internal determinants combine to yield aroused motivation would serve to explain how habitat could lead to an expression of more *n* Achievement in folk tales. (See Table 6.2.) Climate might be conceived as being associated with varying probabilities of success. In the coldest climates, probability of success might be considered very low on the grounds that the people must struggle even to keep alive, whereas probability of successful achievement is optimal in tropical climates where life is "easy," or at least where food can be either picked or grown easily. Moderate probabilities of success might be most apt to occur in temperate regions where man has to struggle somewhat to meet his needs. Then it could be argued that what is being measured in the folk tales is aroused *n* Achievement which is maximal where probability of success is moderate. Or the effect might be direct, as Huntington would argue: invigorating climates may make men feel better or more energetic and they may then conceive more achievement exploits. Both of these interpretations have the advantage of sounding quite reasonable, but the disadvantage of not being very directly testable. How would it be possible to get a direct measure of probability of success in various climates? Or how can we prove that invigorating climates tend to make people think about achievement? Why shouldn't they make them think about love or war?

There is quite a different explanation of the association of climate with *n* Achievement which ties in more closely to our other findings on the intrinsic factors producing *n* Achievement in children. Mother-child households tend to occur more frequently in tropical regions. Using again Murdock's world ethnographic sample, nine of the twenty-three cultures living within 10° of the equator contain mother-child households (39 per cent), whereas only five out of forty-four cultures living further away from the equator (11 per cent) contain mother-child households (chi-square corrected for continuity = 5.34, $p < .05$).[10] Four of the above five exceptions are considered somewhat doubtful by other anthropologists (Ainu, Navaho, Tanala, and Balinese). To turn to the somewhat more general classification we used earlier in establishing the negative relationship between household living arrangements and n Achievement, some form of polygyny is either permitted or encouraged more frequently in hot climates (19 out of 24 cases), as contrasted with nonpolygynous types of families (seven out of 15 cases), chi-square = 4.38, $p < .05$. Stated another way, 61 per cent of the cultures living in temperate climates (mean annual temperature between 40° and 60° F.) are nonpolygynous as compared with only 20 per cent of those living in hot climates. The reasons for this do not lie within the scope of the present inquiry, but one may infer that the connection between climate and n Achievement, and ultimately energy, may be quite indirect and almost accidental in the sense that climate affects household living arrangements, which in turn affect child-rearing practices that modify n Achievement. Here as elsewhere, in dealing with extrinsic factors, one must be very cautious in drawing conclusions about direct effects of environmental variables on motivational level, no matter how reasonable these conclusions seem to be.

The general theme of all our findings in this chapter is that the motivational effects of particular environmental events—physiological, historical, political, or economic—have often been much too easily inferred on the basis of what seems "reasonable." We infer that the Greeks were discouraged by the Peloponnesian War. Why? Because Greece tended to go into a steady decline thereafter. But in terms of actual measurement of Greek achievement motivation, the decline had set in *before* the Peloponnesian War and, as we have argued, may have been produced by the introduction of slaves for rearing Greek children. Or we infer that far from being demoralized by a war, the Germans after World War I reacted in the opposite way. They were stimulated to further effort. How do we know? Because they launched another World War some years later. But inferences about the motivational state of mind of the Germans on the basis of what they did is extremely perilous. Our data suggest their n Achievement level rose between 1925 and 1950 and perhaps even earlier. This may have had little or nothing to do with World War I, or the War may have had an effect quite indirectly by the influence it had on German family life, i.e., in killing off many authoritarian German fathers and permitting their sons to develop high n Achievement.

All our evidence suggests that external events affect motivational levels primarily as they affect the family, or more specifically the values and child-rearing practices of the parents. The family as the nucleus of the social structure is a little like the nucleus of the atom; it is harder to influence by external events than one might expect, and it is often influenced in quite unexpected ways. Certainly tribes that practice or permit polygyny have no intention of lowering n Achievement level. The Methodists were quite disturbed on doctrinal grounds about the tendency of the faithful to get rich. And although they had some glimmerings of an idea of why they did, it is only today that we can see more clearly why the doctrines of Methodism tended to promote values and child-rearing practices in Methodist parents that raised n Achievement levels, which for the various reasons given in Chapter 6 tended both in Britain and America to make Methodists successful in business. One might almost say that history is a record of unintended consequences. The leaders of men operate in terms of certain goals, their success or failure in achieving which are recorded in the daily papers. But these daily events—even major ones like wars—do not directly shape the "tidal waves of history," but only indirectly as they affect the minds of men, or more specifically the values and practices of parents who are rearing the next generation. In terms of conscious policy, a nation may believe that it has accomplished something, and most of its adult citizens may act in terms of such a belief, yet such beliefs and actions may have effects on the motivations and values of the next generation which may undermine or change the very things they thought they had accomplished.

Certainly something like this happened in the case of the ancient Greeks. One can imagine the satisfaction of the average Athenian housewife around 525 B.C. She must have been pleased that the successful wars had made so many slaves available and that her husband's increased income made it possible for them to feed and house several such slaves. They were such a help to her in bringing up the children, and some of them were really quite clever and could teach the children things that the parents could not, for lack of time or the necessary training. Moreover, wasn't it a kind of validation of the very greatness of Greece to have such a large slave population? How could the housewife know that she was contributing to undermining the future of the nation in a far more fundamental way than anything the soldiers or politicians were doing? To be sure she might have been somewhat uneasy at times because there were always Cassandras—old men warning that the moral fibre of the young wasn't what it used to be—but who listened to them? It was such a convenience to have the slaves about, and besides, everybody was doing it.

The illustration is speculative, but the moral behind it is not. If man wants to control his destiny, he must learn to deal less in terms of the supposed reasonable consequences of historical events and more in terms of their often unintended or indirect effects on the motives and values of the next generation.

NOTES AND REFERENCES

[1] Oddly enough, the correlation reported by McClelland and Friedman is the same for most of the sample used by Child *et al.*, but is reduced to zero by four extreme cases. Only 20 cultures were available for analysis of the relationship with *severity*

independence training and *n* Achievement folk-tale content. The correlation between e two variables for all 20 cases is substantially zero as reported by Child *et al.*, but it is ro largely because of a striking reversal in the relationship for the two cases highest *n* Achievement and the two lowest in *n* Achievement (the Comanche and the Papago d the Chiricahua Apache and the Thonga, respectively). Without these four cases, the rrelation for the remaining 16 is a substantial .62. What this suggests, aside from the ual possibility of sampling or coding errors, is that independence and achievement aining may ordinarily go together, but in a few extreme cases they may be strikingly versely related.

[2] There was only one case in one group so that the correlation could not be run.

[3] Nevertheless it might still appear that the Brazilian data are significantly different om those obtained in the United States since the mean age of achievement training ported by United States mothers from the Protestant white middle class is around 50 (Rosen, 1959), or about the same as that reported by the Brazilian mothers. Yet it is recisely in this Protestant middle class that the reverse correlation with *n* Achievement curs in the United States—the *earlier* the achievement training, the higher the Achievement. The inconsistency may, however, be due to a methodological difference the way the questions were asked in the present study and in Rosen's study. As Table shows, the mothers in Brazil were asked "when a son of yours should have learned at," suggesting, if anything, the age at which he should have mastered the behavior question. Rosen, on the other hand, asked "do you think a child before the age of n should be expected to . . ." and "the age begun" was recorded from the mother's swer. Thus, the ages given in the United States and in the other countries are not rictly comparable, since those in the United States tended to refer more to the beginning the behavior in question and those in other countries to the end or completion of astery of the behavior in question.

The data are also not strictly comparable for another reason: Rosen's subjects averaged ound 11 years of age as compared with 16-17 in the present study and Feld (1959) has scovered that mothers' answers to these questions are a function of their sons' ages. Finally, Rosen, who has recently done further studies in Brazil, stresses the fact that ese mothers are very atypical for Brazil as a whole. Presumably because they are embers of the small upper-middle-class élite, they are much stricter on early achieve- ent training than most Brazilian mothers.

[4] It is perhaps worth mentioning that the correlation of age of achievement training th the verbal *n* Achievement score in Japan is −.12, $p \sim .20$, suggesting that the rela- nship may be the same in Japan as it is in Germany and the United States. In general, Japan the verbal measure of *n* Achievement yielded relationships as consistent with eoretical expectation as those obtained with the graphic measure of *n* Achievement, t for the sake of consistency with other countries the figures for the graphic measure ly have been reported.

[5] Unfortunately, *n* Achievement scores are not available on representative samples of otestants and Catholics in Germany, where comparisons can be more legitimately made thout complex interaction effects with class and ethnicity. The difficulty in Germany s with the school system; boys are sorted out into Höhere Schule or Volksschule before is possible to get from them very adequate verbal *n* Achievement scores (around age). Somewhat different tests of *n* Achievement have been administered in both types more advanced schools, and the Catholic boys scored on the average slightly higher both types of schools. Unfortunately, the result cannot be unambiguously interpreted cause a much higher percentage of Protestant boys goes on to the more advanced pe of school (Höhere Schule), as has been demonstrated in Chapter 8. Thus it is en possible that the general Protestant mean is higher, although Catholics score higher both types of schools. Consider the following numerical example: suppose there e five Protestant boys with *n* Achievement scores of 5, 4, 3, 2 and 1 and five Catholic

boys with n Achievement scores of 4, 4, 3, 2 and 1, a situation in which the Protes
boys have slightly higher average n Achievement. Suppose next that the Protestant l
with scores 5, 4, 3 and 2 and only the two Catholic boys with the highest scores (4
4) go on to higher schools. Now if the test is given in the more advanced school,
average of the Catholic boys will be 4 and for the Protestant boys 3.5. If the te
given in the less advanced school, the score for the Protestant boy will be 1 and
the Catholic boys 2. If the same test is not given in the two schools, it is not possibl
determine what the over-all averages of the two religious groups were. The exam
serves to underline the extreme difficulty of making "fair" comparisons of Protestant
Catholic samples because of differing mobility rates.

[6] I am greatly indebted to Andrew Berger and Professor David Bakan for suppl
me with this anecdote.

[7] More recent data (Abegglen and Mannari, 1960) reveal that a higher percentage
business than other types of leaders profess Buddhism as their religion and that aro
36 per cent of them state that their families were of *samurai* origin.

[8] The data used are G. P. Murdock's from *World Ethnographic Sample*. Colum
family and household. The polygyny classification included cultures coded as *m*
in his system and the nonpolygynous those coded as *ce* or *l*.

[9] The data are again from Murdock's *World Ethnographic Sample*. The interpr
tion given them is not the only possible one. They might be regarded as evide
against the hypothesis that slavery lowers n Achievement. The difficulty arises
the lack of any really good historical information on many of these tribes. The hypot
states that high n Achievement should lead to acquisition of slaves which, if t
are used for child-rearing, should eventually lead to low n Achievement in a genera
or two. Contemporary data do not indicate where in the historical sequence a g
culture is. We must assume that enough of them were in the early stage to yield
positive association obtained, but it is still possible to argue that this is not the case
that the whole line of reasoning is in error.

[10] I am greatly indebted to Peter B. Field for supplying me with this analysis.

10

Accelerating Economic Growth

Our analysis has been pursued to its logical conclusion. We have uncovered certain psychological forces apparently making fairly universally for economic development, shown how they alter the activities of individuals in a society, particularly in the entrepreneurial class, and traced their origins to certain beliefs and child-rearing practices in the family. In the course of our study we encountered some great landmarks of historical thinking and came to a better understanding of how most of them represent partial insights into more general phenomena.

Thus the connection seen by Max Weber between the Protestant Reformation and the rise of the entrepreneurial spirit, which provided the jumping off point for this study, can now be understood as a special case, by no means limited to Protestantism, of a general increase in n Achievement produced by an ideological change. The profit motive, so long a basic analytic element among Marxist and western economists alike, turns out on closer examination to be the achievement motive, at least in the sense in which most men have used the term to explain the energetic activities of the bourgeoisie. The desire for gain, in and of itself, has done little to produce economic development. But the desire for achievement has done a great deal, and ironically it was probably this same desire that activated the lower middle-class leaders of the Russian Communist Party as well as the bourgeoisie they criticized so intensely.

The whole view of history shifts once the importance of the achievement motive is recognized. For a century we have been dominated by Social Darwinism, by the implicit or explicit notion that man is a creature of his environment, whether natural or social. Marx thought so in advocating economic determinism, in arguing that a man's psychology is shaped in the last analysis by the conditions under which he must work. Even Freud thought so in teaching that civilization was a reaction of man's primitive urges to the repressive force of social institutions beginning with the family. Practically all social scientists have in the past several generations begun with society and tried to create man in its image. Even Toynbee's theory of history is essentially one of environmental challenges, though he recognizes that states of mind can create internal challenges.

If our study of the role of achievement motivation in society does nothing else, perhaps it will serve to redress the balance a little, to see man as a *creator* of his environment, as well as a creature of it. Much of what the Social Darwinists have taught must be thought through again in terms of a new dimension—i.e., the motives of the men affected by an environmental change or a social institution. A defeat in battle means one thing to a people low in n Achievement, another to a people who are high. Discrimination leads to counterstriving among Jews in the United States who are high in n Achievement, but not among lower-class Negroes who are low. A bureaucracy filled with men high in n Affiliation (Turkey, Italy) is a different kind of bureaucracy from one staffed by men high in n Achievement (the U.S., perhaps Poland). The focus changes. History must be written again, as it was in the 19th century, at least partly in terms of national character, in terms of what a people is trying to do or is most concerned with.

The matter might be left here as a contribution to scientific knowledge and historical perspective except for two considerations, one practical and the other theoretical. On the practical side the pressure is very great to use whatever knowledge is available to accelerate economic development in underdeveloped countries. The countries themselves eagerly want to catch up in their standard of living with the richer countries and many theorists argue that only if they are helped to do so will world peace be realizable, that their high economic aspirations combined with a severe inability to achieve them represent an explosive force in the world community which will tend to erupt into violent or authoritarian shortcut attempts to get what they want. So the scientist cannot help wondering whether what he has learned can be put to some practical use in suggesting policies for accelerating economic development, for humanitarian reasons or even selfish ones, if speeding economic development contributes to world peace.

He is also motivated by a purely theoretical consideration. No matter how carefully he has analyzed the data collected and drawn his inferences from them, he cannot help wondering whether his theory is really correct. The one sure way to find out, the way adopted by all scientific theorists, is to apply the theory in a new situation and see if it predicts the outcome correctly. The test of an hypothesis based on previous research lies always in a new experiment. In a sense then, the test of whether one of our hypotheses is correct, such as that an increase in n Achievement leads to more rapid economic development, would lie in a "social experiment" in which attempts were made to introduce policies that would increase n Achievement in one country to see whether they produced more rapid economic development than in other comparable countries where these policies were not introduced. Such a controlled experiment may not really be possible, but as an ideal it nevertheless gives the scientist a lively interest in thinking through policy implications that might be tried out in a way that would test his hypotheses.

How then would the psychologist speed economic development, assuming for the sake of the argument that the findings reported in previous chapters have sufficient validity to warrant drawing policy implications from them? In the most general sense, the psychologist's chief advice to economists, to politicians, officials or all those concerned with economic development is quite simple: "Pay attention to the effects that your plans will have on the values, motives and attitudes of people because *in the long run* it is these factors that will determine whether the plans are successful in speeding economic development." Such a piece of advice in itself is neither new nor very helpful as it stands. Economists, sociologists and others have always known and have stressed increasingly in recent times the importance of values and motives in speeding up or slowing down the process of economic development.

Early economic theorists like Marshall were very psychologically minded, but from 1870 on there was a tendency for economists to assume an increasingly simple rational psychology of motivation, partly because they felt safer that way and partly because the psychologists were not providing them with any concrete data to work with. Recently economists have begun to speak more openly of the importance of irrational motives (*cf.* Higgins, 1959; Rostow, 1952; Lewis, 1955), but they still have not had the backing of any factual evidence about human motives that a hardboiled economic planner would want to take into account. What is new about the present study is that it does provide such evidence. It is incomplete and doubtless incorrect in particulars, but at least it shows how such information can be systematically collected. Those who want to know more about what to do in a particular country can use the methods adopted here to assess the psychological variables more specifically relevant to their local plans.

But we must try to go further than such general advice on the basis of our own substantive findings. Our suggestions must necessarily be fairly general because we are not dealing with any particular country and also somewhat uninformed because they come after all from a psychologist with only a passing acquaintance with the vast literature and experience that has grown up around policies for accelerating economic development. Suppose we start with the psychologist's frame of reference and ask what should be the psychological objectives of plans and policies aimed at accelerating economic development? What should an agency or a government do that wanted to profit from our findings so as to speed economic growth in an underdeveloped country? In summary form, it should seek (1) to break orientation toward tradition and increase other-directedness, as we have redefined it, (2) to increase n Achievement, and (3) to provide for a better allocation of existing n Achievement resources. It might also strive to accomplish these ends without major simultaneous decreases in n Affiliation and increases in n Power if it is also important to accomplish economic development fairly peaceably. Our findings in Chapter 5 suggested that low n Affiliation and high n Power make up a combination particularly hostile to a peaceable democratic order. Because we know little or nothing about how to affect these motives at the present time, we cannot usefully discuss pursuing this objective further, and must leave the problem to further research. It is somewhat outside the scope of our main inquiry anyway. Let us now consider how to promote each of the other psychological objectives in turn. Then we can review some commonly proposed plans for aiding economic development in the light of our psychological knowledge.

Increasing Other-Directedness and Market Morality

Countries which stress traditional sanctions for insuring conformity in their stories for children have been developing less rapidly economically than those that stress specific new types of interpersonal relations in which the wishes or demands of the other person are a reason for conformity (Chapter 5). Business executives from developed countries are more willing to treat people in terms of their performance rather than their traditional status and to trust strangers in business (Chapter 7). How can this other-directedness or respect for the "impersonal other" be increased? How can the traditional ways of a society most readily be replaced by new norms?

The very first step is to recognize that traditional norms *must* give way to new ones and that the resistance to such change is likely to be very great. Realistic recognition of the need to abandon traditional values has by no means been widespread. There has been much romantic discussion of the traditional peasant way of life and some action toward strengthening it— e.g., the *ejido* movement in Mexico, the Gandhian stress on cottage industry, in some of its aspects. The discussion is romantic, not of course in terms of ultimate values, for who is to say that a simple peasant community achieves less in human happiness than rich industrialized city life? It is romantic in the sense that it believes that peoples will be satisfied with simplicity or backwardness, once they have had contact with advanced material culture and also in the sense that it often takes the stand that developing societies can *both* retain their traditional values *and* develop economically. A passage from Stuart Chase illustrates both points. It was written as advice to the villagers of Tepoztlan in rural Mexico, a generation ago:

"You have in your possession something precious; something which the Western world has lost and flounders miserably trying to regain. Hold to it. Exert every ounce of your magnificent inertia to conserve your way of life. You must not move until you can be shown, by the most specific and concrete examples, that industrialization and the machine can provide a safer, happier more rewarding existence. . . . The United States has nothing to offer you save its medical and agricultural science. Hold to your corncribs, to your economic security. Hold to your disregard of money, of pecuniary thrift, of clocks and watches, of hustle and bustle and busy emptiness. Hold to your damned wantlessness. Hold to your handicrafts, and watch them jealously in the face of tourists and ignorant exporters. When they debase the work of your hands they debase you. . . . When you are sick, ask help from the school-teacher instead of the herb doctor. And if I were you, when and if the new highway comes looping over the mountains into your village street, I would buy all the boxes of extra-sized carpet tacks I can afford." (Chase, 1931, pp. 318-319.)

The advice, though well-intentioned, was obviously unrealistic in almost every particular. The Tepoztecans have by now almost reached the stage where they are ready to accuse Americans like Stuart Chase of trying to keep them in a state of backwardness so that they will not compete with the United States and continue to provide a rural market for its goods. For of course, the road did come over the hill, the carpet tacks were not bought, and with the road came bus service, telephones, eventually electricity, and migration of the men out to work as *braceros* in fields as far away as California and New Jersey. The increased contact with the outside world has raised aspirations greatly. The people have begun to realize they are poor and they don't like being poor. What does it mean to them now to say they should "disregard money," hold to their "wantlessness," and their "magnificent inertia"? They can't now, even if they had wanted to then. Modern technology caught up with them, as it will catch up inexorably with every peasant village in the world eventually.

The Mexicans took certain other advice Chase gave them—as villages everywhere are taking it—and this brought matters to something of an economic crisis. They started going to the school-teacher and the doctor for medical care instead of to the *curandero* or "herb doctor." As a result, Mexican population has doubled since Stuart Chase wrote. With twice as many mouths to feed, traditional handicrafts and traditional small scale agriculture are simply no longer adequate. This is a good illustration of how it is often not possible to adopt only a piece of modern society and reject the rest. It works as a whole as most cultures do—efficiency in health, efficiency in production, high material culture—and backward peoples will have to swallow large chunks of it, if they are to adapt to the changing world. They will have to give up traditional norms and learn to be responsive to new norms established by the group, for the reasons given in Chapter 5. It is no kindness to them to talk of the values of the old way of life. No value judgment is involved in such a statement. The old way of life may *be* better in some ultimate sense.

The point is that if the people want the benefits of the advanced material culture of modern civilization—which they do whenever they come in contact with it, and such contact is inevitable—then they must accept many of the values and other culture patterns which support such a civilization. The psychologist's position here is precisely the same as the public health expert's, when he tells a people that if they want to feel better, they will have to abandon the traditional water sources and dig wells. He does not insist that they have to *want* to feel better. That is their business. Nor does he blur the issue if they plead that they like the old ways of drinking and would like to preserve them and feel better without digging wells. The choice is more obvious so far as health is concerned but it exists so far as values are concerned too. A people *must* break with traditional ways (in the scientist's sense of the word "must") if they are to live at a higher economic level.

Once the need for change in orientation is clearly and unequivocally accepted, the means are not hard to discover. Increased communication is the first necessity—roads, cheap public transportation, electricity, radios, telephones, newspapers, even public speeches where no other means are available (as in rural India). If people are to become other-directed or even to learn about new techniques or new norms, they must somehow come in contact with them. But contact is not enough. The Arabs were in contact with European technological civilization all through the time it was developing but failed to absorb much of it. The Youngs report that degree of contact of 24 Mexican villages with a new factory center "does not predict the particular communities that have changed the most." (1960, p. 367.) The capacity of the community to absorb the change is also important, as measured in the Mexican case by the degree of organization of the village and its "urban life style" (proportion of people who wear shoes). Actually both of these variables reflect the extent to which the people are already favorable to change since the first scale includes such items as "a doctor—eight or more stores" and "electricity in the village."

Use of a doctor, electricity, and shoes represents not "more" organization but a different, more modern kind. Before the villagers patronized the *curandero* and got along perfectly well without electricity and with *huaraches* for footwear. The main question is: what shifts people from the old type of orientation to the new, particularly when the old ways often have strong cultural sanctions supporting them? This is particularly true as one moves from material culture (e.g., footwear) to nonmaterial culture (e.g., methods of curing people). Many poignant stories have been written about the anxieties of the mother who takes a sick child to a doctor rather than the folk-curer for the first time (e.g., Lewis, 1959). She fears that she is doing the wrong thing for the child, or that she will incur the revenge of the spirits or traditional authorities in the community for departing from the old tried and true ways of doing things. She may end up by going to both the new doctor and the traditional "curer."

But such a compromise may not be possible in many areas of life. On the contrary modern ideas may appear directly opposed to religion or to much valued family patterns, and therefore they often encounter very strong resistance. In many underdeveloped countries, modernization is associated with Revolution, Communism, and antireligious feelings—for example, in Mexico and many Latin-American countries, southern Italy, or in parts of the world of Islam. Organized religion may therefore vigorously oppose modernization or any social change, as hostile to its traditional sources of strength in the rural community.

Or modernization may threaten traditional family structure. Goode (1960) reports that generally industrialization has everywhere increased freedom of marital choice (which takes marital arrangements out of the hands of the elders), decreased marriages within kin groupings, increased control of fertility "in the interests of the couple not the kin group," and introduced or maintained high divorce and remarriage rates. Many of these changes will be considered highly undesirable in various countries and will be strongly resisted by local and ecclesiastical authority. Yet as Goode points out, they are probably an inherent part of the modern economic system in the sense that it requires for maximum efficiency a high degree of geographical and social mobility. As we have seen in Chapters 5 and 7, rapid economic development is associated with specificity of relationships to particular others, and with a willingness to judge a man in terms of his performance, not his background or kinship status.

Thus resistance to modernization, particularly in key value areas, is likely to be massive. How can it be overcome? The answer again is simple and straightforward—by an ideological campaign, as the Communists have demonstrated recently, and as religious movements have shown earlier. The *means* of contact—radio, public speeches, the newspapers—must be used to inform people and to prepare them for change. There is little doubt that the fervor with which this is done has an important bearing on its effectiveness.

But where is the enthusiasm for modernization going to come from, if tradition is against it? To some extent it comes from contact with advanced economies, from the simple desires of individuals to fill newly acquired material wants, but increasingly it comes from national pride—from a desire of backward nations to catch up with the rest of the world. It also comes in major sections of the globe from Communism, which contains as a central part of its ideology a strong commitment to overthrowing tradition (particularly as embodied in religion) and introducing modernization and industrialization in every country. Besides nationalism and Communism, various liberal or reform political movements have played an important role in supplying the enthusiasm for change that challenges old ways of doing things. The difficulty here has been that such secular movements, unless they organize themselves more or less as religious movements as the

Communists did in Russia, tend to lack "staying power," to fall apart after the initial revolutionary generation for lack of the kind of supraindividual emotional support that a church provides. Finally, religion itself has supplied much of the stimulus for change. We have been talking about the resistance of religion as if it presented a united front, when in fact all great religions include a variety of different movements, some of which strongly favor modernization. For example, Protestant missionaries have laid the groundwork for change in many countries, as they currently are among the Indians in the state of Chiapas, Mexico. Their primary reason for going abroad may be religious in the long run, but in the short run because they come from advanced economies, they have introduced many new notions about health, education, sobriety, honesty and hard work that contribute directly to economic and social development. As another example, consider the Moslem reform group that has developed in Pakistan largely around the figure of the late great poet, philosopher and religious leader, Mohammed Iqbal. The aim of the movement is to purify Islam of the folk-religious encrustations which in their view have made it a conservative force working largely against social and economic progress. They find strong religious support in the teachings of Mohammed as further interpreted by Iqbal for many facets of modernization such as the emancipation of women. Religions can and have spearheaded change as well as resisted it.

One psychological value of such ideological movements needs particularly to be stressed. They provide an important source of emotional security for people who are rendered rootless and unhappy by the disruption of traditional ways of doing things. They represent a new kind of authority of what it is right to believe and do. Destroying tradition creates anxiety. If the old way is no longer good, what *is* the thing to do? The problem and its solution is nicely illustrated by the situation of an immigrant to the United States. He may realize fairly soon that the old values, the ways of doing things in the old country, no longer apply in this country, but what is he to do about it? He must act according to *some* norms. Of course at first particularly he tends to keep with a group of immigrants from the same country so that the old norms can be followed, but eventually he, or more likely his children, break out of the immigrant group by discovering what the norms of the new country are. Americans have been rather thoughtlessly accused of "conformism" by people who do not appreciate the security that conformity gives to individuals who have been *uprooted* and whose traditional values are often of very little use in guiding their conduct. Nonconformism may be a virtue in a tradition-bound society, but some important source of new norms and conformity is a necessity for a group of individuals bewildered by the speed with which old norms have been shattered. It reduces the conflict and anxiety which come from not knowing what to do at all.

The psychologist accordingly concludes that ideological movements of all sorts are an important source of the emotional fervor needed to convert people to new norms. They are necessary and should be supported in whatever form is politically feasible or most congenial to the country concerned.

But so far the analysis has been at a very general level. Are there specific methods of increasing other-directedness or market morality that a psychologist would regard as likely to be more effective? Because there is no really good evidence on the point, we must content ourselves with proposals that arise from theoretical considerations.

To begin with, an *informed public opinion* as represented in a free press is likely to be very important. It not only provides a guide as to what the new norms are in its editorials, letters columns, and even its comic strips. It also can contribute to a developing conscience as to how to behave in the market place where the traditional sanctions against "immoral" or "asocial" behavior are no longer strong. That is, individuals who are not accustomed to be honest with strangers need some kind of sanctions to prevent them from lying, stealing, and cheating whenever they can get away with it. Mexican filling station attendants provide a small-time illustration. Despite the fact that they have automatic machines for telling how much gas has been delivered and its price, they have discovered many ways of extracting more money from the unwary tourist. They read off the number of liters delivered as the number of pesos due, since the former is larger. They give incorrect change, fail to push the oil measuring stick all the way in, put in one liter of oil and charge for two, wipe out the reading on the meter so that they can "remember" it as more than the customer does, or even tinker with the meter so that it reads incorrectly. On the general prevalence of deception in Mexican rural life, see Lewis (1960). If there is no *inner* control on such behavior, what risk does a dishonest attendant run? What could be done to control such behavior? It is hard to prove charges against him, and police action against so many would be more expensive than allowing them to continue to extract extra money from people "who have more than they need anyway." One generalized answer is "public exposure," writing about the dishonest practices in public in a way that gets back to the people concerned. A major sign of the extent of other-directedness in a country is the freedom and willingness of the press to expose graft and corruption even in high places with impunity and on a large scale. Public "show" trials for such misdemeanors, fully reported in the papers probably have a high "demonstration effect" in the sense that other people engaged in the same practices may begin to feel a vague uneasiness that the "impersonal other" might some day catch up with them too. Vague fear of sanctions from nameless others is certainly one of the sources of morality to strangers.

A second crucial way to break with tradition and introduce new norms is via the *emancipation of women*. A strong feminist movement, like a free press, is a good sign that modernization is making headway in a country.

Psychological considerations as well as the case histories of all rapidly developing countries strongly support this view. The most general explanation lies in the fact that women are the most conservative members of a culture. They are less subject to other influences outside the home than the men and yet they are the ones who rear the next generation and give it the traditional values of the culture. They must be influenced by the mass media or somehow to adopt new values and new norms, if their children are to be effectively brought up in a different way in the next generation. No matter how Westernized Moslem men may become, for example by working in a factory, there is unlikely to be much over-all value and motivational change in the community so long as their wives stay locked up in Purdah insulated from such matters and therefore unable to transmit new values and motives to their children. One reason why the Spanish influence on the Mexican Indian population was limited was because very few Spanish women came to live in the colonies. The men took Indian wives and their children were brought up in a mixed world. The church furthermore concentrated in the early days of the Conquest on converting the men, particularly the sons of the chiefs, so that little value change was transmitted by this route either to the next generation.

Freeing women in the most practical sense means employment of women outside the home. Most underdeveloped countries which have a labor surplus anyway would "panic" at the thought of setting up such a policy objective, but the arguments for it are persuasive. If women leave the home for centers of employment, they are more available to influence from outside sources. They take their new attitudes back into the home and pass them on to the next generation. On the practical side, employment of women has not only been common in the most advanced industrialized nations, but was also stressed in Japan and Russia and is now being stressed in China. In Japan, young girls commonly worked even in the 19th century before marriage in order to accumulate enough money for a dowry, thus exposing themselves to new norms and new experiences that were filtering in through the industrial system. The Communists have acted as if they understood very well that the only way to break up tradition-orientation successfully is to get the women out of the home and into the working force. At any rate they did so in Russia and are doing so now, even if forcibly, in China. In so doing they are acting to produce the psychological changes we have found to be associated with economic development much more effectively than are some of the more democratic underdeveloped countries.

Thirdly, we may refer back to our discussion in Chapter 5 of how other-directedness is learned. There we argued that *group play,* or participation in extracurricular activities was an important way in which children learned to be responsive to the wishes of others. If we take this insight seriously, then a new kind of teacher training becomes important especially for the primary grades where children are learning value attitudes that will guide their behavior toward others throughout their lives. The teachers should be taught the key significance of group participation not as a means to greater learning efficiency—or even to higher n Achievement—but as a means of developing "other-directedness" or responsiveness to peer group norms. It will be hard to get teachers in many traditional countries to understand that group play, group extracurricular activities, group educational projects have anything to do with education, or even more with economic development, but the fact remains that getting the child to pay attention to what others think early in life through such group activities appears to be one of the foundation-stones of political democracy and economic development. Attempts to increase other-directedness need not be limited to children, of course. Conferences, committees or voluntary organizations in which there is free and open group discussion appear to increase other-directedness and they are practically unknown in many of the underdeveloped countries. Riecken (1952) found, for example, that a summer work camp for adolescents in the United States, while it did not change students' attitudes so much in line with its conscious objectives, did increase their other-directedness in the sense that their attitudes shifted toward giving more consideration to group opinion. In a comparison of the test performance of some Arab children who had been to a Western-style nursery school vs. those who had not, in a study to be mentioned below, it was found that their performance on the tests did not differ in significant or meaningful ways, but it was the examiner's impression that their attitudes toward the tests did differ. Those who had been to nursery school, even five years later, appeared more at ease in the situation, adapted more readily to the testing conditions, and were in a sense more "open" to such a strange procedure introduced by an outsider. Early "training" in group play had made them more other-directed, more sensitive and willing to go along with new procedures introduced by a stranger from outside their immediate experience.

Finally, is any kind of strictly *economic* policy likely to increase market morality or other-directedness? Two suggestions come to mind. The first arises out of the long-standing argument as to whether cottage industries should be supported. Spengler states the standard economist's objection: that they are "not likely to contribute significantly to a country's annual supply of capital." (1957, p. 372.) Herman (1957) objects that under certain circumstances, particularly given the right market for high quality goods, such industries may in fact contribute substantially to capital formation. The psychologist enters the picture by asking which of the two types of organization—cottage industries or the factory system—is more likely to break up tradition-orientation and increase other-directedness. On the face of it, drawing individuals out of their homes into *centers of employment* appears more likely to break up traditional value patterns, and to supplant them with new ones based on wage contracts, uniform standards of quality, and the influence of fellow workers on general opinions and beliefs. People in such centers of employment are much easier to reach by the mass media, whether controlled by labor unions, the government, or some private agency, than are individuals separated in their "cottages." In other words, the psychologist would say that leaving aside purely economic considerations altogether, investment in centralized employment rather than cottage industries is more likely to bring about the psychological changes essential to further economic development.

The second suggestion arises out of another traditional controversy. Should investment go into light or heavy industry? It is often argued that people should get used to the modern technical world by gradual stages, that a farmer should go from the digging-stick to the steel-edged plow rather than directly to the motor-driven tractor. Or the best businesses to start are those which do not require the maintenance or servicing of complex machines because these require skills that it might be quite difficult for backward people to learn. Instead, why not capitalize on skills very close to those that they have already? Economic considerations are certainly important in such matters: heavy machinery requires a much greater capital investment and more foreign exchange than do simple tools, but let us forget economics for the moment and consider the psychology of the situation.

Widespread use of *motors* would appear at least on *a priori* grounds to be more likely to induce certain desired attitude changes than simpler tools for the reason that they can be assimilated less easily into traditional ways of doing things. Consequently a man comes forward to make, operate, or service them in terms of his ability to do so rather than in terms of his traditional occupational status. One of the surprising things about Berna's study of entrepreneurs in light manufacturing in South India is his discovery that the entrepreneurs came from "extremely varied backgrounds" (1959, p. 357). When he studied businesses involving the use of machinery he found, contrary to the expectation of some, that not even the majority of entrepreneurs came from traditional merchant castes. There were even Brahmins who traditionally have nothing to do with manual labor of any kind. The motor appears to be a disruptive force which breaks traditional social patterns so that the man most interested or most able is drawn to work with it. He must also learn radical new things that fit less readily into habitual thought and value patterns. A motor is rationally constructed and can be made to run well if it is properly handled, unlike a corn crop which is more dependent on forces outside the man's control. A large motor can give a peasant community a sense of power over nature that it never had before, once it glimpses the great earth moving machines that make roads, the airplanes that annihilate distance, or even the water pump that relieves man of having to carry water by hand.

Peasants do not, of course, immediately adopt the values that a machine appears to foster. They often fail to operate them properly or are unable to fix them if they break down. It does not automatically follow that an un-trained labor force will be "forced" to develop better work habits in a machine-paced or precision-based operation, as Hirschmann argues (see Higgins, 1959, p. 673). As a simple example, an airplane is a complex and expansive piece of machinery that would seem to *require* good maintenance and careful attention to information on how to operate it, if the pilots want to go on living. Yet in one year a local airline in Chiapas, Mexico managed to lose 11 of its 12 airplanes, along with most of the pilots that were flying them. Fatalism, extreme risk-taking, lack of planning and attempts to econ-omize to make more money faster were among the traditional attitudes that were responsible for the catastrophe. Not even the threat of sudden death was enough to change them.

Yet this is not a decisive argument against introducing complex machinery. It represents symbolically the new age, introduces a new kind of social mobility, and ultimately should spread attitudes typical of the modern era. Probably some less drastic form of punishment for mistakes than is involved in an airplane crash would be more effective. In fact, a case could be made for the importance of electricity as an "instructor" in new values. It runs motors, gives mild punishment for mistakes, and above all brings in new information over the radio cheaply, even to nonliterates. Investment in the production and use of electric power may not only be an important index of the speed of economic development, it may also be an important *agent* in producing that development.

Increasing n Achievement

Our empirical evidence on the importance of market morality for eco-nomic development is actually not very strong, resting as it does on a few categories in the children's stories and a few attitude items in the study of entrepreneurs. Nor do we know much empirically about how to change it, though as always in such matters, the less we know empirically the more convincingly we can imagine why it is important and how it can be changed. The case for the importance of n Achievement rests on far more solid factual grounds and extends back into history, down into the lowest levels of development, and out across most modern nations, both Communist and non-Communist. Any country or agency concerned with speeding economic development should be interested in raising n Achievement levels, unless its level is already high (e.g., as in Israel). But how can it be done? Unfortunately, all of the large body of evidence summarized in Chapter 9 goes to show how embedded n Achievement level is in the total culture—in its religion, life style or more particularly in the way its parents raise their children. Changing child-rearing practices on a large scale is not likely to be done easily. The family is the social nucleus of the society, the main carrier of the basic motives and values of the culture. And it may be as hard to alter it intentionally as it was to crack the nucleus of the atom. Perhaps first it would be best to review a few instances where it has been changed, not by intent, but almost by accident when major social events had far-reaching effects on the family and ultimately on *n* Achievement levels without anyone's intending that they should.

Decreasing Father-Dominance

One of the apparent paradoxes in our data is the speed with which national *n* Achievement levels have changed in history (say in Germany between 1925 and 1950) and the slowness with which they should change according to the evidence in Chapter 9 that they are embedded in the family. How can these two sets of facts be reconciled? What happened historically when there were major shifts in *n* Achievement level? Two major social forces appear to have been at work—wars and mass ideological conversions. Let us consider wars first because their effect is hidden, and somewhat more complicated to explain. Wars may well have a marked and sudden effect on *n* Achievement by removing authoritarian fathers from the scene. Recall how father-dominance was shown by Rosen and D'Andrade (1959) in the United States and by Bradburn (1960) in Turkey to be a major source of low *n* Achievement in families where standards of excellence are otherwise high. Recall too how Strodtbeck (1958a) invoked father-dominance to explain the lower *n* Achievement of sons from the upper classes. Their fathers are successful and if they are businessmen tend to have above average *n* Power (Chapter 7). The fathers are likely then, even with the best of intentions, to dominate their sons in a way that lowers *n* Achievement. Abegglen (1958) has given a fuller picture of the family dynamics involved in his study of the life histories of U.S. business leaders who rose from lower-class status. They largely managed to reject their fathers. He states that "there is ample indication from the interview data that the experiences of these men with their fathers was subject to major disturbance. The illness of the father, frequent and prolonged absence or even separation by death or divorce entirely from the father marks most of the life histories. . . . The rejection of the father is not usually a result of a sudden shock, or single traumatic event, but rather the consequence of a more gradual and prolonged, less dramatic but nonetheless effective disillusionment and rupture in the relationship."

But lots of people break with their fathers or have ineffective or remote fathers who do not develop high *n* Achievement or successful entrepreneurship. The behavior and attitudes of the mother are then critical. She is first of all "a strong supporting figure, providing the stability and security necessary to later development and lacking in the father figure. More negatively it may be said that where the mother is strongly nurturant and overcompensating for the difficulties encountered in the relationship with the father, the degree of autonomy, self-confidence, and emotional independence achieved by these men would seem an unlikely outcome. Rather it would appear that the mother of the mobile man is strict and severe in training practices, controlled and moderate in warmth and affection." Furthermore, she has a "well-defined moral code" which makes certain first that the "goal system will not be that of the father nor . . . of his social class," and second that the values of "concentration, effort, and achievement" are emphasized. (Abegglen, 1958, pp. 153-154.) He further stresses the importance in these men's case histories of other adult males such as grandparents or uncles or teachers who to some extent are able to fill the role for the boy of the father who was rejected.

The interesting question raised by these studies is: what general social conditions are likely to promote the absence of the father from the home so that he cannot interfere with the boy's development of high n Achievement? Two such social conditions suggest themselves immediately—the nature of the father's occupation, and major wars. In the first case the father is taken out of the home for long periods of time because of the nature of his work. A prime example of such an occupation is sea-faring. Sailors are notoriously absent from home for long periods of time and cannot exert the kind of supervision over their sons that fathers who live at home can. It should follow that the sons of sailors would have higher n Achievement than other comparable boys, especially in authoritarian cultures where the other factors leading to high n Achievement are present (mothers with high standards of excellence, etc.). A glance at data presented in Chapter 8 and at history tends to support such a hypothesis. High n Achievement cultures tend to travel more which should serve to maintain n Achievement levels high if the fathers are dominant. And the seafaring nations like the Greeks, the early Etruscans, the British, the Japanese, the Scandinavians, the Genoese all appear to have had high n Achievement. One could go further and suggest that some of them decreased in n Achievement because as they got more and more successful they were able to hire or acquire slaves or mercenaries to man their ships from other countries since seafaring kept them away from home too much. It is an ironic twist of history to think that seafaring peoples who acquired slaves from subject nations in the triumph of their success may have caused their own undoing by increasing the n Achievement of those they had conquered and decreasing their own by shifting the balance of which fathers were away from home the most! The hypothesis is of course little more than an educated guess, but it could be checked either historically or at the present time by the type of empirical methods employed throughout this research. It needs careful testing, however, because other factors are known to be important. For example, if the fathers are away from home too early (when the boy is under six), mother-child dependency may result which lowers n Achievement. In Turkey, the fathers of the men with high *n* Achievement were removed from the scene later (from ages 6-14). Also other determinants of *n* Achievement must be present—high standards of excellence and warmth from the mother. Simple removal of the father is not enough as the data on lower *n* Achievement of children from broken homes in Chapter 9 show.

Major wars should also decrease father-dominance by keeping them from home on military campaigns, and by killing off a number of them. Here at last is a factor of sufficient importance and short-range effect to account for the apparent major increases in *n* Achievement level in countries like France and Germany between 1925 and 1950. A whole generation of boys between the ages of 6 and 14 were reared during the 1914-18 war with fathers absent or subsequently with no fathers at all. These are the men who would have reached positions of leadership and authority in the 1950's when our assessment of *n* Achievement levels was made. Perhaps in the relationship of Odysseus and Telemachus, the Greeks have again captured an important theme in human psychology. While Odysseus was away fighting and traveling, Telemachus grew up into a responsible, highly achievement-oriented son! The hypothesis deserves careful checking if only because it provides a way of explaining how *n* Achievement levels can be shifted rather radically in a single generation without the major ideological changes that have sustained longer range trends. Perhaps the classical argument that peace breeds slothfulness and war increases energy (*cf.* De Maistre, 1821) has at least this much truth behind it.

How an underdeveloped country could take advantage of such a possible way of increasing its *n* Achievement level is a little hard to see. The men would have to undertake to become less authoritarian (or be forced into it by feminism), or else start a few wars or promote the merchant marine. Unfortunately, none of these alternatives seems very practicable.

Ideological Factors: the Effect of Protestant Conversion in Mexico

From the beginning religion has been inextricably tied in with *n* Achievement levels. We have traced the connection through Weber's hypothesis linking Protestantism and capitalism, through the association of rises in *n* Achievement level with Protestant revivals in English history, and on down to the type of individualistic, mystical religions practiced by primitive cultures high in *n* Achievement. What the parents deeply and firmly believe *should* affect how they rear their children. Inasmuch as our data are correlational, it does not give insight into which came first—changes in *n* Achievement level or religious reform. It could be argued, as the Waxes very nearly have (1955), that the Protestant Reformation did not *produce* higher *n* Achievement but was itself the product of Mediterranean-style

Christianity being adjusted to fit the needs of a high n Achievement North European ethic.

An opportunity presented itself to check the cause-effect relationship a little more decisively among Indian villages in the state of Chiapas, Mexico. One village was discovered which had been almost totally converted to Protestant Christianity eight or nine years previously. Another was then chosen as a comparison village from the same culture area, which ideologically showed no unusual features—the inhabitants practiced a watered-down version of folk-Catholicism. The hypothesis to be tested is whether the Protestant conversion had raised n Achievement levels and risk-taking behavior among the children in the first village as compared with those brought up in the more traditional community.[1]

First, let us compare the two villages and see what effects the Protestant conversion has had. Both villages are located in rugged mountainous country at an altitude of around 6000 ft and have little contact with Mexican *ladino* culture, since they are accessible only on horseback over mountain trails. Their economy is basically subsistence agriculture and they live traditionally as they have for hundreds of years. The folk-Catholic village is a relatively new one established seven or eight years previously through the liberation of about 45 families of Indian peasants or peons who previously had lived for generations on a large ranch or plantation. They were helped to acquire their own land and to establish their own village and run their own affairs. Miller, who conducted the study, reports "the teacher contrasts the old life and the new in these terms: there was much suffering when the people were on the ranch. Since then there has been much progress—they eat better, they dress better, and they live better. He [the teacher] emphasizes progress and raising the standard of living. The men I talked to emphasized progress toward freedom: now there is no one to order them around, to punish them if they do not obey. They describe the new life as a better one, but they do not seem to think in terms of standard of living." Religiously the people describe themselves as "good Catholics," and forestalled a Protestant missionary's visit several years ago by telling him he would not be welcome. The village is like the Protestant one in the sense that it underwent a change at about the same time that the latter did, except that the change was more one of political freedom than "ideological conversion."

The Protestant Indian village is like the other one in most respects except that the soil is considerably better. It became Protestant through the efforts of an Indian convert who had moved there about eight or ten years previously. After he had been there a while, the villagers invited U.S. missionaries to live with them which completed the conversion of the village and started some conversion in the surrounding villages. The missionaries used recordings in the native Indian language and later translations of the Scriptures. The meaning of conversion to the people is perhaps best summed up in the contrasting images that a villager gives of a Catholic and a Protestant:

"A Catholic is a person who worships images, plays a guitar for their benefit, prays in front of candles, dances, drinks, smokes, believes in witchcraft, goes to the curer when he is sick, and has 2-4 wives. In the old days when they were Catholics they fought with each other, there was a lot of robbery, and there were killings."

"A Protestant is a man who has discovered *El Señor en el cielo* and he worships Him rather than images. He prays directly to Him, he sings hymns in church but doesn't use any musical instruments. He realizes that witches and curers are in league with the Devil, and he goes to the clinic when he is sick."

Obviously conversion has brought with it an internal sense of superiority. The Protestant thinks of himself as having achieved a higher level of religious understanding than the "ignorant" traditional folk-Catholic. Externally the anthropologist observed perhaps four main effects of the Protestant conversion: (1) the Protestants are the only ones in the area literate in their own language (Tzeltal); the reason is religious: since theirs is a religion of the "Book" they cannot fully participate until they can read the New Testament which has been translated into their language for them. (2) The health clinic introduced by the missionaries is an integral part of life in the Protestant village. "The [religious] service was led by the very young man whom I first saw with a microscope in the clinic." (3) The Protestant Church is rigorously ascetic as compared with Catholic churches in the vicinity. "The church is stark. There has been a rigorous elimination of all the symbols associated with folk Catholicism, so Protestants use no crosses, no pictures, no colored paper. Both inside and out the adobe walls are plastered white. A platform is built up in front for the pulpit. The contrast between this and the Catholic church in a nearby center has to be seen to be appreciated." (4) There is group hymn-singing in the Protestant service in the native language. Nearly all of these factors are ones customarily associated with early Protestant conversion and each suggests a reason why Protestant countries may have been helped indirectly by their Protestantism to higher levels of *n* Achievement and more rapid economic development. Insistence on the ability to read the Bible imposes higher standards of excellence and opens the people more to new norms presented in mass media. Medicine represents a "rationalized" treatment of illness previously treated in "nonrational" or magical ways. Religious asceticism prevents savings from being spent in nonproductive ways on decorations for churches and fiestas. Group singing would certainly appear to be one of the ways to encourage people to act together or to become other-directed.

But the empirical question is: what effect did the Protestant conversion of this Mexican Indian village have on *n* Achievement level of its children or the economic welfare of its adults? As we have repeatedly emphasized, it is one thing to argue what effects should be produced, and quite another to test to see if they are actually produced.

The question as to whether the Protestant conversion speeded "economic development" cannot be adequately answered. The Protestant villagers are undoubtedly better off economically than the Catholic villagers, but since their soil is also better, it is impossible to say whether their economic superiority has anything to do with changes in attitudes and motives or simply to the fact that they have superior natural resources. The question as to the effect of the Protestant conversion on motives and values of children can be answered fairly precisely, however, with the data presented in Table 10.1. In the first place it is clear that many more older children,

TABLE 10.1   CHARACTERISTICS OF INDIAN SCHOOL CHILDREN IN A PROTESTANT AND CATHOLIC VILLAGE IN THE HIGHLANDS OF MEXICO

Characteristics		Catholic village	Protestant village	Significance of differences
1. Age	Mean	$N = 32$ 8.75	$N = 46$ 11.37	$t = 4.23, p < .001$
	SD	2.75	2.51	
% boys 13 or older		10	36	$\chi^2 = 4.59, p < .05$
2. Ring-toss game (Boys age 7-12 only)[1]		$N = 17$	$N = 19$	
(a) Number of shifts in position out of 10 throws	Mean SD	1.24 1.83	4.79 1.61	$t = 5.97, p < .001$
(b) Number of successes per person	Mean SD	1.18 1.04	2.32 1.37	$t = 2.74, p < .01$
3. Graphic expression test		$N = 32$	$N = 46$	
(a) Number of scorable units	Mean SD	36.06 13.33	73.39 36.29	$t = 6.31, p < .001$
(b) n Achievement estimate (% above median of deviations from regression of $D-F$ score on $D+F$)[2]		$N = 26$ 38	$N = 16$ 63	$\chi^2 = 2.33, p < .10$ pd

[1] Three Catholic boys in the Protestant village have been added to the Catholic sample.
[2] Only those tests included in which the number of scorable units fell within a range common to both villages (24-55), a range for which regression of $D-F$ on $D+F$ was reasonably linear. The regression equation is $Y = .777X - 5.64$, in which Y is the predicted $D-F$ value and X is the $D+F$ value.

particularly older boys, attend school in the Protestant village. Perhaps the Catholic villagers, being poorer, need their older sons more for work in the fields, but more probably they do not value higher education as much as the Protestant villagers do whose religion demands greater literacy. All the children were given the chance to play the ring-toss game used to assess the moderate risk-taking usually associated with n Achievement (see Chapter 6). Since the older boys were better at the game and there were more of them in the Protestant village, it was decided to limit the comparison to boys aged 7 to 12 only. Girls were eliminated because they were markedly inferior to boys at the game. As predicted on the assumption of their higher n Achievement, the Protestant boys took moderate risks most often, that is, they stood at middle distances from the peg most frequently, 30 per cent of the throws being made between 19 and 51 inches away, 44 per cent between 52 and 84 in. and 26 per cent 85 in. or over (chi-square = 10.60, $df = 2$, $p < .01$). However, the measure was meaningless for the folk-Catholic boys for the simple reason that they adopted a position for the first throw and thereafter hardly ever budged from that position, whether they succeeded or failed. The Protestant boys typically started much further out and moved gradually in toward the peg until they reached a position where they had some success. In Table 10.1 the markedly different approach to the game is reflected in the average number of shifts in position made in each of the two groups out of nine possible shifts. The Protestant boys were much more flexible in adjusting their level of aspiration, or the risk taken, to the experiences of success or failure that they were having. Furthermore, they were on the average significantly more successful in throwing the ring over the peg as would be predicted from their greater flexibility. Certainly their behavior is completely in line with the hypothesis that they are more achievement-oriented and more likely to achieve.

An attempt was made to measure differences in n Achievement directly through the graphic expression test.[2] However, a comparison is nearly impossible because the Protestant children produced records containing many more doodles. There is in fact very little overlap in the distribution of scored units per record and no obvious way of correcting for the difference. On a raw score basis, of course, the Protestant children have much higher D-F scores (higher n Achievement) than the Catholic children but the difference could readily be ascribed to the fact that the Protestant children were somewhat freer in their response to the test ($D - F$ scores correlated with $D + F$ scores .84 in this sample). The z-score correction used in the cross-national study of older boys (see Appendix IV) could not be used because practically all the protocols from the Protestant village fell in the fifth quintile, so that there still would have been practically no correction for length of protocol. A regression based on the whole distribution was also not feasible because it was clearly not linear when the total number of scored units got much above 50 to 60; furthermore, there were no such protocols from the Catholic village. The only reasonable solution appeared to be to use only those protocols from the overlapping portion of the two distributions and to disregard age and sex differences which were not marked anyway in the graphic expression test. Consequently a regression was run of $D - F$ on $D + F$ scores for the range of $D + F$ scores common to both villages (24-55 scored units).[3] Obtained $D - F$ scores were then classified as falling above or below the regression line (as above or below the value predicted on the basis of the regression equation). More of the Protestant children have higher $D - F$ scores than predicted (i.e., higher n Achievement) although the difference does not quite reach accepted levels of significance. What is perhaps more interesting is that in the Protestant sample the dispersion is much greater, both the two or three highest and lowest deviations from the regression line occurring in the Protestant sample. While the general trend in the Protestant group is toward higher n Achievement, there are two or three cases of extremely low n Achievement. It would appear that the marked social change introduced by the Protestant conversion has caused a certain amount of "anomie" or disorganization in the motivational character of the children. The pressure toward change moves the majority in one direction but acts on a few strongly in the opposite direction.

The importance of this study can hardly be overstressed. It represents the closest one can come to a controlled experiment in a social setting. One village was given a certain treatment (Protestant conversion) and another matched village was not. The differences obtained in the way the children reacted would, then, appear to be most probably due to the treatment. Of course it cannot be proved that the n Achievement in the Protestant village was not higher in the first place, which is why they became converted to Protestantism, but the history of the conversion strongly suggests that it was largely a matter of chance that this village was converted. An Indian happened to move there who was himself a convert and from reading the record one has the impression that he would very probably have been as successful in any other village in the vicinity that he had happened to move to. Perhaps as important as anything else in producing the greater achievement orientation in the Protestant village is the conviction the converts have that they are superior to the "ignorant" folk-Catholics around them. Such a feeling ought to lead them to set higher levels of aspiration. It might well diminish as reformist zeal dies away or becomes less salient in countries where Protestantism is clearly the dominant religion. Either of these effects would explain why no over-all differences in n Achievement level exist between Protestants and Catholics in countries like Germany at the present time. In the United States, the Catholics may even be increasing in n Achievement over the Protestants at the present time (Chapter 3) because they, like the Protestants in Chiapas, feel themselves to be a disadvantaged but possibly superior minority.

Catholic and Communist Reform Movements

Certain types of ideological reform or conversion can apparently markedly increase n Achievement at least for a time. It need not be

Protestant, although there are elements in Protestantism as a *protest* movement that make it particularly achievement-oriented and behavior-oriented (involving ethics) rather than belief-oriented (involving dogma and ritual). The reform movement may be Catholic or even Communist. In another part of Mexico, in the city of Monterrey, a "religious revival" within Catholicism may have had a marked effect on the achievement motivation of a key group of businessmen who subsequently played a major part in industrializing the city. Abegglen, in writing a field report on this situation, sums it up as follows:

"There is general consensus in Monterrey that about 30-40 men now aged around 55, control most of Monterrey financially and industrially. They are closely related by kin or marriage, for the most part went to a Jesuit grammar school together back in the 1905-10 period and seem to have scattered during the 1910-17 period when Villa was riding high, typically spending some years in the United States or abroad. They support each other financially and businesswise, and have come up with most of the new activities and ideas that have caused Monterrey to explode population-wise to its present 450,000 and to be a major industrial center. . . . When asked what made the men of Monterrey undertake their new projects from 1936 on, the answer was repeatedly religion. Following the uprising in 1936, a series of religious retreats were held. These were then illegal, as was any religious instruction, but they multiplied rapidly apparently. These businessmen claim that out of this soul-searching came their realization of social responsibility and all of their work for the common people of Monterrey and for their children. One need not take this religious point at face value but these men most vehemently maintain its importance for themselves."

Conversion to Communist ideology may have the same effect. Three types of evidence support such a conclusion. In the first place, party literature, especially for party workers, has been loaded with achievement imagery both in Soviet Russia and Communist China. If one thinks of this as a "front," i.e., as a high level of aspiration set by the people at the top in the hope of getting the rank and file to work a little more strenuously, it must be remembered that the *n* Achievement in children's stories has also been a "front" in several countries discussed in Chapter 3. Yet such ideological commitment to achievement, even when it is apparently not widely shared, has had significant effects on economic development (e.g., as in Turkey).

In the second place, case studies by Bauer (1955) strongly suggest that *n* Achievement may be higher in individuals brought up wholly under the Soviet system since the Revolution than in an earlier generation. Typically in the older person the high levels of aspiration set by the party produce an attempt at rigid conformity with them which actually hides and is a reaction against a basic feeling of weakness and need for dependence derived from earlier upbringing. The younger person, on the other hand, brought up under the high ideals and strong achievement orientation of the Komsomols, may have experiences much like those that produce high n Achievement (see Chapter 9). And in fact he acts and thinks in ways that strongly indicate he has a higher n Achievement. Of course it is always difficult to be sure how "representative" such case studies are and how much the findings obtained from them can be generalized to the whole Russian population.

The third type of evidence is somewhat broader in scope. It is based on the content-analysis of Russian children's readers in 1925 and 1950 for n Achievement, as reported in Chapter 3. The average n Achievement score was .95 in 1925 and 2.10 in 1950, an increase which approaches statistical significance ($t = 1.72$, $p < .10$). By all odds the most probable explanation for such an increase is Communist ideology which has stressed very high standards of achievement both for the country and for its young people. The crucial factor in such reformist movements according to the evidence presented in Chapter 9 on core religious values is that they must stress individualistic achievement rather than passive dependency toward authoritarian forces beyond the individual's control.

Effects of Education on n Achievement

The policy implications of the data on "ideological conversion" are again limited. A country cannot "decide" that it should foster Protestant or Communist missionary movements, effective though they may be in raising n Achievement levels. It can, however, see the importance of a strong achievement-oriented nationalist ideology. And, after all, is it necessary to go the whole way to complete conversion? Case studies suggest that foreign educational influences may be sufficient to increase n Achievement. Many leaders in underdeveloped countries went to missionary schools. For example, Café Filho, formerly president of Brazil, is the son of converted Protestant parents in an overwhelmingly Catholic nation and attended a tiny Presbyterian mission school as a boy. Two of the other three boys who went there with him at the same time are also outstanding figures in Brazil, one a federal senator, the other the president of an insurance company. Political and economic leaders throughout British-dominated countries, from Egypt to India, appear largely to be those who had a British type of education when they were young. The graduates of the American University in Beirut and Roberts College in Istanbul are of key importance in nearly all walks of life in the Middle East. Could these schools be influencing motives and values as well as giving students specific technical education? What empirical evidence there is, however, does not support the hypothesis that such Western-oriented education increases n Achievement.

TABLE 10.2   MEAN n ACHIEVEMENT SCORES (VERBAL) OF MADRAS CITY BOYS AGED
15-17 ATTENDING DIFFERENT TYPES OF SCHOOLS

Religion and school	N	Mean	SD
Moslem New college. Students enter after 11 years of schooling, emphasis on Moslem culture	35	2.40	4.31
Theosophist Besant High School. Run by theosophical society, prepares candidates for teaching, emphasis on Indian culture	20	2.95	4.10
Christian Madras Christian College. Liberal Christian education, run by Scottish missionaries, coeducational, Western atmosphere	24	3.25	4.02
Hindu Hindu High School and Vivekanada College, boys only, emphasis on Hindu tradition and culture	48	5.56	5.44
Government Arts College	24	3.54	4.91

Data kindly supplied by P. V. Veeraraghavan through the cooperation of Major S. Parthasarathy, Sri P. V. Ramamurti, Sri P. Ananthakrishnan, Sri S. Krishnarathnam, Sri C. R. Paramesh, Sri S. Santhanakrishnan and Mr. Syed Sathar Mesh.

Table 10.2, for example, presents some data on n Achievement levels in various types of schools in Madras, India. The boys in the Hindu schools have the highest average level of n Achievement, significantly higher than those in the Moslem school ($p < .01$) and than those in the Theosophist School ($p < .05$). The boys from the Presbyterian School and the Government Arts College fall somewhere in between. Of course these results do not permit a conclusion as to whether the differences are due to selection or education. That is, practically all the boys in the sample were Hindus by religion, so that the school they went to might be determined by social class or caste factors, which in turn had determined their n Achievement levels before they entered school. It is true that the ten Moslem boys in the sample also had a low average n Achievement score (mean = 2.10), just like the boys attending the Moslem School, but even this is not conclusive because of possible selective migration of Moslems out of India into Pakistan. There is certainly no evidence that the Protestant Ethic as represented in Madras Christian College has significantly raised n Achievement levels above what they would be in general government schools or in schools stressing Hindu culture.

Perhaps such schools are not effective in changing motivation because nearly all the boys are still living at home. It was possible to find 25 of them, however, who had lived for one to seven years in a hostel away from home and their n Achievement score was if anything lower (mean = 2.60) than the mean score of 124 boys still living at home (mean = 3.99, difference = 1.39, $t = 1.39$, $p = .20$).

Another type of educational experience that might be supposed on *a priori* grounds to be more effective is provided by the management training courses given largely by or under the guidance of Americans in many underdeveloped countries today, like Mexico, Chile, India, Italy and Turkey. They are enthusiastically recommended by Harbison and Myers (1959) as a means of professionalizing management and generating high level managerial resources. Since they are definitely oriented toward improving by the case method or other means the ability of managers to solve their problems successfully, it might be supposed that they would either increase n Achievement or at least change value attitudes in the direction of those held by managers in the most advanced countries (see Table 7.8). Unfortunately, no careful check has yet been made to see what their effect is. Bradburn (1960) did find that the middle managers attending the Management Training Course at the University of Istanbul did *not* change in their attitudes in the directions predicted, but he did not administer the more sensitive fantasy test a second time. However, he found no difference in n Achievement level when the test was given *before* training to one group and *after* training to another comparable group. If the training had any marked effect, one would have expected the latter scores to be higher. The result is not conclusive, but it is not encouraging either. Those who recommend these courses highly ought to spend some of their energy trying to find out if they have the desired effects.

Perhaps the difficulty with all these studies is that the educational influences which might produce higher n Achievement occur too late in life after character has already been formed. Both psychological theory and research reported in Chapter 9 strongly suggest that the crucial period for acquiring n Achievement probably lies somewhere between the ages of 5 and 10. Perhaps exposure to high standards of excellence and the like will have a lasting effect on n Achievement only if it occurs early in life. An opportunity to check this hypothesis was discovered in Acre, Israel, where a Western-style nursery school for Arab children had been operating for some years. The ring-toss and graphic expression test used in the Mexican village study were administered to 22 four-to-five-year-olds, 12 of whom were in the nursery school, and to 21 ten-year-olds, 11 of whom had been to nursery school.[4] No consistent or significant differences of any kind were found in the data between those who had had the nursery school experience and those who had not had it. The ring-toss results were practically unusable because all of the boys behaved very rigidly as they had in the folk-Catholic village in Mexico. They started throwing at a given distance from the peg and refused to budge from that position regardless of their success or failure and despite reminders from the experimenter that they could stand anywhere they wanted to.

There is some evidence that the nursery school may have a slight effect at the time in the direction of increasing n Achievement, but so far as the older boys are concerned, there are no discernible differences in their test behavior except that the examiner felt that those who had been to nursery school understood the nature of the task somewhat better and were somewhat easier in the presence of a foreigner. Perhaps a nursery school experience is too trivial to affect motivation, but on *a priori* grounds one might well expect that it would: that is, this nursery school, like others in the Western style, stressed warmth and affection for the children, approval for projects "well done," some standards of cleanliness, and group play. The failure of such influences to "take" seems to be due less to inappropriateness for producing n Achievement than to their "partial" character. After all, the nursery school experience is very minor as contrasted with the major shaping influences of the family to which the child returns every day and of the general Arab culture in which he was completely immersed after he left the nursery school. Neither he nor his parents developed an ideology on the basis of the nursery school experience that might have prolonged or intensified its effects.

On balance, exposure to partial educational influences which might increase n Achievement do not appear to be very effective when they are unsupported by "ideological conversion" of the total group in which the experience occurs. There is even some evidence that such partial exposure to other "foreign" value systems may be disruptive and even lower n Achievement. Thus among the Madras city boys (Table 10.2) those attending "deviant" schools have lower n Achievement than those attending the Hindu school, and those removed from home influences and living in hostels also have lower n Achievement. A few of the Mexican Protestant boys received extremely low n Achievement scores. Furthermore, Kerckhoff (1959), in a study of Chippewa school children in Wisconsin, found marked evidence of similar disruptive effects. First he compared the n Achievement scores (verbal) of a comparable group of white and Indian children in the 5th to 8th grades and found as predicted that the white children on the average had higher n Achievement. Then he classified the Indian children as identifying primarily with the white culture, primarily with the Indian culture, or as being mixed in their identification. He found that those Indians who identified with the white culture had the highest n Achievement scores, those who identified with the Indian culture had the next highest n Achievement scores, while it was those of mixed identification who had by all odds the lowest n Achievement scores. Thus there is real experimental support for the observation often made by anthropologists that cultural change may seriously disrupt personality structure. But note that those who identified completely and ideologically with the white culture had higher n Achievement than those who remained "Indian." It was those that were confused in their loyalties whose n Achievement was lowered. The inference seems clear as with the rest of our data that social influences may raise n Achievement level if they are accompanied by "ideological conversion" but lower it if they lead to mixed or confused loyalties. The implications for policy are obvious though somewhat discouraging. Attempts to introduce changes gradually or indirectly without strong ideological conviction and fervor may do more harm than good.

Reorganizing Fantasy Life

One study suggests that the most effective way to increase n Achievement may be to try simply and directly to alter the nature of an individual's fantasies. Burris (1958) attempted to increase the n Achievement level of some college students enrolled in a self-improvement course, by discussing openly with them the achievement imagery (or lack of it) in their imaginative stories. Each student was "exposed" to eight weekly counselling sessions of 40 minutes each, in which he was told that the purpose of the discussion sessions was to "work together toward your understanding what things you wish to accomplish as a result of your school experiences. To get at a clear understanding, we will work out problems which are connected or associated with these objectives; both past and present will be discussed. I will have questions and comments during our discussions which are to help give you topics to talk about . . ." (Burris, 1958, p. 26). The counsellor's comments were based on the presence or absence of different types of statements relating to various aspects of the achievement sequence in the stories they had written prior to entering the course. Matched control groups of students in the course were counselled in terms of how to study or not counselled at all. At the end of the sessions he found, as predicted, that the subjects whose achievement motivation had been openly and intensively discussed with them showed a significant rise in their n Achievement scores in a second administration of the fantasy test. However, one would not put much faith in this finding because the second test may simply have reflected the greater salience of all sorts of achievement-related cues after such an intensive discussion of problems relating to achievement motivation. Their scores may have increased, but do the increased scores reflect a "real" increase in motivation? Burris also checked on their performance in school and found that the subjects whose n Achievement scores had been increased by the counseling sessions showed a significantly greater increase in their grade point average by mid-term of the following semester than had two control groups which had not received the special treatment. He found evidence that the increase in achievement motivation was "real" in the sense that it significantly affected subsequent grades. One study in one country of one particular type of student does not warrant a very broad generalization, but it does suggest that the simplest and most direct method of increasing n Achievement—by working over with a person the kind of fantasies he produces—may be an effective way to produce a change in it.

Theoretical backing for such an hypothesis can be found. By definition fantasy is less tied to specific situational cues than is overt behavior. It transfers more widely to all sorts of new situations. One common criticism of technique-oriented courses—e.g., the case method of teaching management in underdeveloped countries—is that the students understand what is correct in the cases in class but they do not generalize easily to their businesses once they are away from the classroom setting. If they had spent their time in class learning about achievement motivation and learning how to produce achievement-related fantasies, these fantasies might carry over into life situations and instigate activities aimed at producing achievement. If this research shows anything, it is that what people daydream about ultimately affects what they do. It may affect what they do more than what they have learned to do. Thus technique-oriented courses may conceivably be less effective than goal- or fantasy-oriented courses. At least the hypothesis is sufficiently promising to deserve a serious test.

Utilizing Existing n Achievement Resources More Efficiently

From the policy point of view a government or an outside agency apparently cannot do much to stimulate an increase in national n Achievement levels. The methods available are either too uncertain in their effect, require an ideological fervor that must be "real" rather than artificial, or involve actions that would be unacceptable on moral or political grounds. Furthermore, the effects, even if they could be induced, would ordinarily be long-range, affecting the next generation primarily, and most policy makers want to know what they can do *now* to accelerate the rate of economic growth in the next five years. A more practical approach is to start with what high n Achievement is available and to use it more efficiently. All large underdeveloped countries contain hundreds of thousands if not millions of people with high n Achievement even though the over-all average may be low. What can be done to make more effective use of such people?

One obvious approach is to try to get more young men with high n Achievement to turn their talents to business or productive enterprise. As we noted in Chapter 7, the business role is not likely to attract the boy with high n Achievement from the upper classes. Yet the more underdeveloped the country, the more the business leadership has to be drawn from the upper classes. Some mechanism must prevent all the boys with high n Achievement among the élite from electing first to go into the professions (humanities, law, medicine) leaving those with low n Achievement to pursue a business career reluctantly. Probably the strongest argument Harbison and Myers (1959) have for supporting advanced managerial and engineering training is that it will tend to professionalize management and give it high enough prestige to compete with the traditional professions for boys with entrepreneurial talent. It is at least interesting to note that some such process apparently took place in Russia, where executives seem to be more highly trained in economics or engineering than their American counterparts (Granick, 1960).

More directly (and almost certainly more effectively), policies may be pursued which call for the centralization of productive enterprise so that scarce resources of n Achievement or entrepreneurship can be conserved. If there are ten people available for managerial jobs and only one of them has high n Achievement, then the thing to do is organize all business activities under his leadership. If, however, three out of the ten candidates have high n Achievement, then several separate businesses can take advantage of the multiple sources of initiative. One of the obvious ways to centralize productive functions is to put them all in the hands of the government, as the Communists largely did in Russia. They acted as if they knew that their supply of n Achievement was low (as our evidence shows it was) and organized their production to economize on shortages of such talent. The Western democracies have generally been contemptuous of such a centralized system, feeling certain that it leads to inefficiency, but they should remember that they speak from the background of an initially much greater supply of entrepreneurial talent and n Achievement. The approach used by the Russians is much more likely to appeal to other underdeveloped countries which have entrepreneurial talent in short supply, just as the Russians had.

But Communism illustrates by no means the only way to economize on entrepreneurial resources. Hoselitz (1956) points out that historical interest has focused too much on the case of Britain rather than France where economic development followed a different, much more centralized course. The British case applies better to countries where there is a plentiful supply of entrepreneurial talent or n Achievement, the French better to countries where there is not. In France the control and promotion of development was always more centralized than in Britain. In the early stages through Napoleon, "The role of the government always remained paramount. . . . It became the most important institution through which the savings of the nation were collected and utilized for new investment." (Hoselitz, 1956, p. 304.) Later when business had grown too large to remain "under the full tutelage of the State," a major social innovation appeared, the *Crédit Mobilier* of the brothers Péreire, which fulfilled many of the functions formerly performed by the government. The *Crédit Mobilier* was an industrial investment bank which "overcame the shortage of creative entrepreneurs by undertaking the entrepreneurial function itself and reducing many of the actual managers of industrial firms to executors of policies." (Hoselitz, 1956, p. 307.)

The important point about the French example is that other institutional means can be found for economizing on entrepreneurship than the centralized system of state ownership adopted by the Communists. Such a variety of institutional forms of centralization exist that one can be selected that fits a particular national picture best. What is essential to the success of such an institution, however, is a rigorous achievement-related control over who is recruited into operating it or over who is allowed to remain in positions of operating responsibility. How can one be certain that the executives in the institution have high n Achievement? The question is all the more important the more centralized the control over economic development. In an openly competitive situation those with low n Achievement will presumably be gradually selected out by market forces, but in a centralized institution some other mechanism of selection must be present. Historically, the mechanism has sometimes seemed to be a matter of good luck: the brothers Péreire were extraordinarily good entrepreneurs; certain men who rose to political leadership on other grounds, like Ataturk, appear also to have had high n Achievement just by chance. More often entrepreneurial leadership has been provided by middle-class minorities whose sons with high n Achievement were prevented from going into the professions by discrimination (the Jews in various countries, the Protestants in France). In Communist countries the selective factor appears to have been ideological. They did not improve the supply of entrepreneurial talent much by drawing more from the lower classes (Chapter 7) but they set such rigorous production quotas that executives who could not meet them were simply weeded out.

Certainly the performance criterion is effective, but it is hard to apply in many underdeveloped countries where so much of government and business may be controlled by a small number of families. They may simply be unwilling to have their sons "weeded out" for poor performance. It may be more effective to try to control the recruitment process in such countries, to set up standards of n Achievement or past entrepreneurial performance as criteria of eligibility for appointment to a responsible position or for a loan to expand an enterprise.

While it may be hard for the government or the family business in an underdeveloped country to apply rigorous performance criteria in judging its executives, there is no reason why outside agencies could not use such criteria effectively. Many European and American businesses do just this in choosing local managers for their foreign affiliates in underdeveloped countries. Foreign aid programs could do likewise if they insisted as strongly on the proper entrepreneurial or managerial talent for a project as they do on various other criteria, whether political or strictly financial. Investment by a foreign agency in an underdeveloped country should be "in the man as well as in the plan." Careful control must be exercized by some agency over who is put in charge of key enterprises, if a country is to make rapid progress in the face of a generally short supply of entrepreneurial talent. Some more specific suggestions as to how outside agencies can contribute to this problem are discussed at the end of the chapter.

Some Economic and Social Factors in the Growth Process Re-evaluated

The discussion so far has been focused exclusively on the factors found to be important for economic growth in the present study. It has ignored all the economic and social variables considered by many, if not most theorists, to be of major importance—i.e., such variables as rate of population increase, balanced growth, investment criteria, urbanization, natural resources, terms of trade, monetary and fiscal policies, etc. To try to consider them all would be presumptuous and difficult to accomplish without writing another book, but perhaps it will be sufficient to indicate that many of these factors take on new aspects when viewed in the light of our psychological findings. To oversimplify at the outset, they take on *a* new aspect: they can be seen now as *techniques* which are more or less useful depending on the motives and values of the men who try to put them into effect. But let us try to be more specific to give some illustrations of how such a generalization works out in practice, since it sounds banal in its general form.

Resources. "To an economist, capital accumulation is the very core of economic development. . . . Economic development cannot take place without capital accumulation: the construction of irrigation systems, use of fertilizers and better seeds or livestock, land reclamation, building dams, bridges, or factories with machines in them, roads, railways, and airports, ships, and harbors—all the 'produced means of further production' associated with high levels of productivity." (Higgins, 1959, p. 204.) As a descriptive fact, such a statement can hardly be questioned. The difficulty arises when inferences are drawn from it as to the *dynamics* of economic development.

For example, it is sometimes argued that "the endowment of natural resources in [underdeveloped] countries, including farm lands, is a relatively important asset and that differences in stocks of these resources among poor countries are a major variable in determining the growth possibilities of such countries." (Schultz, 1960, p. 7.) What could be more logical than that some countries are poor because they are poorly endowed by nature? They lack water for electric power development, a river transportation system, arable land, or a good climate. Other countries seem to have been favored by nature. They had a strategic position for trade, like Britain, or good land like France, or a favorable man/land ratio like the United States in 1880.

Their capital stock given them by nature to start with appears to have been larger. Yet, as Schultz points out, economists are not at all agreed that natural resources are an important factor in economic growth. Some argue that wealth in land and mineral resources is even a hindrance in that it leads to an overcommitment in these areas and a consequent unreadiness to industrialize. Schultz believes and our data strongly support his conclusion, that what is important is not the variations in the supply of *"existing forms"* of reproducible capital but in *"new and better forms"* of reproducible capital (Schultz, 1960, p. 7). It is *what man makes of his environment* that is real capital. The sea water around the state of Israel was not a valuable natural resource until someone invented a relatively inexpensive way of removing its salt so that it could be used for irrigation purposes. Mexico is sometimes said not to have developed because it did not have a great river transportation system that made national unification and trade easy. But what about the Union of South Africa? It somehow developed without such a river system. The island of Mauritius is underdeveloped and overpopulated. What can it do? Not much with the *existing forms* of reproducible capital. It needs new and better forms. And certainly its initial resources were not so inferior to those of Iceland which enjoys a higher standard of living. It is the human resources that count—in particular the level of achievement motivation.

Or consider another inference that is sometimes drawn from the descriptive fact that capital is so central in economic development. If it is, it would appear to follow logically that the more capital is poured into a country, the more rapidly it will be developed. Some such general line of reasoning seems to have led Millikan and Rostow (1957) to recommend that much larger amounts of foreign aid be made available to underdeveloped countries. Rostow had argued earlier (1956) that development is normally characterized by a "take-off" period into self-sustained growth. What appears to be needed then is a large enough boost in capital from somewhere to move the economy into the take-off stage. The reasoning is persuasive but it neglects the human factor. Intensive studies of incremental capital output ratios, difficult though they are to be precise about, all agree in showing wide variations by country in the amount of capital needed to get the same increase in output. Interestingly enough the variations are fairly closely associated with national n Achievement levels as Table 10.3 shows. The higher the n Achievement level, the less capital was required by a country to produce a given increase in income. Higgins points out (1959, p. 644 ff.) that the incremental capital-output ratios (ICOR) show wide variations from decade to decade within the same country and are unusually subject to error because of conceptual problems in calculating them and because of inadequate economic statistics. Nevertheless it is highly suggestive that despite their inadequacies, they vary so closely with n Achievement level because it makes good theoretical sense that *entrepreneurship can substitute*

TABLE 10.3   RELATIONSHIP BETWEEN INCREMENTAL CAPITAL-OUTPUT RATIOS (ICOR) AND n ACHIEVEMENT LEVELS IN VARIOUS COUNTRIES

Country	ICOR[1]	Rank inverted	n Achievement level (1925)[2]	Rank
Canada	2.7	1	1.58	2
United States	3.0	2	.52	6
Sweden	3.3	3	.92	3
Denmark	3.5	4	.66	5
Australia	3.9	5	1.77	1
Japan	4.7	6	.34	7
Great Britain	5.9	7	.79	4
Netherlands	7.4	8.5	−1.68	9
France	7.4	8.5	−.97	8

Rank order correlation = .63, $p < .05$

[1] From Higgins, 1959, p. 645 for time periods beginning from the 1860's to 1920 and ending so as to include the decade of 1920-30.

[2] Standard scores, from Appendix II.

for capital. Put in simple psychological terms, this means that if entrepreneurial talent is lacking, if people are not motivated to be efficient and to find shortcuts, then any given increase in output will cost more. Nearly every visitor to an underdeveloped country has had the experience of seeing a "conspicuous investment"—say, an expensive hospital with all the most modern laboratory equipment set down in a provincial town where most people are living at a subsistence level. The economic question is whether a way could not have been found, by an achievement-oriented people, to produce nearly the same improvement in health for a considerably lower investment in less spectacular equipment. Certainly China appears to be developing more rapidly than India with less capital required for a given increase in output (Higgins, 1959, p. 727). What the evidence suggests is that China has succeeded to a greater extent than India in mobilizing the energies and ingenuity of her people. Here as elsewhere, it is the human resources that make a large difference in the capital needed to speed up economic development.

Population. Reduction in the rate of population growth has always seemed to be a simple and logical way of accelerating economic development. Countries like India, China and Indonesia appear to be severely hampered in their efforts to increase their standard of living by a population "explosion" caused by decreasing mortality rates without corresponding decreases in the birth rate. Since income is normally computed in per capita terms, it follows that if there are fewer people to divide the existing income, each one will have a somewhat larger share. The extraordinary fact about such a simple and logical idea is that it has so little empirical support. We could find very little evidence in Chapters 1 or 5 that more rapid rates of population growth or even unfavorable man/land ratios have been regularly associated with slower rates of economic development. One possible reason is that population, like resources, must be evaluated in terms of its human quality. Any individual born into a society can be viewed largely as a "mouth" or "a pair of hands," as a consumer or a producer. If he consumes more than he produces he is a liability, but if he produces more than he consumes, he is an *asset*. He makes more of a contribution to income than to consumption in the income per capita ratio. How much he can produce would appear to depend to some extent on what resources are available to him. In this sense, rapid population growth cannot be considered in itself a bad thing in relatively underpopulated countries like those in South America where ample natural resources exist. Yet it should certainly be more of a problem where there are fewer resources to go around as in India. Even in such countries, motivational energy can compensate for high man/land ratios and can find ways to produce or import even food resources that are in short supply (e.g., as in Japan or Israel).

But what harm is there in trying to reduce rate of population growth if it is known that n Achievement level is low (something which certainly cannot definitely be concluded about India, for example, at the present time) and that resources are relatively scarce? Far from causing harm, such a reduction might even create some positive good if one could be sure that the population control measures are most likely to decrease the number of those individuals with nonproductive psychological characteristics such as low n Achievement. But if the birth control policies decrease disproportionately the production of individuals likely to have high n Achievement, then it would have the exact opposite effect of the one intended. Fewer "high producers" or entrepreneurs would be born, and consequently the decreasing rate of population growth might be more than offset by a greater decrease in national productivity. In Japan, the United States, and Italy individuals from the lowest socioeconomic strata tend to have lower n Achievement whereas those from the middle strata tend to have higher n Achievement. It is possible that birth control methods might affect the middle classes more than the "hard to reach" lower classes so that the spread of such methods might actually selectively *decrease* the proportion of people with high n Achievement. Thus it is very important in making birth-control plans to consider what groups are most likely to be affected. One must obviously reduce the number of some kinds of people more than others, yet practically all birth-control policies ignore this problem entirely. No matter how few, the "wrong" kind of people will not produce rapid economic development, nor will the "right" people, no matter how many, block economic development. "Right" and "wrong" mean here, of course, more or less suited in motives and values to the task of economic development.

A favorable economic environment. Economists and other theorists have recognized for a long time that underdeveloped countries have values, motives and social institutions which are not conducive to rapid economic growth. They might be quite willing to accept the evidence presented so far that what many underdeveloped countries lack is enough *n* Achievement or entrepreneurial talent. But when it comes to formulating policies for aiding development, why is it necessary to worry about psychology? Won't certain economic policies gradually foster the kind of personality structure needed? Won't extension of the factory system or machine culture or information about how to make money by industrializing "require" or elicit a class of entrepreneurs who can run the new social institutions? Shouldn't a country worry most about creating *an environment favorable to entrepreneurship?* This is a variant of the Social Darwinist notion that the environment *selects* the kind of people that can succeed in it, or that it is *opportunity* that creates entrepreneurship. Buchanan and Ellis state the case very well as follows: "to contend that the really substantive barriers to development are mainly non-economic is not to deny, however, that these barriers are most surely and easily crumbled from the economic side. Historically the most powerful factor in re-orienting and re-shaping the socio-cultural environment seems to have been the spread of trade and commerce" (1955, p. 407). Trade "offers other outlets for local resources . . . filters in new products, new techniques, new ways of doing things and new points of view . . . weakens the economic base that supports the old values in the traditional social structure" (1955, p. 408).

Marx and Engels presented a somewhat similar analysis in the *Communist Manifesto* over a hundred years ago:

"The discovery of America, the rounding of the Cape, opened up fresh ground for the rising bourgeoisie. The East Indian and Chinese markets, the colonization of America, trade with the colonies, the increase in the means of exchange and in commodities generally, gave to commerce, to navigation, to industry, an impulse never before known, and thereby, to the revolutionary element in the tottering feudal society, a rapid development. . . . Modern industry has established the world market, for which the discovery of America paved the way. This market has given an immense development to commerce, to navigation, to communications by land. This development has, in its turn, reacted on the extension of industry; and in proportion as industry, commerce, navigation, railways extended, in the same proportion the bourgeoisie developed, increased its capital, and pushed into the background every class handed down from the Middle Ages."

The same two points are vividly made in these passages. It is "the market," opportunity for trade, which creates the entrepreneurial class. Then it is this class which, in the pursuit of its objectives, destroys the old social order and introduces new values, new motives, and new social institutions. So if you want to accelerate economic development, *increase trade*, infiltrate the underdeveloped country with "merchant-traders," provide incentives that will induce entrepreneurs to enter the market, provide "a clear picture of the more ample life which additional income will bring" (Higgins, 1956, p. 112). The analysis of how trade has accompanied social change is descriptively quite correct, but the policy implication that trade therefore was largely responsible for change is considerably less certain. It is true that new markets were exploited by entrepreneurs, but it does not follow that a new market opportunity automatically elicits an entrepreneurial response. It is far more likely that the entrepreneur discovered the market opportunity rather than vice versa if the findings reported in this book are valid.

Even without our data, the conclusion seems inescapable from the fact that many more peoples failed to take advantage of "market opportunities" than pursued them actively. Consider just one example. The Arabs in the Middle East have traded with the West all through the modern Industrial Revolution. They have had contact with Western technology, with "new products, new techniques, new ways of doing things and new points of view" all along, certainly in great trading centers like Cairo and Beirut. They have had a "clear picture of the more ample life" for some time. If trade and exposure to new ideas are really effective means of crumbling "old values and the traditional social structure," why has the Arab world been so resistant so long to such influences? Why did the view of the "promised land" of greater wealth not act as a greater incentive "to work harder and better or to take greater risks with one's capital"? (Higgins, 1956, p. 112.)

There are many reasons, of course, why peoples do not respond to the "demonstration effect" of a higher standard of living by behaving as they should to "get ahead." They may have been prevented from doing so by colonial domination, or certain traditional social institutions may have acted as strong deterrents. It would be wrong to conclude that such external influences have *no* effect toward creating an upwardly aspiring group of young people. However, it is equally wrong to infer that external incentives or a favorable environment automatically produce the psychological characteristics needed for a successful middle class. It is even likely that those who are attracted into the market place *primarily* in pursuit of wealth or a higher standard of living are *not* the ones who are most likely to produce economic development. They are not oriented enough toward achievement, toward doing a good job for its own sake. Instead, being focused on rewards, they may stop working when they acquire them, find inferior or dishonest methods of getting them, or refuse to take long-term risks with the money they do earn. Social Darwinism is too simple: a social environment does not directly produce the character structure most adapted to survive in it, as we repeatedly demonstrated in Chapter 9.

Investment criteria. Economists have been particularly challenged by the possibility that some types of investment in underdeveloped areas are likely to be more effective in accelerating development than others. The problem, as Higgins puts it so graphically, is: "Will expenditure on education or on transport in the next few years stimulate the most investment in other fields in subsequent years?" (Higgins, 1959, p. 666.) Certain investments such as construction of an iron and steel plant appear to have more "linkages" with a variety of economic activities or a greater "multiplier effect," and therefore are often assigned a higher priority. But if psychological changes are of key importance, the question shifts to what kind of investment is likely to have the greatest "psychological multiplier effect." This is precisely the question that the first part of the chapter was devoted to answering when various techniques for increasing other-directedness, or *n* Achievement and for using *n* Achievement resources more efficiently were discussed. The psychologist's priorities are for investments that improve communication, take women out of the home, make use of psychological tests or performance criteria to evaluate executives, and reorient school teachers to a new kind of education that stresses group participation and achievement.

Two other types of priorities have been so widely accepted at least as a basis for foreign aid that they deserve a brief review here. The first has concentrated on *technical assistance to agriculture and community development for rural areas.* The United Nations, the United States, the British Commonwealth in the Colombo Plan, private organizations like the Ford Foundation and the American Friends Service Committee, and governments of underdeveloped countries like India have all initiated such aid programs. To some extent they are motivated by welfare considerations: by concentrating on technical aid to agriculture and on improving public health, they certainly have contributed to the well-being of millions of hungry and sick people. However, as Higgins points out, "rural social work" (1959, p. 681), while certainly desirable, should not be confused with economic development. What evidence is there that such technical aid programs should lead to self-sustained economic growth? Actually there is a good *a priori* case that they might be very effective because aid to agriculture appears to be the *easiest way to increase the real income of the largest number of people.* And to an economist higher real income means higher saving which permits higher investment in capital improvements which increases income and so on in a beneficent cycle. The sequence of events may be briefly summarized in the following diagram:

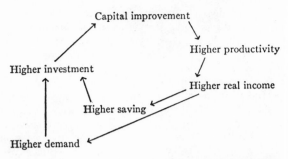

(From Meier and Baldwin, 1957, pp. 319-320)

For example, improved seed (or more technical knowledge about how to plant crops) enables the farmer to produce more. When he sells his crop he then has more income which may enable him to save a little and if farmers everywhere can save, then banks and entrepreneurs have an increase in "real income" to invest in new businesses, or the farmer perhaps can buy a tractor which again improves his productivity, starting the beneficent cycle on a second round. Or if he doesn't save his money he may want to spend it on consumer goods, which should stimulate investment in the industries that produce those goods and thus start a second beneficent cycle. Agriculture is the *easiest* place to produce capital improvement because such things as improved seed can have relatively *large effects* with the *least* disruption of the farmer's normal way of doing things, which makes it easier to get him to accept the change. Aid to agriculture affects the *largest number* of people because by far the largest number of workers in underdeveloped countries are primary producing (in agriculture) and because capital improvements in agriculture are relatively cheap (as compared with building a steel mill, for example) and can therefore be made available by assistance agencies to the maximum number of people. Why shouldn't it receive the highest priority?

The argument is so persuasive that it is easy to see why, when combined with welfare considerations, it has led many agencies in the West to believe that development should focus c agriculture, health, public overhead capital, and technical training. Yet it contains a very simple but fundamental flaw which economists interested in poor countries themselves fully recognize. The beneficent cycle diagrammed is not a simple, automatic chain reaction. It requires individuals who decide to do things at every point in the cycle. The farmer, for example, must not decide to produce less after he has the improved seed because he can now get what he always had with less work. If he produces more, the middleman to whom he sells it must not give him less for it, because there is now a greater abundance (which apparently actually happened when the production of Malayan fishermen was increased by capital improvements; see Firth, 1946). If he has an increase in real income he must not spend it in relatively nonproductive ways such as buying extra land to lie idle or luxury items for his family. If he does want to invest in productive equipment such as a tractor or put his money in a savings bank, effective business entrepreneurs must be available to use the extra savings productively to supply the equipment he wants or to build other industries, and so forth. At every point the operation of the chain of events depends on the values and motives of the individuals in the culture. Classical economic theorists could be satisfied with such a model because they could assume that the people they knew in the countries of the West would act, on the average, in the ways required as opportunities presented themselves. But the precise problem of most underdeveloped countries is that they do not have the character structure, especially the motivational structure, which would lead them to act in the ways required. The model is like a combustion engine without the gas to make it go.

Extensive aid to rural communities in this form may even do some harm in the sense that it greatly increases the rate of population growth and strengthens the most tradition-oriented segment of the society. From the psychological point of view, it does little or nothing to increase other-directedness, exposure to new norms and values, or the supply of entrepreneurial talent. Instead by making traditional agriculture more feasible, it may take some of the pressure off people to change and to find new ways of adapting to a radically different world.

In a second type of aid program, priority is given to *technical or managerial training*. The arguments for it start very close to our own position. What is most lacking in underdeveloped countries is adequate manpower to carry out economic development. But the stress is on training in needed skills rather than on motivation and values, partly because foreign agencies have felt that motives and values were none of their business. The case is clear so far as engineering and other such technical skills are concerned. No matter how many entrepreneurs with high n Achievement are available (e.g., among the Yoruba, Table 3.1), they cannot bring about modern economic development without engineering know-how. They just would not be able to build dams, construct and repair machines, roads, or buildings. Certainly engineering education needs to be improved, because it increases the prestige of related occupations so that they attract more upper-class boys with high n Achievement.

Harbison and Meyers (1959) have recognized that technical skills are also not enough. Executives must be trained in management techniques. Again the point is self-evident. But the importance of creating new motives and values in such managers needs also to be stressed. Otherwise they may learn new techniques but not be motivated to use them or to take risks or be honest. Character education is needed and Bradburn's results (1960), cited above, suggest that ordinary management training courses do not develop character or change values. The problem, of course, is to "develop character" by a means that will not be rejected out of hand as an unwarranted intrusion into a national way of life. The solution lies in presenting openly the psychological evidence that certain motives and values are required for effective economic development. Then the individual is at least faced with a clear decision of what he wants to do—cling to the old values with their associated inefficiencies or seek to acquire the new ones.

A General Plan for Accelerating Economic Growth

Certain policy objectives for aiding development have been proposed and others criticized. Is it possible to go further and propose a general plan framed in terms of such a priority system? The venture is hazardous for a number of reasons: it requires detailed theoretical and practical knowledge; situations obviously differ psychologically, socially, and economically in different countries. Most important of all, the whole point of our argument has been that certain psychological changes must occur before there is likely to be self-sustained rapid economic growth. Having criticized attempts to rely on *external* forces to induce psychological change, can we now turn around and propose a plan in terms of such forces?

There is no real substitute for ideological fervor. A country or at least a significant portion of its élite has got to want economic achievement badly enough to give it priority over other desires. A country cannot be developed from the outside against its will. But having recognized this, we can assume that such a will does exist in most underdeveloped countries, and that even though it could be stronger in many of them, there should be some methods of implementing it that will be more effective than others. That is, even if n Achievement is low in general, some methods ought to be imaginable for discovering and aiding those entrepreneurs who are nevertheless high in n Achievement in a particular country.

As a start, let us look at an instance of "induced" economic development in a backward area, which occurred even without careful governmental or economic planning. Perhaps some lessons can be learned from it of general applicability. In Saudi Arabia, Aramco decided that it wanted to subcontract jobs not directly connected with the production of oil. Despite the fact that the Arabs as Moslems are probably generally low in n Achievement (Table 10.2), the Arab Industrial Development Division of Aramco had no difficulty over the years in locating Arab entrepreneurs, many of whom became quite successful. Perhaps the best way of explaining how the process worked is to let one of the subcontractors tell his story in his own words:

"I am twenty-seven years old and was born in Dammam. Ten years ago my father died; he was a merchant. I went to Bahrein Island for my education, and stayed there seven years. It was there that I learned to read and write English. When I came back from Bahrein, I went to work for Aramco. I had enough money and did not need to work, but my father forced me to work for the company so that I could learn something.

"In 1939 I started first as a telephone operator, because I knew English; after one year I was transferred to the accounting department, then was made Head Clerk. Then I was transferred to the Personnel Recruiting Section as an interpreter in recruiting Arabs. In 1942 my father died, and left me nine people to support—my mother, my three younger brothers, of whom the oldest was twelve; these also include my wife, whom I married when I was fourteen and my three sons. My salary was not enough for my needs, and since my father had left much money, I wanted to spend my time keeping this money busy. So I went into the contracting business.

"I had to learn construction. My first job was making concrete slabs, then grading, then working on the stabilizer, then I moved into real construction, including carpentry, electrical work, and plumbing. . . . Sometimes, as for example last December, I hire as many as four hundred men at once. At present I have one hundred men at Ras Tanura making concrete block buildings, duplexes and seven-unit family apartments. . . ." (Coon, 1955, p. 333.)

Not all the contractors worked on jobs for the company, of course. Some of them started to put in small electric power plants "which served home refrigerators, and then electric shop equipment, and then ice plants. The first ice plant was a one-ton plant built in Al-Khobar in 1948. During the first summer the owner had a hard time selling half of the plant's capacity, except during Ramadhan. But the Ramadhan sales made him decide to double the capacity of the plant the next season. Another bought a plant of one-and-a-half tons' capacity. That year (1949) ice went fast; there were riots at both plants; they couldn't freeze it fast enough." (Coon, 1955, p. 325.)

Coon calls his account of these changes "Operation Bultiste" after the man in Aramco who was initially responsible for giving advice and help to Arab contractors. Apparently it was a successful operation in stimulating entrepreneurial activity—even to starting a taxi service which everyone predicted would fail because Arabs always hitchhiked—which ultimately raised the local standard of living. To be sure the entire development was the result of money which a foreign company put into the area in order to get oil out for sale elsewhere, but some lessons can be learned from this example nonetheless. Let us look at it more closely.

In the first place, the development took place in a very backward, traditional area. Most underdeveloped countries have "leading sectors" usually located near major ports or cities where industrial development plans are focused. Provincial areas are often considered too backward, too lacking in the necessary entrepreneurial skills or social overhead capital—public utilities, communication systems, etc. Yet the example demonstrates that the backward areas have the necessary entrepreneurial talent, and a good case can be made for the likelihood of its being less efficiently utilized than in the urban leading sectors. Individuals with high *n* Achievement in the cities at least have some channels of business opportunity accessible to them, whereas those in the country may have none. To be even more specific, consider the small-time entrepreneurs with high *n* Achievement in Orissa Province, India, listed at the top of Table 7.3. They are doing their best with the opportunities available to them, but how much better they might do if some means were found of aiding them directly. If they worked in the city they would be more likely to discover and utilize existing public or private credit facilities, better marketing procedures, etc. Special development plans aimed at provincial areas are likely to pay larger dividends, precisely because they work to remove inhibitions to successful entrepreneurial activity that are greater than in the cities.

Hoselitz (1958b) has also recommended a program of *rural industrialization* for India, concentrated in towns of 10-20,000 people. He argues that one of its particular virtues is that it provides jobs *where people are* without having to pay the great social overhead cost of moving them to the cities to work. To this we can add that it influences the most traditional sector of the country by introducing new norms and values where they are needed most. By providing centers of employment (as opposed to cottage industry) it moves people out of their homes and exposes them to new ways of thinking and acting in a modern technological society. When such acculturation occurs in the cities, it is apt to be even more traumatic (see Lewis, 1959). Finally rural industrialization avoids some of the disadvantages of large scale, centralized business discussed at the end of Chapter 7. There we saw that everywhere men working for large (usually public) organizations believe more in rules and in status hierarchies, and less in variable rewards or recognition depending on a man's actual performance. So some gain in efficiency should result from organizing productive units on a small to medium size scale.

The second noticeable feature of the Aramco experience is that development occurred through *subcontracting*. To a certain extent this is an extension of the previous point: Aramco decided not to incorporate all the work that needed doing into one large bureaucratic enterprise. Rosenstein-Rodan (1959) has argued that the pattern of industrialization in modern times looks like the reverse of what it was in the past: "Big units come first and induce the subsequent growth of small industrial units around them" (1959, p. 6). This process should be encouraged, if the "few large industrial establishments are not to remain like islands in the sea without any economic diffusion and radiation effects, [which] induce additional industrial growth." The large units "may place subcontracts and orders for small spare parts or intermediate products to other (small and medium scale) firms in the new industrializing region and thereby induce investment in small industrial enterprises dependent on and centering around the big unit." The large firm can provide the means of utilizing efficiently the entrepreneurial talent available in the vicinity just as in the Aramco case. So, as Rosenstein-Rodan suggests, plans for large units can include specifications about subcontracting or financial incentives can be offered by credit agencies for increased subcontracting.

Another less obvious feature of the Aramco development is that it depended to a considerable extent on the capital equipment and technical "know-how" of the large unit. The potential Arab entrepreneur could come to Bultiste for advice as to how to proceed and could make use of public utilities and borrow or rent large equipment introduced by Aramco for its own operations. This idea has been incorporated in a plan for *"industrial zones"* or *"estates"* recommended by Rosenstein-Rodan (1959), Hoselitz (1958b) and others for the promotion of small and medium scale industry in new areas. "In view of the scarcity of capital, the relatively poor transport facilities, and above all, the scarcity of managerial and technical personnel in these places, *combined* factories, rather than single works should be established. In other words, rather than putting five or six different factories, each employing around 50 to 200 persons in different small towns or villages, one big building housing several otherwise independent factories of this size should be established in one place. This means that each 'production center' would actually consist of several departments, each of which produces some different commodity or group of commodities. But the management and technical personnel, e.g., engineers, mechanics, maintenance and repair men could serve the entire establishment, i.e., all five or six departments" (Hoselitz, 1958b, p. 295). Furthermore to save on capital, the industries could use local resources and require only medium technology, "e.g., textiles, leather products, sugar, starch, oils and soaps, paints and varnishes, bicycles and parts, wood products for building purposes, glass and glassware, cement and pottery goods, lanterns, torches, electric lamps, sewing machines, etc." The industrial estate is a means of combining small enterprises to make needed capital equipment (e.g., transportation facilities, utilities) and technical services economically feasible. The government or a private entrepreneur can actually build the facilities for rent thereby preventing land speculation and making the capital needed to get the enterprise going considerably less than if the entrepreneur had had to invest in the building himself. Credit facilities might also be provided that would make development of the estate easier. Enough experience should have been gained from the operation of such estates by now in England, Brazil, India and Italy to plan for their most effective use elsewhere.

A final but key characteristic of the Aramco development is the high *standards of entrepreneurial achievement* implicit in an American subcontracting operation. Subcontracting or industrial estates as mechanisms do not automatically work unless someone is insisting on high standards of performance from the entrepreneurs. An Arab subcontractor who did not produce to specifications undoubtedly in time lost his contracts with Aramco. But as we pointed out in Chapter 7 in discussing the case of the Mexican purchasing agent, such standards are by no means universal. There are many instances of government enterprises in underdeveloped countries which have been allowed to operate inefficiently for years because no effective method for insisting on high standards of achievement has been developed. It is in part for this reason that many people insist on the superiority of the free-enterprise system. It has a built-in mechanism that operates crudely to eliminate inefficient producers. A private business can fail more easily than a publicly owned business, at least in many countries, though not, as we have seen in Communist countries where rigorous production criteria have often been enforced.

The problem then is how to build a mechanism into a development plan for evaluating entrepreneurial performance. A foreign enterprise from a developed country like Aramco usually provides such a mechanism in the standards it sets for its own employees or its subcontracts. Some countries, notably Mexico, have benefitted from the presence of foreign enterprises and have even gone to some lengths to encourage them to set up factories locally recognizing that they can aid development with their better technical knowledge and higher standards of performance. The solution is only a temporary one and has several drawbacks. Sooner or later the underdeveloped country wonders why profits in business done locally should go abroad or why key positions are filled by foreigners, and a move starts toward expropriation of the foreign interests. It can be argued that "development by expropriation" is a technique that will work if a country plays its cards very cautiously, though it is scarcely likely to contribute to international goodwill.

Of course, institutions in the country itself—whether governmental, credit-providing, or entrepreneurial—can and do insist on high standards of performance. They often go to the other extreme and insist on high standards in advance of starting the enterprise. Just as dangerous as no standards is what is sometimes called the "cost accountant's" or "banker's mentality," which insists that an enterprise be thoroughly sound and involve little or no risk before an investment is made in it. Yet it is probably fair to say that Western business has developed by "investing in the man rather than his plan." Many businessmen are not particularly good planners in the technical economist's sense. They merely have had a good idea of what is possible and a better idea of what risks will pay off as they proceeded. Accordingly, stress should be placed on picking the right man—as it was in Aramco, since Bultiste knew the Arabs he was dealing with well—leaving him free to operate if he has a plan that makes a moderate amount of sense, and then evaluating his *actual performance* rigorously after he has had a chance to show what he can do. The psychologist insists, as the businessman is apt to, that the most effective control on an economic development program lies not in the excellence of the plan, as economists are apt to argue (Millikan and Rostow, 1957), but in the excellence of the men selected to carry it out. Some devices are needed both to select the best man to operate it and to eliminate or retrain those who do not perform up to standards.

Subcontracting to Private Business

Putting the problem in this way suggests an approach to foreign aid that international agencies or developed countries might adopt. They can make grants to firms in developed countries to aid similar firms abroad. Let us take the United States foreign aid program as an example. Up to now it has helped underdeveloped countries largely in one of two ways. Either it has made "government to government" loans or gifts based on *plans* for economic development, jointly reviewed, or it has employed personnel in its technical assistance program to give aid and advice to farmers, managers or others in the underdeveloped country.

The first device may be fairly ineffective because the control mechanism is basically the excellence of the plan rather than of the manpower in the country that will carry it out. The second likewise runs into trouble because, however good its technical assistance plans, the government has difficulty recruiting the best American manpower to carry them out overseas, at salaries much below those paid in the private sector. What is needed is more effective selection of manpower both in the United States and in the country it is trying to aid. To accomplish both objectives the U.S. government might subcontract more of its aid plans to U.S. private business so that aid flows on a business-to-business rather than a government-to-government basis. Such subcontracting is already in effect in some technical assistance areas, particularly where aid to foreign universities is involved. The government writes a contract with an American university to aid a particular foreign university. The two universities then work out detailed plans, and personnel can be supplied for overseas assignments by the American university according to needs and established salary schedules. On the whole, the experience with such subcontracts to universities has been satisfactory (Hunter, 1959).

Let us see how a similar arrangement would work between businesses. Suppose that the United States and Brazil decide that the electric power industry in Brazil needs assistance from the United States. Now the U.S. can either give or loan the money to Brazil for this purpose and hope that somewhere in the Brazilian government effective methods exist for selecting the best managers, engineers and the like to use the money. Or the U.S. government can try to recruit an expert to send to advise the Brazilian power industry. Suppose instead the U.S. government (or the U.N., for that matter) signed a contract, let us say, with the Connecticut Light and Power Company to aid the Brazilian power industry. Two advantages would accrue: the U.S. government would have as its representatives in Brazil better men than it could probably employ directly and the American company would be in a position to set manpower standards for the Brazilian company like those set by Aramco in Saudi Arabia. Some of these standards could undoubtedly be set informally by advice and mutual consultation because often an outside agency has an advantage in setting standards: it frees the local company from some of the unpleasant responsibility for enforcing them. But other incentives exist for adopting such standards. For one thing, it tends to insure the continued assistance of the American company but more importantly it lays the basis for a successful appeal to a bank or international loan agency for funds for expansion. The request for such funds would be more likely to be successful if backed by an American company's report on manpower standards and other conditions in the Brazilian power industry.

The advantage of such a plan to the underdeveloped country is that it gets the benefit of the ablest American businessmen, as in the case of Aramco, but without the drawback of foreign ownership of the enterprise developed. The advantage to the United States is that it is "leading from strength"—from the private sector where most of its resources in "know-how" and manpower are located. It will then for the first time be on a par with the Russians, who have on the average sent abler technical assistance representatives abroad because they do not have a private and a public sector. That is, when they want an electric power expert for a project in Ceylon, they ask for nominations from their biggest and best electric power installations in Russia. It would be as if the U.S. were able to get a representative from Detroit Edison to go when in fact it has to try to hire him at a much lower salary.

American business might sometimes object to strengthening its competitors but more often direct competition would not be involved. If one thinks in terms of the small- and medium-scale businesses discussed above as likely candidates for industrial estates, one can think of hundreds of American and European business firms that should be willing to accept contracts to help them get started. Funds for such contracts need not come only from the U.S. government of course. They could be provided by foundations, the underdeveloped countries themselves, or international agencies. U.S. business itself might offer to undertake a few such projects at its own expense as an illustration of what it can do. The plan needs further development to work out its political and economic implications, but at first glance it appears to be a way for foreign aid to flow to underdeveloped countries that takes into account the great importance of highly motivated manpower for the success of any development plan. Furthermore it concentrates on the focal point in development—the entrepreneur and the productive enterprise—rather than on aid to health, welfare and agriculture. Therefore it should give a more lasting boost to the economy. At least it deserves some experimentation as an alternative to existing methods of accelerating economic growth.

So we end on a practical note: a plan for accelerating economic growth through mobilizing more effectively the high n Achievement resources of a developed country to select and work directly with the scarcer high n Achievement resources in underdeveloped countries particularly in small and medium scale businesses located in provincial areas and organized in "productive complexes" to save on scarce capital and manpower resources. While the plan may have defects, it has at least three merits: it suggests an alternative to current aid programs that may be more effective in starting an underdeveloped economy on the path to sustained growth; it provides a method of testing in the hard school of reality the theoretical superstructure from which it is derived; and last but not least, it demonstrates how focussing on psychological objectives and manpower resources can alter thinking about what means are most likely to be effective in producing social change. For in the end, it is men, and in particular their deepest concerns, that shape history.

A Last Word

What, then, did happen to great civilizations like the Renaissance in Florence? The Florentines lost interest in achievement. Their dreams changed. They became more concerned with love and friendship, with art, with power struggles. The dominant Medici family illustrates the shift in motivation from Giovanni, the great merchant banker whose achievement drive led him into all corners of Europe, through Cosimo, *pater patriae,* who consolidated his father's gains, through Lorenzo, *Il Magnifico,* great patron of the arts, to his successors caught in a bloody struggle for pleasure, power and wealth for their own sake. What each generation wanted above all, it got. What saves such a statement from banality is the new fact that the psychologist has now developed tools for finding out what a generation wants, better than it knows itself, and *before* it has had a chance of showing by its actions what it was after. With such knowledge man may be in a better position to shape his destiny.

NOTES AND REFERENCES

[1] I am deeply indebted to Frank Miller for collecting the data and to Professor Evon Vogt for making this study possible.

[2] The scoring of the graphic expression test, for which I am greatly indebted to Elliot Aronson, was of course done "blind," without knowledge of what village the protocols came from.

[3] The Protestant sample available by this criterion (only 16 out of the 46 cases) contained slightly more children aged 11 to 16 (50 per cent) than did the folk-Catholic sample (38 per cent), the remainder in each case being between the ages of 5 and 10. However, the difference is not significant and age has no discernible effect on $D - F$ score in this sample of protocols.

[4] I am much indebted to Norman and Wendy Bradburn for obtaining these data and to the American Friends Service Committee and in particular to William Channel and to Earl McCoy for making this study possible.

FLOW CHART SHOWING INTERRELATIONSHIPS AMONG THE KEY VARIABLES FOUND
TO BE RELATED TO ECONOMIC ACHIEVEMENT

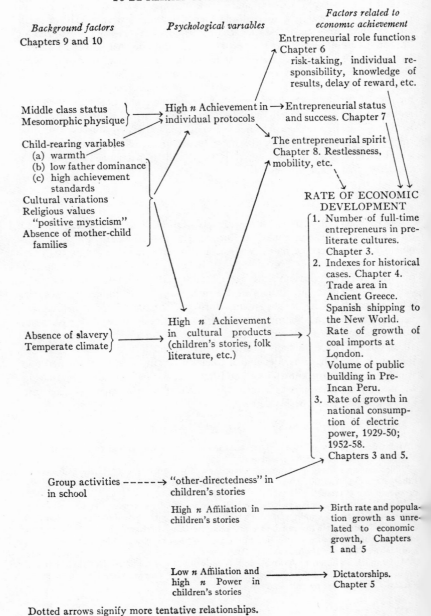

Background factors
Chapters 9 and 10

Psychological variables

*Factors related to
economic achievement*
Entrepreneurial role functions
Chapter 6
    risk-taking, individual re-
    sponsibility, knowledge of
    results, delay of reward, etc.

Middle class status
Mesomorphic physique

High n Achievement in
individual protocols

Entrepreneurial status
and success. Chapter 7

Child-rearing variables
    (a) warmth
    (b) low father dominance
    (c) high achievement
        standards
Cultural variations
Religious values
    "positive mysticism"
Absence of mother-child
    families

The entrepreneurial spirit
Chapter 8. Restlessness,
mobility, etc.

RATE OF ECONOMIC
    DEVELOPMENT
1. Number of full-time
   entrepreneurs in pre-
   literate cultures.
   Chapter 3.
2. Indexes for historical
   cases. Chapter 4.
   Trade area in
   Ancient Greece.
   Spanish shipping to
   the New World.
   Rate of growth of
   coal imports at
   London.
   Volume of public
   building in Pre-
   Incan Peru.
3. Rate of growth in
   national consump-
   tion of electric
   power, 1929-50;
   1952-58.
   Chapters 3 and 5.

Absence of slavery
Temperate climate

High n Achievement
in cultural products
(children's stories, folk
literature, etc.)

Group activities
in school

"other-directedness" in
children's stories

High n Affiliation in
children's stories

Birth rate and popula-
tion growth as unre-
lated to economic
growth, Chapters
1 and 5

Low n Affiliation and
high n Power in
children's stories

Dictatorships.
Chapter 5

Dotted arrows signify more tentative relationships.

References

Abegglen, J. C. *The Japanese factory*. Glencoe, Ill.: Free Press, 1958.
Abegglen, J. C. Personality factors in social mobility: a study of occupationally mobile businessmen. *Genet. Psychol. Monogr.*, 1958, 58, 101-159.
Abegglen, J. C., & Mannari, H. Leaders of modern Japan: social origins and mobility. *Econ. Develpm. cult. change*, 1960, 9, II, 109-134.
Adorno, T. W., Frenkel-Brunswik, Else, Levinson, D. J., & Sanford, R. N. *The authoritarian personality*. New York: Harper, 1950.
Agarwala, A. N., & Singh, S. P. (Eds.) *The economics of underdevelopment*. Bombay: Oxford Univer. Press, 1958.
Alexander, A. P. Industrial entrepreneurship in Turkey: origins and growth. *Econ. Develpm. cult. change*, 1960, 8, 349-365.
Angelini, A. L. *Um novo método para avaliar a motivação humana*. Doctoral dissertation. São Paulo, Brazil: Universidade de São Paulo, 1955.
Aronson, E. The need for achievement as measured by graphic expression. Unpublished master's thesis. Middletown, Conn.: Wesleyan Univer., 1956.
Aronson, E. The need for achievement as measured by graphic expression. In J. W. Atkinson (Ed.), *Motives in fantasy, action, and society*. Princeton, N.J.: Van Nostrand, 1958. Pp. 249-265.
Ashton, T. S. *The industrial revolution*. London: Oxford Univer. Press, 1948.
Atkinson, J. W. Motivational determinants of risk-taking behavior. *Psychol. Rev.*, 1957, 64, 359-372.
Atkinson, J. W. (Ed.) *Motives in fantasy, action, and society*. Princeton, N. J.: Van Nostrand, 1958. (a)
Atkinson, J. W. Towards experimental analysis of human motivation in terms of motives, expectancies, and incentives. In J. W. Atkinson (Ed.), *Motives in fantasy, action, and society*. Princeton, N. J.: Van Nostrand, 1958. Pp. 288-305. (b)
Atkinson, J. W., Bastian, J. R., Earl, R. W., & Litwin, G. H. The achievement motive, goal-setting, and probability preference. *J. abnorm. soc. Psychol.*, 1960, 60, 27-36.
Atkinson, J. W., & Litwin, G. H. Achievement motive and test anxiety conceived as motive to approach success and motive to avoid failure. *J. abnorm. soc. Psychol.*, 1960, 60, 52-63.
Atkinson, J. W., & Miller, D. R. Parental experiences in child training. Unpublished dittoed paper. Univer. of Michigan, 1956.
Atkinson, J. W., & Reitman, W. R. Performance as a function of motive strength and expectancy of goal-attainment. *J. abnorm. soc. Psychol.*, 1956, 53, 361-366.
Atkinson, J. W., & Walker, E. L. The affiliation motive and perceptual sensitivity to faces. In J. W. Atkinson (Ed.), *Motives in fantasy, action, and society*. Princeton, N. J.: Van Nostrand, 1958. Pp. 360-366.

Avery, R. M. Orientations toward careers in business. Unpublished doctoral dissertation. Harvard Univer., 1959.

Barry, H., III, Child, I. L., & Bacon, M. K. Relation of child training to subsistence economy. *Am. Anthrop.*, 1959, 61, 51-63.

Bauer, R. A. The psychology of the Soviet middle élite: two case histories. In C. Kluckhohn, H. A. Murray, & D. M. Schneider, *Personality in nature, society, and culture.* New York: Knopf, 1955. Pp. 633-650.

Beardslee, D. C., & O'Dowd, D. D. Images of occupations. Report #1: occupations project. Mimeographed. Middletown, Conn.: Dept. of Psychol., Wesleyan Univer., 1958.

Behavioral Research Service, *Motive patterns of managers and specialists.* New York: General Electric Company, 1960.

Berlew, D. The achievement motive and the growth of Greek civilization. Unpublished bachelor's thesis. Middletown, Conn.: Wesleyan Univer., 1956.

Berna, J. J. Patterns of entrepreneurship in South India. *Econ. Develpm. cult. change*, 1959, 7, 343-362.

Bindoff, S. T. *Tudor England.* London: Penguin Books, 1950.

Bouquet, A. C. *Comparative religion.* London: Penguin Books, 1954.

Bradburn, N. M. The managerial role in Turkey: a psychological study. Unpublished doctoral dissertation. Harvard Univer., 1960.

Bradburn, N. M., & Berlew, D. E. Need for Achievement and English economic growth. *Econ. Develpm. cult. change*, 1961, in press.

Brown, N. O. *Hermes, the thief.* Madison, Wis.: Univer. of Wisconsin Press, 1947.

Brown, N. O. *Life against death.* Middletown, Conn.: Wesleyan Univer. Press, 1959.

Buchanan, N. S., & Ellis, H. S. *Approaches to economic development.* New York: Twentieth Century Fund, 1955.

Burris, R. W. The effect of counselling on achievement motivation. Unpublished doctoral dissertation. Univer. of Indiana, 1958.

Calvin, John. *Institutes of the Christian religion* (transl. by John Allen). Philadelphia: Presbyterian Board of Christian Education Edition. Volume I.

Chase, S. *Mexico: a study of two Americas.* New York: Macmillan, 1931.

Chaunu, H., & Chaunu, P. *Seville et l'Atlantique* (1504-1650). Paris: Colin, 1955-1959. 11 vols.

Child, I. L., Frank, K. F., & Storm, T. Self-ratings and TAT: their relations to each other and to childhood background. *J. Pers.*, 1956, 25, 96-114.

Child, I. L., Storm, T., & Veroff, J. Achievement themes in folk tales related to socialization practice. In Atkinson, J. W. (Ed.), *Motives in fantasy, action, and society.* Princeton, N. J.: Van Nostrand, 1958. Pp. 479-492.

Childe, V. G. *What happened in history* (Revised). London: Penguin Books, 1954.

Clark, C. *The conditions of economic progress* (3rd ed.). London: Macmillan, 1957.

Cole, A. H. et al. *Entrepreneurship and economic growth.* Mimeographed. Cambridge, Mass.: Social Science Research Council and Harvard University Research Center in Entrepreneurial History, 1954.

Coon, C. S. Operation Bultiste—promoting industrial development in Saudi Arabia. In H. M. Teaf & P. G. Franck (Eds.), *Hands across frontiers: case studies in technical cooperation.* Ithaca, N. Y.: Cornell Univer. Press, 1955. Pp. 307-361.

Cortés, J. B. The achievement motive in the Spanish economy between the 13th and 18th centuries. *Econ. Develpm. cult. change*, 1960, 9, 144-163.

Crockett, H. Achievement motivation and social mobility. Unpublished doctoral dissertation. Univer. of Michigan, 1960.

Cronbach, L. Statistical methods applied to Rorschach scores: a review. *Psychol. Bull.*, 1949, 46, 393-429.

Deane, P. The implications of early national income estimates for the measurement of long-term economic growth in the United Kingdom. *Econ. Develpm. cult. change*, 1955, 4, 3-38.

Deane, P. The industrial revolution and economic growth: the evidence of early British national income estimates. *Econ. Develpm. cult. change*, 1957, 5, 159-174.

deCharms, R. The effects of individual motivation on cooperative and competitive behavior in small groups. Unpublished doctoral dissertation. Univer. of North Carolina, 1956.

deCharms, R., Morrison, H. W., Reitman, W., & McClelland, D. C. Behavioral correlates of directly and indirectly measured achievement motivation. In D. C. McClelland (Ed.), *Studies in motivation*. New York: Appleton-Century-Crofts, 1955. Pp. 414-423.

de Charms, R., & Moeller, G. H. Values expressed in American children's readers: 1800-1950. *J. abnorm. soc. Psychol.*, 1962, in press.

De Maistre, J. *Une politique expérimentale: Paradoxe de la guerre.* (1821). Paris: Librairie Arthème Fayard, 1940.

Dill, W. R., Hilton, T. L., & Reitman, W. R. *Becoming a manager.* Pittsburgh: Grad. Sch. Industr. Admin., Carnegie Inst. Technol., 1961, in preparation.

Dimock, M. E. *Administrative vitality.* New York: Harpers, 1959.

Dollard, J. *Caste and class in a Southern town.* New Haven, Conn.: Yale Univer. Press, 1937.

Dollard, J., Doob, L. W., Miller, N. E., Mowrer, O. H., & Sears, R. R. *Frustration and aggression.* New Haven, Conn.: Yale Univer. Press, 1939.

Douvan, Elizabeth. Social status and success strivings. In J. W. Atkinson (Ed.), *Motives in fantasy, action, and society.* Princeton, N. J.: Van Nostrand, 1958. Pp. 509-517.

Edwards, W. Probability-preferences in gambling. *Amer. J. Psychol.*, 1953, 66, 349-364.

Epley, D. A time for responsibility: time-span and achievement in the University. Unpublished bachelor's thesis. Harvard Univer., 1958.

Fayerweather, J. *The executive overseas.* Syracuse, N. Y.: Syracuse Univer. Press, 1959.

Fayerweather, J. *Management and international operations.* New York: McGraw-Hill, 1960.

Fanfani, A. *Catholicism, Protestantism and capitalism.* New York: Sheed and Ward, 1935.

Feld, S. C. Studies in the origins of achievement strivings. Unpublished doctoral dissertation, Univer. of Mich., 1959.

Firth, R. *Malay fishermen.* London: Kegan Paul, 1946.

Fisher, R. A. *The design of experiments.* New York: Hafner, 1951.

Editors of *Fortune*. *The executive life.* Garden City, N. Y.: Doubleday, 1956.

Fraser, T. M. Achievement motivation as a factor in rural development: a report on research in Western Orissa. Unpublished paper. Haverford, Pa.: Haverford College, 1961.

French, Elizabeth G. Effects of the interaction of motivation and feedback on task performance. In J. W. Atkinson (Ed.), *Motives in fantasy, action, and society.* Princeton, N. J.: Van Nostrand, 1958. Pp. 400-408.

French, Elizabeth G. Motivation as a variable in work partner selection. *J. abnorm. soc. Psychol.*, 1956, 53, 96-99.

French, Elizabeth G.   Some characteristics of achievement motivation. *J. exp. Psychol.*, 1955, 50, 232-236.

Fröhner, R., von Stackelberg, M., & Eser, W.   *Familie und Ehe.* Bielefeld: Maria von Stackelberg Verlag, 1956.

Fromm, E. *Man for himself.* New York: Rinehart, 1947.

Galbraith, J. K.   *The affluent society.* New York: Houghton Mifflin Co., 1958.

Glotz, G.   *Histoire Grecque.* Paris: Les Presses Universitaires de France, 1925. 2 vols.

Godfrey, E. P., & Fiedler, F. E., with Hall, D. M.   *Boards, management, and company success.* Danville, Ill.: Interstate Printers & Publishers, 1957.

Goode, W. J.   Industrialization and family change. Chicago: UNESCO conference on the social implications of industrialization and technological change. Univer. of Chicago, 1960.

Granick, D.   *The red executive.* New York: Doubleday, 1960.

Green, H. B., & Knapp, R. H.   Time judgment, aesthetic preference, and need for achievement. *J. abnorm. soc. Psychol.*, 1959, 58, 140-142.

Groesbeck, B. L.   Toward description of personality in terms of configurations of motives. In J. W. Atkinson (Ed.), *Motives in fantasy, action, and society.* Princeton, N. J.: Van Nostrand, 1958. Pp. 383-399.

Gurin, G., & Veroff, J.   A study of adjustment in a national sample survey. Dittoed paper. Ann Arbor, Mich.: Survey Research Center, 1959.

Gurin, G., Veroff, J., & Feld, S.   *Americans view their mental health.* New York: Basic Books, 1960.

Habakkuk, H. J.   English population in the 18th century. *Econ. Hist. Rev.*, Second series, 1953, 6, 117-133.

Hagen, E. E.   How economic growth begins: a general theory applied to Japan. *Public Opin. Quart.*, 1958, 22, 373-390.

Hagen, E. E.   Population and economic growth. *Amer. econ. Rev.*, 1959, 49, 310-327.

Hagen, E. E.   *How economic growth begins: a study in the theory of social change.* Cambridge, Mass.: Mass. Inst. Technol., 1961, in preparation.

Hall, E. T.   *The silent language.* New York: Doubleday, 1959.

Hann, J.   *Handbuch der Klimatologie.* (Vols. 1, 2, 3) Stuttgart: J. Engelhorn Verlag, 1908, 1910, 1911.

Harbison, F., & Myers, C. A.   *Management in the industrial world.* New York: McGraw-Hill, 1959.

Hauser, P. M.   Demographic indicators of economic development. *Econ. Develpm. cult. change*, 1959, 7, 98-116.

Heckel, H.   Zahlen zum Schulwesen in den Ländern des Bundesgebietes. Dokumentation Nr. 5/1959. Arb. gem. Deutschen Lehrerverbände. Darmstadt, 1959.

Heckhausen, H.   Einige Zusammenhänge zwischen Zeitperspective und verschiedenen Motivationsvariablen. *Ber. 22. Deutsch. Kongr. f. Psychol. (1959).* Göttingen: Verlag f. Psychologie, 1960. Pp. 294-297.

Heichelheim, F.   *Wirtschaftsgeschichte des Altertums.* Leiden: A. W. Sijthoff, 1938. 2 vols.

Herman, T.   Cottage industries: a reply. *Econ. Develpm. cult. change*, 1957, 5, 374-375.

Herrigel, E.   *Zen in the art of archery* (Transl. by R. Hull). London: Kegan Paul, 1959.

Herskovits, M. J., & Herskovits, F. S.   Tales in Pidgin English from Ashanti. *J. Amer. Folklore*, 1937, 50, 52-101.

Heyns, R. W., Veroff, J., & Atkinson, J. W.   A scoring manual for the affiliation motive. In J. W. Atkinson (Ed.), *Motives in fantasy, action, and society.* Princeton, N. J.: Van Nostrand, 1958. Pp. 205-218.

Higgins, B. The "dualistic theory" of underdeveloped areas. *Econ. Develpm. cult. change*, 1956, 4, 99-115.

Higgins, B. *Economic development*. New York: Norton, 1959.

Hill, J. P. Personality and the bureaucratic organization. Dittoed paper. Dept. Social Relations, Harvard Univer., 1959.

Hofstadter, R. *Social Darwinism in American thought* (Revised ed.). Boston: Beacon Press, 1955.

Hoselitz, B. F. Entrepreneurship and economic growth. *Amer. J. econ. sociol.*, 1952, 12, 97-110. (a).

Hoselitz, B. F. Non-economic barriers to economic development. *Econ. Develpm. cult. change*, 1952, 1, 8-21. (b).

Hoselitz, B. F. Social structure and economic growth. *Economia Internazionale*, 1953, 6, 3-28.

Hoselitz, B. F. The recruitment of white-collar workers in underdeveloped countries. *Int. soc. Sci. Bull.*, 1954, 6, 3-11. (a).

Hoselitz, B. F. Sociological approach to economic development. *International Congress of studies on the problem of underdeveloped areas*. Milan: Museo della Scienza e della Tecnica, 1954. Pp. 19-42. (b).

Hoselitz, B. F. Patterns of economic growth. *Canad. J. Econ. Pol. Sci.*, 1955, 21, 416-436.

Hoselitz, B. F. Economic growth and the market. Conference on commitment of the industrial labor force in newly developing areas. Mimeographed paper. New York: Social Science Research Council, 1958. (a)

Hoselitz, B. F. Economic growth and rural industrialization. *Econ. Wkly*, (India) 1958, 291-302. (February 22) (b)

Hoselitz, B. F. Entrepreneurship and capital formation in France and Britain since 1700. In M. Abramovitz (Ed.), *Capital formation and economic growth*. Princeton, N. J.: Princeton Univer. Press, 1956. Pp. 291-337.

Hunter, J. M. Reflections on the administrative aspects of a technical assistance project. *Econ. Develpm. cult. change*, 1959, 7, 445-451.

Huntington, E. *Civilization and climate*. New Haven, Conn.: Yale Univer. Press, 1915.

Huntington, E. *The character of races*. New York: Scribners, 1924.

Inkeles, A., & Rossi, P. H. National comparisons of occupational prestige. *Amer. J. Sociol.*, 1956, 61, 329-339.

Jevons, W. S. *The coal question*. London: Macmillan, 1906.

Jones, R. M. *Studies in mystical religion*. London: Macmillan, 1919.

Kahl, J. A. Three types of Mexican industrial workers. *Econ. develpm. cult. change*, 1960, 8, 164-173.

Kaltenbach, J. E., & McClelland, D. C. Achievement and social status in three small communities. In D. C. McClelland, A. L. Baldwin, U. Bronfenbrenner, & F. L. Strodtbeck, *Talent and society*. Princeton, N. J.: Van Nostrand, 1958. Pp. 112-133.

Katona, G. *Psychological analysis of economic behavior*. New York: McGraw-Hill, 1951.

Katona, G., Klein, L. R., Lansing, J. B., & Morgan, J. B. *Contributions of survey methods to economics*. New York: Columbia Univer. Press, 1954.

Kerckhoff, A. C. Anomie and achievement motivation: a study of personality development within cultural disorganization. *Soc. Forces*, 1959, 37, 196-202.

Keynes, J. M. *The general theory of employment, interest and money*. New York: Harcourt, Brace, 1936.

Klauer, K. J. *Überforderung bei Zeichenaufgaben*. Doctoral dissertation. Johannes Gutenberg Universität zu Mainz. München: UNI-Druck, 1959.

Kluckhohn, C., & Leighton, D. *The Navaho*. Cambridge, Mass.: Harvard Univer. Press, 1947.

Kluckhohn, F. R.   Dominant and substitute profiles of cultural orientations. *Soc. Forces*, 1950, 28, 376-393.

Knapp, R. H.   *n* Achievement and aesthetic preference. In J. W. Atkinson (Ed.), *Motives in fantasy, action, and society*. Princeton, N. J.: Van Nostrand, 1958. Pp. 367-372.

Knapp, R. H.   Attitudes toward time and aesthetic choice. *J. soc. Psychol.*, 1960, in press.

Knapp, R. H., & Garbutt, J. T.   Time imagery and the achievement motive. *J. Pers.*, 1958, 26, 426-434.

Knapp, R. H., & Goodrich, H. B.   *Origins of American scientists*. Chicago: Univer. Chicago Press, 1952.

Knapp, R. H., & Green, H. B.   The judgment of music-filled intervals and *n* Achievement. *J. soc. Psychol.*, 1960, in press.

Kroeber, A. L.   *Configurations of culture growth*. Berkeley: Univer. Calif. Press., 1944.

Kuznets, S.   International differences in income levels: some reflections on their causes. *Econ. Develpm. cult. change*, 1953, 2, 3-26.

Kuznets, S.   Quantitative aspects of the economic growth of nations. *Econ. Develpm. cult. change*, 1956, 5, 5-94.

Kuznets, S.   Underdeveloped countries and the pre-industrial phase in the advanced countries. In A. N. Agarwala & S. P. Singh (Eds.), *The economics of underdevelopment*. Bombay: Oxford Univer. Press, 1958. Pp. 135-153.

Kuznets, S., Moore, W. E., & Spengler, J. J. (Eds.)   *Economic growth: Brazil, India, Japan*. Durham, N. C.: Duke Univer. Press, 1955.

Lamb, H. B.   The Indian merchant. *J. Amer. Folklore*, 1958, 71, 231-240.

Lauterbach, A. T.   *Man, motives, and money: psychological frontiers of economics*. Ithaca, N. Y.: Cornell Univer. Press, 1954.

Lazarsfeld, P. F.   Reflections on business: consumers and managers. Mimeographed paper. New York: Columbia Univer., Dept. of Sociology, 1959.

LeShan, L.   Time orientation and social class. *J. abnorm. soc. Psychol.*, 1952, 47, 589-592.

Levin, H., & Baldwin, A. L.   Pride and shame in children. In M. R. Jones (Ed.), *Nebraska symposium on motivation 1959*. Lincoln, Nebr.: Univer. Nebr. Press, 1959.

Levy, M. J.   Contrasting factors in the modernization of China and Japan. In S. Kuznets, J. J. Spengler, & W. Moore (Eds.), *Economic growth: Brazil, India, Japan*. Durham, N. C.: Duke Univer. Press, 1955.

Lewis, O.   *Five families*. New York: Basic Books, 1959.

Lewis, O.   *Tepoztlan: Village in Mexico*. New York: Holt, 1960.

Lewis, W. A.   *Theory of economic growth*. London: Allen & Unwin, 1955.

Lewis, W. A.   Consensus and discussions on economic growth: concluding remarks to a conference. *Econ. Develpm. cult. change*, 1957, 6, 75-80.

Lipset, S. M.   Some social requisites of democracy: economic development and political legitimacy. Dittoed paper. Berkeley, Calif.: Univer. Calif., Dept. of Sociology, 1959.

Lipset, S. M., & Bendix, R.   *Social mobility in industrial society*. Berkeley and Los Angeles: Univer. of Calif. Press, 1959.

Littig, L. W.   The effect of motivation on probability preferences and subjective probability. Unpublished doctoral dissertation. Univer. of Mich., 1959.

Litwin, G. H.   Motives and expectancy as determinants of preference for degrees of risk. Unpublished honors thesis. Univer of Mich., 1958.

Litwin, G. H.   Achievement motivation, social class, and the slope of occupational preferences in the United States and Japan. Dittoed paper. Dept. Social Relations, Harvard Univer., 1959.

Mackinnon, D. W. Violation of prohibitions. In H. A. Murray, *Explorations in personality*. New York: Oxford Univer. Press, 1938. Pp. 491-501.

Mahone, C. H. Fear of failure and unrealistic vocational aspiration. Unpublished doctoral dissertation. Univer. of Mich., 1958.

Mahone, C. H. Fear of failure and unrealistic vocational aspiration. *J. abnorm. soc. Psychol.*, 1960, 60, 253-261.

Malenbaum, W. India and China: contrast in development. *Amer. econ. Rev.*, 1959, 34, 284-309.

Malthus, T. *An essay on the principle of population*. London: Johnson, 1798.

Malthus, T. *Principles of political economy*. 1820. New York: Augustus Kelly, 1951.

Marshall, A. *Principles of economics* (8th ed.). London: Macmillan, 1930.

Marx, K. *A contribution to the critique of political economy*. New York: International Publishing, 1904.

Marx, K. *Capital* (Edited by F. Engel). Chicago: Kerr, 1926.

Marx, K., & Engels, F. *The Communist Manifesto*. London: Allen and Unwin, 1948.

McClelland, D. C. Some social consequences of achievement motivation. In M. R. Jones (Ed.), *Nebraska symposium on motivation 1955*. Lincoln, Nebr.: Univer. Nebr. Press, 1955.

McClelland, D. C. Risk-taking in children with high and low need for achievement. In J. W. Atkinson (Ed.), *Motives in fantasy, action, and society*. Princeton, N. J.: Van Nostrand, 1958. Pp. 306-321. (a).

McClelland, D. C. The use of measures of human motivation in the study of society. In J. W. Atkinson (Ed.), *Motives in fantasy, action, and society*. Princeton, N. J.: Van Nostrand, 1958. Pp. 518-554. (b).

McClelland, D. C., Atkinson, J. W., Clark, R. A., & Lowell, E. L. *The Achievement Motive*. New York: Appleton-Century-Crofts, 1953.

McClelland, D. C., Baldwin, A. L., Bronfenbrenner, U., & Strodtbeck, F. L. *Talent and society*. Princeton, N. J.: Van Nostrand, 1958.

McClelland, D. C., & Bradburn, N. M. *n* Achievement and managerial success. Dittoed paper. Harvard Univer., 1957.

McClelland, D. C., & Friedman, G. A. A cross-cultural study of the relationship between child-training practices and achievement motivation appearing in folk tales. In G. E. Swanson, T. M. Newcomb, & E. L. Hartley (Eds.), *Readings in social psychology*. New York: Holt, 1952. Pp. 243-249.

McClelland, D. C., Lathrap, D. W., & Swartz, M. An attempt at the estimation of *n* Achievement levels from archaeological materials in a non-Western tradition. Unpublished paper. Care of Lathrap, Dept. Anthropology, Univer. Illinois, 1961.

McClelland, D. C., Rindlisbacher, A., & deCharms, R. C. Religious and other sources of parental attitudes toward independence training. In D. C. McClelland (Ed.), *Studies in motivation*. New York: Appleton-Century-Crofts, 1955.

McClelland, D. C., Sturr, J. F., Knapp, R. H., & Wendt, H. W. Obligations to self and society in the United States and Germany. *J. abnorm. soc. Psychol.*, 1958, 56, 245-255.

Mead, Margaret. *Sex and temperament in three primitive societies*. New York: Morrow, 1935.

Mead, Margaret. Columbia University research in contemporary cultures. In H. Guetzkow (Ed.), *Groups, leadership, and men*. Pittsburgh: Carnegie Press, 1951. Pp. 106-118.

Meier, G. M., & Baldwin, R. E. *Economic development*. New York: Wiley, 1957.

Mejia, G. A. *Genealogies of Antioquia and Caldas* (2nd ed.). Mendellín, Colombia: Ciencia Libreria Technica, 1942.

Merton, R. K. *Social theory and social structure.* Glencoe, Ill.: Free Press, 1949.

Miller, D. R., & Swanson, G. E. *The changing American parent.* New York: Wiley, 1958.

Miller, K. S., & Worchel, P. The effects of need-Achievement and self-ideal discrepancy on performance under stress. *J. Pers.,* 1956, 25, 176-190.

Millikan, M. F., & Rostow, W. W. *A proposal: key to an effective foreign policy.* New York: Harper, 1957.

Mischel, W. Delay of gratification, need for Achievement and Acquiescence in another culture. Unpublished paper. Cambridge, Mass.: Harvard University, 1960.

Morris, C. W. Physique and cultural patterns. In C. Kluckhohn & H. A. Murray (Eds.), *Personality in nature, society, and culture.* New York: Knopf, 1948.

Moss, H. A., & Kagan, J. Stability of achievement and recognition seeking behaviors from early childhood through adulthood. *J. abnorm. soc. Psychol.,* 1961, in press.

Muller, H. J. *The uses of the past.* New York: Oxford Univer. Press, 1957.

Murdock, G. P. World ethnographic sample. Mimeographed table. New Haven: Yale Univer., Dept. Anthropology, 1959.

Nef, J. V. *The rise of the British coal industry.* London: George Routledge and Son, 1932.

Parnell, R. W. *Behaviour and physique: an introduction to practical and applied somatometry.* London: Arnold, Ltd., 1958.

Parsons, T. The motivation of economic activities. In *Essays in sociological theory, pure and applied.* Glencoe, Ill.: Free Press, 1949.

Parsons, T. *The social system.* Glencoe, Ill.: Free Press, 1951.

Parsons, T. Some principal characteristics of industrial societies. In *The Challenge of development.* Jerusalem: Hebrew Univer., 1958.

Parsons, T., & Smelser, N. J. *Economy and society.* Glencoe, Ill.: Free Press, 1956.

Pelzel, J. Entrepreneurship in periods of rapid growth: Japan. In *Entrepreneurship and economic growth.* Mimeographed. Cambridge, Mass.: Social Science Research Council and Harvard Research Center in Entrepreneurial History, 1954.

Pierson, F. C. *The education of the American businessman.* New York: McGraw-Hill, 1959.

Pottharst, B. C. The achievement motive and level of aspiration after experimentally induced success and failure. Unpublished doctoral dissertation. Univer. Michigan, 1955.

Rattray, R. S. *Akan-Ashanti folk tales.* London: Oxford Univer. Press, 1930.

Redlich, F. L. Entrepreneurship in the initial stages of industrialization. In *Entrepreneurship and economic growth.* Mimeographed. Cambridge, Mass.: Social Science Research Council and Harvard University Research Center in Entrepreneurial History, 1954.

Redlich, F. L. Business leadership: diverse origins and variant forms. *Econ. Develpm. cult. change,* 1958, 3, 177-190.

Reed, W. W. The climates of the world. *1941 year book of agriculture.* Washington: U. S. Government Printing Office, 1942. Pp. 665-684.

Reitman, W. R. Motivational induction and the behavioral correlates of the achievement and the affiliation motives. *J. abnorm. soc. Psychol.,* 1960, 60, 8-13.

Ricardo, D. The principles of political economy and taxation. 1817. London: Geo. Bell, 1903.

Ricciuti, H. N., & Sadacca, R. The prediction of academic grades with a projective test of achievement motivation: II. Cross-validation at the high school level. Princeton, N. J.: Educational Testing Service, 1955.

Ricks, D., & Epley, D. Foresight and hindsight in the TAT. Paper read at Eastern Psychol. Ass., New York, April, 1960.

Riecken, H. W. *The volunteer work camp: a psychological evaluation.* Reading, Mass.: Addison-Wesley, 1952.

Riesman, D., with Glazer, N., & Denny, R. *The lonely crowd.* New Haven, Conn.: Yale Univer. Press, 1950.

Roe, Anne *The psychology of occupations.* New York: Wiley, 1956.

Rosen, B. C. The achievement syndrome. *Amer. sociol. Rev.,* 1956, 21, 203-211.

Rosen, B. C. Race, ethnicity and the achievement syndrome. *Amer. sociol. Rev.,* 1959, 24, 47-60.

Rosen, B. C., & D'Andrade, R. G. The psychosocial origins of achievement motivation. *Sociometry,* 1959, 22, 185-218.

Rosenberg, M. *Occupations and values.* Glencoe, Ill.: Free Press, 1957.

Rosenstein-Rodan, P. N. How to industrialize an underdeveloped area. Dittoed paper. Cambridge, Mass.: Center for International Studies, Mass. Inst. Technol., 1959.

Rostow, W. W. *The process of economic growth.* New York: Norton, 1952.

Rostow, W. W. The take-off into self-sustained growth. *Econ. J.,* 1956, 66, No. 261, 25-48.

Ryerson, A. An investigation of child-rearing practices: advice given to layman, 1545-1900. Unpublished doctoral dissertation. Harvard Univer. Graduate School of Education, 1960.

Sawyer, J. E. Entrepreneurship in periods of rapid growth. In *Entrepreneurship and economic growth.* Mimeographed. Cambridge, Mass.: Social Science Research Council and Harvard University Research Center in Entrepreneurial History, 1954.

Scholem, G. G. *Major trends in Jewish mysticism.* Jerusalem: Schocken Publishing House, 1941.

Schultz, T. W. A general view of natural resources in economic growth. Dittoed paper. New York: Social Service Research Council, 1960.

Schumpeter, J. A. *The theory of economic development* (transl. by R. Opie). Cambridge, Mass.: Harvard Univer. Press, 1934.

Sheldon, W. H., Stevens, S. S., & Tucker, W. B. *The varieties of human physique.* New York: Harper, 1940.

Shils, E. The concentration and dispersion of charisma: their bearing on economic policy in underdeveloped countries. *World Politics,* 1958, 11, 1-19.

Shipley, T., & Veroff, J. A projective measure of need for affiliation. *J. exp. Psychol.,* 1952, 43, 349-356.

Simon, H. A. Theories of decision-making in economics and behavioral science. *Amer. econ. Rev.,* 1959, 49, 253-283.

Smith, A. *An inquiry into the nature and causes of the wealth of nations.* 1776. New York: Random House, 1937.

Sorokin, P. A. *Social and cultural dynamics.* Vol. 3. New York: American Book Co., 1937.

Spengler, J. J. Capital requirements and population growth in underdeveloped countries: their interrelations. *Econ. Develpm. cult. change,* 1956, 4, 305-334.

Spengler, J. J. Cottage industries: a comment. *Econ. Develpm. cult. change,* 1957, 5, 371-373.

Spengler, O. *The decline of the West.* New York: Knopf, 1932. 2 vols.

Stepanek, J. E. *Managers for small industry—an international study.* Glencoe, Ill.: Free Press, 1960. (a).

Stepanek, J. E. *Small industry advisory services.* Glencoe, Ill.: Free Press, 1960. (b).

Strodtbeck, F. L. Family interaction, values, and achievement. In D. C. McClelland *et al., Talent and society.* Princeton, N. J.: Van Nostrand, 1958. Pp. 135-194. (a).

Strodtbeck, F. L. Jewish and Italian immigration and subsequent status mobility. In D. C. McClelland *et al., Talent and society.* Princeton, N. J.: Van Nostrand, 1958. Pp. 259-266. (b).

Strodtbeck, F. L., McDonald, M. R., & Rosen, B. Evaluation of occupations: a reflection of Jewish and Italian mobility differences. *Amer. sociol. Rev.,* 1957, 22, 546-553.

Sutton, F. X. Achievement norms and the motivations of entrepreneurs. In *Entrepreneurship and economic growth.* Mimeographed. Cambridge, Mass.: Social Science Research Council and Harvard University Research Center in Entrepreneurial History, 1954.

Sutton, F. X., Harris, S. E., Kaysen, C., & Tobin, J. *The American business creed.* Cambridge, Mass.: Harvard Univer. Press, 1956.

Suzuki, D. T. *Zen and Japanese culture.* New York: Pantheon, 1959.

Teaf, H. M., & Franck, P. G. (Eds.) *Hands across frontiers: case studies in technical cooperation.* Ithaca, N. Y.: Cornell Univer. Press, 1955.

Toynbee, A. J. *A study of history.* (Abridgment of Vols. 1-6 by D. C. Somervell.) New York: Oxford Univer. Press, 1947.

Troeltsch, E. *Protestantism and progress.* (Transl. by W. Montgomery.) Boston: Beacon Press, 1958.

Trollope, A. *North America.* London: Chapman Hall, 1862. 3 vols.

United Nations monthly bulletin of statistics. New York: United Nations Publications.

United Nations statistical yearbooks, 1956-1959. New York: United Nations Publications.

United Nations, *World energy supplies,* 1951-1954, 1955-1958. Series J. No. 2. New York: Statistical office of the United Nations, 1957 and 1959.

Usher, A. P. Spanish ships and shipping in the sixteenth and seventeenth centuries. In E. F. Gay (Ed.), *Facts and factors in economic history.* Cambridge, Mass.: Harvard Univer. Press, 1932.

Veroff, J. A scoring manual for the power motive. In J. W. Atkinson (Ed.), *Motives in fantasy, action, and society.* Princeton, N. J.: Van Nostrand, 1958. Pp. 219-233.

Veroff, J., Atkinson, J. W., Feld, S., & Gurin, G. The use of thematic apperception to assess motivation in a nationwide interview study. *Psychol. Monogr.,* 1960, in press.

Viner, J. The economics of development. In A. N. Agarwala, & S. P. Singh (Eds.), *The economics of underdevelopment.* Bombay: Oxford Univer. Press, 1958.

Warner, W. L., & Abegglen, J. C. *Occupational mobility in American business and industry.* Minneapolis: Univer. of Minnesota Press, 1955.

Watkins, M. H., & Hagen, E. E. *Estimate of world income, 1953.* Cambridge, Mass.: Center for International Studies, Mass. Inst. Technol., 1956.

Wax, M. Ancient Judaism and the Protestant ethic. *Amer. J. Sociol.,* 1960, 55, 449-455.

Wax, R., & Wax, M. The Vikings and the rise of capitalism. *Amer. J. Sociol.,* 1955, 61, 1-10.

Weber, M. *The Protestant ethic and the spirit of capitalism.* 1904. (Transl. by T. Parsons.) New York: Scribner, 1930.

Weber, M. *The theory of social and economic organization.* 1922. (Transl. by A. M. Henderson and T. Parsons.) New York: Oxford Press, 1947.

Wendt, H. W. Motivation, effort, and performance. In D. C. McClelland (Ed.), *Studies in motivation.* New York: Appleton-Century-Crofts, 1955. Pp. 448-459.

Wendt, H. W. On information, season and religion as pre-verbal determinants of some later risk-taking. Unpublished manuscript. Mainz: Joh. Gutenberg Universität, 1960.

White, L. A. *Lewis Henry Morgan: the Indian journals, 1859-62.* Ann Arbor, Mich.: Univer. Mich. Press, 1959.

Whiting, J. W. M., & Child, I. *Child training and personality.* New Haven, Conn.: Yale Univer. Press, 1953.

Whythe, W. H., Jr. *The organization man.* New York: Simon & Schuster, 1956.

Willey, G. R. Prehistoric settlement patterns in the Virú valley, Peru. *Bureau Amer. Ethnol. Bull. 155,* Washington, D. C., 1953.

Wilson, C. The entrepreneur in the industrial revolution in Britain. In *Entrepreneurship and economic growth.* Mimeographed. Cambridge, Mass.: Social Science Research Council and Harvard University Research Center in Entrepreneurial History, 1954.

Winterbottom, Marian R. The relation of childhood training in independence to achievement motivation. Unpublished doctoral dissertation. Univer. Mich., 1953.

Winterbottom, Marian R. The relation of need for achievement to learning experiences in independence and mastery. In J. W. Atkinson (Ed.), *Motives in fantasy, action, and society.* Princeton, N. J. Van Nostrand, 1958. Pp. 453-478.

Woytinsky, W. S., & Woytinsky, E. S. *World population and production.* New York: Twentieth Century Fund, 1953.

Wright, C. W. *Economic history of the United States.* New York: McGraw-Hill, 1949.

Wright, D. McC. Mr. Keynes and the "Day of Judgment." *Science,* 1958, 128, 1258-1262.

Young, F. W., & Young, R. C. Social integration and change in twenty-four Mexican villages. *Econ. Develpm. cult. change,* 1960, 8, 366-377.

Zieger, Oberkirchenrat, Die Religionszuhörigkeit der Studierenden vom Wintersemester 1951/52 an Universitäten, Techn. und sons. wiss. und künstlerischen Hochschulen Westdeutschlands und Westberlins. Amtsblatt der Evang. Kirche in Deutschland, Staatische Beilage Nr. 8, 1953.

variation which is desirable, and either too much or too little would be
less desirable for producing high energy.

Rainfall tends, of course, to go with lack of temperature variation and with
tropical heat, so that, again, shows the same general effect. Cultures with high
_n_ Achievement live in relatively dry climates, whereas those with
low _n_ Achievement live more often in areas of heavier rainfall. Thus the
general picture is quite clear: low _n_ Achievement is associated particularly
with tropical climates, which are very humid and show little temperature
variation. High _n_ Achievement is associated with moderate, dry climates,
which also tend to have poor soil, so that growing conditions for agriculture
are not optimal.

Should we therefore conclude that Huntington's interpretation of such
findings is correct—that climatic conditions invigorate people and encourage
them to think more about achievement? Perhaps, although (as unlike the Yoruba give us pause since they have one of the highest _n_ Achievement levels
recorded. Atkinson's general model of the way external and internal
determinants combine to yield aroused motivation would serve to explain
how habitat could lead to an expression of more _n_ Achievement in folk
tales. (See Table 6.2.) Climate might be conceived as being associated with
varying probabilities of success. In the coldest climates, probability of
success might be considered very low, on the grounds that the people must
struggle even to keep alive, whereas probability of successful achievement
is optimal in tropical climates where food is easy, or at least where food can
be either picked or grown easily. Moderate probabilities of success might be
present only in temperate regions where man has to struggle somewhat
to meet his needs. Then it could be argued that what is being measured in
the folk tales is aroused _n_ Achievement which is maximal where probability
of success is moderate. Or the effect might be direct, as Huntington would
argue: invigorating climates may make men feel better or more energetic,
and they may then conceive more achievement exploits. Both of these
interpretations have the advantage of sounding quite reasonable, but the
disadvantage of not being very directly testable. How would it be possible
to get a direct measure of probability of success in various climates?
How can we prove that invigorating climates tend to make people think
about achievement? Why shouldn't they make them think about love
or war?

There is quite a different explanation of the association of climate with
_n_ Achievement which ties in more closely to our other findings on the
intrinsic factors producing _n_ Achievement in children: Mother-child
households tend to occur more frequently in tropical regions. Using again
Murdock's world ethnographic sample, nine of the twenty-three cultures
living within 10° of the equator contain mother-child households (39 per
cent), whereas only five out of forty-four cultures living further away
from the equator (11 per cent) contain mother-child households. (Chi-

Appendices

Appendix I

How Peter Cut the Rye
(Russia, Third grade, 1929)

Mother had heated up the stove before it was light. She let out the cow and they all went into the field to cut rye. They stopped at the edge of the rye, but Father did not immediately unharness the horse. He took his scythe, tightened the blade, and began to cut rye from the furrows. Peter asked, "Why are you cutting, Father?"

"So that I can put the horse and the wagon in the enclosure."

"Well, let them stand at the edge of the rye. It's better there."

"They can't stand at the edge of the rye. People are going to ride by and they'll knock against the wagon."

Father spoke the truth. He had scarcely finished cutting and he was holding the horse when he looked and along this part of the edge of the rye came Bob's father with his family. Father untied the girth rope around the horse while Peter held the reins. Mother and Mary bound up the rye which had been cut in sheaves. Then, when they had gathered up everything, they all took to cutting and cut until mealtime. After the meal they went to sleep. Peter did not wish to sleep. He looked and there was Bob running along the edge of the rye towards him. He approached and asked quietly, "Do you know how to mow yourself?"

"No," he said, "and do you know?"

"Oh, what a thing to say! A long time ago I learned," said Bob.

Peter became sad because Bob had something to boast about. "Oh, you also don't know how. You're only talking."

"Well, come on. I'll show you."

They went to their wagon. He quietly took the scythe so that no one would hear him. "Well, come on to the other end of the field. If they hear what's going on they'll scold me." They went to another edge of rye.

"Here, now. Watch." Bob began to mow. It was quite true. He knew how. The rye fell nicely in rows and the rows were just as wide as Peter's father's.

"O.K. Give it to me. I'll try," said Peter. Bob wouldn't give the scythe to Peter. "Take your own. You'll break mine and you know what my father will give me then."

"Well, O.K. Come on with me. Then I'll show you that I can mow, too." At his own wagon Peter took his scythe. "It's nothing," he thought, "I'm not going to surrender to you, Bob, even though you are older than I am." They walked a little further. Bob tightened up the blade and straightened out the handle. "Now you cut."

Peter let the scythe swing . . . right into the ground. "Hold it higher towards the tip," Bob said to him. "Cut with the heel and let the tip swing."

Peter reached higher with the tip. The scythe swung to the rye but the rye remained standing in its place. "Take it in little bits, not all at once," said Bob. The sweat was pouring off Peter. He took it in little bits. The rye began to fall but it looked as if an elf had run and danced through the rows. "In better rows. In better rows," yelled Bob. "How is anyone going to bind it up after you? What are you messing things up like that for?"

"It's nothing," said Peter. "The rows are already going better." He cut a wider row. He cut low along the ground itself. "Look how it's going," he said to Bob. "Already I'm taking it almost as wide as my father does."

"Well, go ahead. Go ahead," said Bob. Peter swung with the scythe very wide. Suddenly the blade became tangled in the rye and the handle broke. Peter turned cold all over and at this point Father had just begun to wake up. He got up and he rubbed his eyes. He saw the boys and went to them.

"Oh, here's where we get it!" Peter was frightened. "He'll really give it to me for the handle!"

Father came up, looked the two of them over and saw the broken handle. "Who was clever enough to break the handle?" he said.

"I, Father," Peter answered.

"And who told you to?"

"I was learning to mow."

Father thought a moment and shook his head. "If I gave it to you about the ears, you'd be a sad little tyke around the house. Look, grow a little more and then I'll make you a set of light sized blades." Bob grinned and Peter's father said to him, "What are you laughing at? How many of your father's blades did you break while you were learning to mow?"

When Peter's father said this, Peter's heart became lighter. "Aha," he thought, "it is obvious that it doesn't come to one so easily."

They got a new stick and Father made another handle and again they began to cut the rye.

Don't Ever Owe a Man
[India (Telegu) 1954]

The world is an illusion. Wife, children, horses and cows are all just ties of fate. They are ephemeral. Each after fulfilling his part in life dis appears. So we should not clamour after riches which are not permanent As long as we live it is wise not to have any attachments and just think o

God. We have to spend our lives without trouble, for is it not true that there is no end to grievances? So it is better to live knowing the real state of affairs. Don't get entangled in the meshes of family life.

Just to learn that wife and children are ties of fate, listen to this story: There was once a certain man in a village. As soon as his wife gave birth to a child he took it to the graveyard and placed him in a hole there. After sprinkling some water on the child he asked the child, "Who are you? Why are you born to me?"

The child replied, "Sir, in my last life I used to live selling firewood. One day you purchased a load of it and did not pay me its worth in money. I am born to you so that I can get it." The man asked him, "How much do I owe you?" The child replied, "Two dollars." The man then asked, "Will you go away if I give you two dollars?" The child said, "Yes." As soon as he placed two dollars on the child it died.

Afterwards the man buried him and went home. He did the same for the next three or four children. His wife began to suspect that her husband was burying live children.

One day she asked her husband whether it was fair on his part to do so. Then the man said, "You give me the child this time. I will get it back to you." This time the man did the same thing to the child, as he did to the first one. It told him, "I was an oil monger in my previous life. You owe me money for one pint of castor oil."

The man asked, "Will you go away if I give you a pint of castor oil?" The child said, "Yes." Promising the child that he would give him the castor oil he carried him back to his wife. He gave his wife a pint of castor oil and told her that the child will live while the castor oil lasts. The wife started anointing the child with castor oil. When a small amount of oil was left the child became ill. The illness became worse and the mother, after losing hope that the child would live, took him to the verandah and started crying. The child was fighting for its life. Then the woman went to her husband and said to him, "I can't see him suffering so much. It looks as though it is better if he dies. The pint of oil is gone. Why is he still suffering?"

The man told her, "See whether something is still left in the pot. Clean it well with your hand and rub it on the child." After she did it the child died. From that day she did not oppose whatever her husband did. Again she gave birth to a child. When the man questioned the child, it replied, "Sir, in my last life I deceived you of a couple of thousand dollars. I have come to repay that amount." Then he carried the child back to his wife and said, "This is your son. Look after him carefully. Don't take anything, not even a betel leaf from him. As long as you do that he is your child. If you take anything you won't get him back." So she carried out his orders.

The child grew up and after learning all the arts began earning money. Still his parents never used to take a penny from him. One day after deciding to go to another town on some work, he dressed himself up and took a small bag in his hand and went to the front of his house to get on his horse.

The horse would not allow him to get up. Seeing his mother nearby he asked her, "Mother, hold this bag. After I get on the horse I will take it back." So saying, he gave his mother the bag. Before he could get on the horse, the horse kicked him with its hind legs. Immediately he died. The mother started crying. The father who had gone out returned and after hearing the story, asked his wife to open the bag and see what it contained.

There was exactly two thousand dollars in his bag. He consoled his wife, saying, "You killed your own son by not heeding my words. Why do you cry?"

The Fox Bigger Than an Ox
(French, Second grade, 1922)

The knight making a pilgrimage with his squire had just entered the foreign land. They had left early in the morning, and they hoped they would arrive in Littletown on Little River. On their way, they met a fox who was searching for adventure.

"Heavens!" the knight exclaimed, "this fox seems to be rather big."

"My lord, in the countries I have been riding through before I was in your service, I have seen some, by the faith I hope you have in me, the size of which was far bigger; one of them, as a matter of fact, was as big as an ox."

"It is wonderful fur for a skillful hunter," the knight answered.

Then they went on riding silently. However, after a few minutes, the knight broke the silence and said:

"O Lord! lead us not into the sinful temptation to lie, and give us strength to redeem our mistakes in order that we may cross the Little River without any danger."

"What is the use for this prayer?" the squire asked, surprised.

"Don't you know that all those who have lied during the day, drown in Little River—which we have to cross—unless they recognize their sin?"

They arrived at Small River.

"Is this the famous river in which the liars perish, My lord?"

"No, no, we are far from it."

"Speaking of the fox I was telling you about before, My lord, I've just remembered that he was not bigger than a calf."

"I don't care about your fox."

They went on riding.

"My lord," the squire asked, "what is this water, down there in front of us which we have to cross? Is that Little River?"

"No, no, we will not see it before tonight."

"Anyway, I remember now; that fox was not bigger than a sheep."

As the shade of the mountains grew bigger and bigger, the knight hurried his horse. He perceived Littletown from the distance.

"We will arrive at Little River soon," he exclaimed, "it is the end of our journey for today."

"Little River, Little River," the poor squire whispered quivering from fright. "Ah! My lord, in the name of God I can assure you . . ."

"What do you assure me?"

"That fox we met this morning . . ."

"So what?"

"Well! the one I saw before I was your faithful squire was at least half as big."

"Coward!" the knight answered, "you should learn that the waters of Little River have never drowned the liars, any more than its waters have seen foxes bigger than oxen!"

The Coal Miner and the Gentleman
(Chile, Third grade, 1921)

Peter is very conceited because his father, a very serious, tall gentleman with a black beard, is a great lord of an estate.

Yesterday morning, Peter fought with Bob, one of the smallest boys, the son of a coal miner, and, not knowing what to say to him, because he had no argument, he shouted, "Your father is a shabby man."

Bob blushed and said nothing, but the tears came to his eyes. He told his father what had happened when he got home, and the coal miner, a small black man, arrived in the afternoon with the boy by the hand to lay his complaint before the teacher. Because we were all very quiet when they were talking, the father of Peter, who, as was his custom, was taking off his son's coat, heard his name mentioned and went in to ask for an explanation.

The teacher answered, "This man has come to complain that Peter, your son, has said to his boy, 'Your father is a shabby man.' "

Peter's father wrinkled his forehead and became a little pale. Afterwards he asked his son, "Did you say these words?"

The boy, standing in the middle of the classroom, with his head hanging, before the small Bob, didn't answer. Then the father grasped his arm and made him go forward in front of Bob, so far that they were almost touching, and he said to him, "Ask his forgiveness."

The coal miner tried to interrupt saying, "No, no," but the gentleman would not have it, and he again said to his son, "Ask his forgiveness. Repeat my words, 'I ask your pardon for the stupid, harmful and ignoble words that I said against your father, with whom my father would be very honored to shake hands.' "

Bob's father made a gesture as if determined to say, "I don't want him to."

The gentleman wouldn't have it and his son repeated slowly, "Forgive me for the stupid, harmful . . . and ignoble words that I said against your father, with whom . . . my father . . . would be very honored to shake hands."

Then the gentleman gave his hand to the coal miner who shook it firmly and afterwards, with a sudden shove, threw his boy into the arms of Peter.

"Do me the favor of putting them next to one another," the gentleman said to the teacher.

The teacher put Bob at Peter's bench. When they were together in their places, Peter's father waved, and left.

The coal miner remained, very pensive, looking at the two boys reunited. Afterwards, he went up to the bench and looked at Peter with an expression of love and gratitude, as if he wanted to say something . . . but he said nothing. He stretched out his hand to caress him; not daring to do this either, he satisfied himself by touching his forehead with two rough fingers. At once he went toward the door and turning once more to look back, disappeared.

"Let us remember well what we have seen," said the teacher. "This is the best lesson of the year."

A Little Tree
(Belgium, Fourth grade, 1954)

Once there was in the forest a little tree covered with pointed leaves. "Ah," it said to itself one day, "my neighbors are happy. They have leaves which are pleasing to see. Mine are like needles. Nobody dares approach me. I'd like to have leaves of gold!"

Night came; the little tree dozed, and the next morning, it was transformed! "What joy," it cried, "I'm covered with gold! Not another tree in the forest has a similar garb."

But towards evening a man came up. He threw a fearful look around him, and seeing that nobody was watching him, took off the golden leaves, put them in a sack and fled.

"Oh," said the little tree, "I miss those lovely leaves which glistened in the sunlight. But leaves of glass could be as brilliant. I'd like to have leaves of glass."

That evening it slept, and the next morning it was again transformed. From all its branches hung leaves of glass. "Ah," it said, "this is a pretty attire. My neighbors have nothing like it."

But some black clouds gathered in the sky, the wind rose, the storm burst, and all the glass leaves were broken.

"Alas," sighed the vain little tree, "this foliage that I was ambitious for is very elegant, but very fragile. It would be better to have a garb of good green leaves, fragrant ones."

The little tree slept that night, and the next morning it was dressed as it had wished. But the scent of its fresh leaves attracted the goats, who came to nibble them, and standing up on their hind paws, they nibbled all the way to the top of the little tree and left it entirely bare.

Then, when it went to sleep that night, it longed for its original leaves, and the next morning rejoiced to see them reappear on its branches. They had neither the splendor of gold, nor the luminous transparency of glass, nor the attraction of aromatic plants; but they were solid, nobody came to take them off and the tree kept them throughout all the seasons.

A Strange Salary
(Turkey, Fourth grade, 1954; used since 1943)

1. One day a young man came to the director of a large commercial firm and asked for a job. The director liked the young man's manners and speech. Around those days they needed a person in bookkeeping. Perhaps he could be useful in something. But one had to test him and to observe his knowledge and work closely.

2. The director said to the young man, "All right, I want to give you a job, but first I must put you on a training program. Work with us for a month. If we are satisfied, we shall take you with a regular salary. Of course, you will receive a certain sum for this experimental period. Go and see the bursar, please."

3. The young man left the room.

4. A little later the bursar came to the director. He said, "I've spoken with the young man you sent me."

"How did you find him?"

"He seems like a nice person, but the salary he asked for is very strange."

"How?"

"I offered him a hundred dollars for the experimental month. He did not accept. He said, 'I do not want a flat salary. I must earn my daily pay.' Look at the salary he demands, one cent for the first day."

"What, one cent?"

"Yes, one cent. If we are satisfied, two cents for the second day, four for the third, eight for the fourth. In short, for every day he works well, he wants to be paid twice the amount that he received for the previous day."

The director looked at the bursar in amazement. "How strange! What can he get at the end of the month with this one, two, four cents?"

The bursar shrugged and answered, "Why should we care? As long as he wants it this way."

"All right. If he desires so, let it be so. Let him start tomorrow."

5. The young man was really worthy and conscientious. He worked like

a clock, did all his work with immaculate neatness, and finished everything quickly. He pleased everybody in the bureau by his every act.

6. The month came to an end.

7. The young man went to the bursar and asked for his salary. The bursar raised his head unworriedly. "I have not calculated it yet. Would you please figure it out and bring it to me?"

The young man had already figured it out. He pulled a piece of paper out of his pocket and handed it to the bursar.

The bursar started to read. "According to the conditions agreed upon; namely, one cent for the first day, after that the daily wage being obtained by doubling the amount for the previous day, the sum for the 30-day experimental period is $10,737,418.23."

The bursar's eyes nearly jumped out of their sockets, he looked at the figures carefully again, he paused for a while; then collecting himself, he fixed his gaze on the young man and said loudly, "You seem to have lost your mind!"

"Why? The calculation is obvious. If you want to, please check it over."

8. There wasn't the slightest mistake in the calculations. This was the exact amount the young man had to be paid. The bursar was dumbfounded.

When they went to see the director, the bursar was in no condition to speak. His mouth was dry and his tongue was twisted. He uttered a few incomprehensible words and handed the piece of paper to the director. He too was utterly dombfounded when he read the paper. He gulped a few times, looked at the bursar with knotted eyebrows; but he could not say a word. Even all the capital of the company was not enough to pay this debt.

There was deep silence in the room.

When the young man, who until then had been calmly watching the pitiful condition of the two men, saw that they were unable to speak, he said with a sweet smile on his lips, "When I asked for this salary, I knew perfectly well what it would amount to at the end of the month. I also knew that there wasn't the slightest chance of your being able to pay all this money. My purpose was to show you how attentive I am in financial matters, especially in those that involve long calculations."

The contract was signed that day. The young man joined the company with a fat salary.

Appendix II

MOTIVATION SCORES BASED ON 21 STORIES FROM CHILDREN'S READERS IN VARIOUS COUNTRIES IN 1925

Country	n Achievement		n Affiliation		n Power		Other-directedness Rank[11]
	Mean	Standard score[1]	Mean	Standard score[2]	Mean	Standard score[3]	
Argentina	1.86	.47	1.43	.21	.43	−1.33	21
Australia	2.81	1.77	1.76	−.09	1.24	.39	7
Austria	1.57	.07	1.19	−.30	1.24	1.37	16
Belgium	1.00	−.71	1.57	.51	.76	−.59	22
Brazil[4]	(.29)	(−1.68)	(.95)	(−.81)	(.76)	(−.59)	—
Canada	2.67	1.58	2.38	1.00	1.10	.10	4.5
Chile	1.29	−.32	.86	−.94	1.43	2.00	17
Denmark	2.00	.66	2.19	.67	1.67	1.27	3
England	2.10	.79	2.38	1.00	1.10	.10	1
Finland	1.24	−.38	1.00	−.70	1.29	1.53	2
France	.81	−.97	1.43	.21	1.71	1.35	11
Germany	1.38	−.19	1.57	−.42	1.29	.49	13
Greece	.38	−1.56	2.81	1.75	.71	−.69	14.5
Hungary	1.29	−.32	.86	−1.67	1.48	.88	4.5
Ireland	3.19	2.29	1.95	.25	1.29	.49	14.5
Japan[5]	(1.77)	(.34)	(.77)	(−2.00)	(1.30)	(.50)	—
Netherlands	.29	−1.68	2.14	.58	.38	−1.37	19
New Zealand	1.48	−.06	1.90	.16	.57	−1.60	9
Norway	1.33	−.26	.57	−1.62	.76	−.23	20
Spain	.81	−.97	1.05	−1.33	1.57	1.06	12
Sweden	2.19	.92	1.14	−.40	.57	−.87	23
Union S. Africa[6]	1.05	−.64	1.81	1.02	.57	−.98	6
USSR	.95	−.78	1.00	−1.42	1.62	1.16	10
United States	1.90	.52	2.33	.91	.86	−.39	8
Uruguay	1.48	−.06	.86	−1.00	.81	−.07	18
Mean	1.52						
SD	.73						

MOTIVATION SCORES BASED ON 21 STORIES FROM CHILDREN'S READERS IN VARIOUS COUNTRIES IN 1950

Algeria[7]	.57	−1.91	2.29	2.04	.90	−.31	3
Argentina	3.38	1.84	1.29	−.09	.95	.40	34.5
Australia	2.38	.51	1.24	−.19	.52	−1.03	4
Austria	1.86	−.19	1.14	−1.18	.43	−1.27	31.5
Belgium	.43	−2.09	1.52	.40	.95	.40	21
Brazil[4]	(1.14)	(−1.15)	(.14)	(−2.53)	(.86)	(.10)	—
Bulgaria	2.24	.32	1.24	−.19	1.05	.00	15
Canada (English Catholic)	2.29	.39	2.19	.67	1.24	.39	25.5
(English Catholic)	4.19	2.92	1.95	.25	.90	−.31	—
(French Catholic)	2.00	.00	1.81	.00	.43	−1.27	—

461

MOTIVATION SCORES BASED ON 21 STORIES FROM CHILDREN'S READERS IN VARIOUS
COUNTRIES IN 1950—*Continued*

Country	n Achievement		n Affiliation		n Power		Other-direc-tedness Rank[11]
	Mean	Standard score[1]	Mean	Standard score[2]	Mean	Standard score[3]	
Chile	1.19	−1.08	2.19	1.83	.76	−.23	14
Denmark	1.05	−1.27	1.76	−.09	.86	.10	28
England	1.67	−.44	2.54	1.28	1.10	.10	1
Finland	1.52	−.64	1.71	.81	1.05	.73	12
France	2.38	.51	1.19	−.30	.48	−1.16	29
Germany	2.14	.19	1.29	−.91	1.33	.57	17
Greece	2.29	.39	2.14	.58	.81	−.51	19
Hungary	1.81	−.25	1.24	−.19	.48	−1.17	30
India[8]	2.71	.95	1.24	−.19	1.24	.39	13
Iraq	1.95	−.07	.57	−1.62	2.71	3.39	9
Iran[9]	1.19	−1.08	.19	−2.43	.90	.23	—
Ireland	2.29	.39	1.38	−.75	.90	−.31	11
Israel	2.33	.44	2.90	1.91	.19	−1.76	18
Italy	1.33	−.89	2.00	1.43	.95	.40	33
Japan	1.29	−.95	2.19	.67	.95	−.20	6
Lebanon	2.71	.95	2.10	.51	1.24	.39	36
Mexico	1.57	−.57	1.62	.62	1.19	1.20	23
Netherlands	1.48	−.69	2.19	.67	.71	−.69	39
New Zealand	2.05	.07	1.33	−.84	1.90	1.73	16
Norway	1.71	−.39	1.95	.25	.57	−1.60	38
Pakistan[10]	2.29	.39	1.24	−1.00	−1.33	.57	7
Poland	.86	−1.52	1.43	.21	.48	−1.17	34.5
Portugal	2.10	.13	1.67	.72	.48	−1.17	31.5
Spain	2.33	.44	.62	−1.51	1.86	1.65	2
Sweden	1.62	−.51	1.48	.32	.76	−.23	37
Switzerland							
French	1.71	−.39	1.52	−.51	.52	−1.08	—
German	.95	−1.40	1.05	−.60	1.62	1.16	24
Syria	2.10	.13	1.43	.21	.57	−.87	27
Tunisia[7]	2.14	.19	1.95	1.32	.57	−.98	25.5
Turkey	3.62	2.16	.90	−1.60	.62	−.88	8
Union S. Africa[6]	2.33	.44	1.57	−.42	.86	.10	20
USSR	2.10	.13	1.29	−.91	1.19	.29	22
United States	2.24	.32	2.05	.42	1.38	.29	5
(Catholic)	3.62	2.16	2.33	.91	.90	−.31	—
Uruguay	1.86	−.19	1.57	.51	.81	−.07	10
Mean	2.00						
SD	.75						

[1] Standard scores obtained separately for 1925 and 1950 periods and based on means and *SD*'s for those periods respectively. In the text the mean and *SD* used for the 1950 period is based only on *country* samples (combining the two Swiss samples and omitting the Catholic reader samples in the U.S. and Canada).

[2] Standard scores obtained separately for longer and shorter sets of stories. For stories in a sample above average in length, i.e., 35 lines in length or more, the mean *n* Affiliation score = 1.81,

$SD = .57$. For stories in a sample averaging 34 lines in length or less, the mean n Affiliation score $= 1.33$, $SD = .47$.

[3] Standard scores obtained separately for longer and shorter sets of stories. For stories in a sample averaging 29 lines in length or more, the mean n Power score $= 1.05$, $SD = .49$. For stories in a sample averaging 28 lines in length or less, the mean n Power score $= .83$, $SD = .30$. The break was not made in the middle of the distribution because the correlation of n Power score with length of the stories was confined to the lower third of the distribution.

[4] Not used in the main study; scored separately and open to coding bias.

[5] Based on 13 stories only; not used in the main study.

[6] English readers only.

[7] French readers.

[8] Six Hindi, 7 Telegu, and 8 Tamil stories.

[9] Stories probably too short to provide a valid estimate.

[10] Twelve Urdu and 11 Bengali stories.

[11] Obtained by summing the ranks (for 1925 and 1950 separately) for percentages of stories in a country showing (1) *absence* of institutional pressure, (2) presence of peer interaction pressure, (3) instances in which simple requests or demands are successful in initiating interaction. (See Chapter 5.)

Appendix III

Values Coding System for Children's Stories

In Part One of the system the scorer identifies with Ego. Ego is defined as any character who participates in a major sequence of interaction, involving at least one third of a story. By Ego we mean a person or an animal acting as if he were human (i.e. in a humanlike way). Each character in a story who meets these requirements is to be scored separately in part one of the scoring system. The most important character is scored first.

I. The self orientation (individualistic achievement value complex): take the point of view of the Ego.

    A. STATUS OF EGO. Ego must be classified as either a superior, inferior, or as a peer.

        1. By SUPERIOR we mean any individual who is in a position of authority or superiority relative to others around him. Age, size, social status, or strength are the characteristics which mark off a superior individual.

        Examples:

        King Lion called a council of the jungle animals to see whether they could discover what the great creature was that flew over the jungle a few days before.

        Father tells Peter that if he thinks a dog's life is better than that of a human he ought to try it.

        2. By INFERIOR we mean any individual who is in a position of lesser age, size, social status or strength with regard to others interacting with him.

        Examples:

        A lion cub who is told that man is intelligent while he is only a beast, investigates and finds that it is true, much to his sorrow.

        The loyal little mouse frees king lion.

        3. PEER is to be used under two conditions: the first of these is when Ego's position is not explicitly superior or inferior or when he is both. He must be classified then as a peer. The second meaning of *peer* is when Ego is "one among equals." Here we mean someone of the same age, size, social status, strength, etc.

        Examples:

        Of all the students in the contest, Peter brings in the brightest gift and wins the prize.

Jimmy and Judy didn't know the strokes well enough, and Johnny didn't know how to swim at all. One day Bob put up a pole with a sack attached to it, and Peter and he were sailing.

B. INFLUENCES ON EGO. Ego can be acted upon by a major press of the external world, as classified into four categories or sources of intervention: *fate, nature, man, magic.* The implication is normally that Ego is passively pushed into action by these forces.

1. FATE intervenes. Ego is acted upon by destiny, it is his appointed lot that such and such shall happen or did happen in the past; the thing was preordained.

Example:

The wolf was going to eat the lamb because the lamb called him names a year ago. The lamb protests that she wasn't born a year ago, but the wolf replies that while it may have been someone else, he will eat her all the same. (It's too bad for the lamb, *c'est la vie.*)

2. NATURE intervenes. By this we mean that Ego is acted upon by nature, the world around him or a natural event.

Example:

Peter was on the way to his grandmother's house when the river flooded the road and washed out the bridge, so that he could go no farther.

3. MAN intervenes (or an animal with human characteristics). Here the Ego is acted upon by some other actor, who initiates the action sequence. That is, Ego is "just there," when a second party appears and does something to Ego which has consequences for him.

Example:

The tortoise is carried home by Mr. Fox, for his dinner. Mr. Rabbit follows them and rescues the tortoise from the clutches of the villainous fox.

4. MAGICAL POWERS intervene. Ego is acted on, and is either benefited by or victimized by magic which may be manipulated by another actor in the story.

Example:

Peter-Never-Mind-the-Weather is casually delivering some eggs when a playful fairy tests Peter by making rain fall in the form of cats, dogs, pitchforks, etc.

C. RESPONSE OF EGO. This category is scored only when the Ego is active. Ego can employ any of the following means to reach his goal, whatever it may be. The means is the instrumental activity involved in the action sequence, and all those which occur in the story may be scored.

1. BRAINS—using deceit. This category is scored when Ego uses his brains to deceive another actor, in order to reach his goal. Cleverness, trickery, outwittery, and cunning may be employed.

Example:

The fox flatters the crow into singing, so that she drops the cheese which he eats.

2. BRAINS—no deceit. This category is scored when Ego uses his brains, but with no intent to deceive, in order to reach his goal.

3. BRAWN. Ego can attain his goal either (A) by his external strength and force, i.e., the "big club" or (B) by virtue of his inherent characteristics, i.e., his *native* strength and force.

Examples:

A. The rabbit hit the fox over the head with a cabbage to free his friend the tortoise.
B. The lion rules because he is big and powerful, the acknowledged king of the jungle.

4. HARD WORK. This category is scored when Ego is involved in definite labors, employed for the purpose of reaching his goal. The work may consist of a single supreme effort, or it may be work over either a long or short period of time.

Examples:

Peter was lying in bed and saw something moving in the corner of his room. After gathering up his courage "with a jump he was out of bed, ran across the room, and reached with both his hands into the dark shadow which was still moving back and forth." This is an example of a single supreme effort.

The mother who rescues her baby from an eagle's nest at the top of a mountain in a tremendous burst of energy and willpower is an example of short hard work.

5. MAGIC. Ego invokes magical means to achieve his goal, in the form of spirits, prayer, fantasy, sorcery, and magical manipulations.

Examples:

The good fairy wishes to teach all the children at court a moral lesson. Holding up the horn, he cried, "No boy who has ever been unkind can blow this horn."

An example of fantasy is Mary and Jane at a tea party with their dolls. "Well," says Jane, "this is astonishing! Where do you get your chickens, Madame? In my country they have only two wings." "I buy them in a small town, one hundred miles beyond the moon."

6. OTHER. This category is to be scored when the scorer cannot specify the means in terms of any of the above categories, but yet finds that Ego is doing something instrumental to aid him in reaching a goal.

Example:

Mary is looking at the bunches of flowers. She counts her pennies and buys a bouquet. (Obviously Mary is doing something instrumental but it doesn't fall under the above categories).

D. MOTIVES IN EGO; BIOLOGICAL—OTHER. By this category we mean that Ego undertakes a given activity to attain specific biological goals (food, sex, shelter, water, heat, fuel, and clothing in the sense of protection.) The biological category is scored only when Ego is seeking these supplies as an aid to his basic maintenance in the world—the preservation of his life. If there is any luxury or surplus meaning attached to the items, then the action must be scored as other. Thus by "other" we mean any goal-oriented behavior not falling into the specific biological category.

Examples:

When there was no more porridge in the pot the little old lady set out to search the woods for berries. (biological)

When the maid ran out of caviar, Mrs. Cabot (and/or Lodge, Lowell, etc.) called S. S. Pierce for another barrel. (other)

E. THE OBJECT OF ACTION. In the pursuit of a goal, Ego may either attempt to arouse motive states in, or generally employ the assistance of, another individual. Or he may act on nature.

1. ACTS ON PEOPLE—Ego is active and other people are involved in Ego's sequence of action toward the goal.

Example:

The two Littletownians want to make a business profit and they cheat each other to get it.

2. ACTS ON NATURE—Ego is active but no other person is involved—only nature or the natural world.

Example:

"The children practiced rowing. . . . Mary cut up tiny paper-dolls and placed them in her boat. . . . meanwhile Jimmy loaded wooden pegs on a boat, pretending that he sailed to town with wool."

F. IMPULSE CONTROL: + or −. The meaning of this category is the Ego is inhibiting the desire for self-indulgence as an end in itself, or as anti-social behavior. This suppression has either positive or negative consequences for him in terms of the outcome of the interaction sequence.

Example:

While Peter is lying in bed, he is frightened by shadows in the corner of the room. He decides to investigate himself, rather than calling his mother, who has a headache and should not be disturbed. Peter conquers the situation himself and is glad that he did not call his mother. Thus the situation has positive consequences for him.

This category of impulse control + is exemplified by the Christian ideology of turning the other cheek where the rewards for not expressing hostile impulses are great in the long range view.

Example:

Impulse control −. The good hearted straw takes pity on the ember and swims back to ferry him across the river. In the process, the straw catches fire and the ember drowns. In this case, inhibition of the impulse to let the ember get across on his own steam results in negative consequences for Ego.

G. IMPULSE EXPRESSION: + or −. The meaning of this category is that Ego is expressing impulses aimed at self-indulgence and gratification (egocentric) either in direct rejection of the feelings of others or in indirect neglect of the feelings of others. This expression has either positive or negative consequences for him in terms of the outcome of the interaction sequence (pride-before-a-fall, selfishness are also scored).

Example:

Impulse expression +. In the sory of the mistletoe, the bad fairy dislikes the good fairy and wants to do him in. He manages this by getting a blind fairy to throw a harmful piece of mistletoe at the good fairy. The good fairy falls dead while the bad fairy gets away with his hostile purposes. Here then, impulse expression had positive results in terms of the goals of the bad fairy.

Example:

Impulse expression −. "As they reached the middle of the water, the good hearted straw caught flame and the ember drowned. When the bladder saw that, he laughed so hard he burst. It served him right. Why was he so malicious?"

H. ACHIEVED STATUS: The meaning here is to change one's rank in the social order, relative to other persons, or to gain recognition, by accomplishing some end, i.e., by doing something. The individual is evaluated in terms of his accomplishments or achievements, rather than in terms of his fixed characteristics, given by birth.

Example:

"The sheep, in contrast to the goats, are blessed of God and know neither hunger nor cold, because they sheltered the Saint when he was in trouble and the goats did not."

I. ASCRIBED STATUS: This category implies that the individual is evaluated by fixed characteristics which are given by birth, rather than in terms of his accomplishments.

Examples:

"Then they were sure that she was a real princess, since through twenty mattresses and twenty feather beds she had been able to tell the pea. Only a princess could be so sensitive. Then the prince married her for now he knew that he had a real princess."

"Be careful when you see man, for he is intelligent and we are only beasts."

NOTE: To avoid giving extra credit to cultures that use more descriptive adjectives, each of these last two categories will be scored only once per story.

J. VIEW OF NATURE + or −. Scoring this category must be done in terms of the story as a whole, i.e., it is done only once per story. The classification defines the over-all view that the culture takes of nature. Nature can be perceived as either dangerous or threatening (−) or as in harmony with man, to be conquered, used for recreation and treated as safe (+).

Examples:

(−) Peter went walking. When he had walked a bit more he lost his way and came into a bog, where he began to sink down into the mud. Now he cried for help. "But where did you go?" cried the moon. "Give me light," cried Peter, "I'm lying deep in the bog."

(+) The sun was shining nearly every day, and every day Daddy bathed together with the children and taught them how to swim. (recreation)

K. TOTAL OUTCOME + or −. This category is to be scored for each interaction sequence, in terms of positive or negative consequences for Ego. If the goal is attained, a + score is given; if the action is unsuccessful, it is scored negatively (−).

Examples:

(+) Mr. Rabbit's goal is to free his friend the tortoise from the hungry fox. He distracts the fox and releases the tortoise, who gets away safely. Thus the goal is achieved.

(−) The young lion sets out to find his traditional enemy, man, and fight against him. He is trapped, however, and his two front legs are broken. Thus the total outcome of the interaction sequence is negative because he is thwarted in attaining his goal.

II. The OTHER-ORIENTATION (interaction value complex). Take the point of view of the "other" (another person, society). The task is to induce cooperation, conformity, etc.

L. SOURCE OF PRESSURE: This category defines the type of agent that acts on Ego to conform to society or the group, and specifies the general nature of the pressure in terms of whether it is interpersonal or impersonal.

1. *Impersonal pressure*—The source of pressure to get the person to conform, cooperate, or go along with others is impersonal. That is, a particular other person is not the source of, or reason for, the cooperative act. Instead, pressure comes from any of five sources: the material world, institutional world, moral world, magic world, or material-moral world.

(a) The MATERIAL WORLD as the source of pressure: The material world refers to the natural world, the forces of nature in man's external environment. These forces serve to coerce man into conforming to the standards of the group.

Example:

In Holland the members of the community must work together in a cooperative effort to construct dykes. A failure to do so would result in floods and destruction. The sea serves as a source of pressure.

(b) The INSTITUTIONAL WORLD is a source of pressure. The meaning of the institutional world is that of a force for conformity which is highly generalized, superindividual, persistent over time, and supplying to the actor a set of rules for his behavior. The following are to be considered institutions in this classification:

> The Church (religious)
> The State (political)

The State (economic)
The State (legal)
Private Enterprise and Business (economic)
The Educational System (intellectual)
The Family (social and emotional)

NOTE: the( ) indicate sphere of activity.

All of the above supply Ego with guideposts for action and conformity. The pressure may come from an individual acting in an institutional role i.e. the butcher, the priest, the policeman, but not from any one specific individual acting toward Ego in terms of his unique personality or relationship with him.

(c) The MORAL WORLD as a source of pressure. In this case the force for conformity is supplied by the moral order as a part of man's external environment. The moral order can be defined as a code of behavior, widely accepted by the members of the society, which differentiates "right" from "wrong" action, and is not tied to any one, specific institution.

Example:

The Ten Commandments when no particular religion or God supplies the context.

(d) MAGIC as a source of pressure. In this instance supernatural forces come into play, to force the individual to conform to the society. In the course of influencing events, fairies, devils, angels, etc. may be involved but there can be no reference to personal spirits.

Example:

The emphasis is on conforming to a standard of honesty.—A carpenter drops his axe into the river and is rewarded for telling the water elf the truth about the material composition of his axe. For this he is given a golden axe to replace the wooden one he dropped into the pond. Another carpenter, greedy and dishonest, sets out to deceive the water elf, and loses his own hatchet as well as failing to obtain a golden one. Thus dishonesty is punished by magical means while honesty is rewarded.

(e) The MATERIAL-MORAL world. The meaning of this concept is that the material world serves to reinforce the code of right and wrong conduct as defined by the moral order of the society. Thus any deviations from the moral order will be punished by the natural forces of the external environment.

Example:

Peter knows that it is wrong to steal, yet he takes his neighbor's horse. The next week on the way to the city he is hit by a bolt of lightning.

2. *Interpersonal pressure*—the source of pressure to get the person to conform, cooperate, or go along with others is interpersonal. That is, a particular person or group is the source of or reason for the cooperative act. It can be either individuated or nonindividuated.

(a) NON-INDIVIDUATED: Two people act together, or a group plays together, etc. where there is no explicit evidence that pressures are being exerted on members to conform. In addition, no motives are stated.

Example:

Two people are building a snowman.

(b) INDIVIDUATED: In this case pressure to conform is being exerted by some specific other person. In addition, Ego's role in the social system may in itself supply the pressure to conform. This situation applies only when the role behavior *cannot* be referred to any of the institutions enumerated under L, 1, (b). In the case of pressure supplied by another individual, that individual should be classified as a superior, peer, or inferior. If the discrimination is not possible, the individual should be classified as a peer. (Cf. Part I, A: 1, 2, 3.)

Example:

(Superior)—A small boy is punished by a man much older than himself, because the boy has been cruel to a dog.

(Peer)—In the story of the Jellyfish and the Monkey, the King of the Sea attempts to lure the Jellyfish into his court; "He bids me greet you as his brother and entreats that you will mount upon my back."

(Inferior)—The story of the Mouse and the Cat: The mouse promises to free the cat from the trap in which he was caught, provided that the cat promises never again to harm the mouse and his brothers.

M. MEANS OF PRESSURE: The means or type of pressure to get Ego to cooperate is to be differentiated from the source of that pressure. "Source" specifies the *where* of pressure while "means" or "type" specifies the *how* of pressure.

1. NONE—The person is to cooperate and there is no evidence of a means of pressure.

2. MEANS OF PRESSURE: The means of getting Ego to cooperate involves the application of pressure to conform, and this means of pressure can be divided into five categories:

(a) love
(b) rejection
(c) asks
(d) demands
(e) physical reward and punishment

(a) LOVE: The person cooperates because someone promises love. No hint of rejection can be present, i.e. a threat of loss of love.

Example:

"Help my father beat the barbarians," said the maiden to the knight, "and I will love you forever."

NOTE: *Love* is scored + if the technique is successful and − if it is unsuccessful.

(b) REJECTION: The person cooperates because someone threatens loss of love for not cooperating.

It is important to make the distinction between (a) and (b) when scoring, because the (b) category attempts to tap the dimension of conditional love.

Example:

Peter's parents want him to come home to dinner on time so he can help around the farm, and "if you don't do it we won't love you."

NOTE: *Rejection* is scored + if the technique is successful and − if it is unsuccessful.

(c) ASKS: Someone asks Ego for help, cooperation, or information.

Example:

(Information)—"Where are you going, friend Straw?" asked the Burning Ember. "We are going into the world." "Well let's go together."
(Cooperation or help)—The king needs the heart of a monkey and so he sends the jellyfish to trick the monkey into coming with him to the king's court: "I come to you from the King of the Sea, he bids me greet you as a brother and entreats you to mount my back."

NOTE: *asks* is to be scored + if the technique is successful and − if it is unsuccessful.

(d) DEMANDS: Social pressure is applied to Ego to get him to conform. It may be in the form of demanding, teasing, or shaming.

Example:

"The King of the Sea called to his nearest attendant, who happened to be a jellyfish. The King ordered him to swim at once to the shore and return with a monkey on his back."

NOTE: *demands* is to be scored + if the technique is successful and − if it is unsuccessful.

(e) PHYSICAL REWARDS OR PUNISHMENT: Physical reward means that Ego, by cooperating or conforming, obtains gratification in the form of some kind of specific material or physical benefits. Physical punishment means that, provided that Ego does not cooperate or conform, he subjects himself to material or physical deprivation. In these instances, some specific other person is manipulating the system of rewards and punishments.

Example:

(Reward) "This angel," said the teacher, "is too lovely to be given to any child who is not good and pure of heart." "He who brings me tomorrow the brightest thing on earth shall have the angel for his own."

NOTE: *physical reward* is to be scored + if the technique is successful and − if it is unsuccessful.

Example:

(Punishment)—The lion commands the tiger to divide the spoils of the day's hunt: "Tiger I command, Obey!" The tiger had thought that he had made good shares and he looked at the lion for his approval. The lion raised his paw which was armed with mighty claws and hit the tiger. The tiger fell to the ground shouting with a broken leg. The lion cried, "You do not know how to share."

NOTE: *physical punishment* is to be scored + if the technique is successful and − if it is unsuccessful.

N. MOTIVES FOR COOPERATING: This category is scored when there is some evidence that ego's motives are playing a role in engaging his cooperation. Ego's motivation may be any of five kinds:

> (a) self-interest (X) or (?)
> (b) self-esteem (X) or (?)
> (c) love (X) or (?)
> (d) helping the helpless (X) or (?)
> (e) getting work done (X) or (?)

If there is an explicit statement of Ego's motivation, the category is scored (X) . . . for explicit. But if any inferences are made about the existence of Ego's motivation, then the category is scored (?). Inference here does not mean a high level clinical judgment; rather, the sense is that of a low level guess. For instance, if the story stated that Mary gave her cloak to the poor shivering beggar and nothing more is said, one would score 'Help the Helpless' (?) because while one might think that this motive is at the root of the cooperative act, there is no explicit statement of same. However, if the story stated that Mary gave her cloak to the poor shivering beggar because she felt sorry for him and wanted to help him, the (X) would be scored since there is an explicit statement of the motive.

(a) SELF-INTEREST: The person is to cooperate out of hope of pleasure or fear of pain. The concern here is with self-gratification and indulgence.

Example:

(Self-interest)—Two Littletownians heard that much could be gained by trade and exchange. They decided to cooperate and exchange their houses, each thinking that he would get a "better deal," and outwit the other. (X)

SELF-ESTEEM: The person is to cooperate out of hope of gaining self-respect or fear of failure.

Example:

(Fear of loss of self-esteem)—Peter-Never-Mind-the-Weather had a reputation for being oblivious to weather conditions. He could go out in rain, shine, sleet, or snow. His mother asked him to get some eggs from a neighbor's farm, but changed her mind because it looked like it might rain. Peter went out anyway because he had a reputation to uphold. (?)

(c) LOVE: As in the M scoring category, the person cooperates out of the hope of gaining love or fear of loss of love. However, here there is no external agent responsible for manipulating the variable. The means —the "why" of cooperation is supplied by pressure from within Ego.

Examples:

(Cooperation out of love)—"With pity the sheep made a compact group and among them the Saint could not be seen." (X)

"The eagle has carried off Mary's baby . . . but who is able to scale that dizzy cliff? Mary darted forward and began to make her way up the steep face of the mountain." (?)

Example:

(Cooperation out of fear of loss of love)—Mother could never love a little boy who didn't wash his hands. (X)

(d) HELP THE HELPLESS: This notion most closely corresponds to altruistic charity.

Example:

Mary takes pity on the poor beggar at the side of the road and gives him her cloak. (X)

(e) GETTING WORK DONE: A task is to be completed, a chore accomplished, etc.

Example:

Each day at the beach the children work together to get the boats built so that they can sail out to fish. (X)

O. OUTCOME OF THE STORY: This category is scored either + or −. A plus score indicates that the goal of the cooperative behavior has been successfully attained. A minus score indicates that the goal has not been achieved.

Examples:

(Positive outcome)—By giving the cloak to the beggar, Mary successfully helps the helpless.

(Negative outcome)—The young lion disobeys by not heeding his mother and seeking out man—thus he is punished. Disobedience is not rewarded but has a negative outcome.

Appendix IV

Comparative Validity of Verbal and Graphic Measures of n Achievement in Four Countries

As recorded in Chapter 8, a serious difficulty arose in the research on *n* Achievement correlates among adolescent boys in four countries when it was discovered that the *n* Achievement scores based on fantasy did not correlate appreciably in any of the countries with the graphic expression characteristics repeatedly found by Aronson (1958) to correlate with verbal *n* Achievement in the United States. How was the result to be interpreted? The simplest hypothesis is that Aronson's relationships were either a rare chance occurrence or obtainable only in U.S. college males— i.e., boys with high *n* Achievement do not express themselves graphically the same way abroad.

But there is another possibility—the relationships may not have been obtained abroad because testing conditions for one or the other or both of the two measures may not have been comparable to those in the United States. It needs investigation because studies in the United States have shown that at least the verbal measure of *n* Achievement is easily influenced by situational pressures. If the stories are obtained under achievement-oriented conditions, the *n* Achievement scores are no longer valid measures of individual differences in *n* Achievement in the sense that they now no longer correlate with other behaviors of the individuals (McClelland *et al.*, 1953). Similarly, the graphic expression test may be influenced by the conditions surrounding its administration in ways not as yet investigated.

First, attention was turned to coding errors or testing conditions which may have invalidated the verbal *n* Achievement scores. Coding errors are of course always possible and hard to control when one is dealing with different languages and different coders. The German protocols were coded in German and the Brazilian protocols in Portuguese by judges who had repeatedly checked their scoring reliability against American judges working on the same material in English. The reliability coefficients varied in the range of .72 to .82, which is lower than for protocols rescored in English, but probably as high as can be obtained across two languages because modes of expression in other languages do not fit exactly the coding definitions given in English in the scoring manual. This does not mean, of course, that the coding in the foreign language is less valid. The Indian stories were written in English and the Japanese translated into English so that they could be scored by experienced American scorers whose coding reliability was in the .88 to .95 range. Undoubtedly in this process some errors were introduced but they should not have been large enough to invalidate by themselves the verbal n Achievement scores *within* a country. They would be more likely to introduce noncomparability between countries.

On the other hand, examination of the mean n Achievement scores for the 13 groups tested in Germany strongly suggested that there was considerable variation in the degree of achievement orientation present under presumably standard testing conditions. First, there were marked and significant differences in the mean n Achievement scores obtained for the samples of students tested by the three different administrators used. The average scores were 2.68 for Administrator 1, 4.26 for Administrator 2, and 6.09 for Administrator 3 respectively, all the means being significantly different from each other at $p < .01$. It is true that the first administrator worked in South Germany, the second in Central Germany, and the third in North Germany (see Table 2.4), so that the differences might also reflect a geographical gradient in n Achievement. However, there were wide fluctuations in the average n Achievement scores even among the groups tested by the same administrator in the North. For example, the average score for Group 10 was 4.72 and for Group 11, 7.31 ($p < .05$), although both groups were drawn from schools in the same city.

Second, among the more "aroused" groups—i.e., the six with the highest mean n Achievement scores—five out of six of the correlations of verbal n Achievement with the $D - F$ score from the graphic expression test were *negative* (mean $r = -.085$), whereas in the less aroused groups, six out of seven of the same correlations were positive, as predicted from Aronson's results in the United States (mean $r = .074$, the p of the difference between the two average correlations being about .07 in the predicted direction).

Finally, in one of the 13 groups tested, exactly the same pattern of correlations between verbal n Achievement score and the various graphic characteristics was obtained as had been predicted from Aronson's results. Another class was tested in the same school on the next day by the same administrator with nearly all of the correlations significantly reversed. In Test Group 4 (the first one), the correlation was .26 between verbal n Achievement and the total quartile score (representing all its graphic correlates in the United States), whereas in Group 5 the same correlation was $-.16$, $p < .10$ for the difference in the two correlations. What was the difference in the testing conditions on the two days? The comments of the field director in Germany are particularly revealing:

"In Group 4 a teacher tried to do something about the discipline, which he thought was lacking, but the subjects paid no attention to him. . . . The procedure in Group 5 was somewhat smoother, and discipline perhaps somewhat better than in Group 4. . . . This slight difference appears to have been due to the fact that tests had gotten under way a little late with Group 4, which was the first group tested in the school."

Thus, the boys in Group 4 may have been somewhat more relaxed than in Group 5, at least within the frame of reference of the German school situation. It was only in this more relaxed, somewhat disorderly group that the relationship between n Achievement and graphic expression was obtained that had appeared in the United States data. Conceivably the German school atmosphere, and for that matter the atmosphere in the schools in other countries as well, might have been more achievement-oriented and well-disciplined than in Aronson's American college groups, thus making it more difficult to obtain really spontaneous self-expression either in fantasy or in doodling. The evidence so far presented is at best circumstantial and only suggests such an hypothesis without proving it. It is possible to buttress the argument by referring to the whole tradition of recent American educational theory which has stressed spontaneous self-expression as contrasted with the more disciplined achievement conscientiousness stressed in German and possibly other school systems around the world. But such considerations do not prove that German subjects high in verbal n Achievement would show the predicted types of expressive movements if the testing conditions had been as relaxed as they were in the United States.

They do, however, suggest that if a way could be found of discovering the German boys who remained relaxed despite the generally higher achievement pressure, the predicted relationships should hold for them. The questionnaire administered to the boys in all countries provided a possible means of developing and cross-validating an empirical scoring key for picking out the more and less relaxed ones among them. The average agreement with each of the twenty items on the questionnaire among the four countries was studied to see if it differed on any of them in the four countries as contrasted with the United States. As Table IV.1 shows, agreement is much greater abroad than in the United States with the following two items:

> Item 18. I work like a slave at everything I undertake until I am satisfied with the results.
> Item 19. A child should never be asked to do anything unless he is told why he is asked to do it.

They therefore have promise as a means of picking out more "relaxed" boys abroad, since such boys will presumably disagree with them more just as the boys in the United States do. While the content of the items is on the surface quite different, answers to them correlate positively to an extent as high or higher as between them and answers to most other items in the scale (mean $r = .11$ $df = 1110$, $p < .01$). In all four countries the

TABLE IV.1 AVERAGE AGREEMENT IN FIVE COUNTRIES WITH TWO ATTITUDE ITEMS DEALING WITH "ACHIEVEMENT CONSCIENTIOUSNESS" AMONG ADOLESCENT BOYS (age 15-17)

Attitude items	United States $N = 74$	Japan $N = 175$	Brazil $N = 367$	Germany $N = 398$	India $N = 152$
(Work like a slave)					
mean	4.23	4.93	5.52	5.80	5.89
SD	est. 2.00	1.99	1.67	1.43	1.72
(Don't ask without reasons)					
mean	3.50	5.53	6.05	5.69	5.39
SD	est. 2.00	1.82	1.54	1.74	1.92

Mean differences of the order of .55 and .73 are ordinarily significant at $p < .05$ and $p < .01$ respectively.

Note: The boys expressed their attitude toward the items on a scale of $+3$ (complete agreement) to -3 (complete disagreement) here converted to a scale of 7 to 1.

correlation between them is positive. Furthermore, in the matrix of correlations for the total sample, the correlation between these Items 18 and 19 is higher than it is between Item 18 and sixteen of the remaining items, and than it is between Item 19 and fourteen of the remaining items. The two items "hang together" or tend to be answered similarly by boys in all four countries. Their content suggests an anxious concern with achievement that might well provide a means of distinguishing the more from the less relaxed boys. Those boys who agree strongly with these items should on a priori grounds be those who are more conscientious, and perhaps more anxious about achievement. They say they "work like slaves" and insist on knowing exactly why they are being asked to do something. American boys do not insist as much on either of these points as do the boys from the other countries.

Extreme agreement with these two items was therefore used as a means of dividing the boys into the more and less tense, or the more and less conscientious, at first in a few of the test groups in Germany. It was consistently found as predicted that among the less tense boys, the correlations between verbal n Achievement and the expressive movement characteristics coded were consistently and often significantly in the same direction as Aronson had obtained in the United States. Therefore the measure was used to divide the samples in Japan and Brazil as well as Germany so that the correlations could be computed separately for the two kinds of boys, with the results shown in Table 8.1. On the whole the empirically derived key works reasonably well and the hypothesis is confirmed: among the more relaxed boys the correlations of the verbal measure of n Achievement with the graphic expression variables are the same in all three countries as

Aronson had obtained, with the notable exception of the "unused space" variable as pointed out in Chapter 8. The correlations are much smaller than Aronson's, though many of them are significant and presumably they could be higher if we had a more efficient way of insuring that testing conditions were relaxed in these countries than by picking out boys afterwards who resisted the achievement pressure, on the basis of a couple of questionnaire items not designed for the purpose.

But granted that achievement pressure or conscientiousness is somehow interfering with relationships found under more "spontaneous" testing conditions in the United States, which measure is it affecting? Is it invalidating the graphic expression test, the verbal n Achievement test, or both? The question is of immense importance for the rest of the research because if the verbal n Achievement measure is invalidated by variations in testing conditions, we cannot use it in the rest of research to check abroad on other behavioral correlates of n Achievement previously found in the United States. We can substitute one of the estimates of individual differences in n Achievement based on the graphic expression variables suggested by Aronson, but how do we know that they too are not invalidated by variations in testing conditions? Which is likely to provide the most valid estimate of n Achievement under the circumstances—the verbal or the graphic measure?

The verbal measure has many *a priori* advantages. It has been the instrument used to establish practically everything that is known about n Achievement both at the individual and national levels (see Chapters 3 and 6). What is more, its "face validity" is higher. It makes much more sense to regard a person's achievement-related thoughts as a measure of his need for Achievement than it does the way he doodles on a piece of paper. On the other hand, the evidence rather argues against using the verbal measure of n Achievement in the present experiment. It is well known that it can be easily influenced by situational pressures—in fact, that is the way in which it was originally developed (McClelland *et al.*, 1953). It is also known that under situational arousal, scores of individuals no longer relate systematically to other variables. Furthermore, at least in Germany there are significant variations in mean n Achievement scores from one test group and one administrator to another, which argues strongly that situational factors were operating to modify n Achievement scores at least in that country. Finally, and probably most significantly of all, a preliminary survey of expected relationships of the verbal n Achievement measure to other variables in the study revealed that they were generally insignificant and did not present a picture which confirmed in any significant way the findings repeatedly obtained in the United States. This could, of course, mean that the relationships do not exist in other countries, a matter which the research was primarily designed to investigate, but it might also mean that the verbal measure of n Achievement is not a valid measure of individual differences in those countries under the testing conditions involved.

At any rate it seemed wise to check these same relationships using a measure of *n* Achievement based on the graphic expression variables. Such a measure also has its *a priori* advantages: it is more "culture free" in the sense that difficult decisions about the meaning of language do not have to be made. Unlike imaginative stories, it is not known to be easily influenced by situational pressures. Moreover, the averages for the graphic expression

TABLE IV.2   MEANS AND STANDARD DEVIATIONS OF GRAPHIC EXPRESSION VARIABLES IN FIVE COUNTRIES

Graphic expression variables[1]		U.S. $N = 75$	Japan $N = 175^*$	Germany $N = 411^*$	Brazil $N = 378^*$	India $N = 152^*$
$D + F$	mean	22.25	25.67	33.20	30.35	55.90
	SD	7.64	12.93	12.69	13.59	28.20
$D - F$	mean	8.81	14.81	12.21	15.78	37.66
	SD	9.95	13.21	15.46	12.02	28.05
Diagonals (D)	mean	5.39	3.65	3.90	3.61	5.05
	SD	2.81	2.96	3.06	2.78	4.20
S-shapes	mean	1.31	1.83	2.26	1.85	3.20
	SD	1.60	2.21	2.48	2.35	3.91
Multiple	mean	4.60	3.49	3.54	4.36	11.67
Waves (MW)	SD	1.87	3.12	2.93	3.38	10.44
$D + S - MW$	mean	2.10	1.98	2.65	1.13	−3.34
	SD		4.86	5.12	4.89	10.62
Unused space	mean	17.48	12.42	16.22	15.38	13.69
(mm)	SD	10.45	9.03	10.33	8.44	9.63
Verbal *n* Ach.[2]	mean		8.24	4.60	5.47	3.79
	SD		4.81	5.34	4.24	4.79

* The *N*'s are larger than in Table 2.4 because a rural group of Japanese boys tested are included here but not elsewhere to increase comparability of the samples, and because ages were not available on all subjects.

[1] A brief description of these variables is given in Chapter 8, a complete one in Aronson (1958). All scored units are classified first according to whether the lines are discrete (*D*) or fuzzy (*F*) so that the sum of these two gives the total number of scored units in the protocol which consists of two pages of doodles by the subject. The shape variables—diagonals, S-shapes, and multiple waves—are self-explanatory. Unused space is the sum of the widest margins (unused space in from any side) in mm for the two pages of doodles, using more or less standard paper ($8\frac{1}{2}'' \times 11''$).

[2] The *n* Achievement score is based on stories written to pictures #2 (two men working in a machine shop), #8 (boy in checked shirt at a desk with an open book), #1 (older man talking to a younger man, usually interpreted as father and son), and #9 (man in shirtsleeves at a desk), presented in that order. (See Atkinson, 1958, Appendix III.) By mistake another picture, highly saturated with achievement cues, was presented first in Japan showing a scientist working in a laboratory. The results for this picture are not included but it may have affected the achievement imagery in subsequent stories, though probably not to an extent sufficient to account for the much higher average *n* Achievement score in Japan. Also the pictures were redone in Japan to present Japanese faces and clothing.

variables do not differ significantly from one test administrator to another in Germany, nor nearly as markedly from one test group to another as the mean verbal n Achievement scores.

Let us therefore look at some of the normative characteristics of the graphic expression test, and try to decide which of its scores would be most likely to provide the best estimate of n Achievement. Table IV.2 presents means and standard deviations on all of the graphic expression variables as obtained in the United States, Japan, Germany, Brazil and India. For the sake of comparison the average verbal n Achievement scores for the last four countries are also included. Two facts stand out immediately from a study of these figures. In the first place, the average number of units scored per protocol ($D + F$ score) is significantly larger in all of the four countries than for Aronson's normative group and particularly so for India. The difference could not very well be due to scorer bias since all the protocols were scored by Aronson himself and those for the four foreign countries when they were all mixed together at the same time without identifying marks. The subjects abroad were on the average more productive than in the United States, and more productive in some countries than in others. Either they had more time to see the stimulus designs presented and therefore had seen more to reproduce, or they had more time to doodle, or they were under greater achievement pressure to produce because of testing conditions or internal "conscientiousness," or they were more practiced in scribbling than Aronson's subjects. The first two possibilities very likely explain the much larger number of responses in India, since neither exposure nor reproduction time could be carefully controlled there. The stimulus material, instead of being tachistoscopically presented by a slide projector, was held up briefly for small groups of subjects to see and presentation and reproduction time was controlled by counting rather than by a stopwatch as in the other countries. In fact from this point on it was decided that the graphic expression test results for India were so different from those obtained in other countries—in fact there was very little overlap in the $D + F$ distributions—that they should be discarded as conceivable measures of individual differences in n Achievement in India.

The second point of importance to note in Table IV.2 is that as far as the other three countries are concerned the mean scores on the graphic expression variables differ more or less as they should according to Aronson's findings based on their average differences in verbal n Achievement score. Japan is significantly higher than Germany in verbal n Achievement and also, as predicted from Aronson's results, in $D - F$ score and in amount of space used up. The same is true of Brazil: it is higher than Germany in verbal n Achievement and in $D - F$ score and space used. The trend is reversed only for the raw "shape" scores (Diagonals, S-shapes, and Multiple-Waves), but they are possibly more influenced by the tendency of the Germans to produce more scorable units of all kinds (higher $D + F$ scores). On a percentage basis which crudely corrects for variations in total productivity, the differences among countries in the tendency to scribble various shapes are small and insignificant. The results, like those obtained for the more relaxed boys (Table 8.1), are slightly encouraging in that they show some gross agreement between average verbal n Achievement scores and average scores in graphic expression variables supposedly characteristic of n Achievement. As to which variable is likely to provide the best estimate of n Achievement they cast some doubt on the validity of the shape variables, though the use of Diagonals, on a percentage basis, fares better than S-shapes or Multiple-Waves, just as it does among the more relaxed boys in Table 8.1. Japan has the highest percentage of Diagonals (14.2 per cent), Brazil next (11.9 per cent), and Germany last (11.7 per cent), differences which correspond roughly to the differences in verbal n Achievement scores.

Data on internal reliability and relationships among the graphic expression variables may help decide which will provide the best estimate of n Achievement. They are presented in Tables IV.3 and IV.4 in terms of three main possibilities—line, shape, and space. Table IV.3 presents the usual split-half reliabilities showing how consistently the subject doodled to both stimulus designs with which he was presented. Also over-all estimates are presented at the bottom of the table for the reliability of the particular response characteristic when it is based on the full length test (i.e., for both designs). Table IV.4 presents the intercorrelations of the response characteristics in each country. Since Aronson has found that verbal n Achievement is positively associated with the line $(D - F)$ and shape $(D + S - MW)$ scores,

TABLE IV.3   CORRELATIONS OF GRAPHIC CHARACTERISTICS FOR DESIGN I WITH THOSE FOR DESIGN II

Country	N	Line		Shape		Space	
		Discrete − Fuzzy		$D + S − MW^1$		Unused[2]	
		r	partial r^3	r	partial r^3	r	partial r^3
Japan	134	.39	.13	.11	.08	.68	.66
Germany	391	.39	.32	.17	.15	.70	.69
Brazil	366	.25	.08	.07	.07	.64	.63
Average r		.33	.19	.12	.11	.67	.67
Estimated for doubling the test		.50	.32	.21	.19	.80	.80

[1] Number of diagonals plus the number of S-shapes minus the number of multiple waves.

[2] Unused space, maximum in from any margin.

[3] With total number of scored units in the record $(D + F)$ partialled out.
With $N = 800$, correlations of .070 and .091 are significant at the .05 and .01 levels respectively.

TABLE IV.4 INTERCORRELATIONS OF GRAPHIC CHARACTERISTICS (LINE, SHAPE, AND SPACE)

Country	N	Line $(D-F)$ with shape $(D+S-MW)$		Line with unused space		Shape with unused space	
		r	partial r^1	r	partial r^1	r	partial r^1
Japan	136	.36**	.28**	−.03	.21**	.01	.07
Germany	391	.17**	.10*	−.09	−.04	.11	.14**
Brazil	366	.28**	.26**	−.03	.08	.02	.04
Average		.24**	.19**	−.06	2	.06	.09**

* $p < .05$; ** $p < .01$
1 With total number of scored units in the record $(D + F)$ partialled out.
2 Not meaningful to average these correlations.

and negatively with unused space, presumably the line and shape scores, as representing high n Achievement, should be *positively* correlated (which they are significantly in all countries) and both should be *negatively* correlated with the unused space score characteristic of low n Achievement (which they are not in any consistent way).

Both tables present first order correlations and also partial correlations in which the influence of the number of units in the record has been removed. The purpose of the partial correlations is to attempt to get rid of that portion of a correlation which might be due simply to the greater or lesser responsiveness of the individual. For example, the correlation between the $D - F$ score and the $D + F$ score (i.e., the total number of scored units in the record) tends to be quite high: it is, in fact, .76, $N = 1242$ for the entire four-country sample. Consequently, the $D - F$ scores for the responses to Design I will almost certainly have to correlate highly with the similar scores to Design II simply because of the influence of the subject's over-all "responsiveness." A person who produces few responses to Design I tends also to produce few to Design II, and vice versa, so that correlations between a particular type of response to Design I and to Design II are almost certain to be significantly positive. The partial correlations seem to be an obvious way to eliminate the influence of over-all responsiveness but unfortunately they overdo it. The correlation between any characteristic and the total number of characteristics scored is spuriously high to an indeterminate amount (except for the space variable) because the characteristic is included in the total with which it is correlated. Therefore if the first-order correlations represent an overestimate of the relationships, the partial correlations represent an underestimate. The truth probably lies somewhere in between. With this caution in mind, let us look at each of the types of measures to see which might provide the best estimate of n Achievement.

The *unused space* measure is clearly the most reliable ($r = .80$, Table IV.3) in that subjects are very consistent in the amount of the page they use up in response to the two different stimulus designs. However, it is related to verbal n Achievement only in the more conscientious subjects in the manner predicted (Table 8.1) and it is not negatively related, as predicted, to the shape or line indexes (Table IV.4). Furthermore, it is obviously the most apt to be influenced by quite accidental variables, such as the size of the page used (which was slightly different in Brazil) and mechanical conditions under which the doodling was done (slant of the desk, solidity of support for all surfaces of the paper, etc.). Therefore, it does not seem to be a very likely candidate for the best measure of n Achievement, or even for inclusion in some kind of a total score for estimating n Achievement.

Among the *shape* characteristics, the use of Diagonals is by all odds the most consistently correlated with verbal n Achievement (Tables 8.1, IV.2). but by itself it is such a relatively rare and unreliable index that it was combined with the two other shape characteristics to get an over-all shape index. Even the combined measure has a disappointingly low internal reliability (r around .20, Table IV.3) though it is significantly different from zero. The most encouraging thing about it is that it correlates substantially and highly significantly in all three countries with the line measure ($D - I$ score), as the first two columns in Table IV.4 show. From these sets of figures, we can get the justification for using the shape index as an alternative way of estimating n Achievement from graphic designs on pottery as reported in Chapter 4. Though as we shall see in a moment, the line index is probably the best way of estimating n Achievement from graphic expression, when it cannot be used, as in the pottery studies, there is substantial justification here for using the shape index as a substitute measure since it correlates significantly and substantially with the line measure and also shows some significant positive relationships with n Achievement among relaxed boys in other countries as well as in the United States (Table 8.1).

But how do we know that potters are not under achievement pressure? If they are, wouldn't these very same shapes signify low n Achievement since the correlations in Table 8.1 are reversed for boys high in "achievement conscientiousness"? The argument is not perfectly straightforward, but there are two reasons for doubting that these shape characteristics would ever have a reverse meaning in pottery designs. In the first place, potters seem much more likely to be engaging in spontaneous aesthetic self-expression than the schoolboys tested, many of whom were undoubtedly straining to remember and copy what they saw (according to instructions). This particular type of achievement pressure for conscientious reproduction in a limited period of time does not seem a likely influence on the ceramic artist deciding what designs to put on his pottery. Secondly, we do not know anyway that achievement pressure invalidates the graphic expression variables as signs of n Achievement. It is more likely that it invalidates the verbal measure of n Achievement by raising the scores of some true "lows" above the scores of some true "highs" so that the correlations with the graphic characteristics are reversed. That is, the "false highs" on the verbal measure will now have fewer Diagonals in their records, for example, because they are really "lows" whose scores have been situationally raised by achievement pressure.

Nevertheless, the shape index is not the best candidate for a measure of individual differences in n Achievement among the subjects in our experiment. It is too unreliable, and several of the correlations with verbal n Achievement in Table 8.1 are not even in the predicted direction among the more relaxed boys. The remaining possibility is the $D - F$ score, which is based on the kinds of lines the subjects drew predominantly. It was actually the score developed first by Aronson and which he found to be most consistently related to verbal n Achievement (1958, p. 258). It should be more reliable because it is based on a decision for every scored unit in the protocol. It does, in fact, have a reliability somewhere between .32 and .50 (Table IV.3). Furthermore, it is consistently related at about the same level to verbal n Achievement among the relaxed boys in all three countries (Table 8.1) just as it is in the United States. Finally, it is intercorrelated with the other variables, as it should be if the findings obtained by Aronson are taken as the basis for prediction. That is, the $D - F$ score correlates positively with the number of S-shapes and Diagonals and negatively with the number of Multiple-Waves and with the amount of space left unused at the bottom of the page in every one of the three countries. Table IV.4 summarizes these facts, showing the significant positive correlations of the line score with the combined shape index, and the slight negative correlations with unused space, which however tend to disappear when the first-order correlations are corrected for total responsiveness.

So the $D - F$ score seems by far the most likely candidate for a measure of individual differences in n Achievement based on graphic expression. It still has the disadvantage of being highly correlated with the number of scored units in the record, and to remove this effect for an individual score, it was necessary to convert the raw $D - F$ scores to z-scores as follows. The entire 1242 protocols from all four countries were arranged in order of the number of scored units they contained and divided into fifths. The $D - F$ score means and standard deviations were computed for each quintile and a given raw $D - F$ score converted to a z-score for the quintile in which it belonged in virtue of the number of scored units it contained. See Table IV.5. In short, the z-score indicates whether the $D - F$ score is high or low considering the number of units in the record. The method used is the same as adopted by Child et al. (1958) in correcting n Achievement scores for length of folk tales, or by us in correcting motive scores for length of children's stories as reported in Chapter 3. The correlations of

TABLE IV.5   TABLE FOR CONVERTING RAW $D - F$ SCORES TO $D - F$, z-SCORES BASED
ON 1242 GRAPHIC EXPRESSION PROTOCOLS FROM JAPAN, GERMANY, BRAZIL AND INDIA

$D + F$ quintiles (No. scored units in the record)	$D - F$ scores	
	mean	SD
1. 0-20 units	5.95	6.97
2. 21-26 units	9.23	8.06
3. 27-33 units	12.09	10.73
4. 34-43 units	18.85	12.83
5. 44-170 units	36.52	25.45

Note: An estimate of the subject's n Achievement level can be obtained from his raw $D + F$ and $D - F$ scores as follows: determine which quintile he is in on the basis of his $D + F$ score (the number of scored units in his record), then compute his $D - F$ z-score (the estimated n Achievement score) using the appropriate mean and SD, i.e.,

$$\frac{(D - F \text{ score}) - (\text{mean } D - F \text{ score for that } D + F \text{ quintile})}{SD \text{ for that quintile}} = D - F \text{ z-score}$$

The approximation is of very doubtful validity for protocols falling in the 5th quintile.

the $D - F$, z-scores are now substantially reduced with the total number of units in the record, being .19 for Japan, .13 for Germany, −.08 for Brazil. However, the correlation was still a substantial .49 for India, because nearly all of the Indian protocols fell in the quintile containing the longest records.

Once again, as far as India was concerned, it was clear that the verbal n Achievement measure would have to be used. Fortunately, there were a couple of scraps of evidence that the verbal n Achievement measure might be more valid for the Indian student. Only in India of the four countries was there any sizeable correlation at all between $D - F$ z-score and verbal n Achievement for the total sample ($r = .12$, $p = .07$ pd). This suggests that the Indian student may have been somewhat more relaxed than the boys in the other countries, so that the correlation could be obtained. The impression is confirmed by the fact that the mean agreement of the Indian students with the achievement conscientiousness items is not relatively as high as might be suggested by the figures in Table IV.1 because the Indian students agreed on the average significantly more with *all* the items in the questionnaire than did the boys in the other three countries. So if the mean agreements with these two items for the Indian students are corrected for their over-all greater acquiescence, the mean agreements would be about .50 lower than they are in Table IV.1.

As to the other three countries, both estimates of n Achievement were consistently employed and in general the $D - F$ z-score yielded more significant relationships in accordance with theoretical expectations based on research in the United States. Unfortunately, using the correlates of

the two measures to decide which is the most valid one is like lifting yourself by your bootstraps because the same relationships must be used to
validate both the measure and the theory based on the measure. The issue
gets particularly cloudy if the verbal measure of n Achievement relates to
some variables as predicted and the $D - F$ z-score to others. This happened
in only a few cases, all of them in Japan, but it forced some kind of a decision as to which of the many relationships of n Achievement was most
important and most likely to be universal in all cultures. Priority was actually
accorded, not without misgivings, to the hypothesized greater responsiveness
of individuals with high n Achievement to achievement incentives so far
as performance is concerned, as shown in Table 6.3. It was felt that such a
trend should be as universal as any, and that therefore, the estimate of
n Achievement which reveals such a trend is more likely to be the valid one.
As Table 6.3 shows, the $D - F$ z-score estimate of n Achievement shows
reasonably consistently from country to country that the subjects classified
by it as higher in n Achievement tend to perform better under stronger
achievement incentives (longer odds). No consistent trends of any kind
were found within or between countries for performance under varying
incentives when the verbal measure of n Achievement was used for Brazil,
Germany, and Japan. Furthermore, as the various tables scattered throughout
the book demonstrate, the graphic estimate of n Achievement does yield a
number of other significant and consistent relationships from country to
country that are in accord with the general theory of n Achievement, its
origins and effects on behavior.

Lastly, there is an encouraging bit of evidence that so far as very gross
inter-country comparisons are concerned, the two estimates of n Achievement are significantly correlated. For the sample of 545 boys from all of
the three countries whose mothers happened to be interviewed, the correlation between $D - F$ z-score and verbal n Achievement $= .12$, $p < .01$.
There is no reason to think that the samples of the boys in each country
whose mothers were interviewed were selected in any biased way, so that
the correlation may perhaps be taken as suggestive of a true relationship
which might exist in a "world sample." The same relationship has already
been discussed in Table IV.2, where it is clear that the Japanese boys
averaged highest on both estimates of n Achievement, the Germans lowest,
and the Brazilians in between. But for finer discriminations within a country,
the two measures are not significantly related (except possibly in India),
and do not yield the same pattern of correlations with other variables. A
choice had to be made between the two, and the weight of the evidence is
in favor of the estimate of n Achievement based on the types of lines drawn
($D - F$ score) in Aronson's graphic expression test.

Appendix V

Codes and scores from the cross-cultural study of preliterate tribes.

A. RELIGION CODE

I. Mode of divine contact for average member of religious group
Divine is contacted by the individual

    (a) *Contact made directly through individual's own efforts* (as in mysticism, and not through ritual magic phrases, etc.). "Original" private prayer, contemplation, etc. Scoring weight = +3.

    (b) *Contact made indirectly through the group.* Ritual action in which the Divine acts on the individual (and individual is *not* simply worshipping). E.g., group-induced trances, Quaker meetings, revival meetings, Dionysianism, etc. Scoring weight = +3.

    (c) *Contact made indirectly through fairly precise oral or written traditions.* (e.g., The Bible, Koran, Navaho songs, elaborate ritual superstitions) or in routine ways (e.g., Evil Spirits menace at fixed times or places).

        1. Room for considerable individual interpretation (e.g., Protestant reading of Bible verses). Scoring weight = +3.

        2. Memorization, little or no individual interpretation. Scoring weight = +1.

II. Role of Experts

    (a) Minor or nonexistent. Individual must learn or act by himself. Scoring weight = +2.

    (b) Major teachers of individuals (e.g., Rabbis). Scoring weight = +2.

    (c) *Necessary* mediators; ordinary person cannot perform chief religious duties alone. Special magic attached to Divine Mediator, may be clearly set off by rank (e.g., priests, shamans). Experts *essential* in religious organization. Scoring weight = +1.

III. Objective of Divine-Human Contact (immediate aim)

    (a) *Ethics:* religious service in order to learn right conduct toward others (and toward the world) and to gain divine favor ultimately by action. Scoring weight = +3.

    (b) *Self-Improvement:* holiness; to escape pain, feel better. Buddhism, peace of mind, religion as therapy, heightened awareness, excitement. Scoring weight = +1.

    (c) *Worship:* to please God or Spirits (and gain favor, avoid disfavor) by ritual action, superstitions, taboos, offerings, etc. Scoring weight = +1.

IV. Internalization of Divine-Human Contact

(a) *God or Spirit(s)* may be contacted anywhere and at any time depending on attitude of individual. Objects or places are of minor importance. Scoring weight $= +3$.

(b) *God or Spirit(s)* are contacted chiefly at appointed times and places which may not be permanently sacred and have inter-mediate importance; i.e., there may be religious symbols but they are not necessarily holy. Scoring weight $= +2$.

(c) *Religious practices* organized around sacred objects and places (e.g., images, icons, Mecca, etc.). Shrines, taboo spots, etc. are of basic importance. Scoring weight $= +1$.

Note: Within each of the four categories, a religion must be given at least one check. Often more than one element is present within a category. For example, Christianity emphasizes both worship and ethics and perhaps to a lesser extent, self-improvement. If the elements are of about equal importance both (or all 3) are checked. If one or more of the elements are clearly more important the elements are weighed in order of importance (3:1, 2:1, 3:2:1, etc.). A total score for the category is obtained by multiplying the scoring weight by the emphasis weights, summing these products and dividing by the number of emphasis weights used for the category. For example,

Culture: *Navaho*

I   (a) $\underline{1} \times 3$ (b) $\_ \times 3$ (c_1) $\_ \times 3$ (c_2) $\underline{1} \times 1 = \frac{4}{2} = 2.00$

II   (a) $\underline{1} \times 2$ (b) $\_ \times 2$ (c) $\underline{1} \times 1 = \frac{3}{2} = 1.50$

III (a) $\underline{1} \times 3$ (b) $\underline{3} \times 1$ (c) $\underline{2} \times 1 = \frac{8}{6} = 1.33$

IV   (a) $\underline{1} \times 3$ (b) $\_ \times 2$ (c) $\underline{2} \times 1 = \frac{5}{3} = 1.67$

B. ECONOMIC CODE

I. Presence of entrepreneurs in the culture

An entrepreneur is someone who exercises some control over the means of production and produces more than he can consume in order to sell it for individual (or household) income. Record the percentage of adult males for whom entrepreneurial practices account for:

$\underline{80\%}$ * less than 25% of income (includes subsistence farmers, all service [religious] workers, and wage laborers because they do not control the means of production.)

$\underline{0\%}$ 25%-75% of income.

$\underline{20\%}$ 75% or more of income (includes people who produce for re-sale or trade primarily, though they may have "kitchen gardens," for subsistence). This percentage is to be further broken down into the following categories.

$\underline{5\%}$ traders (people who do not produce, but acquire for resale or rental rather than subsistence or use).

$\underline{0\%}$ independent artisans (shoemakers, smiths, carpenters, etc., when they control the means of production).

$\underline{15\%}$ firm operators. A firm must include capital, management, labor: (e.g., innkeepers, export houses, fisheries, sheep raisers).

* Illustrative figures are for the Koryak

II. Level of capital equipment (e.g., technology) in production and how it is owned

Record the percentage of total tribal income which is derived from production activities employing the three levels of capital equipment. Then break down the percentages according to the fractions of it produced by individually or community owned capital at that level.

	Per cent of income	Individually owned	Community owned
Low (digging sticks, baskets, traps, knives, etc.)	50*	25	25
Medium (fishing boats, cattle, land)	50	50	0
High (large machinery, tractors, etc.)	0	0	0

* Illustrative figures are for the Koryak.

Note: Use the following percentage equivalents for various verbal expressions in the ethnographic literature:

None	= 0%	A number	= 30%
One-two	= 1%	Many	= 50%
A few	= 5%	Nearly all }	
Some	= 10%	Most }	= 80%

C. GAME CODE

The judge recorded in each cell of the following table whether the type of game occurred often (=2) sometimes (=1) or never (=0). Cells were left blank if no information was available. An average index of competitiveness in games was obtained by multiplying the judge's emphasis weights by the scoring weights assigned each cell, summing the products, and dividing by the number of cells in which there was information, as in the example below.

Category		Competitive games		Noncompetitive games	
		Male	Female	Male	Female
Individual	Child	2* × 1	2 × 1	2 × 0	2 × 0
	Adult	2 × 1	2 × 1	__ × 0	__ × 0
Group	Child	2 × .5	2 × .5	__ × −1	__ × −1
	Adult	2 × .5	2 × .5	__ × −1	__ × −1

$$\text{Total score} = \tfrac{12}{10} = 1.20$$

* Illustrative figures are for the Chiricahua Apache.

D. SCORES ON SEVERAL VARIABLES CODED FOR INDIVIDUAL TRIBES

Tribe	Motive z-scores (Veroff)[1]			Religion codes				Competitive game score
	n Achievement	n Affiliation	n Power	I	II	III	IV	
Ainu	.034	.293	.110	2.00	1.50	1.00	1.67	
Aleut	.687	.713	.526	2.00	1.00	1.50	1.67	.75
Aranda	.129	−.323	.107	2.01	1.50	1.67	1.00	.86
Arapaho	.187	.227	−.082	2.67	1.88	1.40	2.17	1.50
Arapesh	−.111	−.230	−.266	1.00	1.50	1.00	1.00	
Araucanian	.128	−.063	.047	2.33	1.50	1.00	2.17	1.50
Ashanti	−.257	−.124	.116	2.00	1.50	1.67	1.50	1.00
Azande	−.209	−.245	.225	3.00	1.67	1.67	1.00	.80
Basuto	−.448	−.037	.048	3.00	1.50	1.33	2.67	.33
Baiga	−.005	.046	.107	2.00	1.50	1.00	1.67	−1.00
Bechuana	.003	−.093	.008					
Chagga	−.182	−.047	−.032	1.50	1.50	1.50	1.67	−.40
Chenchu	−.300	.501	−.071					
Cheyenne	.394	.089	−.145	2.67	1.67	1.00	1.33	.83
Chiracahua Apache	−.258	−.405	.480	2.33	1.50	1.00	2.00	1.20
Chuckchee	.156	−.013	.518	2.20	1.33	1.50	1.67	.33
Comanche	.612	−.306	.364	3.00	2.00	1.67	2.33	1.50
Crow	.229	−.283	.244	3.00	1.67	1.00	2.00	.81
Cuna	.207	−.068	.239	3.00	1.83	2.33	1.83	.80
Hopi	.061	−.045	.399					
Ifaluk (Woleans)	.133	.658	−.183	2.00	1.67	1.00	1.83	.25
Jicarilla Apache	.269	−.135	.074	3.00	1.67	1.00	2.33	1.50
Kaska	−.227	.013	.203	2.00	1.00	1.50	2.00	−.70
Kikuya	−.042	.345	−.348	2.00	1.50	2.00	2.00	.67
Klamath	−.173	.539	−.047	2.00	1.50	1.00	1.00	.50
Konga	−.128	−.006	.395					
Koryak	.189	−.067	.084	2.00	1.33	1.50	1.83	.88
Kurtachi	.023	−.014	−.181	2.00	2.00	1.00	2.00	−1.00
Kwakiutl	.218	.128	.003					
Lepcha	−.108	−.068	.384	1.67	1.50	1.50	1.67	.00
Mandan	.857	.513	−.603	3.00	2.00	1.00	1.83	1.50
Marquesan	.055	−.051	.312	2.00	1.50	1.00	1.67	.83
Masai	.326	.068	.048	2.00	2.00	1.67	1.67	
Mbundu	.126	.476	−.045	2.00	1.50	1.80	2.00	.11
Muria	.115	.433	−.052	2.00	1.50	1.67	2.00	−.14
Nauruans	−.414	.163	.338	2.00	1.00	2.00	2.00	
Navaho	.067	−.381	.125	2.00	1.50	1.33	1.67	1.50
Ojibwa	.043	−.389	−.233	1.50	1.67	1.33	2.00	.00
Paiute	−.022	−.303	−.285	2.33	1.67	1.67	2.33	.80
Papago	.369	−.023	.221	2.17	1.50	1.33	2.00	.90
Puka Pukans	.046	−.278	−.023	2.00	1.00	2.00	1.67	1.00
Tenetehara	−.119	.675	−.162	1.50	1.00	1.50	2.00	
Teton-Dakota	.018	.228	.215	2.50	1.50	1.33	1.67	
Thonga	−.315	−.070	−.429	3.00	2.00	1.33	1.67	.91
Tukuna	−.028	.028	.165	1.00	1.00	1.67	1.67	1.50
Venda	.228	−.118	−.054	2.00	1.33	1.00	1.00	.50
Western Apache	−.097	−.157	.056	2.00	1.33	1.33	2.00	
Wichita	.255	.011	.524	2.33	2.00	1.67	2.00	.33
Winnebago	.273	.321	.204	2.50	2.00	1.33	2.00	1.50
Yoruba	.473	−.027	−.293	2.17	1.33	1.50	2.00	
Zulu	−.097	.108	−.116					
Zuni	.105	.577	−.434					

[1] Based on folk tales (usually 12) and obtained through the kindness of Dr. Irvin Child from a study by Child, Storm and Veroff (1958).

Appendix VI

Questionnaire Used in the Four-Country Study of Adolescent Boys and Their Mothers

STUDENT QUESTIONNAIRE

Here are some statements that people have different opinions about. There are no right or wrong answers. Just mark each one in the blanks at the left, according to the amount of your agreement or disagreement, by using the following scale:

+1 Slight support, agreement   −1 Slight opposition, disagreement
+2 Moderate support, agreement   −2 Moderate opposition, disagreement
+3 Strong support, agreement   −3 Strong opposition, disagreement

Read each item and decide *quickly* how you feel about it: then fill in the number corresponding to the extent of your agreement or disagreement. Put down your first impressions.

1. _____ No sane, normal, decent person would ever think of hurting a close friend.

2. _____ Nowadays with world conditions the way they are, the wise person lives for today and lets tomorrow take care of itself.

3. _____ It is better to go without something than to ask a favor.

4. _____ I set difficult goals for myself which I attempt to reach.

5. _____ The negative opinion of others often keeps me from seeing a movie or play I had planned to attend.

6. _____ Planning only makes a person unhappy since your plans hardly ever work out anyway.

7. _____ There is no such thing as a really permanent friendship. Your friends change with circumstances.

8. _____ If you get bad news it is better to hide what you feel and behave as if you didn't care.

9. _____ There are some people like great artists and musicians who can be forgiven for not being considerate of others, kind to the poor, etc.

10. _____ There is hardly anything lower than a person who does not feel a great love, gratitude, and respect for his parents.

11. _____ It would irritate me very much to have a watch or clock which was off by several minutes every day or so.

12. _____ When a man is born, the success he's going to have is already in the cards, so he might as well accept it and not fight against it.

13. _____ My political opinion is easily swayed by editorials I read.

14. _____ A man with money cannot really learn how to behave in polite society if he has not had the proper upbringing.

15. _____ Respect is due an older man no matter what kind of a person he is.

16. _____ There is no satisfaction in any good without a companion.

17. _____ I often do something just to prove to myself that I can do it.

18. _____ I work like a slave at everything I undertake until I am satisfied with the results.

19. _____ A child should never be asked to do anything unless he is told why he is asked to do it.

20. _____ I enjoy a race or game better when I bet on it.

Please list here any activities (clubs, hobbies, athletics, etc.) you are engaged in outside your regular school work.

_____   _____

_____   _____

_____   _____

_____   _____

_____   _____

What are the three things you would most like to teach your children?

_____

_____

_____

Appendix VII

Questionnaire and Motive Scores in the Cross-Cultural Study of Businessmen and Professionals

INTERESTS AND ATTITUDES

This section deals with your likes and dislikes. Answer all the items. Many of the seemingly trivial and irrelevant items are very useful in diagnosing your real attitude.

Part I. Occupations. Indicate after each occupation listed below whether you would like that kind of work or not. Disregard considerations of salary, social standing, future advancement, etc. Consider only whether or not you would like to do what is involved in the occupation. You are not asked if you would take up the occupation permanently, but merely whether or not you would enjoy that kind of work, regardless of any necessary skills, abilities, or training which you may or may not possess.

Draw a circle around L if you like that kind of work
Draw a circle around I if you are indifferent to that kind of work
Draw a circle around D if you dislike that kind of work

Put down your first impressions.

1.	Advertiser	L	I	D
2.	Auto salesman	L	I	D
3.	Buyer of merchandise	L	I	D
4.	Chemist	L	I	D
5.	Civil Service employee	L	I	D
6.	College professor	L	I	D
7.	Factory manager	L	I	D
8.	Factory worker	L	I	D
9.	Mechanical engineer	L	I	D
10.	Politician	L	I	D
11.	Real estate salesman	L	I	D
12.	Specialty salesman	L	I	D

Part II. Activities. Indicate in the same manner as in
Part I whether you like the following or not. If in
doubt, consider your most frequent attitude. Do not
think over various possibilities. Your first impressions
are desired here.

13. Collecting postage stamps L   I   D
14. Operating machinery   L   I   D
15. Teaching children   L   I   D
16. Teaching adults   L   I   D
17. Being pitted against another as in a
    political or athletic race   L   I   D
18. Raising money for a charity   L   I   D
19. Looking at a collection of rare laces L   I   D

Part III. Comparison of interest between two items.
Indicate your choice of the following pairs by checking
(√) in the first space if you prefer the item to the
left, in the second space if you like both equally well,
and in the third space if you prefer the item to the
right. Assume other things are equal except the two
items to be compared.
Again, just put down your first impressions.

20. Definite salary   ( ) ( ) ( )   Commission on
                                       what is done
21. Work for yourself ( ) ( ) ( )   Carry out
                                       program of
                                       superior who is
                                       respected
22. Work in a large   Work for self
    corporation with   in small
    little chance of   business
    becomming president
    until age of 55   ( ) ( ) ( )

23. Great variety of   Similarity in
    work   ( ) ( ) ( )   work
24. Selling article,   Selling arti-
    quoted 10% below   cle, quoted 10%
    competitor   ( ) ( ) ( )   above competi-
                                       tor

Part IV. Rating of present abilities and characteristics. Indicate below what kind of a person you are right
now and what you have done. Check in the first column
("Yes") if the item really describes you, in the third
column ("No") if the item does not describe you, and in
the second column ("?") if you are not sure.

	Yes	?	No
25. Usually start activities of my group	( )	( )	( )
26. Have mechanical ingenuity (inventiveness)	( )	( )	( )
27. Am always on time with my work	( )	( )	( )
28. Can correct others without giving offense	( )	( )	( )
29. Stimulate the ambition of my associates	( )	( )	( )

Part V. Attitudes. Below are some statements reflecting attitudes towards various matters. Indicate the amount of your agreement or disagreement with each statement by putting a number in the blank at the left according to the following scale:

+1	Slight support, agreement	−1	Slight opposition, disagreement
+2	Moderate support, agreement	−2	Moderate opposition, disagreement
+3	Strong support, agreement	−3	Strong opposition, disagreement

Read each item and decide quickly how you feel about it; then fill in the number corresponding to the extent of your agreement or disagreement. Put down your first impressions.

30. ____I would prefer to work on a project that I could see was getting somewhere, even though it was far from where I usually live and work, among people very different from me.

31. ____I prefer to risk a little to make a lot. That way if you are right one time in five, you are doing all right.

32. ____An article for sale is worth what people will pay for it.

33. ____Seniority should be given greater weight than merit in giving promotions.

34. ____Incentive pay should not be used because workers will overwork and ruin their health or destroy jobs for others.

35. ____In business you can only really trust friends and relatives.

36. ____Workers should not be promoted to managerial jobs even if they are qualified because it would destroy the respect for authority which the workers must have toward management.

37. ____Those who created the wealth of this country worked for success--not for money--for being able to tell a man to go to hell.

38. ____Part of the price one pays in joining any organization today is the sacrifice of decision-making at the individual, personal level, and I, for one, am not willing to pay that price.

39. ____The amount of education a person has should be a factor in determining his pay scale.

40. ____There is hardly any such thing as good luck--that is something people have to make for themselves.

41. ____I approve of a career or job outside the home for married women.

42. ____Planning only makes a person unhappy because your plans hardly ever work out anyway.

43. ____If I have to go to a doctor or lawyer, I prefer someone who is not a close personal friend of mine.

44. ____I feel I waste time and spend it uselessly.

45. ____A good son would try to live near his parents even if it means giving up a good job in another part of the country.

46. ____The most important factor in the success of a firm is the establishment of a reputation for the excellence of its products.

47. ____I work like a slave at everything I undertake until I am satisfied with the results.

48. ____A man with money cannot really learn how to behave in polite society if he has not had the proper upbringing.

49. ____It is remarkable how prayer influences the way things turn out.

50. ____A corporation does things for one reason--profit.

TABLE VII.1 MOTIVE SCORES FOR BUSINESS MANAGERS AND COMPARISON
SPECIALIST GROUPS IN THE U.S., TURKEY, ITALY AND POLAND

Areas and groups	N	Age	n Achievement		n Affiliation		n Power	
		mean	mean	SD	mean	SD	mean	SD
United States								
General Electric managers..........	27	43.0	6.74[1]	4.49	2.63	2.26	6.30	3.05
General Electric specialists	27	43.8	4.77[1]	4.54	2.52	3.06	6.52	2.76
			+1.97**		+.11		−.22	
Turkey								
Middle managers.....	17	33.1	1.76	3.99	4.18	2.30	5.65	3.11
Professionals (educators)	48	27.2	3.52	5.81	3.90	5.16	6.29	4.56
diff..............			−1.76		+.28		−.64	
Italy								
Middle managers.....	68	27.6	4.18	4.13	5.37	3.53	6.21	3.27
Professionals (law, theol., med.).......	107	21.7	2.31	4.31	5.97	3.48	5.25	3.53
diff.			+1.87*		−.60		+.96	
Poland								
Middle managers.....	31	35.9	6.58	5.22	2.16	2.41	5.48	2.84
Professionals (theol., educ.)	48	27.2	4.85	4.98	3.31	2.68	6.35	3.70
diff.			+1.73***		−1.15**		−.87	

[1] $N = 31$.
* $= p < .01$, ** $= p < .05$, *** $= p < .10$ *pd.*

List of Tables

Index